Ferrari

Fourth Edition

Hans Tanner

Haessner Publishing, Inc.
Drawer B
Newfoundland, N.J. 07435

First printed 1959
Reprinted 1960
Revised edition 1964
Revised third edition 1968
New format revised fourth edition November 1974

© Hans Tanner 1959, 1964, 1968 and 1974

Printed in England by J H Haynes and Company Limited.
Bound by The Wigmore Bindery in England

Published in England by G T Foulis & Co Ltd of Sparkford
Yeovil Somerset

Published in North America by Haessner Publishing, Inc.
Drawer B Newfoundland, N.J. 07435

HaeSSNeR

ISBN 0 87799 041 7

CONTENTS

INTRODUCTION

*QUESTION: Mr Ferrari of all the race cars that you have built which is your favourite?
ANSWER: The car which I have not yet created.
QUESTION: Mr Ferrari what has been your greatest victory?
ANSWER: The one which I have not yet achieved.

Ferrari, the Man

THE small office in Modena was crammed to the ceiling with trophies and photos. Enzo Ferrari was conjuring up the scenes of the past. An Alfa Romeo flashing over the bridge at Racenna to win the Circuit of Savio, a young Enzo flushed with victory being presented with the prancing horse symbol by his admirers, a symbol that was to be feared universally in the motor racing world for many years to come.

"Racing is a 'great mania' to which one must sacrifice everything without reticence, without hesitation. No reasoning is valid, for no matter how logical the argument, when the race begins it is less than useless. The only reasoning admitted is that which concerns the race itself, the opponents, the track and the car. When other thoughts emerge or when one begins to spend too much time reasoning logically, it is time to make the break and cut off any relationship with racing, just as one should with all other women when one marries". Thus, the complex man that is Enzo Ferrari sums up why he himself after many victories, decided to withdraw from racing.

Since the day of his retirement he has always maintained this attitude and to him racing represents something obscure, indefinite and indefinable without, in fact, any direct interest for him. For many years he has never been present at any motor race even when his own

creations have been running. He would suffer too much if he were present when one of his beloved machines began to fail, the pain would be too much and he lives in fear of this.

Enzo Ferrari divides his day between his home and his main office in Modena and his factory 16 kilometres away in Maranello. When he enters his office at Modena he goes through large rooms filled with photographs, souvenirs and the hundreds of trophies that are the fruits of many years work. But in one of these offices he always hesitates. Pensive, he remains in the little office that belonged to Dino, his son, for in that room life came to a halt for Enzo Ferrari. Everything remains intact, nothing has been changed since Dino left the office for the last time. On the desk are his pen, an appointment book and, in Dino's place, a photo of the smiling youngster that Dino was during his life.

It was a heavy blow for Enzo Ferrari when his Dino left him forever. He had long been prepared for it and always hoped for a miracle to give his son the health that he lacked. Even in the last moments of Dino's life, father Ferrari would come to his bedside to confide in him his worries and troubles, only with Dino could he open his heart.

But with the death of Dino, nothing changed. Every day Enzo Ferrari climbs into his modest car which waits for him in the courtyard in front of the clients' department; from there he goes to the cemetery and spends a time confiding in his son the details of the new car, the discussions with his team drivers and the doubt that his strength will carry on building new cars to hold off the ever increasing competition from the foreigners. But Dino does not only remain in the memory of his father, his name is recorded on the V 6 cylinder engine. Dino never saw this engine and when it first burst into life, Dino was

*From an interview with the French magazine *Sport Auto* 1974

already gone. When the new car first ran at Modena in the autumn of 1957, Ferrari for once forgot that engines of Grand Prix cars could cause him to suffer, he went to see the race for behind the new car there was for him his beloved son Dino.

FIFTEEN YEARS have passed since the foregoing was written and during those years this book has been revised and gradually brought up-to-date. There has been a great deal of development in both the Grand Prix and Sports Car/Gran Turismo world. Ferrari has had his ups and downs but on the whole he has managed to show that, despite extremely strong competition, he has always been able to keep ahead in one or other of the categories.

In this new and once again completely revised edition will be found the story of Enzo Ferrari from the beginning up to the present day. Much new material and very many new and additional photographs have been included.

In the 1968 revision I wrote that we may well see Ferrari go down in history as another Ettore Bugatti. In the past five years this prediction has been borne out. The mystique has grown by leaps and bounds and many Ferraris are now collectors items fetching much more than their original price. Important collections of Ferraris have come into existence and Ferrari clubs flourish all over the world. In completing these latest revisions, I would like to put in a word of special thanks to Peter Coltrin who took over my position in Modena and has kept in the closest touch with all Ferrari developments through the years. Many of the new photographs are his work and represent a valuable contribution towards the preservation of the history of Ferrari for future generations.

Hans Tanner
Los Angeles 1974

ACKNOWLEDGEMENTS

I would like to take this opportunity to thank all the people whose help made it possible to revise and update this work through the years; In particular thanks are due to Allen Bishop for his work on the new Chapter 13 which traces Ferrari engine design and for the vast amount of work that went into captioning the many additional photos. Stanley Nowak for the research on the 2.7 Ferraris. Chuck Queener and Steve Earle for the research on the 250 GTO. Gerald Roush for research on the 330 LMB. To Geoff Willoughby for his research on the Can Am Cars and Steve Earle once again for additions and corrections to this section. Alan C Bow for his research on the SWB. Ernie Mendicki for information on the Bracco car. Dick Kitchingman for his comments on the book in general. To John Bond of *Road & Track* magazine for permission to quote from articles published by that magazine. To Dean Batchelor for photographic and moral support. Bill Boddy of *Motor Sport* magazine for making available photos from that publication. To all those who were of such great help in compiling previous editions, Luigi Chinetti, Ronnie Hoare, Dr Vicente Alvarez, Charles Lytel, Bernard Cahier, Gordon Wilkins, Jesse Alexander, Federico Kirbus, Jack Faxon, Etienne Cornil and Corrado Millanta.

In this reset and greatly expanded edition, thanks are due to many more. Karl Ludvigsen for photos from the Rodolfo Mailander collection. Eoin Young for photos of the New Zealand specials. Kurt Miska for the use of photos from his extensive collection. Al Hall for photos from his collection. Anthony Bamford for providing photos of the elusive 2 cylinder Ferrari. The late Al Michaelian for all his assistance. Al Bloemker of the Indianapolis Motor Speedway for photos from the Speedway archives. To Henry Pickett who was there when it was all happening. To Briggs Cunningham and John Burgess of the Cunningham Museum for information and advice. To the late 'Pinky' Pinkham and his widow Millie for their great enthusiasm and feel for things 'Ferrari'. To Terry Marder for the laborious job of proofreading. To *Scale Models and Model Cars* magazine for permission to use the three-view drawings from their publication. To the *Autocar* and *Motor* for use of cutaway drawings from their publication. Last but not least are the photographers who contributed to enlarge the photo coverage of this work. Most of the colour is the work of John Lamm, other colour was provided by Henry Austin Clark Jr of the Long Island Automotive Museum, Stanley Nowak and Paul Skilleter of *Motor*. Black and white photography was provided by Peter C Coltrin, Nigel Snowdon, Louis Klementaski, T C March, Guy Griffiths, John Lamm, Stanley Nowak and Rick Busenkell.

Hans Tanner
Los Angeles 1974

CHAPTER ONE
Enzo Ferrari's early history

Racing with Alfa Romeo

IN Valentino Park in the Piedmontese city of Turin stands an old park bench. There is nothing outstanding to mark it, the average passer-by would not know it from the many others that dot the twisty paths. To Enzo Ferrari the bench has a particular attachment and when in Turin he occasionally visits the park to spend a little time sitting there. It is his bench of memories.

One day in 1947 he sat there and cried. Raymond Sommer had just won the Turin Grand Prix with the 1500cc supercharged Ferrari. Enzo cried tears of satisfaction, it was the first victory of the Grand Prix car that bore his name.

Sitting there, memories come to mind of another day many years before when he had first made his aquaintance with the bench, brushing off the snow in the bitter winter of 1918—19. Then his eyes were filled with tears of despair.

It all began in a house on the outskirts of Modena in 1898. The winter was bitter as only winter in the Po Valley can be.

On February 18th Enzo Ferrari was born, the snow was so deep that his mother could not go into town to register his birth until the 20th which according to Italian law at that time became his official birthday.

Father Ferrari had a small metal workshop which adjoined the house. In this shop he constructed axles and roofs for the Italian railways, the small room over the workshop was shared by Enzo and his older brother, Alfredo.

At that time the internal combustion engine had already gone through its birth pangs and Enzo was fortunate in having a father who was one of the first in Modena to acquire a car. On every opportunity he would ride in the unreliable, bone-shaking machine that soon so completely absorbed his interest. In those days to talk about cars was the same as talk of satellites and astronauts to the boys of the present age. When he was ten years old, Enzo Ferrari had his first taste of motor racing. His father and elder brother took him to the circuit of Bologna which was run on the old via Emilia. There he watched Vincenzo Lancia set the fastest lap and Felice Nazzaro win at the then fantastic speed of 60 miles per hour.

A year later there was another event for him to see. This time he went on his own as the race was being held at Navicello, some three miles away from his house. He hiked through the fields to get to the event which was known as the 'Mile Record'. Conditions for the drivers were none too good and men with buckets of water washed down the dirt road before each group of competitors took off.

Enzo chooses a career

At this time Ferrari had three great ambitions, to be an opera singer which was quickly forgotten due to lack of an ear for music; a sporting journalist, which he later attempted without making a great mark; and to become a racing driver. After seeing his first races he was determined to follow the latter course and by high pressure salesmanship he induced his father to teach him how to drive the family car by the time he was thirteen.

Father Ferrari wanted his son to become an engineer but Enzo who had no great liking for school was more interested in working with his hands, a decision that he was later to regret.

His father's business had been expanded to take on automobile repair work and there Enzo built up his mechanical knowledge. Covered from head to foot in grease he dreamed of emulating the exploits of Lancia and Nazzaro.

The shadow of the first world war fell on

them and Enzo was called to arms. He was posted to the 3rd Mountain Artillery but in those days there was no selective service, it went purely by age group. When Enzo proudly announced to his sub-lieutenant that he was a mechanic the officer decided that he was a "wise guy" and put him to work shoeing mules.

Eventually he was allowed to work on his beloved motors and this helped inspire him to greater enthusiasm. Aircraft and motors were the future. The Wright brothers had started it and now the Capronis were unloading their cargoes of death from the skies.

A new hero, Francesco Baracca, whose daring exploits with his Nieuport and Spad fighters, sent enemy after enemy cracking out of the skies, captured the imagination of the Italian public. Everything in the world that mattered seemed to be driven by the motors that Enzo loved so much.

Invalided out of the army

There were dark moments when his father died, this was followed by the death of his brother Alfredo who had contracted an illness at the front. It was Enzo's turn and he was struck down by illness. He was rushed to the military hospital at Brescia for an operation and from there he ended up in a camp near Bologna, a group of miserable huts where the hopeless cases were sent.

Recovery was slow, the army had no further use for him, but something of value came out of his military stint in the shape of a letter of introduction to Fiat from his Colonel.

It was the winter of 1918–19 and it was bitterly cold. Full of hope Enzo made his way to Turin where he presented himself at the offices of Fiat with his letter.

The interview was brief and bitter. Fiat, he was informed, was too small to absorb all the invalids of war. Enzo was out in the street on his way to make his first acquaintance with his park bench.

There was no work anywhere for the young Ferrari and he quickly ran out of the small inheritance his father had left him.

Then lady luck smiled and he ran into a man of Bolognese origin named Giovanni who found Enzo to his liking and offered him a job as a tester. The war had stopped the production of passenger automobiles in Italy and Giovanni specialised in modifying Lancia light truck chassis into something that could be used for a passenger car. It was Ferrari's job to test them and drive the bare chassis to Milan where the bodies were built onto them.

During this period he came to know many famous racing drivers of the era, Felice and Biaggio Nazzaro, Cagno, Salamano and many others.

As his salary increased so did his confidence. His greatest stroke of luck came when on one of his trips to Milan he met Ugo Sivocci, an ex-racing cyclist who had become chief tester with the Costruzioni Meccaniche Nazionali or C.M.N. as it was known. Sivocci got on well with the young Ferrari and they became firm friends. Sivocci was instrumental in getting a job for Ferrari with the C.M.N. workshops and Ferrari transferred to Milan which was fast becoming the centre of automobile development. C.M.N. was a reasonably prosperous undertaking as they had built four-wheel-drive tractors for artillery trains during the war.

After the end of the conflict they had turned to producing passenger car chassis and were using left over bits from Isotta Fraschini to build up engines to fit in these chassis.

A start in motor racing

With C.M.N. Ferrari had his first taste of competition. One of his first jobs was to assist Sivocci to accompany one of the motor cycle riders in the North-South Rally. Their rider won but not until Ferrari and Sivocci had performed some hectic repairs when their man crashed a short way from the finish at Naples.

Ferrari's opportunity came at the end of 1919, he ran in the Parma-Poggio di Berceto hill climb. Antonio Ascari won and Enzo came in fourth. C.M.N. entered him in the Targa Florio of the same year. He and Sivocci set off from Milan driving the same car that they were to use in the race as finances were somewhat restricted. They had a shaking but temporary holdup in the mountains of southern Italy when they ran into deep snow and were set upon by wolves.

Enzo always carried a revolver with him and succeeded in putting the wolves to flight and

Palermo was made in time for the race.

The Targa Florio did not work out too well for Ferrari, he had trouble almost at the start when his fuel tank strap broke and it took a long time to fix. As a result he dropped to last place in the classification. By dint of some heroic driving he made up some of the lost time but he was really out of luck. As he approached a town on the circuit he was stopped by the local 'Carabinieri' and told that he and the other competitors behind him would have to wait. The local governor was making a speech in the market square through which the race passed. They would not be allowed to proceed until the speech was over. All protests were in vain and it was a long time before they were allowed to continue. They had strict instructions not to pass the governor's car on the road and several miles passed before that worthy turned off to give them the road. Enzo shouted some unprintable comments about Italian politicians and raced towards the finishing line. When he arrived, to put it into his own words, "The timekeepers and spectators had already left on the last train to Palermo."

Alfa Romeo

An offer from Alfa Romeo took him away from C.M.N. and a short while later he was able to repay his friend, Sivocci by having him transfer to that company too.

At the beginning Alfa Romeo had their ups and downs but Ferrari and Sivocci the 'gung ho' kids made a worthy addition to the Alfa team which already included the serious Antonio Ascari and amateur opera star, Giuseppe Campari.

With Alfa Romeo, Ferrari returned to the Targa Florio and this time it was a different story, he placed second overall with the great Campari behind him.

Together with Sivocci he was entered by Alfa Romeo in the Coppa delle Alpi. The Alfas were not on their best form and Sivocci had to be content with 4th whilst Enzo Ferrari lost a close battle with Sailer's Mercedes for 5th place.

In the meantime, team mates Ascari and Campari were keeping the Alfa colours flying and with a great effort Ferrari began to show his real ability on the very difficult Mugello circuit run on the Futa Pass. He took the 4.5-litre car to win ahead of his companion Sivocci. From there he went on to an equally important victory on the Aosta Grand St. Bernard hillclimb still with the unwieldy 40/60 model Alfa. At Alfa Romeo, Ferrari became more than a racing driver. His enthusiasm and devotion to the company was quickly noticed and he was given a type of undercover assignment to find technicians which Alfa badly needed. At that time Alfa Romeo had only one designer whose assistant's actual profession was that of pharmacist.

First Ferrari brought his closest friend, Luigi Bazzi from Turin. Since that day Bazzi has always been with Ferrari and works at Maranello to this day.

Through Ferrari's efforts a new figure came on the scene. A man with cold eyes and tremendous energy, sporting an old fashioned 'Re Umberto' moustache and perched on his head an equally old-fashioned bowler hat. The man was Vittorio Jano. Ferrari had never met Jano but had to rely on Bazzi's description of the man to formulate his plans to entice Jano away from Fiat.

Ferrari was more than successful, not only did he come back with Jano but several other important Fiat technicians. Just how valuable these men were to Alfa Romeo can only be gauged by the tremendous numbers of victories by the P2 and P3 Alfa Romeos.

In 1923 Alfa Romeo produced their model 'R L Sport' a much improved version of the 'R L' of the previous year. With this car Ascari won the 3-litre class of the Targa Florio whilst Sivocci took the 4.5-litre class with the old 40/60.

The prancing horse

On June 17th 1923 came an important occurrence in the life of Enzo Ferrari. He was entered by Alfa Romeo to run in the Circuit of Savio at Ravenna. During this race he put up an amazing exhibition of driving — he annihilated all opposition. When he came in there was no one else in sight and with his 3-litre he not only won the race overall but set the lap record against much more powerful opposition. The crowd went wild for the young Modenese driver, they broke down the police cordons and carried him off on their shoulders. Before the noise of applause and congratulations had died down, a man pushed his way through the crowd, as he reached Enzo he shook his hand warmly and invited him to his home. It was the father of Francesco Baracca the famous Italian fighter ace who shot down 35 adversaries in the 1914—18 war. Francesco Baracca had used a yellow shield in the centre of which was a prancing horse emblem, as his personal badge. It was a badge dreaded by his enemies until the day in 1918 when Baracca's career ended. The family was sent the prancing horse emblem on a piece of aeroplane fabric. The invitation by Baracca's father had a reason, the Baracca family wished to present Francesco's badge to Enzo Ferrari as a symbol of his courage and audacity.

With Enzo Ferrari, the prancing horse badge became famous again, first on Ferrari's personal racing cars, then as a badge of the famous Scuderia Ferrari and finally as the emblem of the cars that Enzo built bearing his own name.

The group of enthusiasts at Alfa Romeo led by Ferrari decided that Alfas must do things in grand style for 1924. Ferrari's organization was to become invaluable. Whilst Jano and Bazzi worked in the test house and on the drawing board, the team was backed up by the enthusiasm of Ascari, Campari and Sivocci. Jano was working on a 2-litre as the international formula had been adopted with that limit and in the spring of 1924 on the Parma-Poggio di Berceto road, a favourite testing place, people several times saw Antonio Ascari driving a strange looking car still unpainted; that was the only indication of Alfa Romeo's big plans. At the circuit of Cremona the new car appeared and astounded everyone by leaving all the other competitors far behind and by being timed at over 125 m p h on the Cremona straight.

Personal success as a racing driver

Ferrari continued to do well for Alfa Romeo. He won the Pescara race beating the whole Mercedes team that was fresh from its victory in the Targa Florio. In this event Ferrari was only driving an RLS Alfa, team-mate Campari had the P2 model and team orders were for Campari to take on the Mercedes. However, things worked out differently, Enzo shot straight into the lead, after a few anxious glances in the rear view mirror to see if Campari was coming up, Ferrari decided to press on. It was fortunate that he did so as Campari had broken down and, had it not been for Ferrari's effort, the Mercedes Benz would have gone unchallenged. From 1927 on, Fiat decided to withdraw from competition but other adversaries of Alfa Romeo were still strong. Enzo Ferrari became more and more involved in organizing the team but continued to race as much as he could. In January 1924 he won the Gargano hillclimb setting a new record and taking the 3-litre class as well. He repeated his win at the circuit of Savio coming in ahead of Foroni's Itala and Nuvolari's Chiribiri.

In the years that followed, Ferrari suffered from continual ill health which curtailed his racing activities but when he did race it was always with satisfying results. At Padua, on the circuit of Polesine, he again beat Nuvolari setting a new record of 108.1 k p h. At Pescara he won the race again and at Modena, his home town, he really set people talking when he first won the 1500-cc event, ahead of Marinoni's Alfa, and then won the unlimited class with his 1500, being faster than the 2- and 3-litres and setting a new record.

The loss of Antonio Ascari in the French Grand Prix was a great blow to Alfa Romeo and the little group of enthusiasts but under the sympathetic direction of Prospero Gianferrari all the team exerted themselves to the full and one Alfa Romeo success led to another.

With ill health worries and hard work in organization Ferrari had little time for racing but he was back on the scene again in 1928. In the 1500-cc class at the circuit of Alessandria he came in first, ahead of Tonini's Maserati, at the same time setting the fastest lap. At Modena he again emerged victorious with the 1500 repeating his previous achievement of setting a faster time with his little car than the 2- and 3-litres and proceeding to beat his own fastest lap putting it from 107 k p h to 121 k p h. All did not always go so smoothly and on his own favourite Mugello circuit he had to take a back seat to the almost invincible Materassi with his Talbot and at the same time was beaten by Presenti's Alfa Romeo. He was in action again in

1929 but the season began very badly. At Verona for the circuit del Pozzo he could do no better than 5th behind the Bugattis, Delages and Maseratis. The next race went just as badly, at Mugello he arrived 8th behind several well-known names, Brilli-Peri, Morandi, Pintacuda, Varzi, Campari and Biondetti, but again he managed to come in ahead of Nuvolari.

The Scuderia Ferrari

One evening in a restaurant in Bologna, enjoying the wonderful food for which that town is famous, an idea was born, Enzo Ferrari with the Caniato brothers from Ferrara and Mario Tadini, future "King of the Italian hill climbers", mulled over the idea of forming a private racing team. Ferrari's three companions agreed to go into partnership with him and so on December 1st 1929 the "Scuderia Ferrari" was born.

Enzo Ferrari ostensibly left Alfa Romeo although his ties with the Milanese company remained very close. He became Alfa Romeo distributor for Emilia, Romagna and Marche provinces and based himself at Modena. Ferrari continued to race on occasions, he took third place at Alessandria behind Varzi and Zanelli and drove an 1100-cc Talbot to second places at Montenero and Pescara in 1931.

Ferrari's wife announced that Enzo was about to become a father, and when his son, Dino, was born in January 1932 he decided to retire from racing permanently; to be a father was a great responsibility and he must work to assure a future for his son.

The first Ferrari publication. It was a monthly magazine bearing this logo

CHAPTER TWO

The Scuderia Ferrari as official Alfa Romeo Team

IN the years of his direct association with Alfa Romeo Enzo Ferrari had shown a tremendous ability for organization, and an equally fervent enthusiasm for all that was connected with racing and sports cars. Thus when Alfa Romeo decided to withdraw from racing no one was surprised to hear that the whole of the Alfa Romeo material was to be handed over to Ferrari who would be responsible for keeping the name of the Milanese firm in the limelight.

When the Scuderia Ferrari was founded at Modena on December 1st 1929, Alfa Romeo announced 'The Scuderia Ferrari will have at its disposal all the Alfa Romeo racing material which will be maintained with the assistance of the parent firm. The new organization will be independent, but closely connected by mutual interests to the Milan headquarters, the name and prestige of the Alfa Romeo marque will be in the hands of the Modenese concern. The Scuderia Ferrari will not limit itself to participating solely in a schedule of racing, but will also have the responsibility of the care and maintenance of customers' racing and sports cars.'

Together with this authority some of the Milanese firm's best technicians and equipment were transferred to what had been a small garage in the Via Emilia at Modena.

With the transfer of all the material and personnel, Ferrari immediately began to rebuild his modest establishment, and before long a two-storey building was erected, formed of two wings, one being for the maintenance of customers' cars and the other for the preparation of the Scuderia Ferrari's cars for the racing team. Two Shell pumps graced the front of the building, and a large badge showing the radiator grille of a racing car with the name Alfa Romeo underneath it was attached to the wall; under the sign, in big white letters was written 'Scuderia Ferrari.'

In the front part of the building were the offices between which was situated the first of several notorious 'waiting' rooms where millionaires and future racing champions were to await the pleasure of Enzo Ferrari.

Eduardo Weber

For 1930 Ferrari based his racing programme on the still successful P2 Alfa Romeo, and for sports car racing he had the choice of three different versions of the 1750-cc model. It was at the beginning of this season that Enzo Ferrari called on his friend Edoardo Weber from Bologna. Together the two men applied the first twin-choke carburetters to the Alfa Romeo racing designs, a system that was to remain for high performance cars until the present day.

During the season he had to face Bugatti and Maserati, the traditional opponents of the Alfa Romeo. Already however there began to be signs of increased German interest in racing, and Mercedes Benz were producing some large capacity 'monsters' to challenge the Italian opposition. The Germans employed light alloys as much as possible and relied on highly tuned engines in preparation for the all out attack on Grand Prix racing that was to take place at a later date.

The Mille Miglia 1930

Mercedes Benz had cast an envious eye on the great Italian classic, the Mille Miglia and the publicity to be gained by winning this event was growing by leaps and bounds every time it took place; a first place for a German car and driver would do much to boost the prestige of the 'master race.' Mercedes sent a 6-litre car for the 1930 edition of the event, the drivers being the

16

great Caracciola and Werner. The Scuderia Ferrari relied on the smaller 1750-cc 6-cylinder supercharged Alfa Romeo and Enzo divided his team into two groups. Group No. 1 was led by Nuvolari and Guidotti and comprised Campari/Marinoni and Pirola/Guatta. The second group were led by Varzi and Canavese with Ghersi/Cortese and Mazzotti/Maggi making up the rest of the team. Enzo Ferrari however had a problem with his team, something which would arise many more times in the future of his racing activities. He had too many primadonnas, and Nuvolari made it clear that he was more interested in beating Varzi than he was in beating the German challenge. Varzi did not make any comments, but everyone knew he would drive the car to its absolute limits to beat the 'Mantovano.' Campari was bellowing "I'll show them all!" Immediately the race started the duel between Varzi and Nuvolari began. Nuvolari started 10 minutes behind Varzi but by the first control at Bologna he had cut this down to 9 minutes and now led the 'Mantovano' by one by 1 minute. However to his surprise he found he was not leading for in front by one minute was Luigi Arcangeli with a Maserati. At The Florence control Nuvolari maintained his one minute lead over Varzi but by the time Poggibonsi was reached, Varzi had made up two minutes and now led the 'Mantovano' by one minute. At Rome the two cars dead-heated and the Maserati disappeared. The pace was fast and furious neither driver willing to give in to the other and Enzo Ferrari was going crazy with worry for fear that both drivers would wreck their cars in the fight. At Terni, Varzi was ahead, at Spoleto Nuvolari was again in the lead, at Perugia and Gubbio it was a dead heat. At Tolentino Nuvolari had once again pulled out a one minute lead. However there was a dramatic change after Ancona, on the return to Bologna, for Varzi was 6 minutes behind Nuvolari and after the arrival at Brescia, Varzi was asked why this had happened. He was furious, for Enzo Ferrari had had enough of this battle and at Ancona, Varzi had been informed by the mechanics that he was comfortably in the lead and so he had begun to take things easy. When he got to Treviso he found out the true position and gave up trying as he was convinced that the

information given him at Ancona had been a manoeuvre to give Nuvolari the victory. Varzi realized his error in trusting others when racing was concerned and he never forgave himself for it, always remembering this lesson in every race he ran after that.

A Nuvolari legend

It was in this Mille Miglia that the story arose that Nuvolari had caught Varzi by putting out his lights and sneaking up on his team mate to pass him just before Brescia. However Varzi's story was different. On the long descent of Arsie, Varzi's co-driver, Canavesi, saw the unmistakable lights of a 1750 Alfa Romeo a long way behind and he turned to Varzi and shouted "It's him." Varzi immediately realized that he had lost the best part of the 10 minutes starting advantage which he had over Nuvolari and decided that it was useless to attempt to regain the lost ground so close to Brescia. Nuvolari did put out his lights to try and sneak up, but he did not pass Varzi until Peschiera at 5.20 in the morning, at which time the sun was beginning to rise.

Nuvolari thus came in as winner, but in the heat of battle with Varzi, the German opposition had been completely forgotten. The team of Caracciola/Werner suffered a crushing defeat being over one hour behind Nuvolari at Brescia. Nuvolari set the first over 100 k p h average with a new record of 100.45 k p h.

The life of the P2 Alfa Romeo was fast coming to an end since the day five years previously when Antonio Ascari had taken it to its first victory at Cremona. Jano decided to make some final alterations to the P2 and put extra weight on its rear axle, removing the streamlined tail and adding a spare tyre. Varzi drove this car at the Targa Florio, and was out for blood after the Mille Miglia affair. Both Nuvolari and Campari were there with the 1750 Mille Miglia type Alfa Romeos, but Varzi made no mistakes this time and came home first, breaking the record for the Targa Florio by over 20 minutes and giving the Scuderia another great victory to its lists. Nuvolari had some trouble with his car and could do no better than 5th behind Campari. Louis Chiron was second with a 2.3-litre Bugatti but more than two minutes behind the flying Alfa Romeo. Despite its victory, the race marked the last appearance of the P2 Alfa Romeo. Varzi, still furious about the Mille Miglia, left the Scuderia Ferrari and joined Bugatti.

The 2.3-litre Alfa Romeo

In 1931 the Germans were back. This time Carraciola and Sebastian turned out with a 7-litre Mercedes and months of practice and preparation were undertaken. The Scuderia Ferrari also had plans for something new and the 2.3-litre Alfa Romeo was the result. Two of these cars were entered for Nuvolari and Arcangeli whilst Campari and Borzacchini had the well-tried 1750-cc models. Unfortunately the new 2.3-litre cars were not ready until the very last moment and Ferrari was to pay dearly for the tardy preparation.

The rapid and powerful German car had no trouble outdistancing the Italian opposition on the initial straights, but as the twisty section of the race was reached the Alfa Romeos began to make up ground rapidly. At Rome Nuvolari was delayed time and time again with blown tyres but as he fell by the wayside, the other Alfas took over. Borzacchini took the lead followed by Campari and Arcangeli, also delayed by tyre stops was in third place. Campari then put on the pressure and at Gubbio took the lead from Borzacchini; after Gubbio, Arcangeli with the swift 2.3 was going full steam again and by Bologna held a firm lead of over 4 minutes ahead of the Germans. The tyres began to give trouble again and Arcangeli losing ground fast was passed again by Campari. After Arcangeli's retirement only Campari was left to hold off the German challenge but on the final straight leading to Brescia the tremendous power of the monster Mercedes told and Carraciola swept by the gallant Campari to give Germany its first win in the Mille Miglia.

For the 1931 Grand Prix season Ferrari had Nuvolari, Borzacchini, Arcangeli and Ghersi. Bugatti employed Varzi, Chiron, Bouriat and Conelli while Mercedes used Caracciola and Stuck. At this period there were many rumours that Campari was retiring from racing to take up an operatic career, but finally he himself put an end to these reports by announcing that he had no

intention of abandoning racing and that opera was just his hobby. That year both Bugatti and Maserati had built, for the big races, cars that gave over 230 b h p and Ferrari decided to counteract these multi-cylinder monsters with one of his own. Consequently two 1750-cc engines were fitted together to make a 12-cylinder and the car was successfully tested at the Coppa Acerbo at Pescara where Campari had an easy win with it. Two cars were prepared for the G.P. of Monza with Campari and Nuvolari named as drivers. In the early evening before the race, Arcangeli insisted on trying out one of the cars and coming out of the underpass and entering the fast curve, lost control and crashed to his death. Nuvolari with the other car nevertheless had good fortune during the race and finished well ahead of Fagioli's 3-litre Maserati and the 2.3 Alfa of Borzacchini. However Varzi with the 4.9-litre Bugatti set the lap record. Nuvolari won the Montenero race for Ferrari and Borzacchini took a first place at Avellino. Campari and Borzacchini shared a second place in the Grand Prix of the ACF and Nuvolari and Borzacchini tied for second place at Spa.

Targa Florio 1931

In the Targa Florio, Nuvolari once again got the better of Varzi. The race was run in the pouring rain and Nuvolari had taken care to put on mud guards which gave him a decided advantage over Varzi's Bugatti and ensured a comfortable win.

Varzi openly admitted that he would have rather driven for Ferrari than for Bugatti. He felt that Nuvolari always had an advantage over him in the sense that the 'Mantovano' was driving an Italian car, but he claimed that he could not do otherwise as Jano had a marked preference for Nuvolari, and he, Varzi, was still haunted by the 1930 Mille Miglia incident.

In the final event of the season, the Grand Prix of Brno, Nuvolari was lying third when the leading car of Fagioli went off the road striking the base of an overpass bridge causing it to collapse. Nuvolari and Varzi being close behind ran into the wreckage and were eliminated, and, with the mechanical breakdown on Borzacchini's car, Louis Chiron was left to win the race for Bugatti.

It was during this period of great rivalry between Nuvolari and Varzi that interesting comments were made on the difference in their personalities. Giovanni Canestrini, doyen of Italian motoring journalists, notes 'Archille Varzi was always the picture of elegance, his carefully pressed blue overalls, his specially made racing gloves and his goggles, the cleaning of which drove his personal mechanic Bignami to near desperation. He always carried two pairs of goggles plus a rain vizor and was slave to many minute peculiarities. He could not stand even the slightest noise from the body work of a racing machine and the car had to be immaculate, polished and perfect. He was never seen at the wheel of a car that had any dents or scratches in it or that was not shining like new.' Of Nuvolari, Canestrini writes 'Nuvolari was similar to Varzi only in the regularity of his racing uniform. He always wore his racing overalls tight at the ankle, a yellow shirt and a white leather racing cap on which he pinned an image of the Madonna bound with the Italian tricolor. Later when he was given a small golden tortoise by Gabriele D'Annunzio, he made it his emblem and always wore it on his shirt. Nuvolari's opinion about the cars he raced was briefly "The cars are always all right so long as he could drive them fast.'

The P3 Alfa Romeo

1932 was to be a significant year for the Scuderia Ferrari. Jano had finished the design of his 2650 Tipo B Alfa Romeo better known as the P3. This car was expressly designed as the answer to Bugatti's big 4.9-litre, and with it began the domination of Nuvolari and all that was left for Varzi and the Bugatti, were a few lap records during the season.

The Mercedes opposition for the 1932 Mille Miglia was seriously weakened as Ferrari had taken the precaution to sign on Carraciola for his team. Nevertheless Ferrari was faced with a strong enough team made up of Broschek and Sebastian as well as Varzi with the 2.3 Bugatti. The Germans had set a new course record the previous year and Ferrari was very interested in getting it back for Italy.

The 2.3-litre cars had undergone a considerable amount of development and started as strong favourites. After only 100 kilometers had been run the Alfas began to pull away from the Mercedes, Bugatti and Lancia opposition, but instead of a procession, a tremendous battle amongst the members of the same team ensued. Nuvolari, Caracciola, Campari and Borzacchini alternated in the lead. In the end it was Borzacchini who came in first, a complete triumph for Alfa Romeo who took the first seven places, with Strazza's Lancia 8th ahead of four more Alfas. The record set by Carraciola the previous year was pulverized being taken from 101.17 k p h to 109.88 k p h by the winning car.

After the success of the 2.3 Alfa Romeo in the Mille Miglia, it continued to give the Scuderia Ferrari victories in the 24 Hour Race of Spa, The 24 Hours of Le Mans, The Targa Florio, Grand Prix of Finland and the Grand Prix of Marseilles.

For the Grand Prix of Monza the new P3 Alfas were pitted against the latest Maserati, the model V5, a 16-cylinder monster of 5-litres giving out over 350 b h p from its supercharged engine. The big Maserati was driven by Fagioli and the Scuderia Ferrari were represented by Nuvolari, Campari and Carraciola. The Maserati was more powerful but the Alfa was much lighter and easier to handle. In the first heat for the race, Nuvolari and Fagioli fought bitterly only a few yards apart. In the corners the Alfa pulled away but on the banking the Maserati forged ahead, the two cars passing the grandstands side by side. The battle grew hotter and hotter and everyone waited for something drastic to happen. Just before the end of the heat Nuvolari in a frantic attempt to stay ahead spun on the curve where Alberto Ascari was to lose his life many years later. He regained the road but was well behind Fagioli, in second place. Before the final there was an incident which nearly caused the cancellation of the race. Fagioli and Nuvolari had a bitter quarrel, each accusing the other of deliberate blocking and as a result Alfa Romeo threatened to withdraw from the race. The public, hearing this, caused such a disturbance that the French Revolution must have seemed quiet by comparison. The troubles were hastily patched up and the two adversaries went arm in arm to the starting grid.

The action seen in the first heat was repeated in the final. Nuvolari had given his car such a thrashing trying to outpace the Maserati that it was falling apart, consequently he took over Campari's car and the beefy opera singer had to be content with the half-wrecked car. The race did not last very long as the big Maserati began to fail. Things looked set for another Nuvolari victory but just a few laps before the end a fuel line broke on the 'Mantovano's' car and it looked as if the Maserati would win after all. Only at the last moment was the honour of Scuderia Ferrari and Alfa Romeo saved, when Carraciola in response to a frantic signal squeezed by the slowing Maserati to take first place.

Nuvolari's year

During the season Nuvolari won race after race. He won the Grand Prix of the ACF, the Targa Florio, the Coppa Acerbo at Pescara, the Grand Prix of Avellino, the Montenero race at Leghorn, the Monte Carlo Grand Prix and was placed second in the German Grand Prix and third at Masaryk. Of the other members of the Scuderia Ferrari, Carraciola won both the German Grand Prix and the Eifelrennen, being placed second at Monaco and Pescara, and third in the Grand Prix of France. Borzacchini was second in the Targa Florio, second in the Grand Prix of France and Montenero and third in the German and Italian Grands Prix.

The Mille Miglia of 1933 proved another triumph for Nuvolari and the Scuderia Ferrari. Varzi was missing from the entry list and Nuvolari had a comparatively easy win. His only opponent was Borzacchini but the latter was out of the race at Narni with mechanical trouble.

At Monte Carlo Nuvolari met his arch rival Varzi again. Other entries included such great names as Chiron, Lehoux, Dreyfus, Trossi and Etancelin, but already after a few laps these aces had fallen behind. At the start of the race Varzi with the Bugatti jumped into the lead, Nuvolari's Alfa close behind. On the fourth lap Nuvolari got by into first place, after another four laps Varzi was back into the lead which he in turn held for two laps, then it was Nuvolari again and so it went on for the whole of the race. Despite their tremendous pace both men were looking for weak points in each other's driving and in the machines. On the 93rd lap, with 7 laps to go to the end of the race, the pace increased furiously. The two cars had been lapping at 2 min. 6 sec. and suddenly on the initiative of Nuvolari the times dropped to 2 min. 2 sec. only to be immediately matched by Varzi. Again the time was improved to 2 min. 1 sec. by Nuvolari only to be equalled once again by Varzi. On the 98th lap Nuvolari was ahead, but when passing the start-finish line and braking for the Gasometer hairpin, Varzi left his braking to the last possible minute and managed to squeeze past the 'Mantovano.' Together they swept up the hill towards the Casino corner, by a brilliant piece of driving Nuvolari nosed ahead of Varzi as they negotiated the tricky corner. As they shot out of the tunnel it was Nuvolari ahead and when they crossed the line a new record of 2 min. flat was announced for the 'Mantovano'; no sooner however was the news out that it was announced that Varzi had covered the same lap in 1 min. 59 secs. Everyone waited excitedly to see which car would be first out of the tunnel on the last lap. There was a flash of blue and Varzi's Bugatti crossed the line the winner, the Alfa had disappeared to show up later puffing along in a cloud of smoke, Nuvolari seated on the tail of the completely spent car. Borzacchini saved Ferrari's honour with a second place.

A week after the Monte Carlo event, Nuvolari was after Varzi again, this time at the Circuit of Alessandria. Varzi had a marked advantage, having won the event every year for the three preceding years. Nuvolari had ample revenge and came in first leading two other members of the Scuderia Ferrari, Trossi and Brivio, across the line.

The Tripoli G P Lottery

In 1933 it was decided to hold a tremendous lottery in conjunction with the Grand Prix of Tripoli, the winning ticket being worth over 100,000 U.S. dollars (at 1974 values).

Unbeknown to the organizers, a meeting took place in Rome when Borzacchini, Nuvolari and Varzi met with the holders of the tickets that pertained to their cars. The owners of the tickets tried to come to an arrangement to 'fix' the race with the drivers and divide the lottery money but neither of the three would hear of it. All had the same reply: 'I intend to run my race as I see fit.' Nevertheless the story hit the newspapers and caused much alarm amongst the other drivers. On the eve of the race one thing was certain, all the drivers were out to get the 'Three Musketeers' as they had been nicknamed, for they were convinced that Nuvolari, Varzi and Borzacchini had made a deal amongst themselves.

When the race began it seemed that everyone was working against the three. Birkin's Maserati went into the lead followed by Nuvolari, Campari, Varzi, Fagioli and Borzacchini. The race was running at an average speed of 111 m p h when on the fourth lap Campari swept by Nuvolari and Birkin into the lead. Borzacchini slowed to a halt in his pit with a broken gearbox, so one of the 'musketeers' was already out. Varzi was now running on only seven cylinders and on the fifth lap Campari was 9 seconds ahead of Birkin, 14 seconds ahead of Nuvolari and 57 seconds ahead of Varzi. Varzi stopped at the pits for a plug change knowing that Nuvolari and Birkin would have to stop for fuel whereas he would not. Nuvolari kept himself within striking range of his Scuderia Ferrari team mate, Campari, at the same time pulling ahead of Birkin. After 14 laps Campari made a pit stop and retired, and whilst Birkin made his pit stop Varzi went by into second place. After 20 laps he was only 18 seconds behind Nuvolari and when the 'Mantovano' made his expected pit stop Varzi was out in front. But suddenly the unforeseen happened. As Varzi changed over to his reserve tank, the valve would not work. Frantically Varzi worked on it slowing all the time. Nuvolari seeing that he was in trouble went after him as hard as he could. It was the last lap and Varzi finally had the valve functioning but Nuvolari was already by. Varzi tried hard to make up ground and tucked in behind the flying Alfa. Coming up to the finishing line Varzi was still behind but with superb judgment and using the slipstream tow that he was getting to great effect. Varzi managed to beat Nuvolari over the line by a nose.

Nuvolari went on to win the 24 Hours of Le Mans with Raymond Sommer also with a Scuderia Ferrari Alfa. He then took a first in the Eifelrennen and at Nimes, where a newcomer to the Scuderia, Guy Moll, first made his appearance, he took third place and later repeated with another third place at Nice. Brivio won the Targa Florio and the Swedish Grand Prix for the Scuderia, whilst Nuvolari and Borzacchini were placed first and second in the Tunis Grand Prix. Campari had gone to Maserati and soundly beat the Scuderia Ferrari in the French Grand Prix at Montlhery. Nuvolari, who for some time had been discontented with the Scuderia Ferrari, saw the victory of his ex-team mate and started to think seriously about driving the new car for the Maserati team. Flushed with his success he now began to have ideas of independence from the Scuderia. He was taking badly to the strict control that Enzo Ferrari exercised over the team; he claimed that his prestige was suffering because of Ferrari's control and one day openly went to Enzo and told him he wanted the name of the team altered from 'Scuderia-Ferrari' to 'Scuderia Nuvolari-Ferrari.'

Nuvolari goes to Maserati

It was clear that under such circumstances an agreement could not be reached and so in July 1933 Nuvolari and his ever present 'little brother,' as the Italians called Borzacchini, left the Scuderia Ferrari to join Maserati. Enzo Ferrari reconstituted his team by taking on Fagioli and Louis Chiron, and took back Campari from Maserati. To these top names were added those of Moll, Siena and Brivio.

Ferrari was quite satisfied at his choice when Fagioli beat Nuvolari in the Italian Grand Prix finishing 40 seconds ahead of the 'Mantovano's' Maserati and setting a new lap record of 115 m p h and a record for the 500 miles at 108 m p h.

It was in this race that the Scuderia Ferrari entered Trossi with the 4.5-litre Duesenberg, but this news could not attract the public's attention away from the expected duel between Campari with the Ferrari Alfa and Borzacchini with a Maserati, the latter out to show up his former team. The first heat was interesting enough, Trossi led the race until a piston broke spreading oil on to the track. Czaykowski's 4.9 Bugatti then led the heat despite an all-out effort by the Scuderia Ferrari's up-and-coming young driver, Guy Moll who put in a lap at 122 m p h. Everyone waited eagerly for the second heat to see the battle between Borzacchini and Campari. Borzacchini was first off, closely followed by Campari, but on the first lap it was Balestrero's car which came round first. Campari had over-taken Borzacchini on the banking and being at the absolute limit, had been unable to hold on and had gone over the rim of the banking. The unfortunate Borzacchini, in an attempt to avoid Campari also went over the top of the banking. Campari was killed outright and Borzacchini died twenty minutes after having been taken to hospital. The day was further marred when in the final, Czaykowski crashed to his death with his Bugatti.

After his win in the Italian Grand Prix, Fagioli went on to win Pescara for the Scuderia and to take second place at San Sebastian and Masaryk, both these latter races were won by Louis Chiron also with a Scuderia Ferrari car. At the beginning of 1934 the Scuderia Ferrari was once again reorganized. Nuvolari had made up his mind to stay with Maserati but Varzi had finally broken away from Bugatti. Thus Enzo Ferrari made up his team with Varzi, Chiron and the promising Moll. Bugatti too, had reorganized his team, the new leader being Benoist with Wimille and Brivio as team mates.

Mille Miglia 1934

For the Mille Miglia Nuvolari began to show his true inclinations. Instead of going to Enzo Ferrari to ask him for a car he went to see his old friend Vittorio Jano. Jano and Nuvolari came to an agreement and Jano promised that he would get him a specially prepared 2.3-litre Alfa Romeo.

When Varzi heard this he went screaming to Ferrari who, however, wisely decided to hold off arguing with Jano and with a smile told Varzi not to worry, that his Alfa Romeo had been bored out to 2.6-litres.

Varzi started the race four minutes behind Nuvolari and he used this as a tactical advantage. Varzi based his plan of action on catching up with Nuvolari and then staying there behind him, watching him all the time, with the know-ledge that he would by then have almost a full 4 minutes advantage over 'Jano's pet' as Varzi called him. Varzi forgot all about the others in the race, he was after Nuvolari's blood. He was so busy with the Nuvolari problem that he did not even notice that Tadini in another of the Scuderia Ferrari Alfas had pulled out a 5 minute lead and that a completely unknown driver Bonetto, was also ahead. Bonetto running his first race nearly caused the end of Scuderia Ferrari. With his old Alfa loaded up with spares and tyres, he had set off on the Mille Miglia without any practice, and over the Futa Pass found himself in the lead. Enzo Ferrari had established a refuelling stop on top of the Futa Pass and seeing the Alfa come flying up the road, Enzo naturally thought it was his ace driver. Fearing that Varzi had missed the fuelling stop, Ferrari threw himself into the road in front of the Alfa, waving his arms frantically. Bonetto looked him straight in the eye without lifting his foot for a second and Enzo Ferrari found himself in a roadside ditch plastered with mud.

Bonetto's run did not last much longer, a tree taking care of the reshaping of his chassis.

In the meantime Varzi had made up 3 min. 38 secs. on Nuvolari and after Bologna he caught and passed his rival, who let him by with a shrug of his shoulders. Nuvolari was in trouble due to the tyres he was using which were unsuitable in the wet. After Florence however the road conditions improved and Nuvolari set about regaining on his rival. When Nuvolari caught him Varzi tucked in behind and, watching him like a hawk, never let him get away. In their battle the two of them overtook Tadini, and by Rome were only 1 minute behind the leader. At Terni, Nuvolari took advantage of a quick fuel stop to regain time, being only 2 min. 45 secs. behind but from Terni to Perugia he lost ground and was back to 3 minutes behind. Between Terni and Ancona, Varzi began to have trouble with a slipping clutch and Nuvolari, driving like a madman, reduced the interval to 20 secs. When he heard this, it spurred him on to even greater effort and from Ancona to Bologna he pulled out all the stops and had a lead over Varzi of 2 min. 49 secs. When Varzi stopped to refuel, Enzo Ferrari was waiting for him to give him the news; he also gave him the weather report and

Varzi made a quick decision. Four rain tyres were mounted on the wheels and the eight spark plugs were replaced for ones that would give better performance at high r p m for the fast section of the race that was coming up.

The stop dropped him to 4 min. 30 secs. behind Nuvolari, but for Varzi the race was already in the bag. The rain had started to fall in torrents and he knew the 'Mantovano' would be in difficulty. By the time they got to Venice, Varzi had an 8 second lead and as they went over the Laguna bridge, the two adversaries were side by side. Nuvolari waved Varzi on and settled back to make the best of his second place. Further behind, Louis Chiron displaced the tiring Tadini to take third and so bring up another Scuderia Ferrari triumph.

German opposition intensifies

1934 marked the appearance of the all-out German opposition in the shape of Mercedes Benz and Auto Union. Despite the advanced design of the German machinery, the year was nevertheless to be one of great success for the Scuderia Ferrari. Varzi won at Allessandria, Montenero, Tripoli, Nice, Penya Rhin and in the Targa Florio and was placed second at Biella, Avus, and in the Grand Prix of France. Louis Chiron was first at Casablanca, Marne and in the French Grand Prix, he came second at Monaco, Penya Rhin and Alessandria and third at Tripoli, the Eifelrennen and in the Grand Prix of France. Trossi won Biella and Vichy, being third at Nice and sharing third places in the French Grand Prix with Moll and the Italian with Comotti. The young Guy Moll won at Monaco for the Scuderia and was second at Montenero, Tripoli and Marne.

In the Grand Prix of Alessandria, won by Varzi, Nuvolari was all out to beat his adversary but sliding on a wet road went out of control, crashing and breaking a leg. Varzi was more than relieved to have his rival out of the way for the Grand Prix of Tripoli, and the Scuderia Ferrari entered a team made up of Varzi, Trossi, Chiron and Moll. The most feared rival of the Ferrari team was Taruffi who had taken the place of Nuvolari in the Maserati team, and who was at the wheel of the tremendously fast type V5 16-cylinder Maserati. At the start of the race it was

Taruffi who jumped into the lead, running at an average speed of over 124 m p h. He was followed by Varzi and Chiron with Alfas bored out to three litres but at the Mellaha corner Taruffi's brakes locked and he went careering off the road in the attempt to slow the monster down.

With Taruffi out and with Moll held up with a blown tyre, Chiron and Varzi decided to take things easy especially as both were suffering from slight clutch slippage. Guy Moll, who had been given a specially good engine by Enzo Ferrari, made up time fast on the two leaders. When Chiron had to slow as his oil pressure was dropping on the last lap, Moll went by him and sat on the tail of Varzi. On the last corner before the finishing lap Moll tried to cut in on the inside of Varzi's Alfa but Varzi was too old a hand at the game and cut him off nearly sending him off the road. Moll was furious and accused Varzi of deliberately trying to run him off. Enzo Ferrari put a stop to this quarrel and told Moll to behave himself and obey team orders in the future.

Moll was back in favour for the Avus race and Ferrari gave him a special streamlined car. The race also marked the return of Nuvolari who had had his car prepared so that he could drive it with only one foot as his other leg was still in plaster. Despite the appearance of the new 16-cylinder Auto Unions, Moll won the race with the streamlined car at 125 m p h.

The strategies of Louis Chiron

Ferrari realized that when the new German cars found reliability his Alfa Romeos would be completely outpaced. There was nothing he could do about it except run the cars for the rest of the season and have Jano plan something new for the future. For the French Grand Prix Chiron and Ferrari put their heads together. The German cars put up some very fast early practice times and although the top Scuderia Ferrari drivers thought they could equal them, Ferrari's decision was to run several seconds slower than they could do in order to get the Germans over-confident. At the start of the race Chiron jumped ahead and led the amazed Germans, he then fell back a little and suddenly got out in front again. The Germans had to push their machinery to the limits and the strategy worked out for all their cars blew up and the Scuderia Ferrari took the first three places with Chiron, Varzi and Trossi.

Chiron again played tricks with the Germans in the German Grand Prix. He set a very fast time in practice which the Germans could not equal and caused them to work all night to change axle ratios. The next time out he again went faster until finally the wily Neubauer, racing manager for Mercedes Benz, sent spies out all around the circuit only to find that Chiron had been cutting off the whole Harussel section by going up the steep test hill and consequently considerably shortening the circuit; Neubauer furiously had the short-cut blocked. Chiron was unable to get away with any tricks in the actual race but nevertheless finished third.

For 1935 the writing was on the wall. Fagioli was taken on by Mercedes Benz, Taruffi went to Bugatti and Nuvolari was finally back with the Scuderia Ferrari, a situation which caused Varzi to go over to Maserati and later to Auto Union.

Wolves in sheeps' clothing

In 1935 the Scuderia Ferrari was to triumph once again in the Mille Miglia. This time it was with the diminutive, square-jawed, Carlo Pintacuda, one of the few drivers who have won the Brescia classic more than once. Both Varzi and Pintacuda, when they presented themselves at the technical inspection, caused an uproar. Pintacuda arrived with nothing less than a Grand Prix Alfa Romeo, transformed slightly and equipped with mudguards and lights sufficient to meet the race regulations. Varzi did the same only he presented the latest type 3.7-litre supercharged Grand Prix Maserati similarly adapted. Of this type of Maserati there were only four models in existence, and the Alfa was unique, having had its engine bored out to 3 litres. Della Stufa, who was Pintacuda's co-driver, was so cramped in his makeshift seat that he had to run the whole race with one arm round Pintacuda's shoulder. Many people criticized these two entries, claiming that they were not in the spirit of the race which originated for series-built sports cars. The complaints were of no avail as the cars complied with the written regulations. Nevertheless the event was known as 'The race

of the two against the hundred.'

Varzi was quickly out of the picture, after only 50 km he began to have trouble with his Maserati and was forced to retire. Pintacuda ran like clockwork for the whole of the distance, coming in 38 minutes ahead of second place man Tadini and breaking Varzi's record of the previous year. During the 1935 season the Scuderia still had their fair share of success mainly due to the brilliance of Nuvolari. The 'Mantovano' won the German, Nice, Pau, Montenero, Biella and Turin Grands Prix, but there was a noticeable absence of Grand Epreuve wins. Nuvolari also took second at Masaryk and shared his second place in the Italian Grand Prix with Dreyfus. Dreyfus won the French Grand Prix and was placed second at Monaco and Pau. Brivio won the Targa Florio, took seconds at Montenero and Turin, and thirds at Monaco and Pescara. Chiron had to be content with second places at the Avus, Grand Prix de France and the Targa Florio, and sharing a second place at Nice with Dreyfus. Chiron scored a third at Masaryk, Trossi a third at Montenero and Pintacuda a third at the Turin Grand Prix.

For the Coppa Acerbo at Pescara, the Scuderia Ferrari entered Varzi, Moll, Chiron and Ghersi, as Nuvolari had decided to run for Maserati in this event. Mercedes entered Fagioli, Caracciola and Henne; Auto Union had Stuck and Sebastian whilst the Maserati factory entered Nuvolari and Zehender.

In the rain it looked as if the Italian cars might have an advantage over the Germans, but on the first lap it was Caracciola ahead of Stuck who was in turn leading Varzi. On the third lap Varzi set a new lap record and passed Stuck who was shortly afterwards passed by the Mercedes of Fagioli. Varzi's efforts did not last long for on the fourth lap he was forced to change a rear tyre and then found that he had gearbox trouble. This left three German cars leading. With Nuvolari in the first Italian car over 1 minute behind the Germans, Enzo Ferrari decided to throw Guy Moll into the battle. He also decided to call in Ghersi and have Varsi take over the car. When Varzi restarted he was over 5 minutes behind the leader, Caracciola. Shortly afterwards Stuck retired with engine troubles and Nuvolari made a stop to repair a broken oil

(Top) Ferrari on a CMN, during 1919 Targa Florio. He ran 1st in his class
(Middle Left) Enzo Ferrari in an Alfa Romeo RL 3000 at Ravenna 1923. He set the fastest lap and it was at this race that he met the father of Francesco Baracca whose symbol has been carried by the Scuderia ever since
(Middle Right) Ferrari and Siena in an Alfa Romeo 6 cyl RL/SS at Pescara, Coppa Acerbo July 1924
(Bottom) Targa Florio 1920. Sivocci (21), Ferrari (20) and Campari (34)

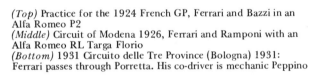
(Top) Practice for the 1924 French GP, Ferrari and Bazzi in an
Alfa Romeo P2
(Middle) Circuit of Modena 1926, Ferrari and Ramponi with an
Alfa Romeo RL Targa Florio
(Bottom) 1931 Circuito delle Tre Province (Bologna) 1931:
Ferrari passes through Porretta. His co-driver is mechanic Peppino

(*Top*) Ferrari after winning the 1932 Bobbio-Penice Race with Vallisi in an Alfa Romeo 1750

(*Bottom*) 1st in class, Circuit of Modena 1927. Ferrari and his 1500-cc 6 cyl Twin Cam Alfa Romeo. Giulio Ramponi is standing by the cockpit

(Top) Cuneo-Colle della Maddalena 1930. Left to right: Luigi Arcangeli, Tazio Nuvolari on car and Enzo Ferrari
(Middle) The first building of Scuderia Ferrari at viale Trento Trieste, Modena 1929
(Bottom) The Alfa Bimotore Record Breaker with Nuvolari driving. The car was built by the Scuderia Ferrari workshops in Modena

LA SCUDERIA FERRARI

MODENA

Pubblicazione Illustrata

Conto Corrente Postale

19 Maggio XIV

(Top Left) Later Scuderia Ferrari changed the format. Here it is just before the Second World War

(Top Right) 1934 refuelling at the Coppa Acerbo. Note Enzo Ferrari in the background

(Bottom) 1933 The Scuderia Ferrari raced this 4.5 litre Duesenberg. It was driven by Trossi and was duelling for the lead when the engine blew up, in the ill fated Monza GP in which Campari, Borzacchini and Czaikowski were killed. Whitney Straight took it to England at the end of 1933. The car is in Brooklands guise in this photograph

(*Top*) 1935 Coppa Acerbo, Nuvolari driving
(*Middle*) 1934 French Grand Prix. Louis Chiron in the 1934 - 1935
3.2 litre P3 Alfa Romeo. This car won against the might of Mercedes
and Auto Union. Scuderia Ferrari cars came second and third
(*Bottom*) The 'Flying Fox' Louis Chiron in a 1934 P3 Alfa Romeo

(*Top Left*) Achille Varzi at the wheel of an Alfa Romeo in front of the Scuderia Ferrari, Modena
(*Top Right*) In 1935 Rene Dreyfus won the French GP and was placed 2nd in the Monaco GP for Scuderia Ferrari
(*Bottom*) Ferrari's first Formula 1 Grand Prix win. 1948 Gran Premio d'Italia, Sommer (Ferrari 28) and Villoresi (Maserati 40)

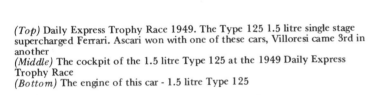

(*Top*) Daily Express Trophy Race 1949. The Type 125 1.5 litre single stage supercharged Ferrari. Ascari won with one of these cars, Villoresi came 3rd in another
(*Middle*) The cockpit of the 1.5 litre Type 125 at the 1949 Daily Express Trophy Race
(*Bottom*) The engine of this car - 1.5 litre Type 125

tube. The times down the Montesilvano straight gave some idea of the differences in speed between the German and Italian cars, Caracciola and Henne with their Mercedes recorded 181 m p h, Chiron's Alfa 170 and Nuvolari's Maserati 155 m p h Varzi in his attempt to catch up set one lap record after the other, Caracciola still in the lead damaged his car when he went off the road and Fagioli had to stop for fuel, so Moll found himself in the lead. Varzi by now was only 25 secs. behind Henne. Chiron came into the pits to change a plug and whilst the car was being refuelled, a mechanic tested the plugs with a screwdriver and a resulting spark set fire to the car; Chiron threw himself out of the blaze to extinguish his flaming overalls and it took over ten minutes to control the fire. Moll was still leading 32 seconds ahead of Henne who was in turn followed by Varzi with Fagioli 62 seconds behind. The following lap Moll had troubles and slowed and Varzi took the lead having passed Henne. Fagioli also passed Henne but Varzi was out of luck again, a burst tyre dropped him back leaving Fagioli to lead Moll by 50 seconds. Moll tried everything he knew and set a lap record which pulled him up to 37 seconds behind Fagioli. The next lap however tragedy struck. Moll, in the act of lapping Henne, tried to pass him on the Montesilvano straight and crashed to his death thus depriving the Scuderia Ferrari of its most promising driver.

Nuvolari returns

For the German Grand Prix Nuvolari returned to the Scuderia Ferrari, and Ferrari fielded a team of cars bored out to 3.2-litres driven by Nuvolari, Chiron, Brivio and Balestrero. The task seemed hopeless against the might of the two German organizations. Mercedes fielded Caracciola, Fagioli, Lang, Von Brauchitsch and Geyer, whilst Auto Union had Rosemeyer, Varzi, Stuck and Pietsch. Caracciola with four victories on the Nurburgring already behind him, took the lead at once but Nuvolari kept the Alfa right on the heels of the Mercedes. Behind Nuvolari came Fagioli, Rosemeyer, Von Brauchitsh and Chiron. Nuvolari however had no illusions and dropped back in the hope that Rosemeyer and Caracciola would battle it out

and eventually retire. After six laps three Mercedes were leading, Caracciola, Fagioli and Von Brauchitsch; Rosemeyer was the only Auto Union driver left and was running behind the rival organization's cars. As the rain stopped Nuvolari decided to make his attack and went by one after another of his opponents. On the 11th lap he stopped for fuel just about the same time as Von Brauchitsch and Rosemeyer, and it seemed that the time consumed in the stop would decide the race. The Scuderia Ferrari's fuelling hose broke and it seemed all was lost, Nuvolari's stop had taken 30 seconds longer than Rosemeyer's and 40 longer than that of Von Brauchitsch. Nuvolari did not give up and with a tremendous effort overtook Rosemeyer on the next lap; he then set about catching Von Brauchitsch, setting a new record every lap. The pace was too hot for the Mercedes' tyres to last out, and when two laps from the finish Nuvolari was 32 seconds behind, Neubauer fearing excessive tyre wear signalled Von Brauchitsch to slow down. The German's tyres were on the canvas, yet all was still set to play the German anthem. But Brauchitsch had paid the penalty, his tyre had blown in the Karussel. It was a moment of great triumph for Nuvolari and Enzo Ferrari.

Bazzi's Bimotore

The Bimotore was conceived by Luigi Bazzi, one of the best technicians in the history of the racing game. He joined Alfa Romeo in 1922 after a term in Fiat's experimental department and took over as head of Alfa Romeo's racing department. In 1933, he joined Scuderia Ferrari and became the right-hand man to Enzo Ferrari.

After the traditional year-end banquet of the Scuderia Ferrari on 16th December 1934 at Modena, there was a quick meeting of Ferrari's closest collaborators. The purpose was to examine the international situation in automobile racing. At this meeting Bazzi came up with the suggestion that a powerful car could be built in an extremely short time utilizing the coupling of two engines, thus the 'Bimotore' concept was born.

Enzo Ferrari put the idea before the directors of Alfa, who approved the project and assigned one of their designers, Arnaldo Roselli, to develop the design and carry out the drawings necessary for construction.

The idea of having one engine in the front and one in the rear of the car with the clutch, gearbox, transmission and driving position between them was certainly an ingenious layout. Bazzi was able to obtain favourable weight distribution and utilized units completely tested by Alfa Romeo. The resultant car was powerful and had an adequately small frontal area.

The 'Bimotore' used two of the famous 'Monoposto' Alfa Romeo Tipo B engines with their capacity increased to 3165-cc. Each engine gave 270 b h p at 5,400 r p m. The specific output of these engines was extremely high for the time at 85 b h p per litre, about 10 b h p/litre higher than the Auto Union record engine of 1934 which had a maximum of 375 b h p from its five litres.

The Tipo B engine was a classic eight-cylinder inline with the cylinders made up of two aluminium-alloy groups with steel forced-in liners. The crankshaft was also in two pieces joined at the centre by a flange with the cam drive gears located in the central position. Also located at this point were the takeoffs for the superchargers and other auxiliaries such as magnetos, water pump and oil pumps. The crankshaft was counterweighted, and it was supported on 10 bearings. Valve actuation was by means of twin overhead camshafts. The cams transmitted through tappets directly to the valves. On the left hand side of the engine, centrally driven, were the two Roots-type superchargers and the two vertical Weber carburetters. On the right side were located the gear pumps for pressure and scavenge of the oil, the water pump and the Bosch magneto. On the same side were the exhausts, the water and the oil tubing.

Two 'Bimotores' were built. The first, driven by Nuvolari, had the two 3165-cc eight-cylinder engines, for a total capacity of 6330-cc. Bore and stroke were 71 x 100 mm and each engine put out 270 b h p at 5400 r p m for a total of 540 b h p. The second car driven by Chiron, had two 2905-cc eight-cylinder engines (bore and stroke 68 x 100 mm) each rated at 260 b h p at 5,400 r p m giving a total of 520 b h p from 5810-cc.

The Transmission system

The clutch and gearbox were mounted in unit on the front engine. The hub of the clutch and the shaft of the gearbox were constructed to allow the shaft linking the two engines to pass through it. The clutch was of the dry type with steel and duralumin discs. The gearbox was a constant mesh three-speed unit with a reverse. The differential was placed behind the gearbox. At the tail of the gearbox, and behind the differential, was the point of junction for the two engines, which could be engaged or disengaged by a lever. This facilitated starting from cold or was used when drive from the front engine only was required. On the crankshaft flange of the rear engine there was a vibration damper.

The rear engine was situated behind the driver's seat and fixed to the chassis by twin transverse members. On these were attached two robust oscillating parallel arms. On these were the housings of the conical couplings that transmitted drive to the wheels. Each wheel, linked by a short halfshaft to the housing, could therefore oscillate as in the swing axle system. At the rear, the car was suspended on two semi-elliptic leaf springs attached to the oscillating independently-sprung wheels on the Dubonnet system.

Hydraulic drum brakes were mounted at all four wheels and there was a mechanical hand brake on the rears.

The cooling of the engines was by means of a front-mounted radiator. On the sides of the car were two interconnecting fuel tanks which were sufficient to give the car a range of 300 kilometers.

The body was in aluminium with duralumin bracing. A fin was incorporated in the headrest to assist in stabilizing the car at high speed.

The dimensions and weights of the car were as follows: Wheelbase 110.2 in.; front and rear track 54.3 in.; ground clearance 5 in.; height 54.7 in. Front tyres were 5.50 x 20, rears 6.50 x 21. Dry weight was 2205 lb and with fuel, oil and driver it weighed 2888 lb.

The prototype of the car was presented to the press on 9th April 1935 and the day after it was tested on the Brescia-Bergamo Autostrada by Attilio Marinoni, the Scuderia's chief tester.

Tyre troubles

Nuvolari also tested it at the same time and was able to immediately reveal the car's high performance. That afternoon the 'Bimotore' was taken to Monza where it checked out perfectly from a mechanical and road holding point of view. The car made its debut in the 9th Tripoli Grand Prix on 12th May 1935 with the participation of the two cars. The first was driven by Nuvolari who had the 6330-cc model, and the second by Louis Chiron who had the 5810-cc version of the car. During the race neither of the cars had mechanical trouble, but problems came from tyres (Nuvolari changed eight and Chiron changed six). This was caused by the weight handicap of the 'Bimotore' over the competition's lighter cars. The fastest lap of the winner, Caracciola, was 136.77 m p h, while Nuvolari's fastest lap was 133.78 m p h. The Bimotores finished in fourth and fifth places.

Fifteen days later, on 26th May, the two Bimotores were entered in the GP of the Avus in Germany. There were two elimination heats of 100 km. each and a final of 200 km. Fagioli's Mercedes took first overall in the final with Chiron's Bimotore in second place. Chiron crossed the finishing line with the tread of one of his tyres completely gone. Nuvolari was unable to run in the final as during the heat he had been forced to make a pit stop with a blown rear tyre. At the Avus there were no mechanical problems with either car.

After these results, Enzo Ferrari decided to attempt the breaking of some world speed records. To reduce weight, the side tanks were removed and substituted by a single small tank. The headrest and fin were also reduced in weight and size. To improve the aerodynamics of the car, aluminium discs were fitted on all wheels and, with a few other minor modifications, the total weight saved was 80 kg.

The record attempt was made on 15th June by Tazio Nuvolari on a section of the Firenze-Mare Autostrada. He was able to set two new international records; the flying kilometre at 199.92 m p h and the flying mile at 200.77 m p h and 304.50 metres at the average of 208.91 m p h. The records were previously held by Hans Stuck who had set them at Lucca in Italy on 15th February 1935.

One of the two Bimotores was sold in England in 1936 and in 1937 was raced by Austin Dobson. It was purchased in 1937 by Peter Aitken who converted it into a single-engined car. In this form it reappeared in several races in the immediate post war period.

Scuderia Ferrari 1936

For 1936 Ferrari made up his team of Nuvolari, Brivio, Tadini, Pintacuda and Farina. The Mille Miglia was again a triumph for the Scuderia with Brivio winning, Farina second, and Pintacuda third.

During the season Nuvolari won at Penya Rhin, Montenero, Hungary, Milan, and the Vanderbilt Cup. He took second place in the Eifelrennen and the Italian Grand Prix, Brivio was placed second in the Montenero race at Leghorn, and took third places in the German Grand Prix, Eifelrennen and Vanderbilt Cup.

Farina was 3rd at Penya Rhin and the Milan Grand Prix and Pintacuda took a second place at Tunis. The Scuderia Ferrari was winning less and less races. In the Tripoli Grand Prix it was Varzi again with the Auto Union, he passed his team mate Stuck on the last but one lap and finished 4 seconds ahead of the German. In this race the new 12-cylinder Alfa Romeo made its first appearance, it was 4106-cc and gave 380 b h p, the three new cars being given to Nuvolari, Brivio and Tadini whilst Pintacuda had an older model. The car had been built to meet the German challenge but from the beginning showed itself incapable of performing the task. Apart from the lack of speed, the cars were troubled with tyres as had been the Bimotores and it was left for Pintacuda to come in as the first Italian car behind the Germans. In all the Scuderia Ferrari had to change 30 tyres on their cars during the race. The Scuderia ran into trouble during practice when Nuvolari was badly bruised and suffered from a cracked vertebra. However he was quickly back on the scene and took the 12-cylinder Alfa to a victory at Penya Rhin beating Caracciola by three seconds. Later he also won in the Hungarian Grand Prix finishing ahead of Rosemeyer.

In the Vanderbilt Cup Nuvolari made no mistake, he dominated the race from start to finish lapping everyone except Wimille and Brivio. Farina who was for a long time in third place crashed against a protective barrier and was forced to retire. Brivio ran for a long time in second place but had a nine minute pit stop which let Wimille ahead but Nuvolari ended up 12 minutes ahead of the French champion and no less than 25 minutes ahead of Mauri Rose.

In 1938 things went from bad to worse. The saving grace was the Mille Miglia, won again this year by Pintacuda with a Scuderia Ferrari Alfa Romeo, Nuvolari won the Milan Grand Prix with Farina second and Brivio won the Turin Grand Prix with Farina second and Trossi third.

The 3 Litre Formula

The new Formula of 3-litres caused a big change in the Italian racing world. The public attendances at Monza had dropped from around the 70,000 mark to less than 20,000 due to the German superiority. Ugo Gobbato who had become the director of Alfa Romeo decided it was time to begin an all out effort to combat the Germans and consequently he decided to form 'Alfa Corsa', a new team to be run directly under the control of the Alfa Romeo factory. All the material belonging to the Scuderia Ferrari, including the new Type 308, an 8-cylinder three-litre, was transferred to Milan. Drivers taken on were Nuvolari, Farina, Sommer, Tadini, Pintacuda, Severi, Emilio Villoresi and Siena. Nuvolari was given the new three-litre to try out at Pau where he met opposition in the shape of Caracciola and Lang. During practice Nuvolari's car developed a fuel leak and the car burst into flames; Nuvolari saved himself by jumping out of the car. When he saw Enzo Ferrari he exclaimed "I don't want to race again, the fire frightened me too much. How can one protect oneself from it?" Nuvolari confirmed his decision later in Milan and took a trip to the USA. Tripoli was run without him and turned out to be yet another German triumph. The 12-cylinder Alfa Romeo could do no better than 4th place driven by Raymond Sommer.

The 1938 Mille Miglia saw the arrival of a new star on the scene. Clemente Biondetti with an Alfa Romeo won the event setting a new record that was not to be beaten until 1953, by Giannino Marzotto with a 4.1 Ferrari. During this edition of the Mille Miglia a Lancia driven by Bruzzo crashed into the crowd at Bologna and two days later the government declared that the Mille Miglia on public roads was finished.

After an abortive attempt to run the Mille Miglia from Tripoli to Torbruk the 1939 event was abandoned to take place in 1940 on a closed circuit Brescia, Cremona, Mantova, Brescia.

It was in this race that two new names came to the public view, one, a man, was Alberto Ascari, son of the famous Alfa Romeo driver Antonio Ascari, and the other, even more significant, a car by the name of Ferrari. Enzo Ferrari at last was independent and on the threshold of a new era in motor racing.

ENZO FERRARI had announced his three types of cars, the 125 Sport, 125 Competizione and 125 Gran Premio in the winter of 1946 - 47. When the Type 125 appeared it was an immediate success but there were no signs of the Gran Premio. There was a great deal of speculation, as Ferrari had indicated that he was returning to the International racing scene, after a long absence, and that the comeback would be with a revolutionary car bearing his own name. The public, however, had to wait until 1948 before they saw the first of these cars. Ferrari entered a full team in the Italian Grand Prix of that year which was held at Turin. His drivers were the well known aces Prince Bira, Raymond Sommer, and Nino Farina.

Everyone commented on the strange-looking cars, they were very small with a wheelbase of 7 ft 1 in. and a track of 3 ft 11 in., as opposed to the 158 Alfa Romeo's wheelbase and track of 8 ft 2 in. and 4 ft 5 in. Fifteen-inch wheels were used instead of the more usual seventeen-inch type and the cars looked rather ugly.

Colombo's engine design

This finally was the car designed by Gioacchino Colombo who had closeted himself with Enzo Ferrari for many months to produce something new in the world of motor racing. The Colombo-designed engine was remarkable for being the first car since 1907 to compete in Grands Epreuves with an engine having a larger bore than stroke. However, the engine was disappointing in one way. It had an exceptionally large piston area of 44 sq in. and 10,000 r p m was theoretically obtainable without exceeding 3,500 ft/min piston speed. In actual fact the maximum r p m attained with the engine proved to be no more than 7,500 r p m,

consequently the power output was no greater than that achieved by cars with less cylinders and lower piston area. As a result of this it was decided to concentrate on a particularly small and light chassis frame.

During practice for the Turin Grand Prix the Ferraris behaved themselves very well, Sommer being placed in the front row of the starting grid, Farina in the second row and Bira in the fifth row.

The race showed the potentialities of the new cars, Sommer in the pouring rain took on the Alfa Romeos and the Maseratis. He lay a close second behind Wimille on the latest Alfa Romeo and had a tremendous battle with Villoresi's latest Maserati; Farina followed up strongly in 4th place and Bira lay just behind Farina. An altogether satisfactory beginning with a brand-new car. Sommer only lost his second place to Villoresi by a car's length and it was rather obvious that the Maserati had been forced over its limits.

The next outing of the 125 Gran Premio was at the Garda races where Farina took the car to a comfortable win.

The 1948 racing season ended rather badly for Ferrari when he entered two cars for the Monza Grand Prix. Both cars started in the second row, driven by Farina and Sommer. Although the cars performed well while they were running, it was not Ferrari's day as Sommer had to fall out when in third place, his retirement being caused by illness. Farina was able to hold on to fourth place until his transmission gave out.

The main engine casting of these cars was in light alloy and contained supports for a seven bearing crankshaft. This casting contained the water jackets for the twelve inserted wet liners which were grouped in two banks of six at an included angle of 60 degrees. These liners had a flange at their base, to provide a water seal, and were closed at their top by a siluminum light-alloy cylinder head, there being one camshaft per bank. Each combustion chamber contained two valves inclined to an included angle of 60 degrees. Inlet valve diameter was 1.26 in. and exhaust valve diameter 1.18 in.

Each valve was closed by a pair of hairpin valve springs lying in a fore and aft plane and actuated by a rocker arm from the single overhead camshaft centrally mounted. The spark plugs were inserted into the inlet side of the head. A single Weber, Type 40DO 3/C carburetter fed the single Roots-type supercharger which ran at 1.22 times engine speed, the supercharger discharging into a central manifold. The camshafts were chain driven, and also provided drive for the twin magnetos.

Slightly domed pistons gave a compression ratio of 6.5 : 1. The connecting rods were placed side by side on a crank pin measuring 1.77 in. diameter. The division of the big ends was angled so that the upper half of the rod might be withdrawn upwards through the cylinder bores. The crankshaft was heavily counterweighted and a gear-type pump, mounted at the front of the engine, fed oil into the crankshaft and through internal passages to the mains and the big ends.

The running gear and suspension

A five-speed gearbox was in unit with the clutch housing, all the gears being in constant mesh and of the helical-pinion type.

An open propeller shaft transmitted drive to a fixed bevel box and an intermediate gear was used so that the propeller-shaft line was considerably below the centre line of the halfshafts.

A transverse spring having a master leaf 38 in. long was mounted beneath the frame in front and connected through levers to a system of unequal length wishbones. Damping was provided by the use of Houdaille vane-type shock absorbers.

The swing-axle principle was employed for the rear suspension so that exposed halfshafts were fitted with inboard joints only, whilst a single radius arm was inclined inwards from the hub to a pivot on the frame. A single transverse leaf spring ran behind and was mounted below the halfshafts, the length of the master leaf being 36 in. The first models of the 125 Gran Premio employed a system of torsion bars for the rear suspension, this however was changed to the above system of suspension. On the final models this was again changed with the leaf spring being mounted high. The Ferraris' last appearance that season was at the Barcelona Grand Prix where Bira and Farina made up the team with a Spanish driver Pola. Bira showed the potentialities of the car by leading the race but all three cars retired eventually with mechanical troubles.

The 'Thinwall Specials'

During the winter Ferrari set about finding more reliability for the cars and improving the handling characteristics which were not of a very high order. He sold two of the first cars to private owners, both English, one to Peter Whitehead and the other to Tony Vandervell, the latter's car becoming the first of the series of well-known 'Thinwall Specials.'

Also during the winter there had been a big change at Ferrari. Enzo Ferrari had for some time been negotiating with the two Maserati aces, Ascari and Villoresi, and was successful in obtaining their services for the 1949 season.

The factory began their Formula 1 season with a team of two of the modified cars at Spa for the Belgian Grand Prix. The cars were very fast but only managed 2nd and 3rd places, an unsupercharged Talbot winning because of better fuel consumption, the Ferraris having to stop to refuel. It was a lesson which Ferrari kept in the back of his mind and used to good effect at a later date. The team of Ascari and Villoresi next appeared at the Swiss Grand Prix where the cars were running even better than before and the team was rewarded with 1st and 2nd places. At Rheims only Villoresi was present with a works car but did not last long. Villoresi made up for the failure in the Rheims race with a victory at Zandvoort, Ascari breaking a stub axle on his car.

Ascari and Villoresi then took the cars to Silverstone for the *Daily Express* meeting where there was a fierce battle with Farina's Maserati which ended when Farina collected a straw bale just as he was passing Ascari who won the race with Villoresi third. Farina and his Maserati renewed the Silverstone battle at Lausanne where the Ferrari factory was represented by Ascari and Cortese, the latter having temporarily replaced Villoresi. This time Farina had the upper hand and Ascari finished 2nd, Cortese could not do better than 4th.

The Type 125 Two-stage

Setting a fashion for the future, Ferrari and Colombo were planning something new for the Italian Grand Prix at Monza. It was rather obvious that Ascari and Villoresi were hard pressed to deal with the rapid Maserati of Farina so everyone expected the single-stage supercharged Ferrari to be fitted with a two-stage layout, it was even rumoured that Ferrari would go immediately to a three-stage system. No one was, however, quite prepared for the almost completely new car that appeared for practice. A two-stage layout was used with two Roots-type blowers mounted one above the other in front of the block, the top blower feeding the usual Ferrari intake manifold running in the V of the two heads. The big surprise was the twin overhead camshaft per bank layout being gear driven instead of chain as on the earlier engine. Single ignition per cylinder was employed, the plugs being fed by magnetos. The engine, however, remained the same basic Colombo layout, insofar as the block, crankshaft and connecting rod design was concerned.

The chassis, while based on the earlier model, was built specially for the car and the wheelbase was increased from 7 ft 1 in. to 7 ft 10 in. whilst the track underwent a change from 3 ft 11 in. to 4 ft 2½ in. Although the suspension members were somewhat modified the system of double wishbones with single transverse leaf spring coupled to the top wishbone by a tubular link was retained. At the rear, swing axles were used as on the earlier model and the transverse leaf spring was mounted above the axle as had been done on the last of the single-stage models. Modified two-leading-shoe drum brakes were used, and the car had much lower and cleaner lines than its predecessor. The 1498-cc engine had a compression ratio of 6.5 : 1 with an output of 300 b h p at 7500 r p m; this was later increased to 315 b h p at 7800 r p m on a further development of this type which used a De Dion rear axle layout. The 5-speed and reverse gearbox was still in unit with the engine whereas on the later De Dion type it employed only 4 speeds and reverse in a gearbox/differential unit on the rear axle.

When the De Dion model was introduced it was again decided to make chassis alterations. The wheelbase was shortened again from 7 ft 10 in. to 7 ft 8 in. but the track remained the same. The De Dion rear axle was used in conjunction with a transverse leaf spring and the De Dion tube was located by a roller running in a vertical guide on the rear frame cross member, with a bronze pad in a guide on the differential casing. A ZF differential assembly was also used and parallel radius rods ran forward to the chassis frame from the hub carriers.

Two of the two-stage supercharged cars appeared for the Grand Prix of Italy together with the two single stage cars. The team this time was made up of Ascari, Villoresi, Bonetto and Sommer, the former two had the two stage cars and the latter the older models. Ascari had no trouble in setting the pace and led the race from start to finish. Villoresi had less luck going out with a broken gearbox. Of the older cars Sommer struggled around to take 5th place whilst Bonetto, despite or because of some spirited driving, blew up his car. During the season the factory team was backed up, in European races, by Peter Whitehead's privately owned car which, after it had undergone modification to the rear springing, turned out to be much to Whitehead's liking, from the handling point of view, and he had a certain amount of success with it in various races. His most notable performance being in the French Grand Prix where he set the lap record but was robbed of an apparently certain win in the last few laps when the gearbox gave out; nevertheless he managed a creditable 3rd position. The Vandervell car after its crash at Silverstone was not seen again during the season.

The 1950 Season

For the 1950 season Ferrari was already making his plans for an attack on the Alfa Romeo supremacy with an unsupercharged design but for the first part of the season the supercharged models had to be the team's mainstay. At Pau the first race of the 1950 season, Villoresi and Sommer made up the team with the older single stage cars. The results were satisfactory and Villoresi finished a comfortable 2nd with Sommer an unhappier 4th.

The big encounter between Ferrari and Alfa Romeo came at the San Remo Grand Prix. Ferrari naturally fielded the strongest team possible, Ascari and Villoresi with the two stage cars and Sommer, Serafini and Vallone with the single stage machines. It was immediately clear that even the new Ferraris were no match for the rejuvenated 158 Alfa Romeos and Villoresi did well to finish 2nd after Ascari had his engine seize.

The next appearance of the team was at Monaco with Ascari and Villoresi in the new cars and Sommer driving a single stage. On the first lap however Farina's Alfa spun, coming out of the tunnel, on some sea water that had come over the wall and a fantastic multiple collision resulted. Only Fangio amongst the Alfas got through unscathed, Ascari and Villoresi were delayed in the mix up and never saw Fangio again; nevertheless Ascari was placed 2nd but Villoresi retired with rear axle trouble.

The short chassis De Dion axle car made its first appearance in the Swiss Grand Prix, the car being driven by Villoresi. However both Ascari and Villoresi retired early on in the race, Ascari with engine failure, and Villoresi with axle breakage.

At the Belgian Grand Prix only Villoresi appeared with a supercharged car for the team as Enzo Ferrari was already beginning his experiments with his unsupercharged designs. Villoresi had the swing axle car used by Ascari at the Swiss Grand Prix and placed it 6th, behind teammate Ascari on the new unblown 3.3-litre. This was the end of the 1500-cc supercharged car as far as Ferrari was concerned. One two stage car was sold to Vandervell and it made an appearance at Silverstone with Ascari driving but it went very poorly and Ascari spun off the road. The car disappeared from the scene as quickly as had the first 'Thinwall Special.'

Peter Whitehead had in the meantime been supporting the team again to the best of his ability and put up some excellent performances, his best results being a 3rd place at Silverstone and a win in the Ulster Trophy. However, as the Italian Grand Prix at Monza approached, it was becoming clear that Ferrari had lost all interest in his supercharged models and was putting all his efforts into producing the unsupercharged 4.5-litre car.

When the 4.5 Ferrari took the lead from Farina's Alfa in the Italian Grand Prix, the supercharged Ferraris were already a memory of the past.

CHAPTER FOUR

The unsupercharged Formula 1 cars

ENZO FERRARI spent some time in the winter of 1949, weighing up the pros and cons of Formula 1 racing. Although his new 12-cylinder two-stage supercharged car showed great promise, he was not exactly convinced that it was the answer to the Alfa Romeos. He had for some time been watching the big French Talbots giving him trouble as they would run through the whole of the Grand Prix distance without refuelling, whereas his cars always had to stop due to their high consumption. The Talbot was repeatedly doing well against much more powerful cars, so, if a really efficient unsupercharged engine were built, taking advantage of the 4.5-litre maximum, and that could run through a race without refuelling, it would without a doubt become a match for the highly tuned Alfa Romeos. The Alfas suffered from a tremendously high fuel consumption which would always force them to stop and here Ferrari was to have the edge.

Ferrari engages Lampredi

Ferrari on the recommendation of Professor Carlo Ruini of the Le Reggiane aircraft factory hired Aurelio Lampredi for his design department in September 1946. At that time Lampredi was 29 years old and was given the title of junior designer. Lampredi was not too happy with Ferrari and when an offer came six months later to join Isotta Fraschini to redesign that company's new rear-engined Monterosa, he took the opportunity and left Ferrari.

Despite their new designs Isotta were headed fast for financial troubles and Enzo Ferrari fully appreciative of his former employee's talents offered him a new contract at much better terms. Ferrari had conceived the 12-cylinder Type 125 Grand Prix car with the consultation service of Ing. Gioacchino Colombo and one of Lampredi's first tasks was to translate the studies into drawings.

His next major job was to produce a Formula 2 car on the basis of the 1.5-litre supercharged version. Lampredi retained the Colombo-type engine and designed a completely new chassis with rear-mounted gearbox, limited-slip differential and De Dion layout that was to be the standard for Grand Prix chassis design for a number of years to come.

Ferrari was looking for someone to replace Colombo as designer and it took him a while to realize that he already had a first class designer in Lampredi right under his nose.

Lampredi tried to convince Ferrari to go all out with the supercharged concept in Formula 1 but Ferrari was adamant and insisted on the unsupercharged approach. Lampredi consequently set about designing the 'Lampredi type' 12-cylinder Ferrari engine beginning with the 3.3-litre Type 275, which made an encouraging debut in the Belgian Grand Prix at Spa in 1950 where Ascari placed 5th.

Lampredi was born at Livorno on the 16th June 1917 and was the son of a machine shop superintendent. He received his technical education at Livorno and Fribourg in Switzerland. He progressed from a beginning as a draftsman at Livorno Naval shipyards to working in the engineering department of Piaggio's aircraft engine department before moving to Carrara. There he worked with a steel manufacturer designing heavy industrial tooling. From there he moved to the Le Reggiane company at Reggio Emilia, a stone's throw from Modena. At Le Reggiane he worked on such exotic projects as an 18-cylinder inverted W engine with many interesting features such as three-stage supercharging, direct fuel injection and four valves per cylinder. Another of the projects that he was involved in was an H 24 fuel-injected engine. All this esoteric work prepared him well for his future position with Ferrari and it was at Le Reggiane that he came into contact with Professor Ruini who was to recommend him to Ferrari.

Successor to Colombo

Colombo having left Ferrari, Lampredi took over and immediately set to work on an unsupercharged design, the whole thing being kept very quiet. It was therefore a great surprise to everyone when at Spa in 1950 a 3.3-litre 12-cylinder unsupercharged car made its appearance driven by Ascari. This gave everyone an indication where Ferrari was heading, the car being an interim model that later was developed to a 4.1-litre and finally the full 4.5-litre.

At Spa the car was not particularly fast being some 12 seconds slower than the Alfa Romeos and 2 seconds slower than the fastest Talbot. At the Geneva Grand Prix in July of the same year the capacity of the 3.3-litre car was raised to 4.1-litres, this time being only 2 seconds a lap slower than the Alfa Romeos and considerably faster than the Talbots. Finally for the Italian Grand Prix the 4.5-litre appeared.

4.5 litre V-12

Lampredi in designing the 4.5-litre made full use of the information gained from the Colombo designed single-cam V12 and the layout of the new engines was basically similar to the smaller 1.5 and 2-litre designs a common feature being that a larger bore than stroke was used. The crankcase of the Lampredi types was split on the centre line of the crankshaft. As some difficulty had been experienced with the seals used on the detachable heads of the 1500-cc types, the bigger engine was given a threaded recess, machined around the combustion space, into which the cylinder liner was screwed. As a result each head with the liners and water jacket could be bolted to the crankcase with only one joint at the base of the liner away from the combustion area. Sealing at the base consisted of two O rings around each liner, near their bottom ends.

The two cylinder heads were light-alloy castings with inserted valve seats and two valves per cylinder, inclined at an included angle of 60 degrees. The diameter of the inlet valve was 1.625 in. and the exhaust valve 1.465 in.

Each valve was closed by twin hairpin-type springs having ten effective coils (instead of Colombo's 8) of 1.26 in. in diameter and a wire thickness of 0·157 in. The crankshaft ran in 7 Vandervell bearings. This type of bearing was first used experimentally on the Type 125 and 166 engines. The results of the experiments showed that this type of bearing gave a noticeable improvement in mechanical efficiency as well as having greater length of life and reliability. The front end of the crankshaft provided a drive for a roller chain which transmitted to the camshafts, there being one shaft per bank of cylinders.

Vandervell bearings were also used for the big ends which were 1.73 in. diameter. The Borgo light-alloy pistons were steeply domed and gave, by use of different crowns, compression ratios running from 11:1 to 14.5:1. Gudgeon pins attached them to H-section connecting rods which were connected on the crankpins to lie side by side. Lampredi immediately adopted connecting rods whose caps were split horizontally instead of the angled Colombo design. This was partly due to the fact that there was no possibility of withdrawing the piston/rod assembly upward through the block.

The two banks of cylinders were at an included angle of 60 degrees and the firing order was 1, 7, 5, 11, 3, 9, 6, 12, 2, 8, 4, 10. On the 3.3-litre the 4.1-litre and the first 4.5-litres, ignition was by one plug per cylinder, but the final models employed two plugs per cylinder. On the single-ignition types two Marelli magnetos mounted vertically at the back of the block were used but the twin-ignition types had two aircraft-type magnetos mounted horizontally at the front of the engine.

The single-ignition engine gave about 330 b h p at 6500 r p m but in its final form for European racing the twin ignition engine had the output raised to 380 b h p at 7500 r p m whilst the Indianapolis derivative of the twin ignition car again had its output raised to 430 b h p at 7500 r p m.

Carburetters and lubrication

On the earlier versions three downdraught Weber 40 DCF carburetters were used each carburetter being of the twin-choke type. Later on the Indianapolis cars and on the special 4.5 that appeared at Albi and Buenos Aires three four-choke Weber 40 IF 4/C carburetters were fitted giving the effect of one carburetter per cylinder. The carburetters received air from an external scoop let into the top of the bonnet. The carburetters themselves were fed by two Fimac pumps, one situated on the right hand frame member below the driver's seat and driven by a belt from the propeller shaft, drawing from the rear mounted tank, the other fitted on the engine and driven from the front of the right hand camshaft. Lubrication was by wet sump with an external oil radiator, there being an oil pump of the gear type transversely mounted at the nose of the crankcase. Delivery from the pump was partially through the oil radiator with a thermostat preventing delivery to the radiator core until the oil reached a certain temperature. There was also a spring-loaded relief valve from the exit so that in fact the oil cooling system was under a very low pressure. Oil was delivered to the main bearings through a gallery pipe bolted to the main bearing caps. From this there were branches to each of the seven main bearings. The crank pins were cross drilled and the sump contained two gallons of oil.

The transmission

Power was transmitted through a metallic multi-disc clutch and from there was carried by means of the propeller shaft to the gearbox/differential unit at the rear axle. (The prototype 3.3-litre had the gearbox in unit with the engine as a normal swing-axle long chassis was used having been derived from the earlier Formula 2 type frame.) Two spur gears were used for the final drive which enabled a low entry line for the propeller shaft into the four-speed gearbox. The gearbox/differential unit was split lengthwise at its centre and a wide range of final and indirect ratios was provided. Nevertheless with this split housing, a considerable amount of time was necessary to change axle ratios. Drive to the wheels was by means of two universal-jointed halfshafts and ample provision was made for

lubrication of the gearbox/differential unit. Radius arms were in pairs lying parallel one above the other to take engine torque and brake reaction, the wheel position being governed by a De Dion tube. It was controlled by a fixture on the front side of the tube in a slot on the back of the gearbox/differential housing; this was coupled with a roller on the back edge of the tube which engaged with a slot fixed to a tubular arch extending between the rear ends of the side tubes of the frame. The suspension was effected by a single transverse leaf spring. At the front there was a transverse leaf spring which connected to the bottom link of the wishbone layout. Both front and back springs were of similar construction with six leaves apiece having a width of 1.77 in., and damping all round was by means of Houdaille shockabsorbers. The steering box was located on the off side part of the front cross member, it was a normal worm and wheel type with 1 7/8 turns from lock to lock. An articulated steering column connected the box with the steering wheel. A conventional 3-piece track rod was used, a heavy drop arm pivoting round the left hand side of the cross member with a fixed track rod joining it to the steering arm. Short swinging arms were connected to the steering pivots. The brake drums were equipped with vents on their surface and were heavily finned on their periphery; their mounting was such that they projected into the airstream inboard of the wheel to ensure maximum cooling effect. They were of the two leading shoe type which have a central guiding member to eliminate any servo shoe effect. The front and rear brakes were operated by separate master cylinders.

The Indianapolis cars

The frame was made up of two parallel side members of oval tubular structure. On the first cars these were 4.7 in. deep and 2.25 in. wide; on the Indianapolis cars for 1952 these dimensions were increased but on the special model for the 1953 Indy, the dimensions were much reduced as space frame principles were employed. A round, 3 in. diameter tube formed the cross bracing behind the clutch housing, the front bracing being taken care of by a built-up plate which also acted as a locating member for the suspension units, a third cross brace was provided by a built-up cross piece behind the halfshafts. From the time of the introduction of the 4.5-litre the body shape had been altered several times.

The prototype 3.3-litre had a wheelbase of 7 ft 10 in. which was reduced to 7 ft 6 in. for the 4.1 and 4.5 models, however for the Indianapolis cars the wheelbase was again increased to 7 ft 8 in. with a wider track of 4 ft 3½ in. front and 4 ft 3 in. rear as opposed to the 4 ft 2 in. front and 4 ft 0 in. rear on the earlier 4.5 types.

When the prototype 3.3-litre car first appeared at Spa the unsupercharged engine was fitted into a swing-axle long-wheelbase chassis. Ascari drove the car into 4th place staying ahead of Villoresi in the two-stage supercharged model. The car appeared again for the Grand Prix of Rheims where it practised with the team drivers; however the circuit was considered too fast for the car and it was withdrawn before the race. Two cars appeared for the Grand Prix des Nations at Geneva, one was the 3.3-litre but the other was already of 4.1-litres capacity. Both Ascari and Villoresi made a great impression during practice and took 2nd and 3rd places on the front row of the starting line up. The cars had now been fitted with the 7 ft 6 in. De Dion chassis and in the race Ascari went into the lead. Of the Alfa Romeo team only Fangio got by Ascari. Villoresi unfortunately had a bad crash whilst lying 5th with only seven laps to go, whilst Ascari was clinging tenaciously to Fangio having lost only some 30 seconds in 50 laps. Just after Villoresi's crash Ascari was in trouble with water coming from one of his exhaust pipes, so Alfa Romeo were left a clear field. From then on Ferrari abandoned all work on the two-stage supercharged cars and one of them was sold. The Ferrari team disappeared from the scene for a few weeks and there was feverish activity to prepare for the all important race at Monza.

The Italian Grand Prix 1950

For the practice period of the Italian Grand Prix two new cars both 4.5-litres appeared on the scene to be driven by Ascari and Serafini. In practice Ascari unofficially broke the lap record and Alfa Romeo were extremely worried despite the fact that they had done some high pressure work themselves to increase the output of their engines. This however was only achieved at the expense of fuel consumption, as the engine also required a great deal of alcohol in the fuel to assist in internal cooling.

The pace at the start of the event was terrific, Ascari really showed that the new car could go and began a tremendous battle with the Alfa Romeos, passing into the lead for two laps. At the end of the 22nd lap, however, the Ferrari disappeared much to the joy of the Alfa team. It was not the end of the story; Serafini, who had been running in 6th place, came in for a change of tyres and Ascari took over. Driving as only Ascari could, he worked his way back into 2nd place which he kept until the end of the race. The 4.5 Ferrari demonstrated very effectively that at last here was an unsupercharged car that could comfortably match the speed of the 1500-cc supercharged Alfa Romeo, so long dominator of the Grand Prix world.

For the final race of the European season at Barcelona Alfa Romeo were absent, already having won the world championship. Ferrari turned out three cars for this event. Two 4.5-litres for Ascari and Serafini, and the 4.1-litre Geneva car for Taruffi. The three cars were in the lead immediately and finished the race in the order of Ascari, Serafini and Taruffi.

Although at the end of the 1950 season the Alfa Romeos were still unbeaten, it had been a close thing and the future looked bright for Ferrari in 1951. To him it was a friendly rivalry but nevertheless a serious affair. He was pitting a team of cars of his own manufacture against Alfa Romeo whose cars had been designed in the offices of the Scuderia Ferrari at Modena and he was against an organization that he himself had spent many years perfecting.

Preparations for 1951

The winter was spent hard at work sorting out minor problems and further increasing the output of the cars. A twin-ignition cylinder head was being worked on to give even more horse power as Ferrari knew full well that Alfa Romeo would not be resting on their laurels. He knew what the possibilities were of increasing the performance of the 158 Alfa Romeo and decided that it would not be a foregone conclusion that the 4.5-litre cars would beat their supercharged rivals with any great ease, so the maximum effort went into the production of the 1951 version of his car.

At the beginning of 1951 for the race at Syracuse, Ferrari entered Ascari and Villoresi with the 1950 cars which indicated that the 1951 models were not just modified 1950 types but something completely new. Ascari and Villoresi, in the absence of the Alfa Romeos, completely dominated the race but Ascari retired ten laps from the end with overheating, leaving Villoresi to win.

The identical cars went to Pau with the same effect of Ascari and Villoresi leading with the greatest of ease. However Ascari was again destined to break down, this time with transmission troubles, so Villoresi again emerged the winner.

A big clash between Alfa Romeo and Ferrari was expected at the Grand Prix of San Remo, so the new 1951 Ferrari made its appearance in the hands of Alberto Ascari. The car was equipped with the twin-ignition cylinder head and modified brakes with stiffer drums and back plates. The 1950 cars were also present with Villoresi and Serafini. As it happened Alfa Romeo decided, at the last minute, not to compete and the Ferraris had a clear run. Ascari won with ease. Villoresi had a small excursion off the road which put him out, leaving Serafini to take 2nd place.

Again it was hoped that Ferrari and Alfa Romeo would meet, this time at Silverstone, but when it was announced that the race would be run in heats, Ferrari decided he would be at considerable disadvantage, Alfas not having to refuel in the short heats, so he decided not to compete. One Ferrari, a 1950 model, was present driven by Reg Parnell; this car had been sold to Tony Vandervell. Under strange circumstances, in a race that was stopped when the track was flooded by a tropical rain storm, it actually won. The Alfas had slowed down to a crawl to avoid damaging their engines which were fitted with a very low-mounted air intake to the carburetter-supercharger unit and might have been flooded in some of the deep pools that formed on the circuit. However the victory was not taken seriously.

The Swiss Grand Prix

The big encounter came at Berne for the Swiss Grand Prix. Two of the new cars were entered supported by a 1950 car, the latter was however, fitted with the 1951 brakes. Ascari and Villoresi had the new cars and Taruffi was brought into the team to replace Serafini on the third car. Things did not work out exactly as planned and Ascari was burnt in the Formula 2 race. As he was feeling off form he handed over his new car to Taruffi and himself took over the 1950 car. In the pouring rain, Ascari limped around in constant pain and was never in the picture, then Villoresi took the other car off the road after only 13 laps, so only Taruffi was left to look after the Ferrari fortunes. Taruffi that day drove one of his most determined and brilliant races. He had been sitting in 3rd place and had Farina, world champion of 1950, ahead of him. Relentlessly he pursued his rival and one lap from the end passed him taking 2nd place behind Fangio; altogether an outstanding performance.

At Spa the Ferrari team turned out for the first time with three of the 1951 cars and the line up was Ascari, Villoresi and Taruffi facing the Alfa Romeo competition. Alfas hoped to put distance between themselves and the Ferraris on the very rapid Belgian circuit by sheer speed, as they had again increased the output of their engines. It was however a very close thing as both Ascari and Villoresi finished on the same lap as the winning Alfa. In the early stages of the race the Ferraris had even been able to lead the Alfas but Taruffi went out with transmission troubles.

The French Grand Prix

The battle was renewed at the French Grand Prix at Rheims. There was a change in the team as Taruffi was otherwise engaged and Ferrari decided to take on 'Pepe' Gonzales, a close friend and fellow countryman of Fangio. Ferrari was soon to find out that his decision was an excellent one and he never had cause to regret his choice. This was rather unfortunate for Taruffi who was automatically relegated to 'fill in' man for the team.

The cars that appeared at Rheims were

somewhat modified having reshaped bodies and a curved windscreen to replace the former aero type screen. The battle was hot and furious. The Alfas and Ferraris came by on the first lap at tremendous speed in a close bunch and all the other competitors were already a long way behind so that for a while it seemed as if two completely separate races were being run on the same circuit. After ten laps Ascari coasted in with a broken gearbox. The fight continued relentlessly with Alfas also having their troubles. Gonzales came in to take on a little fuel after 34 laps and Ascari took over the car which was lying in 2nd place. However Ascari could not catch Fangio and had to be content with maintaining his 2nd place. Villoresi followed up in 3rd place whilst there was an amusing race for 4th place between Parnell in Vandervell's 1950 Ferrari which was creeping along with a broken transmission and Farina's Alfa which had chronic magneto troubles and was barely moving on what sounded like one cylinder, Parnell took fourth place from Farina by a short head, the former world champion beating the side of his car to urge it on to greater speed.

Ferrari vanquishes Alfa Romeo

Finally came the long awaited day of Ferrari's triumph over the all-conquering Alfa Romeo. At Silverstone Ascari and Villoresi had the 1951 cars but Gonzales had to make do with a 1950 model. In practice Gonzales shook everyone with the first ever 100 m p h lap on the Silverstone Circuit and Alfa Romeo could do nothing about it. Fangio tried everything but his best time was one second slower.

From the start of the race a tremendous battle developed between the two Argentine drivers, but Enzo Ferrari's planning finally bore fruit. When the Alfa Romeo stopped for fuel, the race was lost and the best that Fangio could do, despite a superb exhibition of driving, was to trail home over one minute behind his fellow countryman. Ascari had fallen out with a broken gearbox but Villoresi consolidated the triumph by coming in 3rd.

Once defeated, the Alfa Romeo team collapsed in chaos and for the next world championship race on the Nurburgring only Fangio remained cool and collected. Ferrari had added Taruffi to their already powerful team and there was no question about the result; Ascari winning, Gonzales, Villoresi and Taruffi taking 3rd, 4th and 5th. It was Fangio's skill which saved the face of Alfa Romeo and prevented them from being annihilated.

At Pescara where Alfa Romeo did not enter, new boy Gonzales recorded another win for the prancing horse team, Ascari having had troubles. Driving a 1950 car, he broke the rear axle on the first lap and after taking over Villoresi's car did the same on that, leaving Gonzales running alone.

Alfa return to the attack

Bari was the next encounter between Ferrari and Alfa Romeo. Ferrari were very confident. However they forgot the superb exhibitions of which Fangio was capable and the Argentine driver placed his Alfa Romeo into the lead at the start and was never challenged; Ascari and Villoresi broke down again and it was left to Gonzales to take 2nd place behind Fangio.

For the Italian Grand Prix Ferrari fielded three brand new cars for Ascari, Villoresi and Gonzales. These cars, with the twin ignition heads, were fitted with a reshaped body that was fitted with a curved windscreen and high headrests faired into the tail. Taruffi was also in the team but with an earlier type twin ignition car, and the Ferrari lineup was completed by the Brazilian driver Chico Landi who was down to drive the prototype 2.5-litre 4-cylinder, but for the actual race used a 1950 type 4.5-litre.

Landi retired on the first lap with transmission troubles but the rest of the team really got to grips with the Alfa Romeo team. Towards the end of the race Alfa Romeo was completely beaten and in a hopeless position when Farina set about giving one of his driving exhibitions. He threw the howling Alfa round the Monza circuit in a manner that had everyone gasping and for a time it really looked as if he would save face for Alfa Romeo. A stop for fuel, necessitated by a split tank, ruined the chance of this and Alfa Romeo were relegated to a 3rd place. Ascari and Gonzales were 1st and 2nd, Villoresi and Taruffi were 4th and 5th.

Barcelona

The last race of the European season was, as usual, Barcelona. From practice times it looked as if the race would just be another assertion of Ferrari's superiority as Ascari was some 1.5 seconds faster than Fangio. However it was not to be, the Ferraris were beset by tyre troubles which slowed them down. Villoresi blew up his engine and Taruffi fell out with a chassis fault. Ascari was in continual trouble with tyres struggling to keep his 4th place, only Gonzales was able to give any showing of real form, but the best he could do was 2nd. Fangio won and with it whisked the world championship from under Ferrari's nose. Alfa were jubilant and announced their retirement from racing.

This announcement was to cause the premature death of Formula 1 racing, as organizers were unwilling to run races just for Ferrari to beat a few antiquated Talbots and Maseratis. Although some Formula 1 races were to be run in 1952, it was on a reduced scale and it was decided that the world championship of drivers would be based on the results of Formula 2 races.

The Indianapolis cars

Due mainly to some very active promotion work by Ferrari's American agent, Luigi Chinetti, three of the 4.5-litre cars were ordered by American customers to run at Indianapolis, Ferrari and Ascari got together and decided that this would be an excellent opportunity for a 'European attempt' at the famous American track.

Consequently during the winter work began on the Indianapolis cars. The first move was to produce a new chassis with a wheelbase of 7 ft 8 in. with a front track of 4 ft 3½ in. and a rear track of 4 ft 3 in., in other words a general enlargement all round. The frame was strengthened by welding a triangulated system of small diameter tubes on top of the normal side members. The bonnet line of the cars was lowered with the provision of a large mid-bonnet air scoop intended to give some ram effect to the ingoing air. Much work was done on the engine and the power was finally raised to 430 b h p.

The Indianapolis cars made a preliminary outing in what was to be the only Italian Formula 1 race of the year at Turin. Ascari and Farina had the first two Indianapolis models whilst Villoresi had an earlier engine mounted in the Indianapolis chassis. These three were joined by Taruffi driving the prototype 2.5-litre 4-cylinder. The Ferraris naturally went into line ahead formation but things did not work out altogether to the team's satisfaction. Ascari was leading when, three laps from the end, his fuel tank split; Farina had trouble with his gearbox and then went off the road trying to catch his teammates, so Villoresi won, with Taruffi in the 4-cylinder prototype in 2nd place.

The next appearance of these cars was at Indianapolis where Ascari qualified at 134.308 m p h. The other three cars belonging to the Grant Piston Ring Company, Howard Keck and Johnny Mauro, did not fare too well and none of them qualified for various reasons. The Keck car was fitted with fuel injection and did record a lap at 134.2 m p h but Keck withdrew the car as his driver was faster on the second Keck car with the Offenhauser engine.

Ascari made a fairly good impression during the race but the car was obviously not suited to the track, his run ending with a hub seized and the wheel collapsed.

Formula Libre

The only other outing that the works made with the 4.5-litre during 1952 was when they sent Villoresi to England for the Formula Libre races at Silverstone and Boreham.

At Silverstone the Ferrari ran against the BRMs but these latter cars as usual broke down, Taruffi winning with Vandervell's 'Thinwall' Ferrari whilst Villoresi brought the works car home 2nd, ahead of Landi's privately owned 4.5 Ferrari. At Boreham, Villoresi won the race with Landi's private car 2nd.

Apart from Vandervell's car, Ferrari had sold 4.5-litre cars to Rosier and Landi, both of which raced with mixed success. The most outstanding result being Rosier's 1st place at Albi with Landi 2nd after the BRMs had retired. Mr Vandervell's 'Thinwall' was seen on several occasions with various drivers and it was the only really successful privately owned car.

The 4.5-litre was destined to make two more outings for the factory during the 1953 season.

There was one race in Buenos Aires and the Albi Grand Prix that were run under Formula Libre rules. The car that was sent to Argentina was a very much cleaned up version of the twin ignition 4.5. The body in fact closely resembled a much larger version of the 2-litre 4-cylinder, with the exception that it had an air scoop in the middle of the bonnet. In the Buenos Aires Grand Prix Ascari recorded fastest lap in practice, but in the race itself he had trouble and retired after a few laps with oiling problems.

This particular car was seen once more for the Albi Grand Prix where it faced a full team of BRMs and Mr Vandervell's 'Thinwall' Ferrari driven by Farina. Ascari really pulled out the stops in this race and for a few laps was breathing right down the neck of Fangio's leading BRM; he was so close to the green car that it looked as if the tail of the BRM was several times actually in the Ferrari's air intake. But this did not last for long and the 4.5-litre pulled into the pits with engine and gearbox smoking. The Vandervell car did not go very much farther than the factory one, Farina pulling into the pits soaked with hot oil. The plodding Rosier saved the day for Ferrari when he brought his private-ly owned car in 1st and when the BRMs again had troubles, one of them crashing badly. From then on the factory never again raced the 4.5-litre car, so ended an era in motor racing, a period that had seen the end of the Alfa Romeo domination of the Formula 1 world. The achievement of this gave Enzo Ferrari a great deal of satisfaction, he had laid his plans care-fully and had reaped the benefit.

Mile Record

In 1953 another variation of the 4.5-litre made an appearance. Luigi Chinetti ordered a special car for Indianapolis. The car had the standard 4.5-litre twin-ignition engine but in a short wheelbase space-frame chassis with much strengthened hubs. The car went to Indianapolis but did not qualify, mainly due to American drivers who could not handle the car properly. The car disappeared from the scene until 1956 when Chinetti took it to Daytona Beach where the Ferrari was driven by Bob Said to a record of 170 m p h for a two way mile and 174 m p h for the one way run, a speed which still stands unbroken at the time of writing. The car was then used by Carroll Shelby under Chinetti's sponsorship to win some major American hill climbs. Its last appearance was at Indianapolis 1957 where Farina used it as a practice car for his Indianapolis attempt with the Bardahl 6-cylinder Ferrari.

1952
1953

Alberto Ascari

CHAPTER FIVE

The Formula 2 Ferrari, 12-cylinder and 4-cylinder cars

DURING the 1946-47 period, Enzo Ferrari announced the construction of three new types of car all to be called the 125, the three models were to be the 125 Sport, the 125 Competizione and the 125 Gran Premio. The last named was the first supercharged single seater whilst the 125 Sport was the first all enclosed sports car. The Type 125 Competizione, a 1500-cc car with the 12-cylinder engine having a bore and stroke of 55 x 52.5 mm was destined to be the forerunner of the tremendously successful 12-cylinder Formula 2 cars.

The Type 166

The 1500-cc Competizione was a rather stark two seater with an ugly body resembling the 125 Gran Premio, but having detachable cycle type wings. The early cars suffered a great deal with oiling plugs but were nevertheless eminently successful. Competition was fierce in those days with most of the top-line drivers competing in any little local races just to get their hand in again after the long period of inactivity caused by the war. The 125 won at Parma, Rome, Vigevano and Varese and Nuvolari took it to his last victory at Forli. However the competition from the A6G Maserati was becoming very strong as this car had been bored out from 1500-cc to 2-litres. Ferrari decided to do the same and two new models were announced in December of 1947, the Type 166 Sport and Type 166 Corsa. The Type 166 Corsa had made its debut in 1947 with Sommer at the wheel and had been an immediate success with a victory at Turin. The new cars had the bore and stroke altered to 60 x 58.8 mm giving a capacity of 1992-cc. The Sports was quoted at 90 b h p and the Corsa at 130 b h p.

The first of the 166 Corsas still retained the two seater body although a second seat was not fitted, the extra space being faired over. The car was equally as successful as its forerunner the Type 125.

Sommer won the Petites Cylindres race at Rheims and followed up with a win in the Formula 2 race at Florence, Farina won the Garda race and Landi was victorious at Bari. Luigi Chinetti used one of the earlier cars with the cycle type wings to win the 12 Hours of Paris.

During 1948 Ferrari began to look to the future with his 2-litre cars and the next Corsa model was made up of the 166 engine fitted into the 125 Gran Premio chassis. This was to be the 1949 car. Villoresi and Ascari joined the ranks of the Ferrari drivers and the results began to pour in. Villoresi won at Luxembourg, Garda, and Brussels, Ascari led a 1, 2, 3, 4 procession at Bari supported by Cortese, Bonetto and Landi. At Naples Vallone was first and Bonetto second, Villoresi won the Grand Prix of Rome with Taruffi, Cortese and Rhigetti all on Ferraris following. Cornacchia was first at Senigallia and Fangio led another procession home at the Monza Grand Prix with Bonetto, Ascari, Landi and Cortese supporting. Bracco was unbeatable in hill climbs and Ascari showed his ability by leading Tadini home on a similar car at the Petites Cylindres race at Rheims.

Formula 2-De Dion

Ferrari however was not satisfied with the makeshift arrangement of a 2-litre unsupercharged engine in a 1500-cc supercharged type chassis. He had already decided the future of his Formula 1 cars and adopted similar plans for the Formula 2 cars; a completely new chassis was to be built incorporating a De Dion rear axle. These cars were prepared for the 1950 season with a formidable team of Ascari, Villoresi and

Sommer lined up to drive them. The short chassis 1949 cars utilizing the Formula 1 frame had always been a little difficult to handle and often showed a tendency to crab on the straights. Towards the end of the season a longer chassis of 7 ft 10 in. was used instead of the original one of 7 ft 1 in; this new chassis retained the swing axle layout and the car had its 5-speed gearbox in unit with the engine. For his De Dion chassis Ferrari once again altered the wheelbase reducing it to 7 ft 6 in. and having a track of 3 ft 11½ in. compared to the 3 ft 10 in. of the swing axle short chassis car and the 4 ft 2½ in. of the long chassis model. In the new car the gearbox was moved back to become a unit with the differential housing. The front suspension remained similar to that used on the swing axle cars being by double wishbones with a transverse leaf spring attached to the upper arms. The rearward sweeping De Dion tube was located by twin tubular radius arms running parallel to the chassis frame, the drive from the differential being by means of two halfshafts universally jointed at either end, a transverse leaf spring and Houdaille shockabsorbers completing the assembly. The chassis frame was similar to the tubular ladder frame used on the earlier cars but was lower and lighter and the number of gears was reduced to four. A much more shapely body was fitted on the car and the radiator grille although still retaining the Ferrari egg-crate style was a distinct improvement on the earlier, almost vertical type.

The 1950 Season

During the 1950 season only the works team used these cars whilst many other drivers relied on the 1949 type short chassis model. The short chassis cars were still very successful during the season in the hands of the Argentine team of Fangio, and Gonzales whilst Bracco, Tadini, Cortese and Vallone also ran them as private entries. On occasions the works team made an outing with the short chassis cars and also used the 7 ft 10 in. chassis on one occasion. Villoresi and Vallone ran the long chassis swing-axle car at the Grand Prix of Rome and brought them home 2nd and 3rd behind Ascari's De Dion car. At Erlen, Villoresi and Vallone took first two places with the short chassis models, Tadini

placed the same car 2nd at Modena and Cortese took the short chassis to another win at Naples.

The Formula 2 De Dion car made its first appearance at Pau for the Formula 1 race, Ascari driving it amongst the bigger cars purely to see how it would go. Although very fast, there were various troubles and the day ended with a broken universal joint. With the Pau experience behind them Ferrari set about curing the road-holding problems and from then on, although there were occasional troubles, the car went on to a tremendous success. Ascari began the winning run with a victory at Modena and scored another win at Mons; Villoresi won at Monza and Sommer easily came in first in the Formula 2 race at Berne. Ascari continued with a first place at Rome and another at the Petites Cylindres race at Rheims. Two cars were entered at Rheims but Villoresi's broke its rear axle; a defect which was repeated at Bari where Ascari and Villoresi shared a car. One of Ascari's most impressive performances was at Zandvoort where he placed the Formula 2 car 3rd in the Formula 1 Grand Prix. The rear axle trouble recurred at Geneva and Serafini took over Villoresi's place in the Formula 2 team when the latter was seriously injured in the Geneva Formula 1 race. Mechanical trouble put Serafini out at the Nurburgring but Ascari went on to win with the greatest of ease and the two ended the season with a 1, 2 victory at Garda.

The 4-cylinder Formula 2

Although virtually unbeatable in the Formula 2 class, Ferrari began to notice that on many occasions his cars were being given uncomfortable competition by such rival marques as HWM, Simca Gordini and Cooper. With the engagement of Aurelio Lampredi as chief engineer it was decided to start on a new conception of a Formula 2 car and abandon the 12-cylinder engine. The 12-cylinder lacked torque on twisty circuits and Lampredi chose a 4-cylinder design to compensate for this. In the meantime Ferrari had decided to continue racing the 12-cylinder cars in 1951 Formula 2 events but found that his Formula 1 plans were advancing more rapidly and with more success than originally anticipated so that the Formula 2 programme had to be somewhat limited. However before the

Formula 1 season got underway he sent his top drivers to the three Formula 2 races at Marseilles, Monza and Genoa. Ascari won at Marseilles whilst Villoresi took both the races at Monza and Genoa but the competition had been close and Ferrari was considering the disposal of the cars. The Marzotto family, bankers from Valdagno, who had been very active for some time racing sports Ferraris, expressed an interest in these cars and consequently Giannino Marzotto and Mario Rafaelli, also of the Marzotto team, used the cars at Rome. Rafaelli won and Marzotto was third. The Scuderia Marzotto then purchased the cars, as Ferrari had announced his withdrawal from Formula 2, and they were taken to Rouen where Giannino Marzotto won the race, Rafaelli breaking his rear axle.

For the Formula 2 race at Naples, the Ferrari team borrowed the cars for Ascari and Villoresi to drive; Marzotto was only too willing to come to this arrangement as he did not find driving the single seaters at all to his liking. Ascari won but Villoresi retired with the second car and Marzotto was not seen again as there was some friction between the Scuderia Ferrari and the Scuderia Marzotto when it was found that Ferrari would be returning to the Formula 2 scene with the 4-cylinder cars. Gonzales borrowed one of the De Dion 12-cylinder cars at the end of the season for the Modena Grand Prix and finished 2nd behind Ascari's 4-cylinder prototype.

The 1951 Season

Several private owners ran various versions of the Formula 2 cars during 1951. The Ecurie Espadon from Switzerland had two swing-axle cars driven by Fischer and Staechlin, Peter Whitehead used his long chassis Formula 1 frame fitted with a 2-litre engine and Franco Cortese ran a short chassis car with a special engine fitted with stub exhausts.

Just before Lampredi's idea of building a 4-cylinder engine had been accepted by Ferrari, he had planned to build a twin-cam version of the 12-cylinder Formula 2 engine based on his work with the 1500 two-stage supercharged Grand Prix design. The bore and stroke were altered to 63.5 x 57.8 mm but the design was shelved on approval of the 4-cylinder project.

Lampredi at work

During the winter of 1950-51 Ferrari had again been looking into the future. He had appointed Lampredi as his chief engineer to replace Colombo who had gone to Maserati to work on their new Grand Prix design. Although very busy with the development of his 4.5-litre unsupercharged Formula 1 projects Ferrari had carefully weighed up the many proposals and suggestions for the future Formula 1 which was due to change in 1954. With his projected 4-cylinder he could look forward to achieving two objects at once. One, to recommence activity in the Formula 2 field which he had previously and reluctantly decided to forgo in favour of a more extended Formula 1 campaign, and the other virtually to force the issue with the FIA to limit the 1954 Formula to 2.5-litres unsupercharged, causing him a great saving in the development of his cars. The premature appearance of a 2.5-litre unsupercharged car would be a method of leading the way to those that were still in doubt as to the future of Formula 1. With Lampredi he reasoned that the 4-cylinder would give him more torque out of corners than the 12, and if the Norton motor-cycle engine (at that time master of the motor cycling world) could be made to give 100 b h p per litre so could his projected 4-cylinder engine.

Prototype 2.5 litre

By spring of 1951 the first 4-cylinder engine was on the test bench, two versions being prepared, a 2-litre with a bore and stroke of 90 x 78 mm and a 2.5-litre with a bore and stroke of 94 x 90 mm. As it was, the 2.5-litre came into being first and made its initial appearance at Bari with Taruffi driving. It made an excellent impression and was seen again once more that year at Monza. The 2.5 served as the test bed for the chassis intended for the 2-litre, the same principles as used in the 12-cylinder De Dion car being employed although the chassis was considerably shorter.

In designing the engine of this car Lampredi used very few of the previously accepted Ferrari principles except his practice of eliminating head gaskets. The engine comprised a very deep light alloy crankcase which housed the five Thinwall bearings to support the crankshaft. At the front end of the engine, driven by the nose of the crankshaft, was a train of gears which at the bottom drove the water and oil pumps. A second train ran up to drive the twin overhead camshafts, the train also had provision for the driving of the magnetos. At first, the magnetos were mounted horizontally at the front, but soon both 4-cylinder engine designs had their ignition systems mounted vertically at the front.

To make an effective gas and water seal the four steel liners were screwed into recesses surrounding the combustion chambers, the cylinder head being cast integrally with the water jackets, each liner had a flange at the bottom with two rubber O-rings to provide an oil and water seal.

Two valves per combustion chamber were fitted, closed by two hairpin valve springs, the included angle being 58 degrees. Light-alloy inverted tappets were fitted between the valves and the camshafts and controlled by double coil springs. The peak performance of the engine varied between 7000 and 7500 r p m at which revs the first engines gave about 160 b h p. Ferrari, wishing to produce a car to go the whole Grand Prix distance without refuelling, settled on a 80 : 20 petrol/alcohol mixture which gave a consumption of about 12 m p g under normal usage. All versions of the 4-cylinder engines used DCOE Weber carburetters.

A considerable gain over the previous 12-cylinder engines was achieved in combustion efficiency by the adoption of two plugs per cylinder. A great deal of research work went into the exhaust system; the first system adopted being the use of a single straight pipe. This was followed by the use of stub exhausts and the later adoption of pipes from cylinders 1 and 4 and 2 and 3 joining into a large diameter pipe just in front of the driver's cockpit.

Because of the large size of the combustion chamber and the small quantity of alcohol used in the fuel, a great deal of planning went into the internal cooling. The water pump discharged directly into a passage cored inside the centre main bearing housing, the water being then distributed upwards to the cylinder head. From the head the water was drawn off by four riser pipes, bolted down to passages cored between the twin spark plug seatings and offset to the inlet side of the head. Although at first the maximum output of the engine was very creditable it fell short of expectations and consequently an extensive development plan was put into action to push up the output closer to the desired 100 b h p per litre.

A notable feature of these engines was their very high standard of reliability and the fact that the peak of the torque curve was reached at a little under 5000 r p m.

A multi-disc clutch transmitted power to the four-speed gearbox; the gears rear-mounted were carried in a vertically-split light-alloy housing. The main and layshafts were positioned side by side and drove a crown wheel and pinion. The same housing accommodated two spur gears which embraced a ZF limited slip differential.

A De Dion type rear axle was employed, the tube of which passed behind the main drive casting which embodied a groove providing transverse location for the halfshafts and hubs. By using two parallel radius arms on either side of the car it became unnecessary to articulate the De Dion tube. A transverse leaf spring was mounted low down at the back of the car and damped by two Houdaille shockabsorbers. The front suspension was also by means of a transverse leaf spring, mounted very low down at the front end of the frame and on the first models was connected to the upper members of the unequal length wishbones by an articulated rod, the later cars were fitted with a two-master-leaf spring attached directly to the lower wishbones. A full length kingpin was placed between the wishbones and a separate link used to connect the Houdaille shockabsorbers. Both front and rear springs were supported at two points, the front location being designed to ensure understeer. The articulated steering column passed down the left hand side and was connected to a worm and wheel steering box through three universal joints. The transverse steering linkage involved a sleeve arm and two short track rods mounted ahead of the front wheel centres.

There was a very marked offset between the

wheel centre and the projection of the kingpin; this allowed the achievement of the greatest practical diameter for the brakes, made possible deep fins to provide adequate drum stiffness and also allowed the fins to be exposed to maximum air flow. The light alloy drums with bonded linings were of 13.8 in. diameter and gave a friction lining area of 245 sq in. Two leading shoes were employed for both front and rear drums, a light alloy trellis attached to the back plate gave a central guiding point for each of the stiff light-alloy shoes.

A steel frame was employed with oval frame members which were 4.4 in. deep, 2.15 in. wide and had a wall thickness of 1.5 mm. This frame was cross braced by large tubes at the front and the back and smaller tubes placed just behind the engine and ahead of the gearbox. A strong superstructure was built up around the front of the driver's cockpit and U section longitudinal tubes were carried fore and aft to give additional stiffness.

The driver in this car was seated centrally above the fixed propeller shaft. In the tail there was a 33 gallon fuel tank and the total weight of the car was 1200 lb (543 kg).

The car made its first appearance at the Grand Prix of Bari driven by Taruffi; for this race it had the 2.5-litre engine fitted and it finished a creditable 3rd. It was next seen, still with the 2.5-litre engine, at the practice for the Grand Prix of Italy at Monza where it was driven by all the members of the team plus Chico Landi who was due to drive it in the race. However he used his own 4.5-litre and the 2.5 was sent back to the factory.

At the end of the season the car made its first appearance as a 2-litre with both Ascari and Villoresi having the new types for the Modena Grand Prix. Both cars showed an outstanding superiority over the 12-cylinder De Dion type driven by Gonzales, but he finished second when Villoresi had a breakdown.

A World Championship F2

Although rumour had it that Ferrari would run both the 12s and the 4s during the 1952 season, the 12 for fast circuits and four with its greater torque for the twisty courses, it was not to be so. He decided to go all out with the 4-cylinder, a policy that was to pay dividends. The old Formula 1 of 4.5 unsupercharged and 1500-cc supercharged had in effect come to a premature end with the withdrawal of Alfa Romeo and Ferrari was the only one left with an effective Formula 1 car. It also became evident that Formula 2 races would take the place of the majority of the events scheduled for Formula 1 and that consequently the World Championship would be based on Formula 2. This was just to Ferrari's liking and he set about sweeping the board with a vengeance.

Farina, out of work after the withdrawal of Alfa Romeo, was engaged for the Ferrari team to join Ascari, Villoresi and Taruffi, this being the team fielded for the first race on the European calendar at Syracuse. The cars had been somewhat modified since their first appearance at Modena and they gave a clear indication of what could be expected from them in the future. Villoresi was the unfortunate one, his car catching fire on the starting line from a carburetter blowback. Restarting later he managed to finish in 7th place whilst Ascari, Taruffi and Farina took the first three places, in that order.

That season a group of races were organized in France known as the French Grand Prix series, for which the same drivers had to be nominated. For the first race at Pau, Ferrari sent Ascari, Villoresi, and Scotti, Taruffi staying at home and Farina having been injured at Turin. Scotti was no great success and spun off immediately whilst Ascari and Villoresi held the first two places until Villoresi spun and bent his car. Nevertheless despite being able to take it easy Ascari was able to lap within 1 m p h of his lap record set with the 4.5-litre the previous year. Farina rejoined the team for Marseilles but Villoresi was out of luck again and was eliminated with a faulty carburetter. Farina took the lead when Ascari stopped to change tyres but in an attempt to show up the No. 1 team man he spun off leaving Ascari to win easily.

With Ascari at Indianapolis and Villoresi hurt in a road accident, for Naples Ferrari fielded a team of Farina, Taruffi and Andre Simon, the latter having been very impressive with Gordinis. The cars ran 1, 2, 3 with Farina leading Taruffi and Simon, until Simon crashed.

The same team put in an appearance at the

Swiss Grand Prix at Berne and everything looked set for another Ferrari sweep with Farina hopefully taking the much needed world championship points in the absence of Ascari. But it was not to be. Farina, in his enthusiasm, broke his car and then took over Andre Simon's car and did the same thing, leaving Taruffi a clear winner.

For the Paris Grand Prix Villoresi returned to the team which was still made up of Farina and Taruffi. Farina was way back so he handed over to Simon the reserve driver and took over Villoresi's car which was better placed; once again he took to the woods and being helped back to the track was disqualified allowing the faithful Taruffi to record another win.

For the Grand Prix of the Monza Autodrome Ascari returned to the team, Villoresi had a bad day and it was left to Ascari, Farina and Simon to take the first three places in heat 1. Ascari went out with engine trouble in the second heat leaving Farina and Simon to keep Ferrari ahead despite some opposition from Maserati. The total time of the two heats counted for the final result which gave Farina 1st place and Simon 2nd.

Beaten by Gordini

The Grand Prix of Europe that year was at Spa and again the Ferrari team showed its superiority for Ascari won easily with Farina 2nd but Taruffi for once crashed. Then came Rheims and here the confident Ferrari team were severely shaken. Behra's Gordini jumped into the lead and Ascari did everything possible to overtake the French car without success. The only result was that the Ferrari began to overheat from excessive slipstreaming. Villoresi had already retired and Farina trailed a long way behind. Ascari in exasperation handed over to Villoresi and the battle was as good as finished. Ascari took his car back again later but the Ferrari team was at last beaten, Farina finishing a poor 2nd and Ascari 3rd.

At Rouen, however, the team was back on form and the result was Ascari, Farina and Taruffi in the first three places. At Sables d'Olonne it looked like the usual Ferrari procession but even before the race Ascari was unhappy. He had a great dislike of black cats

and on going to the garage he found no less than a litter of 5 black kittens nesting in his seat. The intruders were summarily evicted and Ascari stamped out of the garage in a poor mood. Nevertheless the race began with the usual 1, 2, 3. Then Harry Schell spun his Maserati after the engine had deposited all its oil on a tight corner of the track; Ascari and Farina were next on the scene and a bad crash followed. Farina was trapped under his car and an instant later several more cars joined in the pile up but he was freed without injury. Villoresi who had been lying further back came up to save the day and record yet another Ferrari win.

The British Grand Prix saw Ascari 1st and Taruffi 2nd but Farina had persistent plug trouble and finished 6th. Ascari completed his hat-trick of wins on the Nurburgring when the team went there for the German Grand Prix. He stopped for oil two laps from the end which let Farina into the lead but Ascari made no bones about who was No. 1, and before the next lap was over he was back in the lead having made up over 14 seconds on a furious Farina. Taruffi in 3rd place broke his De Dion tube on the last lap and dropped to 4th letting Fischer, a private Ferrari owner, into 3rd.

In the next event of the French Grand Prix series Ferrari sent Ascari, Farina and Simon to Comminges. Ascari, after leading, broke his car but took over from Simon to win with Farina 2nd. At Zandvoort it was Ascari, Farina and Villoresi in the first three places.

In the Italian Grand Prix at Monza they were, however, to receive another unpleasant surprise. The team for the race was Ascari, Farina, Villoresi, Taruffi and Simon but it was Gonzales' Maserati that took the lead and nothing that the Ferrari team tried could catch the flying 'Bull of the Pampas'. Fortunately Gonzales had to refuel and Ascari squeezed by whilst the Argentine driver was in the pits; once in the lead he stayed there but none of the other members of the team could make any impression on the Maserati and Villoresi finished 3rd, Farina 4th, Simon 6th and Taruffi 7th.

At the Grand Prix of Modena Ferrari decided to try out his newly acquired driver Mike Hawthorn who, however, had an accident with his Cooper Bristol and his place was taken by local driver Sighinolfi. Ascari although leading broke his own car and took over Sighinolfi's. In the meantime Villoresi leading the race was very hard pressed by the Maserati of Gonzales who finished an uncomfortably close 2nd with Ascari 3rd. After the race there was a big argument as Gonzales had rather obviously been baulked by Carini's HWM, a situation which had in fact robbed the Maserati of victory.

During this season Ferrari had also produced some Formula 2 cars for sale, a policy which he was later to regret, due to complaints that the customers' cars were not nearly as fast as those of the factory. The truth in fact was that the customers were not as fast as the factory drivers. Nevertheless the dissatisfaction later caused Ferrari to stop the policy of selling Formula cars to clients.

The Ecurie Espadon from Switzerland obtained two cars for Rudolf Fischer and Staechlin, the latter however completely wrecked his car whilst Fischer put up a very good performance during the whole season to finish up fourth in the world championship. Louis Rosier the French champion was another customer and later the Ecurie Francorchamps from Belgium purchased one, as did the well known sportsman from Northern Ireland, Bobby Baird. These cars met with mixed success, the only notable performances being by Fischer who won the Eifelrennen, and the Avus race, and Rosier who won at Cadours.

Alberto Ascari was declared World Champion for 1952 and Ferrari could look back on the season with complete satisfaction.

The 1953 Season

Everyone began to wonder what new car Ferrari would pull out of the bag for the 1953 season but when the cars turned out for the Argentine Grand Prix there was no noticeable difference. He had concentrated on the engine output and had virtually left it at that.

Hawthorn had replaced Taruffi and now joined the team of Ascari, Farina and Villoresi. His first race for Ferrari was the Argentine Grand Prix where he was placed 4th, Ascari winning and Villoresi taking 2nd whilst Farina had one of his all too frequent crashes.

For the first race of the European season at

Syracuse, Ferrari turned out a full team of Ascari, Farina, Villoresi and Hawthorn and from practice times it looked as if the race would be another Ferrari sweep. However things worked out differently in the actual race. Ascari was the first to blow up his car, when Hawthorn was slightly involved when Tom Cole crashed with the Cooper Bristol. Hawthorn was wearing a short-sleeved shirt and when he went through the sheet of flames thrown up by Cole's burning petrol tank Hawthorn was burnt on the arm and elbow so that after a few more laps he handed over to Ascari. Needless to say Hawthorn never again raced in sleeveless shirts.

Ascari continued the race but blew up Hawthorn's car and as Farina and Villoresi blew up too the whole team were out leaving De Graffenried in a Maserati to win. The trouble was later traced to faulty material in the valve springs, a situation which was quickly rectified in time for the next race at Pau. Ascari, Farina and Hawthorn made up the team for this race and from the outset the Ferraris were so much superior to their competitors that team manager Ugolini decided to have the cars run in close company, the drivers switching the lead from lap to lap in order to give the public something to see. However as things worked out Farina seemed to take a great objection to Hawthorn leading and always made an effort to take the lead when Ascari let the young Englishman by; as a result of these tactics he managed to spin his car on the downhill stretch and stall the engine making it impossible for him to restart. He was last seen beating his car with his fists. Ascari and Hawthorn continued to record an easy 1st and 2nd.

Teaching the customer

During practice there had been an interesting occurence. Enzo Ferrari was getting a little fed up with the continual complaints by the customers that their cars were not as fast as those of the team. The Ecurie Francorchamps car was present at Pau having been completely rebuilt and brought up to factory specification during the winter. Laurent however was very much slower than the team and consequently started to complain. As a result of his complaints, Hawthorn was asked to try the car as he had done some testing on it previously at Modena. Hawthorn was not only quicker with the private car than with his own works car but put up the fastest time of the day, 2/10ths of a second faster than Ascari. From then on customers were a little more careful before they complained.

Hawthorn was sent to England with a car for the International Trophy race whilst Ascari, Farina and Villoresi went to Bordeaux. Farina was out of the running again with a broken gearbox whilst Ascari and Villoresi filled the first two places. Hawthorn with the lone car won with ease at Silverstone and then carried on to Northern Ireland for the Ulster Trophy which again he won with ease.

In the meantime the other three team members were at Naples where they had trouble from the Maseratis. Nevertheless Ascari did hold the lead for a time only to have his throttle control break, the repair of which cost him so much time that he dropped to 5th in the final results. In the absence of Ascari, Farina showed his real ability taking on the Maseratis and beating them in great style. Villoresi was not in the picture and had to be content with a 4th place.

For the World Championship meeting at Zandvoort the whole team was together once more. Again in practice the Maseratis showed themselves to be potential dangers but during the race itself Ascari and Farina had the upper hand. Villoresi was out with fuel feed troubles and Hawthorn finished 4th, much to the annoyance of Ugolini who was quite pointed in his displeasure. Hawthorn's reply was that he was not going to go over what he considered to be his limits just for the sake of a 1, 2, 3 finish.

The next championship race was at Spa and for the first time there was only one Ferrari in the front row, Ascari was sandwiched between the Maseratis of Fangio and Gonzales and that was the last he saw of them. The Maseratis went far into the lead and although Ascari was really trying, pulling away from the rest of his team, the Maseratis lost him completely. Suddenly however the Maserati bolt was shot and both cars were out leaving the Ferraris back in their usual 1, 2, 3 position. Nevertheless not everything went smoothly from there on, Farina

broke his engine and Hawthorn split a fuel line, as a result he made several visits to the pits to take on fuel. Villoresi moved up into 2nd place whilst Hawthorn dropped to 6th.

Mike Hawthorn's triumph

The Maserati menace was present again at Rheims for the next World Championship event and it was here that Ugolini was to have cause to regret his unkind words to Hawthorn. Mike Hawthorn that day showed his true potential as one of the finest drivers in the world. The race developed into one mad battle between Ferrari and Maserati and the fight was not won until the last corner when Hawthorn slipped inside Fangio and led him over the finishing line by a car length. The nose of Gonzales' Maserati was level with Fangio's cockpit to take 3rd place and Ascari was half a car length behind Gonzales, Farina and Villoresi making up 5th and 6th.

At Silverstone for the British Grand Prix Ascari had a particularly good day, the Maseratis were unable to challenge him but the rest of the team did not have things so easy and finally Farina came in 3rd and Hawthorn 5th.

The Nurburgring, scene of the German Grand Prix, was Ascari's favourite, he always arrived 5 days before the race and spent every day going round and round the track in his Fiat 1400. He made no bones about the start and let the Maseratis fight it out with his team mates. However luck was not with him that day and just before coming to the straight he lost a wheel. He continued to drive back to the pits on his brake drum whilst Farina swept by into the lead. After the wheel had been fixed Ascari continued but naturally was way behind. Ugolini decided that Championship points must if possible be gained by Ascari, called in Villoresi and gave his car to Ascari, Villoresi then took over Ascari's car in which he finished 8th. Ugolini's plan went wrong when Ascari blew up Villoresi's car in the attempt to catch up. Farina was however equal to his task and began to pull away from the Maseratis to win with Hawthorn 3rd.

In the Swiss Grand Prix the Ferraris took complete control again from the Maseratis, Ascari, Farina and Hawthorn were in front set for a 1, 2, 3 victory but Ascari had to stop with

(Top) Swiss GP at Berne 1949, Villoresi with the 1.5 litre single stage car. This car had a modified rear suspension
(Middle Left) The Type 125 2-stage supercharged car of Villoresi at Monaco 1950. He retired after being second, with rear suspension troubles
(Middle Right) Sommer at the Monaco GP 1950. He is in the single stage supercharged V12 car. Starting in row 4 he finished 4th behind Fangio (Alfa Romeo), Ascari (Ferrari Type 125 2-stage supercharged) and Chiron (Maserati)
(Bottom) Carlos Menditeguy with the 2 litre supercharged single cam-per-bank Ferrari at Buenos Aires

(Top) Peter Whitehead's long chassis swing-axle hybrid Ferrari. It could take either a 1.5 litre supercharged or a 2 litre unsupercharged engine. The bonnet intake is for the unsupercharged engine although when the photo was taken it was fitted with the Formula 1 engine

(Bottom) Villoresi in the Ferrari 3.3 litre was involved in a crash with Farina's Alfa Romeo. Ascari in a similar car retired with engine trouble after holding second place. GP of Nations, Geneva 1950

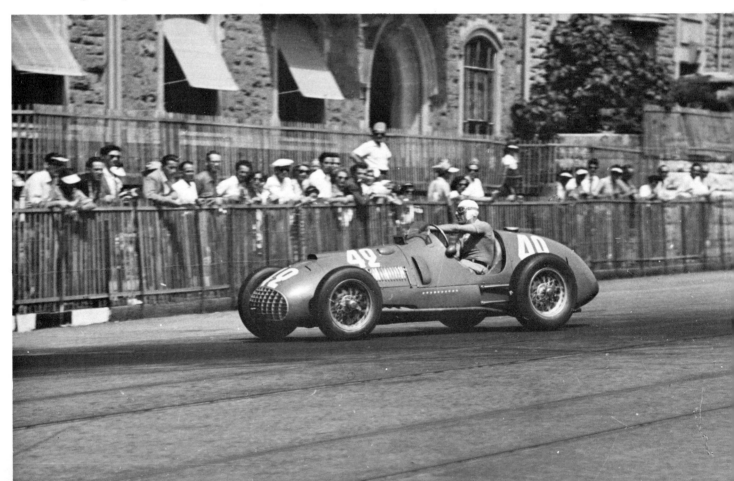

(*Top*) Taruffi driving the 4.1 litre unsupercharged Formula 1 GP
Ferrari in the 1950 Penya-Rhin GP
(*Middle*) Ascari and Villoresi at Monza with the new 4.5 litre twin ignition
cars, the day that the Alfa Romeos were decisively beaten. Ascari (1st),
Gonzales (2nd) and Villoresi (4th)
(*Bottom*) Left to right: 'maestro' Nello Ugolini - Ferrari team manager, Ing.
Aurelio Lampredi - chief designer, Luigi Villoresi, Enzo Ferrari, Alberto
Ascari all around the twin ignition 4.5 litre Formula 1 Ferrari

(Top) Gonzales with the 4.5 which ended the Alfa
Romeo supremacy at Silverstone
(Bottom) The engine of the single ignition 4.5 litre
Ferrari at Silverstone

(Top Left) Villoresi, Gonzales and Ascari. The team which beat the Alfa Romeo at Silverstone July 1951

(Top Right) Ron Roycroft racing the 4.5 litre at Wigram, in New Zealand 1958. In the 1957 season he was the only local driver to lead the Super Squalo Ferraris

(Middle Left) The first appearance of the Indianapolis 4.5 litre version. Here Ascari (left) and Nino Farina at the Valentino GP (Turin) 1952. Both retired to leave Villoresi to win in a similar car

(Middle Right) Gonzales with the 4.5 Ferrari passes on the inside of the Alfa Romeo of de Graffenried, Barcelona 1951

(Bottom) Ascari with the 4.5 Indianapolis Ferrari 1952

(Top) Ascari's 4.5 spinning off due to broken wheel spokes during the 1952 Indianapolis 500. It was the only 4.5 Ferrari to qualify
(Bottom Left) Villoresi with the modified Indianapolis Ferrari at Boreham
(Bottom Right) The Grant Indianapolis Ferrari which did not qualify, with driver Johnny Parsons, here on display at Torreys Pines

(Top) Farina at the wheel of the Chinetti Indianapolis Ferrari. He, amongst several other drivers, was unable to qualify the car
(Bottom) The Indianapolis/Daytona/Monza Chinetti owned 4.5 Ferrari. Farina and others tried to qualify for the 1954 Indianapolis 500 with it. At Daytona, Bob Said set a New Speed Record. At Monza it was driven by Harry Schell, Carroll Shelby raced it to some minor successes. The car is now restored and is used in some vintage car events

(*Top*) Gabriele Besana in the pits at Buenos Aires in 1948. The Ferrari Type 166C has been stripped of headlights and wings (cycle type) for the Formula Libre race

(*Middle*) Stagnoli with the Zagato bodied Ferrari 2 litre 12 cyl at the Monza GP 1951, passing the HWM

(*Bottom*) Formula 2 race GP Autodrome Monza, 26 June 1949. Bonetto leads Ascari and Fangio. Fangio won

a clogged carburetter and when he rejoined the race he had dropped to 3rd. His two team mates were plodding along following team orders when Ascari suddenly put down his foot and went sailing by them to win yet another Grand Prix, Farina was purple with rage and even Ugolini was not too pleased. Villoresi was never in the picture making several pit stops for water.

It was just before the Italian Grand Prix that Ferrari announced that he would retire from racing which naturally caused an uproar but, in most of the circles in the know, this was not taken too seriously. At Monza, despite these threats of retirement, two brand-new Formula 2 cars made their appearance and were tried by all members of the team. However for the race Ascari, Farina, Villoresi and Hawthorn were all driving the models used all the year.

The Monza race was one that will long be remembered. The front group of Ascari and Farina with the Ferraris and Fangio and Marimon with the Maseratis circulated in such close company that they seemed tied together. The race, just as at Rheims, was settled when, on the last corner of the last lap with everyone trying their hardest to take the lead, there was a sudden mix up as Ascari and Marimon shot off the road and Fangio cut through to give Maserati their first important win, with Farina hot on his heels, Villoresi brought up 3rd, and Hawthorn with an obviously much slower car, 4th.

So once again Ferrari could look back to a very satisfactory season. Alberto Ascari was World Champion for the second time and although competition from Maserati had been very stiff, Ferrari had only been beaten once by the rival marque.

The 1954 Season - The Type 553

Despite the threats of withdrawal from racing, Ferrari had nevertheless prepared something new, bearing in mind that the Formula was changing for 1954 and that Formula 1 was to be reinstated with a limit of 2.5-litres unsupercharged. For the Italian Grand Prix at Monza an entirely new Ferrari appeared on the scene. It was known as the Type 553 and was the first Ferrari Grand Prix car to utilize the space frame principle of construction. The new model employed the other 4-cylinder engine designed by

Lampredi with a bore and stroke of 93 x 73.5 mm with a cubic capacity of 1997-cc. Two valves per cylinder were used but at a much greater angle than on the previous Type 500 engine. The twin overhead camshafts were driven by a train of narrow spur gears from the nose of the crankshaft, combined with a bevel gear for the water pump and two magnetos. These were mounted low in front of the engine and were driven by an idler gear. The two magnetos fed two plugs per cylinder and two twin choke Weber 50/DCO carburetters were bolted to a sub-frame on the chassis and attached to the cylinder head by means of flanged rubber tubes. As pannier tanks were fitted, the exhaust pipe was made to rise up and over the tank and so the pipe ran very high past the driver's cockpit.

The steering box was placed in the centre of the main transverse structure on the front of the chassis, this structure also acted as a point for the attachment of the front suspension members. The front suspension was by means of unequal length wishbones at the ends of which were ball joints attached to the stub axles, taking the place of the more normal kingpins. A thin leaf spring was mounted under the chassis, the ends of which were attached to the lower wishbones, there being a rubber block insert between the wishbones and brackets extended from the chassis frame. Rear facing steering arms were linked by jointed track rods to a central steering arm projecting backwards from the steering box.

At the back of the space frame structure was the differantial/gearbox assembly which was cast as a unit, the drive to the shafts being taken out of the back, upwards through a pair of spur gears and forwards to the crownwheel and pinion, the transmission shaft from the engine entering the assembly at a very low point. The final drive was by means of universally jointed halfshafts, the hub carriers being attached to a forward running De Dion tube which passed in front of the differential/gearbox housing instead of behind as on the type 500 cars. A transverse leaf spring mounted high above the axle was employed and was attached to the hub carriers by short links, the spring being located in the centre by a bolt and pairs of rollers on either side.

Lampredi decided to use pannier tanks to do away with the effects of fuel consumption on handling characteristics that arose with a large rear mounted fuel tank, this gave rise to a very wide body and the car was immediately nick-named the 'Squalo' or shark.

At Monza before and during the practice period all the members of the team tried out this car. Ascari was fairly satisfied with it but all the drivers preferred to take the well-tried type 500 for the race, two of the new model 553s being given to Maglioli and Carini to drive. As Maglioli had a distinct dislike for Grand Prix cars and Carini was by no means a top class driver, nothing very much could be expected from the new cars. Maglioli finished in 8th place whilst Carini's car was withdrawn after many pit stops.

CHAPTER SIX
The 2.5-litre Formula 1 Ferrari

Juan Manuel Fangio

12 Cylinders

DURING the winter of 1950/51, Ferrari decided to experiment further with unsupercharged Grand Prix car designs. The Swiss driver Rudolf Fischer had indicated his interest in a special car, so Ferrari produced a 2.5-litre version of the well known 2-litre 12-cylinder Formula 2 engine. This power plant, with a bore and stroke of 68 x 58.8 mm, was mounted in a long-wheelbase swing-axle chassis, Ferrari preparing the car for the first race of the European season.

He was, however, not content to watch the results from Fischer alone and set about building a second car for his works team. This car had the same engine but fitted into one of the chassis prepared for the two-stage supercharged Formula 1 engine, with a De Dion rear axle.

Both these cars made their first appearance at Syracuse, the first of the European season's races and frequently used by Ferrari for trying out new ideas. The factory car was driven by Dorino Serafini into an excellent 2nd place whilst Fischer followed up strongly with 3rd place. Both cars appeared again at Pau where things did not go too well; Serafini retired, something being wrong with the steering and Fischer, after some troubles, finished 6th.

Fischer then went on to San Remo and again he took an excellent 3rd place. There was less opposition in the race at Bordeaux and Fischer took the opportunity really to go racing and make sure of 2nd place.

Fischer was very happy with the car but at the Swiss Grand Prix had a setback which could not be blamed on the car itself. In the rain he was constantly having to wipe the inside of his visor free of muddy water which also splashed over his glasses but in wiping them clean he smeared some oil on them. The result was that he could

see even less clearly and consequently dropped further and further back, finally to finish 11th. Fischer made up for his poor run at Berne with a good 4th place at Zandvoort. He then finished off his season with a 1st place at the Freiburg hill climb and a 6th place behind the works cars in the German Grand Prix.

The factory 2.5-litre car had not been seen again after the Pau race and Fischer, wishing for a 4.5-litre, the 2.5-litre 12-cylinder used in the Swiss race was reconverted to a 2-litre to serve as a second car for some of the Formula 2 events. However, the withdrawal of Alfa Romeo and the prospects of no Formula 1 racing in 1952 caused Fischer to think again and he purchased one of the new 4-cylinder designs instead.

4 Cylinders

Ferrari had taken the decision to build a 4-cylinder Formula 2 car as the 12-cylinder models were being challenged very seriously on some circuits. Originally it was intended to use these cars for certain races and rely on the 12s for others but when Ferrari saw the outputs and performance in tests of the car and being aware that the 1952 season would see Formula 2 races counting for the world championship, he decided to go all out with his 4-cylinder design. He also had a good idea that the future Formula 1 would be limited to 2.5-litres so at the same time as he designed the 2-litre he also produced a 2.5-litre version which differed only from the smaller engine in having a bore and stroke of 94 x 90 mm compared with 90 x 78 mm for the 2-litre. The 2.5-litre engine was in fact the first to go on the test bench and it was run at the Bari Grand Prix with Taruffi driving. This first appearance showed the car to have great potential and served to test the chassis intended for the 2-litre car. Taruffi faced very strong opposition at Bari and, despite this, brought the car home 3rd. Mr Ferrari was very satisfied. The 2.5-litre made another appearance that year at the practice for the Grand Prix of Italy. All the members of the Ferrari team had a go with the car and Ferrari himself had decided to let Chico Landi, the Brazilian champion, drive the car in the race. Landi covered quite a distance with the car in practice but at the last minute Ferrari put him in a 4.5-litre 12-cylinder and the 2.5-litre was returned to the factory.

The 2.5-litre 4-cylinder differed very little from the 2-litre version. As in the 2-litre a deep light-alloy crankcase was employed containing five Vandervell Thinwall bearings. The nose of the crankshaft provided the drive, through a train of gears, to the oil and water pumps and upwards to the twin overhead camshafts and magnetos. The principle of using four steel liners screwed into the block to eliminate a head gasket was adhered to, the head being cast integrally with the water jackets. Two rubber O-rings were used near the bottom end to provide an oil and water seal.

Two valves per chamber were used, each actuated by two hairpin valve springs. Light alloy inverted tappets were fitted between the valves and the camshafts, and controlled by double coil springs. The prototype engine gave 200 b h p at 6500 r p m this being raised to 230 b h p at 7500 by relying on a new bottom end and connecting rods with strengthening webs running down the sides and round the bearing caps. Ferrari again used his idea of getting a better fuel mileage by settling on an 80 : 20 gasoline alcohol mixture. For this engine Ferrari also decided to use two plugs per cylinder and the exhaust system on the prototype was by means of a straight pipe running along the side of the car; only once did the car appear with the stub exhausts that were common on the 2-litre and this was in a special tryout by Fischer when the engine was fitted to his 2-litre chassis.

The same careful thought to cooling had been given to the 2-litre and similarly the 2.5-litre had the water pump discharging directly into a passage cored in the centre main bearing, the water then being distributed upwards to the cylinder head. From the head the water was drawn off by four riser pipes bolted down to passages cored between the twin spark plug orifices and offset to the inlet side of the head.

A multi-disc clutch transmitted power to the four-speed gearbox, the gears of which were carried in a vertically split light-alloy housing, the main and layshafts were positioned side by side and drove a crownwheel and pinion. The same housing accommodated two spur gears which embraced a ZF limited-slip differential.

A De Dion rear axle was employed the tube of which passed behind the main drive casting which embodied a groove to provide for sideways location of the axle and wheel hubs. Through using two parallel radius arms on either side of the car, it was not necessary to articulate the De Dion tube. A transverse leaf spring was mounted low down at the back of the car and was damped by two Houdaille shockabsorbers. The front suspension was by means of a transverse leaf spring mounted very low down at the front end of the frame and was connected to the upper wishbone by an articulated rod. A full length kingpin was placed between the wishbones and a separate link was used to join the Houdaille shockabsorbers. Both front and rear springs were supported by two points, the front location being designed to ensure understeer. The two-piece steering column passed down the left hand side and was connected to a worm and wheel steering box through three universal joints. The transverse steering linkage involved a slave arm and two short track rods mounted ahead of the front wheel centres.

There was a very marked offset between the wheel centre and the projection of the kingpin, which allowed the achievement of the greatest practical diameter for the brakes and made possible the deep fins to provide adequate drum stiffness and also to allow the fins to be exposed to the maximum air flow. The light alloy drums with bonded linings were of 13.8 in. diameter and gave a friction lining area of 245 sq in. Two leading shoes were employed for both front and rear drums, a light alloy trellis attached to the back plate gave a central guiding point for each of the stiff light alloy shoes.

A steel frame was employed with oval frame members which were 4.4 in. deep and 2.15 in. wide and had a wall thickness of 1.5 mm. This frame was cross-braced by large tubes at the front and the back and smaller tubes placed just behind the engine and ahead of the gearbox. A strong superstructure was built up around the front of the driver's cockpit and longitudinal tubes were carried fore and aft to give additional stiffness.

The driver in this car was centrally seated above the fixed propeller shaft. A 38 gallon (143 lt) tank was mounted in the rear. The car weighed 1250 lb (562.5 kg.).

During 1952 the 2.5-litre made only one appearance when an engine was given to the Swiss driver Fischer for the Maloja hill climb. It was purely in the nature of an airing and Fischer won easily with the engine fitted into his 2-litre chassis. This was the only time that the car appeared with stub exhausts which made themselves famous for burning the seat out of an unwary policeman's trousers.

The 1953 Season

The first appearance of the 2.5-litre with a full team of drivers was at Buenos Aires in 1953. Three engines were taken along to fit into the 2-litre chassis for the Buenos Aires Grand Prix which was Formula Libre; Farina, Villoresi and Hawthorn took the first three places after Ascari's 4.5-litre Ferrari had fallen out.

The cars appeared again when Farina and Hawthorn took them to Rouen for the Formula Libre race. It was a walkover for Ferrari, Farina being 1st and Hawthorn 2nd, the latter setting the fastest lap.

Ferrari decided to give the promising young sports car driver, Umberto Maglioli, who had recently joined the team, a tryout on the Grand Prix car. Consequently Enzo Ferrari chose the rather difficult Susa Mont Cenis hill climb and sent the 2.5-litre there. Maglioli performed fairly well in his first attempt with a Grand Prix car and put up second fastest time of the day. At the same time, Ferrari decided to send Hawthorn to England with the other 2.5-litre but, at Silverstone in the Formula Libre event, things did not go so well and the car was withdrawn after a few laps with overheating.

The 1954 Season - The Type 625

The following year, 1954, the new Formula 1, of 2.5-litres unsupercharged, came into force

and Ferrari seemed well prepared, for besides having the much-tested 2.5-litre 4-cylinder engine in the 2-litre chassis, he was working on an entirely new car which had made its prototype appearance in the last race of 1953 as a 2-litre.

The 1954 car, known as the Type 625, very closely resembled the 2-litre car of the previous year, in fact the only noticeable difference was in the fitting of Weber 50 DCOA/3 carburetters, mounted on a framework welded to the chassis frame and coupled to the engine by rubber hoses to eliminate the transmission of engine vibration to the carburetters. The other change which had actually taken place during the previous season was the elimination of the linkage between the front leaf spring and the top wishbone, the spring now being linked directly with the lower wishbone.

Team changes

At this period Enzo Ferrari lost the services of Ascari and Villoresi who went to Lancia. Farina and Hawthorn were left for his team along with the well known Argentinian driver Froilan (Pepe) Gonzales who signed on.

The first race of the season was the Argentine Grand Prix and the cars immediately showed themselves faster than the new Maseratis driven by Fangio and Marimon. However, in the tropical storm that descended on the track, the combined mastery of Fangio and the road holding of the new Maserati, were the downfall of the Ferrari team. Fangio gained 12 seconds a lap and despite a tremendous effort by Hawthorn, who showed much more ability in the wet than his team mates, Fangio swept by into the lead. The Maserati almost lost its lead again when the track dried out but another rainstorm sealed the fate of Ferrari, Farina finished 2nd and Gonzales 3rd.

Again in the Buenos Aires Grand Prix Fangio was the danger but he was quickly eliminated and Hawthorn took command and led until the last lap when his engine blew up, Maurice Trintignant in Louis Rosier's private Ferrari winning and the Maserati of Mieres holding Farina out of second place. Trintignant's brilliant drive earned him a place in the Ferrari team much to the annoyance of Rosier who had counted on Maurice to be his team mate in the Scuderia Auvergne.

The first European outing of the team was at Syracuse where Farina, Hawthorn and Trintignant used the Type 625 whilst Gonzales drove the new experimental Supersqualo. Farina won with Trintignant second, but Hawthorn was involved in a crash early in the race which destroyed not only his car but that of Gonzales as well.

Three cars were prepared by the factory for the race at Pau, the team being made up of Gonzales, Farina and Trintignant, Hawthorn being out of commission after his Syracuse accident. All looked set for another Ferrari victory but things did not go according to plan. Farina was the first in trouble, badly denting the nose of his car by running into another competitor with the result that he had to stop to beat out the bodywork as it was touching the steering. Gonzales in the meantime had taken the lead with Trintignant 2nd and again things looked set, when Gonzales' engine blew up with a big bang and Trintignant was left in a comfortable lead. The Ferrari team had not however reckoned with Behra and the Gordini. Already once previously Behra had upset the prancing horse stable when he beat the full team at Rheims. That day at Pau was to be another indication of the French motor cyclist's skill and he relentlessly pursued Trintignant's Ferrari. A few minutes before the end of the race Behra passed the Ferrari and all Trintignant could do was to be satisfied with his 2nd place supported by Farina in a poor 5th position.

Farina returned to Italy to run in the Mille Miglia during which he had a serious accident and, with Hawthorn still suffering from bad leg burns, the Scuderia was reduced to Gonzales and Trintignant. These two were sent to Bordeaux where they ran 1st and 2nd with ease for most of the race. Towards the end Trintignant's Ferrari began to go sick and he dropped back into 3rd place, his 2nd place being taken by Manzon in a private Ferrari.

Silverstone

The International Trophy at Silverstone followed and Ferrari decided to give Umberto Maglioli another try-out on the Grand Prix car.

He sent two of the Type 625 models for Trintignant and Maglioli and the new 555 Squalo for Gonzales who won his heat with it whilst Maglioli took 4th with the 625; in the second heat Trintignant won from Parnell in a privately owned Ferrari. There was a scene in the final when Gonzales' new car refused to start. The Argentine driver consequently took over Trintignant's car and Trintignant took over Maglioli's. Gonzales had no difficulty in winning the final but Trintignant with a rather obviously slow car could do no better than 6th.

Umberto Maglioli did not like driving the Formula 1 cars, much preferring the big sports models but he had to be included in the team due to the absence of Farina and Hawthorn. He was sent with the other two team drivers to the Bari Grand Prix and for once things went well. Gonzales winning ahead of Trintignant but with Maglioli a poor 7th.

For the Belgian Grand Prix, the original team was together again although neither Hawthorn nor Farina were 100 per cent fit. Out of the factory team only Hawthorn and Trintignant were given the 625 models whilst Farina and Gonzales had the Type 555. Trintignant put up a fine performance and brought his car in 2nd behind the flying Maserati of Fangio. Hawthorn had a less satisfactory experience. The guard over his exhaust pipe broke away and let exhaust fumes escape into the driver's cockpit. Overcome by the gases Mike just made it back to the pits where he had to be lifted out of the car. Gonzales took over having already blown up his own car and proceeded to gain 4th place.

Farina was lost to the team again when he had another serious accident whilst testing at Monza, so the team was once more without his services for the French Grand Prix. For this race only Trintignant used the 625, both Hawthorn and Gonzales having the new 555. The race was marked by the first appearance of the Mercedes Benz streamlined Grand Prix cars. These cars set such a tremendous pace that the opposition was completely annihilated. The 555s did not go very far and even the 625 of Trintignant blew up its engine.

It was left for Manzon's privately owned Ferrari to save the day, he took 3rd place but a very long way behind.

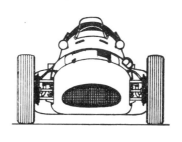

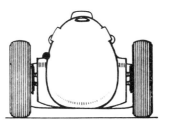

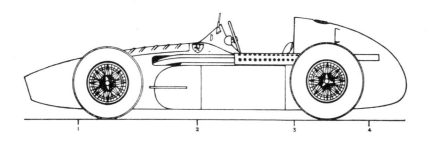

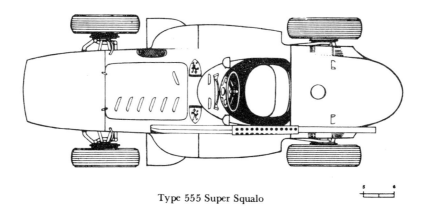

Type 555 Super Squalo

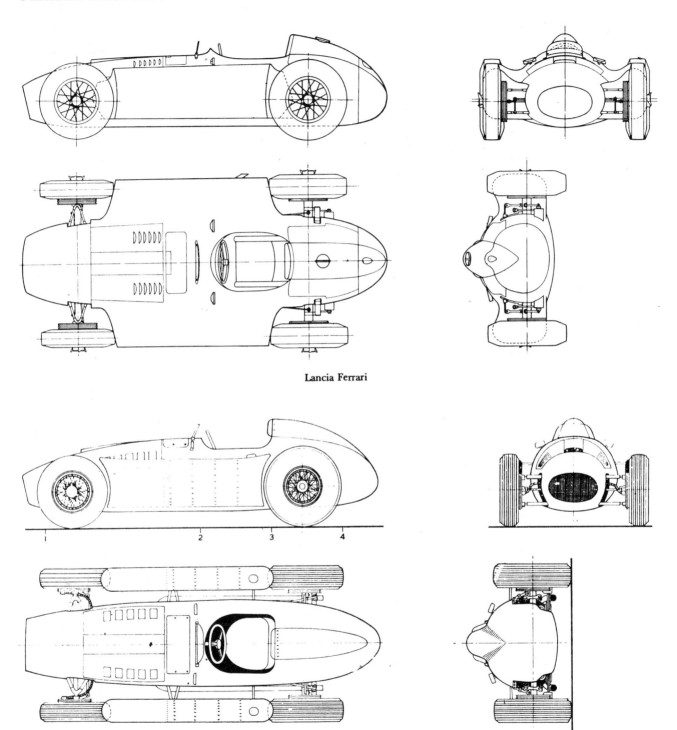

Lancia Ferrari

Lancia D50

The Mercedes challenge

Ferrari was not very happy with the situation. The 625 types were being forced to their maximum in an effort to deal with the opposition, the new 555 Squalo being miserably unreliable. As a result he embarked on some emergency measures to try to balance things out. The 625 chassis was as much liked by the team drivers as the 555 chassis was disliked, but the engine of the 625 lacked the power to compete successfully in the face of the new Mercedes challenge. Ferrari therefore decided to combine the best points of the 625 and the 555 engines, using the reliable bottom end of the former and the cylinder head of the latter designed to give more power. The new engine had its valves at an included angle of 100 degrees and the bore and stroke were altered to 100 x 79.5 mm from the original 94 x 90 mm. Weber 58 DCOA/3 carburetters were fitted in place of the 50 DCOA/3s. This engine could be recognized by square-edged cambox covers.

This engine was first tried out at Rouen fitted into Hawthorn's 625 chassis. Trintignant had a normal 625 and during the race the two cars easily held 1st and 2nd places, putting up a great demonstration, but both had to stop for a small amount of fuel, a thing most unusual for Ferrari, and then, when it looked like a certain 1st and 2nd, Hawthorn's engine broke its crankshaft leaving Trintignant an undisputed 1st.

For Silverstone a complete team of 625 models was prepared all fitted with the new engine and all incorporating changes to the steering necessitated by the wider cam boxes.

It was the second appearance of the new Mercedes Benz and everyone expected another walk over. However, Mercedes found themselves hampered by the all-enveloping body of which Gonzales took full advantage and led the race from start to finish much to Enzo Ferrari's delight. Hawthorn came 2nd and Trintignant 5th.

For the relatively unimportant race at Caen, Trintignant was given a factory car as the event counted towards the French Championship. The engine fitted was the earlier 625 but it was mounted in one of the chassis prepared for the new engine. Trintignant after a battle with the Maseratis won the race comfortably.

German Grand Prix

For the German Grand Prix Ferrari decided to keep his troublesome Squalos at home and sent a team of four 625 models. The team was made up of Gonzales, Hawthorn, Trintignant and Taruffi. The latter two had ordinary 625s. Taruffi using the modified chassis but with the early engine and Trintignant having a completely unmodified car with the early engine. Gonzales and Hawthorn had the latest thing from the factory. Bottom ends from the promising Type 735 Monza sports model were used in conjunction with the heads from the Type 555 fitted with the same wide angle valves and Weber 58 DCOA/3 carburetters as used on the Hawthorn car at Rouen.

Gonzales, upset by the death of his friend Marimon during practice, could only get into the second row of the start but Hawthorn put up second fastest time of the day and was next to Fangio's Mercedes on the starting line. The rest of the team were further back, Trintignant in the 3rd and Taruffi in the 5th row.

At the start of the race it looked as if it might well be a repeat of the Silverstone result. Gonzales was in the lead like a flash and came thundering by in first place on the first lap. Fangio however used the superiority of his Mercedes and his own knowledge of the Nurburgring to great effect and passed the hard working 'Pepe' who stuck to 2nd place for some time and then suddenly seemed to lose interest and fell back. In the meantime Hawthorn was already out with a broken axle and Taruffi had been slowed by a blown out tyre. Finally Gonzales was called in and his car was handed over to Hawthorn who drove a brilliant race, pushed the Ferrari as fast as it would go and overtook the Mercedes which was in second place a few laps from the end, thus placing himself in a very satisfactory position. Trintignant too put up a good performance catching the ailing Mercedes just before the end to take 3rd whilst Taruffi finished 6th.

For the Swiss Grand Prix the 555 reappeared, two of them keeping company with two of the 625 models. Manzon crashed one of the 555s and Maglioli as junior member of the team had to take the other one as it was not going too well. Gonzales drove a new model 625 with a high tail and headrest, whilst Hawthorn and Trintignant had the normal-bodied 625s; all three cars used the 735/555 engine introduced at the Nurburgring. Gonzales again put up a tremendous show but the Mercedes opposition was too much and he could only finish 2nd. Trintignant brought his car into 3rd place only to have his engine blow up whilst Hawthorn went out with fuel pump breakage.

Enzo Ferrari was still not satisfied with the performance of the cars and obviously something had to be done. For the Italian Grand Prix at Monza, he was able to obtain the services of Ascari as the new Lancia was not ready, and for him he produced yet another variation of the 625, this time with a complete Type 555 engine fitted. Hawthorn had the ordinary model 625 but with the Rouen type engine having the 625 bottom end and the 555 head; Trintignant had a similar car but with extra fuel tanks fitted. Maglioli was given an original Type 625 without the modifications and with a normal 625 engine.

Ascari seemed very happy to be with Ferrari and put up a tremendous exhibition of driving, battling with the Mercedes of Fangio and the Maserati driven by Moss. He led the race at half distance but the effort was too much for the engine and it gave up with a big bang. Trintignant had very little luck and was forced to stop with various troubles, finally coming in 5th, whilst Hawthorn scored an excellent 2nd place although never having been in the Prix ride, thankfully handed over to Gonzales who had blown up his Type 555. By violent driving, having pushed the car up into 3rd place and his job being done, Gonzales handed back to Maglioli who held the place until the finish of the race.

The end of the 1954 Season

The final event of the season was at Barcelona where the troublesome 555 Squalo finally won a race in the hands of Hawthorn. The factory sent Trintignant with a 625 fitted with the 555 engine and Maurice put up an excellent performance despite full teams of Mercedes, Lancia and Maserati. He took the lead several times but his

run ended when he went out with a broken gearbox. With the end-of-season success of the 555 Squalo, it looked as if Ferrari would be abandoning the type 625 altogether preferring to develop the 555 and work on his new 6-cylinder in-line GP design as well as the 2-cylinder Monte Carlo project.

However, for safety's sake, he decided to send the revamped 625 models to Argentina to give him more time to work on the Squalo.

Realizing that the cars would probably be inadequate, several modifications were made on them. The front suspension that had worked so well on the Squalo which had won at Barcelona, was employed for all the cars, this comprised new double wishbones and coil springs. The rear suspension also underwent change. The De Dion was retained but the leaf spring was mounted above the differential unit, a 5-speed gearbox being fitted and all the cars having the 555 engine. All three cars had redesigned bodies and exhaust pipes which now ran downwards and along the bottom of the body instead of up high by the driver's cockpit as before. A stubbier tail was designed and at the front the nose plunged further down rather like the Squalo. One of the cars was fitted with the high tail and headrest first used on the 625 at the Swiss Grand Prix.

The 1955 Season - Argentina

The Argentine Grand Prix that year was a confusing affair with drivers stopping time and time again for relief from the heat. Gonzales was right amongst the leaders fighting a furious battle and often jumping into the lead but he had to stop and Farina, who himself had come in to hand over to Maglioli, took over from the Argentine driver. Trintignant blew up his car but found that it was not the end of his day's racing as he was immediately called upon to help with relief driving on the two remaining cars. The Gonzales Ferrari took 2nd and the Farina car was placed 3rd behind Fangio who had gone the whole distance in his Mercedes without relief.

In the final race of the Argentine Temporada the 625s were fitted with 750 Monza engines for the Formula Libre race.

The modified 625s made their first appearance in Europe at the Grand Prix of Turin where they were noticeably outclassed. Farina was out quickly with a broken gearbox and Trintignant blew up his engine whilst in a comfortable 4th position. Harry Schell, the newcomer to the team, was not very happy in his first drive being a very long way behind and finally finishing in 5th place; it seemed that this must surely be the end of the type 625. It came rather as a surprise, therefore, when the cars again appeared at Monte Carlo in company with the 555 Squalos. For this race both Trintignant and Farina chose the 625 but again Farina had an unlucky day. His car was damaged on the first lap causing him to spend some time in the pits having the body-work beaten out, and he was able to get no higher than 4th in the final classification. The big surprise however, came from Trintignant. At first Fangio's Mercedes had been leading until its engine broke, then Moss on the second Mercedes led until the same trouble eliminated him. Next it was Ascari with the Lancia but he crashed into the sea. Mieres took over for a short time but his Maserati broke its rear axle, then Musso for a brief period, his Maserati also breaking, so that Trintignant was a very surprised 1st which he kept until the end of the race, giving Ferrari an unexpected victory in the Grand Prix of Monaco which was also the Grand Prix of Europe that year.

The end of the 625

Nevertheless Ferrari had no illusions about this victory and the cars appeared only as practice hacks at Spa and Zandvoort; the end had come. The 625 had its last fling at Aintree for the British Grand Prix. Eugenio Castelotti had joined the team after Ascari's death had caused Lancia's retirement from racing and the team for the British race comprised Hawthorn, Trintignant and the young Italian. Castelotti's transmission broke, Trintignant blew up his engine and Hawthorn came in to hand over to Castelotti; the result was a 6th place and the end of the road for the 625.

During the season another 625, modified to this 'Tipo Argentina' as it was sometimes known, made an appearance. This car was driven by the Marquis de Portago who was making his debut in a Grand Prix car. The car itself was an earlier 625 with the 4-speed gearbox but with the latest engine and 'Argentine' bodywork. He

had very little success due to the unreliability of the engine and finally had a crash with it at Silverstone. Two of the cars ended up in Australia with 750 Monza engines fitted for the Formula Libre races in that country.

THE 4-CYLINDER SQUALO AND SUPER-SQUALO TYPES

At the Grand Prix of Italy held at Monza in 1953 a new type of Ferrari made its first appearance. Known as the type 553 it retained the 4-cylinder engine and, although it was a 2-litre, it was obvious that this was Ferrari's future Formula 1 car. The 2.5-litre Formula came into existence in 1954 and Monza was the last race for the 2-litre World Championship. Ascari and Villoresi spent a great deal of time in practice, trying out the new car, but could not record times as fast as with the older Type 500 so the two prototypes were given to Maglioli and Carini to drive in the race. As usual Maglioli was not very happy in the Grand Prix car and motored quietly into 8th place whilst Carini had trouble with his car finally pulling in to retire it, accompanied by much arm waving and fist shaking.

After the Monza race, the 2.5-litre made its debut on the Modena test track, the car being known as the Type 555 'Squalo' or shark.

Lampredi, in designing this car, had retained the 4-cylinder engine but the 553 2-litre and the 555 2½-litre engines differed in many ways from the Type 500 2-litre and Type 625 2.5-litre. In the 2-litre 553, Lampredi had used a bore and stroke of 93 x 73.5 mm which was enlarged to 100 x 79.5 for the Type 555 and gave a total capacity of 2,496-cc. Two valves per cylinder were mounted at the included angle of 100 degrees and were operated by twin overhead cam-shafts driven from the nose of the crankshaft through a train of narrow spur gears. The magnetos, being mounted low down at the front of the engine, were driven by the first idler gear of the train. Although the bottom end of the Type 555 was much stronger, most of the prin-ciples of water passages, oil ducts, seals and liner location employed on the 500 and 625 were adhered to in the 553 and 555 designs. The same type of deep light-alloy crankcase as used in the earlier engines was retained but there were several modifications to the crankshaft supports. The webbing was made more rigid and the crankshaft having enlarged bearings. The water and oil pump drives were similar and the four steel liners were recessed into the combustion chamber as on the Type 500. The engine also utilized the flange at the bottom of the liner with two rubber O-rings providing an oil and water joint.

100-degree opposed valves were closed by two hairpin valve springs and light alloy tappets were fitted between the valves and the camshafts, the tappets being controlled by double coil springs one inside the other.

Special Type 58 DCOA/3F (F standing for Ferrari) Weber carburetters were produced for this engine and mounted in two pairs on the offside of the engine. The method of attachment used on the 625 was again employed whereby the carburetters themselves were mounted on a frame bolted to the chassis member. Flanged rubber tubes linked them to the cylinder head, thus eliminating engine vibrational effects on the carburetters.

Chassis changes

The chassis of this car was built on the space frame principle. At the front, a main box structure was used with a transverse bridge to hold the centrally mounted steering box. At the ends of this bridge were placed the suspension units which comprised unequal length wishbones attached by means of ball joints to the wheel hubs replacing the kingpins and bushes on the 500 and 625 models. A thin leaf spring was mounted transversely underneath the chassis, the ends of which were attached to the lower wishbone, this together with a rubber block, mounted between the wishbones, provided the springing mechanism for the front end.

The chassis at the rear was wedge-shaped and served to contain the gearbox differential unit. The casting of this unit allowed a very low transmission line and the final drive was taken out of the rear upwards through a pair of spur gears and forwards to the crown wheel and pinion. Silent bloc bushes supported the sub-frame to which the gearbox differential casing was bolted. Double universally jointed halfshafts transmitted the drive to the wheel hubs, each wheel hub carrier being attached to the De Dion tube running across the car in front of the gearbox/differential unit instead of behind as on the earlier cars. The tube was located by a block running in a vertical guide. Two radius rods either side were provided for axle location running forward and being attached to the chassis. A transverse leaf spring was used, mounted above the rear axle assembly and connected to the hub carriers by short links. Location of the spring on the chassis was by a central bolt and pairs of rollers either side, these having an effect on the roll stiffness and allowed the tail to be broken loose more easily.

Four separate exhaust pipes were used, numbers one and four and two and three being joined together, the twin tubes then further joining into one large bore tailpipe. As pannier tanks were used on this car, the exhaust pipe swept up and over these tanks so that the pipe was high up by the cockpit. The pannier tanks were linked to a small capacity tank in the tail.

Steering was provided by arms running rearwards from the front hub carriers and coupled by jointed trackrods to the central steering arm projecting out of the rear of the steering box. The steering box was linked to the steering wheel by a single universally jointed column running down the centre of the engine.

Quick-change axle ratios

By running the De Dion tube in front of the gearbox/differential housing, the reduction gear housing was left behind the axle unit and made easily accessible. Also the small fuel tank taking up very little room enabled the axle ratios in the car to be changed very quickly as opposed to about an 8 hour job on the earlier cars where the tank had to be dismounted, the transmission shaft and halfshafts disconnected and the whole gearbox/differential unit taken out before the casing, which was split centrally, could be opened.

First racing appearance of the 555 Squalo was at Syracuse in 1954. Farina and Gonzales were down to drive the cars but Farina, who was not used to the handling which differed greatly from the earlier models, due to the concentration of the weight within the short wheelbase, did not hesitate to make known his dislike for the car and was very cheerful when he managed to blow up his engine during practice. As a result he drove the older Type 625 and only Gonzales started with the 555. Early in the race Hawthorn, blinded by a shower of hay thrown up by another car, crashed into a wall and caught fire. Gonzales arrived on the scene, stopped his car and leapt out to help Hawthorn who was in fact already out and safely over the wall putting out his burning overalls. Whilst Gonzales was looking for Hawthorn his car rolled forward into Hawthorn's blazing wreckage and caught fire too ending in the total destruction of both cars. Altogether an unfortunate beginning for a new car.

The 555 made its next appearance at Silverstone where Gonzales drove it in the first heat of the International Trophy. The tubby Argentinian driver put up a tremendous show driving flat out in the wet to lead the heat from start to finish. It looked as if the new car was really in order when misfortune struck and the mechanics, whilst trying to start the car for the final, found the engine seized solid.

Back at the factory some modifications were made to the car, the engine being moved forward in the chassis by 50 mm (2 in.). With these modified cars Farina and Gonzales were sent to the Belgian Grand Prix at Spa. The cars behaved very well and Gonzales made second fastest practice time with Farina 3rd. Things did not however work out too well for Gonzales withdrew almost immediately with engine trouble, and Farina, although at times leading the very rapid Maserati of Fangio, went out at half distance with ignition trouble.

At the French Grand Prix which followed, the 555 Ferrari met for the first time the new Mercedes Benz which made a serious addition to the opposition, especially as Mercedes No. 1 driver was Fangio. Also opposing them was a powerful Maserati team with Ascari and Villoresi, on loan from Lancia, driving for the other Modenese factory.

Ferrari sent two fo the Type 555 for Gonzales and Hawthorn. Practice times were disappointing but during the race Gonzales set off after the flying Mercedes being the only one of all the others that could keep anywhere near the two German cars. Hawthorn, further back, had his engine blow up after ten laps and shortly after-

wards Gonzales was out with a burst oil line. The 555 had failed again.

The unreliability of the engines under stress was a real problem and Ferrari sent the older 625 models to both the British and the German Grand Prix. Maglioli took one of the cars to Pescara but it broke down on the first lap of practice and the car was withdrawn when Maglioli had to return home because of family matters.

Ferrari showed a certain lack of confidence in the cars when they arrived at Berne for the Swiss Grand Prix. Although the cars had undergone modification having wider front brakes and engine alterations, they were given to the junior drivers Maglioli and Manzon. Manzon did not like the car at all and during practice crashed - destroying the car. Maglioli, just as unhappy with his 555, drove around quietly to take a poor 7th place.

The all-important Italian Grand Prix saw the appearance of only one Type 555 although the old 625 given to Ascari was also fitted with a type 555 engine. From the beginning Ascari with the older-chassied car led and Gonzales was right amongst the leaders with his Type 555 but again he was forced to retire although this time not with engine failure but with a broken gearbox.

Practical development of the 555

After the Monza failure Enzo Ferrari set about a very intensive development plan for the Type 555 and every day one of the cars could be seen at the Modena Autodrome testing longer and shorter wheelbases, alternative steering and different springs as well as experiments with fuel weights and larger tanks in the rear.

As a result, for the Spanish Grand Prix at Barcelona, only one 555 made its appearance to be driven by Hawthorn. This car was however much modified from the original. The engine oil passages were again altered and stronger connecting rods used. Valves were altered and a smaller diameter exhaust system came into use.

Front suspension did away with the transverse leaf spring which was replaced by small coil springs with an anti-roll bar running under the front of the car. The track rods were changed to revert to the original 625 type and the upper wishbone was widened. Several minor alterations were made to the rear axle and the general opinion was that the car handled in a much better manner.

Hawthorn, despite the presence of full factory teams of Mercedes, Lancia and Maserati, was able to get into the lead early on and, after swapping places with Trintignant for some laps, went on to record a convincing win for Ferrari. At last the 555 Squalo had behaved itself. During the winter of 1954 — 55 Ferrari decided to send a team of the earlier Type 625 cars to Argentina to allow him to concentrate on his Type 555. During its period of winter development several further changes were made from the Barcelona-winning model and the new car was known as the 'Supersqualo.'

The Supersqualo

The Supersqualo had a completely new chassis frame utilizing two large diameter tubes with tubes of smaller diameter forming a type of superstructure to carry the rear suspension, body and tanks. Pannier fuel tanks were still retained but a larger rear tank was fitted. A dropped radiator mounting gave a much lower bonnet line with a longer, wider and flatter nose than used on the previous year's models.

The 555 Supersqualo made its first appearance at Turin. Farina drove the car in practice but despite having covered hundreds of laps at the Modena circuit to get used to it, he still did not display any enthusiasm for the car. During practice it broke an oil line and finally Farina decided he would take the old 625 instead.

The next appearance of the team with the Supersqualos was at Bordeaux, when Farina and Trintignant were listed to drive them. Again in practice Farina broke an oil line and during the race was forced to retire with gearbox trouble after only a few laps. Trintignant had a difficult time keeping up with the Maseratis and he finally handed over to Farina who put on the pressure but all he succeeded in doing was to spin out so he handed back to Trintignant and the car was finally retired being very far back in the field.

It was rather obvious that when the Supersqualos were taken to Monte Carlo no one in the team wanted to drive them and they were finally

dumped on Harry Schell, a newcomer to the team, and Taruffi who had been called on at the last moment to make up numbers. Farina and Trintignant again preferred the antiquated 625 models. Schell only went half way being very unhappy with the car and finally retired with a blown piston; Taruffi equally unhappy with his car puttered around at the tail end of the field and came in to hand over to reserve driver Paul Frere who continued to drive round as best he could with the gearbox giving trouble, finally handing the car back to Taruffi.

Belgian Grand Prix

Ferrari decided to send a full team of Supersqualos to the Belgian Grand Prix at Spa. For this race he chose Farina, Trintignant and Paul Frere, the latter having an intimate knowledge of the course and showing great promise in Grand Prix cars. Long tapering noses were fitted to the cars for this high speed circuit, rather resembling the 1958 Vanwall.

Farina managed a 4th fastest time in practice and during the race took 3rd place after having been a steady 4th for most of the race; Frere showed that the Ferrari confidence had not been misplaced and brought his car in 4th whilst Trintignant, still in poor health after an accident at Monza, finished 7th having had several minor troubles.

In view of this performance things looked brighter for the future and the team was sent to Zandvoort with renewed enthusiasm. There was however to be a big shuffle in team drivers; Castelotti who was left without a job when Lancia decided to give up racing after the death of Ascari, was included in the Ferrari team. Hawthorn too made his way back to the Modenese team after having decided that the Vanwall was going nowhere that season. Farina, who was still having trouble with the leg burns he sustained the previous year at Monza, decided to retire from racing, so only Trintignant was left of the original team.

Zandvoort with the rejuvenated team turned out a great disappointment. Although Hawthorn put his car into the second row for the start, none of the cars went well during the race, Trintignant broke his gearbox and retired, Castelotti managed to push himself up to 5th and Hawthorn had pit stops, first with gearbox trouble then with a broken-off exhaust pipe and finished back in the field in 7th position.

Lancia hands over to Ferrari

With Lancia out of racing the momentous announcement was made that all the Lancia material would be handed over to Ferrari. This certainly looked like a very useful shot in the arm even if Ferrari did not like to play around with cars that were not of his own design or manufacture.

The Lancias were taken to the Grand Prix of Italy at Monza as No. 1 cars for the Scuderia Ferrari and the Supersqualos were there mainly for practice. However things worked out differently and after a practice accident to Farina, who had decided to make a comeback and try the Lancia machinery, it was decided to withdraw the Lancias and the team again relied on the Supersqualos. With Jano from Lancia and Massimino, formerly of Maserati and Alfa Romeo, joining the Ferrari design staff some quick improvement work had been done on the 555 Supersqualo; Massimino quickly sorted out some handling problems and a new 5-speed gearbox was built in time for Monza. Now for the first time it seemed that the Supersqualos had turned into decent racing cars. However it was all too late and the Supersqualo was destined for the graveyard as the new Lancia material offered much greater opportunities for development.

Castelotti put up a brilliant showing at Monza trailing the two leading Mercedes Benz, nevertheless steadily losing ground; he was finally involved in a close fight with Musso's Maserati until Musso broke his car and Castelotti won his 3rd place back, never again relinquishing it for the rest of the race. Hawthorn was less fortunate with the breakage of his gearbox mounting causing his retirement, whilst the unhappy pair, Trintignant and Maglioli, trailed around at the back of the field finishing 6th and 8th.

The end of the Supersqualos

It was the last time that the Scuderia Ferrari ran the Supersqualos. All work now concentrated on the Lancias and the 4-cylinder designs were quickly forgotten.

Two of the Supersqualos were fitted with Type 860 Monza sports car engines of 3.5-litres and were sent out to Australia for the Formula Libre races with Parnell and Whitehead. The cars were purchased by private owners after the races and remain in private hands.

THE V8-CYLINDER LANCIA/FERRARI.

Towards the end of the 1955 season, Ferrari found himself at a very low ebb. The turn of the tide had begun when Ascari and Villoresi left him the previous year to go to Lancia. The whole matter was accelerated by the appearance of the new Mercedes Benz and during the 1955 season, it needed no genius to see that Ferrari's cars were nothing but outdated also-rans, a situation which he had once experienced in his Alfa Romeo days.

With the death of Ascari and Lancia's withdrawal from racing, the situation seemed no better until the encouraging announcement that all the Lancia material would be handed over to Ferrari who would at the same time absorb the technical and design staff.

Jano's Lancia engine

Back in January of 1954, at the Caselle Airport of Turin, Ascari had taken the first test ride in the new Grand Prix Lancia. This new creation of Vittorio Jano, although a 90-degree V8 design of 2.5-litres, was nevertheless a direct derivative of the earlier sports cars. The chain drive to the cams was one of the major similarities with the double roller chain for each head running straight across between the two cam sprockets and then over an adjustable idler placed just below the left hand cam sprocket of each bank.

The other similarity in this engine was in the cylinder head structure. There was a deep external web crossing between the cam boxes just above the centre of each combustion chamber. Between each cylinder bank there was a stud going down into the block and there were eight more studs along each side of the detachable head.

The Lancia had wet liners inserted in a one-piece block and crankcase. The water jackets of adjacent cylinders were completely separate except for a cross passage at the top just below the head face. The jackets were structurally joined by two planes of fore-and-aft webs, and were tied to the crankcase by lateral webbing.

Jano, to avoid liner distortion, used a method which employed a flange on the liner which met the cylinder head through a gasket. Just ¾ of an inch below the top was a shaped and notched flange which aligned with a counterbore in the cylinder casting. Between these two flanges, right at the top of the liner, all the stress of the cylinder head seal was absorbed. From this point down, the liner only had to guide the piston and took no compression stresses. Seal at the bottom of the cylinder was assured by a close fit plus two rubber O-rings grooved into the liner.

As a result of this, the liner could be made very thin for light weight and high rate of heat transfer. Water speeds and jacket capacity were low to keep temperatures up and wall friction down, the coolant coming in through manifolds low at each side and exiting through ducts alongside the inlet valve seats. Distribution was directed around the valve seats and around a finned section of the exhaust valve guide.

The water pump itself was driven from a small gear train at the nose of the crankshaft and had an integrally cast duct to the cylinder manifolds. Mounted vertically ahead of the front suspension, the radiator had a thick core and integral top and bottom tanks.

Each cylinder head and its joint seal was treated as a unit in itself, the water jackets acting only as structural supports.

The bottom of the block was machined off at the centre line of the crankshaft and the five main bearings were backed up by deep thick webs, the heads and cylinder block being cast in Siluminum.

The main bearing caps were very heavy, each one had two big studs close in and two smaller ones further out which connected the webbed cap firmly to the block. All the strength of this bottom end was in the block and main bearing caps, plus the machined crankshaft.

The engine sump, therefore, was purely a collector for oil to feed the dry-sump system. A high-volume scavenge pump was mounted low down at the front, taking in oil through a series of collectors hung from the main bearing caps. An oil reservoir was in the tail of the car and a core type radiator was mounted in the front of the left hand outrigger with a scoop on the outside. The pressure pump was offset to the right of the crank nose and was integral with the top of an oil filter housing. This engine had practically no external pressure oil feeds. The main artery of the lubrication network was a gallery which ran from the front to the back of the block in the centre of the V. Each main bearing was fed by a short duct down through the web. Passages up through the water jackets and head joints fed ducts drilled across the heads which in turn delivered pressure oil to the camshaft bearings and valve mechanisms.

The cylinder head was detachable and to take full advantage of this, two-bolt rod big ends were split diagonally so that they could be extracted up through the cylinders.

Originally the pistons were high domed with full skirts carrying five piston rings each, one being below the gudgeon pin. Heavy ribs under the crown curved down to carry loads to the gudgeon pin bosses. Very shallow cutaways for valve head clearance were used.

The valve gear

The prototype Lancia engines had long slim fingers separating the cam and valve stem end; hairpin springs were fitted to keep the stems short and valve weight down. But Jano decided that this system was too heavy for his liking and later on in the development it was abandoned. Compact tappets were used, being of a simple mushroom type screwed directly to the valve stem and on some of the engines there was a surrounding collar for extra security. Valve clearance was easily set by rotating the tappet in relation to the valve and locked by a series of notches under the pressure of the coil valve springs.

Due to the detachable heads there were no mechanical restrictions on the valve dimensions. The valves were large with thick stems, the inlet valve having a diameter of 46 mm (1.81 in.) and the exhaust 44 mm (1.75 in.). Both had bronze seat inserts and were angled at 40 degrees to the cylinder centre line. The inlet valve stem was an inch longer to allow room for a large diameter port from the carburetters.

The prototype engines had special Weber carburetters made to fit with the design but the engines when seen in competition used Solex Type 40 PII. These were of the twin choke type and fed by a fuel line network down the centre of the group. Use was made of a finned, temperature pickup bulb placed high between the two rear carburetter intakes where it would pick up maximum heat from underbonnet air. The air came in through a duct in the top of the nose instead of through a conventional scoop.

Twin Marelli magnetos were driven off the back ends of the inlet camshafts and protruded through the firewall into the cockpit. The prototype car had two small cowling airscoops leading to each one of the magnetos. These were changed to a single scoop leading to both that could be opened or shut at will.

At the back of the engine was a small cover for oil sealing and a direct connection to the propeller shaft which, like the engine, was inclined from right front to left rear.

The transmission was immediately behind the driver and all its shafts plus the integral differential were aligned across the car.

The input countershaft was at the bottom, the mainshaft at the centre and the spur driven differential was at the top. At the left of the ribbed case was an integral housing for the dry multiplate clutch which drove the countershaft. The clutch cover plate housed a pair of bevel gears which took up power from the prop shaft and which had an extension for the starting motor.

The gearbox had five forward speeds, first being used only as a starting gear; Porsche-type synchromesh was used on the top four. Gears were selected with a gateless lever on the right hand side of the car and transmission to the box was through twin rods.

A hydraulic cylinder, operated by the left foot of the driver, actuated the clutch through a small slave cylinder at the rear which pulled the withdrawal lever against a coil spring in tension.

The section of the casing for the differential was sufficient to prevent pressure buildup and allowed for a large range of axle ratios. A ZF type differential was used.

In the case of the Lancia, the drive went through U-jointed halfshafts which were very small in diameter. Both universals were of the simple Hooke type and length changes were permitted by sliding splines which rode on ball bearings.

The frame and suspension

In his design Jano used the engine and gearbox to give support to the frame. Tubing of about 1½ in. diameter was used to form a simple truss-type frame. To link up the front cross member and the cockpit superstructure, Jano designed special lugs on the front and back of each cylinder head to bolt on to the structure. There were additional lugs at the bottom of each head which linked with mounts on the bottom frame members. Two boxed towers were built up each side just ahead of the engine and these served as mounts for the suspension. These two mounts were connected crosswise by large upper and lower tubes whilst the back mounts were traced by smaller diagonal tubes. Behind the driver's cockpit, the frame extended to the large transmission casting which in turn served to support the transverse leaf spring and the locating block for the De Dion tube. Small tubes and perforated sheet metal webs were additional aids to stiffness around the cockpit itself.

Fuel tanks and weight distribution

Jano spent much time on studying roll centres, weight transfers and distribution. To keep the front/rear weight distribution constant he devised the system of having the main bulk of fuel in the outrigged pontoon tanks with a small additional tank behind the driver's head.

For the front suspension Jano used equal length parallel wishbones, these being made out of welded-up tubes with forged connections. The outer ends were ball-jointed into the forged spindle and vertical support. At the outer ends of the bottom arms were enclosed rollers which located the main leaf of the transverse spring. The result was initially low stiffness per wheel, which could be increased by screwing down two out-rigged stops above the small top leaf. The front arm of each wishbone extended inboard of its pivot as a drilled I section lever. Flanges on the bottom levers acted against rubber buffers on the lower crossmembers to limit upward wheel travel, while the upper levers worked the plungers on the vertically placed tubular shock absorbers. These units were there because that was the best place to feed stress into the chassis without adding more bracing.

At the rear a small light De Dion tube curved behind the differential and was located in one plane by parallel trailing arms mounted inboard on each side. The sliding block for lateral guidance was bolted to the frame, the guide hanging below the De Dion tube. Springing was by a transverse leaf spring, clamped in the centre and working on rollers below the hubs. This spring was in fact more flexible in operation than the roller mounted type used in the Ferraris.

Jano mounted his tubular shockabsorbers about one foot apart in the centre of the car in a vertical plane. Links and rocker arms actuated them from the top and a third rocker joined them at the bottom.

Brakes and steering

As there was no space left for inboard brakes, conventional outboard brakes were employed, but having four shoes per wheel. Drums were very wide and heavily finned but no scoops to the backing plates were used.

The steering wheel led through a short shaft to the steering box mounted just behind the dashboard. The steering arm pushed a long drag link down the centre of the engine V which rotated a bell crank vertically pivoted to the upper cross member. The bottom arm of the bell crank turned the wheels through a split track rod and drilled I section steering arms. The rear brakes had a system of cable application controlled by a small lever in the cockpit.

The Lancias first made their appearance under the Scuderia Ferrari colours at the Grand Prix of Italy at Monza. Castelotti joined the Ferrari team and was entered with a Lancia together with Farina and Villoresi.

In practice the cars showed more than adequate speed but trouble with tyres on the high speed banking had the whole team worried and Enzo Ferrari decided it was too risky to have them run under these conditions and consequently withdrew all three cars.

The gift of the Lancia material plus the offer of financial assistance from FIAT naturally put Ferrari into a much better position than he expected at the end of the 1955 season.

The Ferrari Supersqualo and Type 625 were outdated and there seemed nothing new up Ferrari's sleeve although Lampredi made an abortive attempt to bolster up his sadly failing reputation by designing a 2-cylinder engine which could have been mounted in a new type of chassis and used for racing on twisty circuits. He had also designed a 6-cylinder engine to replace the four on the faster circuits but nothing looked promising and the designs were shelved.

With the Lancia material, Ferrari had new hope and decided on a complete reorganization of his Scuderia. Lampredi left and Bellentani of Maserati was retained to act as personal supervisor of the Grand Prix cars. Jano remained in a design consultant capacity and the well known Massimino was also called in as a consultant. Ferrari then employed a promising newcomer, Ing. Andrea Fraschetti, to join the already formidable design staff and the scene was set.

Fangio joins Ferrari

The withdrawal of Mercedes Benz left Fangio free and he was immediately employed to lead the team. Farina had retired from racing so Ferrari obtained the services of the promising young Maserati driver, Luigi Musso who, together with Castelotti made up the Italian element of the team, and a further promising driver was added by the engagement of Peter Collins. During the winter the original Lancias underwent a certain amount of modification at the Ferrari factory where they did away with the idea of using the engine as a main brace for the frame and added bracing struts leading from the bulkhead to the front cross member.

Ferrari did not favour the idea of the pannier tanks and installed his main tank in the tail of the car, retaining small reserve tanks in the front ends of the panniers. The pannier tanks themselves were blended into the main part of the body and the four exhaust pipes each side were guided through the pannier to finish in megaphones just in front of the rear wheels.

At the rear of the car a transverse leaf spring,

mounted above the gearbox/differential unit, replaced the original spring mounted below this unit and Houdaille shockabsorbers took the place of the Lancia telescopic type. These shock-absorbers were mounted on chassis extensions which carried the fuel and oil tanks. At the front an anti-roll bar was fitted together with Houdailles. These cars made their first appearance in the Argentine Grand Prix and showed themselves to be extremely fast. Fangio, although breaking the engine of his own car, took over Musso's and continued to win the race. A week later the cars were out again at the Mendoza Grand Prix which had replaced the Buenos Aires Grand Prix on the calendar. Fangio had no trouble at all in winning this event.

The next modification on the car was to remove the small reserve tanks still carried in the panniers and locate them either side of the chassis frame. At Syracuse, for the first race of the European season, Fangio had this latest type whilst Musso and Castelotti drove the same types as used in Argentina but Collins, as junior in the team, had to be content with an unmodified Lancia. Fangio again led the other team members to a certain victory.

Fangio and Collins were sent to Silverstone with two of the modified cars but received a bad shock when the Vanwall ran away from them and both the cars went out with clutch trouble.

The two other drivers, Castelotti and Musso, were sent to Naples where Castelotti was due to drive the modified car that had been fitted with a Massimino designed swing axle layout but for the race this was dispensed with. Musso whilst in the lead had his engine break and Castelotti retired early on in the race with no oil pressure.

The 1956 Season - Monaco

For the Grand Prix of Monaco, Castelotti had the car which still retained the reserve tanks in the panniers but Fangio, Collins and Musso had the further modified cars with the tanks in the main body of the car. Castelotti went out early with a disintegrated clutch and Fangio, in a frantic attempt to catch the flying Maserati of Moss, spun his car badly denting it and disturbing the De Dion location. Fangio stopped and handed over to Castelotti and Collins was flagged in to hand over to the maestro. Fangio

turned on the heat and began to chase Moss relentlessly. Despite this, and the fact that he closed the gap considerably, he was unable to catch the Maserati before the end of the race and had to be content with 2nd place.

The team was reduced in numbers when Musso had a bad accident with a Ferrari sports car during the 1,000 km of the Nurburgring, and for the Belgian Grand Prix he was replaced by Paul Frere, a driver whom Ferrari particularly liked to use for the very fast Spa-Francorchamps circuit due to his intimate knowledge of the track.

The fifth car was taken along to keep the Belgian organizers happy and given to Belgian driver Andre Pilette. This car was painted in the Belgian colours but the Ferrari team did not show excessive interest in the entry.

Fangio quickly bettered his Mercedes Benz records on the circuit, but during the race Moss, with the Maserati, again showed the Ferrari team his heels; however Fangio got past him and pulled out into the lead and, when the Maserati lost a wheel, the team were in a 1, 2, 3, 4 order. Castelotti went out with transmission trouble and shortly after Fangio had the same thing happen. Collins was then installed in 1st place without anyone left to challenge him whilst Frere eliminated the last Maserati hope by passing Behra into 2nd place. Pilette was out of the picture finishing a poor 6th.

An over-square V8 engine

Bellentani, on instructions from Ferrari, had been experimenting with a different bore and stroke on the V8 engine and all the cars prepared for the Grand Prix of Rheims had the new engine with the bore and stroke of 76 x 68.5 mm instead of the previous 73 x 73 mm of the original engines. With Musso still absent from the team, Ferrari decided to try out two young drivers, Gendebien who had driven once before in the team at Buenos Aires and the very promising Spaniard 'Fon' De Portago.

Fangio, Collins and Castelotti placed themselves in the front row of the grid and, from the start, toured round in a close bunch changing the order from lap to lap. Unfortunately a small miscalculation had been made in the pits and Harry **Schell** in the Vanwall suddenly appeared on the scene. Everyone thought he was a lap behind but when it was found that he was challenging the Ferraris for the lead, there was some frantic signalling to the complacent three. The boys had to resort to some hectic driving to stay ahead of the flying Schell and things were very uneasy until finally the Vanwall failed. With Fangio in the lead all seemed set but in the meantime both Gendebien and De Portago were out, the first with clutch trouble and the second with a seized gearbox. Next man in trouble was Fangio who split a fuel line, and the time lost in repairs dropped him back to 4th. Try as he would he could not make up the lost time and had to be content with 4th place whilst Peter Collins went on to win his second World Championship event with Castelotti 2nd.

When the team made its next appearance for the British Grand Prix at Silverstone the drivers were Fangio, Castelotti, Collins and De Portago, Musso still being unfit. The cars were not too convincing in practice, and things looked little better in the race. When the BRMs broke down, Fangio went into the lead but Collins was out with no oil pressure. De Portago was well placed so Collins took over his car whilst Castelotti bent his car and came into the pits to retire. De Portago insisted on taking over but was black flagged after two more laps as the officials were afraid that the car was dangerous. Portago waited at the finish and pushed the car over when Fangio crossed the line. Fangio was 1st, the Collins/De Portago car 2nd and the Castelotti/De Portago car 10th.

German Grand Prix

At the Grand Prix of Germany on the Nurburgring, the next event, the cars put up a fine showing, Fangio and Collins being obviously faster than the Maserati opposition and were quickly installed in 1st and 2nd places. Castelotti was already out with magneto trouble and Musso, now back with the team but not too fit, was called in to hand over to the other Italian. Collins was forced to retire when it was found he had a fuel leak which was almost asphyxiating him and he took over De Portago's car. Both Collins and Castelotti tried hard to make up the lost ground but the result was that both of them spun off, the cars being too

damaged to continue. Once again Fangio came in 1st.

For the Italian Grand Prix at Monza six cars were entered, the sixth member being Wolfgang Von Trips, a driver who had shown tremendous promise during the season and who had given Ferrari some nasty moments during the Mille Miglia with his 300SL Mercedes. In practice both Collins and Fangio threw treads and Von Trips on his first Grand Prix outing went off the road completely destroying the car.

There was a great deal of apprehension in the team after the practice due to the tyre problem. At the start, however, both Castelotti and Musso threw caution to the winds as they were after each other's blood for the Italian Championship. After only a few laps both Musso and Castelotti blew their tyres but Fangio and Collins held back to save theirs and the race became a battle between the new offset-engine Maserati of Moss and the two Ferraris of Fangio and Collins. De Portago although driving carefully also had a tyre burst on the banking and the resulting damage caused him to retire. Castelotti, back in the race did nothing to subdue his pace, but he paid the price of his folly when another tyre burst and he was lucky to escape with broken front suspension. Collins was the next in tyre trouble and had to change, then Fangio was out with broken steering. The mechanics worked hard to replace the broken pieces, cannibalising De Portago's car and Castelotti took over. At half distance Collins came in for a tyre check and it was then that he made a gesture which allowed Fangio to take the 1956 World Championship. Although Fangio did not expect it, Collins offered his car to the Maestro who set off to do the best he could. When the Maserati stopped for fuel Musso was in the lead much to the joy of the Italian crowd. The Maserati was back into second place and Fangio running in third place trying to catch Moss but being very careful. Only a few laps from the end Musso's steering broke and he narrowly missed crashing into the pits; with his retirement went his hopes for a World Championship race win and the Italian Championship for 1956. Castelotti plodded on to finish 8th.

The new Maserati won but Fangio was 2nd thus assuring his fourth World Championship title.

Plans for 1957

Naturally during the winter of 1956/7 a great deal of work was undertaken at the Maranello factory. Ferrari was making big plans for the 1957 season and virtually set about cornering the market in drivers. His first setback, however, came when Fangio chose to drive for the rival Modenese Maserati factory so he decided to make up for the lack of his star by having all the promising young drivers, who were available, tied to him by contract.

Hawthorn, having had enough of his exploits with the British cars, returned to the team and was in company with Peter Collins, Castelotti, Musso and De Portago. Other drivers engaged were Von Trips, Gendebien, Trintignant, Phil Hill and Perdisa.

During the winter the V8 engines again underwent a change and Bellentani and Bazzi produced a new model with a bore and stroke of 80 x 62 mm as opposed to the former bore and stroke of 76 x 68.8 mm. Carburetter layouts were experimented with and Webers produced a new type specially built for the V8 engine. However the cars prepared for the Argentine Grand Prix retained the Solex type but with a modification to the adaptors which improved the flow from the carburetters to the head ports. New chassis were produced closely following the original Lancia design but substituting large dimension tubes where Lancia had used twin small diameter tubes. The superstructure round the cockpit was altered completely and the new chassis did away with the necessity of the bracing struts between the front crossmembers and the cockpit superstructure. After the Monza experiences, Ferrari did away with the Lancia steering arms and replaced them with solid forgings. One of these new models also sported unequal length wishbones, the chassis pivot point naturally being repositioned. The panniers carrying the exhaust pipes were retained and the cars looked very little different from the 1956 model.

For the Argentine Grand Prix Ferrari nominated Hawthorn, Collins, Castelotti, Musso, Perdisa and Gonzales as drivers; the latter was taken on at the request of the organizers so as to have an Argentinian driver in the team. The Argentine trip was disastrous and from practice times it looked as if no progress had been made since the previous year, the cars being seemingly underpowered. Hawthorn, Musso and Collins were out of the race with broken clutches; Castelotti suffered from a broken halfshaft and lost a wheel; Collins took over from Perdisa, the latter being very reluctant to make the change-over and Gonzales, who was still not fit after an accident sustained a long time ago at the Tourist Trophy, came in to hand over to De Portago. The Spaniard continued to take fifth place whilst Collins was back in the pits to hand over to Von Trips who finally brought the car in 6th.

The Grand Prix of Buenos Aires held two weeks later again saw the Ferrari team in the field. Although the cars were running better, Castelotti could obtain no better than 3rd place in the first heat with Hawthorn 4th and Musso 5th. Collins shared his car with Masten Gregory who had been given a drive due to his brilliant performance in winning the 1,000 km sports car race the week before.

In the second heat both Hawthorn and Castelotti had alternated in the lead but dropped back to let Collins win. The Maseratis got by Hawthorn who finished 4th, with Perdisa 5th.

The final result, achieved by adding together the times of the heats, placed Ferrari 3rd, 4th, 5th, 7th and 8th.

First appearance of the new car

In the early spring after the Argentine races Ferrari was working on another new model but in the meantime Castelotti was killed at Modena whilst testing one of the cars back from Argentina. Perdisa decided to retire from motor racing and take up selling cars so at the beginning of the European season the Ferrari team was already reduced in numbers. For the first race of the European season at Syracuse, Ferrari fielded two cars driven by Musso and Collins. It was also the first appearance of the new 1957 car. This car employed the Ferrari type chassis that had been introduced in Argentina but had the front suspension changed to unequal length wishbones, combined with coil springs. The familiar pannier tanks were abandoned and the result was a completely new slim line for the 1957 car with four snake like exhaust pipes ending in megaphones running along the side of the body.

Although the cars made the fastest time in practice they were no real match for the Vanwall of Moss during the race and it was only when Moss broke down that the two Ferraris were firmly established in 1st and 2nd places.

With no serious opposition at Naples Ferrari took the opportunity to do some experimenting. He sent Hawthorn and Collins in the V8 cars and Musso with the completely new V6 Formula 2 car.

Both V8 cars had the old-style body with the panniers carrying the exhaust pipes but both of them were considerably modified.

Hawthorn had one of the old Lancia chassis frames which had been lengthened by 10 cm to accommodate his long legs. At the front a complete Supersqualo Ferrari suspension layout was welded to the chassis frame, being of the double wishbone and coil spring type with long kingpins in the place of the Lancia ball joint layout. Ferrari Supersqualo steering was also adapted to this unit. During practice this car appeared with the Supersqualo type brakes but a changeover was made, the Ferrari type backing plate being retained and the Supersqualo brake drums being replaced by the wider finned Lancia drums.

Experimental swing-axle layout

On the Collins car Ferrari experimented with a rear-end layout incorporating swing axles, similar to that tried at Naples the previous year. Massimino had made some modification and it was hoped that this would be the answer for twisty circuits. The two swinging halfshafts crossed over at their inner ends and were mounted on ball joints, while the ends were welded to hub carriers from a De Dion tube, the normal fore-and-aft location by double radius rods being retained. Very short coil springs were fitted instead of the previous year's transverse leaf spring, to this was added an anti-roll bar.

Collins set the fastest time in practice but Hawthorn's car had seized splines on one of the halfshafts and after being repaired it was found that Hawthorn could lap at the same speed as Collins. During the race the two British drivers took turns at leading until Hawthorn had the line to the fuel pressure gauge break and lost

some time in the pits for repairs. This let Musso in the Formula 2 car into 2nd place but Hawthorn put his foot down to regain his lost position. He broke the lap record several times in his attempt to catch Musso passing the Italian driver just before the end of the race. Ferrari decided to do away with the swing axle layout and it was never again used.

De Portago is killed

Whilst preparations were under way for the Monaco Grand Prix, Ferrari suffered another serious setback when 'Fon' De Portago was killed in the Mille Miglia. Portago being somewhat of a celebrity apart from his motor racing activities, the accident attracted a great deal of publicity mostly detrimental to Ferrari. Not only had Ferrari lost his most promising driver but he had to face the wrath of the Italian newspapers who thoroughly enjoyed and exploited the opportunity to attack the 'murderous' sport, naturally, without having any idea of what they were talking about.

For the Monaco race Ferrari turned out with Collins, Hawthorn, Trintignant and Von Trips. Musso was unable to race as he was still suffering from a serious illness that had laid him low before the Mille Miglia. Ferrari sent a total of six cars for the practice, four for the race and one V8 for practice plus the V6 Formula 2 car.

All the V8 models except the practice car had the slim body without the panniers similar to Musso's car at Syracuse.

Hawthorn's long chassis car from Naples had the body style altered from the pannier type to the slim Syracuse type. Another car similar to Hawthorn's was also present and both this and the Hawthorn car had a new exhaust system with reversed cones on their megaphones; Ferrari using a little bit of motor cycle practice. No conclusive results were achieved by this and the only real effect was to dampen the tremendous blare of noise from the megaphones.

The practice car with the panniers was a 1956 model.

Ferrari troubles started in practice. Collins was out in Hawthorn's car which had the Supersqualo front suspension when he lost control out of the chicane and rammed into a large iron bollard, the car being too damaged to race. The rest of the team were continually changing cars and putting in a great deal of time with the Formula 2 car as well. Hawthorn found the 1956 practice car much to his liking, especially as he fitted fairly well into it and elected to drive the car in the race.

Trintignant was given the other reversed cone car whilst Collins and Von Trips had the normal megaphone type.

Monaco

At the beginning of the race things looked promising, with Collins right behind the Vanwall of Moss, but after only a few laps Moss in the leading Vanwall crashed into the wooden poles of the chicane barricade throwing the poles across the track. Collins ran right into these poles and skidded through the sandbags into another bollard. Fangio, with the Maserati, got through unscathed followed by Brooks, who jammed on his brakes and Hawthorn who was following rammed a front wheel of the Ferrari against a rear one of the Vanwall. The shock sheared the front suspension sending the whole unit, wheel, drum and hub, sailing into the yacht harbour. Hawthorn skidded out of control his car landing right on top of Collins's wrecked car, fortunately without damage to the drivers. Two Ferraris already out and Fangio was comfortably in the lead set for another Grand Prix win.

Ferrari hopes now rested on Von Trips and Trintignant. Von Trips was well placed in third position but was obviously unable to make up anything on Brooks who held 2nd place with a Vanwall. Trintignant was further back having a lot of trouble shaking off the smaller fry and getting the nose of his car dented in the process. He finally moved up to fifth place but trouble with his magnetos caused him to stop at the pits and dropped him back again; when he rejoined the race it was with a misfiring engine. In the meantime, Von Trips had been called in to hand over to Hawthorn but the latter was unable to make up any time on Brooks as he found the driving position much too cramped for him; he was quickly back in the pits and the car was returned to Von Trips who was then assured of 3rd place.

Just before the end of the race, whilst Von Trips was going up the hill to take the Casino

bend, his engine blew up in a big way and he crashed in the same spot where his co-national, Hans Hermann, had piled the Mercedes into the wall the previous year. On returning to the pits he informed a pale team manager that the engine, clutch, gearbox and chassis frame were broken. Trintignant was continuing as best he could finishing the race 6th and last, probably the only time that Ferrari had the humiliation of finishing in last place.

Next setback for the Scuderia Ferrari was when Von Trips crashed badly on the Nurburgring with a Gran Turismo car and there was little hope of his participation for the rest of the season.

Ferrari had a great deal of work to do to replace all the damaged cars, but for Rouen he was back with four cars. Musso was fit again so he rejoined the team with Hawthorn, Collins and Trintignant.

Hawthorn had his own long-chassis car and the other three had cars all fitted with the Ferrari-designed chassis.

Musso was fastest of the team in practice and during the race led Fangio for some time but was eventually forced to give way to the Maestro. Collins came up from behind and passed Musso but dropped behind again when he had gearbox trouble. Hawthorn was not in the picture having a hard time fending off the BRM of McKay Fraser. Finally Musso finished 2nd with Collins a long way behind in 3rd place and Hawthorn even further back in 4th place.

When the team turned up at Rheims, it did not look very convincing. Hawthorn had a long chassis car which turned out to be one of the Monaco wrecks that had been repaired; Collins had a 1956 type Lancia/Ferrari and Musso, to everyone's surprise, was driving the oldest of Lancia/Ferraris.

As Hawthorn did not like the handling of his long-chassis car, it was given to Gendebien to drive and Mike took the unsatisfactory car he had driven at Rouen.

Musso surprised everyone by pushing the old 'heap' into 2nd place at the start but was unable to make any impression on the rapid Vanwall of Moss. Collins was early out of the race with a blown engine, then it was Hawthorn, who had been holding on to 3rd place, who disappeared with a damaged engine. Fortunately for Musso, the Vanwall broke down and he sailed into the lead which he retained unchallenged to the end but before the victory was accomplished, Ferrari had another car break down when Gendebien also went out with engine trouble.

British Grand Prix

For the British Grand Prix at Aintree, Ferrari entered Hawthorn, Collins, Musso and Trintignant. Hawthorn with his long chassied car and the others in the 1957 models which had run at Rouen. At the last minute there was a changeover, Trintignant finishing up with Hawthorn's car and Hawthorn taking over Collins' 1957 car.

Hawthorn put up a great show and held grimly on to second place but just as Behra's Maserati blew up and Hawthorn would have taken 1st place but one of his tyres picked up a piece of the Maserati's disintegrated clutch and the tyre went flat. Hawthorn thinking that the De Dion had broken pulled into the pits to retire but the mechanics, seeing the trouble, changed the wheel and sent him out again. However his stop had put him back into 5th place. The team eventually took 2nd with Musso, Hawthorn coming in 3rd and Trintignant was a very poor 4th, these positions having only been gained by the fact that the opposition broke down.

German Grand Prix

At the Nurburgring the Ferrari engineers finally obtained adequate power from the engine and Hawthorn and Collins qualified for the front row with Musso, the only other team member for this race, further back on the grid. All three drivers used the Ferrari chassied 1957 models, Hawthorn having used his long chassis car only in practice. For the first two laps the two Ferraris were out in front with Hawthorn leading Collins but when the old maestro, Fangio, pushed his Maserati in front, the two Ferraris dropped back content to take 2nd and 3rd places. The unexpected happened and Fangio stopped. It was then that the Ferrari team manager made a very bad tactical error for, thinking that Fangio had broken down, he signalled the two Ferrari drivers that they were 1st and 2nd and were to go easy. Fangio had in fact not broken down but was in the pits taking on fuel. The Maserati rejoined the race whilst the two Ferrari drivers were having fun changing the lead to amuse the spectators. Fangio with the extra fuel and new tyres did not at first seem to be able to make any impression on the Ferraris and was in fact losing ground but then he pulled all his experience out of the bag and really put his foot down; he began to carve large chunks off the Ferrari lead and, before the Ferrari pit realized it, was right on the tail of the two British drivers. A sensational lap of 9 min 17 secs, the first time in the history of the Nurburgring that 9 min 20 secs had been broken, sent Fangio sweeping by the two Ferrari drivers to win another World Championship event, and left a rather embarrassed Hawthorn and Collins with 2nd and 3rd place respectively.

Ferrari threatens retirement

Pescara was the next World Championship event and Ferrari announced that, after all the difficulties he had had with the Italian press and Government officials resulting from the Mille Miglia accident of De Portago, he would withdraw from racing.

Under pressure from the organizers and Luigi Musso, Ferrari relented at the last moment and allowed the Italian driver to have a car which went to Pescara as a private entry. Naturally Hawthorn and Collins took a very poor view of this and it was to give rise to a good deal of difference of opinion between the two British drivers and the lone Italian.

Musso, eager to show that he was without a doubt No. 1 of the Ferrari team, decided that he would show everyone how the Ferrari could really go and, placed in the front row, Musso led for two laps in the race before being passed by Moss but his oil tank was already beginning to break loose. He ignored frantic signals from the pits where the team manager could see the damage and before he realized what had happened his engine seized from want of oil.

As was expected, Ferrari did not go into retirement for very long and there was a full team entry for the Italian Grand Prix at Monza. Ferrari lined up Hawthorn, Collins and Musso, with a fourth car for Von Trips who had made a fairly rapid recovery after his Nurburgring accident.

(Top) Bonetto's first race for Ferrari at San Remo 1949. He drives a 2 litre GP GP Roma 1950. Villoresi achieved second place in the 2 litre 12 cyl swing axle car
(Middle) Vallone came third in the 1950 GP Roma again in a 2 litre car
(Bottom) Mario Rafaeli of the Scuderia Marzotto won the 1951 GP Roma with a 2 litre swing axle car

(Top) Prix de Geneve 1950. Serafini in the 2 litre de Dion
Ferrari. He finished 3rd to Trintignant and Simon in Gordinis
(Middle) Ascari in the new de Dion axled 12 cyl 2 litre about to
overtake Vallone in his 2 litre swing axled car
(Bottom) Cortese's special stub exhaust Ferrari at the
Schauninsland Hillclimb 1951

(*Top*) Ascari won the 1950 GP Roma with the de Dion axled 2 litre 12 cyl

(*Middle*) The Formula 2 Ferraris being prepared for Ascari and Villoresi at Marseilles 1951
(*Bottom*) Dino Ferrari

(*Top Left*) Ascari at Modena in the prototype 4 cyl 2 litre, 1951
(*Top Right*) Farina with the Type 500 4 cyl during the Swiss GP 1952. Usual team leader Ascari is at Indianapolis
(*Middle*) Reims 1952. The long nosed Formula 2 Ferrari received its only defeat here
(*Bottom*) 8 June 1952, GP Autodrome Monza. Guiseppe Farina won with a stub exhaust Ferrari Type 500

(Top Left) Silverstone 1952. Ferrari's line-up, from left to right:
Ugolini (pointing) mechanic Nicolini, Taruffi, mechanic Marchetti,
Farina, chief mechanic Meazza and Ascari
(Top Right) The winner was Ascari. Silverstone 1952
(Middle Left) Mike Hawthorn's first Ferrari test, Modena
1952
(Middle Right) Buenos Aires 1953. Mike Hawthorn's first
race with Ferrari
(Bottom) Farina wins the 1953 German GP with the Type
500 4 cyl 2 litre

(Top) The 1953 line-up for the British GP. Ascari, Gonzales (Maserati), Hawthorn and Fangio (Maserati)

(Middle Left) Maserati's only major victory of 1953, and the last race under the 2 litre Formula. Italian GP 1953. Here Ascari and Farina lead the Maseratis of Fangio and Marimon. Marimon collided with Ascari on the last corner of the last lap allowing Fangio to win

(Middle Right) Alberto Ascari, World Champion 1952 and 1953 with the Type 500 Ferrari

(Bottom) The 553 Squalo Ferrari in 2 litre form at the Italian Grand Prix. It can be seen how the pannier fuel tank necessitated running the exhaust pipe at shoulder level, with a large protective guard

(Top Left) Taruffi in the 2.5 litre 4 cyl Prototype at the Valentino GP 1952. He finished 2nd behind Villoresi's Indianapolis 4.5
(Top Right) The 4 cyl engine of that car
(Middle Left) The short chassis 4 cyl Ferrari at Monza, during practice. It was the first Ferrari to have an outside high-level exhaust pipe
(Middle Right) Mike Hawthorn in action with the Prototype 2.5 litre 4 cyl at Silverstone
(Bottom) Froilan Gonzales during British GP practice at Silverstone 1954

(Top) Rouen 1954. Mike Hawthorn with the Type 625

(Middle Left) Hawthorn, 1955 British GP, Aintree. Type 625A; this model was superceded by the Supersqualo which turned out to be a far less successful model

(Middle Right) Farina in the Prototype 2.5 Supersqualo at Modena 1955

(Bottom Left) The only event at which the long nosed Supersqualo was used. Farina at Spa 1955

(Bottom Right) Reims 1954. Gonzales with his Type 555 Supersqualo

Top) Peter Collins in the Lancia-Ferrari at Monte Carlo 1956
Left) The four cylinder engine of the Type 555 Supersqualo
Middle Right) Fangio won the 1956 British GP in this Lancia-Ferrari
Bottom) The Lancia D50 as first modified by Ferrari

(*Top*) On test at Modena in December 1956. This is the prototype 1957 car
(*Bottom*) 1957 Buenos Aires. Mike Hawthorn in the second half (in cooler clothes)

(*Top*) Hawthorn in practice for the 1957 Monaco GP in the reverse cone V8 Ferrari
(*Bottom*) Hawthorn using one of the 1956 style V8 Lancia-Ferraris at the Naples GP of 1957. He finished second to Collins also Ferrari mounted

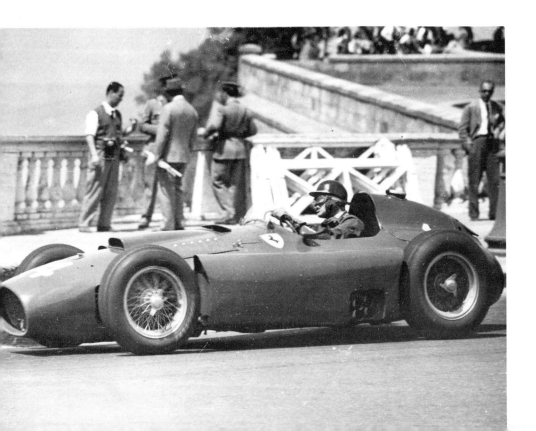

(Top) V8 Ferrari. Musso at Rouen 1957
(Bottom) German GP 1957. Hawthorn in the V8 Ferrari

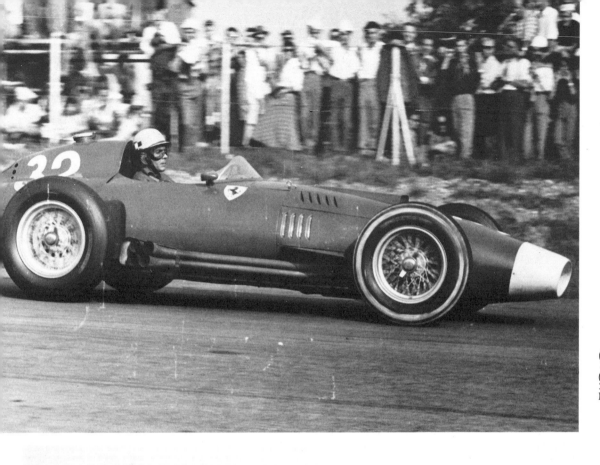

(Top) Musso at Monza in 1957 in the V8 Ferrari
(Bottom) The prototype 246 Dino in 2.2 litre form. Modena 1958

(Top) Luigi Musso testing the first 246 Dino at Modena in
1957
(Middle) Severi testing the Type 156 Dino V6 Formula 2
(Bottom) Phil Hill testing the Type 156 Formula 2 car at
Monaco during practice 1957

(Top) Von Trips in practice at Monaco 1957 with the Type 156
(Bottom) Unloading the Type 156 at Monaco 1957

(*Top*) 1958 Monaco GP, Hawthorn in the Type 246 Dino
(*Middle*) 1958 Monaco GP, Von Trips in the Type 246 Dino
(*Bottom*) 1958 Belgian GP, Hawthorn in the Type 246 Dino

The cars made a poor impression during practice and were left behind by the Vanwalls and Maseratis. The fastest Ferrari was that of Collins who was in the second row of the starting grid.

Two of the cars had modified air intakes on the bonnet, the intake coming forward on to the nose of the car and ending in a flared opening just above the Ferrari badge. These two cars were driven by Hawthorn and Collins.

During the race the cars were towards the back of the field and Hawthorn was even challenged and passed by the old Centro Sud Maserati driven by Bonnier. Collins, leading the Ferraris, was lapped by both Moss and Fangio but due to many breakdowns eventually moved up to 3rd place. However just as he seemed safe for 3rd place, his engine gave out with a broken valve and Hawthorn, who had eventually repassed Bonnier, moved up to 3rd. Again this looked safe but a broken fuel pipe sent Hawthorn into the pits. After the repairs he was back down to 5th position. Von Trips had by then moved up to 3rd but a long way behind Moss and Fangio, and in the meantime Hawthorn had lost his 5th place to Harry Schell's Maserati.

The end of the Lancia/Ferraris

It was the last appearance of the Lancia/Ferraris and a week later the shape of things to come was seen at the Modena Grand Prix when both Collins and Musso appeared with the V6 cylinder engined Formula 2 cars, the V6 engines having been bored out to 1860-cc.

When for the final event of 1957 at Casablanca the team turned out with the V6 Dino cars with the 2.4-litre engine it clearly indicated that the era of the V8 Lancia/Ferrari was past.

CHAPTER SEVEN

The V6 Dino Formula 1 and 2 cars

Mike Hawthorn

FERRARI had experienced excellent results with his Formula 1 Lancia/Ferraris during 1956, again winning a world championship. However, he was still thinking how nice it would have been had he won the championship with cars that were 100 per cent his own manufacture. Before very long the V8 cars would be obsolete and something new had to come. In 1957 the new Formula 2, limited to 1500-cc, would come into force and Ferrari decided to put some ideas on paper that could possibly be used for a future 100 per cent Ferrari Formula 1 car. He set about designing a true Grand Prix for his Formula 2 model which would be robust enough to allow further development, relying on a very powerful engine of a new design to give him maximum performance from the car.

Massimino, Jano, and to an extent, Ferrari's son Dino developed a V6 concept. Young Dino died before the design became a reality, and since then, all V6, and some 8-cylinder Ferraris have been known as 'Dino'.

Work went ahead with the new project and before the end of 1956 the new V6-cylinder engine was ready for the test bench.

Came 1957 and the Formula 2 Ferrari was eagerly awaited. During April of that year a new exhaust noise could be heard running up and down the Maranello-Abetone road as Martino Severi, the chief tester, made the initial trials; later in the month Peter Collins and Mike Hawthorn had their first go in the car at the Modena autodrome.

The V6 Formula 2

Naples was running a Formula 1 race and combined with it was the first Italian Formula 2 event. It was there that the Formula 2 Ferrari made its debut. Luigi Musso drove the car as both Collins and Hawthorn were driving Lancia/Ferraris in the Formula 1 event. In alignment all the team drivers had a go and much to everyone's surprise, the little car registered 3rd fastest time. During the race it had no trouble staying in 3rd place and went up to 2nd place when Hawthorn stopped at the pits; it was only by dint of tremendously fast driving that Hawthorn was able to catch the small Ferrari again. For its first race the car had been very impressive.

The engine of this car was entirely new for Ferrari, a very compact 65 degree V6 design in the formation of two banks of three cylinders. The two cylinder blocks were staggered relative to one another with the left block slightly ahead of the right one. Driven from the front of the short rigid crankshaft were the oil pump, water pump and fuel pump as well as four overhead camshafts. Two 14 mm spark plugs were situated in the centre of each combustion chamber and these were fed by two magnetos mounted on the front of each inlet camshaft. Later engines had one magneto mounted on the rear. Three down-draught twin-choke Weber carburetters were placed in the V of the two banks. Three exhaust headers per bank fed into single tail pipes. All castings were Siluminum light alloy and lubrication was dry sump.

The bore and stroke was 70 x 64.5 mm giving a capacity of 1490-cc. The compression ratio was 9.5 : 1 as the engine was intended to run on petrol (doped fuel was officially passe' as of the 1958 season) and 180 b h p was obtained at 9,000 r p m.

In chassis layout the whole thing was in the nature of a scaled down Formula 1 car. The frame had two main members of large diameter tubes, with a superstructure of smaller tubing forming a part of the whole unit providing torsional rigidity. It was not a pure space frame with all members in tension or compression, nor was it a simple ladder type frame relying on the inherent strength of the tubes, but it was a combination of the two. The 6-cylinder engine was offset to the left as it was on the Formula 1 Lancia/Ferraris. At the rear of the chassis was a 4-speed and reverse gearbox/differential built in unit, the gearbox shafts being transverse to the centre line of the car, as on the Formula 1 car. The small diameter propeller shaft ran diagonally across the bottom of the cockpit entering the gearbox through bevel gears, whilst the propeller shaft line was projected rearwards beyond the bevels, ending in a starter dog, exactly as the Lancia/Ferrari so that the same portable starter could be used for Formula 1 or Formula 2 models. After passing through the gearbox the drive was raised to the differential by spur gears and to the wheels by universally jointed half-shafts.

Adapted from Formula 1

Front suspension was by double wishbones with coil springs interspersed and an anti-roll bar, while Houdaille shockabsorbers were neatly fitted to the chassis frame under the bottom wishbone. These triangular wishbones were of unequal length, the top one being shorter, and they ended in short vertical king pins instead of the ball joints as on the Formula 1 cars, the two small king pins being joined by a forged stub axle member. The front brakes were built from existing components, the back plates and shoes being from the Formula 1 Lancia/Ferrari, of the thin cast-iron type, these two units being adapted into the design of the front end of the Formula 2 car. At the rear a De Dion layout was used, the construction of the components and basic design following Formula 1 practice, with the De Dion tube running across the car behind the gearbox/differential unit. However instead of having the centre location of the tube mounted low, with the ball fixed to the chassis and guide below the tube, the Formula 2 design had the guide attached to the chassis and ball on the centre line of the tube, thus giving fixed roll centre height. The ends of the tube were located by forward facing double radius rods, with spherical pivots, and suspension was by a high mounted transverse leaf spring and Houdaille

shockabsorbers as on the Formula 1 cars. The rear brakes were constructed especially for the small car but followed normal Ferrari practice, having wide drums with thin cooling fins. The driving seat was mounted slightly to the right of the cockpit and the steering wheel was quite high and nearly vertical, the column running across the top of the engine to the steering box which was mounted on top of the chassis by the left hand side suspension unit on the prototype. This was changed over to the right on later cars. As the car was intended for full length Grand Prix it carried a 37 gallon fuel tank which was contained in the tail with another tank mounted in the cockpit alongside the driver's left leg. Oil carried in a container attached to the rear of the main fuel tank and the bodywork followed the lines of the Formula 1 Lancia/Ferrari, with the exhaust pipes running low alongside the body and ending in megaphones just ahead of the rear tyres. With 15 in. wheels fitted, the overall effect was a scaled down Formula 1 car and from a distance it was very difficult to recognize the little car from its big brother.

Handling demonstrated at Monte Carlo

After its first successful outing at Naples, the car was next taken to the Grand Prix of Monaco where it kept the Formula 1 cars company. All four of the team drivers spent a considerable amount of time driving the car in practice and everyone was satisfied with its handling for although it lacked power compared with the Formula 1 Ferraris on the uphill sections, it was, if anything, faster on the downhill parts. Despite the fact that its lap times were not as good as the Formula 1 Ferraris, it was nevertheless considerably faster than many of the other marques of Formula 1 cars. Ferrari had taken the car along to Monte Carlo just to see what everyone thought of it although he had no actual intention of running it in that race, the next appearance being scheduled for the Formula 2 race at Rheims where the car was to be driven by Maurice Trintignant. In the race Trintignant was faced by a whole host of super-lightweight British cars that made the Ferrari look rather out of place. On power it was more than a match for its rivals but during the race their lightweight despite less power made the

British cars formidable opponents. The battle was terrific and Trintignant certainly had no easy time but the pace finally was too hot for the opposition which fell by the wayside and Trintignant went on unchallenged to record the car's second victory in two appearances.

Although the car did not appear again that season in Formula 2, a second 1500-cc model was built. The second car differed from the prototype in having the two magnetos mounted on the rear of the inlet camshafts and, in consequence, the steering column was turned to the right of the engine with the steering box mounted by the top of the right hand front suspension unit instead of the left hand one. This second car underwent testing at the Modena autodrome with disastrous results. Ing. Andrea Fraschetti, Ferrari's promising young addition to the design staff, was driving it when suddenly the car went off the road and turned over. Fraschetti died from his injuries a day later.

Formula 1 development

Enzo Ferrari had not been too happy with the performance of the Lancia/Ferraris during the season. The only time they went really well was at the German Grand Prix but even then the cars were relegated to 2nd and 3rd place by an error of pit strategy. In Ferrari's mind the time had come to do away with the Lancia material and set about using his Formula 2 design to the full. The 1500-cc V6 cylinder block was adopted and bored out to 1860-cc retaining the original crankshaft assembly and tests were carried out at Modena and Monza comparing the performance of this type with the Lancia/Ferrari. The 1860-cc model was found to be slightly faster and much easier to handle, Ferrari therefore decided to profit by the Modena Grand Prix to give his latest idea an airing. On the original Formula 2 car there had been a large air intake on top of the bonnet which somewhat restricted the view of the driver so the second car, with the bored out engine, was provided with a perspex fairing round the carburetter intakes the top of which was left open. The earlier Formula 2 car underwent the same modification but traces of the original intake could still be seen just in front of the windscreen. The exhaust system was also modified and long thin pipes were extended over the rear axle, to end in megaphones.

These two cars made their appearance at Modena to be driven by Collins and Musso. The race was held in two heats and during the first, Musso was hard on the heels of Behra's Maserati and set up a lap record. Behra's larger engined car, however, pulled away and Musso took 2nd with Collins 4th. In the second heat, Musso did not really try to catch Behra being content with his 2nd place whilst Collins had a wheel to wheel battle with Schell on the other factory Maserati, Collins' car being not quite fast enough to pass the Maserati driver and thus ending up again in 4th place.

Ferrari was so satisfied with this performance that the whole team of Ferrari/Lancias was stacked into a corner and high pressure work began to prepare a team of V6-engined cars for the last Grand Prix of the season at Casablanca. One completely original Lancia D50 remains in the Turin Automobile Museum.

The original Formula 2 prototype was now fitted with an engine enlarged to 2.2-litres whilst a new experimental block of 2417-cc capacity was produced. The most interesting factor at Casablanca was that the Ferraris were running on aviation spirit whilst the rest of the field were still on their special fuel mixtures. So Ferrari was once again ahead of everyone in his tests for the forthcoming season. For the Casablanca race Collins had the 2.4-litre and Hawthorn the 2.2. Although the Ferraris' practice times were slower than some of the opposition, they had a decided advantage in that they had a much lower fuel consumption, with their engines burning avgas, and they consequently carried much less fuel than their competitors. Collins quickly brought home this advantage and came round with a big lead on the first lap. However everyone seemed to be unwell that day and Collins and Hawthorn were no exceptions, both driving with attacks of Asian flu and high temperatures. Collins spun out losing his 1st place and later hit a straw bale which put him out whilst Hawthorn burnt a piston and was forced to retire.

Ferrari, as usual, had had the foresight to try out his new cars before the end of the season and, as a result, was well prepared for the Argentine 'Temporada.'

The Type 246 Dino

For the two races in Buenos Aires he sent out four cars, three of them were the latest type 246 Dino cars which had the 2.5-litre V6 engines fitted into the Formula 2 chassis and the fourth car was the one used at Casablanca by Hawthorn being the original Formula 2 car modified and fitted with the 2.2-litre engine. They were now officially named Dino in memory of Ferrari's son.

During practice for the Argentine Grand Prix there was a great deal of changing about with carburetters for Ferrari had taken out complete sets of Solex and Weber carburetters for the V6 cars. It was found that the Solex gave better performance at the top end but eventually for the race Webers were fitted as better low end performance was preferred for the Buenos Aires circuit.

Fangio, with the Maserati, set the fastest practice time on his home ground with 1 min 42 secs. Hawthorn however took the second place with 1 min 42.9 secs and Collins was third fastest.

Ferrari troubles started when Collins broke a halfshaft on the starting line but Hawthorn went straight into the lead whilst Musso went by Moss into 4th place. Before long Fangio passed Hawthorn and Musso was forced to give way to the amazing little Cooper of Moss who moved up into 3rd place and set off after Hawthorn and overtook him. Hawthorn then stopped and complained of failing oil pressure but after an inspection he took off again. Moss had the little Cooper firmly in the lead when Musso suddenly became aware that he was catching the Englishman. Fangio had stopped and dropped back whilst changing tyres and the Italian driver tried everything he knew to catch Moss but his effort had come too late although less than 3 seconds separated them when they crossed the finishing line.

At the Buenos Aires Grand Prix, held two weeks later, things did not look too promising as Hawthorn was only 4th on practice times, Collins and Musso were 5th and 6th whilst the 2.2-litre to be shared by Von Trips and Hill was 7th fastest. Von Trips was to drive the car in the first 30 lap heat and Phil Hill in the second heat.

Hawthorn however again went straight into the lead with Musso 3rd and Von Trips 4th. In the wet, Von Trips put up a tremendous performance to take the lead, but when he overtook Fangio he was so surprised at having passed the World Champion that he looked round and whilst doing this he lost control, the car crashed and was totally wrecked but fortunately without injury to the German driver. Hawthorn won the heat from a very disgruntled Fangio with Musso 3rd.

In the 2nd heat Hawthorn broke a halfshaft and Musso took the lead but, when he spun his car, Fangio went ahead leaving the Italian to come in 2nd.

Goodwood 1958

Ferrari sent Hawthorn to England for the Goodwood meeting where he gained a place in the front row of the grid. During the race Behra went into the lead and pulled away from Hawthorn but his BRM ran out of brakes and rammed the chicane. Moss with the Cooper had made a very poor start but began catching Hawthorn. When Moss went into a spin Hawthorn was left to win with ease.

Musso also made a lone venture and had no difficulty in winning the Syracuse Grand Prix in the face of very little opposition.

Another solo effort was that by Collins who took one of the Dino 246 cars to Silverstone for the *Daily Express* trophy. Having obtained a place on the front row at the start, he had no difficulty in winning and setting a lap record of 1 min 40 secs jointly with Behra's BRM.

The first European outing of the full Ferrari team in 1958 was at Monaco where four cars were sent for Hawthorn, Musso, Collins and Von Trips. Two of the cars had a new type chassis, with the lower frame member strengthened, whilst the other two had the normal Formula 2 type frame; the cars were equipped with a new type of brake drum of alloy with cast-iron liners. The original windscreen-like 'Perspex' covers over the carburetters were replaced by a new type which completely covered the carburetter air intakes and had an opening at the rear instead of the more usual air intake at the front.

Practice times showed the BRM and Vanwall opposition to be faster than the Ferraris and at the start of the race Hawthorn was lying 6th but he then made a stupendous effort to pull up to 3rd place and, after Behra's leading BRM went out, he challenged Moss for the lead. Moss and Hawthorn had a tremendous battle with the Ferrari and the Vanwall alternating in first place. This came to an end when the Vanwall broke down leaving Hawthorn comfortably in the lead with a new lap record of 1 min 40.6 secs but, just as the result seemed set, the fuel pump broke loose and Hawthorn was forced to retire leaving Trintignant's Cooper leading. Ferrari made efforts to speed up Musso in 2nd place but try as he would he could only carve fractions of a second from the lead of the Frenchman's car. When Trintignant put in a few fast laps just to show that he could go faster, Ferrari signalled Musso to let him go and hold 2nd place. In the meantime Collins had suddenly decided that he was not going to have the Italian driver finish ahead of him and pulled out the stops but, despite some frantic driving, he found he had left his effort too late and was unable to catch Musso. Von Trips had been circulating for over half the race with his brake pedal broken off and the remaining spike of metal had worn through his shoe giving him a great deal of pain; just before the end of the race his gallant drive came to an end when his engine blew up. Musso was 2nd and Collins 3rd.

Three of the 246 Dinos were sent to Zandvoort for the Dutch Grand Prix, to be driven by Hawthorn, Collins and Musso. Two of them had the strengthened chassis whilst the third had one of the original Formula 2 frames. In practice the cars were very disappointing with Hawthorn, the fastest of the team, in 6th place with a 1 min. 39.1 secs opposed to Lewis Evans' fastest time of 1 min. 37.1 secs, Collins registered 1 min. 39.3 secs and Musso 1 min. 39.5 secs.

During the race the performance of the Ferraris was very poor and they were never really in the picture. Hawthorn was trying his best but the car did not handle properly for the circuit and seemed to lack speed. Collins broke his gearbox and Hawthorn after a hard drive finished 5th with Musso 7th. In all it was the poorest performance given by Ferraris for a long time.

For the Belgian Grand Prix Ferrari sent four cars for Collins, Hawthorn, Musso and Gendebien. At the request of the organizers Gendebien's car was painted in the Belgian national colour of yellow. In practice the Ferraris more than made up for their poor performance at Zandvoort. On the very fast circuit they showed that they had more than adequate speed and Hawthorn turned in the fastest lap of 3 min. 57.1 secs, a speed of 133.04 m p h; Musso registered 3 min. 57.5 secs and Gendebien 3 min. 59.3 secs.

Although Moss went straight into the lead, it was the Vanwall of Brooks that was ahead on the first lap. Moss, missing a gearshift, had over-revved his engine. Collins and Gendebien were 2nd and 3rd, but Collin's engine gave out and Gendebien spun, having a great deal of trouble getting out of other cars' way and restarting. Hawthorn was established in 2nd place but could not catch Brooks although he set a new lap record of 3 min. 58.3 secs, a speed of 132.36 m p h. Musso was unfortunate in having a tyre burst, the car crashing but fortunately without serious results to the driver. Brooks won but Hawthorn had netted another 2nd place plus fastest lap points towards his World Championship.

The French Grand Prix

Ferrari sent five cars to Rheims for the French Grand Prix, to be driven by Hawthorn, Collins, Musso, and Von Trips. One of the five cars was the Type 156 Dino V6 Formula 2 car, similar to the model that had won the Formula 2 event at Rheims the previous year with Trintignant. This car had been modified since its previous appearance by the fitting of telescopic shockabsorbers similar to those used on the Formula 1 cars.

Of the four Formula 1 models, three were the type with the redesigned stronger chassis whilst the car driven by Musso retained the original layout as used on the Formula 2 car. All of these cars were fitted with a new type of front coil spring with telescopic shockabsorbers fitted down the centres of the coils; again the cars appeared with the big metal cowlings over the carburetter intakes instead of the 'Perspex' type originally used.

Peter Collins was down to drive the Formula

2 car but when the race started it was obvious that the Porsche single seater was more than a match for the car. Moss with the Cooper worried Behra's Porsche for a while before breaking down and leaving Collins with a comfortable 2nd place. Collins was completely outpaced by the Formula 2 Porsche, although he was equally superior to the other types of Formula 2 cars. In practice for the main event, Hawthorn quickly broke the lap record set by Fangio's Ferrari the previous year at 2 min. 25.8 secs, setting a new time of 2 min. 23.9 secs the first day. The final day of practice saw all the Ferrari team turn on the speed, Hawthorn recording an astounding 2 min. 21.7 secs with Musso slightly slower at 2 min. 22.4 secs.

As a result of this both Hawthorn and Musso were in the front row of the starting grid with Collins right behind them in the second row. Before the first lap was finished, Hawthorn was in the lead and it took Musso only until the second lap to get ahead of Harry Schell's BRM into 2nd place. Collins moved up to 3rd but went up an escape road when a piece of metal jammed behind his brake pedal. Hawthorn was building up a big lead from everyone except Musso who was hanging on only a few seconds behind. Then disaster struck Musso who took a curve too fast and crashed off the road subsequently dying from his injuries. Von Trips, who had made a poor start, worked his way through the field and Collins was beginning to catch up again. Hawthorn was having a perfect day and just before the end set up a new lap record of 2 min. 24.9 secs; Von Trips was a good 3rd behind the Vanwall of Moss, and Collins, just as it looked as if he would be 4th, ran out of fuel and had to push the car home losing his place and dropping to 5th.

The British Grand Prix

After the success at Rheims, Ferrari decided to send only three cars to Silverstone for the British Grand Prix. All three cars were of the 246 Dino type with the strengthened Formula 1 chassis. Hawthorn's car had the curved windscreen cut away and replaced by a small aero screen. The cars of Collins and Von Trips had large fuel tanks in the cockpit whilst that of Hawthorn had a tail tank only. During practice

the Ferraris were slower than the fastest Vanwall, BRM and Cooper so that only Hawthorn was in the front row, with a time of 1 min. 40.4 secs, Collins was in the second row with 1 min. 40.6 secs and Von Trips in the third with 1 min. 42.0 secs.

Collins made a brilliant start and took the lead on the opening lap; Moss tried everything that he knew to pass the flying Ferrari, but was being followed closely himself by Hawthorn. Before long Moss was out with a broken engine and Ferraris were 1st and 2nd. Hawthorn came into the pits for oil but was off again without losing his 2nd place. Von Trips was having less of a good time than the others and his brakes were giving him constant trouble. When he finally came into the pits to have them fixed it was found that his engine bearings had gone and the car was retired.

Collins won with ease and Hawthorn took a comfortable 2nd and also setting the fastest lap.

Ferrari decided to enter only two cars in the Grand Prix of Portugal which was the next World Championship event. He sent a normal 246 Dino car with the Formula 1 chassis for Hawthorn and Von Trips had the car which first appeared in the 500 Miles of Monza as a 3-litre. This car had the Formula 1 chassis, a Dino 246 engine but with coil spring rear suspension and side mounted oil tank.

Hawthorn in practice registered second fastest time with 2 min. 34.26 secs only .05 sec. behind the Vanwall of Moss. Von Trips was considerably slower and qualified for the third row with a 2 min. 37.04 secs. Hawthorn went into the lead at the beginning of the race but on the twisty, true road-type circuit his brakes could not match the disc type on the Vanwall and he had to slow and let Moss pass. Von Trips had been holding 3rd place but he too was passed by a disc-braked British car. Hawthorn dropped further and further back and finally had to stop at the pits to have his brakes readjusted. Hawthorn set out to regain his 2nd place and set a new lap record of 2 min. 32.3 secs, but before long he was out of brakes again. When the BRM broke down he went back into 2nd place to make certain of some more valuable points for the World Championship. He very nearly messed things up when he spun on the last lap and stalled his engine. He was only able to restart by pushing the car, in reverse, off the circuit and then driving back on at the point he had left it, a close thing for as it eventually turned out this could have cost him the world title of 1958. Von Trips brought the coil spring car home 5th.

German Grand Prix

For the German Grand Prix, Ferrari turned out with a team made up of Hawthorn, Collins, Von Trips and Phil Hill who was entered to drive the Formula 2 car which was to run in the F2 race held concurrently with the Grand Prix of Germany.

Hawthorn, Collins and Von Trips had the type 246 Dino cars, all of them having the stronger Formula 1 type chassis. One car was equipped with forged top wishbones whilst the others had the tubular type top and bottom. Houdaille shockabsorbers were fitted on all the three team cars with spring-tension adjusters for the front coil springs on all the models. A fourth car appeared in practice, this being the car that had appeared at the 500 Miles of Monza with the coil spring suspension at the rear instead of the transverse leaf spring. This car had been driven by Phil Hill at Monza where it had been fitted with the 3-litre V6 Dino engine. For the Nurburgring race it had the normal 246 Dino engine and the oil tank had been removed to the side of the scuttle from its original tail position. This car did not use Houdaille shock-absorbers but had telescopic types all round.

The Formula 2 car was identical to the one used at Rheims with the lighter chassis. It employed the Type 156 Dino engine and Houd-aille shockabsorbers were fitted, replacing the telescopics tried out at Rheims. During practice the car appeared with alloy type ribbed brake drums which were changed for the actual race to a set in cast-iron.

During practice the top drivers had Fangio's remarkable lap time of 9 min. 17.4 secs. in view, but it was expected that this time would be beaten as there had been slight improvements to the surface of the circuit. Hawthorn in the first day's practice got down to 9 min. 21.9 secs. and then in the final practice period set an amazing time of 9 min. 14 secs. Collins got down to 9 min. 21.9 secs. which also placed him in the

front row, whilst Von Trips was in the second row with a 9 min. 24.7 secs. and Hill, the fastest of the Formula 2 cars, in the third row at 9 min. 48.9 secs.

It was expected after the two Scuderia Ferrari victories at Silverstone and Rheims, and bearing in mind Hawthorn's practice time, that there would be no catching the blonde Englishman. It was therefore quite a surprise when Moss went straight into the lead and began to pull away with ease. It was a great relief to Hawthorn and Collins when the Vanwall broke down and left the two Ferraris in 1st and 2nd places. Von Trips was dropping back with almost non-existent brakes and Phil Hill was right amongst some of the Formula 1 cars, leading the F2 category by a long way. Hawthorn and Collins played at switching the lead as they had done the previous year but they were in for as big a shock as had happened on the other occasion. Tony Brooks with the Vanwall was catching them fast and using his disc brakes to advantage on the twisty sections of the circuit. He finally passed both Ferraris into the lead. Then disaster struck the Ferrari team. Collins, in attempting to pass Brooks again, went off the road and was fatally injured and on the next lap Hawthorn's clutch gave out forcing him to abandon his car on the circuit. Hill who had been comfortably leading the Formula 2 category spun on some oil and then began to suffer from oil being sprayed on to his rear tyres from a broken breather tube; this made the Ferrari almost impossible to control and he dropped further and further back to finish 9th overall and 4th in the F2 category. The only Ferrari left running in the Formula 1 race was Von Trips who brought a completely brakeless car home 4th.

Monza: Ferrari fits disc brakes

For the Italian Grand Prix at Monza, Ferrari sent four cars to be driven by Hawthorn, Von Trips, Gendebien and Phil Hill, the latter making his first appearance in the Ferrari Formula 1 team. These four cars were quite a mixed batch. Hawthorn was given one of the Formula 1s, with strengthened chassis which had a set of Dunlop disc brakes fitted. These brakes had been fitted originally on Peter Collins' privately owned 250 Gran Turismo and with assistance from Dunlop they had been adapted to the Formula 1 car in an attempt to solve the disadvantages in braking from which Ferrari had suffered both in Portugal and at Nurburgring.

A new type of V6 Dino engine was also tried out for the first time under racing conditions. This engine, known as the Type Dino 256, had a bore and stroke of 85 x 72 mm giving a total capacity of 2451-cc as opposed to the Dino 246 with a bore and stroke of 85 x 71 mm.

A second car was present also with the strengthened Formula 1 chassis but fitted with the Dino 246 engine and with drum brakes of a new type. Both these cars used Houdaille shock-absorbers. The third car was equipped with the lighter Formula 2 chassis, it also had a Dino 246 engine, the new type drum brakes and Houdaille shockabsorbers. The fourth car was the ex-500 Miles of Monza car with the coil spring rear suspension. This car had a revised rear suspension, in that the coil springs were much longer and were mounted on a bracket that extended below the De Dion tube. It was equipped with telescopic Koni shockabsorbers and also had the new type drum brakes which instead of being in cast iron were of bi-metal composition with an alloy casting surrounding a steel liner.

During practice the cars appeared with the metal air intake for the carburetters, but for the race itself all the cars used the Plexiglass cover.

During practice it was found that the Ferraris were not as fast as the Vanwalls although Hawthorn managed to get in the front row of the start with a lap in 1 min. 41.8 secs., thus beating the previous year's practice lap record. The other three Ferrari drivers had the second row to themselves being very close on times. Gendebien with 1 min. 42.5 secs., Von Trips 1 min. 42.6 secs. and Phil Hill with 1 min. 42.7 secs.

At the start, the Vanwalls jumped into an immediate lead whilst Hawthorn was off slowly having had to jab his clutch to prevent himself from stalling. Gendebien had difficulties as well and added to them he was rammed in the back by Brabham's Cooper. The troubles however were not over as, going into the Lesmo corner, Von Trips crashed into the back of Schell's BRM and both cars hurtled off the road being completely wrecked, Schell and Von Trips luckily

got away with scratches plus a damaged knee for the German driver.

Despite the fast start made by the Vanwalls, it was Phil Hill who was leading by the Ascari curve. When the cars roared by the pits, Hill had several car lengths over a very surprised Moss and Lewis Evans. Hawthorn was already up with the leaders and tucked in behind the two Vanwalls, being followed equally closely by the Vanwall of Brooks.

Hawthorn soon passed quickly by Moss and Lewis Evans and was after the flying American. By the fifth lap Hawthorn was in the lead but Gendebien was in the pits examining his rear axle; after consultation the car was retired with a bent De Dion tube resulting from the collision with the Cooper. Phil Hill, in 2nd place, had a tread strip off his tyre and had to pull into the pits. Hawthorn was repassed by Moss but pressed him very closely. Then the Vanwall went out with a broken gearbox and Hawthorn pulled away to a fairly comfortable lead. Hill worked his way back to 3rd place and then into 2nd. When Hawthorn came in to change tyres at half distance Hill went by in the lead but, when Phil Hill came into the pits to change a rear wheel, Hawthorn was out in front again although he was challenged for some time by Masten Gregory with his Maserati. Whilst Hill was in the pits he was passed by Brooks who now set out after Hawthorn whose clutch was beginning to sound worn and the Vanwall was making up time fast; ten laps before the end of the race he was by the Ferrari driver. Hill was also catching Hawthorn fast but the team manager slowed him down so that he would not take valuable World Championship points from the Englishman and the American finished his first Formula 1 race in 3rd place 4.1 seconds behind Hawthorn.

Casablanca

The final Formula 1 race of the 1958 season was held at Casablanca and there was much speculation as to who would be the next World Champion. Hawthorn was leading on points but could still lose the title if he did not take second place and provided that Moss won and set the fastest lap. Naturally, as expected, there was to be a lot of team play with both Ferrari and Vanwall trying to cause the other marque to break.

For this final event, Ferrari sent three cars to be driven by Hawthorn, Phil Hill and Gendebien. Hawthorn had the same car that he had used at Monza with the strengthened Formula 1 chassis, the Dino 256 engine and the Dunlop disc brakes. Phil Hill had the Formula 2 chassis with a Dino 246 engine and the bonded-alloy drum brakes whilst Gendebien used the coil-spring rear suspension car which was the same as at Monza except for the fitting of Girling disc brakes.

Things looked promising when Hawthorn set the fastest lap with 2 min. 23.1 secs. in practice. Phil Hill tried the Hawthorn car but did not make good time with it as he could not get used to the disc brakes; nevertheless with his own drum-braked car he put himself in the second row with a time of 2 min. 24.1 secs. whilst Gendebien was in the third row with 2 min. 24.3 secs.

At the start of the race Phil Hill set out after Moss trying to get him to blow up the Vanwall. The Ferrari got by on the straight but on braking the Vanwall was by again. This game continued until Hill finally went up the escape road trying to outbrake Moss; Hill was quickly back on the road and repassed Hawthorn who was waiting behind to see what would happen but the American could no longer get close enough to Moss to worry him. Hill at least tried to steal the point for the fastest lap with a new record of 2 min. 23.3 secs. but Moss showed that he was master of the situation and put the record down to 2 min. 22.5 secs. Towards the end of the race Phil Hill, who was still in 2nd place, was given a signal from the pits to let Hawthorn by into 2nd, although he was almost 40 seconds behind the American. The Vanwall won but Hawthorn was secure in 2nd and took the World Championship, with Hill bringing up 3rd place. The only Ferrari driver not to finish was Gendebien whose car went off the road on an oil patch, the car being wrecked and the driver suffering from a few broken ribs.

Mike Hawthorn: Champion

Mike Hawthorn had won the 1958 World Championship for Ferrari but it had been a close thing. Vanwall had taken the constructors' championship with wins by Moss at Zandvoort, Portugal and Morocco, and Brooks at Spa and Monza. Ferrari's only Grand Epreuve victories throughout the year had been with Collins at the British Grand Prix and Hawthorn at the French Grand Prix. Hawthorn in fact won the championship by virtue of his 2nd places scored at Spa, Silverstone, Monza and Morocco, and his fastest laps at Monaco, Spa, Rheims, Silverstone and Portugal.

Hawthorn throughout the season had been on top form and was quite capable of tackling the Vanwall opposition, as was demonstrated by the many lap records he set both in practice and in the various races. However, it was clear that the Vanwall was in many respects the superior machine and in the hands of Moss, Brooks and Lewis Evans it was indeed a formidable opponent; one of the main reasons for its superiority were the Vanwall disc brakes. Hawthorn by dint of brilliant driving was almost always able to outpace them for the fastest laps while his brakes were in good condition, but the combination of first class drivers and the disc brakes beat him in many races. Ferrari did fit disc brakes to Hawthorn's car at the end of the season but by then it was too late to have any effect on the outcome of the Championship.

The 1959 Season - Ferrari needs more drivers

Ferrari decided to stick to the 246 and 256 Dino models for the 1959 season and things looked hopeful for another World Championship as Vanwall, the main opposition to Ferrari, had retired from competition. As it turned out there were several factors that were not in Ferrari's favour. Another British marque, Cooper, had come into the limelight with surprise victories at Buenos Aires and at Monaco and were likely to constitute a new danger for 1959 season. Added to this was the tragic loss of Musso, of Collins and, during the winter in a road accident, of Mike Hawthorn. Von Trips and Ferrari by mutual consent had decided to part company so Ferrari was left with the problem of reorganizing his team completely. His only two remaining team members were Phil Hill who lacked experience in Grand Prix cars and Gendebien who was also not in the champion class of Grand Prix drivers. Phil Hill had put in some brilliant performances which indicated that he might well become a top flight man but there was little

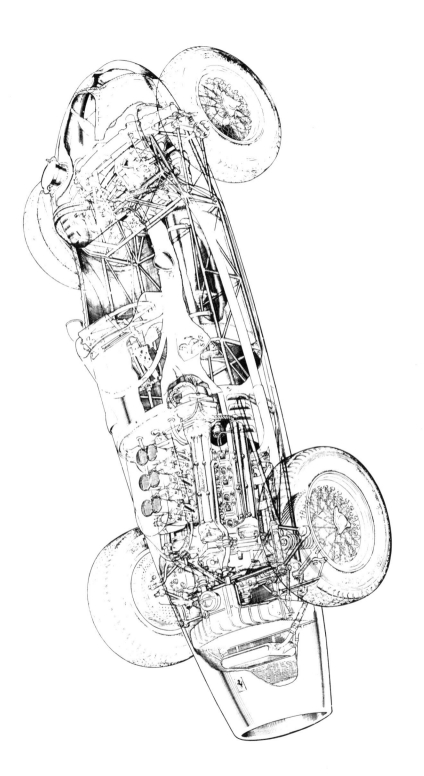

Cutaway drawing of the 246 Dino

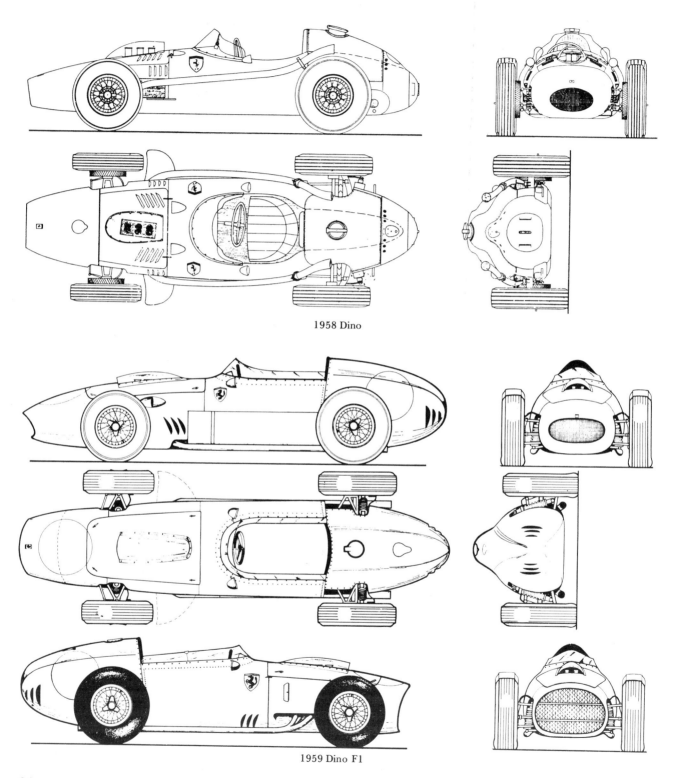

1958 Dino

1959 Dino F1

hope for Gendebien to become anything but a team filler.

The retirement of Vanwall left Tony Brooks free and Ferrari was quick to avail himself of the services of this brilliant Englishman. He also added another British driver, Cliff Allison, who had shown promise with the Lotus during the previous season. However, it was too much to expect Allison to be a serious contender for the World Championship in his first season with Ferrari. To round off his team Ferrari included Jean Behra, a very experienced driver who had rendered good service to Gordini, BRM and Maserati in the previous years but who had a difficult temperament and who had yet to prove his full worth by winning a Grand Epreuve. In all, the team looked adequate.

Fantuzzi's bodywork

The V6 Dino was modified to tackle the new season. With the arrival of Fantuzzi who had been Maserati's body builder and responsible for the admirable lines of the 250 F Maserati, the rather ugly Ferrari took on new lines that were considerably more pleasing. The upswept exhaust pipes were changed to run alongside the body level with the underside of the car, with their outlets behind the tank, instead of running above the rear suspension; experiments took place to aim at better gas extraction with a device called the 'snap' turbo exhaust which was supposed to give better fuel consumption and increased performance. All the cars were fitted with the Dunlop type disc brakes and with Dunlop tyres. Coil-spring rear suspension with Koni telescopic dampers replaced the transverse leaf springs and Houdaille vane type shock-absorbers. Throughout the season the Ferrari showed that it was by no means the best car from the point of view of roadholding but indicated a marked superiority in power over its adversaries.

Monaco

The Argentine 'Temporada' was not held in the 1959 season so the first meeting with the British opposition was at Monaco. Ferrari sent Behra, Brooks and Phil Hill with Formula 1 cars and Cliff Allison with the 1500-cc Formula 2 car as a Formula 2 event was being held in con-

junction with the Grand Prix. All three of the Formula 1 cars had the new chassis, disc brakes and the coil spring/telescopic damper rear end. The attractive slim bodies that had been seen on test in Modena were replaced by a short nosed type that made the cars look like open mouthed whales. The reason for this was to give better cooling on the twisty circuit. Ferrari had also learnt that long slim noses at Monaco were likely to be crumpled in the first-lap rush to the 'Gasometer' hairpin.

In practice only Behra of the team was able to qualify for the front row of the grid, his time being 1 min. 40 secs. whereas Brooks with his Ferrari was unable to equal his previous year's time with the Vanwall of 1 min. 39.8 secs. and had to be content to share the second row with Phil Hill after setting a time of 1 min. 41 secs. However, as it turned out, all the Formula 1 Ferraris succeeded in improving on the best Ferrari time set the previous year by Hawthorn of 1 min. 41.5 secs.

In the Formula 2 race held concurrently with the Grand Epreuve there were only three cars admitted; Von Trips with the new Porsche, Allison with the Ferrari and Halford with the Lotus. The outcome of the Formula 2 event was eagerly awaited as a pointer for the future events of this type. In practice all three had been very close with Von Trips at 1 min. 43.8 secs., Allison 1 min. 44.4 secs. and Halford at 1 min. 44.8 secs. As it turned out, this race never took place as Von Trips spun on some oil on the second lap and crashed into the other two Formula 2 cars thus eliminating all of them from the race.

Behra led from the start of the race but Moss was right on his tail with Brabham in the other Cooper also close behind. Although Behra led until the twenty-first lap it was obvious that he was having a hard time staying ahead of Moss and at times it seemed that Moss could have passed him easily but preferred to stay behind and push the Frenchman to the point of blowing up. This is precisely what happened for on the twenty-fifth lap the engine of Behra's Ferrari exploded and thereafter the two Coopers dominated the race. After Moss had gone out with gearbox trouble it was left for Brabham to win his first World Championship event with

Tony Brooks bringing his Ferrari into 2nd place. Phil Hill put up a very spirited performance spoilt only by four spins which dropped him to 4th place at the finish.

Slim bodies for Zandvoort

The next event entered by Ferrari was the Dutch Grand Prix at Zandvoort. Here the cars appeared with the slim bodies and their weight reduced to 540 kg. Nevertheless in practice it was obvious that the Ferraris were as unsuited to the Dutch circuit as they had been the previous year. The team was made up of Brooks, Behra, Phil Hill and Allison. Only Behra was up amongst the main opposition gaining a place in the second row with a time of 1 min. 36.6 secs. Brooks was in the 3rd row, Phil Hill in the 5th and Allison in the 6th and last row. Nevertheless, all of the team except Allison bettered Hawthorn's best Ferrari lap set the previous year of 1 min. 39.7 secs.

At the start of the race Behra fought like a lion in an endeavour to get up to the front but the best he could do was fourth place. He fell back to sixth and then managed to struggle back up to 5th where he finally finished one lap behind the winning BRM of Bonnier. Behra's team mates fared worse than he did. Brooks had to stop because he was losing too much oil, Phil Hill managed a poor 6th place and Allison finished in 9th place ahead of last man De Beaufort in a sports Porsche.

The French Grand Prix

Rheims was the scene of the French Grand Prix and before this championship event a Formula 2 race was held. Ferrari sent the Formula 2 car for Allison to drive but he was unable to live up to the record set by Trintignant and Collins in the two previous years. Allison was easily dominated by the Cooper Borgward of Moss and the TecMec Porsche of Hans Herrman until he retired two laps before the end of the race. There were high hopes in the Ferrari camp as Rheims was a circuit where the power of the Ferrari could make itself felt. For this event the team was joined by the promising young American driver, Dan Gurney, who was making his début in European Grand Prix racing.

Practice showed that Ferrari had the right to be optimistic for both Brooks and Phil Hill broke Hawthorn's lap record of 2 min. 21.7 secs. with times of 2 min. 19.4 secs. and 2 min. 19.8 secs. which gave them both front row positions. Behra also broke the Hawthorn record with 2 min. 20.2 secs., and Gurney did well for the first time in a G.P. car with 2 min. 21.9 secs. The big shock came when Brabham managed to insert his Cooper amongst the Ferraris with a 2 min. 19.7 secs., an improvement of some 8 seconds over his previous year's time. Behra was left at the start but again showed his determination; thrilling the French crowd he made up the lost ground and by the twenty-fourth lap was in 3rd place. Gurney went out at the twentieth lap with his radiator pierced by a stone and Behra's run came to an end on the thirty-fifth lap with a burnt piston. Tony Brooks had jumped into the lead immediately and made himself comfortable some distance ahead of the others. Behind him Phil Hill was switching places with several drivers until the twenty-fifth lap when he firmly installed himself in 2nd place. The Ferraris showed clearly that they were the fastest cars and were not to be denied when the circuit suited them.

Driver problems

Things back in Modena were not running very smoothly. For some time the somewhat mixed team had not been combining as a team should. Behra did not approve of the Commendatore's system of not appointing a No. 1 driver and always strove to give the impression that he was actually the first team driver. He also required a great deal of modification to be done on his own car and it was even hinted in the French press that Behra was telling Ferrari how to build his cars. At Rheims came the incident where Behra struck team manager Tavoni in a fit of temper and matters were not helped by the French press siding with their favourite, Behra. Summing up, Behra's record for Ferrari showed no great advantage for the Modenese firm so Ferrari and Behra parted company. Enzo Ferrari was not in the least bothered to lose the Frenchman as he had already found an excellent replacement in the shape of Gurney. On top of this problem came further trouble with the Italian labour unions and Ferrari was unable to get his cars ready in time for the British Grand Prix at Aintree. This event gave Brabham yet another victory on his route to the World Championship.

Avus suits the Ferraris

The German Grand Prix of 1959 was held at the banked Avus track in Berlin, despite a great deal of criticism about the unsuitability of the circuit. The Avus allowed high speeds and gave a definite advantage to the Ferraris. Allison came out the fastest in practice with 2 min. 5.8 secs. followed by Brooks, 2 min. 5.9 secs. Moss showed that the Cooper was in the running with a 2 min. 6.8 secs. ahead of Gurney's 2 min. 7.2 secs. Phil Hill was the slowest of the Ferraris with a 2 min. 7.6 secs. However, during the two heats and the final there was no doubt about the outcome. Both Moss and Gregory on a works Cooper tried their utmost to tail the flying Ferrari only to have their own engines blow up.

In the first heat it was Ferrari 1, 2 and 3 with Brooks, Gurney and Hill. The second heat was the same with the order Brooks, Hill and Gurney. The final classification was 1st Brooks, 2nd Gurney, 3rd Hill. Brooks set a lap record of 2 min. 4.5 secs. just to show that even during their record laps in practice the Ferraris had something in reserve. The average speed of the new lap record was 148 m p h.

For the Portuguese Grand Prix at Monsanto, Ferrari sent only three cars for Brooks, Hill and Gurney. Again Ferrari had the same troubles of roadholding that had appeared at Zandvoort and it was left to newcomer, Gurney, to put up the best performance of the team with a time of 2 min. 8.0 secs. Nevertheless, he was some 5 seconds slower than the fastest practice lap by Moss on the Cooper. Phil Hill also managed to get down to 2 min. 8.0 secs. which put him completely off form and was in a poor 4th row position with a fastest time of 2 min. 11 secs.

During the race Phil Hill had one of his few accidents; it was slight but enough to eliminate the car. Tony Brooks trailed home a pathetic 9th being last but one. Gurney in some measure saved the day by bringing the car in 3rd but he was a complete lap behind the winner, Moss.

The Italian Grand Prix 1959

For the Grand Prix of Italy, Ferrari hopes were again high as the Monza track suited their high speed. They were in for a shock when Moss with the Cooper set the fastest lap at 1 min. 39.7 secs. Brooks was back on form and managed 1 min. 39.8 secs. but found himself sandwiched between two Coopers when Brabham lapped in 1 min. 40.2 secs., pushing the Ferraris of Gurney and Hill into the second row and those of Allison and Gendebien into the third row. There were high hopes of victory by Brooks but this was short-lived when the British driver retired with clutch failure on the first lap.

The race developed into a battle between Hill, Moss and Gurney, Brabham being content to sit back and finish to assure him of the World Championship. Despite the tremendous pressure put on him by the two Ferraris, Moss was unruffled and when the Ferraris had to stop for tyres, Moss was firmly in the lead, a position which he held until the end of the race with Hill bringing the Ferrari into 2nd place and Brabham's Cooper displacing Gurney for 3rd. Allison and Gendebien finished in 5th and 6th places respectively.

The first Grand Prix of the United States was held at Sebring. This event saw the return of Von Trips to the Ferrari team. Gurney was already in the process of signing with another organization so Ferrari preferred to use Von Trips who had agreed to sign on once again with the Italian team for 1960. The entries for the United States Grand Prix were therefore made up of Brooks, Hill, Allison and Von Trips. Ferrari found that the Sebring circuit was as unsuited to the cars as had been Zandvoort and Monsanto. The best performance by the team was the practice time of Brooks of 3 min. 5.9 secs., exactly 5.9 seconds a lap slower than Moss with the Cooper. It was by no means a happy situation for Ferrari; Brooks started in the second row with Von Trips, Allison and Hill having the third row to themselves with times of 3 min. 6.2 secs., 3 min. 6.8 secs. and 3 min. 7.2 secs. respectively. The car that Brooks was driving was the latest thing from the Ferrari factory having the chassis shortened by 100 mm and having independent rear suspension by means of wishbones and coil springs.

It was an unfortunate race for Ferrari. Brooks had a collision with Von Trips on the first lap and dropped to 15th place. Phil Hill retired on the ninth lap with the brakes not functioning and Allison was out on the twenty-fourth lap with a broken clutch. Brooks managed to work his way back into 3rd place whilst Von Trips struggled around finally to take 6th. With his 3rd place at Sebring, Tony Brooks took 2nd place in the World Championship with 27 points to Brabham's 31 but in the constructors' championship Ferrari was beaten by Cooper by 53 points to 38.

When the 1960 season came along Ferrari decided to retain the 246 and 256 Dino models as the F I A had decreed that the change in formula would take place in 1961. Ferrari realized that his front engined cars would be outclassed by the British Cooper and Lotus but he still had the edge in sheer power over his adversaries. All his efforts during the season would be towards the preparation for the new formula of 1500-cc in 1961.

1960 — A change of drivers

During the winter of 1959 — 60 there were many rumours that Ferrari had produced a rear engined car, but these were strongly denied by the Maranello sources. For 1960 Ferrari had once again to reorganize his team. Brooks left to drive for the Yeoman Credit Cooper team as he realized that it would be even more difficult for him to try for the World Championship with Ferrari in 1960 than it had been during the previous season. Gurney, Ferrari's promising newcomer, left to join BRM as that company offered greater financial remuneration. Ferrari had already signed on Phil Hill and Allison and at the end of the 1959 season Von Trips had rejoined the team. To these three Ferrari added another American, Richie Ginther, who had had a great deal of experience in Ferrari sports cars in the USA. Ginther did a great deal of testing for Ferrari and the Commendatore was sufficiently impressed to give him a place on the team. Gendebien, apparently unhappy with the few drives he had been given the previous season was shopping around for a Cooper to drive, so Ferrari was left with a team that was not so

strong as he had been used to in the past.

During the winter, many attempts were made to improve the front-engined Dino and a general switchover from the De Dion rear-end layout to the wishbone i r s was made. Experiments were also conducted with a single-cam-per-bank Dino engine which gave more power in the lower ranges but was down on power at the top where the twin-cam-per-bank Dino engine excelled. This engine was mounted in the short chassis model which at first had the De Dion rear-end layout but nothing was seen of this car during the 1960 Grand Epreuve season.

Argentina again

The Argentine season was once again back on the calendar and Ferrari sent four cars for Hill, Allison, Von Trips and Ginther. Ginther's car was fitted with a 3-litre Dino engine for the Buenos Aires Grand Prix, a Formula Libre event to be held after the Argentine Grand Prix and it was there that Ginther was to make his debut for the team. However, there was some last minute shuffling about and the 3-litre engine was pulled out of the car and a 246 Dino substituted and the car given to one-time Ferrari team driver, Froilan Gonzales, leaving Ginther without a ride.

Two BRMs, a Lotus and a Cooper were faster than the Ferraris in practice and Allison, Hill and Von Trips had the second row to themselves being almost 3 seconds slower than Moss who put up the fastest time. Gonzales was in the third row which he shared with World Champion Brabham, Harry Schell and Trintignant, all on Coopers. During the race Allison showed that the past season with Ferrari had given him adequate training and he brought his car home in an excellent 2nd place behind McLaren on the works Cooper. The rest of the team did not fare so well, Von Trips was 5th, Phil Hill 8th, three laps behind the winner; Gonzales finished 10th.

Monaco

For the first race of the European season at Monaco, Ferrari produced three of the front-engined Dinos with i r s and a new five-speed transmission. Drivers were Hill, Von Trips, Allison and Ginther, the last to drive the new rear-engined prototype. Practice times were fantastic and showed that there had been great improvements in the cars. All the qualifiers broke the previous year's lap record. Von Trips was the fastest of the Ferrari team with a time of 1 min. 38.3 secs. which broke the previous year's lap record by 1.5 secs. but was only good enough to place him in the third row for the start. Ginther and Hill both registered the same time of 1 min. 38.6 secs. which gave them the fourth row to themselves, Ginther showing that the new rear-engined car, if not faster than the front-engined type, was certainly not slower.

During the race Phil Hill moved back into the second line group being unable to keep up with the tremendous pace set by the leaders. Von Trips was further back, having had trouble when oil in the undertray caught fire. Ginther was running a steady race with the rear-engined prototype, showing both his and the car's potential. Von Trips' car gave out with a broken clutch and Ginther's car broke its transmission but both of them crossed the finishing line to be classified 8th and 6th respectively. Phil Hill by dint of some dogged driving managed to take 3rd place. However Monaco was an unhappy race for Ferrari, for Allison had a serious accident in practice which put him out for the rest of the season just when he was showing promise of being one of Ferrari's best drivers.

Zandvoort – A poor performance

At the Grand Prix of Holland it was intended to enter the rear-engined Ferrari again but it was found that time was so short that it would be impossible to get the car ready for the event. Hill, Von Trips and Ginther were entered in three i r s front-engined Dinos. As on previous occasions at Zandvoort the Ferraris were most unhappy. Ginther caused a surprise by being the fastest of the Ferrari team but both he and Phil Hill only just managed to better the previous year's time for a Ferrari set by Behra at 1 min. 36.6 secs. with times of 1 min. 36.3 secs., and 1 min. 36.4 secs. respectively. Von Trips was slower than Behra's time with 1 min. 36.7 secs. This placed the two fastest Ferraris in the fifth row and Von Trips in the sixth. Phil Hill retired on the fifty-sixth lap with his engine blown and Von Trips and Ginther were placed 5th and 6th, the usual poor Ferrari performance on the Dutch circuit.

The next race in the calendar was the Belgian Grand Prix at Spa and because of its high speed nature there was some hope for a good Ferrari performance. Ferrari entered three of the front-engined cars having decided to prepare the rear-engined model purely for 1500-cc events in anticipation of the new formula. Despite Ginther's excellent performance he was dropped from the team both for 'political' reasons and to give a tryout to the Belgian driver Willy Mairesse. The other two cars were to be driven by Hill and Von Trips.

Optimism at Spa

Practice times gave reason for some optimism in the Ferrari camp. Phil Hill qualified for the front row with a time of 3 min. 53.3 secs., being almost 4 seconds faster than Mike Hawthorn's previous lap record set with the Dino Ferrari in 1958. Nevertheless, Hill was 3.3 seconds slower than Brabham's Cooper. Neither Von Trips nor Mairesse were able to beat the old Hawthorn record and started in the fourth and fifth rows. Phil Hill put up a fantastic performance during the race and tackled Brabham with gusto. At half distance Hill was 11 seconds behind the World Champion and was beginning to cut down on his lead. Von Trips was slowed with a defective clutch and Mairesse was still getting the feel of his first Grand Prix ride. Hill managed to cut down Brabham's lead to 8 seconds but Von Trips had the misfortune to have a universal break which nearly caused a serious accident. Just as Hill was really getting to grips with Brabham, his fuel line to the instrument panel broke and started a small fire. The resulting stop at the pits dropped Hill to 5th place. Mairesse was out of the race shortly afterwards with a blown engine and Von Trips was already out with clutch trouble. Hill managed to make up time and finally finished in 4th place.

The French Grand Prix

There were high hopes again for the French Grand Prix at Rheims. Ferrari again sent the same team as at Spa; Hill, Von Trips and Mairesse, Ginther still being left out. In practice Phil Hill took a front row position with a time of 2 min. 18.2 secs., beating Tony Brooks' Ferrari time of 2 min. 19.4 secs. of the previous season. Brabham again provided an unpleasant shock when he registered a time almost 2 seconds faster than Hill. A more pleasant surprise for Ferrari was that Mairesse seemed to have got the hang of the G P car extremely well breaking Brooks' time to qualify for the second row with Von Trips in the third row.

From the start of the race there was a tremendous battle between Brabham and Phil Hill with the lead changing lap after lap. When Hill made a mistake and had to take to the escape road it was Von Trips who moved up to challenge Brabham. Before long the incredible Hill was up in front again passing Von Trips and tailing Brabham by a hairsbreadth. Mairesse went out with transmission failure, and on the twenty-ninth lap Hill's Ferrari coasted into the pits with the same trouble. On the thirty-first lap Von Trips was also in the pits with the same trouble and the Ferrari challenge was at an end. However, both Hill and Von Trips were classified, Von Trips 11th and Hill 12th.

First failure at Silverstone

For the British Grand Prix at Silverstone, Ferrari sent only two cars, both front-engined Dinos for Hill and Von Trips. Ferrari had won every British Grand Prix held at Silverstone since 1951 so the two drivers had a high standard of performance to live up to. It was obvious in practice that the two Ferraris were deficient in roadholding compared with the British machinery. Von Trips qualified for the second row with a time of 1 min. 37 secs. and Phil Hill was in the third row with a time of 1 min. 37.8 secs., both of them a good deal slower than Brabham's fastest practice lap of 1 min. 34.6 secs. During the race the two Ferraris toured around in the middle of the field without ever looking as if they could get into the picture. Phil Hill led Von Trips but just before the end Von Trips put on a spurt and passed his team mate to take 6th place with Hill 7th — an altogether disappointing performance.

The 1960 German Grand Prix was held as a 1500-cc race so that the Porsches would be on more even terms with the British cars. As a result Ferrari did not compete.

His next outing was at Oporto for the Portuguese Grand Prix. Again only two cars were entered for Hill and Von Trips, both being front-engined Dinos. In practice things were not very encouraging for the Ferraris, with both drivers qualifying for the third row, Von Trips with a time of 2 min. 28.4 secs. and Hill with 2 min. 28.42 secs. The fastest lap of the practice session was set by Surtees' Lotus at 2 min. 25.5 secs. Phil Hill put up a spirited performance during the race but Von Trips hit the straw bales on the first lap and crumpled the nose of his car. Phil Hill battled valiantly in fourth place moving up to third when Gurney began to have trouble with his BRM. When Moss stopped for plugs Hill moved into second place but was passed by Brabham. He fought back but his efforts resulted in hitting a kerb, he then missed a shift because of clutch trouble and the Ferrari's run was at an end. Von Trips had made up some time and was involved in a furious fight with Clark's Lotus for 3rd place, but the Lotus stayed ahead and Von Trips had to be content with 4th.

The Italian Grand Prix

The Italians had decided to use a combination of the road circuit and the banked track at Monza for the Italian Grand Prix. The idea was to give the Ferrari a sporting chance to win the event. The idea backfired, the British constructors boycotting the event as they considered the use of the banking dangerous. Added to this was the fact that Coopers had nothing to lose by not competing, Brabham already held the World Championship for drivers and Cooper already had the constructors' championship in the bag.

Monza in this way turned out to be a Ferrari benefit as all opposition was second rate. There was a moment when it seemed that even the Ferraris would not run as Enzo Ferrari withdrew the whole team as a protest at the way his mechanics had been manhandled and obstructed by the local police but when an official apology was made the cars were back on the track. For the first time the Ferraris had been entered by Societa per Azioni Esercizo Fabbriche Automobile E Corse (SEFAC) the new Ferrari company. Three front-engined Dino cars were sent for Hill, Ginther and Mairesse. Von Trips was given the prototype rear-engined 1500-cc car as there was a 1500-cc category being held concurrently with the Formula 1 event.

There was no question about the Ferrari superiority during practice: Phil Hill recorded 2 min. 41.4 secs., Ginther 2 min. 43.3 secs. and Mairesse 2 min. 43.9 secs., the best time by the opposition was by Cabianca's Cooper/Ferrari (a Cooper chassis with a 4-cylinder type Super-squalo Ferrari engine built by the Scuderia Castelotti) with 2 min. 49.7 secs. Von Trips in the Formula 2 car was also well up, being nearly 8 seconds a lap faster than the works Porsches.

At the start it was Richie Ginther who took the lead, followed by Phil Hill. Von Trips was beaten on the start by the Porsches but by the second lap the Formula 2 Ferrari was by and settled down into the slipstream of Mairesse's Formula 1 Ferrari. After sixteen laps Ginther had to stop for rear tyres; he was followed in by Hill who changed three and then stalled on trying to rejoin the race, this gave Ginther a 25 second lead. When Mairesse came in to change three wheels Ginther took over in giving Von Trips a tow. Hill took the lead again when Ginther had to change two more tyres. When Hill came in to change two more tyres the mechanics performed the job so fast that he did not lose his lead. Mairesse also made another stop for tyres and complained of a failing transmission. The procession continued and the Formula 1 cars came in 1st, 2nd and 3rd in the order Hill, Ginther and Mairesse. Von Trips came in first of the Formula 2 cars a full lap ahead of his opposition.

The Dino's retire

Phil Hill thus became the first American since Jimmy Murphy to win a European Grand Prix; his average speed was a new record of 132.07 m p h and he also set the lap record of 136.64 m p h. It was the swansong of the front-engined Dino Ferrari; the cars were not entered in the final event of the season, the United States Grand Prix, so the Dinos were retired after the Monza event.

CHAPTER EIGHT
The rear engined Grand Prix types

Phil Hill

FERRARI'S resistance to building a rear-engined car was extremely strong. He was used to being a leader in the motor racing field and did not like copying others' ideas. He had resisted disc brakes when his own designs were unsuccessful and almost jeopardised the 1958 World Championship because of his reluctance.

The front-engined Formula 1 cars were able to hold their own on the fast circuits in 1959 — 60 but were totally unable to match the British cars on the twistier circuits. Ferrari felt that his front engined designs would be able to compete in the remaining two years of the 2.5-litre Formula 1 but progress of his rivals was faster than anticipated. Quickly he initiated some studies of the Cooper chassis which had been purchased by Centro Sud and at one time there were rumours that he was giving Centro Sud a V6 engine to mount in one of the Cooper chassis in exchange for the other frame which he would use for his experiments, this however, never materialized.

Suddenly one morning a rear engined Ferrari appeared on the Modena test track with chief tester Martino Severi at the wheel. All was not well at this first test and Severi found that both front wheels would lift off the ground under hard acceleration.

Impressive practice at Monaco

A short while later the new car appeared at Monaco where Richie Ginther was scheduled to drive it. There it was announced that the prototype had a 2.1-litre engine fitted, just in case it was a failure, but those in the know were aware that it had the normal 246 Dino engine. During practice at Monaco the car was quite impressive, Ginther recorded a time of 1 min. 38.6 secs., the same time as Phil Hill in the front engined Ferrari and only 0.3 of a second slower than Von Trips who set the

fastest Ferrari time. Apparently the bugs had been sorted out.

During the race the car went well enough and despite breaking a ring-gear tooth, it was given 6th place in the classification. An improved gear was fitted in time for the Dutch Grand Prix at Zandvoort but there had been no time to work on the engine. The car was extensively tested and by the time the race came round it was beginning to blow oil through the breathers due to worn rings and consequently did not start.

At this time Ferrari decided to abandon work on the 2.5-litre rear engined type and run the rest of the season with the front engined cars, the idea being that all development work should then be concentrated on the 1.5-litre rear engined version for the new Formula 1 in 1961.

Preliminary tests were done with the Jano-designed V6 1500-cc engine that had been used in the front engined Formula 2 cars, this engine had the bore and stroke of 70 x 64.5. Chiti however had already begun work on a modified version of this engine and retaining the 65-degree V layout. Chiti however had changed the bore and stroke to 73 x 58.8 which gave a shorter stroke and reduced the corrected piston speed at 9,000 r p m from 3,970 to 3,860 feet per minute. The second version was an engine with the 120-degree V angle which allowed for a lower body line.

The 2.5-litre prototype was drastically modified to turn it into a 1500-cc rear engined prototype. The chassis frame was shortened at the rear by eliminating the extension that held the clutch throwout cylinder, a new unit being fitted on to the rear of the gearbox to perform this function. The headrest was trimmed down and this in turn forced a relocation of the magnetos. The fuel tanks were repositioned and the driver's seat was moved further downwards in the frame. With the new 1500-cc engine fitted, Von Trips tested the car at the Modena Autodrome and two days later it appeared for practice for the Solitude race in Germany to take on the Porsches on their home ground. The car was an immediate success and Von Trips won. Ferrari continued to experiment extensively with this car and special mounts were made to take the Lotus type long parallel radius-rod suspension. On the Ferrari this system reduced rear roll stiffness and induced more rear wheel toe-in. This suspension was only used experimentally, not actually being employed on the finalized car but the rear wheel hub carriers were redesigned to give a small amount of permanent toe-in.

At the same period of testing, the front suspension was given the new geometry that had been tested on the front engined cars. Up to then the front wheels had always passed through a range of positive camber during their vertical travel. By angling the top wishbones downwards towards the centre of the car it was possible to preserve negative camber at all times on the outside wheel in a corner and in this manner improve the front end's 'sticking' characteristics.

The multiple pivots for the rear suspension attachments were also used to preserve negative camber and to keep the roll centre high at the back end. The front suspension layout raised the front roll centre to some five inches above ground level.

A prototype test raced at Monza

Ferrari planned to put the 246 Dino or a 256 Dino engine into this 1500-cc prototype, if the British cars were entered at Monza but the British constructors boycotted that race and so Ferrari decided the event would present a perfect test for the 1500-cc version. The car was therefore prepared with the 65 degree Chiti engine, the only modifications being the substitution of a smaller radiator which allowed a smaller air intake in the nose and the addition of air scoops for the driver and the magneto which had been running hot. For Monza the car was fitted with an auxiliary fuel tank and had no difficulty in winning the 1500-cc class, a long way ahead of any opposition, with Von Trips driving.

The car appeared again for the Modena Grand Prix in company with a front engined 1500-cc car. Von Trips drove the rear engined prototype and Ginther the front engined car. Von Trips had a tremendous battle with Bonnier's Porsche, the lead changing several times on each lap. Just before the end, Von Trips' brakes began to fail and he had to drop behind and let Ginther, in the front engined car, take up the challenge. The front engined car was not up to the job and Porsche had their revenge, Ginther finishing a close second and Von Trips an equally close third.

After the Modena race the car went back to the factory to be converted to 1961 specifications which included a new body.

The 1961 cars

While all this testing was going on Ing. Carlo Chiti had been working on the second version of his modified Dino engine, the one with the 120-degree V. By the time the Italian Grand Prix at Monza came round, Chiti had already made substantial progress with what was to be Ferrari's power plant for the 1961 season.

The reasons for going to the 120-degree layout were mainly that this configuration gave the best rotational balance that could be expected from a V6. Slightly higher engine speeds could be expected with the same factor of reliability. The rear engined layout of the new cars permitted the low wide configuration which would have been impractical with the front engined cars. The 120-degree engine would not have fitted in the space between the front wheels and it would have been impossible to provide enough steering lock for the front engined car. The rear engined design allowed for the wider angle which gave a lower rear body line and provided a great deal more room for either the carburetters or fuel injection equipment plus the possibilities of straight intake passages.

The new engine was also required as the original Dino powerplant, although very small by the standards of the era was in effect larger than it need be, as it was designed as a 2.5-litre. As a 1500-cc the engine was trimmed to 265 pounds, some 55 pounds lighter than the 2.5-litre 65-degree V6.

The Type 156

To reduce the weight of the 156 engine Chiti achieved a saving by shortening the connecting rods and reducing the diameter of the big ends. The rods, following Ferrari racing practice, were machined from large forging blanks and retained the two-bolt big ends. The wide angle layout allowed for a certain simplification of the crankshaft design and a consequent reduction of weight. Chiti retained the simple deep sided crankcase construction which terminated in a very wide finned oil pan that was so shallow that it served for little more than a cover plate. The pressure and scavenge pumps were driven from the front end of the crankshaft and a new innovation in the shape of a disposable oil filter was placed vertically at the front of the engine. The oil gallery layout followed the earlier Dino, running down the centre of the V with transfer passages to the heads at the back of the block.

One major difference between earlier Dinos and the Chiti designed 120-degree engine was that the cylinder bank offset was transposed. Jano in the first Dino, followed the Lancia system of off-setting the left hand bank ahead of the right hand bank. Chiti reversed this and moved the right bank ahead of the left one. This change-over was apparently not for any specific technical reason and was probably more to bring the 120-degree design in line with all previous Ferrari V12 models. Internally the Chiti engine differed from the older Dinos in that experience with the earlier engine had been well heeded and resulted in a certain amount of simplification in the new power plant. Each cylinder head was held down by eight studs instead of the original twelve. Chain drive to the camshafts was retained, but between the cam sprockets, the chain was made to run straight across as on the V8 Lancia, instead of being drawn down around an additional idler sprocket.

Each bank had its own double-roller chain system, driven from two half-speed gears on the nose of the crankshaft. The twin distributors splayed out at 120-degrees in front of the block were also driven by these gears through spiral pinions.

On the tension side, between the drive and intake cam sprockets, the right hand chain passed over an additional sprocket which served no purpose until the advent of fuel injection, having its own access plate which would allow a fuel injection pump to be driven and placed in the V of the cylinders. The Weber carburetters used on this engine were specially constructed experimental instruments with three throttle bodies cast in one unit.

Although the cylinder head structure was simplified it was almost 100 per cent Dino in layout. The wide cam lobes still acted on the broad mushroom tappets which Jano designed, the tappets screwed directly on to the valve stem for guidance and clearance adjustment. The coil valve-spring layout was also retained. However, Chiti departed from Dino practice of machining both cam housings in the same plane, returning to the technique of making the cut at right angles to the respective valve stems. Valve inclination was 28 degrees from the vertical for the intakes and 32 degrees for the exhausts, giving a total included angle of 60 degrees, unchanged from the earlier Dinos.

Development of the new engine

Only one exhaust valve size was planned on this engine, 34 mm. Two intake valve diameters were allowed for to produce different power curves as desired, the two measurements being 38.5 mm and 42 mm. In examining the gas velocities that follow from Ferrari's large intake valve and using the parameters of 195 and 260 feet per second gas speed, for peak torque and peak power respectively, the result was engine speeds of 7,200 and 9,600 r p m for the smaller valve and 8,700 and 11,600 r p m for the larger valve. Since the engines quoted power peak was at 9,500 r p m it would seem that the smaller valve layout was intended to match that peak and to provide good torque whereas the larger valve layout was intended to increase the power curve at the top end at the expense of the lower end performance.

Both these valve sizes were designed for the 65-degree and the 120-degree engine layout and initial power outputs for both types of engines were calculated at 160 to 170 b h p for the smaller valve and 180 to 190 b h p for the larger valve. These outputs were increased through development in the 1961 to 1963 period.

Because of the better balance of the 120-degree engine it produced slightly more power due to the raising of the safe rev limit from 9,500 r p m to 10,000 r p m which is an increase from 4,080 to 4,300 ft per min of corrected piston speed.

These impressive outputs were consistent with that which the 65-degree engine was giving in 1960. On test the two 1.5-litre units gave 172 and 177 b h p. With the dimensions at this period the V6 had a piston area of 39 sq. inches which was very good for such a design. The prototype went through 50 hours of bench testing without any problems being found and it proved itself to be just as reliable on the racing circuits during 1961.

The gearbox and final drive on the rear-engined Ferrari was somewhat unusual although at a glance it resembled the components used on other rear engined designs. The gearbox was relocated behind the rear wheel centre line.

However, instead of being placed in unit with the engine, the multiple-disc clutch was carried out in the open at the back of the box, driven by a long shaft that extended from the engine underneath the gearbox. This kept the clutch well ventilated and arose probably because of the many failures experienced by Ferrari with the enclosed Lancia/Dino designs. This layout also made it easy for the attachment of the required ring gear and starter. This system, too, permitted a lower mounting of the engine which had a very shallow dry sump. The drive line had other features. The drive shaft to the clutch was not designed for torsional absorbtion. This function was controlled by a large coupling which contained eight rubber elements that were under compression when the engine was pulling the car. The engine was further ahead of the rear wheels than, mechanical considerations required. This allowed for correct weight distribution and for the possible installation of the longer Intercontinental engine in the event that the formula would ever become popular, which as we now know, was not to be the case. The torsion coupling was fitted, where the clutch would normally have been housed, in a cast forward extension from the gearbox.

The gear train up to the clutch from the engine shaft was readily interchangeable. To change the overall gear ratios, the entire clutch and back cover plate complete with its built-in hydraulic clutch withdrawal caliper was taken off. The two gears were laid out so that the ratio provided would never be higher than one to one and most often would be a reduction between unity and two to one, so that the clutch and attached input shaft to the gearbox would usually run at less than engine speed. The primary or input shaft of the all-indirect gearbox was placed on the right and slightly below the centre line of the secondary or output shaft, which directly drove the spiral bevel final drive gears. The box housed five constant-mesh forward speeds on the earlier cars and six on some of the later experimental models, all without synchromesh, and was equipped with its own pressure lubrication system.

In-board rear brakes

Dunlop disc brakes were used as on previous Ferraris but without the radial drilling encountered on early Dinos. A new innovation was the mounting of the discs inboard at the rear whilst the front discs were in the conventional outboard layout.

The halfshafts were fitted with two Hooke type universal joints apiece and near their inner ends had ball type sliding splines. The rear hubs were carried in simple hollow light alloy suspension posts.

The prototype rear engined car had tubular rear wishbones and forged wishbones at the front but the later rear engined models had the forged members replaced by welded up tubular parts mounted at new angles. Ball joints were still used at the outer pivots but the forged vertical suspension post was completely redesigned to incorporate added stiffness and to serve as a better attachment for the rearward facing steering arm. The rear suspension wishbones were adjustable both in length and the location of their inner pivots, which allowed for experimentation in the setup.

On the prototype, the Cooper system of mounting the front anti-roll bar within the transverse frame tube was followed, connecting it to the suspension through splines, trailing levers and vertical links. However, for the 1961 cars the trailing levers were made about 1½ times as long to decrease the roll stiffness with the same size anti-roll bar.

An anti-roll bar was also fitted at the back end of the 1961 car but its centre diameter was very small and its effect therefore minimal.

The rack-and-pinion steering was placed at the driver's feet together with a 12 volt battery with a small booster cell attached. A transverse steering damper was activated by the left end of the steering rack.

The oil reservoir was located just behind the radiator. The core of the radiator was in three sections, either side being for water and the centre strip for oil.

The twin nostril nose section was something brought over from Maserati by Fantuzzi who left the Maserati company to take on the Ferrari body work after he had built three of the so-called 'piccolo' Maseratis. This type of Maserati had bodies which bore a twin nostril nose designed by the author of this book who in turn copied the idea from the ill-fated Sacha Gordine Formula 1 car.

Ferrari made wind tunnel tests on this type of nose and found that it gave better penetration than a conventional single scoop.

The 1961 Season

For the 1961 season Enzo Ferrari had a strong enough team comprising Phil Hill, Wolfgang Von Trips and Richie Ginther.

Chiti's new 120-degree engined car made its first appearance at Monaco to be driven by Ginther who was Ferrari's chief tester. Phil Hill and Von Trips had similar chassis but with the Chiti modified 65 degree engine installed.

The results with the 120-degree car were extremely satisfying and Ginther was the fastest of the Ferraris with a time of 1 min. 39.3 secs. only .2 sec. behind the fastest time of practice set by Stirling Moss. Phil Hill was in the second row with a 1 min. 39.8 secs. and Von Trips was in the third row with an identical time to Hill but as he recorded his time after Hill he had to take the third row place.

Richie Ginther went straight into the lead but was closely pressed by Stirling Moss who passed him on the 14th lap. Von Trips was held back with a faulty throttle. Team orders allowed both Phil Hill and Von Trips to pass ahead of Ginther

but when it was found that neither of the two drivers could tackle Moss, Ginther was given the go ahead signal. On the 32nd lap Ginther went by Von Trips and by the 75th had caught Phil Hill. Ginther then set off in full pursuit of Moss and the Lotus, closing on him all the time. By the 81st lap Ginther had closed to 4 seconds of Moss but the British driver was on top form and used all his virtuosity to stay ahead, crossing the line 3.6 seconds ahead of the young American. Phil Hill followed in third and Von Trips in 4th place. It was altogether a satisfactory result with three Ferraris starting and three finishing within the first four places.

For the next race of the World Championship circus at Zandvoort, Ferrari sent three of the cars equipped with Chiti's 120-degree engine, the drivers being the same as at Monaco: Hill, Ginther and Von Trips. This time it was like the old days of the Ascari, Volloresi, Farina era. The whole of the front row was made up of Ferraris, all the more surprising as Ferrari had been notoriously unsuccessful on the Dutch circuit over the previous years.

Phil Hill and Von Trips both recorded 1 min. 35.7 secs., with Hill again taking the leading position from Von Trips due to setting the time earlier. Ginther was next with 1 min. 35.9 secs. All the Ferrari lap times were faster than the previous year's best set by Ginther in the 2.5-litre Dino of 1 min. 36.3 secs.

Von Trips jumped into the lead at the start and remained there until the finish with no one to challenge him. Phil Hill had more of a problem and had a tremendous battle with Jim Clark's Lotus for over two-thirds of the race, finally shaking off the green car to place second. It was Stirling Moss' turn to chase Richie Ginther and he did a masterful job slipstreaming the third Ferrari driver and passing him on the last lap to take fourth place. Again it was a satisfactory result for Ferrari with all three cars again finishing and collecting 1st, 2nd and 5th places.

The three 120-degree cars again showed up for the Belgian Grand Prix at Spa to be driven by Hill, Ginther and Von Trips, they were joined by a fourth car painted yellow and handled by Olivier Gendebien, the Belgian driver. The Ferraris completely dominated practice although they could not record as fast times as had been

(Top) Hawthorn won the 1958 French GP at Reims and set the fastest lap. This was the most significant race of the year as the point for fastest lap was the one which clinched Hawthorn's 1958 World Championship

(Middle) Modena Autodrome 1959. Tests on the new Fantuzzi bodied Dino F1. Far left leaning on the counter is Tavoni, the team manager. Right, in the helmet, is Jean Behra with Fantuzzi on his right. The two in hats are Ing. Amorotti, Ferrari and Cav. Luigi Bazzi

(Bottom) Jean Behra, 246 Dino, leads Moss in the great duel during the first part of the 1959 Monaco GP

(*Top*) Tony Brooks in the 246 Dino at the chicane, Monaco GP 1959
(*Middle*) Phil Hill, Monaco GP 1959, the 246 Dino at the 'Tabac'
(*Bottom*) September 1960, Modena GP and the Formula 2 Ferrari

(*Top*) Von Trips in the Formula 2 Dino at Syracuse 1960
(*Middle*) Phil Hill, Monaco GP 1960, 246 Dino
(*Bottom*) Von Trips, Monaco GP 1960, 246 Dino

(Top) The first rear engined prototype Ferrari after its first and unsuccessful test, Modena 1960
(Bottom) Monaco 1960, the prototype rear engined Type 246 Dino

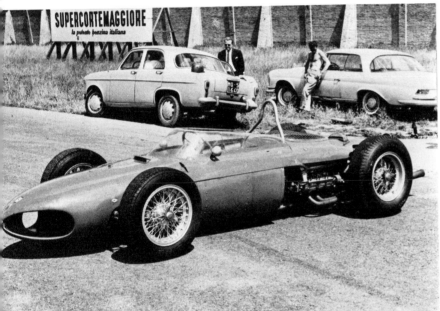

(Top Left) Richie Ginther in the rear engined Ferrari in the 1960 Monaco GP
(Top Right) The Ferrari F1-61 using the 65 degree engine here at Monaco
(Middle) The Ferrari F1-61 using the 120 degree engine during tests at Modena
(Bottom) The prototype 1961 65 degree V6 Ferrari on test at Modena

(*Top*) Ginther driving the prototype V6 at Modena
(*Middle*) The F1 61 120 degree V6 Ferrari at Monza 1961
(*Bottom*) Baghetti wons the French GP at Reims 1961 with
the 65 degree Ferrari. It was a surprise win for the new
driver who edged the Porsches out by inches

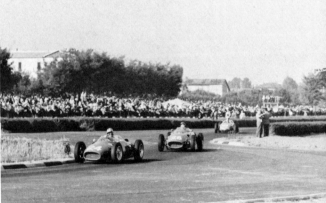

(Top) September 1960, Modena GP, the 1500-cc Formula 2 Ferrari
(Bottom Left) Bandini testing the 'Nurburgring' F1 Ferrari at Modena 1962
(Bottom Right) The rear engined 1500-cc F2 prototype driven by Von Trips leads the 1500-cc F2 front engined car driven by Ginther through the esses at the Grand Prix of Modena

(Top) The modified 'Nurburgring' Ferrari, a post
season experimental car. Here is Surtees in November
1962
(Middle) Surtees driving the 1963 Ferrari with Bosch
fuel injection
(Bottom) John Surtees at Stowe, Silverstone in the
1963 British GP

set by the 2.5-litre Ferraris on the rapid Spa circuit. Phil Hill took pole position with a time of 3 min. 59.3 secs., exactly 6 seconds slower than he had been with the 2.5 Dino the previous year. Von Trips recorded a 4 min. 1 sec. and Gendebien made up the front row with a time of 4 min. 03.0 secs. Ginther was in the second row with a time of 4 min 06.1 secs. having been beaten for 4th time by Surtees' Cooper by 0.1 sec.

A Ferrari triumph

On the race day the Ferrari performance was tremendous, the four Maranello cars strung themselves out in the first four places awaiting the team manager's decision on the order in which they should finish. Hill led on lap one but was passed by the yellow Ferrari of Gendebien much to the delight of the Belgian crowd. By lap three Hill was in the lead again and the following lap Von Trips also passed the Belgian. On lap six Gendebien really put his foot down and passed both the Ferrari aces to regain the lead but by lap nine the two red Ferraris had swept by him again. On lap 12 Ginther also moved ahead of the Belgian and matters settled down except for some switching around between Hill and Trips which finally ended on the 25th lap with Hill taking the lead for good. And so they finished, Hill, Von Trips, Ginther, Gendebien, a complete Ferrari triumph. For the Grand Prix of the A C F at Rheims it was expected that Ferrari would have another sweeping victory. The three 120-degree cars were once again in the hands of Hill, Von Trips and Ginther but the Gendebien 65-degree car repainted red was given to promising newcomer, Giancarlo Baghetti, surprise victor of both the Syracuse and Naples Grands Prix.

Once again the Ferraris had the front row to themselves. Phil Hill was the fastest with 2 min. 24.9 secs., 6.7 seconds slower than his previous year's time with a 2.5-litre car.

Von Trips was next with 2 min. 26.4 secs. and Ginther with 2 min. 26.8 secs. The newcomer Baghetti was further back on the unfamiliar circuit with a time of 2 min. 30.5 secs. which placed him in the 5th row.

Hill, Von Trips and Ginther went straight into the lead. Moss made a valiant attempt to slip-stream them but it was to no avail. Baghetti circulated in 11th place behind the best of the Lotus, BRM and Cooper drivers. Von Trips took the lead on the 13th lap from Hill, whilst Baghetti by dint of hard driving had worked his way up to 4th. Just as everything seemed set for another 1, 2, 3, 4 victory for Ferrari, Von Trips pulled into the pits with a hole in his radiator, this despite the fact that precautions had been taken to fit protective grilles. On the thirty-eighth lap Phil Hill spun and could not restart his engine with the button so he lost one lap in push-starting his car, a procedure that was against the rules but was overlooked by the officials. This left Ginther in the lead but on the 41st lap he too was in the pits with his radiator completely blocked with asphalt and stones. So it was left to the inexperienced Baghetti to try and save the day for Ferrari. The young Italian was set a difficult task as he was badly harassed by the two Porsches of Bonnier and Gurney. The hot pace forced Bonnier to drop back leaving Gurney to fight it out as he had at Syracuse. On the last lap Gurney committed a tactical error and passed Baghetti into Thillois corner, this allowed the young Italian to slip-stream the Porsche along the finishing straight and pull by Gurney to cross the finishing line fractions ahead.

Phil Hill finished 9th but set a new lap record of 123.888 m p h. It was lucky that Ferrari had Baghetti as his cool and collected driving saved the day. The other Ferrari drivers had only themselves to blame for their failure as their tactics of keeping close company had thrown stones, gravel and asphalt into each others air intakes with the results already noted.

British Grand Prix

For the British Grand Prix, held at Aintree, Ferrari sent the three 120-degree cars for the usual trio, Baghetti was entered with the 65-degree model with which he had won at Rheims. All the Ferrari drivers were new to the Aintree circuit but on the opening of practice, with a strong wind blowing, both Ginther and Phil Hill recorded 2 min. 00.8 sec. a time shared with Bonnier's Porsche. Von Trips was further back with a time of 2 min. 01.4 secs. and Baghetti way back with 2 min. 06.0 secs.

On the second practice session all three Ferrari drivers improved their time to 1 min. 58.8 secs., which they again shared with Bonnier's Porsche. Baghetti also improved his time but was still far back with 2 min. 02.0 secs. On the following day the track was wet and the times were slower and both Moss and Salvadori registered times faster than the Ferrari drivers. When it came to the final practice session it was raining heavily and the Ferrari team showed that even under these adverse conditions they were superior to their rivals, and registered the three fastest times of 2 min. 05.8 secs., 2 min. 06.2 secs. and 2 min. 06.4 secs. for Hill, Von Trips and Ginther respectively. Baghetti was not so happy about the rain and recorded 2 min. 12.8 secs.

Bonnier took the pole position away from the Ferraris as he had recorded his time first, he was flanked by Ginther and Hill with Von Trips in the second row all with identical times. Baghetti's time gave him an 8th row starting position.

Conditions at the start were atrocious, rain was setting the track awash and it was almost impossible to see.

By the end of the first lap the three Ferraris were already in the lead, Bonnier having found that the Porsche handled badly in the wet. Phil Hill led Von Trips and Ginther and only Moss was able to keep up with the Ferraris. Moss began to chase Ginther and went by him on lap six. Von Trips was challenging Hill and Moss was challenging Von Trips. Trips passed Hill into the lead and then on the tenth lap Moss succeeded in getting ahead of Hill too to take second place. Both Von Trips and Moss pulled away from Hill and Ginther. As the rain came to a halt Baghetti who had been running in the middle of the field crashed at Waterways. As the track dried Von Trips took advantage of a spin by Moss to increase his lead and Ginther pressed Hill and passed him. Moss appeared to have trouble and Ginther passed him on lap 37. By lap 44 Phil Hill was by Moss as well and on the following lap the Lotus retired to leave the way clear for the Ferraris. The only alteration was that Hill replaced Ginther in second position on the 48th lap and Ferraris were once again 1, 2, 3, in the order Von Trips, Hill, Ginther.

German Grand Prix 1961

For the German Grand Prix at the Nurbur-gring Ferrari entered four cars, the three 120-degree models for his regular drivers and the 65-degree type for Mairesse.

During the first practice session Bonnier with the Porsche surprised everyone by beating Stirling Moss' lap record (with the 2.5-litre Vanwall) of 9 min. 9.2 secs. Bonnier's new figure was 9 min. 06.6 secs. Hill recorded the best Ferrari time and was second fastest at 9 min. 10.2 secs. Von Trips could only manage 9 min. 23.5 secs., Ginther 9 min. 23.8 secs. and newcomer Mairesse 9 min. 32.7 secs.

During the second practice session Phil Hill caused a sensation, Bonnier's new record was completely shattered with a Ferrari time of 8 min. 55.2 secs., no less than 14 seconds better than the Moss record with a 2.5-litre car. Both Mairesse and Ginther also improved their times, the Belgian recording 9 min. 15.9 secs. and the American 9 min. 16.6 secs. During the last practice session Von Trips improved his time to 9 min. 05.5 secs. but Ginther, Hill and Mairesse were slower.

His lap record gave Phil Hill the pole position, Von Trips was in the 2nd row and Ginther and Mairesse were in the 4th row, not the usual line up as in other races. At the start it was Brabham in the new V8 Cooper Climax that took the lead followed by Moss, Bonnier, Gurney and Phil Hill in the first Ferrari. Brabham left the road when he hit a puddle of water on the first lap and Phil was getting into his stride sweeping by Bonnier and Gurney, he then passed Moss into the lead but the Englishman was by again, shortly after the Karussel, and led the Ferrari by 1.5 seconds at the start/finish line. Von Trips was the next Ferrari up in 6th place followed by Ginther in 8th. Moss drove as only he could and began to increase his lead over Phil Hill, Von Trips moved up to 3rd behind his teammate and Ginther moved up to 6th. Moss pulled out to a 10 second lead over Hill and the duel was on. Ginther dropped back from his 6th place to 8th and Mairesse moved up from 10th to 6th. On lap 6 Phil Hill recorded a 9 min. 09.7 secs. to Moss' 9 min. 13.4 secs. Ginther dropped another place to 9th and Mairesse maintained a steady 6th. On the same lap that Hill was putting the pressure on to Moss, Von Trips started to put the pressure on to Hill recording 9 min. 08.1 secs. thus setting a new lap record. On the 7th lap however, Moss came back with a spurt and broke Von Trips' new record with a 9 min. 05.4 secs., Phil Hill almost matched this with a 9 min. 06.9 secs. but Von Trips was in great form and reclaimed the record with 9 min. 04.3 secs.

Moss also had something more up his sleeve and turned another lap record on lap 8 in 9 min. 02.8 secs. Von Trips in his assaults on the lap record had passed team mate Hill into second place and was going hell bent after Moss; again he broke the new record with 9 min. 01.6 secs., with Hill close behind at 9 min. 03.3 secs.

Moss was a fraction slower on his next lap but the incredible Von Trips lowered the record once again with 9 min. 01.1 secs. Hill followed with a 9 min. 03.0 secs. which gave him a 0.4 second pickup on Moss but did not bring him closer to Von Trips. On lap ten Moss pulled out all the stops and turned 9 min. 01.2 secs. not quite fast enough to get the record and Trips replied with an electrifying 8 min. 59.9 secs., the first official under 9 minute lap set on the Nurburgring. His triumph was shortlived for Phil Hill also had decided to pull out the stops and came round with a 8 min. 57.8 secs. which put him right on Von Trips tail. Moss continued lapping in 9 min. 01.4 secs. and Von Trips repeated his 8 min. 59.9 secs. Mairesse lost his secure 6th place when he spun and retired and Ginther moved up to 8th. On the last but one lap Phil Hill overtook Von Trips but was still some 14 seconds behind Moss. On the last lap a tremendous battle for second place developed between Von Trips and Hill both of them slid on a rain puddle and went sideways losing some more time to Moss, Von Trips straightened out the quickest and beat Hill over the line by 1.1 seconds. Ferrari had been beaten by the virtuosity of Moss as they had at Monaco, Moss had won despite the fact that the Ferrari was a superior machine. At least the Ferrari team had the satisfaction of setting a new record together with 2nd, 3rd and 8th places.

Italian Grand Prix

With the Italian Grand Prix coming up Enzo Ferrari decided to give the promising young Mexican driver, Ricardo Rodriguez, a tryout on the team. The three regular team members were given the 120-degree cars and Rodriguez had the 65-degree model, Baghetti also joined the lineup this time with a new 120-degree type. In addition to these cars Baghetti's old 65-degree model from Rheims was there as a practice car for the whole team. The Italian race was once again held over the combined road and banked track circuit and the overall record stood to the credit of Phil Hill with a 2.5-litre Dino at 2 min. 41.4 secs. a time that would be difficult for the smaller 1.5-litre cars to beat. There were two practice sessions and Ferrari immediately showed that they were going to be a dominating force on the very fast circuit. Ginther came out on top with a time of 2 min. 46.8 secs. only 4.4 secs. slower than the 2.5-litre record. Hill followed with 2 min. 48.9 secs. and Rodriguez surprised everyone by being next with the 65-degree car in 2 min. 49.6 secs., Von Trips followed with 2 min. 50.3 secs. and Baghetti was considerably slower with 2 min. 53.4 secs.

On the second day's practice Von Trips pulled up into first place with 2 min. 46.3 secs., and the young Rodriguez again shook everyone by setting second fastest only 0.1 sec. slower than the German driver. Ginther was slower than his best but Phil Hill improved his time to 2 min. 47.2 secs. whilst Baghetti also jumped a lot of other competitors to register 2 min. 49.0 secs. which was only beaten by one non Ferrari this being Graham Hill's V8 BRM which was a non-starter in the race. The line up for the Monza race was a grid with two cars per row instead of the more usual 3, 2, 3 system. Von Trips and Rodriguez were in the front row with the German on the pole. Phil Hill and Ginther shared the 2nd row and Baghetti was in the 3rd row.

At the start of the race Rodriguez was already moving and all the Ferraris except for Baghetti were quick to follow. As the cars passed by the pits after completing the road part of the circuit Phil Hill was in the lead followed by Ginther, Rodriguez and Clark's Lotus followed in turn by Von Trips, Brabham on the V8 Cooper Climax and Baghetti. As they returned to the road circuit and moved down to the curve before the main straight Clark tried to pass Von Trips who had moved ahead of him in the meantime and the two cars touched. Clark overturned without damage to himself but Von Trips' car crashed into the fence, taking the lives of 12 spectators, the extremely popular Von Trips losing his own life in the process. The race continued without the Ferrari team drivers being aware of what had happened and Hill led Ginther, Rodriguez and Baghetti in a Ferrari procession. By the fourth lap Baghetti had closed up with the other three team cars and set the fastest lap at 2 min. 48.4 secs. Only Brabham in the V8 Cooper was able to keep up with the flying Ferraris. The two leading Ferraris switched positions to provide some entertainment for the crowd, Ginther led on lap 4, Hill on lap 5, Ginther lap 6, Hill lap 7, Ginther laps 8 and 9, Hill lap 10, Ginther laps 11, 12 and 13 and then Hill went permanently into the lead.

All the Ferraris were setting a fast pace lapping in the 2 min. 50.0 secs. region but the pace began to tell even on the Maranello cars. On the 14th lap Rodriguez was in the pits and the oil level was checked before the car was pushed away. Baghetti pulled in only a few seconds later and was immediately retired with clouds of smoke coming out of the engine. The Ferrari team manager consequently slowed both Hill and Ginther who proceeded to circulate some 3 seconds a lap slower having a comfortable 25 second lead over their nearest opponents. Ginther began to drop behind Hill and it was noticed that Moss was beginning to make up ground on the Ferrari, on the 24th lap the Ferrari's bolt was shot and Ginther retired in a cloud of smoke. A worried Ferrari team manager informed Hill that Moss was now only 18 seconds behind but Hill had the situation well in hand and turned a 2 min. 49.6 secs. and several laps at 2 min. 50 secs. followed by another 2 min. 49.3 secs. on the 29th lap, 2 min. 49.1 secs. on the 30th lap, 2 min. 49.8 secs. on the 35th lap and 2 min. 49.4 secs. on the 37th lap, before easing off to lap at 2 min. 53.0 secs. to 2 min. 54.0 secs. for the remaining laps, Moss having broken down, and leaving Hill with a 30 second advantage over his nearest rival. As he crossed the finishing line Phil Hill became the first American world champion, but the day was

clouded for Ferrari with the death of Von Trips and the breakage of his three other cars. The last event of the season, the American Grand Prix, was run without Ferrari participation as he had already clinched both the drivers' and manufacturers' world championships.

In the drivers' championship Phil Hill was 1st with 34 points, the unfortunate Von Trips remained second on the list with 33 points, Ginther was 5th with 16 points, Baghetti 9th with 9 points and Gendebien 13th with 3 points.

In the manufacturers' championship Ferrari netted a total of 40 points to Lotus 32, Porsche 22, Cooper 14 and BRM 7.

The 1962 Season - Ferrari is in trouble

For the 1962 season Ferrari had high hopes of repeating the successes of 1961. The loss of Von Trips had left him with Phil Hill, since Richie Ginther had taken a contract with BRM. However at the end of the 1961 season Ferrari had given a try out to Ricardo Rodriguez who showed himself a capable driver. Ferrari made up his team with this young Mexican plus the two Italians, Giancarlo Baghetti and Lorenzo Bandini, the latter recruited from the ranks of the Scuderia Centro Sud. In all it was not the best team that Ferrari had ever fielded as only Phil Hill could really be called experienced, the other three showed a great deal of promise but lacked maturity. The team was not Ferrari's only problem for 1962. In an argument with one of the senior members of his staff there had been an unfortunate falling out which resulted in what amounted to the whole of the top echelon of Ferrari's staff taking sides against him. Ferrari had always been inflexible with staff problems and as a result of his unwillingness to back down, all his top men left him. This created no small problem as most of these men had been either hand picked or carefully trained over a period of years to form a top-notch organization. Ferrari was left without Chief Designer, Commercial Manager, Team Manager, Chief Tester, Foundry Manager and General Manager. It was a tough proposition to replace them but he did. This factor combined with the fact that the British had finally produced engines comparable in power and reliability with

Maranello products plus a great deal of trouble with the Italian labour unions caused Ferrari to have one of his most disastrous seasons in 1962.

At his annual press conference in Modena, Ferrari announced that the 1961 Grand Prix car would remain basically unaltered for the 1962 season. The main difference was to be the utilization of a 4-valve-per-cylinder head and a new six-speed transmission which was located between the engine and the final drive instead of being overhung behind the differential as on previous models. The six-speed gearbox car was seen at the beginning of the season with No. 1 driver, Phil Hill at the wheel. This car had the track increased from 3 ft 11¼ in. to 4 ft 1 in. The 4-valve-per-cylinder engine never materialized during the 1962 season and Ferrari relied mainly on his 1961 cars.

Two races that were not world championship events began the 1962 season, Ferrari entering cars for both events.

Brussels Grand Prix

The first was the Grand Prix of Brussels and Willy Mairesse prevailed on Ferrari to send him with a car. Ferrari provided Mairesse with a 1961 chassis fitted with a 65-degree engine, however the old car was equipped with one of the latest 6-speed gearboxes.

As practice was held in the wet, the previous year's record was not broken but the fastest time of day was set by Jim Clark with his Lotus at 2 min. 3.1 secs. Mairesse was fourth fastest with a time of 2 min. 4.7 secs.

The race was held in three heats with all the competitors running in each heat. In the first heat Graham Hill, with the BRM, took the lead from the start but was challenged by Mairesse and Moss. The BRM went on to win the heat with Moss second and the lone Ferrari third.

In the second heat it was Mairesse who led at the start but he was quickly passed by Moss. The Belgian driver spun the Ferrari, in his attempts to keep up with Moss, dropping to 5th place. Mairesse however, was on top form and quickly made up ground and when the Moss Lotus broke, the Ferrari went on to win with a comfortable advantage over the other competitors.

In the final heat Bonnier with his Porsche held a lap one lead but on the next lap Mairesse was by and had no difficulty winning. The other non-championship event at the beginning of the season was the Pau Grand Prix. SEFAC decided to enter two cars for Ricardo Rodriguez and Lorenzo Bandini to drive in order to give the two newcomers some additional experience before the championship events began. Rodriguez was given a 1961 car with a 120-degree engine and Bandini had a similar chassis with a 65-degree engine.

Rodriguez was almost two seconds slower in practice than Jim Clark who lapped in 1 min. 32.5 secs.; nevertheless the young Mexican was in 2nd place on the grid.

At the start of the race Rodriguez took the lead with Bandini circulating in 5th place. On the 8th lap Rodriguez lost first place and began to slow up, finally dropping to 4th. When Jim Clark retired, Rodriguez was let up into 3rd place and back to 2nd on Bonnier's retirement.

Netherlands Grand Prix

The first race of the 1962 world championship season was held at Zandvoort. Phil Hill had the 1962 car with the centrally mounted gearbox and the wider track; Baghetti and Rodriguez were sent with two of the 1961 cars with 120-degree engines.

In practice 10 cars beat Phil Hill's previous year's record of 1 min. 35.7 secs. to show how much progress had been made by the British designers. Phil Hill with the new car managed to record 1 min. 35.0 secs. so was the only Ferrari driver to better the previous year's record. Rodriguez turned in 1 min. 36.1 secs. and Baghetti in 1 min. 36.3 secs. With these times Hill was in the 4th row and the two other Ferrari drivers in the 5th row for the start. Phil Hill ran in 5th place at the start and moved up to 4th during his battle with Surtees' Lola. At half distance Phil Hill was in 2nd place after the retirement of McLaren and Clark but was too far back to catch the leading BRM of Graham Hill. Baghetti was holding down 5th place whilst Rodriguez was involved in several shunts. Phil Hill's oil pressure began to fall and slowing up he was passed by Trevor Taylor's Lotus. When Innes Ireland crashed, Baghetti moved up to 4th and Rodriguez crashed again five laps from the end, this time bending the car too much to continue.

It was not a very promising beginning to the championship season as it had been obvious that the No. 1 cars of BRM, Lotus and Cooper were faster than the Ferraris.

Monaco Grand Prix

For the next championship event, held at Monaco, SEFAC Ferrari sent five cars for Hill, Mairesse, Bandini, Baghetti and Rodriguez. Only two of the cars had been officially invited and so the other three had to qualify. As a result of these proceedings Bandini started with Hill and Mairesse but Baghetti and Rodriguez remained spectators. Phil Hill drove the central gearbox 1962 car during practice but all three of the cars that appeared on the starting grid were the 1961 type 120-degree engined cars.

During practice Jim Clark with the Lotus broke the lap record with a time of 1 min. 35.4 secs. with Mairesse the fastest of the Ferraris in 1 min. 36.4 secs. an improvement of some 3 seconds over Richie Ginther's fastest Ferrari lap the previous year. Mairesse qualified for the 2nd row, Hill for the 3rd and Bandini for the 4th.

There was a big mix up at the start with several cars crashing at the Gasometer hairpin. Fortunately the three Ferraris managed to get through unscathed. Mairesse was off in second place but spun at the Station hairpin. Phil Hill was dicing for 4th place and Bandini followed in 6th. Phil Hill moved up to third but was himself passed by Brabham. Mairesse in his accident had damaged his suspension and was running way behind. When Graham Hill's leading BRM broke its engine Phil Hill moved ahead of Brabham again to take 2nd place behind McLaren. The American Ferrari driver began to pile on the pressure to catch McLaren in the works Cooper but the task of making up 17 seconds with only 7 laps to go was too much, nevertheless Phil Hill made a tremendous attempt and had reduced the difference to 3 seconds when the cars entered their last lap. The Cooper crossed the line first but Hill was second just 1.3 seconds behind. Bandini followed in 3rd place and Mairesse was classified 7th although he had broken his engine on the 91st lap.

Belgian Grand Prix

There were hopes that Ferrari would repeat the previous year's win on the very fast Spa circuit where the four Ferraris entered had swept the board in 1961. SEFAC Ferrari entered four cars to be driven by Phil Hill, Mairesse, Baghetti and Rodriguez with Bandini along as a reserve. The Ferrari team were in for a big disappointment; Graham Hill set the fastest lap with a BRM of 3 min. 57.0 secs. and the best that Phil Hill could do was 3 min. 59.6 secs. which was 0.3 sec. slower than his fastest lap in 1961. The Ferrari drivers found that the cars were in fact some 7 m p h slower than the previous year's cars. Phil Hill's time was the fourth fastest qualifying time and Mairesse was 5th with 3 min. 59.8 secs. Rodriguez recording 4 min. 01.0 sec. and Baghetti 4 min. 08.0 secs. These times placed Phil Hill in the second row, Mairesse and Rodriguez in the 3rd and Baghetti in the 6th.

Mairesse put up a very spirited show being fifth at the start but mixed things with the lead group. Phil Hill and Rodriguez were with the second group of cars, being placed 7th and 8th.

On the 4th lap Mairesse passed Trevor Taylor into the lead but lost it to the Englishmen on the following lap, on lap 6 Mairesse was ahead again. Phil Hill and Rodriguez began to move up but Baghetti retired with ignition troubles.

Both Taylor and Mairesse were passed by Jim Clark and Mairesse dropped to third. When Taylor spun, Mairesse was back in second place but could make no impression on Clark. The Mairesse/Taylor battle was renewed until both cars touched and crashed. Taylor's Lotus was totally destroyed and Mairesse's Ferrari caught fire and was completely burnt out; all this without serious consequences for the two drivers although the Ferrari driver was kept out of racing for the main part of the season. Neither Phil Hill nor Rodriguez could catch the leading Lotus and second place BRM so they contented themselves with an almost photo-finish for 3rd and 4th places, the American beating the Mexican by a nose. After the Belgian Grand Prix Ferrari had troubles at home with the labour unions and as a result the cars could not be prepared in time for the Grand Prix of the A C F held at Rouen. Phil Hill attended the race to see fellow Californian, Dan Gurney win his first major race and to see himself fall still further behind in world championship points standing.

British Grand Prix

The troubles were not over by the time the British Grand Prix at Aintree came round, but by dint of some hard work one car was prepared for Phil Hill to race, the other drivers having to remain sidelined.

SEFAC Ferrari sent the central gearbox car and Phil Hill had his time of 1 min. 58.8 secs. in view from 1961. He had difficulty in practice and was very unhappy with the car, nevertheless he improved his 1961 time by 2.6 seconds registering 1 min. 56.2 secs. There had been such a tremendous improvement in the British cars that even the 2.6 seconds faster than the old record was not nearly good enough. Jim Clark in the Lotus set a new record of 1 min. 53.6 secs. and Phil's time placed him in the 5th row with 11 cars faster than his best.

In the race Hill had a terrible time, his car was still not handling properly and he ran well back, not even figuring in the first 10. After a great deal of struggling he finally moved up to 9th place before he retired with distributor trouble.

German Grand Prix

After the poor showing at Aintree, Ferrari sent four cars to the Nurburgring for the German Grand Prix, Phil Hill had the same car that he had used at Aintree with the centrally mounted gearbox. Baghetti had the 1961 120-degree type. Ricardo Rodriguez was sent with an old 65-degree model and Bandini had the 156/62/P model, a completely new car that was supposed to be Ferrari's latest 1962 model and built to take the 4-valve engine. However, despite rumours to the contrary, the 4-valve engine did not make its appearance at the Nurburgring and the new car had a 1961 type 120-degree engine fitted into it.

The Type 156/62/P

The new car was most noticeably different in its bodywork. The 1961 type twin nostril nose section was replaced by one with an oval intake that somewhat shortened the body and made it look much more like the then current Lotus and Cooper cars. The rear lower engine panels were left off to give better cooling and to reduce weight, and the lateral tanks were modified to give a smoother line. Another noticeable difference was the changeover to the inclined seat that was popular with the British constructors instead of the more usual upright seat fitted to previous Ferraris.

The car was also modified in the chassis department. At the front the two upper tubes of the frame were carried straight to a point above the hubs of the wheels instead of descending obliquely, this served to eliminate the flexing which was found due to the weight of the radiator and oil tank.

At the rear of the chassis frame, the transverse tube was arched upwards to act as a support for the differential unit.

The gearbox was moved further back, being similar in layout to that used in the 1961 car but discontinued in the 'one off' 1962 model. The lower part of the chassis frame was lengthened with large tubes inclined backwards to serve as a 'nest' for the gearbox.

Suspensions were also altered. There was a modification to the upper wishbones of the front suspension; the wishbones being given a lower locating point than on the previous models. The front and rear anti-roll bars were retained but, on the rear suspension, the bar acted on the lower wishbone instead of the upper as on the earlier models. The lowering of the front wishbones necessitated the addition of long rods from the extremities of the front anti-roll bar to the point of attachment on the wishbone. An alteration was also made to the exhaust system, the new car having much shorter final pipes, megaphoned to end just beyond the rear wishbones.

At the Nurburgring the Ferrari drivers had Phil Hill's time of 8 min. 55.2 secs. as a standard but their hopes of equalling this time were doomed to failure. The first big shock was that Gurney with the 8-cylinder Porsche broke the Ferrari record with a time of 8 min. 47.2 secs. and both Graham Hill and Jim Clark also recorded better times than the old record. When the Ferraris went out to try and match these times the results were most disappointing. The fastest member of the team was Rodriguez who recorded 9 min. 14.2 secs., some 19 seconds slower than the previous year's best Ferrari time. Phil Hill tried out the new car but was very happy to hand it over to Bandini and try to get amongst the leaders with his older central gearbox model. With this car he recorded a very poor 9 min. 24.7 secs., Baghetti followed with a 9 min. 28.1 secs. and Bandini showed that the new car was far from right with a time of 9 min. 39.7 secs.

The results of practice left the Ferrari drivers with positions in the 3rd row (Rodriguez), the 4th (Phil Hill and Baghetti) and the 5th (Bandini).

Phil Hill made a good start and initially held third place but he began to fall back in the rain-soaked conditions. Bandini brought the new car's run to a quick close by sliding off the road at the Karussel on the first lap. At the fifth lap Phil Hill was in the pits to have his vizor cleaned. Rodriguez moved up to 7th place on the first lap and up to 5th on the 4th lap. On lap 5 he was overtaken by Jim Clark but kept the oldest model Ferrari going well till the end of the race. Baghetti was most unhappy in the wet conditions but improved his position through other cars retiring. Phil Hill was out with a broken wishbone so that the final results were Rodriguez 6th and Baghetti 10th altogether a very unsatisfactory performance for Ferrari.

Italian Grand Prix

For the Italian Grand Prix at Monza Ferrari turned out in full force. Phil Hill had his central gearbox model, Baghetti and Rodriguez were given the 120-degree types, Bandini had to be content with the 65-degree car. Willy Mairesse marked his return to competition after his pile up in Belgium by driving the new car with the reclining seat. The 24 valve engine failed to materialize.

Mairesse showed that he was in good form by setting the fastest of the Ferrari times at 1 min. 42.8 secs. His effort was of no avail and there were nine British cars faster with Jim Clark taking the pole position at 1 min. 40.3 secs. Mairesse was followed by Rodriguez at 1 min. 43.1 secs., Phil Hill at 1 min. 43.4 secs., Bandini at 1 min. 44.3 secs. and Baghetti 1 min. 44.4

secs. These times gave Mairesse a place in the 5th row, Rodriguez the 6th, Phil Hill the 8th and Baghetti and Bandini in the 9th, showing that the Ferrari would have to go very hard indeed if they were to have any chance whatsoever to repeat the previous year's victory.

The BRMs of Graham Hill and Richie Ginther showed much greater speed and were quickly out in front. Mairesse was able to join in a battle with the second group of cars driven by Gurney, McLaren, Ireland, Maggs and Bonnier. The third group of cars saw a similar battle between Rodriguez, Baghetti and Phil Hill.

Phil Hill made repeated pit stops and fell further and further behind, Rodriguez had trouble with his engine and the car slowed noticeably, the Mexican retiring with ignition failure. Baghetti moved up to third place on his home circuit but spoiled everything by spinning off and losing several places. Bandini was plodding around at the back of the field whilst Mairesse was putting up a gallant show to try and put his Ferrari amongst the leaders. On the last lap he passed McLaren's Cooper for 3rd place but the Cooper driver slipstreamed the Ferrari and pulled by the red car across the finishing line to regain third. Baghetti finished 5th, Bandini 8th and Phil Hill a very dissatisfied 10th.

Drivers' dual gives Ferrari a 1, 2 finish

The Grand Prix of the Mediterranean held at Pergusa was not a world championship event but Ferrari decided to send Baghetti and Bandini with two cars to ensure that SEFAC would take the Italian Formula 1 championship. The wisdom of this decision was questioned as the rivalry between Bandini and Baghetti was well known. As it turned out the race was a wheel-to-wheel fight between the two Italians and it was touch and go that either of them finished. Both cars had their tachometers reading over 10,000 r p m and both had their radiators almost completely blocked because of their close-company tactics. Bandini arrived at the finish with several holes in his radiator and almost no water. Both drivers had the 120-degree models and Bandini set the fastest practice lap at an average speed of 136 m p h. This record was equalled by Baghetti on his 37th lap and was again equalled by Bandini

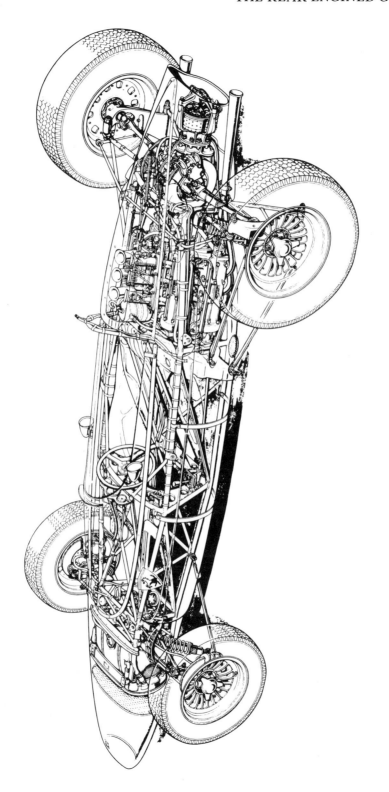

Cutaway of the 1963 V6 F1 Ferrari

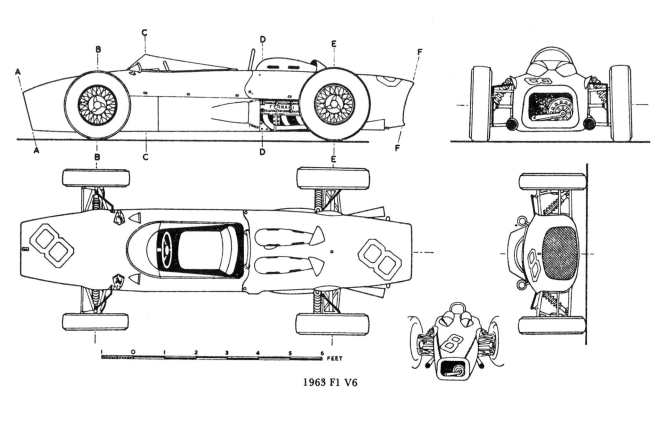

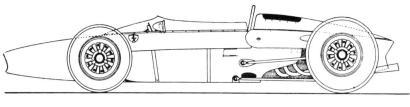

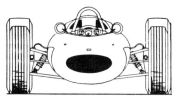

1963 F1 V6

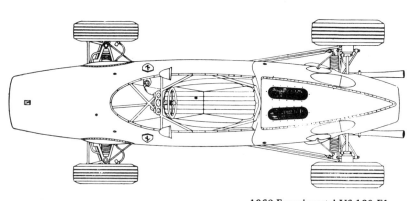

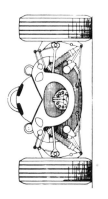

1962 Experimental V6 120 F1

on the 50th and last lap when he came from behind and pipped Baghetti for first place on the finishing line to give Ferrari his only 1, 2 result of the season.

Ferrari withdraws from Formula 1

After this event Ferrari sent a letter addressed to Giancarlo Baghetti, Lorenzo Bandini, Phil Hill and Ricardo Rodriguez announcing that he would withdraw from competition for the rest of the season, the text of the letter was:

The present position once again makes it impossible for us to carry out the plans established since Monza to construct four new Formula 1 cars.

Due to the lack of the indispensable collaboration by our workmen, for reasons that have their origin in a national problem and not one that originates in our own organization, we see ourselves forced to renounce future races.

We will continue within the limits of the reduced timetable to work on the development of the prototype Formula 1 car in the hope that we will be able to make use of the experience in the future. The above has been communicated to you in the case that you should desire to find other means to compete in the remaining races. This may be done with the sole reservation that you use the conventional accessories, that is: Dunlop-Shell-Marchal-Ferodo.

We thank you for your collaboration during the present racing season and regret that in the field of Formula 1 we were not able to produce means to compare with our constructions for Gran Turismo, Sports and Prototypes. With my best wishes,

signed, Enzo Ferrari

So ended a most disastrous season for Ferrari with not a single world championship event falling to the Maranello factory. In the constructors' championship Ferrari finished last but one with 18 points, behind BRM, Lotus, Cooper, Lola and Porsche.

In the drivers' championship Phil Hill finished 6th with 14 points, Baghetti 11th, Rodriguez 12th, Bandini 13th and Mairesse 14th.

The SEFAC Ferrari racing team received a complete overhauling at the end of the disastrous 1962 season. Phil Hill and Baghetti left to join the newly formed ATS team run by the 'Ferrari Rebels.' Ricardo Rodriguez lost his life in an accident during practice for the Mexican Grand Prix and Bandini rejoined the reconstituted Scuderia Centro Sud of Mimmo Dei.

Ferrari decided to alter the system of driver contracts and made up his mind that all works drivers would be full employees of the factory and be required to help in the development and testing.

A new model for 1963

Consequently he engaged John Surtees, seven times world motor cycling champion, Willy Mairesse and Mike Parkes for his purpose, indicating that he did not foresee the running of as many team cars as in the past. The cars for 1963 received a thorough going over and the new model was seen after the 1962 Monza event. Both Ing. Jano and Ing. Rocchi, joint designers of the chassis, were present. The problems studied were most efficient roadholding to allow a greater margin of adhesion in high-speed curves, and to examine the possibilities of improving frontal area.

The test car underwent 13 different coil spring changes and an 'Indianapolis' setup was also tried in reverse as all the Monza corners are right handers.

On the new car various anti-roll bars were tried the front bar being attached by a vertical link to a rear-facing plate welded into the V extremity of the top wishbone. At the rear the anti-roll bar was attached by an even longer vertical link to the lower wishbone at a point where the coil spring originally had its location.

On the front of the chassis itself an extra member was added to give additional strength. This member ran from the front of the top side member to intersect the diagonal crossmember.

In the attempt to improve the frontal area, the front coil spring/damper units were moved further inboard. The positions of the brake calipers on the front brakes were also altered, on the test car the calipers were mounted at the rear of the disc instead of at the front as on the Nurburgring prototype.

Other alterations were the removal of the carburetter air intake scoops at the front of the bulges on the rear deck and their repositioning on the side and rear of these bulges.

With the assistance of Surtees and Parkes the car underwent further major modifications during the winter of 1962 – 63 and two cars were ready in time to race at the Daily Express Trophy in early May 1963. These cars were similar in external looks to the Monza prototype but in fact possessed a more compact and lighter multi-tube frame. At the front end, the well-tested double wishbone and coil spring/damper layout was retained but at the rear there was a major change, there being a lower wishbone pivoted on the chassis at its apex, a single upper transverse arm and two long radius arms completed by coil spring/damper units.

Ferrari retained the inboard brakes at the rear but for the first time fitted alloy wheels instead of the traditional wire types. These wheels were of his own design and manufacture with five pin drive and knock-off type hub nut.

There was still no sign of the 4-valve-per-cylinder engine but the V6 120-degree engine was fitted with Bosch high pressure fuel injection, the pump being located in the V of the cylinders and being driven by a toothed belt.

The air intakes had big trumpets and in common with the Lucas low pressure system used on the British engines, the Bosch type had slide throttles with one plate for each group of 3 inlets.

A new type 6-speed gearbox was fitted between the engine and the final drive unit, operated by a left hand gear lever in the cockpit. The driving position was very reclined, the driver's feet being under the rack and pinion steering.

Daily Express Trophy

For the International Daily Express Trophy race SEFAC Ferrari entered two cars for Surtees and Mairesse both of them being the new types. After the poor performances in 1962 it was wondered if Ferrari could get back again to his tremendous performances in 1961 and the Daily Express Trophy would certainly show what

could be expected for the World Championship events later in the season.

In practice it was Innes Ireland with a Lotus BRM that set the fastest lap of 1 min. 34.4 secs. Although he did not manage a place on the first row of the grid, Surtees placed in the second row with a time equal with Jim Clark's Lotus of 1 min. 36.2 secs. Mairesse qualified for the third row at 1 min. 38.0 secs. compared with the fastest Ferrari time by Von Trips in the 1960 Silverstone event of 1 min. 37.0 secs. with the front engined 2.5-litre Dino. At the start Surtees was in 5th place but quickly began to show that the new Ferrari was a force to be reckoned with; on the second lap he moved up into third spot. Mairesse, less familiar with the circuit than the British driver was circulating in 12th place chasing Bandini's Centro Sud BRM and Bonnier's Cooper. It was noticed that there was blue smoke coming from Surtees' engine but the ex-motorcycle champion pressed closely on the tail of second man McLaren. On laps 2 and 4 Surtees went round in 1 min. 36.0 secs., better than his practice time and on lap 10 succeeded in passing McLaren for second place to sit on the tail of the leader, Clark. Mairesse in the meantime overdid things in passing Bandini's BRM and spun into the ditch at Stowe. Clark began to draw away from Surtees but Surtees was also outdistancing the remainder of the field. Clark pulled out to a six second lead and then on the 28th lap Surtees' cloud of smoke vanished and it was only a question of time before the Ferrari retired, as FIA regulation forbade the addition of oil. On the 31st lap the Ferrari's promising race was over and Surtees coasted into the pits.

It had been a failure, but the performance of the new car in its first outing gave Ferrari and the mechanics a morale boost and high hopes for the championship events the first of which was to be held at Monaco a few weeks later.

Monte Carlo

SEFAC Ferrari again entered only two cars for the Monaco Grand Prix. These were to be driven by Surtees and Mairesse, Surtees having his Silverstone car and Mairesse having a brand new one as there had not been time to repair his own after the crash in England. The first practice sessions saw the two Ferraris running with special sawn-off noses in an effort to avoid the usual dented air intakes on the first lap scramble. Unfortunately these shorter noses caused overheating problems and the two Maranello cars returned with the original slim noses. Jim Clark with the Lotus set the fastest lap with a time of 1 min. 34.3 secs. but Surtees was not far behind being 3rd fastest qualifier in 1 min. 35.2 secs. with Mairesse in the 3rd row at 1 min. 35.9 secs. which gave him seventh best time. The second group of six cars all being within .9 of a second of each other, the race promised to be a real tussle.

During the last practice session Surtees nearly eliminated himself from the race when he had brake failure and bounced against both sides of the chicane, damaging a wheel and a wishbone. However, the Ferrari still seemed as strong as ever. It was quickly repaired and had no trouble in being on the line for the start.

At the start of the race there was a pitched battle between Graham Hill and Ginther on the BRMs and Clark in the Lotus with Surtees' Ferrari close behind. After Clark passed Hill into the lead the Ferrari driver began to put the pressure on to the two BRMs and, after 28 laps, passed Ginther to take 3rd place. The second Ferrari of Mairesse never got going really well. Although the Belgian moved up to 6th place he was forced to retire before half distance with transmission troubles.

In the meantime Surtees had set his sights on Graham Hill and from laps 40 to 48 began seriously to challenge the 1962 World Champion. Finally on lap 57 Surtees moved the red Ferrari ahead of the BRM going into Ste. Devote and the battle continued. Clark had a lead of 10 seconds on Surtees. On lap 63 Graham Hill managed to wrest 2nd place away from Surtees again and just then the Ferrari began to slow. Surtees had noticed that his oil pressure was falling so he began using 500 r p m less in the attempt to save his engine. The engine began to sound rough and Surtees was being spattered with oil. As a result of this the 2nd BRM driven by Ginther began to make up time on the Ferrari and by lap 75 was by the red car. It was McLaren's turn to challenge Surtees and on lap 79, Surtees was another place back in 5th spot. When Clark spun, Graham Hill moved his

BRM into the lead with Ginther 2nd, McLaren third and Surtees' Ferrari fourth. Surtees found to his surprise that the oil pressure had stabilised and made up his mind to try and displace McLaren from third place. He piled on the pressure and in the attempt set a new lap record of 1 min. 34.6 secs. McLaren went as hard as he could and equalled the record on his next lap. With two laps to go, Surtees was only 2 seconds behind and despite the oily state of the track he turned in another lap record of 1 min. 34.5 secs. but it was not good enough and McLaren crossed the line 1.3 seconds ahead of the Ferrari.

Belgian Grand Prix

Ferrari again entered two cars only for the Belgian Grand Prix at Spa and once more his two drivers were John Surtees and Willy Mairesse. Mairesse could always be counted on to put up a good performance on his home ground circuit especially as he was a great favourite with the Belgian crowd. The practice period saw very stormy weather but there was no rain during the actual practice runs. All competitors had Brabham's 3 min. 51.9 secs. lap record as a standard but as this had been set with a 2.5-litre Cooper it seemed unlikely that it would be broken by the smaller cars. Graham Hill set fastest practice lap with a time of 3 min. 54.1 secs. with Dan Gurney in a Brabham next fastest. Mairesse lived up to expectations on the Spa circuit and recorded third fastest with 3 min. 55.3 secs. Surtees surprisingly was only able to manage 10th fastest time. At the start it was Jim Clark from the third row who went into the lead and set a pace that only world champion Graham Hill could match. On his first lap Clark was already 16 seconds ahead of all the field except for Hill. Mairesse made a good start and inserted his Ferrari into third place behind Hill's BRM, having passed Jack Brabham in the process. In trying to catch up with Hill, Mairesse spun off and it was Surtees' Ferrari that took up the challenge battling with Brabham and McLaren for third place. However, this group was already over half a minute behind the leader, Clark.

Surtees moved up into third place but he was 46 seconds behind Clark and 36 seconds behind Graham Hill, his nearest adversary was Gurney some 20 seconds behind him. In the meantime Mairesse trying to make up time retired the Maranello car with gearbox troubles, causing Surtees to abandon too. It was not a very satisfactory result, the Ferraris were doing better than the previous year in that they were matching the British cars' performance but now they were not reliable enough.

Netherlands Grand Prix

For the next World Championship event held at Zandvoort, Ferrari again sent two cars one for Surtees and the other for the Italian driver Scarfiotti, winner of Le Mans. In practice Scarfiotti was not in contention and Surtees managed to put up fifth fastest time of 1 min. 33.0 secs. compared to Jim Clark's 1 min. 31.6 secs. which was better than Phil Hill's time of the previous year of 1 min. 35.0 secs.

At the start it was the same story as at Spa, Clark went straight into the lead with Surtees running in 6th place. On the second lap Surtees moved up to 5th place and was shortly battling with Maggs for fourth. Scarfiotti was doing the best he could in his first Formula 1 race and was holding down 8th place. When Graham Hill stopped at the pits for repairs and Brabham had throttle troubles, Surtees moved the Ferrari into second place, but he was a long way behind the leader Clark and on the 60th lap he had the experience of being lapped by the Lotus driver. Surtees was being pressed by Gurney's Brabham and on the 63rd lap made a mistake and spun letting the American driver into second place. Surtees carried on in third place for the rest of the race where he finished with Scarfiotti in 6th. This time the Ferraris had shown reliability but not enough speed.

British Grand Prix

For the British Grand Prix, held at Silverstone, Ferrari sent only one car to be driven by John Surtees. Surtees' practice time was one second faster than his best lap in the earlier Silverstone event, the new time being 1 min. 35.2 secs. Nevertheless, it was only good enough to give him fifth best practice time, Clark's Lotus having recorded 1 min. 34.4 secs., Gurney, Graham Hill and Brabham also being faster than the Ferrari.

During practice both Surtees and Ing. Mauro Forghieri realized that it would be touch and go whether the car would be able to go the whole race distance without refueling. Forghieri wisely decided that they would have to fit a supplementary tank and set about designing one on the spot. This was no easy task as there was little enough room in the already cramped car. Forghieri came up with a drawing to place the tank between the driver's leg and Surtees himself, with the aid of a mechanic, did the manufacturing and welding of the tank which was finished at 1.00 a.m. on the morning of race day. Forghieri and the mechanic did the installation so that Surtees could get some sleep and by 4.00 a.m. the car was ready.

The race settled down with Clark running away from everyone. Surtees fought it out with Graham Hill for second place and managed to pass and pull away from the BRM. Misfortune struck and Surtees began having trouble with his gearbox, this allowed Graham Hill to repass him for second place, but the Ferrari driver was still capable of keeping the British car well in his sights. On the last lap it was Graham Hill's turn to have bad luck, the BRM ran out of fuel and the Ferrari recaptured second place, while Hill coasted over the line to take third. The pre-race decision to mount the extra tank had been right, BRM had not taken the same precaution and had paid the price.

In summing up the British Grand Prix an Italian journalist said that it reminded him of a story about the famous racing cyclist Fausto Coppi. Coppi had easily won the race, but second place man was wild with delight and went around shouting "I've won, I've won". When someone pulled him aside and reminded him that Coppi had in fact finished a long way ahead of him the cyclist replied "Oh yes, I know, but he's completely out of our class so I've won".

So it was at the British Grand Prix with Jim Clark first and Surtees the winner over the rest.

French Grand Prix

In the French Grand Prix held at Rheims Ferrari once again sent two cars for Surtees and Scarfiotti. During practice which was held under wet conditions Scarfiotti hit a deep puddle at

140 m p h and after a series of wild slides crashed into a telegraph pole, the car was wrecked, Scarfiotti suffered a fractured knee, leaving Ferrari with only the Surtees car with which to take on the British horde. The remaining Ferrari showed speed enough and Surtees recorded 2 min. 21.9 secs. which hansomely beat the previous year's absolute lap record for 1.5-litre cars of 2 min. 24.0 secs. This gave Surtees the fourth fastest qualifying time with Clark the fastest at 2 min. 20.2 secs. During the race the lone Ferrari's run did not last long and on the 12th lap Surtees brought the car in with a faulty fuel pump, one lap later he was back in the pits this time to retire, leaving Clark's Lotus to notch up yet another World Championship win.

For the German Grand Prix held at the Nurburgring Ferrari once again sent two cars, one for John Surtees and the other for Mairesse.

Surtees' car differed from that of Mairesse in having a new body shape for the rear of the car. Mairesse's car was more slender, rather like a Lotus whilst Surtees' car had the rear of the body widened with a larger opening for the clutch and gearbox. The wider body necessitated the addition of small plates that were bulged to accommodate the roll bar and the rear spring location. Both Ferraris had a new type of alloy wheel, the modified version being without the eared knock-off hub cap. The new wheel was fixed with five nuts; this new layout saving in weight about 500 grams per wheel.

German Grand Prix

At the Nurburgring the Ferrari drivers were out to make up for the poor showing of the Maranello cars on that track the previous season. None of the team had been able to equal Phil Hill's 1961 record of 8 min. 55.2 secs. and had been a long way off Gurney's record with the Porsche in 1962 of 8 min, 47.2 secs. However, in practice Surtees showed quickly that the Ferrari was back on top form with an excellent time of 8 min. 46.7 secs. a time which was only beaten by the incredible Jim Clark who set a time of 8 min. 45.8 secs. It seemed that Ferrari would do extremely well on the German circuit as the nearest of the opposition, Bandini with the

BRM, could only manage a time of 8 min. 54.3 secs. The second Ferrari driven by Mairesse qualified 5th fastest with a time of 9 min. 03.5 secs. These times gave Surtees a place in the front row and Mairesse a place in the second. At the start both Ginther with the BRM and Clark with the Lotus made fast getaways and by the time half of the first lap had been run the order was Ginther (BRM), McLaren (Cooper), Clark (Lotus) and Surtees in 4th place with Mairesse in 8th place, Maggs, Graham Hill and Ireland separating him from his team mate. On the second lap there was excitement in the Ferrari pit. Surtees passed in the lead some 30 yards ahead of Clark's Lotus, both cars being a long way ahead of next man McLaren. Mairesse failed to pass, he had been caught by a violent gust of wind while all four wheels were off the ground. The car went completely out of control Mairesse being fortunate to be thrown out as the car was completely destroyed. Mairesse, however, was out for the rest of the season with a broken arm and wrist as well as a damaged knee. At the third lap Surtees was still in the lead but Clark was slowly closing the gap. On the fourth lap Clark passed Surtees having a ten yard lead on the Ferrari on passing the start/finish line. The following lap the picture changed again; Surtees moved ahead of Clark who had evidently forced his car too hard in the attempt to stay ahead of the Ferrari. Surtees increased his lead lap by lap and was never again challenged. The Ferrari crossed the line in first place to record the marques' first win of the 1963 season and the first win on the German circuit for seven years.

Surtees also set a new lap record of 8 min. 47.0 secs. and beat the race record set by Stirling Moss in 1961 of 148.5 k p h with a new time of 154.2 k p h.

Mediterranean and Italian Grand Prix

For the Mediterranean Grand Prix held at the circuit of Pergusa, Ferrari sent only one car for Surtees. The event did not count towards the World Championship and he had no real opposition. Surtees went into the lead at the start and never lost the lead. He easily broke the record set in 1962 by Bandini of 128.2 m p h with a new speed of 130.4 m p h to give Ferrari their second win of the season. For the Italian

Grand Prix, Ferrari was short of drivers with Mairesse and Scarfiotti injured, so he took the opportunity to invite Lorenzo Bandini of Centro Sud back into the fold. Bandini had been putting up some excellent performances with Centro Sud's BRM but Mimmo Dei, as always, did not put any obstacles in Bandini's way to a better drive. Before the Monza event Ferrari had announced his car for the 1964 season. The unveiling of the new model caused a certain amount of comment as the design was quite advanced. Ferrari had gone over to the mono-coque system of construction that was pioneered by Colin Chapman in Formula 1 racing. A completely new engine was also shown, being a V8 in layout. This marked Ferrari's first departure from a V6 type in almost seven years of Formula 1 design.

The new car was sleeker than the 1963 version and the 90-degree V8 had Bosch high pressure fuel injection, transistor ignition and was quoted as giving 220 b h p at 11,000 r p m. The bore and stroke of the new engine were 64 x 57.8 mm giving a cubic capacity of 1,487-cc. The main part of the Ferrari monocoque structure was the forward section which was fabricated and riveted in a manner similar to aircraft construction. This structure comprised two lateral tanks moulded round a top and bottom tube, the tubes being staggered in a vertical plane. The twin tubes on either side served to carry the oil and water from the engine to the radiator and back. The two side structures were joined together by a floor panel and further linked by four bulkheads, the front ones being pierced to allow for the drivers legs. At the rear instead of using a triangulated sub-assembly of tubes, Ferrari used the engine, gearbox and differential as an integral part of the frame, these units being attached directly to the rear bulkhead.

Suspension units were brought within the body wherever possible and at the front the spring/damper units were completely inboard as on the Lotus. The Ferrari engineers aimed at getting a smaller maximum cross section than the Lotus. The original plans called for a car that would be some 2 cm smaller than its British rival, but Ferrari insisted on more pilot comfort and the cross section came out to 70 cm which

was 1 cm more than the Lotus. The new car had a front track of 3 ft 8 in., a rear track of 3 ft 7 5/8 in. and a wheelbase of 6 ft 4 in.

Monza

For Monza Ferrari sent the 1964 monocoque car for Surtees to drive, however the car was not equipped with the V8 engine and used a modified version of the 120-degree V6. The engine of this car had a new type of piston, transistor ignition and a new type of injector pump. With the modifications the r p m was raised to 11,000 the engine giving 210 b h p on the bench. A normal 1963 car was given to Bandini and there were high hopes of a repeat of the Nurburgring victory when John Surtees took the new car round the Monza circuit in 1 min. 37.3 secs. the previous best by a 1.5-litre Ferrari time ever on the road circuit in a race 1 min. 39.8 secs. by Tony Brooks with the 2.5-litre Dino in 1959.

Surtees with this time was 1.2 secs. faster than the next best qualifier Graham Hill. Bandini qualified for the third row with a time of 1 min. 40.1 secs. the 6th best time.

Right from the start of the race Surtees and Clark renewed their Nurburgring battle, it was wheel to wheel with the Ferrari having a slight advantage and with Bandini's Ferrari also well placed in the 'secong group' made up of himself, Brabham, Ginther and Ireland; but on the 17th lap Surtees' run came to an end when his engine broke. With the retirement of Bandini with a broken clutch shaft the British cars had it all their own way and Clark went on to win and clinch the 1963 World Championship.

Watkins Glen

Although Clark had taken the World Championship with his win at Monza, Surtees had a battle going on for 2nd place with BRM driver Richie Ginther and Ferrari sent three cars for the United States Grand Prix at Watkins Glen. Two of the cars were the tubular chassis model, one being for Bandini and the other as a practice car. The monocoque car from Monza, still with the V6 engine mounted, was sent for John Surtees to drive.

The first practice session saw Surtees turning a time of 1 min. 15.7 secs. which was third fastest behind Jim Clark's Lotus (1 min. 15.0 secs.) and Dan Gurney on the Brabham (1 min. 15.5 secs.). Bandini's best lap was 1 min. 21.2 secs. In the second practice session Surtees lowered his time to 1 min. 14.4 secs. and Bandini registered a 1 min. 17.2 secs. but in the meantime Jim Clark had recorded 1 min. 13.6 secs., Graham Hill on the BRM 1 min. 13.7 secs. The third practice session on Friday saw John Surtees register a 1 min. 13.6 secs. Graham Hill improved his time on the fourth and last practice session on Friday to 1 min. 13.4 secs. and Bandini took the Ferrari round in 1 min. 15.8 secs. These times by the Ferrari drivers were not improved as the practice sessions continued. The monocoque Ferrari of Surtees broke down with a fault in the engine due to an imperfection in the casting of the block. This meant that Surtees had to use the practice car with which he returned a creditable time of 1 min. 13.7 secs.

The starting line up saw John Surtees in the front row which he shared with Graham Hill and Jim Clark.

Richie Ginther got the BRM off to a good start and took the lead but Graham Hill, with the No. 1 BRM, was in the lead on the first lap with Dan Gurney in the Brabham second, closely followed by Surtees in the tubular chassis Ferrari.

Surtees moved up and began to challenge Graham Hill. At ten laps Surtees was in the lead followed by Graham Hill, Dan Gurney and Jack Brabham in another of his own cars. Bandini held the second Ferrari in 11th place just behind Bonnier's Cooper. At 40 laps the order of the leading three was unchanged but Ginther had replaced Brabham for 4th, Bandini had moved up to 9th place but was being challenged by Jim Clark who had stalled at the start and lost over one lap changing batteries. By 60 laps Surtees was still in first place with Graham Hill second and Ginther on the second BRM having taken

over third when Gurney broke down. Clark had moved ahead of Bandini who moved up to 8th due to Gurney's retirement. At 80 laps Surtees was averaging 109.49 m p h and was 14 seconds ahead of Graham Hill who had slowly dropped back, Bandini moved up to 6th place. All of a sudden it was all over for Surtees when a valve spring broke. Because of Surtees' retirement, Bandini moved up to 5th place where he finished at the end of the race. Ginther therefore took a firm lead over Surtees for 2nd place in the world drivers' championship.

Although Ferrari announced that the V6 Dino engine had reached the end of the line and would not be used again in Grand Prix racing, he changed his mind for the beginning of the 1964 season. He said that he would have a total of six Formula 1 cars for the 1964 world championships with Surtees and Bandini as his team drivers. Two of the V6 engines, fitted into the monocoque chassis unveiled at Monza 1963, would be held as reserve cars for the season whilst the cars that would do the work would be the new V8 and flat 12-cylinder engines fitted into the monocoque chassis. Two each of these cars being made, the V8 to be used for the short twisty circuits and the horizontally opposed 12 for the fast circuits like Rheims, Spa and Monza. Since the overall dimensions of these engines were similar they were completely interchangeable.

The flat 12 is basically the four-cam 12-cylinder supercharged engine of 1950 cut in half and laid out in horizontally opposed formation. Two different bore/stroke dimensions were tried for this engine: 55 x 52.5 mm with a displacement of 1498-cc, this being the bore and stroke of the original supercharged engine, and 56 x 50.4 mm with a displacement of 1489-cc. The latter engine was reported to have given 225 b h p on the bench. The V8 had a bore and stroke of 64 x 57.8 mm, displacing 1487-cc and reputedly gave 220 b h p at 11,000 r p m.

CHAPTER NINE
The Championship contest 1964 to 1973

John Surtees

THE last world championship event of the 1963 season was the South African Grand Prix on December 28th. Ferrari sent three cars, a practice car with the older V6 engine in a tubular chassis and two of the latest V6 monocoques for Bandini and Surtees.

The troubles that had plagued the Ferraris at the Mexican Grand Prix had been sorted out to a certain extent by minor modifications to the suspension and chassis. Because of the sandy conditions of the East London circuit, the steering joints on all three cars were heavily greased and sealed in plastic covers. The monocoques differed only in that Surtees' car had a long shaped windscreen while Bandini's had a short upright one.

On practice, the target was Clark's 1 min. 28.9 secs. practice lap set the previous season and Surtees started off with a 1 min. 32.4 secs. Handling problems were encountered with both new cars and Surtees elected to stick with it and sort out the trouble while Bandini transferred to the tubular chassis model.

Despite the handling problems Surtees was the first to break 1 min. 30 secs. with a time of 1 min. 29.8 secs. and Thursday's practice ended with the Ferrari holding the fastest time.

Bandini recorded 1 min. 33.4 secs. with the new car and ended up with a 1 min. 31.0 secs. in the tubular chassis car.

During the evening, the Ferraris were modified and set lower at the front but, during the two practice sessions on Friday, Surtees was unable to equal his previous time, recording 1 min. 30.2 secs. in the morning and 1 min. 30.8 secs. in the afternoon.

Bandini took out the monocoque again on Friday and got down to 1 min. 30.2 secs. in the morning and 1 min. 31.5 secs. in the afternoon. He had a final run in the practice car but could do no better than 1 min. 33.0

secs. and, as a result, he decided on the monocoque for the race.

Clark, Brabham and Gurney had all bettered Surtees' first day mark with the Lotus' fastest at 1 min. 28.9 secs. this put the two Ferraris in the second row behind the Lotus and the two Brabhams.

Two hours before the start, an electrical fault occurred in Surtees' car and the Ferrari mechanics worked frantically to fix it. Just as the cars were being wheeled on to the grid, the Ferrari was finally coaxed to function properly.

The flag fell at 3 p.m. and Brabham took the lead. First time round, Clark had taken over first place with Surtees second, followed by the two Brabhams of Brabham and Gurney.

While the Brabham team were trying to pass Surtees, Clark increased his lead and by lap 6 Brabham and Gurney had slipped past the Ferrari. Surtees forced his way past Brabham on lap 8 and held third position. Further back, Bandini fought with Maggs and Taylor with the Ferrari ahead on laps 5 and 6, Maggs and Taylor getting past on lap 7.

At the halfway mark Clark had a comfortable lead with Gurney 2nd and Surtees 3rd. Then, on lap 43, Surtees coasted into the pits his engine having blown up in a large cloud of smoke. Taylor and Maggs had to pit, allowing Bandini to move up to 5th, a position which he held until the end of the race.

The 1964 Championship trail began at Monaco on May 10th. Ferrari entered two cars for Surtees and Bandini. The British driver had the latest monocoque V8 and the Italian a V6 as was run in the latter part of 1963.

Practice times, on the tight Monegasque circuit, were as close as ever, the first nine cars all being within two seconds of the fastest time of the day set by Jim Clark's Lotus at 1 min. 34.0 secs. Surtees qualified the V8 for the second row at 1 min. 34.5 secs. and Bandini was in the third row at 1 min. 35.5 secs.

At the start it was Clark, Brabham and Graham Hill, with Gurney displacing Surtees from 4th. Surtees held on to 5th place until lap 12 when he began to have gearbox trouble. He was passed by Ginther's BRM and on lap 13 dropped to last but one, retiring on lap 16 with a broken gearbox.

Bandini started 7th and lost three places on the 1st lap. He regained one place when he passed Phil Hill on lap 3 but the American repassed him on lap 7. Bandini then began a steady climb in the standings, taking 8th on lap 14, 7th on lap 18, 6th on lap 30, 5th on lap 53, 4th on lap 63 before transmission trouble slowed him and forced him to retire on lap 68. Although he was not running at the end of the race, the distance he had covered classified him in 10th and last place.

Dutch Grand Prix

The second race of the 1964 season was the Dutch Grand Prix at Zandvoort on May 24th. For this event Ferrari entered two monocoque V8s for Surtees and Bandini.

Practice times, as at Monaco, were very close and Gurney nosed out Clark for the fastest qualifying time of 1 min. 31.2 secs. Surtees was in the second row of the grid with 1 min. 32.8 secs. and Bandini in the fourth row with 1 min. 35.0 secs.

At the start Bandini, as at Monaco, was passed by several drivers and dropped to 15th. He passed Baghetti's BRM into 14th but his engine was already running rough with fuel injection problems and, on lap 11, Baghetti repassed the Ferrari before it finally retired on lap 21. Clark and Graham Hill were off first with Gurney behind them, Arundell came by Surtees to take 4th but was repassed by the Ferrari on lap 3. On lap 9, Surtees was by Gurney into 3rd and on lap 22 he moved the red car by Graham Hill's BRM into 2nd where he kept it for the rest of the race. He was unable to make any impression on Clark and finished nearly 1 minute behind the winning Lotus.

On June 14th, the racing circus moved to Spa-Francorchamps for the 24th Belgian Grand Prix. Two cars were entered for Surtees and Bandini, both being V8s. Gurney set a sensational 3 min. 50.9 secs. practice record and no one else was able to approach the time. Surtees was second fastest on the first day but had to settle for a place in the second row of the start at 3 min. 55.2 secs. Bandini was once again in the fourth row with a time of 3 min. 58.8 secs.

The first lap was hectic, with Arundell's Lotus leading. The British car was almost immediately passed by Gurney's Brabham, with Surtees not wasting any time and pressing by into second place. Surtees set after Gurney and a battle was on. The Ferrari swept by on lap 3 but the battle was over as quickly as it had begun and the Ferrari fell back through the pack with a broken engine to retire on lap 4.

Bandini started in 9th place and promptly lost this place to Phil Hill. When Surtees retired, Bandini was back in 9th which he held until lap 11 when his engine began to give trouble and he too was forced to retire. The race was marked by the fantastic finish with Gurney, looking a certain winner, running out of fuel, followed in turn by the next leader McLaren whose battery ran out and finally Clark winning but running out of fuel before he realised he had won.

French Grand Prix

The 1964 Grand Prix of The Automobile Club de France returned to the Rouen-Les Essarts circuit. Ferrari sent the usual two cars for Surtees and Bandini.

Clark in the new Lotus 33 was fastest in practice at 2 min. 09.6 secs., but this time Surtees was on the front row with a 2 min. 11.1 secs. Bandini in the second Ferrari qualified for the third row with a time of 2 min. 12.8 secs. Surtees held third place at the start, behind Clark and Gurney, but on the third lap he was in the pits with engine trouble. The mechanics got the car going again and Surtees restarted last-but-one to complete two more laps before retiring with a broken engine. Bandini, for once, gained a place at the start but on the second lap made up for it by losing two places. Because of Surtees' pit stop and Graham Hill's spin, Bandini moved up to 7th on lap 4 but was back down to 10th by lap 7. He remained in 10th place until lap 27 when he was passed by Mike Hailwood in the Lotus BRM but, because of Clark and Ireland's retirements, he went up to 9th place which he held until the end of the race.

British Grand Prix

The European Grand Prix for 1964 was also the British Grand Prix and it was held for the first time on the Kentish circuit of Brands Hatch. Again Ferrari sent his usual pair of Surtees and Bandini.

Clark was the fastest in practice, with the Lotus turning a time of 1 min. 38.1 secs., Graham Hill and Dan Gurney filled out the front row with Surtees Ferrari in the second row, having set a time of 1 min. 38.7 secs. Bandini sat in the third row with a time of 1 min. 40.2 secs. Clark took the lead from the start and held it for the rest of the race. Gurney was second, on lap 2, but dropped right back so that, by lap 3, the pattern for the remainder of the race was settled in the order Clark, Graham Hill and Surtees.

Bandini moved steadily up through the field to 4th on lap 18, holding this place until lap 66 when he was passed by Brabham, and eventually finished in 5th place.

German Grand Prix

The German Grand Prix was held on the Nurburgring on August 2nd. Ferrari sent two monocoques, a V8 for Surtees and a V6 for Bandini. Surtees was in his element, on the tricky Nurburgring, having his motorcycling experience plus the 1963 Grand Prix win and a 1,000 km victory behind him.

He had no trouble in taking pole position on the grid with a time of 8 min. 38.4 secs. Clark and Gurney were next to him and Bandini, who had worked really hard with the V6, filled out the front row with a time of 8 min. 42.6 secs.

Bandini was first off but Clark was by on the return road, behind the pits, and as they swept onto the main part of the circuit the order was Clark, Gurney, Surtees, Graham Hill and Bandini.

The first time past the pits, Clark led Surtees but, by the time the next lap was completed, the Ferrari was in front. Gurney moved ahead of Clark on lap 3 and challenged Surtees, taking the lead on lap 4. By lap 5 Surtees was back in the lead, the battle was close but Surtees went on to win by over a minute.

Bandini as usual lost several places at the beginning of the race and had to go through the tedious business of regaining some of them. From 7th on lap 2 he went to 6th on lap 3. On lap 8 he improved his position to 4th, passing Jack Brabham in the process, but the Australian fought back and forged ahead on lap 11, just before retiring the car on lap 12. This retirement and Gurney's troubles put Bandini up into 3rd place where he finished.

John Surtees' average was 96.56 m p h and he set a new lap record of 8 min. 39.0 secs. (98.30 m p h).

Austrian Grand Prix

The first ever, Austrian world championship Grand Prix was held at the Zeltweg airfield on August 23rd.

The circuit was in very bad condition and the situation had a marked effect on the race. Ferrari sent the V6 for Bandini and the V8 for Surtees.

Graham Hill was fastest in practice, with a time of 1 min. 09.8 secs. and Surtees was second best with a time of 1 min. 10.1 secs. Bandini recorded 1 min. 10.6 secs. which placed him in the second row. There was a large number of breakages in practice because of the roughness of the circuit but everyone effected repairs in time.

At the start, Gurney led in the Brabham but, by lap 2, Surtees had the Ferrari ahead of the Brabham and kept it there until lap 7 when the rear suspension broke and Gurney was back in the lead. Bandini, from lap 2 onwards, held 3rd place moving into 2nd when Surtees dropped out. On lap 8 he was displaced by Clark and stayed 3rd behind the Lotus until lap 41 when Clark broke his final drive. On lap 48, Gurney's car became difficult to control as the chassis had broken and Bandini was never again challenged on his way to his first Grand Epreuve win.

Italian Grand Prix

For the 1964 Italian Grand Prix at Monza, on September 6th, Ferrari as usual made a greater effort than at the other races during the season. He sent a V6 for Scarfiotti, two V8s for Surtees

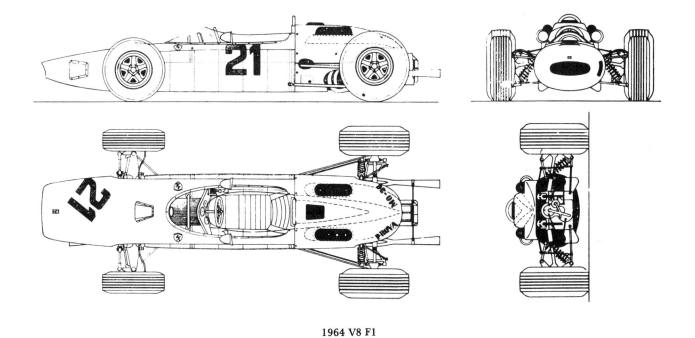

1964 V8 F1

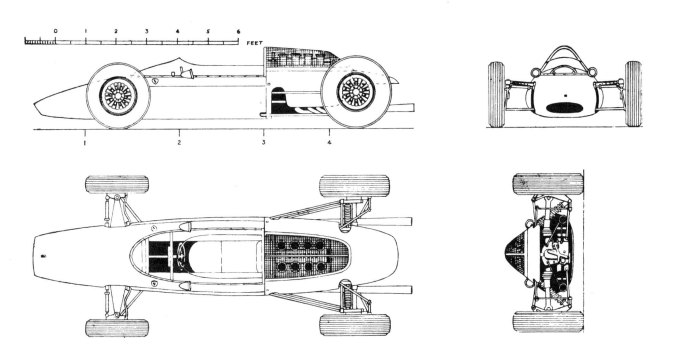

1964 V8 Monocoque

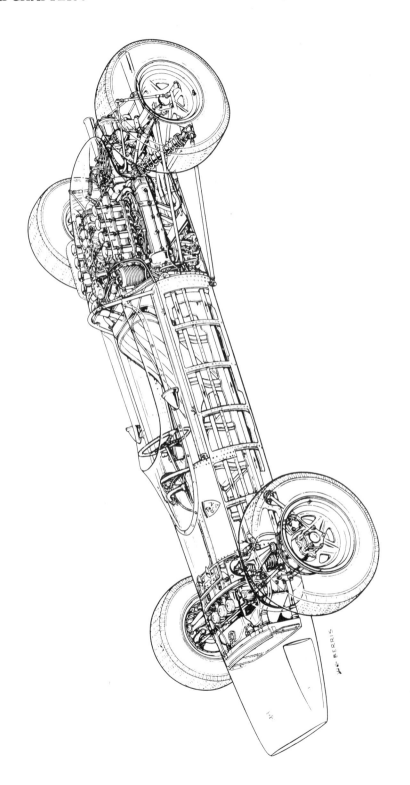

1964 Formula I V8 Ferrari with the tubular chassis

and Bandini and the new flat 12. The 12 was driven by Bandini during practice but it was decided not to run it in the race.

Surtees was in great form after his Nurburgring victory and his near-win in Austria. He set a new lap record of 1 min. 37.4 secs. to take pole position on the grid. Bandini qualified for the third row in 1 min. 39.8 secs. and Scarfiotti was in the seventh row with a time of 1 min. 41.6 secs. The race was extremely exciting as a tremendous battle developed between Gurney and Surtees. Gurney took the first lap but Surtees was out in front from lap 2 until lap 6 when Clark joined in the fight and Surtees suddenly found himself 3rd. On lap 7 he was back in 2nd place and on lap 8 he led the race again. On lap 10 Gurney had the lead; lap 11 it was the Ferrari; laps 12, 13 and 14 went to the Brabham, 15 to Surtees, 16 to Gurney. From lap 17 to 21, the red car stayed in front and then it began again, the lead changing 14 times more in the following 35 laps. On lap 57, Surtees established himself in the lead for good, the Gurney challenge ended on lap 69 when Gurney fell back through the field with troubles in the Brabham.

Bandini also put on a great show, switching places repeatedly with Ginther for 3rd place towards the end of the race. The Italian crowd roared its approval when he pushed by his opponent's BRM on the last lap, making certain of the 3rd place. Scarfiotti plodded along in the V6 finally finishing 9th.

Surtees averaged 127.78 m p h and set a new lap record of 1 min. 38.8 secs. (130.18 m p h). The win at Monza put Ferrari into the lead for the Manufacturers' Championship and put John Surtees into a very favourable position for a World Championship.

U.S. Grand Prix

The 1964 US Grand Prix was held at Watkins Glen, New York. Surtees and Bandini were entered by North American Racing Team instead of by the factory and the four cars, two V8s, one V6 and one flat 12 were painted in blue and white American colours. Ferrari was apparently having a disagreement with the Automobile Club of Italy and as a result had the cars entered by the American team.

During practice Clark's Lotus took the pole position with 1 min. 12.6 secs. with Surtees in a V8 Ferrari next to him at 1 min. 12.7 secs. and Bandini's Flat 12 in the 4th row at 1 min. 13.8 secs. At the start Surtees' Ferrari leapt into the lead and increased it to 5 seconds. Clark had dropped to 4th at the start but quickly recovered and took the lead from Surtees. However, Surtees stayed close behind with the two cars nose to tail. On lap 44 Clark had fuel injection trouble and Surtees regained the lead only to lose it to Graham Hill's BRM on the next lap.

A spin by Surtees gave the BRM an even greater advantage and so it ended with Graham Hill leading Surtees 39 to 34 points in the World Championship with only the Mexican GP to go.

Mexican Grand Prix

For the Mexican GP Ferrari retained their blue and white colours and the cars were again entered by NART. John Surtees drove the V8, Bandini had the flat 12 and Pedro Rodriguez was given the V6.

Fastest time in practice was set by Jim Clark at 1 min. 57.2 secs. with Gurney's Brabham 2nd, Bandini third at 1 min. 58.6 secs., and Surtees fourth at 1 min. 58.7 secs.

Clark was off first at the start with Gurney behind him, Bandini held 3rd place but was 8 seconds behind. Surtees was in 10th place but from the second lap he began to move up. Graham Hill fought with Bandini for 3rd place and finally headed the Ferrari. By the 20th lap the two Ferraris were running in 4th and 5th places. The situation was tense as Surtees had to finish 2nd and beat both Clark and Hill to become World Champion and at this stage of the race both Clark and Hill were ahead of him. Bandini constantly fought with Hill in an attempt to tire out the BRM driver and on the 30th lap the Ferrari and the BRM collided pushing Hill into the guard rail and crushing his tailpipe. Hill lost a lap in the pits for repairs and his World Championship chances were gone as Surtees moved into 3rd place only to be repassed by Bandini's 12 which demonstrated greater power in the high altitude of Mexico City. With one lap to go for Jim Clark to clinch his World Championship, the Lotus slowed and

Surtees moved into second place behind the winner Dan Gurney. As a result Surtees won the World Championship for Ferrari by 1 point from Graham Hill and 8 points from Clark.

1965
South African Grand Prix

The South African Grand Prix, held on 1st January 1965, became the season's first championship race. Ferrari sent two cars for Surtees and Bandini, Surtees having the V8 and Bandini the flat 12. Surtees went well in practice, turning a time of 1 min. 28.1 secs. which put him in the centre of the front row, next to Jim Clark, who was fastest with 1 min. 27.2 secs. Bandini qualified the flat 12 for the third row of the grid with a time of 1 min. 29.3 secs.

At the start of the race, Clark took immediate command and was never really challenged. Surtees dropped to 5th on the first lap but by lap 5 was firmly in 3rd position. Bandini fell to 8th place and moved up to 7th on lap 6, a position which he held until lap 34.

Surtees remained third, chasing the team of Clark and Spence in very slippery conditions. When Spence spun on lap 60 Surtees went ahead, Bandini's pit stop dropped him far behind and he was classified as 15th some 19 laps behind the winner. Surtees took second place 29 seconds behind Clark.

The 1965 Monaco Grand Prix was held on May 30th. Ferrari nominated Surtees and Bandini and sent three cars, a flat 12 for Bandini and two V8s for Surtees.

The first day of practice, on Thursday, was held in the rain and times were slow. Surtees had different types of Dunlop tyres on his two V8s but was unhappy with both cars. All three Ferraris used short fibreglass nose cowlings in anticipation of some denting which is the rule rather than the exception at Monaco. The flat 12 overheated somewhat in practice and, for the race, the fibreglass nose was replaced with one even more abbreviated and made out of aluminium.

Fastest lap of the day went to Graham Hill's BRM at 1 min. 37.1 secs. with Bandini and the flat 12 Ferrari going well to record second best at 1 min. 37.5 secs., only three cars breaking the 1.40 mark. Surtees was very dissatisfied with a time of 1 min. 49.3 secs.

For Friday's practice the weather improved and so did the times. Stewart's BRM took top honours with 1 min. 32.9 secs. and Bandini took the 12 down to 1 min. 33.2 secs. to record third fastest. Surtees was still experiencing engine tuning problems, nevertheless, he got down to 1 min. 34.0 secs. which was fifth fastest. During the final practice session on Saturday, the weather was perfect and Bandini recorded a 1 min. 33.0 secs., which was third fastest and placed him on the second row of the grid. Surtees' V8 finally began to run properly and he recorded 1 min. 33.2 secs. which placed him on the third row.

Dry, cool weather prevailed for the Grand Prix on Sunday. The two BRMs of Hill and Stewart jumped into the lead followed by Bandini and Surtees with Brabham right behind. The two BRMs drew away from the two Ferraris at the rate of about 1 second per lap with Brabham pressing Surtees. Hill had to take the escape route to avoid another car that he was lapping on lap 25, this let Stewart into the lead with Bandini and Surtees coming up to 2nd and 3rd. Surtees seemed content to follow Bandini and not to pass him. Brabham was pressing hard and got by Surtees, setting his sights on Bandini. Stewart spun and Bandini took the lead going as fast as he could to hold off Brabham. On lap 34 Brabham passed Bandini into the *Gazometre* hairpin and shut the door on him. Graham Hill was now back in the fray and making up time fast. Surtees, warned of Hill's approach, began to speed up and close on Bandini. Then Brabham's engine broke and Bandini was back in the lead with Surtees and Hill hot on his heels.

At 50 laps, the order was the same but by lap 53 Hill had forged ahead of Surtees and went after Bandini. Hill outbraked the Ferrari at the *Gazometre* and the Ferraris were back in 2nd and 3rd places. Hill continued at a tremendous pace, pulling away from the Italian cars.

Surtees made his move on lap 78 and passed Bandini. There was no hope of his catching the BRM as Hill was breaking the lap record with regularity finally leaving it at 1 min. 37.7 secs. on lap 82.

Having been passed by his team mate, Bandini slowed to conserve fuel and to hold on to 3rd, as 4th place man Stewart was a long way behind.

The colour photograph overleaf shows, of course, the ex-Peter Whitehead 1½ litre supercharged Ferrari, not 4½ litre

Ferrari Type 166C (no. 004C) now in the Long Island Automotive
Museum USA

The ex-Peter Whitehead 4½ litre green Ferrari at the Donington
Museum England

The streamlined V8 Ferrari at Reims in 1956

Luigi Chinetti driving a Ferrari type 166 at the 50th anniversary of the
Le Mans Retrospect Race. (A Type 166 won the 1949 Le Mans 24
Hour Race)

The engine of the Ferrari Type 412MI

The Formula 1 Ferrari 312 B/3 at Monaco in 1973

Nikki Lauda in the Ferrari F1 car in the 1974 British Grand Prix

A 4.4 litre 6 cylinder Type 121 LM car
The Ferrari 4.4 litre Type 121 LM engine

A Type 250 Testa Rossa Ferrari
A PininFarina Ferrari 250MM coupe

The ex-Tom Cole 2.7 Ferrari after restoration. When Cole raced it, it
had a blue and white colour scheme

(*Top Left*) The V8 Ferrari of Surtees leads the 1963 US GP at Watkins Glen
(*Top Right*) The 1963 - 1964 Formula 1 monocoque Ferrari V6 with Surtees aboard at Modena September 1963
(*Bottom*) The fuel injected V6 Formula 1 engine of the 1963 - 1964 season

(Top) John Surtees leaving Druids corner at Brands Hatch, 1964 British GP, in the Type 158 V8
(Middle) World Champion 1964, John Surtees with the V8 Ferrari which was placed 2nd in the 1964 US GP at Watkins Glen
(Bottom) Bob Bondurant in the V8 Ferrari in the 1965 US Grand Prix

(*Top Left*) The F1/65 V8 Fromula 1 Ferrari
(*Top Right*) Ferrari F1/65 V8
(*Middle Left*) The Flat 12 Ferrari F1/65
(*Middle Right*) Bandini in the Flat 12 leads Surtees in the V8 at Monaco 1965
(*Bottom*) The Formula 2 Type 166 Dino V6 engine

(Top Left) The 1966 V12 36 valve Ferrari with engine
cover in place
(Top Right) The 1966 V12 24 valve Ferrari engine
(Middle) The 1966 Formula 1 Ferrari V12 (36 valve)
(Bottom) Scarfietti with the 3 litre V12 winning the
Italian GP in 1966

(*Top*) Surtees with the 3 litre V12 winning the Belgian GP in 1966
(*Middle Left*) Bandini with the V6 2.4 litre car finished 2nd in the 1966 Monaco GP
(*Middle Right*) Surtees leads the 1966 Monaco GP in the 3 litre V12
(*Bottom*) The 1966 V12 Ferrari. This shows the engine/transmission units and the inboard disc brakes

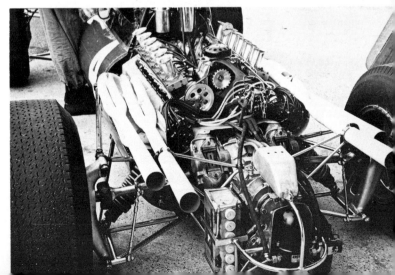

(*Top*) Another angle of the 36 valve V12 engine
(*Middle*) The V12 engine/transmission unit of the 1967 Formula 1 Ferrari
(*Bottom*) The two 3 litre Ferraris dominated the 1967 Syracuse GP. Parkes with the 1967 engined car leads Scarfiotti with the 1966 engined car

(Top) US GP Walkins Glen 1967. Chris Amon with the lightweight F1 Ferrari. It had a gearbox derived from the Formula 2 unit
(Middle) Mike Parkes led the 1967 Daily Express Trophy Race from the start to finish in the 3 litre V12
(Bottom) Amon and his 48 valve Ferrari. Here at Mexico he was a strong 2nd when he ran out of petrol two laps from the end

(*Top Left*) No. 25 Jacky Ickx in the Dino V6 F2.
Crystal Palace 1968
(*Top Right*) Tino Brambilla, Thruxton 1970. F2 Dino
(*Middle Left*) An extra oil-cooler for the Ickx Ferrari.
South Africa 1968
(*Middle Right*) 60 degree V12 Formula 1 Ferrari,
September 1969
(*Bottom*) The Ferrari F1 312 B1

As Hill started his last lap, Surtees coasted around to the finishing line completely out of fuel. This gave Bandini 2nd place in the race and a disgruntled Surtees was classified 4th.

After the Monaco race there was an obvious state of unfriendliness in the Surtees/Ferrari camp. Some unfortunate recriminations in British and Italian newspapers created a situation that was steadily to deteriorate through the 1965 — 66 season, ending with Surtees eventually leaving the Ferrari team.

French Grand Prix

For the first time since 1948 the Grand Prix of the A C F was not held at the regular circuits of either Rheims or Rouen-Les Essarts. The race was held on 27th June 1965, at Clermont-Ferrand on the tricky twisting five mile Charade circuit.

Ferrari sent Surtees with a V8 and Bandini with the flat 12. Clark's Lotus set the standard with a time of 3 min. 18.3 secs. and Bandini qualified the 12 at 3 min. 19.1 secs. which put him on the front row. Surtees, with an identical time to that set by Bandini, was in the second row as he had set his time later than his team mate.

Clark made it clear that he was master of the track, taking the lead at the start of the race and holding it to the finish. Stewart, after jockeying with Bandini, did the same for second place and Surtees, after falling to 5th place on lap 2, moved up to 3rd on lap 5 and stayed there for the rest of the race. Bandini ran 5th until lap 10 when he fell to 7th. He finally lost a wheel on lap 37 but was classified as a finisher in 8th place.

British Grand Prix

Silverstone, the traditional postwar home of the British Grand Prix, was the venue of the 1965 event, the race being held on July 10th. For the first time in the season both Surtees and Bandini were driving flat 12 Ferraris.

Clark again set the pace with a time of 1 min. 30.8 secs. Surtees qualified for the second row with 1 min. 31.3 secs. and Bandini in row three with 1 min. 32.7 secs. Clark pulled another of his start-to-finish races and Graham Hill moved by Ginther's Honda on lap 1 to take 2nd and

hold it to the end. Surtees pulled up to 3rd on lap 3 but on lap 36 was challenged and passed by Spence in the second works Lotus. Surtees repassed the green car but on lap 41 the Lotus was ahead again. On lap 42 Surtees made a determined effort and held on to his 3rd place until the end. Bandini was out of the race on the third lap with engine problems.

Dutch Grand Prix

The 14th Dutch Grand Prix was held at Zandvoort on July 18th. The Ferrari team being present with a flat 12 for Surtees and a V8 for Bandini. Graham Hill's BRM set the fastest lap in practice and Surtees qualified for the second row with 1 min. 31.0 secs. Bandini was slower qualifying for the fifth row with 1 min. 33.1 secs.

Ginther's Honda led from the drop of the flag. Surtees made a bad start coming round in 7th place on the first lap. Bandini did just the opposite and gained several places coming round in 9th place.

By lap 6 the lead pattern was set with Clark taking his 'usual' position. On lap 9 Surtees passed Spence into 6th place but was himself displaced by Hulme on lap 12. Bandini dropped two places when he was passed by McLaren and Rindt and stayed in 11th place until lap 34 when he moved ahead of his two opponents and, further, pulling past Spence's Lotus into 8th place on lap 37.

Surtees passed Ginther on lap 19 and steadily held on to 6th place until lap 52 when the Honda repassed and stayed ahead. Spence and Rindt moved ahead of Bandini again but Rindt's retirement on lap 49 let the Ferrari up one place. On lap 59 Bandini went by Spence and held off the Lotus until the last lap, when Spence squeezed by, leaving Bandini to finish 9th; Surtees finished 7th.

German Grand Prix

The German Grand Prix was held, as usual, on the Nurburgring; the 27th edition of the race being scheduled for 1st August 1965. Surtees was entered in a flat 12 Ferrari and Bandini in a V8. Everyone had their sights on the 8 min. 39.0 secs. (98.338 m p h) lap, set the previous year by Surtees' V8 Ferrari. Impressive as the Ferrari record had been, Clark made short work of it and turned 8 min. 22.7 secs. for the fastest time of the practice session. Surtees went round in 8 min. 27.8 secs. to take the fourth position on the front row of the grid. Bandini took the V8 round in 8 min. 33.8 secs. to place on the second row.

In the race, Clark showed his practice form and took the lead, running first from start to finish. Surtees ran into gear selector problems on the first lap and came by at the back of the field, finally dropping to last place and trailing at the end of the field until lap 12 when the problems became too great and he retired the car.

Bandini was up to 5th at the end of lap 1 but a spin coming out of the *Karussel* dropped him to 12th; he continued and through the retirement of several other cars he moved up in the standings to finish 6th.

Belgian Grand Prix

The 1965 Belgian Grand Prix took place at the traditional Spa-Francorchamps circuit on June 13th. Ferrari entered Surtees and Bandini, sending the same three cars that had appeared at Monaco, the flat 12 for Bandini and the two V8s for Surtees.

Practice on the Friday was from 5 p.m. to 7 p.m. for the works entries only, this gave the top-notch drivers a clear run, unhindered by the slower private owners.

Immediately, the times went under the 4 minute mark; Graham Hill, fresh from his Monaco victory, recorded best time of the day with the BRM in 3 min. 48.0 secs. Surtees followed with 3 min. 49.5 secs., a time equalled by the second BRM of Stewart; Clark was next with 3 min. 49.7 secs.

Bandini's Ferrari had been detuned to get better fuel consumption and the Italian driver was not too happy with the fast and tricky Belgian circuit; his time of 3 min. 58.5 secs. was the slowest time of the day except for Bucknum's Honda.

On the Saturday practice session, Bandini got down to 3 min. 54.0 secs., but Surtees could not repeat his time of the day before, his best being 3 min. 51.0 secs. This left Surtees in the third

row for the start and Bandini way back amongst the private owners in row six.

At 3.30 p.m., just as the race was about to start, it began to rain. At the start it was Hill's BRM in the lead, followed by Clark's Lotus, Stewart's BRM and Surtees in the V8 Ferrari.

First time round, Clark had snatched the lead with Surtees holding down 4th and Bandini running at the back of the pack. By lap 6, Ferrari hopes were finished, Surtees retired with a blown engine and Bandini was tailing along dismally in 10th place. Because of a retirement, he moved up to 9th where he stayed until the finish of the race.

Italian Grand Prix

The final World Championship race of the European Season was held on September 12th at Monza for the Italian Grand Prix.

Ferrari added Vaccarella and Scarfiotti to his regular entries, Surtees and Bandini, and produced three flat 12 cars, one being brand new, and one of the V8 cars.

The V8 was assigned to Vaccarella, and as Scarfiotti did not show up, Surtees had a choice of two flat 12 cylinder cars.

The 12 cylinder Ferrari engines had been modified with a new type of cylinder head with a different inlet port angle. The long intake stacks, with the Lucas injectors in them, were angled outwards instead of being vertical and all four Ferraris had new type brake calipers.

There were two practice sessions of 3½ hours each on Friday and Saturday. On Friday Surtees took out his own 12 cylinder but quickly ran into engine problems and changed over to the new car left vacant by Scarfiotti. With the new car, Surtees had no trouble in getting down to 1 min. 37.0 secs. being 0.8 secs. faster than Clark's Lotus and 0.9 secs. faster than the amazingly quick Honda of Bucknum. Bandini followed up with 1 min. 38.4 secs. and Vaccarella, slower, at 1 min. 40.2 secs.

On the Saturday Surtees improved his time to 1 min. 36.1 secs., but was beaten for the pole position on the grid by Clark's 1 min. 35.9 secs. Bandini also improved his time to 1 min. 37.2 secs. giving him a position in the second row. Vaccarella took the V8 round in 1 min. 38.9 secs. to secure a place in row six. As Surtees went out on to the starting grid, the hydraulic

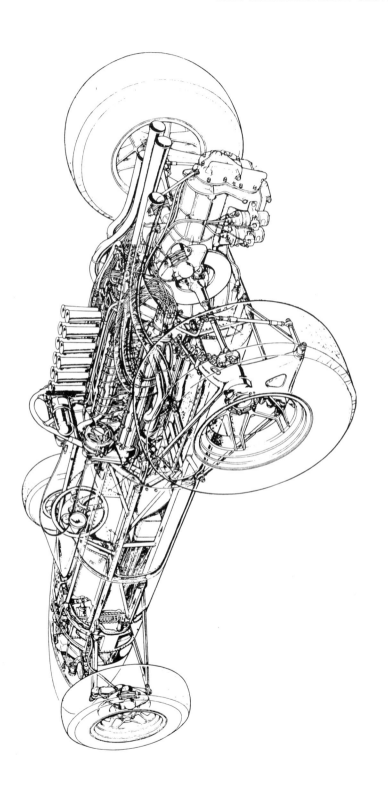

Cutaway drawing of the 1966 V12 Ferrari Formula 1 car

Dino 166

F1/1966

mechanism of his clutch was malfunctioning. Quick work by the mechanics seemed to fix the trouble but when the flag fell Surtees got away slowly and was left behind by the leaders.

On the first lap, it was Clark's Lotus, Hill and Stewart, on BRMs, and Bandini's Ferrari; Surtees having dropped to 14th. Surtees' clutch went solid and he was forced to shift gear without it. Despite these problems he began to make up time fast and moved through the field. Bandini was overtaken by Gurney's Brabham and dropped to 5th and Surtees quickly displaced him from that position. Surtees then got between Gurney and Hill, putting him into 4th place, then slipped past Hill into 3rd. On the 11th lap, both Stewart and Surtees passed the leader, Clark, and for a short period Surtees inched ahead of Stewart to take the lead. Stewart regained 1st place and held it for six laps. Vaccarella was engaged in his own furious battle further back in the pack with Bonnier and Gardner.

The lead changed from lap to lap between Clark, Stewart and Hill who had moved up again, Surtees slipping into 2nd and 3rd places as positions switched several times per lap in this furious battle.

The situation seemed to settle down with the two BRMs in front, with Clark tailing them closely. Surtees a few yards back, followed by Gurney and Bandini. Only 1.5 seconds covered the first six cars. At 33 laps, the lead group lapped the Vaccarella, Bonnier, Gardner battle and Surtees' clutch began to slip badly. He limped around the rest of the lap to pull into the pits and retire. Bandini gave up trying to stay in the fight with the first four and settled down in 5th place. Vaccarella retired with a broken valve, and, when Clark retired, Bandini moved up to 4th where he finished.

US Grand Prix

The 1965 Grand Prix of the United States took place at Watkins Glen on October 3rd.

A week before the race, Surtees had a bad accident driving his Lola T70 in Canada and his injuries laid him up for a considerable time. Bandini thus assumed the role of team leader and took over Surtees' flat 12 with his own flat 12 as a spare car. The two other Ferraris running were officially entered by the North American Racing Team although they were under the supervision of Ferrari team manager Dragoni and were worked on exclusively by the Ferrari mechanics. The two NART entries were the flat 12 for Pedro Rodriguez and a V8 for Bob Bondurant, making his debut in Grand Prix racing. Practice was split into two four-hour sessions, on the Friday and Saturday before the race. The figure to shoot for was the previous year's fastest race lap of 1 min. 12.7 secs. Bandini was out early and repeatedly switched cars. He ended up with the fourth fastest time of the day. Rodriguez went out to show Bondurant the way round; apparently Bondurant had a difficult time learning the circuit as he covered more than 150 laps during the two practice sessions. On the Friday, Bondurant's best lap was 1 min. 15.1 secs. which he improved to 1 min. 12.9 secs. on the Saturday. Rodriguez was making no impression at all and the best he could do was his Saturday time of 1 min. 13.45 secs., while Bandini managed a 1 min. 12.05 secs. on Saturday. These times left Bandini in the third row for the start, Bondurant in row seven and Rodriguez in row eight.

At the start it was Graham Hill in the BRM followed by Clark's Lotus and Stewart's BRM. Bandini was next, leading a bunched up group that included Spence, Brabham and Gurney. Bondurant and Rodriguez were in the 'third' group with Ginther, Bonnier, McLaren and Siffert. Gurney began to move up, passed Brabham and Spence, and went after Bandini just as rain and a heavy wind started on lap 12. Graham Hill took the lead when Clark retired with a broken piston. Gurney was 2nd, some 14 seconds back, and Bandini 3rd close behind Gurney; in the rain, Jack Brabham moved up fast passing both Bandini and Gurney. Bandini was also passed by Rindt's Cooper but towards the end of the race he put on pressure and regained his place from the Austrian driver when the Cooper developed gearbox trouble. The pits gave the 'Go' sign to Rodriguez and the Mexican made a determined effort, going by Rindt with six laps to go. Graham Hill performed the 'hat trick' by winning his third USA Grand Prix in a row; Bandini finished 4th, Rodriguez 5th and Bondurant 9th.

Mexican Grand Prix

The 1965 Mexican Grand Prix was held at the Mexico City circuit on October 24th. Ferrari sent three cars, that had been at Watkins Glen, for Bandini with Scarfiotti replacing Bondurant on the team and Pedro Rodriguez in the third car that was actually entered in the name of the North American Racing Team and identified with a blue and white stripe down the centre of the car. All three Ferraris were fitted with the flat 12 engines, two new engines having been flown in from Modena for Bandini's use arriving on the Thursday before the race.

The Rodriguez car, as it was officially a NART entry, was not affected by Ferrari's Dunlop contract and the opportunity was seized to switch to Firestones to see how the car handled. There were practice sessions on Friday and Saturday with everyone trying desperately to tune their engines for Mexico City's 7,000 ft altitude.

Before Rodriguez had a chance to evaluate the Firestone tyres he crashed, after losing a rear wheel. The car was badly damaged and, despite a great deal of effort, it was not ready in time to make the starting line-up on the Sunday. The mechanics did some experimental work with shorter megaphone exhausts but it was Bandini's turn to go off the road when he slid on the banking, hit the guard rail and cracked the front wheel flange. Before he crashed, Rodriguez had turned a time of 1 min. 59.06 secs., Bandini 1 min. 57.71 secs. and Scarfiotti 2 min. 01.84 secs. against the fastest time of the day by Gurney's Brabham at 1 min. 56.24 secs.

On Saturday, with his car still in pieces, Rodriguez went out in Scarfiotti's car and turned an identical 1 min. 59.06 secs., his previous day's performance. Scarfiotti in the same car was faster at 1 min. 58.93 secs. and Bandini was down to 1 min. 57.31 secs. compared to Jim Clark's fastest time of the day 1 min. 56.17 secs.

On race day, the weather was perfect but Rodriguez's car was still unfinished so he took over Scarfiotti's despite the fact that the Italian had been consistently faster.

Bandini's time qualified him for the fourth row of the start and Rodriguez was in the seventh row. The end of the first lap saw Ginther's Honda pulling away into a healthy lead followed by Stewart's BRM, Spence with the Lotus, Gurney's Brabham, Hill's BRM and Bandini, the first of the Ferraris. Bandini succeeded in passing Hill but Hill went by again on the 4th lap pulling steadily away from the Ferrari. Bandini, after he had lost ground to Hill, seemed to slow a little and was immediately challenged by Rodriguez. The Mexican driver was displaced by Siffert's Brabham but, on the next lap, Rodriguez was ahead again. The two Ferraris then engaged in a fierce battle, with Bandini staying ahead until lap 14 when the Mexican went by, much to the satisfaction of the Mexican spectators. The battle went on for 12 more laps with the two Ferrari drivers switching position several times. In the battle they caught up with Stewart's BRM that was suffering from a slipping clutch.

At half way Bandini got into a slide and wiped out the nose of his car against the rubber tyre markers that lined the course. He went into the pits where a spare nose piece was fitted but, while the mechanics were still working on it, Rodriguez joined his team mate in the pits with his flat 12 engine running rough. The trouble was diagnosed as a faulty rectifier that in turn resulted in a flat battery. A new battery was quickly fitted but Rodriguez was last-but-one when he rejoined the race. As the race drew to a close the two Ferraris circulated in 7th and 8th position with Rodriguez last and Bandini last-but-one. On the final lap Bandini had to slow down considerable as his engine was almost out of water and Rodriguez was able to get by. It was the first time for a long while that Ferraris had placed last and last-but-one.

1966 Syracuse

Syracuse was the venue of the first Formula 1 race of the 1966 season, the event being held on May 1st. Ferrari entered two cars, for Surtees and Bandini, whose only real opposition was from the Brabham team, the rest of the field being made up of private owners. Surtees had the new V12 cylinder 3-litre Ferrari and Bandini with a V6 Dino 246 with a displacement of 2.4 litres. In practice, the time to beat was the old record set by Clark in a 1.5-litre Lotus of 1 min.

46.0 secs. Surtees had no difficulty in breaking this time and easily recorded 1 min. 42.3 secs. Bandini was also below the old record with 1 min. 43.9 secs. This placed them in the first two positions on the grid, as the Brabham challenge never materialized. At the start, Surtees' engine was running rough so it was Bandini who took the lead. After three laps, Surtees engine had cleared the plugs and he swept by Bandini and was never challenged from the rest of the race. The Ferraris finished first and second with Bandini 24 seconds behind his team mate. Surtees also set a new lap record of 1 min. 43.4 secs. (118.92 m p h). It was a promising first outing for the new 3-litre 12-cylinder and Ferrari had high hopes of a championship season.

In 1966 the new 3-litre Formula came into force. Great things were expected of Ferrari because of his extensive experience with 3-litre V12 engines added to the fact that John Surtees, as number one driver, was capable of taking on anyone in championship races.

For the new formula, Ferrari produced, as expected, a V12 engined car. The chassis was a semi monocoque with tubes employed for various purposes. One tube ran back all the way along the engine outriggers to provide solid attachment points for the four engine mounts. By previous Ferrari standards the car looked large but in fact the dimensions were modest with a wheelbase of 7 ft 9.7 ins., a front track of 4 ft 9.5 ins. and a rear track of 4 ft 8.7 ins. The 3-litre twin cam per bank V12 was developed from the 3.3-litre sports car engine. It was only basically identical to the 3.3-litre as the castings were new from the ground up. Lucas fuel injection was featured with long intake trumpets, the intakes being in the centre of the Vee and the exhausts, a bundle of tuned 'snakes' coming up from either side of the engine to end in four mild megaphones.

Two Marelli coils were mounted on either side of the five-speed gearbox which was a direct derivative of that used on the P2 sports car, added to this were two distributors.

The suspension was derived from the P2, the units being scaled down accordingly and at the same time slightly strengthened.

Monaco Grand Prix

The first World Championship race of 1966 was held at Monaco on May 22nd. For the event, Ferrari sent two 3-litre V12s and the 246 Dino V6 for drivers Surtees and Bandini.

The Ferraris did not show up for the Thursday practice, as their transporter had been held up in the thick Italian national holiday traffic.

On Friday morning, practice was from 8 to 9 a.m. Surtees and Bandini were out early with Surtees immediately amongst the fastest in the V12 car, Bandini using the V6. In the final practice session in the afternoon, Ferrari produced the second V12 for Bandini.

Surtees' V12 was the one he had used at Siracuse and Silverstone, and Bandini's was brand new. Both cars were fitted with 15 in. rear tyres and used quick change knock-off hubs. Ventilated disc brakes were fitted to both cars but, on one occasion in practice, the pads on one of Surtees' rear brakes were on fire when he stopped at the pits.

After practice, Bandini decided to use the V6 car for the race as he had recorded 1 min. 30.5 secs. with it, giving him fifth place on the grid in the third row. Surtees took the V12 around in 1 min. 30.1 secs. to take second place on the grid to Clark's Lotus which had recorded 1 min. 29.9 secs.

The race began at 3 p.m. on Sunday and Surtees shot ahead of Clark who was jammed in first gear. Surtees led the first lap closely followed by Stewart's BRM, Bandini holding 7th place.

By five laps, Surtees and Stewart, still in close company, had pulled well away from the field but on lap 13 Surtees realized that there was something amiss with his rear axle as he rounded the *Gazometre* hairpin and waved Stewart ahead. Surtees toured round for the rest of the lap and came in to let the mechanics have a look. He then did one more lap before retiring with a broken self-locking differential.

Stewart now led, followed by Rindt's Cooper Maserati and Graham Hill's BRM with Bandini in the V6 Ferrari up to 4th place. As Bandini was informed of Surtees' retirement, he began to press, pushed by Hill to take 3rd and started to attack Rindt for 2nd. By lap 20, Bandini was past. Stewart was still leading comfortably and Bandini was being closely pressed by Hill and Clark, the latter having made a sensational recovery after his first lap delay. The 2nd, 3rd and 4th place cars were slowly closing the gap on Stewart, having reduced the margin from 31 seconds to 27 seconds. Clark broke a hub and Hill spun leaving Bandini secure in 2nd place, the Italian closed the gap on Stewart to 18 seconds and finally to 12 seconds at which point Stewart put on the pressure and set a new lap record. Bandini could do no more so he eased off to make certain of 2nd place, finishing 40 seconds behind the BRM.

Silverstone

The 1966 International Trophy was held at Silverstone on May 11th and Ferrari sent one car for John Surtees to drive. The car was the one that had been used at Siracuse. Surtees was a firm favourite to win the race but had a surprise when Brabham at the last minute turned a faster practice lap. From the start of the race it was all Brabham who led for the whole 35 laps. Try as he might Surtees could not catch the Australian and had to be content to finish 2nd, 7 seconds behind Brabham.

Belgian Grand Prix

The Belgian Grand Prix was held on the traditional Spa-Francorchamps circuit on 12th June 1966. Ferrari sent three cars for Surtees and Bandini, two of the V12s with the 2.4-litre 246 Dino in reserve, but Bandini elected to run the smaller engined car in the race and the new V12 remained unused.

In practice, Surtees showed he was the complete master of the tricky Belgian circuit, recording 3 min. 38.0 secs., the closest the opposition could come was a 3 min. 41.2 secs. by Rindt in the Cooper Maserati. Bandini in the V6 qualified for the second row of the start with a time of 3 min. 43.8 secs.

Rain threatened at the start of the race and when the flag fell Surtees spurted ahead. The rain came with an unexpected suddenness and at Malmedy the lead group was involved in a multiple spin that eliminated several of the top cars. Surtees was ahead of this melee and came by on the first lap in first position followed by Brabham, Bandini and Ginther.

Bandini snatched the lead from Surtees at the end of the second lap and Rindt, who had spun with the crowd, was making up time fast in the wet. By lap 3 he was 3rd behind Bandini who had been ousted from his lead by Surtees. On lap 4, the Cooper Maserati passed the Ferrari and dominated the race until lap 24 when his limited-slip began to give trouble. Surtees speeded up and passed the Cooper Maserati, continuing to win in 2 hrs. 9 min. 3 secs. at an average speed of 113.93 m p h. He also set the fastest lap at 4 min. 18.7 secs. an average of 121.91 m p h. Bandini rounded out an excellent day for Ferrari by coming in 3rd, one lap behind Surtees.

French Grand Prix

The Grand Prix of the A C de France was held on 3rd July 1966 at Reims. After the arguments at Le Mans and Surtees and Ferrari had parted company, the British driver joined the Cooper Maserati team. Ferrari replaced Surtees with Mike Parkes, the Surtees V12 being handed over to Bandini and a new car built, being longer in the cockpit and front section to accommodate the tall Englishman.

In the absence of the Ferrari team during the first practice session on the Wednesday, Surtees in his new mount easily broke the Reims lap record by 6 seconds leaving it at 2 min. 10.7 secs., a time that was thought by all to be very difficult to beat.

On the Thursday, the Ferrari team made their appearance and, after a few laps to settle down, Bandini began to shake the opposition getting closer and closer to Surtees' time and then getting below it with 2 min. 10.1 secs., 2 min. 09.8 secs. and 2 min. 09.2 secs.

Surtees and his team mate Rindt got together to pull a fast one on the Ferraris; by using Rindt to 'leapfrog' into Bandini's slipstream Surtees was able to record 2 min. 08.4 secs., which left him holding fastest time of the day although, for racing purposes, it could be discounted as being an artificial figure.

Parkes showed the Ferrari potential by immediately getting down to 2 min. 11.9 secs. in his new car and finally recorded 2 min. 10.2 secs.

On Friday Graham Hill finally got the new

H16 BRM running well to record 2 min. 09.2 secs. Surtees in turn could not repeat his previous day's figure as was to be expected and recorded 2 min. 10.6 secs. but the BRMs time spurred the Ferrari drivers into action.

Parkes broke the 2.10 mark with 2 min. 09.1 secs. and Bandini on his first flying lap turned 2 min. 08.8 secs. then 2 min. 08.2 secs. and finally left the record at 2 min. 07.8 secs. No one, other than Surtees and Hill, had been able to break the 2.10 mark, which left the Ferraris in a strong position. Bandini and Parkes therefore held the two outside positions on the front row with Surtees' Cooper Maserati between them.

The Sunday of the race was extremely hot and, as 'Toto' Roche dropped the French flag, it was Bandini's Ferrari that took the lead closely followed by Brabham. The challenge from Surtees failed to materialize as the car slowed immediately after the start.

On lap 1, it was Bandini with Brabham in his slipstream followed by Parkes' Ferrari. Bandini covered his first flying lap in 2 min. 13.6 secs., a new race lap record. Bandini increased his pace in the effort to get away from Brabham, finally leaving the lap record at 2 min. 11.3 secs. He drew away from Brabham while Graham Hill had pushed the V8 BRM right behind Parkes, the two being engaged in their own private fight. On several occasions Hill had the nose of the less powerful BRM ahead of the Ferrari but Parkes managed to hold his advantage. When Hill's camshaft broke, it left the second team Ferrari secure in 3rd place. Bandini opened up an 18 second lead over Brabham who had also drawn away from Parkes.

On lap 32, Bandini's throttle cable broke and the Ferrari slowed to a halt at the hairpin. With a length of wire from a straw bale he made a connection to the throttle linkage and was able to restart and return to the pits for lengthy repairs. This left Brabham in the lead with a 40 second advantage over Parkes. Bandini rejoined the race 11 laps later, he was now so far back that he could not even cover the number of laps needed to qualify for classification. Although he finished with the car running in top form he was not listed in the results. As the race drew to a close Brabham eased off and led Parkes' Ferrari over the line by 9.5 seconds.

Dutch Grand Prix

The 1966 Dutch Grand Prix was held at Zandvoort on July 24th. Ferrari entered two 3-litre V12s for Parkes and Bandini. They were the same cars that the team had used at the French Grand Prix but had undergone detail modifications. Guards had been fitted around the rear of the gearbox to protect the battery, ignition coils and fuel pump. The rear suspension uprights had extra lugs to enable different radius arm positions to be obtained. The windscreens were slightly modified with new deflectors and the lower front wishbones were plated.

There were three official practice sessions. One on Friday morning, the second Friday afternoon and the third on Saturday morning. In the Friday morning session Bandini lapped at 1 min. 32.4 secs. and Parkes at 1 min. 34.5 secs., so neither driver approached Clark's previous year's lap record of 1 min. 30.6 secs. During the afternoon session, both drivers improved their times, Bandini recording 1 min. 30.0 secs. and Parkes 1 min. 31.0 secs., Brabham, however, was down to 1 min. 28.4 secs.

On the Saturday, practice had hardly begun when Bandini hit some oil and spun off, slightly injuring himself. Parkes continued to improve his times, ending up with a 1 min. 29.0 secs., which placed him in the second row of the start alongside Dan Gurney. Bandini's car was straightened by dint of some all night work and his time gave him a position in the fourth row, alongside ex team mate John Surtees.

At the start, the two Brabhams of Hulme and Brabham and the Lotus of Clark sprinted off from the rest. Parkes was running in 5th place and Bandini in 9th. On the 11th lap, Parkes lost control, headed for the sand dunes and managed to demolish Rindt's stationary Cooper Maserati. Bandini did the best he could but after 23 laps he was already one lap behind the leaders. Bandini did manage to pull away from Surtees' sick car but shortly afterwards the Ferrari went into a violent spin when a front brake locked, Bandini continued at a reduced pace and finally finished 6th, some three laps behind the winner, Jack Brabham.

German Grand Prix

The 1966 German Grand Prix was held at the Nurburgring on August 7th. Ferrari entered three cars, two V12s for Parkes and Bandini and the V6 2.4-litre for Scarfiotti.

Practice was held in two sessions on Friday, morning and afternoon, and one session on Saturday morning. Much to the other two drivers' surprise, Scarfiotti in the smaller V6 was the fastest of the Ferrari team on Friday morning turning 8 min. 28.8 secs., compared to Stewart's fastest time of the morning with the 2-litre BRM of 8 min. 26.0 secs. Bandini recorded 8 min. 30.7 secs. and Parkes 8 min. 39.7 secs. The privately entered V12 Ferrari engined Cooper also qualified but managed only a miserable 10 min. 39.7 secs. Just as practice was ending, Scarfiotti lost control of his car and crashed, fortunately without too much damage.

None of the Ferraris practised on the Friday, as at 4 p.m. the starting time, it began to rain and the track remained soaked for the 1½ hours allotted.

On Saturday morning, the inimitable Jim Clark, with a 2-litre Lotus, set a new practice record of 8 min. 16.5 secs., a time that was only approached by Surtees' Cooper Maserati. Scarfiotti was again the source of surprise, his repaired V6 turned 8 min. 20.2 secs. which gave him a place on the front row of the starting grid. Bandini improved his time to 8 min. 21.1 secs. which gave him the middle of the second row, with Parkes next to him at 8 min. 21.7 secs.

The morning of race day was dull and wet and as the cars lined up the rain was falling steadily. As they sped off the line, it was Surtees in the Cooper Maserati, Brabham and Bandini. As they headed towards the start/finish line, for the first lap, it was Brabham who led Surtees and Rindt; Clark, Gurney and Bandini, who had dropped back, being only slightly ahead of team mate Parkes. On the second lap, the Ferrari pair were also passed by Graham Hill. By lap 6 the Ferrari team were a disgruntled 8th, 9th and 10th, with Bandini leading Parkes and Scarfiotti. On lap 10, two of the Ferraris were eliminated when the fuel injection went awry on the V6 and the V12 of Parkes skated off the road. Bandini continued to finish 6th, over 8 minutes behind the winner Brabham.

Italian Grand Prix

Held at Monza on 4th September 1966, the Italian Grand Prix once again attracted a larger than usual entry from Ferrari.

Three new factory cars were entered for Bandini, Parkes and Scarfiotti with a fourth car, the 2.4-litre Dino on loan to Giancarlo Baghetti who was contracted to the Parnell Racing Team.

Parkes and Scarfiotti had no trouble in qualifying for the first two places on the grid, their only challenger was Clark's H16 BRM-engined Lotus. Parkes turned 1 min. 31.3 secs. and Scarfiotti 1 min. 31.6 secs., with Bandini in the second row at 1 min. 32.0 secs., the Italian being slower as he spent most of practising running-in his engine. Baghetti qualified for the seventh row with a time of 1 min. 35.5 secs.

At the start, Bandini took the lead but was forced to pit on lap 2 with fuel, from a broken connection, soaking him. Parkes led at the end of lap 2 but fell back to 4th on lap 4 when Brabham took the lead. At the 8th lap Brabham retired with an oil leak and Parkes made up ground to retake the lead, holding it until lap 12 when once again he dropped to 4th, Scarfiotti being the new leader. On lap 18 Scarfiotti was firmly in the lead and Parkes back in 2nd place, only to be displaced on the next lap by Surtees' Cooper Maserati and on the following lap by Hulme's Brabham. On lap 26 he was by his two opponents and challenged Scarfiotti, taking the lead on lap 27. On lap 28 Scarfiotti and Surtees went by again but then the Cooper Maserati started to slow with a fuel leak. The struggle then went on for 2nd place with Hulme and Parkes changing places 12 times in 22 laps.

Parkes did an excellent job of keeping Hulme away from Scarfiotti. Bandini retired with ignition troubles on lap 34.

Scarfiotti became the first Italian to win since Ascari's victory in 1952, his average was 135.48 m p h, covering the 68 laps in 1 hr. 47 min. 14.8 secs. He also set the fastest lap in 1 min. 32.4 secs. (139.20 m p h). Parkes finished 2nd, six seconds behind, and Baghetti was not classified as he had covered less than 90 per cent of the total distance.

U.S. Grand Prix

The United States Grand Prix was held at Watkins Glen on 2nd October 1966. Despite the fact that the race had the largest purse of the whole Grand Prix season, Ferrari elected to send just one car for Lorenzo Bandini; the two other entries originally nominated were withdrawn. The V12 had the latest 3-valve heads with two intakes and one exhaust.

Practice sessions were held on the Friday and Saturday before the race and the target was the previous year's record of 1 min. 11.16 secs. set by Jim Clark. Practice on the Friday was hectic with Hill, Stewart, Brabham, Surtees, Rindt and Ginther all breaking the 1.10 mark. The session ended in particular satisfaction when Bandini set the fastest lap of the day at 1 min. 08.67 secs.

During the Friday session Bandini further improved his time to 1 min. 08.57 secs. but was displaced from pole position by Brabham's 1 min. 08.42 secs. and, towards the end of the practice, lost his first row position when Clark turned the H16 BRM-engined Lotus in 1 min. 08.53 secs.

Bandini had his revenge at the start of the race; he made a brilliant start and dived between the two green cars to lead the pack up the hill. At the end of the first lap, it was Bandini some yards ahead of Clark, Ginther's Honda, Brabham and Surtees' Cooper Maserati. On the second lap, Bandini had increased his lead. Brabham then slipped into second place and was soon at Bandini's heels with Clark and Surtees right behind. On lap 9 Surtees displaced Clark and on lap 10 Brabham took the lead from Bandini. As the leaders began to lap the tailenders, Brabham and Bandini swept past Arundell's Lotus but Surtees was baulked and a contact of cars resulted which cost Surtees three laps in the pits. On lap 19 Bandini retook the lead from Brabham but it was all over on lap 35 when a piece of plug fell into the cylinder and the engine blew.

Mexican Grand Prix

The last event of the 1966 season was as usual, held at Mexico City. Ferrari chose not to participate as nothing of importance could be gained in the world championship standings.

Surtees by virtue of one first for Ferrari and his points with Cooper Maserati for the rest of the season clinched 2nd place in the championship behind Jack Brabham but it was a valueless position for Ferrari. His best placed drivers were Parkes and Bandini who tied for 8th overall with 12 points and Scarfiotti 9th overall with 9 points. Not a very satisfactory ending to what promised to be a great year. No doubt the discussion about Surtees and Ferrari will be brought up many more times on the subject of what kind of a season it could have been.

1967

Race of Champions

The British Racing and Sports Car Club, together with the *Daily Mail,* revived the Race of Champions for 1967 and the event was held at Brands Hatch on March 12th.

Ferrari sent three cars, for Amon, Bandini and Scarfiotti; all three cars were V12s and one had a new engine.

All the hopes of Ferrari were pinned on Amon who had the reputation of being one of the fastest drivers on the tight circuit. However, he had a car accident on his way to the circuit, bruising his arm and right ankle. During the practice sessions he gave it a try but found he had to drive with one hand and his braking was limited by his injured ankle. He felt he was not sufficiently fit to drive in the race and Ferrari withdrew his entry.

While Scarfiotti drove a 1966 car, Bandini had the latest model from Maranello, unfortunately ignition troubles were encountered. Practice was held in two sessions on the Saturday before the race and Dan Gurney, on the Eagle-Weslake, set the standard to beat at 1 min. 32.2 secs. Of the Ferrari drivers, Scarfiotti turned 1 min. 34.2 secs. to qualify for the 3rd row of the starting grid and Bandini lapped in 1 min. 34.8 secs. which placed him in the fifth row. Amon's best time, despite his tremendous handicap, was 1 min. 34.6 secs., which showed his potential, had he been fit. The Pearce-Ferrari, driven by Chris Lawrence, qualified last at 1 min. 43.8 secs.

The race was held as two heats of ten laps each and a final of 40 laps.

In the first heat, neither of the two works

Ferraris were in the picture; Scarfiotti finished 6th and Bandini 10th; the winner of the heat being Dan Gurney's Eagle-Weslake. The second heat saw Gurney the winner once more with the Ferraris improving their positions slightly; Scarfiotti finished 4th and Bandini 9th. In the final, Gurney and Brabham fought it out, up front, and Bandini began a remarkable pursuit from his poor starting position in the back of the field; by half distance he went past Siffert to take 3rd place. Bandini started to gain on the two Eagles of Gurney and Ginther and, when Ginther retired, Bandini took over 2nd place. He pressed as hard as he could but just missed catching Gurney, finishing 0.4 seconds behind the winner. Scarfiotti brought the 1966 car home in 5th place.

B R D C Trophy

The British Racing Drivers Club Daily Express Trophy meeting was held at Silverstone on April 29th. As the Monaco Grand Prix date was very close the entries were below standard for the Silverstone event. Ferrari sent just one car for Mike Parkes to drive having the long chassis 1966 built specially for him mated to a 1967 engine.

In practice it was Stewart with the lone BRM H16 set the fastest lap in 1 min. 28.2 secs. with Parkes second fastest at 1 min. 29.8 secs. In the second practice session Stewart was again fastest at 1 min. 27.8 secs. and Parkes again followed in 1 min. 28.0 secs. On the third session Parkes changed from 10 inch rear rims to 12 inch and tried Firestone tyres, with this combination he equalled Stewart's time. Parkes took the lead immediately from Stewart and, by the third lap, the Ferrari and the BRM had pulled out a lead over all the rest of the competitors. Then Parkes began to pull away from Stewart as the track became slippery. Parkes was from then on able to set his own pace, the others being out of sight. The Ferrari crossed the line some 17 seconds ahead of second place, Jack Brabham having averaged 185.73 k p h for the 52 laps.

Monaco Grand Prix

The Monaco Grand Prix on May 7th was the first of the World Championship events held in Europe in 1967.

Ferrari originally had three entries but took advantage of only two of them for Bandini and Amon. Both of the cars had the new 36-valve engine with the central exhaust pipes and both had new nose cowlings and miniature windscreens with the rear view mirror faired in. Very large air scoops had been fitted to the front brakes and there was a small scoop for the driver's feet and two large intakes for the inboard-located rear brakes.

The time for everyone to go after, in practice, was Bandini's race lap record of 1 min. 29.8 secs. and on the Thursday afternoon practice session Bandini turned 1 min. 30.4 secs. and Amon 1 min. 34.1 secs. with Jackie Stewart's BRM fastest of the day at 1 min. 29.5 secs. Scarfiotti was listed as a non starter. On the Friday morning, Bandini was slower with a time of 1 min. 33.0 secs., but Amon improved his time to 1 min. 30.8 secs.

Saturday saw Bandini make a tremendous effort and turn a lap in 1 min. 28.3 secs. but it was not good enough to match Brabham's time of 1 min. 27.6 secs. Amon again improved his time to 1 min. 30.7 secs.

The excellent time by Bandini placed him on the front row with Brabham but Amon was in the 7th row.

Bandini jumped into the lead at the start and as the first lap was completed Bandini led Hulme's Brabham, Stewart's BRM, Surtees' Honda and Gurney's Eagle-Weslake. At the chicane there was some fast shuffling and flying dust with Hulme and Stewart diving past Bandini; two laps later Gurney moved the Eagle-Weslake ahead of Bandini who was now fourth; Amon was right at the back of the pack. When Gurney broke his fuel pump drive, Bandini went back into 3rd place and when Stewart broke his ring and pinion gear, Bandini was 2nd behind Hulme at a distance of 15 seconds. Surtees was trying to get the Honda past the Ferrari but with no success. Bandini began to press Hulme and reduced the gap to 7 seconds but Hulme was equal to the effort and kept his lead consistent at about 8 seconds and not allowing the Ferrari to approach any closer. At half distance it was still Hulme followed by Bandini with Amon now moved up to fourth place behind Bruce McLaren. By the 70th lap Bandini began to show signs of tiredness after the tremendous pressure he had tried to put on Hulme. On lap 82, as the Ferrari took the chicane, it struck one of the wooden barriers and went out of control, it climbed the straw bales and landed upside down in the middle of the road with the driver trapped underneath. The car immediately caught fire and by the time Bandini could be rescued he was very seriously injured and died a few days later. The accident threw a cloud over the proceedings and Amon's fine drive into third place was almost overlooked.

Syracuse Grand Prix

Normally the Syracuse Grand Prix is the first event of the European season but, for 1967, the organizers scheduled their race for May 21st which put it right in the middle of clashing seasonal activities. As a result of this, the only works team present at the Sicilian race was a two-car entry from Ferrari plus a mixed bag of five other cars.

Ferrari entered Scarfiotti and Parkes, the latter having a 1966 car with a 1967 engine, and Scarfiotti used the 1966 car with which he had won the Grand Prix of Italy. Scarfiotti's car had the exhausts on the outside of the head while Parkes had the exhausts on the inside of the Vee, both engines having the three-valve-per-cylinder layout.

The Syracuse record was held by Surtees at 1 min. 42.3 secs., set the previous year with the prototype 3-litre Formula 1 car. In practice, Parkes turned 1 min. 41.6 secs. and Scarfiotti 1 min. 41.7 secs., the nearest competitor being Siffert's Cooper Maserati at 1 min. 44.2 secs.

These times naturally meant that the two Ferraris sat on the front row of the grid and from the start the two red cars ran in close formation. Then on the last few laps they slowed down and took the chequered flag in a dead heat, having covered the 308 kilometers in 1 hr. 40 mins. 58.4 secs. Scarfiotti was credited with the fastest lap in 1 min. 41.0 secs., an average speed of 121.71 m p h.

Dutch Grand Prix

The Dutch Grand Prix was held at Zandvoort on June 7th. Ferrari sent four cars for Amon, Scarfiotti and Parkes. The fourth car was a 1966 model to be used as a spare, a completely new car was sent for Scarfiotti while Parkes had his long 1966 car with the 1967 engine and another 1967 model for Amon. Ferrari had practised on the Dutch circuit before official practice began and seemed elated at the time turned. Official practice began on the Friday morning and the standard to beat was Jim Clark's old 1500-cc Formula 1 record of 1 min. 30.6 secs. On Friday morning, Parkes recorded 1 min. 30.5 secs. and Scarfiotti 1 min. 30.3 secs., only Amon being able to get well below the old record with a 1 min. 27.9 secs. Fastest lap of the morning was Hulme's Brabham at 1 min. 26.8 secs. and the Ferrari effort somehow seemed to be lacking in spirit.

In the afternoon session, Parkes improved his time to 1 min. 27.6 secs., Scarfiotti got down to 1 min. 28.6 secs., and Amon to 1 min. 27.1 secs. In the final session on Friday only Parkes improved his time with 1 min. 27.4 secs. During the Saturday practice session, all three drivers again improved on their times Amon with 1 min. 26.9 secs., Parkes with 1 min. 27.0 secs., and Scarfiotti with 1 min. 27.9 secs. Surtees with the Honda was fastest of all with 1 min. 24.6 secs., showing that the Ferraris were definitely lacking. These practice times put Amon and Parkes in the fourth row of the start and Scarfiotti in the sixth.

At the start, it was Graham Hill with the Lotus-Cosworth, followed by Brabham, Rindt with the Cooper-Maserati, Gurney with the Eagle-Weslake and Amon, the first of the Ferraris, hounded by Clark's Lotus-Cosworth. Hulme moved up to pass Amon and Gurney. When Gurney headed for the pits, Amon moved up but was quickly passed by Clark thus falling back to 6th place. In 7th place was Rodriguez with a Cooper-Maserati, in 8th Stewart with the BRM and Parkes with the second Ferrari in 9th, Scarfiotti following up in 11th place.

When Hill dropped out, Amon moved up into 5th place and began to challenge Hulme. Rindt fell out with suspension trouble, this let Hulme and Amon up into 3rd and 4th places and their battle continued, Amon trying everything to get by; he could get alongside the Brabham but could not pass it and Amon had to be content with 4th place supported by his team mates Parkes in 5th and Scarfiotti in 6th places.

Belgian Grand Prix

The 1967 Belgian Grand Prix was held at Spa on June 18th. Ferrari ran the same three cars that had been used in the Dutch Grand Prix by Amon, Parkes and Scarfiotti. Practice was held on Friday and Saturday with Surtees record of 3 min. 38.0 secs. set with a 3-litre Ferrari the previous year, as a standard.

On the Friday Parkes got below this figure, recording 3 min. 36.6 secs., he was followed by Amon at 3 min. 36.8 secs. but Scarfiotti, who was not quite at home on the circuit, recorded 3 min. 42.1 secs.

The following day saw Parkes slower with 3 min. 36.9 secs. but both Amon and Scarfiotti improved their times, Amon turning a fast 3 min. 34.3 secs. and Scarfiotti 3 min. 37.7 secs. but compared to Jim Clark's fastest time of the day of 3 min. 28.1 secs., the Ferraris still had to go faster if they were to have any hope of challenging the 'Flying Scot'. At the start, Clark shot off the line and led up the hill after *Eau Rouge,* he was followed by the Cooper-Maserati of Rindt, Stewart's H16 BRM and the two Ferraris of Parkes and Amon. On the tricky left hand bend at *Blanchimont,* Parkes went into a wild slide, the car overturning and throwing him out by the side of the road, he suffered a broken leg and a broken wrist, putting him out of action for some time.

Parkes' accident was reported to the Ferrari pits by Surtees, as he retired his Honda, and Amon plodded on rather unenthusiastically after having witnessed the Parkes accident. Gurney moved his Eagle-Weslake up to 3rd place while Amon was involved in a dog-fight with Brabham, Rindt and Rodriguez while much further back Scarfiotti duelled with Spence in the second H16 BRM. Amon and Scarfiotti were given the sign 'PARX OK' but at that moment Amon was rather busy as Rodriguez had passed him and was spraying oil over the Ferrari.

As Clark pulled into the pits, the order became Stewart, Gurney, Brabham, Rodriguez, Amon, Rindt. When Clark re-entered the race, he was a long way back keeping company with the Scarfiotti Ferrari. Scarfiotti was forced into the pits with a cracked hydraulic pipe on his rear brakes and lost a great deal of time. After Brabham blew his engine, Amon made a determined effort to push ahead of Rodriguez and put himself firmly into 3rd place which he held until the end of the race. Scarfiotti was 11th although not officially classified.

British Grand Prix

The British Grand Prix was held at Silverstone on 15th July 1967, and Ferrari sent just one car for Chris Amon to drive. It was expected that the British GP would see the debut of the new lightweight Ferrari with the four-valve-per-cylinder engine but, as it turned out, Amon had the earlier model with the three-valves-per-cylinder. In practice, Amon lapped at 1 min. 26.9 secs., which compared with Jim Clark's time of 1 min. 25.3 secs. (123.53 m p h). Amon's time placed him in the second row of the start between Surtees' Honda and Gurney's Eagle. At the start, the two Lotus 49s of Jim Clark and Graham Hill pulled away from everyone followed by Jack Brabham and Amon with the Ferrari, these in turn being tailed by Gurney's Eagle, Stewart's BRM and Surtees' Honda.

At the end of ten laps, Hulme had brought the second Brabham through the field and displaced Amon from 4th position. On lap 26 Graham Hill took the lead from Clark and the two Lotuses had the race well in hand. Hulme was now third with Brabham fourth and Amon's Ferrari 5th followed by Rodriguez with the Cooper-Maserati, these being the only cars on the same lap as the leader. Hill first had suspension trouble and then blew his engine, as a result everyone moved up a place. As the race drew to a close, Amon made a determined effort and began to push Brabham, it took him a long time to get by the Australian which ruined his chances of snatching second place from Hulme. Once by Brabham, Amon increased the pace, he had seven seconds to make up but it was too late and Hulme crossed the line 3.8 seconds ahead of Amon who had to be content with third.

French Grand Prix

The 53rd Grand Prix of the Automobile Club de France was held July 2nd. The French classis once again switched circuits and for the first time was held on the Bugatti circuit at Le Mans.

It was a poor and unpopular choice for such an important event, the circuit being just over 4 kilometers in length and more suitable for Formula 3 than Formula 1.

Ferrari was in bad shape for drivers as Parkes was out after his Spa accident and Scarfiotti had shown some reluctance to continue Formula 1 racing after the accidents to Bandini and Parkes. So it was left to Amon to uphold the Ferrari colours. Two cars were sent, both with the 36-valve V12-cylinder engines. A short blunt radiator air intake was tested during practice but the car appeared with the normal long type for the race. Amon, after practising with both cars, decided to use chassis No. 0005 for the race, this being a newer car than 0003 which was the reserve.

On the Friday, Amon registered a time of 1 min. 39.3 secs. with only Brabham (at 1 min. 37.9 secs.) and Hulme (at 1 min. 38.0 secs.) faster. On the Saturday, Amon improved his time to 1 min. 38.0 secs. but the new Lotus entries took the day with Graham Hill fastest at 1 min. 36.2 secs. Amon's time gave him a starting position in the middle of the third row of the grid. Graham Hill took the lead and Clark quickly moved up through the pack so that by lap 7 Clark was 1st, Hill 2nd, Brabham 3rd, Gurney 4th, Amon's Ferrari 5th and Hulme 6th. As Hill broke down, Hulme passed Amon but shortly afterwards was repassed by the Ferrari. Hill's retirement was followed by that of Clark enabling Amon to hold the Ferrari in 3rd place behind Brabham and Gurney. Hulme was a constant menace and overtook the Ferrari on lap 30. When Gurney retired, the Ferrari was back to 3rd but unable to make an impression on Hulme. All Amon could do was to hold on to 3rd place until the end but even this was not to be; the accelerator pedal came adrift on lap 48 and the Ferrari's run was over.

German Grand Prix

The 1967 German Grand Prix was held at the Nurburgring on August 6th. Ferrari sent two cars for Chris Amon, one being the latest type with engine weight reduced slightly and the gearbox with the selector rod, on top of the box, running forward through the V of the engine to a rocking arm just behind the seat of the driver, this arm being in turn controlled by a right hand shift in the cockpit. The second car used the heavier earlier type of gearbox with the gear selector rod located along the right hand side, through the chassis sponson. On the Friday morning practice session, Amon was out in the new car, his fastest time was 8 min. 44.7 secs., the fastest time of the session being set by the Honda of Surtees at 8 min. 25.0 secs. Biggest surprise of the practice session was the amazing time set by the Formula 2 Matra-Cosworth of Ickx who recorded 8 min. 27.5 secs.

On the Friday afternoon, Amon improved his time to 8 min. 20.4 secs., and Denny Hulme set the fastest time of the session at 8 min. 13.5 secs. The astounding Ickx recorded 8 min. 14.0 secs. in the four-cylinder Formula 2 car.

On Saturday morning, Amon recorded no time as he had to pull off with a faulty fuel pump in the new Ferrari. A big fuss was caused when the organizers announced that any damaged cars on the track could not be retrieved until after some national and Formula 5 races had been held. This meant all night work for several other teams beside Ferrari.

Amon's time gave him a position in the 3rd row of the grid, some 16 seconds slower than the fastest qualifier, Jim Clark.

On the first lap, Clark's Lotus led from Hulme's Brabham, Gurney's Eagle, Brabham, the Eagle of McLaren, Surtees' Honda, Stewart's BRM and Amon's Ferrari in 8th. Clark had problems with a slow leak in the rear tyre and Gurney took over the lead from Hulme, Brabham and Steward. Ickx embarrassed both Amon and Surtees by pushing the Formula 2 Matra ahead of the 3-litre Ferrari and Honda. As Amon's fuel load lightened and the tyres became bedded in, he went by the Formula 2 car and tucked in behind Brabham to begin another battle in which the wily Australian used every trick in the book to keep the Ferrari behind, much to the consternation of Ferrari team manager, Franco Lini, who turned purple and shook fists.

Gurney looked set to win and was running well when a universal broke and Hulme took the lead, followed by the battling Brabham and Amon a long way behind. Hulme crossed the line some 40 seconds ahead of Brabham who held off Amon by 0.5 seconds to make it a 1, 2, 3 for the 'down under' drivers.

Canadian Grand Prix

The first Canadian Grand Prix was held at the Mosport circuit at Toronto on 27th August 1967.

Ferrari entered only one car for Chris Amon, this being 0005 with the three-valve light alloy engine, however, the car was reputed to weigh only 1,157 lb.

Unofficial practice was held on the Thursday before the race with the official sessions on Friday and Saturday. The Ferrari went well and on Thursday the three fastest were Gurney, Clark and Amon. Gurney recording the only under 1 min. 24.0 secs. lap.

On the Friday, Amon had difficulty in repeating his previous day's performance. He did a great number of laps and changed suspension settings frequently but the best he was able to record was 1 min. 24.0 secs. On the Saturday, Ferrari fitted Firestone tyres with a lower profile that altered the effective gear ratios and necessitated the changing of the gearbox. With the new box in place, Amon found some difficulty in selecting 3rd gear but eventually he recorded 1 min. 23.3 secs. to place in the second row for the start, alongside Dan Gurney's Eagle.

Race day was spoiled by low cloud and occasional drizzle. Just as the warming up lap began, the drizzle returned making the track extremely slippery. Amon had the embarrassment of spinning the Ferrari at 50 m p h on his warming up lap and, as the flag fell, a cautious field took off at a slow pace trying to get the feel of the track conditions. As they came round on the first lap, Amon was in last place, having spun again and having no adhesion at all on the slippery track.

When the track dried out, Amon was able to move up to 9th but the weather worsened again and it was only by the retirement of other cars that Amon was able to finish 6th.

Italian Grand Prix

The Italian Grand Prix was the next event in the 1967 world championship season. For once, Ferrari did not have his usual raft of entries, limiting himself to producing a brand new car,

plus an earlier model, for Chris Amon to drive. Ferrari driver Scarfiotti was entered in one of Dan Gurney's Eagles and Ferrari was roundly criticized by the Italian press for not entrusting his cars to any Italian drivers. Ferrari replied to this with the comment that whenever an Italian driver was killed in a Ferrari it was classed as a national disaster and the press would then make all kinds of attacks on him, however, the Italian press seemed to have a more callous attitude when it came to foreign drivers. A second point was that there were no Italian 'professional' drivers anymore. Scarfiotti, Vaccarella and Baghetti were all fine drivers but looked on motor racing as more of a hobby than a job.

The new Ferrari with the 48-valve engine weighed in at 1130 lb. The twin overhead camshafts per bank were very close together. In the new engine, Ferrari reverted to single ignition with a central spark plug, the exhausts being mounted in the V of the engine. The inlet tracts were unusual, being outside the heads and of downdraught type, the ports being considerably curved to accommodate this location. The quoted output was 403 b h p, with fuel injection beneath the throttle slides. The Ferrari mounted ventilated discs which would seem to be unsuitable at Monza but despite some discussion they were retained for the race.

The first day of practice was very hot and Jim Clark lost no time in showing his class, recording 1 min. 28.5 secs., a new unofficial record. Chris Amon tested air scoops to pressurize the induction system and was out with a 3-valve and a 4-valve Ferrari at different times. As a result of his practising, Amon recorded 1 min. 29.35 secs., fourth best time on the first day. The next day, a thunderstorm prevented faster times and Amon's best was 1 min. 30.0 secs. just before the deluge. The first day's time placed Amon in the second row of the grid, alongside Dan Gurney's Eagle.

There was a mess up at the start; as the front line moved from the dummy grid, they took off before the flag fell and several drivers were left behind.

Halfway round the first lap, Gurney led Brabham and Amon but, by the 3rd lap, the slow starters were up with the lead group. Clark and Hill forced their Lotus entries into first and second, with Gurney, Brabham and Hulme following, and the Ferrari down to 8th just ahead of Surtees' Honda and Scarfiotti's Eagle. Amon moved up one place when Gurney broke a con rod. The first group of Clark, Hill, Brabham and Hulme moved away from the second group of Stewart, McLaren and Amon, and by 10 laps, Rindt in the Cooper-Maserati joined the fight and Surtees also joined in the melee. With Clark in the pits, the order was Hill, Brabham, Hulme, Surtees and Amon. When Hulme fell out, Amon moved up to 4th but shortly afterwards he pitted to check his rear suspension and tyre pressures, as the car was weaving. This dropped him to 6th place. As the leader completed the 60th lap, Amon was in again to have a loose damper bracket tightened; the delay putting him completely out of contention, his final position was 7th and last.

U.S. Grand Prix

The United States Grand Prix took place on 1st October 1967 at Watkins Glen, New York. Ferrari entered one car for Chris Amon to drive. It was a new one, the major change being in the transmission department which was derived from the Formula 2 car. It was here that considerable weight was saved over the older type Formula 1 gearbox. The new lightweight also used a new type of inboard brakes. Unfortunately the Ferrari's real potential was not shown in practice as the new ram scoops over the fuel injection air intakes consistently came loose as the car touched 160 m p h on the straight. The scoops were removed for the race and Amon recorded 1 min. 06.64 secs. (124.50 m p h) to qualify fifth fastest behind Graham Hill, Clark, Gurney and Brabham. This placed him in the third row of the two-by-two grid, alongside Denis Hulme.

Amon ran in 5th place for the first three laps with Graham Hill leading the race from Gurney and Clark. On the fourth lap, Amon was passed by Hulme's Brabham but on lap 10 the Ferrari displaced Jack Brabham to regain 5th. On lap 16 he finally had revenge for the whole season of battling with the Brabhams when he passed Denis Hulme and went on to challenge the leaders, never again to be challenged by the

Brabhams during the race. On lap 21, Amon was by Gurney and closely tailed the Lotus duo of Graham Hill and Jim Clark. Amon's Ferrari was never less than one second behind Hill who was staying ahead of Clark by inches. Hulme was already 20 seconds behind Amon and Brabham another four seconds behind that. On lap 65 Amon and the Ferrari finally forced their way past Graham Hill for 2nd place. On lap 76 Graham Hill retook 2nd and held on until lap 84, when his clutch began to be a real problem, and Amon went ahead again. It lasted until lap 95 when Amon disappeared; he had had fluctuating oil pressure for the whole race and the engine quit with bearing failure with only 12 laps to go.

Mexican Grand Prix

The Mexican Grand Prix was the last of the World Championship Events of the 1967 season. Chris Amon represented Ferrari and put up an excellent showing in practice qualifying second fastest behind Jim Clark's Lotus which gave him a position on the front row of the grid.

At the start of the race it was Graham Hill who led Amon and Clark with third fastest qualifier Gurney already eliminated as he had punctured his radiator on the exhaust pipe of the slow starting Lotus of Clark. Clark passed the Ferrari on lap 2 and then went into a lead for which he was never challenged. On Graham Hill's retirement on lap 14 Amon took over 2nd place and had no difficulty in holding it. With the end of the race in sight and some 40 seconds down on Clark, Amon's Ferrari began to suffer from vapour lock which forced him to limp round the track for the last two laps and salvage a 6th place after a really fine drive.

This left Ferrari in fourth place for the 1967 constructors championship behind Brabham, Lotus and Cooper-Maserati. Amon took fourth place in the drivers' standings behind Hulme, Brabham and Clark with 20 points total. Parkes had 2 points and Scarfiotti 1, these two being right at the bottom of the list.

It could be said that the season was satisfactory enough for Ferrari. The car showed its true abilities towards the end of the season and Chris Amon certainly tried hard enough to win for Maranello.

1968

South African Grand Prix

The first race of the 1968 season was the South African GP held at Kyalami on January 1st.

Ferrari entered three of the V12 3-litre cars. No. 8 for Chris Amon, No. 9 for Jacky Ickx and No. 10 for Andrea de Adamich.

Fastest practice lap was by Jim Clark in a Lotus Ford at 1 min. 21.6 secs. De Adamich qualified for the 3rd row at 1 min. 23.6 secs. with Amon next to him at 1 min. 23.8 secs. and Ickx in the 5th row with 1 min. 24.9 secs.

De Adamich moved his car up to 8th place by the 5th lap and to 7th by lap 12 before crashing on lap 13. Ickx moved up to 9th on lap 7 and 7th on lap 13, 6th on lap 24, 5th on lap 44 before he retired with a broken oil line.

Amon started in 7th place, moved up to 5th on lap 13 maintaining his position until lap 43 when he moved up to 4th in which position he finished the race.

Spanish Grand Prix

The Spanish Grand Prix was held at Jarama in Barcelona on 15th May 1968, Ferrari entered cars for Amon (No. 19) and Ickx (No. 21).

Amon was most impressive in practice qualifying for the pole position at 1 min. 27.9 secs. with Ickx recording 1 min. 29.6 secs. for a position in the 3rd row. Ickx ran 9th at the start but retired on lap 13 with ignition trouble while Amon held 3rd at the start and moved up to 2nd on lap 13. He moved into 1st place on lap 16 and firmly held it until his fuel pump gave out on lap 57.

Monaco Grand Prix

At Monaco on May 26th there were no Ferraris present because of major strikes in Italy.

Belgian Grand Prix

The next appearance of the Ferraris was at Spa-Francorchamps on 9th June 1968 for the Belgian Grand Prix, Chris Amon was in No. 22 and Jacky Ickx in No. 23.

Lotus had introduced the spoiler tail at Monaco, based on the American Chapparal wing but at Spa, Ferrari was the first with a realistic aerofoil in Grand Prix racing. Ing. Forghieri's system was to mount a small aerofoil high in the airstream and positioned practically above the rear wheels. Ferrari drivers reported increased stability and the Firestone tyres were found to be running a bit above normal temperature so it could be assumed that the aerofoils were indeed effective.

Amon recorded fastest lap in practice at 3 min. 28.6 secs. with Ickx at 3 min. 34.3 secs. placing both Ferraris on the front row.

Amon led from the start but was passed by Surtees' Honda before retiring on lap 8 with a damaged oil radiator. Ickx ran 3rd until lap 4 when he was passed by both Stewart and Rodriguez. As the race progressed he fell as low as 6th but continued on to the finish finally taking 3rd place.

Dutch Grand Prix

The Dutch Grand Prix was held at Zandvoort on 23rd June 1968, Ferrari again entered two cars Amon in No. 9 and Ickx in No. 1. Amon once again set the fastest lap at 1 min. 23.54 secs. for the pole position with Ickx in row 3 at 1 min. 24.42 secs. Stewart proved to be master of the race and Ickx finished 4th with Amon 6th.

French Grand Prix

The Grand Prix of France was held at Rouen Les Essarts on July 7th. Two Ferraris were entered one for Amon (No. 24) and the other for Ickx (No. 26). Ickx recorded 1 min. 57.7 secs. to place in the front row next to Stewart and Rindt while Amon qualified at 1 min. 57.8 secs. in the second row.

Ickx led from the start holding off Stewart until lap 18 when he dropped to third but by lap 20 he was back in the lead which he held until the finish, giving Ferrari a convincing victory. Amon had mixed fortunes and finally finished in 10th place.

Brands Hatch

At the British Grand Prix, held at Brands Hatch on 20th July 1968, the two Ferraris were again entered for Amon (No. 5) and Ickx (No. 6). Amon's practice time of 1 min. 29.5 secs. placed him on the front row of the grid alongside Oliver and Hill while Ickx 1 min. 31.0 secs.

placed him in the 5th row. Amon started in 4th place, moved up to 3rd when Hill retired on lap 27. He then moved ahead of Siffert into 2nd on lap 37 only to be passed again by the Swiss on lap 42. Siffert continued to win the event, Amon taking 2nd place behind him. Ickx who had started in 11th place moved up to 3rd when he finished.

Nurburgring

The German Grand Prix was held at the Nurburgring on 4th August 1968. Two cars were entered, No. 8 for Amon and No. 9 for Ickx. Ickx showed tremendous potential by recording 9 min. 04.0 secs. for the fastest lap in practice while Amon was second fastest at 9 min. 14.9 secs. The time closest to the Ferraris was that of Rindt whose third fastest time was 9 min. 31.9 secs.

As it turned out Stewart took the lead from the start and held it for the rest of the race, while Graham Hill did the same for second place. Amon ran in a firm 3rd place until lap 12 when he crashed. Ickx brought his Ferrari home in 4th place.

Monza

The Italian GP was held at Monza on 8th September 1968. At Monza, the Ferraris sported perhaps the most sophisticated aerofoil control system where the actuating piston was operated by oil pressure from the engine. The wing had two positions, horizontal and minus 15 degrees. Other variation inputs were from road speed and brake line pressure.

Ferrari again had two cars entered, No. 9 with Amon and Ickx with No. 8. Fastest lap in practice was by Surtees' Honda at 1 min. 26.07 secs. Amon qualified for No. 3 position on the front row at 1 min. 26.21 secs. and Ickx for the second row at 1 min. 26.41 secs.

Amon started 4th and moved into 2nd place before he was involved in a crash on lap 9 while Ickx drove a steady race to finish 3rd.

Canadian Grand Prix

The Canadian Grand Prix was held at Mont Tremblant on 22nd September 1968. Ferrari entered only one car, for Chris Amon (No. 9) and he qualified for the middle of the 1st row at 1 min. 33.8 secs. Amon led the race until lap 72 when his transmission gave out.

Watkins Glen

At the US Grand Prix, held at Watkins Glen on 8th October 1968, Amon's Ferrari (No. 6) was joined by newcomer Derek Bell (No. 7). Andretti's Lotus Ford made fastest practice lap at 1 min. 04.20 secs. with Amon at 1 min. 04.37 secs. in the second row and Bell at 1 min. 07.06 secs. in row 8. Bell retired on lap 14 with overheating and Amon, after holding 3rd place until lap 10, retired on lap 59 with a broken water pipe.

At the Mexican Grand Prix held on 3rd November 1968, the two Ferraris were entered for Amon (No. 6) and Ickx (No. 7). Siffert's Lotus Ford was fastest in practice at 1 min. 45.22 secs., but Amon was next to him on the front row at 1 min. 45.62 secs; by contrast Ickx could do no better than 1 min. 49.24 secs. to qualify for row 8.

Ickx retired on the third lap with ignition trouble and Amon on lap 16 with overheating.

1968 proved to be a year of great promise for Ferrari with the cars showing the performance to do extremely well but the season proved to be relatively fruitless due to a plague of minor problems. It was commented that Chris Amon had to be the unluckiest driver of the year.

1969
South African Grand Prix

The first race of the 1969 World Championship series was held in South Africa at Kyalami on March 1st. Ferrari entered a single V12 for Chris Amon. The car differed from the late 1968 model by having a single rear wing and a wider frame to accommodate the new engine with outside exhausts. The fuel tanks were also larger.

Brabham set fastest lap at 1 min. 20.0 secs. and Amon qualified for the second row at 1 min. 20.5 secs. At the start Amon ran in 7th place until lap 5 when he dropped back to 9th. He made his way up to 5th place by lap 33 but retired the following lap with a broken engine.

Spanish Grand Prix

The first race of the European season was the Spanish Grand Prix held at Barcelona on 4th May 1969. Ferrari again entered a solitary car for Chris Amon. During the first practice session

Amon was fastest at 1 min. 27.6 secs. and later improved his time to 1 min. 26.2 secs. Rindt's Lotus eventually proved faster with a time of 1 min. 25.7 secs. but Amon held his place in the centre of the front row. Rindt leapt into the lead and pulled away from Amon who held a firm second place. Rindt crashed on lap 19 and Amon inherited the lead to hold it until lap 56 when his engine gave up.

Monaco Grand Prix

The Grand Prix of Monaco was held on 18th May 1969. Ferrari entered a single car for Amon (No. 11). Stewart set the fastest lap in the Matra Ford at 1 min. 24.8 secs. and Amon placed the Ferrari on the front row of the grid next to Stewart at 1 min. 25.0 secs. At the start Stewart took the lead with Amon behind him. Amon remained in 2nd place behind the Matra Ford until lap 17 when the Ferrari retired with differential troubles.

Dutch Grand Prix

The Dutch Grand Prix was held at Zandvoort on 21st June 1969. The CSI had banned the wings which had been the cause of serious accidents during the Spanish and other Grands Prix and all the team turned out with mini wings that were part of the bodywork. Ferrari entered one car for Amon (No. 8) and had two variations of mini wings at hand. Fastest lap in practice was set by Rindt's Lotus at 1 min. 20.85 secs. with Amon qualifying for the second row at 1 min. 22.69 secs. Amon came round on the first lap in 4th place only to drop to 5th place on the second lap and to 6th place on the 7th lap. He regained 5th on lap 17 and continued to battle for the rest of the race. He moved up to 4th on lap 27 but it was a back and forth battle and he ended the race with a creditable 3rd place.

French Grand Prix

The French Grand Prix was held at the Charade circuit at Clermont Ferrand on 6th July 1969. Ferrari sent one car for Chris Amon (No. 6). The fastest practice lap was set by Stewart in the Matra Ford at 2 min. 00.6 sec. Amon qualified for the 3rd row of the starting grid at 2 min. 04.2 secs. Stewart took the lead at the start and

held it throughout the race to win. Amon was 5th on lap 1, dropping to 6th on lap 4. On Hulme's retirement he moved back up to 5th on lap 13 and 4th on lap 22 when Rindt retired. He held this place until his engine gave up on lap 30. However he was classified 10th and last.

British Grand Prix

The British Grand Prix was held at Silverstone on 19th July 1969. Ferrari sent a lone car for Amon (No. 11). Rindt's Lotus was fastest in practice at 1 min. 20.8 secs. and Amon qualified for the second row at 1 min. 21.9 secs. Rindt took the lead from the start with Amon 6th and dropped to 9th by lap 13 finally to retire with gearbox trouble on lap 45.

German Grand Prix

For the German Grand Prix there were no Ferraris entered and the next appearance of the Ferrari team was at Monza for the Italian Grand Prix.

Italian Grand Prix

The Italian Grand Prix was held on 7th September 1969. It was supposed to have been the debut of the new flat 12 Ferrari but the engine broke while Amon was testing the car at Modena and for Monza Ferrari entered an elderly V12 for Brambilla (No. 10). Brambilla's times were less than encouraging so Rodriguez was given the car for the race. Even the fiery Mexican could do little with the car and with a time of 1 min. 28.47 secs. qualified for the 6th row of the grid. During the race Rodriguez was never in contention and gained places mainly due to other cars retiring and finally finishing in 6th place.

Canadian Grand Prix

The Canadian Grand Prix at Mosport was held on 20th September 1969. It was a repeat of Monza for Ferrari only the old V12 (No. 6) was entered and Rodriguez qualified for the 6th row at 1 min. 20.5 secs. He was never in the running and fell out of the race on lap 37 with no oil pressure.

US Grand Prix

The US Grand Prix was held at Watkins Glen

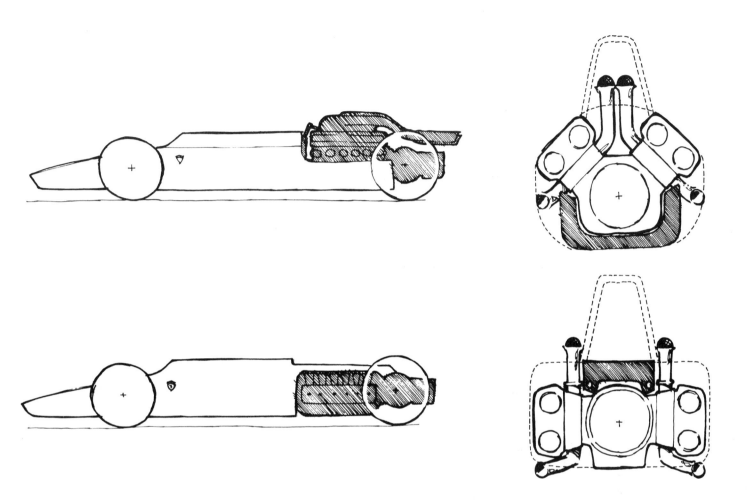

The top drawing shows the mounting of the 3 litre V12, whilst the lower shows that of the flat 12 3 litre

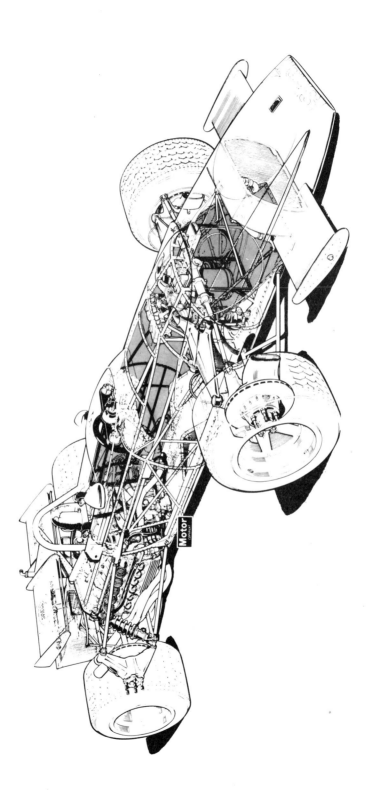

The 1970 Ferrari 312B cutaway

on 5th October 1969. It was a repeat of the two previous debacles. The single V12 was entered by NART for Rodriguez (No. 12) and he qualified at 1 min. 5.94 secs. for the 6th row of the grid. Again he was never in the running and due to multiple retirements finished in 5th place.

Mexican Grand Prix

The Mexican Grand Prix on 19th October 1969 saw the same NART-entered V12 for Rodriguez (No. 12) but the results were even worse than on the previous occasions. Despite the fact that it was his country's Grand Prix and for this reason spurred himself to every effort, Rodriguez qualified at 1 min. 49.46 secs. for the 8th row in last but one place. Again during the race he was never in contention and finished 7th because of the retirement of other cars.

So ended an altogether poor year for Ferrari with Chris Amon 12th in the World Championship and Pedro Rodriguez 13th equal from his combined points with Ferrari and BRM.

1970

South African Grand Prix

The South African Grand Prix was held at Kyalami on 17th March 1970. Ferrari sent one of the flat 12 cars for Jacky Ickx (No. 17) who recorded 1 min. 20.0 secs. in practice to qualify alongside Rindt in the second row of the grid. The fastest lap had been set by Stewart in his March Ford at 1 min. 19.3 secs. Ickx ran in 2nd place for four laps and then fell back finally retiring on lap 61 with a broken engine.

Spanish Grand Prix

The Spanish Grand Prix was held at Jarama on 26th April 1970. Again Ferrari sent a flat 12 (No. 2) for Ickx. The car recorded 1 min. 24.7 secs. in practice to qualify for the third row of the grid. Brabham recorded fastest lap at 1 min. 23.9 secs. Ickx was eliminated in a spectacular 1st lap crash in which the Ferrari was destroyed by fire.

Monaco Grand Prix

The Monaco Grand Prix was held on 10th May 1970. The lone Ferrari flat 12 was again driven by Ickx who recorded 1 min. 25.5 secs. in

practice to qualify for the 3rd row of the starting grid compared to the 1 min. 24.0 secs. set by Stewart for pole position. Ickx ran in 5th place until he was eliminated by a broken driveshaft on lap 12.

Belgian Grand Prix

For the Belgian GP which was held at Spa Francorchamps on 7th June 1970, Ferrari sent two of the flat 12 cars. Ickx had car No. 27 and Giunti No. 28. Fastest lap in practice was by Stewart in the March Ford at 3 min. 28.0 secs. Ickx qualified for the 2nd row of the grid with 3 min. 30.7 secs. and Giunti in the 3rd row with a time of 3 min. 32.4 secs. Ickx ran in fifth place at the start moving up to 4th on the 4th lap he maintained this position until lap 7, when he dropped two places; by lap 19 he was back up in third place only to drop way back to finish 8th and last. Giunti worked his way up from 14th on the 1st lap to 6th by lap 15 but a spin at La Source dropped him back again. By steady driving he regained his position holding 6th on lap 25, 5th on lap 26 and moving up to 4th on the last lap.

Dutch Grand Prix

The Dutch Grand Prix was held on 21st June 1970. Ferrari again sent two flat 12 cars for Ickx (No. 25) and Regazzoni (No. 26). Ickx qualified for the 1st row of the grid with 1 min. 18.93 secs. compared to Rindt's pole position time of 1 min. 18.30 secs. Regazzoni was in the third row with 1 min. 19.48 secs. Ickx took the lead at the start but was quickly passed by Rindt. Ickx held second place until lap 50 when a flat tyre forced him to pit and dropped him to 4th place. On lap 58 he moved back up to 3rd, a place which he held to the end of the race. Regazzoni was in 9th place at the start but rapidly moved up into 6th place by lap 6. He moved up to 5th on lap 24 and 4th on lap 32. By lap 52 he was 3rd but was repassed for 3rd by Ickx on lap 57 to finish 4th behind his Belgian team mate.

French Grand Prix

The Grand Prix of France was held at Clermont Ferrand on 5th July 1970. Ferrari entered two 312Bs for Ickx (No. 10) and Giunti (No. 11). Ickx recorded the fastest practice lap and sat on the pole with a time of 2 min. 58.22 secs. Giunti qualified for the 5th row with a time of 3 min. 01.85 secs. Ickx leapt into an immediate lead followed closely by Beltoise in the Matra Simca. Ickx led for 14 laps and then retired with a burnt valve. Giunti was never in the picture and finished in 14th place.

There was a story behind Ickx's retirement. In practice after Ickx had set a very fast time it was found that his engine had poor compression on one cylinder, probably due to a stone being ingested from the track. The mechanics tried to repair the situation without taking the engine out and turned the valve on its seat. However, that did not cure the situation. Ickx tried the spare car just before the race but it had not been set up for the circuit and handled poorly so Ickx chose to drive the car with the questionable engine instead.

British Grand Prix

The British Grand Prix was held at Brands Hatch on 19th July 1970. Ferrari entered two 312Bs for Ickx (No. 3) and Regazzoni (No. 4). Rindt set the fastest lap at 1 min. 24.8 secs. but Ickx was also on the front row with 1 min. 25.1 secs. Regazzoni qualified for the 3rd row of the grid at 1 min. 25.8 secs. As the flag fell, Brabham led from the first row but Ickx passed him into Paddock Bend and began to pull away. Ickx led through lap 7 when he retired with a broken transmission. Regazzoni ran in 6th place and moved up to 5th when Ickx retired. On lap 13 he was overtaken by both Stewart and Beltoise but repassed Beltoise on lap 24 and regained his place from Stewart on lap 32. On lap 54 he moved up to 4th place when Oliver retired and remained in this position until the end of the race.

German Grand Prix

The German Grand Prix was not held as usual on the Nurburgring because of a safety dispute with the drivers. The event was held instead at Hockenheim on 2nd August 1970. Ferrari entered two 312Bs for Ickx (No. 10) and Regazzoni (No. 15). Ickx took pole position with a time of 1 min. 59.5 secs. and Regazzoni placed in the second row with 1 min. 59.8 secs.

On the first lap it was Ickx in the lead followed by Rindt and Siffert with Regazzoni 4th. At the halfway mark Rindt pulled out into the lead while Ickx fell to second but by the next lap (26) Ickx was back in first place. Regazzoni then duelled with Rindt for 2nd place, but Regazzoni's gearbox seized just before the pits. Rindt then challenged Ickx for the lead and the lead changed five times during the last 10 laps. With 2 laps to go Ickx hesitated when Rindt took to the grass and the Austrian Lotus driver won from the Ferrari by 7/10 of a second.

Austrian Grand Prix

The Austrian Grand Prix was held at Zeltweg on 16th August 1970. Ferrari sent three of the 312Bs for Ickx (No. 12), Giunti (No. 14) and Regazzoni (No. 27). Rindt's Lotus set the fastest lap at 1 min. 39.2 secs. but Regazzoni qualified next to him on the front row with 1 min. 39.7 secs. and Ickx in the 2nd row at 1 min. 39.8 secs. Giunti was in the third row with 1 min. 40.3 secs. As the flag fell Regazzoni leapt into the lead with Rindt 2nd but at the end of the 1st lap Ickx was in second place, Rindt was 3rd and Giunti's Ferrari 4th. On the 2nd lap Ickx took the lead with Regazzoni holding 2nd and the order remained the same until the end of the race to give Ferrari a tremendous comeback victory. Giunti was passed by Rindt but regained 3rd place when Rindt retired. A pit stop on lap 38 for a wheel and tyre change dropped Giunti to 10th but by lap 40 he was back in 9th, on lap 48 he moved up to 8th and on lap 51 to 7th where he finished one lap behind his victorious team mates.

Italian Grand Prix

The Italian Grand Prix was held at Monza on 6th September 1970. Ferrari again entered three of the 312Bs for Ickx (No. 2) Regazzoni (No. 4) and Giunti (No. 6). Ickx took pole position with a time of 1 min. 24.14 secs. Regazzoni qualified for the 2nd row at 1 min. 24.39 secs. and Giunti for the 3rd row at 1 min. 24.74 secs. Ickx led from the start and held 1st for 3 laps then the lead began to switch in the usual Monza manner between Ickx, Rodriguez, Stewart and Regazzoni. In ten laps the lead changed 4 times and during the whole race the lead changed at least 28 times. Ickx retired on lap 26 with clutch

(*Top*) Marie Andretti wins the 1971 South Africa GP with the Ferrari 312B (No. 1/002)
(*Bottom*) Barcelona 1971, first lap, first corner. 312 Bs of Ickx and Regazzoni

(*Top*) Regazzoni. Monaco 1971
(*Bottom*) Ickx with the Ferrari 312 B2 (No. 006) winning the
1971 Dutch GP

(Top) Regazzoni. Ferrari 312 B. Brands Hatch 1971
(Bottom) Andretti. German Grand Prix 1971

(Top) The cockpit of Regazzoni's Ferrari 1971
(Bottom) Mario Andretti with the winning 312 B2
Ferrari in the Questor GP Ontario, California 1971

(*Top*) Questor Grand Prix 1971. The front suspension
(*Bottom Left*) Monza September 1973. The F1 312 B2. Ickx stands second from left, on his left is Ing. Colombo and then Ing. Rocchi
(*Bottom Right*) 1972 Ferrari F1 312 B3

(Top) The first version of the 1973 F1 312 B3
(Middle) The second version of the 1973 F1 312 B3
(Bottom) Monaco 1973. Ickx with the 312 B3 Ferrari

(*Top*) Monaco 1973. Merzario with the 312 B3
(*Middle*) Niki Lauda with the 1974 Ferrari F1 B3. Here
at the Fiarano test track is the Argentine GP car
(*Bottom*) Louis Rosier with the first version of his
converted GP car at Buenos Aires 1000 Km 1954. The
car finished 7th but suffered from overheating

(Top Left) Louis Rosier's 4.5 litre single seat Ferrari after its second rebodying by Scaglietti. The car retains its central driving position
(Top Right) Practice at Buenos Aires 1956. Fangio in the experimental V8 Lancia engined Super Squalo Ferrari
(Middle) Briggs Cunningham's 4.5 litre Ferrari with glycol cooled brakes
(Bottom) A special prototype. A Lancia engine in a Ferrari Super Squalo chassis

troubles and Giunti had already retired with a broken engine on lap 15. With 8 laps to go Stewart took the lead but on lap 54 Regazzoni passed him and led to the finish giving this relatively newcomer his first Grand Prix win and another first for Ferrari.

Canadian Grand Prix

The Canadian Grand Prix was held at Mont Tremblant on 20th September 1970. Ferrari entered two of the 312Bs for Ickx (No. 18) and Regazzoni (No. 19). Stewart qualified with the best time at 1 min. 31.5 secs. and Ickx was next to him on the front row at 1 min. 31.6 secs. Regazzoni was in the second row at 1 min. 31.9 secs. Stewart led from the start with Icks second and Regazzoni 6th. Stewart pulled out a lead on Ickx who in turn was well ahead of Rodriguez in 3rd place. Regazzoni moved up to 5th on the 8th lap and into 4th on lap 18 then to 3rd on lap 23. When Stewart retired Ickx took the lead and Regazzoni moved to second and the pair were never headed for the rest of the race to give Ferrari another convincing 1, 2 victory.

US Grand Prix

The US Grand Prix was held at Watkins Glen on 4th October 1970. Ferrari entered two 312Bs for Ickx (No. 3) and Regazzoni (No. 4). Ickx was fastest in practice with a time of 1 min. 03.07 secs. with Regazzoni in the 3rd row at 1 min. 04.30 secs. Stewart led at the flag from Rodriguez with Ickx third and Regazzoni 4th. Ickx moved to second and Regazzoni to third but Regazzoni had to pit with ignition troubles and to change a front tyre, this dropped the Swiss driver way back. Ickx while in second place pitted with a fuel breather losing fuel and when he rejoined the race he was 12th. Ickx quickly made his way back through the pack and finished 4th, while Regazzoni could do no better than 13th.

Mexican Grand Prix

The Mexican Grand Prix was held on 25th October 1970. Ferrari entered two of his 312Bs for Ickx (No. 3) and Regazzoni (No. 4). Regazzoni set the fastest practice lap at 1 min. 41.86 secs. and Ickx was in the second row at 1 min. 42.41 secs. The race started over 1 hour late because of the impossibility of controlling the crowd. Regazzoni led the first lap but by the 2nd lap Ickx was in the lead. Regazzoni dropped to 3rd when he hit his ignition switch during a gear shift but on lap 13 moved back into second when Stewart's car hit a dog. From then on the two Ferraris had it all their own way to finish 1st and 2nd. Ickx earned 40 points and Regazzoni 33 points in the World Championship. Rindt was declared World Champion despite his death at Monza as no one had surpassed his total of 45 points.

1971

South African Grand Prix

The first of the 1971 World Championship series was held at Kyalami in South Africa on 6th March 1971 where Ferrari sent three drivers, Mario Andretti, Jacky Ickx and Clay Regazzoni along with four cars. Three of the cars were the normal 312B models and the fourth a new 312B/2. This latter car was a further development of the promising 312B design by Mauro Forghieri. It had smaller frontal area than the earlier version and had a wedge shape to it. The tub of the chassis was made of 16 gauge alloy to comply with the 1972 rules and still used the internal tubular strengthening.

The rear brakes and suspensions were moved inboard while the front suspension followed the previous year's layout although employing different geometry. Top forged rocker arms were used with a wide based lower wishbone with inboard mounted Koni shockabsorbers.

The rear suspension was new and as there was no room to mount the spring damper units in a vertical position, a system was devised to mount them horizontally across the back of the engine with a bell crank top wishbone and a single top radius rod together with a wide-based non-reversed lower wishbone.

On its first appearance at Kyalami there was some finalizing to be done with a question whether to make the wheelbase 90.8 in. or 92.76 in. with a track of 54.5 in. Unfortunately Regazzoni completely demolished the car in testing before the race and the Ferrari team had to rely on the 312Bs. Andretti had car No. 002

which was last raced by Giunti at Monza, Ickx had 001 and Regazzoni 004.

In practice Stewart's Tyrrell Ford set the fastest lap at 1 min. 17.8 secs. Regazzoni qualified for the front row of the starting grid with 1 min. 18.2 secs., Andretti for the second row at 1 min. 19.0 secs. and Ickx for the 3rd row at 1 min. 19.2 secs. Regazzoni took an immediate lead from Fittipaldi's Lotus with Ickx Ferrari 3rd. Regazzoni began to pull out a lead but on lap 17 Hulme outbraked Regazzoni to take the lead. After the halfway mark both Surtees and Andretti passed Regazzoni. Ickx had dropped to 9th. Andretti was in good form and passed Surtees when the British driver began to have gearbox troubles. Andretti closed on Hulme and when the race was almost over Hulme had a bolt detach from the rear suspension and Andretti went by into the lead which he retained to the finish to give Ferrari the first victory of the season and for Andretti his first victory for Ferrari. His time was 1 hr. 47 min. 35.5 secs. an average of 112.367 m p h. Andretti also set the fastest lap at 1 min. 20.3 secs. an average of 114.321 m p h a new record. Regazzoni finished 3rd and Ickx finished 8th.

Spanish Grand Prix

The Spanish Grand Prix was held at Monjuich, Barcelona on 18th April 1971. Ferrari again entered three 312Bs for Ickx (No. 4) in 312B No. 003, Regazzoni (No. 5) in 312B No. 004 and Andretti (No. 6) in 312B No. 002. Ickx set the fastest practice lap at 1 min. 25.9 secs., Regazzoni was second fastest at 1 min. 26.0 secs. and Andretti qualified for the 3rd row of the grid at 1 min. 26.9 secs. Ickx took an immediate lead but he was passed by Stewart who pulled away from the Ferrari. On lap 12 Regazzoni pitted with fuel pump problems only to find that the back end of his car was on fire. Regazzoni retired and Andretti was hounding Rodriguez for 4th place. Stewart held a 4 second lead over Ickx and eventually extended it by another 4 seconds. Andretti began to trail flames and was called in for a fuel pump replacement which cost him 8 laps. Later a loose union caused another fire and Andretti parked the Ferrari on the track. Ickx pressed hard and closed the gap to within 3 seconds with 10 laps

to go but Stewart won with 2.3 secs. advantage over the Belgian driver who had set a new lap record at 1 min. 25.1 secs., an average of 99.64 m p h. Regazzoni officially retired on lap 13 with engine trouble and Andretti on lap 50 with a defective fuel pump.

Monaco Grand Prix

For the Monaco Grand Prix on 23rd May 1971, Ferrari sent three 312Bs for Ickx (No. 4) 312B No. 006, Regazzoni (No. 5) 312B No. 005 and Andretti 312B No. 002. Stewart set fastest lap at 1 min. 23.2 secs. with Ickx next to him on the front row at 1 min. 24.4 secs. Regazzoni recorded 1 min. 26.1 secs. for a place in the 6th row. Andretti had trouble in practice with a shaft seizing in the injection pump and as a result was only able to do one lap of practice under dry conditions. Despite every effort he failed to qualify for the race. Stewart led the Monaco Grand Prix from start to finish and Ickx ran a steady third behind Siffert until lap 29, when they were both passed by Peterson. Siffert's retirement let Ickx up into 3rd place where he finished. Regazzoni retired on lap 24 with a broken rear suspension.

Dutch Grand Prix

The Dutch Grand Prix was held at Zandvoort on 20th June 1971. Ferrari entered three 312Bs for Ickx (No. 2) 312B/2 No. 006, Regazzoni (No. 3) 312B/2 No. 005 and Mario Andretti (No. 4) 312B No. 003. Regazzoni went off the road in practice when a rear tyre went flat and Andretti had a bad crash when one of his rear tyres went flat. Larger rear wheels were fitted to eliminate this as the Firestones were pulling away from the rims. Ickx set the fastest practice lap at 1 min. 17.42 secs. and Regazzoni qualified at 1 min. 17.98 secs. for the second row with Andretti in row 7 with a time of 1 min. 20.32 secs. The track was rain soaked and the drivers were given 15 minutes familiarization before the start of the race. Andretti's Ferrari developed fuel pump trouble at the start and he retired on lap 6 after having made an excursion into the sand with a defective pump.

Ickx took an immediate lead followed by Rodriguez and on the second lap Regazzoni moved ahead of Stewart into 3rd place. On lap 8 Rodriguez took the lead and stayed there until lap 29 when Ickx went ahead again but only for one lap. On lap 31 Rodriguez held the lead but Ickx was back in front on lap 32 and stayed there for the rest of the race. He covered the 70 laps in 1 hr. 56 min. 20.09 secs., an average speed of 94.06 m p h. Ickx also set the fastest lap at 1 min. 34.95 secs., an average speed of 98.783 m p h. Regazzoni finished in 3rd place despite a spin at Tarzan corner in which he lost the whole of the nosepiece of his car.

French Grand Prix

The Grand Prix of France was held on the new Paul Ricard circuit at Le Castellet on 4th July 1971. Ferrari sent two cars, for Ickx (No. 4) 312B/2 No. 006 and Regazzoni (No. 5) 312B/2 No. 005. Stewart's Tyrrell Ford was fastest at 1 min. 50.71 secs., but the two Ferraris occupied the next two places on the front row of the grid with Regazzoni at 1 min. 51.53 secs. and Ickx at 1 min. 51.88 secs.

Ickx was pushed off at the chicane and fell to 8th while Regazzoni held 2nd place to Stewart who led from start to finish. Ickx pressed hard but on lap 4 his crankshaft broke and on lap 20 Regazzoni slid on some oil and hit the guardrail breaking a wheel.

British Grand Prix

The British Grand Prix was held at Silverstone on 18th July 1971. Ferrari entered two 312Bs for Regazzoni (No. 5) and Ickx (No. 4). Regazzoni had equal fastest time with Stewart at 1 min. 18.1 secs. but held pole as he set his time first. Ickx turned 1 min. 19.5 secs., which placed him in the 3rd row of the starting grid.

Regazzoni jumped into the lead with Ickx right behind him but during the first lap Stewart overtook Ickx and set out after Regazzoni. On the 4th lap Stewart outbraked Regazzoni and took the lead which he held to the finish. Siffert's BRM passed Regazzoni but the Ferrari regained 2nd place on lap 14 and held it until Regazzoni's retirement with engine trouble on lap 48. Ickx held 4th until lap 38 when he had to stop with a blistered tyre which dropped him into 12th place. He had moved up to 9th place when he too retired with engine problems on lap 51.

German Grand Prix

The German Grand Prix was held at the Nurburgring on 1st August 1971. Ferrari entered three 312Bs for Ickx (No. 4), Andretti (No. 5) and Regazzoni (No. 6). Stewart set the fastest lap at 7 min. 19.0 secs. and Ickx was second fastest at 7 min. 19.2 secs. Regazzoni qualified for the second row at 7 min. 22.7 secs. and Andretti for the 6th row at 7 min. 31.7 secs.

Ickx led at the start but already at the north curve Stewart went by and pulled away from the Ferrari. Ickx went into a slide and broke his battery against the earth bank. Regazzoni took over second but was passed by Siffert. On Siffert's retirement Regazzoni was back in 2nd place but was in turn passed by Cervert. Andretti moved up steadily and the two Ferraris finished 3rd (Regazzoni) and 4th (Andretti).

Austrian Grand Prix

The Austrian Grand Prix was held at Zeltweg on 15th August 1971. Ferrari sent two 312Bs for Ickx (No. 4) and Regazzoni (No. 5). Siffert's BRM set the fastest lap at 1 min. 37.44 secs. with Regazzoni qualifying for the 2nd row at 1 min. 37.90 and Ickx for the 3rd row at 1 min. 38.27 secs.

At the flag Siffert went into the lead which he held for the rest of the race. Regazzoni was second and Ickx 4th. Regazzoni battled with Cervert the two switching 2nd and 3rd places. On lap 8 Regazzoni's engine broke. Ickx's engine had already lost its tune and from lap 3 onwards he began to fall back steadily until he retired on lap 31 with a broken engine.

Italian Grand Prix

The Italian Grand Prix was held at Monza on 5th September 1971. Two cars were entered by Ferrari. Ickx (No. 3) in 312B No. 004 and Regazzoni (No. 4) in 312B No. 005. Amon was fastest in the Matra Simca at 1 min. 22.40 secs. with the Ickx Ferrari second fastest at 1 min. 22.82 secs. Regazzoni qualified at 1 min. 23.69 secs., giving him a place in the 3rd row.

Regazzoni made a lightning start and took the lead. He held it for three laps and then in the typical cut and thrust of Monza racing he came by in 4th place on the fourth lap. Ickx was never in contention and retired on lap 15 with a broken transmission. On lap 9 Regazzoni was back in the lead but dropped again to 4th before he too retired with a broken transmission on lap 17.

Canadian Grand Prix

The Canadian Grand Prix was held at Mosport on 19th September 1971. Ferrari entered three cars for Ickx (No. 4) in 312B/2 No. 006, Regazzoni (No. 5) in 312B/2 No. 005 and Andretti (No. 6) in 312B/2 No. 007. Stewart set the fastest lap at 1 min. 15.7 secs., but the Ferraris were not at their best. Ickx qualified for the 5th row at 1 min. 16.5 secs. and Andretti next to him at 1 min. 16.9 secs. Regazzoni was in the 7th row with a time of 1 min. 17.5 secs. Ickx came by in 7th place on the first lap, Andretti was 11th and Regazzoni 13th. Regazzoni moved up one place but went out with a broken engine on lap 7. Ickx moved up as high as 4th but gradually fell back to finish 8th while Andretti finished 13th.

US Grand Prix

The US Grand Prix at Watkins Glen was held on 3rd October 1971. It was the last of the year's series as the Mexican Grand Prix had been cancelled. Ferrari sent three cars but only two were used as Andretti had to drive at Trenton in a USAC race which had been postponed from the previous weekend. Regazzoni (No. 5) had 312B/2 No. 005 and Ickx (No. 32) had 312B No. 004.

Stewart set the fastest lap at 1 min. 42.642 secs. Regazzoni was in the 2nd row at 1 min. 43.002 secs. and Ickx in the 3rd row with 1 min. 43.843 secs. At the start Regazzoni ran in 4th place and Ickx in 6th. On the 5th lap Ickx moved up to 5th and on lap 9 passed Regazzoni for 4th. On the 14th lap Ickx went by Hulme taking 3rd and on lap 17 passed Stewart for second place. Ickx began to close up on Cevert who was leading. The Belgian Ferrari driver set a new lap record at 1 min. 43.474 secs. (average 117.495) and came within two seconds of the leader. Ickx made no further progress as his alternator came adrift and on lap 49 he was in the pits to retire. Regazzoni finished in 6th place. Stewart won the World Championship and of the Ferrari drivers Ickx was 4th with 19

points. Regazzoni 7th with 13 points and Andretti 8th with 12 points.

1972

Argentine Grand Prix

For the first time in 12 years the Argentine GP once again became the first Grand Epreuve of the racing season.

It was held on 23rd January 1972 at the superb Buenos Aires Autodrome. Ferrari retained his previous year's driver Jacky Ickx, Clay Regazzoni and Mario Andretti. For the Argentine event Ferrari sent three cars, No. 5 for Regazzoni, No. 6 for Ickx and No. 7 for Andretti.

They were basically the same as the previous year's cars but considerable modification had been made in the suspension department. At the front, inboard suspension was used as on the 1971 cars but a wider track and different geometry was used. At the rear the inboard system with horizontally mounted rear suspension was replaced with a conventional wishbone and link system giving a wider track and consequently made the car easier to set up.

As the Argentine organizers had elected to use circuit No. 9 there were no previous records to judge by for this was the first time the circuit had been used. On the Thursday there was an unofficial practice and Regazzoni came out the fastest at 1 min. 15.7 secs. On Friday there were two practice sessions. In the first Ferrari elected to carry out their full-tank testing and the times recorded were Regazzoni 1 min. 16.77; Ickx 1 min. 16.95 and Andretti 1 min. 17.07 secs. During the second session, which gave the team an opportunity to run under cooler conditions, Ickx set the fastest time of day with 1 min. 13.56 secs. Andretti also broke the 1 min. 14 secs. mark with a time of 1 min. 13.98 secs. and Regazzoni recorded 1 min. 14.13 secs.

On Saturday there were two sessions again. Regazzoni improved his time to 1 min. 13.28 secs. during the second session, while Andretti improved to 1 min. 13.61 secs. during the same session. Ickx was unable to improve on his previous day's time. These times placed Regazzoni in the third row of the start, Ickx in the 4th row and Andretti in the 5th. The pole was held by the Argentine driver Carlos

Reutemann at 1 min. 12.46 secs. with Jackie Stewart next to him at 1 min. 12.68 secs. The Ferraris were unable to challenge the leaders Stewart and Reutemann, Regazzoni running 5th and Ickx making a slow start. Andretti's engine was giving trouble, large flames coming out of his car's exhaust. A series of pit stops did not remedy the situation and Andretti was black flagged at 21 laps. At half distance, Ickx had passed Regazzoni but his car was smoking badly, the two Ferraris running in 5th and 6th places.

The race ended with a win for Jackie Stewart with the Ferraris in 3rd and 4th places with Ickx ahead of Regazzoni. Their showing was not very impressive having obtained their positions more by the retirement of other cars than anything else.

South African Grand Prix

The South African Grand Prix was held at Kyalami, between Johannesberg and Pretoria, on 4th March 1972. Ferrari entered three of the 312B/2 models, the cars having new nose sections.

Ickx was allocated No. 6, Regazzoni No. 5 and Andretti No. 7. Practice was held in three sessions and Stewart in the Tyrrell dominated all three of these sessions. On the Wednesday he recorded 1 min. 17.0 secs., with Ickx and the Ferrari 2nd fastest at 1 min. 17.7 secs. Regazzoni recorded 1 min. 18.5 secs. and Andretti 1 min. 19.0 secs. On Thursday Stewart was again fastest with both Ickx and Regazzoni recording 1 min. 17.8 secs. and Andretti at 1 min. 18.2 secs. During the Friday session, Stewart was once again fastest while Regazzoni made a special effort and brought his time down to 1 min. 17.3 secs., Andretti was down to 1 min. 17.5 secs., while Ickx remained slow at 1 min. 18.8 secs.

This placed Regazzoni in the centre of the front row behind Stewart and Fittipaldi. Andretti and Ickx were positioned in the 3rd row behind Hailwood's Surtees and Hulme's McLaren. Regazzoni made a slow start and Hulme dashed into the lead ahead of Stewart and Fittipaldi. On lap 2 Stewart took the lead, followed by Hulme and Fittipaldi with Andretti the first Ferrari up in 6th place.

The Ferraris were not on good form and the engines were apparently about 1,000 r p m down compared to their performance in practice. Regazzoni and Andretti circulated disconsolately in 7th and 8th places with Ickx further behind.

Regazzoni had a tyre go soft and in stopping to replace it dropped to 12th place, while Andretti made a valiant effort and challenged 4th place Ronnie Peterson's March. With six laps to go Andretti squeezed by Peterson and finished 4th while Ickx struggled to 8th place and Regazzoni two laps down in 12th place. Altogether it was not a very encouraging expedition by Ferrari.

Spanish Grand Prix

The first race of the European Grand Prix circuit was held at Jarama near Madrid on Monday 1st May 1972. The previous complaints about the organization and its promotion of the 1970 Spanish Grand Prix had been sorted out and the race was scheduled for the Monday as it was a national holiday.

The Ferrari team had three of the 312B/2 cars. Ickx used No. 6, Andretti took over Regazzoni's No. 5 while Regazzoni had No. 8, a completely new car. Andretti's usual No. 7 was kept behind at the factory. The cars were modified having the oil tanks removed from behind the driver's head to the gearbox at the rear of the car. Another new feature was the use of a headrest fairing which extended to the rear of the car.

The first practice session was on Saturday during which the fastest lap was set by Emerson Fittipaldi's Lotus at 1 min. 19.75 secs., this being the only car to break the 1 min. 20 secs. mark. Ickx recorded 1 min. 20.58 secs., Regazzoni 1 min. 21.21 secs. and Andretti 1 min. 21.84 secs., the latter achieved his time in only 5 laps at which time his engine broke. The other two Ferrari drivers completed 31 and 30 laps respectively to obtain their times. On Sunday's practice, Ickx set the fastest lap at 1 min. 18.43 secs. with Andretti at 1 min. 19.39 secs. and Regazzoni at 1 min. 19.71 secs. This placed Ickx on the pole position of the starting grid with Andretti next to Jackie Stewart in the 2nd row and Regazzoni in the third row.

At the start, Hulme's McLaren led from the

first row, followed by Stewart, Regazzoni, Ickx, Fittipaldi and Andretti. On lap 5 Stewart took the lead followed by Hulme and Ickx. Then Fittipaldi passed Stewart and on lap 15 Ickx did the same, moving the Ferrari into 2nd place. Andretti moved by Hulme to take 4th place but the Ferrari engine broke shortly afterwards while Fittipaldi opened up a 5 second lead over Ickx.

A light shower of rain and a special type Firestone tyre allowed Ickx to close right up on Fittipaldi but the rain did not persist and Ickx was unable to pass the leader. Fittipaldi extended his lead over the Ferrari. Further back, Hulme in 4th place ahead of Regazzoni, had trouble slowing down and retiring and letting the Ferrari up into 4th place. With one third of the race to go, Fittipaldi had a 9 second lead over Ickx. The Ferrari's tyres were giving out and any hopes that Ickx might have had of challenging the Brazilian driver for the lead were over.

Stewart, in third place, lost his nose cowling and came into the pits to find his radiator damaged, this let Regazzoni into third place.

Fittipaldi won by 19 seconds over Ickx, with Regazzoni in 3rd place, one lap behind the leader. Fastest lap of the race was set by Ickx on lap 52 at 1 min. 21.01 secs. (151.283 k p h); a new record for the track.

Monaco Grand Prix

For the Monaco Grand Prix on 14th May 1972, Ferrari entered only two cars, as Andretti was due to race at Indianapolis. Three cars were actually sent, Regazzoni was back in No. 5 and Ickx in No. 6, the new No. 8 that had been driven by Regazzoni in Spain was used as a spare car.

On the Thursday practice, Ickx recorded 1 min. 23.3 secs., which was fastest time of day, with Regazzoni at 1 min. 23.8 secs. being fourth fastest behind Hulme and Stewart. On the Friday Ickx improved to 1 min. 21.6 secs. and Regazzoni to 1 min. 21.9 secs. but they were both beaten by Fittipaldi's Lotus at 1 min. 21.4 secs. although no one else broke the 1 min. 22 secs. mark.

On Saturday the rains came and practice times dropped. Ickx recorded 1 min. 48.3 secs.,

and Regazzoni 1 min. 46.8 secs. Ickx then took out the later car No. 8 and recorded 1 min. 45.3 secs. which turned out to be fastest time of day which gave some idea of how bad conditions really were.

The rain was pouring down for the start and it was Beltoise with the P160 BRM who beat Ickx into Saint Devote to take the lead. Beltoise made the most of being in the lead and clear of the spray by opening up a wide lead over Regazzoni, Fittipaldi and Ickx.

After 20 laps, Beltoise comfortably led Ickx and Regazzoni with Fittipaldi in 4th place losing ground to the two Ferraris. At this stage Stewart closed up on Regazzoni and passed him to take third. Stewart then proceeded to close up on Ickx but spun and dropped behind Regazzoni again.

Stewart made another attempt to tackle the Swiss Ferrari driver and this time it was Regazzoni's turn to make a mistake, he spun into the barricade damaging the car sufficiently to put it out of the race. Stewart had ignition problems and slowed, being lapped by Beltoise and Ickx. Beltoise continued to lead until the finish beating the Ferrari over the line by over 1 minute.

Belgian Grand Prix

The 1972 Belgian Grand Prix took place on the new Nivelles-Baulers circuit on June 4th. The Nivelles circuit was a far cry from the challenging Spa circuit on which previous Belgian GP had been held and in fact turned the event into just another 'autodrome' type race.

Ferrari sent three cars and two drivers. Ickx had 312B/2 No. 6 and Regazzoni 312B/2 No. 5, with 312B/2 No. 8 in reserve. During the first practice session, the Ferraris were predominant, both Ickx and Regazzoni setting identical times of 1 min. 12.00 secs. This state of affairs lasted until Fittipaldi in the Lotus got into his stride and turned fastest time of the day in 1 min. 11.60 secs., relegating the Ferraris to 2nd and 3rd fastest. On the first session on Saturday, Fittipaldi again took fastest with 1 min. 12.52 secs., while Ickx turned 1 min. 11.90 secs. and Regazzoni equalled his time of the previous day at 1 min. 12.00 secs.

During the 2nd Saturday session, Fittipaldi

continued his dominance with 1 min. 11.43 secs., Regazzoni being close behind at 1 min. 11.58 secs. and Ickx at 1 min. 11.84 secs., being beaten by Hulme in the McLaren at 1 min. 11.80 secs. This placed Regazzoni in the centre of the front row of the starting grid, between Fittipaldi and Hulme, with Ickx in the 2nd row alongside Cervert in the Tyrrell-Cosworth.

At the start, Regazzoni led Fittipaldi, Ickx and Hulme. On the 9th lap Fittipaldi took the lead from the Ferraris and started to pull away from the Swiss driver. On lap 31 Cervert's Tyrrell also passed Regazzoni having inherited third place from Ickx when the Belgian's throttle linkage went out of adjustment. On lap 58 the surviving Ferrari was eliminated when Nanni Galli with the new Tecno crashed and Regazzoni was unable to avoid the fracas, hitting the Tecno and damaging the Ferrari badly enough to put it out of commission.

French Grand Prix

The 1972 French Grand Prix was held on July 2nd at the Charade circuit at Clermont Ferrand.

Ferrari sent three cars, No. 6 for Ickx with No. 5 as a spare car for the Belgian driver. Nanni Galli was on loan from the Tecno team for this event and he was given No. 7. All three cars were reworked to give improved suspension and control at the rear. This was achieved with a new lower wishbone with a rearward running strut from the hub carrier upright mounting to a bracket located under the gearbox. The positive lower positioning of the upright permitted the elimination of a twin forward leading radius arm setup and the substitution of a single unit. This single arm ran from the top of the upright to a location behind the cockpit and above the engine. Because Charade is a low speed circuit, the narrow style nose cowling was used. New airfoils were fitted further behind the normal location and the head fairing extended further to the rear being cone shaped.

The first practice was on the Friday and the practice record stood to the credit of Ickx who had set it in 1970 at 2 min. 58.27 secs. During the Friday session Ickx recorded 2 min. 59.4 secs. with Ferrari No. 5 and 2 min. 56.8 secs with No. 6. However, fastest time of the day went to Cervert with the Tyrrell at 2 min. 55.4 secs.

Galli recorded 3 min. 02.0 secs. On Saturday Ickx recorded 2 min. 57.7 secs. with No. 5 and 2 min. 59.5 secs. with No. 6, with Galli recording 3 min. 03.8 secs. Fastest time of the morning session was Amon's Matra Simca at 2 min. 54.7 secs.

During the second practice session on Saturday, Ickx used No. 5 and recorded 2 min. 55.1 secs., while Galli improved slightly to 3 min. 00.7 secs. Fastest time was again Amon's Matra Simca at 2 min. 53.4 secs. This gave Ickx a position in the second row of the start beside Stewart and behind Amon and Hulme. Galli qualified for the 10th row.

At the start of the race, Amon led and at the end of the first lap it was Amon, Hulme, Stewart and Ickx Ferrari in 4th place. The leading three drew away from the Ferrari and Fittipaldi with the Lotus began to move up on the Belgian. After 19 laps the Lotus was challenging the Ferrari for fourth place. At 20 laps Amon pitted which allowed everyone in the lead group to move up one place. Ickx was driving hard and was putting his wheels off the road in the effort to stay ahead of the Lotus. Fittipaldi bided his time and Ickx's tactics resulted in the Ferrari pitting with a flat tyre on lap 29. This put an end to any Ferrari hopes and Ickx finished in 11th place, one lap behind the winner Stewart, while Galli finished in 13th place also one lap behind.

British Grand Prix

The 1972 British Grand Prix took place at Brands Hatch on July 15th.

Ferrari entered cars for Ickx, Andretti and Nanni Galli. Galli was replaced at the last moment by Andrea Merzario as Galli was required by his contract to drive the Tecno. Andretti because of his US racing commitments was a non starter. Ickx had No. 5 Ferrari with No. 6 as a reserve and Merzario was allocated No. 7. All the cars were slightly modified, the front mounting of the rear airfoil being altered to give a steeper angle of incidence.

On the first practice session on Thursday, the time to aim for was the existing record of 1 min. 23.8 secs., and only Fittipaldi, Ickx and Revson were able to break this time. Fittipaldi was the fastest at 1 min. 22.9 secs. with Ickx using

Ferrari No. 5 at 1 min. 23.4 secs. Merzario recorded 1 min. 26.0 secs.

During the second practice session on Thursday it was Stewart who was fastest at 1 min. 22.4 secs. Ickx recorded 1 min. 22.9 secs. with No. 5 and 1 min. 23.6 secs. with No. 6, Merzario recorded 1 min. 23.9 secs. with his car.

During the Friday practice Ickx was the fastest of all, turning a lap at 1 min. 22.2 secs., with Ferrari No. 5, in Ferrari No. 6 he recorded 1 min. 25.3 secs. and Merzario in No. 7 turned 1 min. 25.9 secs. During the final practice session on Friday, Fittipaldi turned a 1 min. 22.6 secs., while Ickx recorded 1 min. 24.3 secs., in No. 5 and 1 min. 25.1 secs. in No. 6. Merzario improved his time to 1 min. 23.7 secs. in No. 7. As a result of these times, Ickx was on the pole with Fittipaldi next to him in the front row. Merzario was in the 5th row next to Carlos Reutemann in a Brabham.

At the start Ickx led into Paddock Bend and by the second lap had established a lead over Fittipaldi, the two in turn having a considerable lead over the rest. From there on the race continued with the Belgian and the Brazilian drivers increasing their lead over the others steadily. Stewart was third with Merzario's Ferrari holding 13th place. On the 23rd lap the leaders were baulked and Stewart closed up. Ickx braked heavily, throwing Fittipaldi off his pace which let Stewart dash by into 2nd place.

On lap 30 Merzario pitted to replace a flat tyre. Fittipaldi retook 2nd place from Stewart on the 34th lap. Fittipaldi began to press Ickx and the Belgian was already in trouble with a leaking oil cooler which caused his oil pressure to fluctuate. On lap 49 Ickx gave up and both Fittipaldi and Stewart went by. Merzario was trying his best and moved up in the standings, at the end of the race he was in 6th place, one lap behind the winner Fittipaldi.

Austrian Grand Prix

The Austrian Grand Prix was held at the Osterreichring at Zeltweg on August 13th. Ferrari sent three cars, No. 5 for Ickx and No. 7 for Regazzoni; No. 6 was held as a spare car for Ickx.

Regazzoni's car was modified with air collector boxes on either side to duct cold air to the inlets. This layout was unusual as the radius arms on each side from the rear suspension run across the top of the inlets. Because of this, the intake boxes had to enclose the radius arms. A leather boot was fitted around the radius arms at the point where it ran through the end of the intake box.

The Ferraris were plagued with vapour lock and in the attempt to rectify the situation, extra electric fuel pumps were fitted to keep the collector tank full. The pipes were re-routed and insulated but it served no real purpose and the Ferraris would only run a few laps at full performance. Every different gasoline was tried to no avail.

The first practice was on Friday during which Regazzoni lapped in 1 min. 37.20 secs. and Ickx in 1 min. 38.28 secs., compared to Fittipaldi's time with the Lotus of 1 min. 35.97 secs.

During the Saturday practice Ickx recorded 1 min. 37.33 secs., while Regazzoni was able to record fastest time of day as the Ferrari ran well enough for sufficient time to enable him to achieve a 1 min. 36.04 secs. lap. This gave Regazzoni 2nd place on the starting grid next to Fittipaldi. Ickx was positioned in the 5th row of the 2 x 2 grid alongside Ganley's BRM.

At the start, Stewart took the lead from the 2nd row with Regazzoni in 2nd place. The Ferrari was already in trouble hesitating out of the corners and holding up the rest of the group. Fittipaldi was third man up and on lap 5 he went by the Ferrari to take 2nd place. Ickx was running badly in 14th place. On lap 9 Hulme passed Regazzoni for 3rd place and it was all over for the Ferrari. Regazzoni gave up on lap 13 and Ickx on lap 20, both with the same problem in the fuel system that had plagued them in practice. Fittipaldi's black and gold Lotus recorded yet another victory.

German Grand Prix

The German Grand Prix was held at the Nurburgring on July 30th. Ferrari undertook some testing several weeks early and as a result the rear suspension layout and geometry was modified. The new type was first tried out at Clermont Ferrand and the same system used for the Nurburgring event with Ing. Forghieri present to observe the results.

Ferrari entered car No. 5 for Ickx, Regazzoni in No. 7 and Merzario in No. 8. There were two sessions of practice on the Friday with drivers having both to qualify and to try for grid positions. The time to beat was the previous year's best for the cleaned up circuit set by Cervert at 7 min. 20.1 secs. Merzario had a moment when he lost control of his car and hit the bank. During the first Friday session Stewart was fastest at 7 min. 17.20 secs., while Ickx turned a 7 min. 21.99 secs., Regazzoni 7 min. 24.60 secs. and Merzario 7 min. 25.90 secs.

During the second Friday session, Ickx left no doubt as to his ability, recording an outstanding 7 min. 10.0 secs., almost 5 seconds faster than the next best time by Fittipaldi. Regazzoni was very much slower and Merzario was unable to record a time because of his crash.

On Saturday Ickx continued to show that he was master of the Nurburgring by consistently lapping under 7 min. 10 secs., ending up with a 7 min. 07.00 secs., only Stewart and Fittipaldi were able to break the 7 min. 10 second mark besides Ickx. Regazzoni's best was 7 min. 13.4 secs. and Merzario recorded a 7 min. 30 secs., after his car was repaired. Ickx had the pole for the 2 x 2 grid with Regazzoni in the 4th row and Merzario in the 11th row. As the cars rushed into the South Curve it was touch and go as to who would take the lead. Ickx proved to have the best line and took the lead ahead of Peterson's March and Regazzoni's Ferrari.

At the end of the first lap Ickx had a 3 second lead having covered the opening lap in 7 min. 29.1 secs. Fittipaldi displaced Regazzoni from 3rd place and on the second lap Ickx was down to 7 min. 20.7 secs. On the third lap the race settled down with Ickx way out in front, then Peterson and Fittipaldi close together followed by Regazzoni with Stewart on his heels. Merzario was back in the pack involved in a battle for 16th place. Ickx's 3rd lap was covered in 7 min 19.0 secs., extending his lead to 10 seconds.

On lap 4 Ickx improved his time to 7 min. 16.7 secs., while Stewart was still trying to get by Regazzoni. On the 6th lap Ickx turned 7 min. 16.2 secs. and by half distance he seemed certain of victory if nothing happened to his car. Regazzoni still held off Stewart. On the 8th lap

Ickx continued his record breaking run with a 7 min. 14.7 secs. extending his lead to 15 seconds over Fittipaldi. Peterson's spin let Regazzoni and Stewart into 3rd and 4th places. On the 10th lap Fittipaldi's Lotus began to smoke and Regazzoni closed up. The gearbox of the Lotus gave out and started a minor fire as Regazzoni took over second place.

On Ickx's tenth lap he recorded 7 min. 13.6 secs., and by lap 11 he had a 46 second lead although the Ferrari did not sound as good as it had previously. Merzario pitted with low oil pressure but was told to continue and try to finish. Stewart was still on Regazzoni's tail trying to pass, at *Hocheichen* he made his move and the two cars touched wheels, Stewart came off second best and spun out breaking a right front suspension. Regazzoni was now free to run a comfortable race in second place.

Ickx won in 1 hr. 42 min. 12.3 secs., 187.7 k p h with Regazzoni second in 1 hr. 43 min. 00.6 secs. and Merzario in 11th place, 1 lap behind to give Ferrari his most outstanding result of the 1972 Grand Prix season.

Italian Grand Prix

The Italian Grand Prix was held on 10th September 1972 at Monza. The circuit was changed from the previous year's race by the addition of chicanes at the Vialone or Ascari curve and on the pit straight leading into the Curva Grande. The new Ferrari 312B/3 was tested, the design having a new chassis, suspension and bodywork to conform with the 1973 CSI regulations on fuel tank protection and width. Engine and gearbox were basically the existing units. However, the car was deemed unready for the Monza event and Ferrari sent three of the B2 types, No. 5 for Ickx, No. 7 for Regazzoni and No. 8 for Andretti. The three cars had the narrow nose cowlings with the side fins instead of the full width type cowling.

Many drivers had difficulty with the new chicane setup which slowed the times over 10 seconds compared to the previous year's times. Andretti put his wheel on the curb of the chicane and spun.

Stewart was fastest during Friday's practice at 1 min. 35.82 secs. with Ickx second fastest at 1 min. 36.0 secs. Regazzoni 5th fastest at 1 min.

36.52 secs., and Andretti 7th fastest at 1 min. 36.86 secs. On the Saturday the weather was very hot and Ickx recorded 1 min. 35.63 secs., Regazzoni 1 min. 35.83 secs. and Andretti 1 min. 36.32 secs. This put Ickx on the pole, Regazzoni in the second row and Andretti in the 4th row of the 2 x 2 starting grid.

Stewart, who shared the front row with Ickx, broke at the start and Ickx took an immediate lead with Regazzoni 2nd and Andretti 4th, the Ferrari being split only by Fittipaldi's Lotus. On lap 14 Ickx let Regazzoni by to take the lead but on lap 17 Regazzoni found Pace's March in the way at the exit of the chicane and brushed the March, breaking the Ferrari's left rear suspension and setting a minor fire which was quickly controlled. However, the Ferrari was out of the race. Ickx retook the lead and on lap 23 Andretti pitted to change a flat right front tyre.

The Lotus of Fittipaldi did not seem to be able to make up anything on the Ferrari and just as the scene seemed set for the rest of the race Ickx's engine quit and he coasted to the pits on lap 46. A short-circuit had eliminated all the electrical system. It was left for Andretti to finish 7th for Ferrari, 1 lap behind the winner Fittipaldi.

Canadian Grand Prix

The Canadian Grand Prix was held at Mosport on 24th September 1972. Ferrari entered three cars, No. 5 for Ickx, No. 6 for Merzario and No. 7 for Regazzoni. However, Merzario was withdrawn at the last moment and No. 6 was held as a spare car. The previous record for the circuit stood to Ickx in a Brabham set in 1969 at 1 min. 18.1 secs. Stewart had lapped in practice at 1 min. 15.3 secs. in the 1971 event.

First official practice was on Friday during which Ickx went off the road and damaged the Ferrari's suspension. Stewart recorded fastest lap at 1 min. 14.5 secs. Ickx best was 1 min. 19.3 secs., but Regazzoni clocked a 1 min. 15.3 secs.

On Saturday morning it was Revson who was fastest in the McLaren at 1 min. 13.6 secs. while Ickx was back on the track with a 1 min. 14.7 secs., while third fastest was Regazzoni in 1 min. 15.2 secs. On Saturday afternoon, Peterson was fastest at 1 min. 14.0 secs. Regazzoni improved to 1 min. 14.5 secs. and Ickx dropped back to 1

min. 15.9 secs. The practice times gave Ickx and Regazzoni positions in the 3rd row for the start.

At the start it was Peterson, Stewart and Revson with Ickx in 4th place and Regazzoni in 6th. Ickx moved up to 2nd but by lap 20 he had passed Revson and Fittipaldi. At the halfway point Ickx had to pit with a punctured front tyre and to have the electrical system attended to. Stewart then led Peterson, Revson and Fittipaldi with Regazzoni in 5th place. As Peterson fell out and Fittipaldi had problems, Regazzoni moved up to 3rd on lap 57 but with seven laps to go he was involved in a spin when he found his way blocked by another driver. The incident dropped him to 5th while Ickx, after his pit stop, could manage no better than 12th place.

US Grand Prix

The United States Grand Prix was held at Watkins Glen on 8th October 1972. Ferrari entered three cars with Andretti in No. 6 and Ickx and Regazzoni having their Canadian GP cars Nos. 5 and 7 respectively. On the Friday, Jackie Stewart was fastest in practice at 1 min. 40.48 secs. Regazzoni was the best of the Ferraris at 1 min. 41.95 secs., with Andretti at 1 min. 42.48 secs. and Ickx at 1 min. 42.60 secs. The bad weather on Saturday morning prevented any good times, Peterson's March was fastest at 2 min. 05.29 secs. and Ickx second fastest at 2 min. 06.69 secs; the other two Ferraris did not run.

In the afternoon conditions were better, fastest time being set by Carlos Pace at 1 min. 55.37 secs. with Regazzoni at 1 min. 55.88 secs., Andretti 1 min. 58.31 secs. and Ickx at 2 min. 00.24 secs. These times placed Regazzoni in the 2nd row, Andretti in the 4th row and Ickx in the 5th row for the start.

At the start Stewart led with Regazzoni rushing through to take second place but clashing with Reutemann and Revson. On the first lap, however, the Ferraris came round in 5th, 6th and 7th places with Ickx leading Regazzoni and Andretti. By the 23rd lap, Andretti was slowed with tyre problems while Regazzoni fell back to 11th when his exhaust system began to break up, losing him considerable power. Ickx hung on to 6th place and

Andretti increased speed in the rain. Two laps from the end, Ickx was up in 4th place but he had an exhaust break off and drag on the ground sending up showers of sparks, as a result Peterson beat the Ferrari over the line by a fraction and Ickx had to be content with 5th, Andretti was 6th one lap behind and Regazzoni 8th, also a lap behind.

At the end of the 1972 season Ferrari announced the construction of a new Formula 1 car to be known as the F1/B3, this was to retain the well known 12-cylinder Boxer engine but the chassis was to be completely new.

The B3 was totally built at Maranello under the supervision of engineers Colombo and Forghieri and photos of the new car appeared in the motoring press.

The car was tested at Fiorano and Misano, a great deal of the testing being done by Merzario.

After the tests the car suddenly went into limbo and was conveniently forgotten. Ferrari not unnaturally had no apparent comments.

Local opinion has it that the very short wheelbase was one major defect making the car very tricky to handle.

The name F1/B3 was then applied to a totally new design which is described further on in the text when it made its appearance in the 1973 Spanish Grand Prix.

Whatever happened to the abortive B3/72 design is as yet not known but in true Ferrari tradition there is very little doubt that any useful parts were used for the construction of something else.

1973

Argentine Grand Prix

The Argentine Grand Prix was held at Buenos Aires on 28th January 1973. While still working on the development of the new B3, Ferrari sent out two of the previous year's B2s Nos. 005 and 008 for Ickx (race number 18) and Merzario (race number 20) respectively.

Regazzoni's BRM set the fastest lap at 1 min. 10.54 secs. with Ickx qualifying for the 2nd row of the grid at 1 min. 11.01 secs. and Merzario for the 7th row at 1 min. 12.39.

Ickx ran in 5th place at the start and had a great dice with Revson's McLaren for that place until the Ferrari had tyre problems. Ickx was

further delayed by a broken throttle rod but managed a creditable 4th place with a stuttering engine. Merzario brought the 2nd Ferrari home in 9th place.

Brazilian Grand Prix

The Brazilian Grand Prix was held at Interlagos at Sao Paulo on 11th February. Ferrari sent the two cars from Argentina. Ickx again had 312B/2 No. 005 (race number 9) and Merzario 312B/2 No. 008 (race number 10).

Ronnie Peterson's Lotus set fastest lap at 2 min. 30.5 secs. with Ickx qualifying the B2 on the front row at 2 min. 32.0 secs. Merzario qualified for the 7th row at 2 min. 37.7.

During the race Fittipaldi's Lotus dominated from start to finish but with Ickx well up with the front runners until the 4th lap when he picked up a piece of glass in his right rear tyre which began to deflate. When Ickx finally had to pit to replace the tyre he was by mistake given one of Merzario's tyres which was one inch narrower. This did not help roadholding and Ickx lost his chance to tackle the leaders. Nevertheless the Ferraris ran well through the race, Merzario finishing 4th and Ickx in fifth place.

South African Grand Prix

The South African Grand Prix was held at Kyalami on 3rd March. It was hoped that the new B3 would be ready in time but it was not so and Ferrari sent one of the B2s that had run in Argentina (No. 005) for Ickx and No. 006 for Merzario, the other Argentine car (No. 008) having been returned directly to Maranello.

On the Wednesday practice, fastest lap was by Hulme's McLaren at 1 min. 16.42 secs. Merzario turned 1 min. 18.46 and Ickx 1 min. 19.08. On Thursday, Merzario recorded 1 min. 18.45 secs. and Ickx 1 min. 19.03. On the Thursday too, Ickx decided to try out Merzario's car and with the car bearing the number 9T (Ickx having race number 8 and Merzario race number 9) he improved his time to 1 min. 17.16 secs. On the Friday he continued to practice in No. 9T and recorded 1 min. 17.58. After this he made his decision to use Merzario's car for the race.

Merzario, on Friday used Ickx car bearing the No. 8T and turned 1 min. 17.64 secs; one of these times compared to Hulme's fastest on

Friday at 1 min. 16.28. Ickx placed in the 5th row at the start and Merzario in the 6th row.

On the 2nd lap of the race the South African driver Charlton began a chain accident and Ickx made contact with Regazzoni's BRM and was forced to retire with a damaged wheel.

After the clean up, Merzario was in 8th place and by attrition amongst the others, moved up to 6th place. A spin dropped him back to 8th and finally after some more dropouts he finished 4th, one lap behind the winner Stewart.

Spanish Grand Prix

The Spanish Grand Prix was held at Montjuich Park at Barcelona on 29th April. The lap record had been set by Ickx at 1 min. 25.1 secs. in 1971 and was the standard to beat.

The new Ferrari 312/B3 finally made its appearance but due to the unsatisfactory results during testing at Monza, Merzario's entry was withdrawn and both new cars (Nos. 010 and 011) were at the disposal of Ickx who began practice on Friday in No. 011 which had side radiators and bore race number 8, entry number for Merzario. Ickx then switched to No. 010 which bore race number 7. He covered only a few laps before he had ignition failure. He had recorded 1 min. 26.9 secs. in 011 and 1 min. 24.6 secs. in 010 compared to Peterson's Lotus which was fastest at 1 min. 23.4.

On Friday afternoon Ickx recorded 1 min. 24.2 secs. in 010 and on Saturday 1 min. 23.5 secs. also in 010. This gave him a position on the third row of the 2x2 grid for the start.

At the start Ickx ran in 9th place involved in a battle with Follmer's Shadow but on lap 36 the Ferrari's brakes had begun to fail and the time lost in bleeding the system in the pits dropped him so far back that the completion of the race just became an exercise in testing the new car. Ickx finished 12th and last covering 69 laps to the winner Fittipaldi's 75 laps.

The 1973 F1 Ferrari

The new Type 312B/3 Ferrari which made its first appearance at the 1973 Spanish Grand Prix was unique in Ferrari history as it was a true monocoque as opposed to the previous Ferrari technique of using tubing with aluminium sheet wrapping around a structure which Ferrari himself referred to as an 'Aero monocoque'.

Due to the constant strikes and trouble with the Italian Metal Worker's Union, Ferrari had the first two monocoques built at T.C. Prototypes at Northampton, England. The Maranello workshops completed the assembly of the car.

The front suspension was made up of wide-based wishbones and fabricated rocker arms sprung by inboard spring/dampers.

A pair of triangular magnesium castings were bolted to the front of the monocoque and served as locations for the pivot point of the rocker arms, an anti - roll bar and the steering rack.

Also attached to these castings was a tubular structure providing the location for the forward mounting point of the lower wishbones. This structure also carried the clutch and brake master cylinders and in the case of the front radiator car (No. 010) carried the radiator core, No. 011 having been designed with side radiators.

The front uprights carried outboard ventilated disc brakes tucked into the wheels and additional cooling to them was provided by scoops.

At the rear, a magnesium bridge-type casting was provided at the extremities of which were located the outboard spring/damper units with extra strengthening from tubular supports. The casting also located the gearbox to which were attached the inboard ventilated disc brakes.

The gearbox drove through shafts splined at the inboard end. Long radius rods located on the chassis gave additional support to the rear uprights.

The lower part of the suspension was achieved by reversed wishbones mounted under the engine together with rear-facing tie rods located by a casting bolted to the gearbox.

The method of hanging the engine from a beam as in the Type B1 and B2 Ferraris was abandoned and the engine of the B3 was a completely stressed member.

Immediately behind the back of the monocoque and the engine, a cast magnesium sandwich plate was provided. Two engine bearing plates were bolted to this and the engine in turn bolted to this structure. The sandwich plate had holes in it to allow the rollover bar to be fitted, this bar having both front and rear support bars.

The steering wheel was mounted vertically to the ground, the shaft running longitudinally to a point about 12 inches from the wheel at which point a universal joint connected it at a steep angle down to the rack.

Fuel was carried in the monocoque in tanks both sides of the drivers hips.

During early tests it was found that the side radiator car gave trouble with overheating. An attempt was made to improve this by extending the ducts but this proved to be no solution. One car was therefore converted to a front-radiator system and body changes resulted. A new nose with an air cooling opening was fitted and new side panels were required.

The newly required deformable structure rule was solved by Ferrari by providing a detachable sandwich made of foam and fibreglass.

At the time of writing, nothing was available on the new engine, however, some external differences could be seen, the alternator being relocated at the top of the engine and the methods of attachment of the engine indicated that there were probably some changes in castings to accommodate the convenience of attachment.

Belgian Grand Prix

The Belgian Grand Prix was held at Zolder on 20th May. Ferrari entered Ickx and Merzario but the latter was a non-starter. Ickx had the two B3s No. 011 having been changed from side to front radiators and had a new oil tank and scavenging system piping which proved to be unsuitable. No. 010 sported a new airfoil mounting of sheet steel replacing the tubular-type mounting. The fastest lap on Friday was by Fittipaldi's Lotus at 1 min. 26.08 with Ickx at 1 min. 27.31 secs. On Saturday, Ickx improved to 1 min. 25.87 and further improved to 1 min. 23.10 although Peterson's Lotus had taken the pole at 1 min. 22.46 secs. This gave Ickx a place in the 2nd row of the start but he had to stop with a sudden drop in oil pressure and it was found that a needle from a bearing had found its way into the oil pump and seizing it sheared the drive. The pump assembly from the spare car was fitted but in the race the car retired after 6 laps with exactly the same problem. The culprit was a timing case bearing failing and shedding

another needle roller into the oil pump.

Monaco Grand Prix

For the Monaco Grand Prix on 3rd June Ferrari entered two of the new cars race number 3 for Ickx (312B3 No. 010) and race number 4 for Merzario (312B3 No. 011).

On Thursday, the fastest qualifier was Stewart at 1 min. 28.5 secs. with Ickx 3rd fastest at 1 min. 29.3. Merzario recorded 1 min. 30.3 secs.

On Friday Stewart improved to 1 min. 27.5 and Ickx, after registering a time of 1 min. 40.4 secs, hit the kerb and damaged his front suspension. Merzario recorded 1 min. 29.8 secs. and Ickx turned out in Merzario's car with the number 4T painted on it and turned a 1 min. 31.4.

On Saturday, Ickx original car was fixed and he improved his time to 1 min. 28.7 secs. with Merzario at 1 min. 29.3.

These times gave Ickx a position in the fourth row and Merzario a position in the 8th row of the starting grid.

At the start, Ickx was up in the lead group and was in 3rd place when the Ferrari broke its right hand drive shaft at the splines on lap 45. Merzario was way back and retired on lap 59 with low oil pressure.

Swedish Grand Prix

In 1973 Sweden held her first Formula 1 Grand Prix race, the venue being Anderstorp on 17th June.

Ferrari sent two of his B3s for Ickx (race number 3) car No. 010 and car No. 011 being marked T3.

Ickx did not use 011 at all, doing his practising in 010.

Fastest lap on Friday was set by Cervert's Tyrrell at 1 min. 24.740 secs. Ickx recorded 1 min. 26.778 secs. which he improved during the afternoon to 1 min. 26.168. On Saturday morning he further improved to 1 min. 25.869 secs. and recorded a 1 min. 25.604 on Saturday afternoon. This gave him a place on the 4th row of the start but the performance of the B3 was uninspiring, Ickx finally finishing in 8th place.

French Grand Prix

The 1973 Grand Prix of France was held at the Paul Ricard circuit at Castellet on 1st July.

Ferrari entered Ickx and Merzario and sent 3 cars. A completely new B3 No. 012 for Merzario and 010 and 011 for Ickx.

Early during practice, Ickx spun and damaged the rear aerofoil and 010 was repaired with parts from 011.

On the Friday, fastest lap was set by Stewart's Tyrell at 1 min. 48.37 secs., with Ickx at 1 min. 51.44. Ickx at 1 min. 51.44. Ickx also turned a time in 011 bearing the number 3T at 1 min. 51.92.

On the Saturday, Merzario turned 1 min. 51.17 and Ickx 1 min. 51.70, after which his car was torn down as the fibreglass under the monocoque had come loose.

During the Saturday afternoon practice, Ickx turned 1 min. 51.48 secs. and Merzario 1 min. 51.53. This placed Merzario (number 4) in the 4th row of the starting grid and Ickx (number 3) in the 5th row.

At the start, Merzario had problems starting his car and as a result ran in the back of the field. Ickx did not seem to be showing any enthusiasm, running around in 8th place, and it was not until Stewart came by to lap him that he began racing. This late effort took some effect and he placed 5th at the finish, Merzario finishing 7th.

British Grand Prix

The 1973 British Grand Prix was held at Silverstone on 4th July, Ferrari entered two cars for Ickx and Merzario but only Ickx made an appearance.

Ickx used car 010 (race number 3) and kept 012 (race number 4) as a spare car.

Fastest time on the Friday practice session was by Hulme's McLaren at 1 min. 16.5 secs., with Ickx turning 1 min. 18.9. On Saturday Peterson's Lotus was fastest at 1 min. 16.3 and Ickx could not improve his previous day's time, recording 1 min. 19.2 secs. This placed Ickx in the 8th row of the starting grid and during the race he was never among the leaders and having to content himself with dicing with some of the lesser lights. He finally finished in 8th place.

Dutch Grand Prix

The Dutch Grand Prix was held on 29th July at Zandvoort. Ferrari was still trying to sort out the problems which had made the new B3s so uncompetitive in the previous races and as a result there was no entry from the team in the Dutch event.

As the season progressed it became apparent that all was not well with the new B3. Jackie Ickx in an interview with Mike Doodson published in *Autosport* on 9th August 1973, revealed his dissatisfaction. He mentioned that he was unable to do well with the car and gave the example that he was only 20th fastest at Silverstone. He felt that the car was very difficult to drive, stating 'You can't feel what it wants to do. It is relatively unpredictable and it is not possible to be competitive in Formula 1 today with a car like that.'

The matter came to a head and Ickx met with Ferrari to determine the future. The situation was amicably settled with Ferrari agreeing to release Ickx from his contract and allowing him to freelance.

The Ferrari programme called for extensive attempts to improve the situation concerning the B3 and Ickx would be free to test and even rejoin the team by mutual agreement.

Ickx had already indicated that he would not be with the team in 1974 and it was therefore of no great value to either parties for him to be included in the development of a car that he would not be driving during the 1974 season. He quoted difficulties in communication with Ing. Colombo, the development engineer of the B3, and stressed that the only way a present day Formula 1 team could be successful was as a tight knit family. In the circumstances, it would be better to part company so that neither party would suffer.

Ickx had also faced serious criticism in the Italian Press which accused him of having lost interest and the will to win. Ickx performance on the Nurburgring for the McLaren racing team successfully put paid to these allegations.

German Grand Prix

The German Grand Prix was held at the Nurburgring on 5th August but the Ferraris of Ickx and Merzario were non-starters. Because of his discussions with Ferrari, Ickx was freelancing and drove for the McLaren team.

Austrian Grand Prix

The Austrian Grand Prix was held at Zeltweg on 19th August 1973.

Ferrari sent one B3 for Merzario No. 011 (race number 4). After the dismal performance of the B3 in previous events Ing. Forghieri had been given chassis No. 011 to see what he could do to improve matters. He applied knowledge gained from his work with the 1973 Sports/Prototype cars.

The car was completely revised and the front radiator system dropped and replaced by thin radiators fitted on either side of the cockpit the air being taken in low between the wheels and exhausting out of the top of the side sponsons. Additional cooling was provided by passing the water from the engine through finned tubes in the sponson.

The saddle type oil tank over the transmission that had been part of the aerofoil was modified to be along the right hand side of the engine and an oil cooler was fitted to the left.

The Boxer-engine double-duct layout was modified from the previous position of one air intake on each side surrounding the suspension rods.

A new chisel shaped nose with a large full-width aerofoil above it was fitted and a large central airscoop was provided to perform the function of the double air intake system to the engine. The scoop internally split and ducted the air horizontally to the intakes of the two banks of cylinders. The suspension geometry had also been changed.

The car performed well and Merzario recorded 1 min. 36.42 secs. compared to Fittipaldi's Lotus time of 1 min. 34.98. This placed Merzario in the 3rd row of the starting grid.

However, Ferrari had problems breaking the first engine after only two laps of practice. The replacement engine lost power and the 3rd engine was not much better. During the race, Merzario, running briefly in 4th place, collided with Cervert's Tyrrell. The Ferrari continued to run very well in 6th place but the engine was beginning to lose power and Merzario eventually finished in 7th place.

Italian Grand Prix

The 1973 Italian Grand Prix was held at Monza on 9th September, Ferrari entered Merzario in a B3 (race number 4), car No. 012.

Ickx was hired back on the team as a free-lancer in Ferrari No. 010 (race number 3).

Merzario qualified at 1 min. 36.37 secs. for row 4 of the 2 x 2 starting grid and Ickx was in row 7 at 1 min. 36.99. In the race, Merzario crashed on lap 2 and Ickx could do no better than 8th.

Canadian Grand Prix

The Canadian Grand Prix was held at Mosport on 23rd September 1973. Ferrari entered just one car for Arturo Merzario (race number 4).

Merzario qualified for the 10th row of the starting grid and the Ferrari was never impressive, finishing in 15th place.

US Grand Prix

The Grand Prix of the USA was held on 7th October at Watkins Glen, New York.

Ferrari entered a lone 312/B3 for Merzario as Ickx was again freelancing and driving for Iso.

Merzario qualified at 1 min. 41.455 secs. compared to Peterson's Lotus time of 1 min. 39.651 for the pole position. This placed the Ferrari in the 5th row of the 2 x 2 grid and, in the race, the Ferrari did not distinguish itself, finishing in 16th place.

Summary

To sum up the 1973 Grand Prix season there is no doubt that it was one of the worst that Ferrari had experienced.

In the earlier part of the season when Ferrari was running the earlier 1972 312B/2s (Argentina, Brazil and South Africa) at least the results were adequate. A Ferrari started in the front row of the Brazilian Grand Prix and the two cars finished 4th and 5th.

In Argentina a Ferrari started in the 2nd row and finished 4th.

In the South African Grand Prix a Ferrari started in row 5 but finished 4th.

Then the new 312B/3 appeared at Barcelona and started in the 3rd row finishing 12th and last, not a very auspicious beginning.

At the Belgian Grand Prix the B/3 started in the 3rd row which gave some encouragement but the car did not finish.

At Monaco it was a 4th row start but both cars failed to finish.

In Sweden another 4th row start and an 8th place finish.

At the Grand Prix of France a 4th row start with a 5th place result.

At the British Grand Prix an 8th row start and an 8th place finish. There were no entries in the Dutch or German GPs while attempts were made to make the cars more competitive.

At the Grand Prix of Austria a 3rd row start was achieved with a much modified car the result was a 7th place finish.

At Monza, on home ground, things were just as bad, a 4th row start and an 8th place in the results. In Canada things deteriorated even more, a starting position in the 10th row and a 15th place finish. In the USA Grand Prix a 5th row start and a 16th place finish. It was a disastrous year to say the least. The parting of the ways with Ickx became a certainty when, towards the end of the 1973 season, Ferrari announced that his drivers for 1974 were to be Regazzoni and Lauda.

After the announcement that Ferrari had signed on Regazzoni and Lauda for 1974, there was some furore in the Italian Press about the dropping of Merzario from the team. Apparently Ferrari was dissatisfied with the performance of the Italian driver and a parting of the ways came about.

Another major event at the end of the season was the re-emergence of Ing. Forghieri who had been dismissed by the Italian press as 'being on the way out'. Apparently this was not so and it was Ing. Colombo who was 'out', being re-assigned by FIAT Company to take a position with their other subsidiary OM.

CHAPTER TEN
Experimental and special Ferraris

IN the more than twenty eight year period in which Enzo Ferrari has been building cars bearing his own name his fertile mind has been responsible for the production of over 260 different models of single-seater racing cars. As is to be expected, in the production of these models there have been many experimental types, some being successful and others a failure. Ferrari has never been hesitant in putting his ideas into concrete shape rather than arguing the pros and cons in theory on the drawing board. His system has proved itself more than satisfactory in most cases although in others he undoubtedly made mistakes.

With their successes in international racing it is not surprising that much has been written about Ferrari.

However, very little has been said about the designs that eventually led to the known successful models. Even less is known about the projects that were tested and then pigeon-holed. The main reason for the lack of information on the experimental Ferraris has been Modena and Maranello's own reticence to admit that they produced something that did not work.

Experimental cars that have proved successful are also difficult to trace as the factory usually maintained a tight security guard on these designs and often as not the cars only appeared briefly on the Modena test track before being returned to the factory to be completely modified in the light of new information. Despite these difficulties, information has leaked out and former employees of Ferrari have been less hesitant to talk after they have found employment elsewhere. From these and other sources it has been possible to put together an accurate picture of behind-the-scenes development and it is a subject which because of its interest is worth while discussing at length.

The Experimental and Special Ferraris produced can be arranged into four groups:

1. Experimental cars that were raced and used in the development of a definite type;

2. Cars built for special purposes or to customers' special order;

3. Experimental designs that were never seen on the race track and which were shelved;

4. Specials produced independently from the factory but based almost entirely on Ferrari components (only the Thinwall Special Ferrari has been considered for discussion in this group).

Of these four groups the first is the most important in the history of Ferrari. Here we find the acceptance of a basic idea and its development through various stages to a highly successful end product, a process which lacks the colour of the weird and wonderful 'one off' experiments that comprise the second and third groups, but which is none the less a fascinating study for the racing enthusiast.

The Type 375 F1

The most outstanding example of the first group is the development of the type 375 F1 4.5-litre Ferrari, a car which caused a definite change in the history of motor racing. In the evolution of this car, several stages, each with varying success, were passed before the final goal was reached.

The car of the later type 500 2-litre 4-cylinder was an immediate success and its only development was to 'improve the breed', consequently we find an absence of experimental types of this model.

The development of type 625 2.5-litre unsupercharged actually began before that of the 2-litre although the 2.5-litre Formula came after the 2-litre Formula 2. It was just an example of Ferrari's anticipation which kept him in the lead in the early days of his career as a constructor. The 2.5-litre unsupercharged prototype was an immediate success and did away with the need for further experiments both in the 2.5-litre and 2-litre categories, although naturally these designs were subject to continual improvement.

The Squalo and Supersqualo

After this series of first-rate designs we come to Ferrari's greatest failure, the Squalo and Supersqualo models. Ferrari had realized the need for replacement of the highly successful but ageing 4-cylinder unsupercharged cars and decided to embark on a new design. Two experimental type 553 2-litre cars were produced in time for the last of the old 2-litre Formula races at Monza; these served as prototypes for the type 555, 2.5-litre cars for the forthcoming season and were the only experimental cars produced for this unsuccessful series. The failure of these cars was due to Ferrari abandoning the system which had served him so well with the development of the 4.5-litre. Instead he was willing to throw a makeshift design into the fray in the hope that he could stem the decline of the old reliable types 500 and 625. His project was not radical enough to meet the advanced opposition from Maserati, Lancia and Mercedes Benz.

Although the Squalo and Supersqualo looked impressive and different to the spectator, the new designs were nothing more than a rehash of the 500 and 625 models. They utilized the same basic engine and suspension with a chassis that was purely a tubular ladder-type frame with a superstructure for additional strength. In this way, the design could not hope to compete with the more advanced multi-tube and spaceframe designs from other factories.

No further experimental types of the Squalo and Supersqualo were built although there were many engine, chassis and suspension changes.

The Squalos represented a stale period in Ferrari thinking as it was rather obvious that no amount of minor modification could turn an inherently poor and already out-of-date design into a race winner. The situation was saved for

Ferrari in two ways, one, by the fortunate gift of the Lancia material after that company decided to withdraw from racing and two, by a house cleaning in the technical department with the appointment of new consultants and designers.

The Lancia equipment provided Ferrari with yet another world championship, but the fact that the cars were not his own product did not altogether please Ferrari. He planned to rebuild the Lancia design completely. In doing so he produced two experimental cars which merit only brief discussion as they were of minor importance and neither contributed anything to the final true Ferrari version of the Lancia. The 1957 performance of the V8 Ferraris showed that the 'new blood' was not up to the task. Both Hawthorn and Collins commented after the final race of the season that the cars were in fact slower than the 1956 Lancia-based version. The solution was again to change some of the staff, the most important being the appointment of Vittorio Jano as consultant.

The 246 Dino

The result was the beginning of another upward trend for Ferrari with the birth of the 246 Dino model. The engine design represented a considerable advance which would stand Ferrari in good stead for some time, but the rest of the car was nothing remarkable. The new engine nevertheless gave the car a sufficient advantage to win another world championship for Ferrari. In the production of the 246 Dino design, Ferrari followed his old policy of putting an experimental car in the field. Once again the system met with success but no more experimental types were forthcoming for a long time until Ferrari was forced into the realization that the front-engined Dino design was no longer able to deal with the more advanced British chassis designs. Finally Ferrari broke down on his anti-rear-engined stand and after a year playing around, measuring Cooper and other chassis he once again threw an experimental prototype in the field.

Once more the basic idea was a success and eventually led to the 1961 World Championship. His apparent superiority in the 1961 season caused him to be totally unprepared for the surprise of the 1962 season. British technology in the engine design department had caught up with his designs and as he was already behind in chassis development, his cars had to take a back seat again..

In the second group of cars, those built for special purposes and to customers' special order represent a totally different facet in the history of Ferrari. This group includes various cars designed to run in the Indianapolis chassis. This project showed that Ferrari never had any real grasp of the problems set by the Indianapolis track; as a result all the efforts ended in failure.

Also included in this group are the odd assortment of special cars built to customers' requirements. Ferrari was always extremely reluctant to produce single-seater cars to special order, mainly because the production of such cars interfered with the work on his own factory Formula cars. Added to this was the fact that Ferrari had very little confidence that customers could do much good for the factory's name with such productions. On some occasions when he did feel that something could be gained he agreed to produce special cars for events in which the factory did not intend to participate.

At best, these cars were always a compromise, no great thought went into their design and they were usually made up out of already available parts.

In the third group we find the experiments which Ferrari is least willing to discuss. Here are the engines intended for racing boats, experimental Indianapolis engines and the complete failures.

GROUP 1 – EXPERIMENTAL CARS USED IN DEVELOPMENT

Enzo Ferrari's 1.5-litre two stage supercharged car showed great promise but Ferrari was not altogether convinced that it was the answer to the all conquering 158 Alfa Romeo. He had for some time been watching the big French unsupercharged Talbots. On many occasions he had been bothered by these lumbering cars which ran through the average Grand Prix without refuelling. His supercharged cars always had to stop for fuel and often as not

the Talbots were able to take advantage of this and come out the winners. With these Talbot successes against much more powerful cars Ferrari began to realize that a really efficient unsupercharged engine taking advantage of the 4.5-litre limit, would be more than a match for the fuel-hungry Alfa Romeos.

The 275 F1

The problem was dropped on the desk of a new man Aurelio Lampredi who had replaced Colombo as chief designer. The Swiss driver Rudolf Fischer had been negotiating with the factory to buy a car for Formula 1 events and Ferrari saw his opportunity to do some extensive experimenting. He convinced Fischer to take a special car, hinting that better things would be available if the Swiss went along with the idea. Fischer's special car was made up of a swing-axle long wheelbase chassis from one of the 1.5-litre supercharged cars, and a highly tuned 2.5-litre V12 cylinder sports car engine. It was known as the type 212 F1.

Not content with waiting for results from Fischer's car, Ferrari ordered a second model built with the same type of engine but going a step further by using a De Dion chassis which had originally been designed for the 1.5-litre twin stage supercharged car. Both cars made their debut at Syracuse; both showed promise the factory car placing 2nd and Fischer's 3rd.

Fischer continued to complete a satisfactory season, regularly placing in the prize money. The factory car ran once more at Pau where it retired with steering troubles.

After Pau Ferrari made up his mind; the 2.5-litre had served its purpose and was put into retirement; preparations were made to build a new car. For this second stage of Ferrari's plan a 3.3-litre engine was prepared with a bore and stroke of 72 x 68 mm. Only two of these engines ever existed, the second being used for a 'one off' sports car. The 3.3-litre engine was fitted into a swing-axle long wheelbase chassis because the De Dion chassis from the 2.5-litre was being modified for use at a later date. This 3.3-litre type 275 F1 made its first appearance for the Belgian Grand Prix at Spa. It was significant that Ascari preferred it for the race to the supercharged 1.5-litre. He drove the 3.3-litre to 5th place ahead of Villoresi who had the latest supercharged model. The 275 F1 was then sent to Rheims but the circuit was considered too fast for the car and it was withdrawn before the race.

The 340 F1

While these tests under actual racing conditions were going on, Ferrari was busy building yet another version, the type 340 F1, this time a 4.1-litre. This capacity was obtained by increasing the bore to 80 mm and leaving the stroke at 68 mm as in the 3.3-litre. A completely new chassis was designed for the new model based on the experiences with the 2.5-litre De Dion version. The wheel base was reduced to 7 ft 6 in. with the front and rear tread of 4 ft 2 in. and 4 ft 0 in. respectively. This new car appeared at the Grand Prix des Nations at Geneva in company with the 3.3-litre, the latter having been modified and installed in the De Dion chassis from the dismantled 2.5-litre. Geneva marked the end of the line for the 1.5-litre supercharged Ferrari, the two unsupercharged prototypes put up a tremendous performance taking 2nd and 3rd places on the starting line up in the face of a full team of Alfa Romeos.

The race itself was not so fortunate for Ferrari. Ascari put up a sensational performance only to retire a few laps from the end with a blown head gasket. Only Fangio of the Alfa team had been able to get by Ascari and even then could not pull ahead by more than half a second per lap. Villoresi also ran close company to the Alfas but had a serious crash seven laps from the end. Despite their non-finish at Geneva, great things were expected at Monza for the Italian Grand Prix. The Alfa Romeo camp's confidence was badly shaken when Ferrari announced that the 4.1-litre was being relegated to No. 3 team car. The spearhead of the attack would be two completely new 4.5-litre models.

Ferrari used the same chassis he had adopted for the 4.1-litre; in the engine department a new crankshaft was fitted increasing the stroke to 75.5 mm which, with the bore of 80 mm, gave a capacity of 4498-cc. The pace at the start of the race was terrific. Ascari showed in no uncertain terms that Ferrari's theory had been right. The unsupercharged car led the whole of the Alfa Romeo team but retired on the twenty-second lap much to the relief of the Alfa Corsa organization.

However, the battle was not over. Serafini, who had been running in sixth place, was called in and Ascari took over working his way up into 2nd place by brilliant driving, a position which he held until the end of the race.

With their victory at Monza, Alfa Romeo already had the world championship in the bag so they decided to avoid the Ferrari opposition at Barcelona and rest on their laurels. Ferrari had a field day in the Spanish event, finishing 1, 2, 3, 3rd place being taken by the 4.1-litre Geneva car but it was the last appearance of this model.

For the 1951 season Ferrari produced a more advanced version of the 375 F1 with twin plugs per cylinder and during the season the 'invincible' Alfa Romeo was finally beaten. Alfa Romeo ended the 1951 season with another world championship but then permanently withdrew from racing, causing the premature end of the 1.5-litre supercharged and 4.5-litre unsupercharged formula. Alfa Romeo had no choice but to follow this course as it was obvious that if they continued to run for another season they would be heavily defeated by Ferrari.

For the next two years the world championship was run with Formula 2 cars, a field in which Ferrari was to prove supreme. The development of the successful 2-litre designs actually took place while work on the 4.5-litre was also progressing. Ferrari had had a great deal of success with his 12-cylinder 2-litre in Formula 2 events and the combination of Ascari and the 2-litre proved to be a winner on the majority of occasions. Nevertheless, Ferrari found that the opposition was, often as not, finishing too close for comfort. The 12-cylinder car was faster than its competitors but it lacked performance low down in the r p m range. Ferrari had noticed in particular the performance of the 4-cylinder HWM and decided that a really efficient

4-cylinder design would be the answer. Ferrari also had an idea that the future Formula 1 would be with a 2.5-litre limit and as a result he embarked on a dual operation. His plan was to build a race winner for the 2-litre Formula and at the same time have a 2.5-litre design ready and tested before the new Formula 1 came into being.

The Types 500 and 625

As it happened the 2.5-litre design was ready first and was used as the test bed for both cars.

The smaller type 500 had a bore and stroke of 90 x 78 mm giving 1980-cc and the larger type 625 had the dimensions of 94 x 90 mm giving 2490-cc. Stirling Moss had been engaged to drive the prototype 625 in the Bari Grand Prix but after Moss had blown up one of the engines on test at Modena Ferrari felt that he would be better off with a qualified engineer, Taruffi, testing out his new model. In the Bari event the prototype was quite impressive. Taruffi bringing it home in 3rd place.

The prototype appeared again in practice for the Grand Prix of Italy, the car being driven by all the members of the team. Ferrari, urged by Fangio, decided to let the Brazilian driver, Chico Landi, run it in the race but at the last moment changed his mind and substituted a 4.5-litre. The 2.5-prototype had served its purpose and went back to the factory where it was modified to take the 2-litre engine. In its 2-litre form the prototype made a surprise appearance at the Modena Grand Prix and Ascari had no difficulty in winning the event a long way ahead of the factory 12-cylinder Ferraris and the new Maseratis.

A further experiment was tried during the 1952 season. The 2.5-litre engine from the prototype was given on loan to Rudolf Fischer who had purchased a type 500 for the world championship events. Fischer had the engine installed in the 2-litre chassis and had no difficulty in winning the Maloja hill climb thus clinching his Swiss National Championship.

After the event the 2.5-litre engine was returned to the factory.

It became increasingly obvious that Ferrari had guessed right and that the future Formula 1 would in fact be with a 2.5-litre limit. The Formula Libre event scheduled for the beginning of 1953 at Buenos Aires gave Ferrari the opportunity to make some further tests. He had three new 2.5-litre engines built and these were sent out to Argentina with the 2-litre team cars. In the period between the Argentine Grand Prix and the Formula Libre Grand Prix of Buenos Aires the 2.5-litre engines were installed in the 2-litre chassis.

Farina, Villoresi, and Hawthorn drove the cars in the events and took the first three places with no difficulties.

Of the three cars, two had the 2-litre engines replaced after the Buenos Aires race but Ferrari decided to keep one in 2.5-litre form to use when the opportunity presented itself in European competition. This remaining car was given to newcomer, Umberto Maglioli, to drive in the Susa Mont Cenis hill climb. Maglioli performed well enough for his first drive in a Grand Prix car and registered 2nd fastest time of the day.

In the meantime, Ferrari had built a further 2.5-litre. This car differed very little from the previous models except for refinements in bodywork and the use of twin choke carburetters instead of individual carburetters per cylinder. Ferrari sent Mike Hawthorn to England for the Formula Libre event at Silverstone but the car had to be withdrawn after a few laps with overheating.

Ferrari sent both the 625 models to the Rouen Grand Prix which was being run as a Formula Libre event. Hawthorn drove the older 'Buenos Aires' car and Farina had the car which Hawthorn used at Silverstone now known by Ferrari as the 'definitive prototype'. The two ran away from all opposition, Farina finishing 1st with Hawthorn in close company.

1954, The new Formula

The following year, 1954, the new Formula 1 of 2.5-litres unsupercharged came into effect. It was quickly apparent that, despite Ferrari's precautions to have the cars tested and ready, other people were also making advances. There was a strong rumour that Mercedes Benz were coming back into racing, and the new 250F Maserati showed its potential when it defeated the 625 Ferrari in the first of the races held under the new Formula. Ferrari had been aware that this situation would arise and consequently he had decided to begin work on a new design whilst the 1953 season was still in progress.

The Type 553

Modena had been alive with rumours about a new super design that would take care of the Germans if they decided to show their faces. When the two Ferrari prototypes appeared at Monza they were a disappointment in all but external looks. Ferrari, with high-pressure work, had completed the two cars in time for the last event of the 2-litre Formula, fitting them with 2-litre engines so that they could be given a run in competition well ahead of time. When these type 553 models appeared they were very impressive, being low, squat and having much better lines than the earlier types 500 and 625. A new 4-cylinder engine with a bore and stroke of 93 x 73.5 mm instead of 90 x 78 mm of the type 500 was fitted. Unfortunately, closer inspection revealed that, for all the looks, Ferrari's thinking had not advanced very far. The chassis was a revamped version of the type 500 with some additional strengthening in the form of a tubular superstructure. Suspension had not been changed, remaining the classic Ferrari double wishbone and leaf springs at the front and De Dion and leaf spring at the rear.

Even the engine turned out to be nothing more than a rehash of the type 500 with a new cylinder head with wider angles on the valves.

The major difference between the 553 and the earlier models was that the De Dion tube passed in front of the differential/gearbox housing instead of behind as on the type 500. Added to this, was a stepped-down take up for the transmission shaft which enabled the seating position to be lowered. Another difference was the use of pannier tanks, Lampredi, the designer, attempting to do away with the effects of fuel consumption on handling. The top drivers of the team tried out the two prototypes in practice

but quickly abandoned them to return to the faithful type 500 for the race. The two 553s were turned over to Carini and Maglioli, neither being by any means a top driver, so hope for the new cars was not very high. Carini retired after a poor performance and Maglioli finished a long way back in 8th place.

The following year the car appeared as a 2.5-litre in which form it was known as type 555 Supersqualo. Ferrari was to pay dearly for this poor design and it is amazing that he persisted so long when it regularly put in one miserable performance after another. Only once in its long life did the 555 perform with any credit: Hawthorn won the Spanish Grand Prix with a version that had coil spring front suspension. In all the Squalo and Supersqualo design had the undistinguished record of 1 first place, 2 third places, and 14 retirements out of 24 entries.

It was indeed fortunate for Ferrari that the Lancia company decided to hand over the whole of their Grand Prix racing department to him at the end of the 1955 season. Ferrari had nothing new up his sleeve, all his experiments during the year having been failures. With the Lancia material available he decided on a complete shakeup of his organization.

Despite the 'new look' it was an uneasy year for the Maranello factory. Maserati opposition was strong and it was touch and go to win the world championship. Ferrari was never very happy with the fact that he was getting results with the designs he had inherited and during the season the Lancia material underwent a great deal of modification. The chassis was redesigned and the engine completely rebuilt until virtually all that was left of the Lancia design was the V8 layout.

The new engine had a bore and stroke of 80 x 62 mm as opposed to the Lancia D50's 76 x 68.8 mm. The new car was known as type 801 and could really be called a true Ferrari although outwardly it bore some resemblance to the Lancia D50.

The Type 801

For the 1957 season Ferrari lost Fangio to Maserati and it soon became evident that the type 801 Ferrari was no real advance over the

Lancia/Ferrari of the previous season, in fact both Hawthorn and Collins commented that they thought the cars were actually slower, as the 1957 season progressed, and that Bellentani was making no headway. However, Jano and Fraschetti had been hard at work on new projects whilst Massimino had some ideas of his own.

At the Naples Grand Prix, the new V6 Dino already described in Chapter 7 naturally stole the limelight but the two 801 models that were present were also something different. Hawthorn's car used an original Lancia chassis which had been lengthened by 10 cm. At the front a complete Supersqualo Ferrari suspension layout was welded to the chassis frame, being of the double wishbone and coil spring type with long kingpins in the place of the Lancia ball joint layout. Ferrari Supersqualo steering was also adapted to these units. During practice this car appeared with Supersqualo brakes but for the race a changeover was made, the Ferrari backing plates being retained and the Supersqualo drums being replaced by the wider finned Lancia drums.

Massimino also made some radical changes on Collins' type 801, a swing axle layout was used in place of the De Dion. The two swinging half axles crossed over at their inner ends and were mounted on ball joints, while at the outer extremity they were welded to hub carriers taken from a De Dion tube, the normal fore and aft location by double radius rods being retained. Short coil springs and an anti-roll bar replaced the previously used transverse leaf spring. Massimino hoped that this layout would be the answer for twisty circuits like Naples and Monaco but the car proved no faster and the experiments were abandoned.

Ferrari then developed the Dino, producing versions of increasing capacity, as described in Chapter 7, until the 1959 season saw the beginning of the decline of the front engined Dino but he was unwilling to bring out a new design as the formula was due to change in 1961. However, the realization that despite the Dino's power advantage over the British opposition the V6 model could no longer match the performance of the rear engined cars, forced Ferrari's hand.

A move towards rear engines

Early in 1960 a rear engined car appeared on the Modena test track. First results were not very encouraging but by the time the Monaco race came round, Ferrari was confident enough to enter the car which Ritchie Ginther tried out in that event. The fact that he was only 0.3 sec. slower than the fastest time of the Ferraris set by Von Trips showed that Ferrari had overcome the majority of the difficulties experienced with the new design. The car retired with a broken transmission and was scheduled to appear at Zandvoort for the Dutch Grand Prix.

By then Ferrari had already decided to forget the possibility of using the rear engined car for the rest of the Formula 1 season and to concentrate instead on preparing the rear engined design for the forthcoming Formula 1 of 1500-cc. His forethought again paid dividends.

The fortunes of the front engined Dino declined steadily but the completely modified rear engined car, now fitted with the 1500-cc type 156 Dino engine, won a convincing victory at the Grenzlandring. At Monza it ran again and finished a long way ahead of any other 1500-cc opposition, but it met with defeat on home ground at Modena when it was beaten by Porsche after a race-long battle.

When the new formula commenced in 1961 Ferrari was on top again, his rear engined type 156 won the World Championship with Phil Hill driving.

In 1962 the situation changed again, the British constructors had at last caught up in engine design and Ferrari suddenly found himself outclassed as he had never been before.

Mike Costin in his book *Racing and Sports Car Chassis Design* said 'Recent sports and racing Ferraris show the very considerable influence of British chassis designers, although it would appear sometimes that the lessons learned this way are not fully understood'. This warning was not heeded at Maranello and Ferrari performance suffered as a result during 1962. The results of the 1962 season clearly indicated that Ferrari had to meet the greatest challenge he had had to face since he began with his own cars more than fifteen years earlier.

An analysis showed that despite his long run of success Ferrari could have done better by more adventurous thinking. The situation in motor racing had at the time forced him to make a much greater effort to maintain his position in the field than he had done in the past.

Special & Experimental Ferraris

According to the official Ferrari project register the following engines were categorized as experimental:

No	Type	Cyl	B/S	Unit cc	Total cc
39	735S	4IL	102 x 90	735.4	2941.6
47	625FI	4IL	94 x 90	624.6	2498.3
48	700	4IL	99 x 90	692.8	2771.2
60	(115) 256FI	6IL	82.4 x 78	416	2496
61	(116) 252FI	2IL	118 x 114	1246.7	2493.4
69	(123)	6IL	100 x 90	706.8	4241.1
70	(124)	4IL	110 x 90	855.3	3421.2
71	(127)	6IL	97.5 x 78	582.3	3494.2
72	250 Sup	12V	68 x 68	246.9	2963.5
86	(128) 260	12V	75 x 58.8	259.8	3117.2
87	Exp	8V	74 x 72.2	310.5	2484.2
97	(139) 2985	8V	81 x 72.8	375.1	3000.8
98	1965	6V	77 x 71	330.6	1983.7
99	2265	6V	81 x 71	365.8	2195.2
106	2965	6V	85 x 87	493.7	2962.1
109	196 GT	6V	77 x 71	330.6	1983.7
110	(144)	12V	75 x 68	287.1	3445.9
111	256 FI	6V	86 x 71	412.4	2474.5
112	(152)	6V	84 x 72	399.0	2394
113	(153) 1565	6V	72 x 64.5	262.6	1575.6
120	(155)	6V	85 x 72	408.5	2451.1
121	(159)	12V	77 x 75	349.2	4190.4
122	(161) 854	4IL	65 x 64	212.3	849.5
123	(162) F.IntCont	12V	75 x 71	313.6	3764.0
124	(163) 330GT	12V	77 x 71	330.6	3967.4
125	(164) 950	4IL	67 x 69	243.2	973.0
127	156 F2	6V	73 x 58.8	246.1	1476.8
133	250 Inj	12V	73 x 58.8	241.1	2953.2
134	246 Inj	6V	85 x 71	402.9	2417.3
141	(164bis) 1000	4IL	69 x 69	258	1032
142	(165) 1600GT	6V	73 x 62	259.5	1556.8
145	156FI 65°	6V	81 x 48.2	249.4	1496.4
146	156FI 120°	6V	73 x 58.8	246.1	1476.6
148	276S	6V	90 x 71	451.7	2710.2
154	296 P	6V	87 x 82	487.5	2924.9
170	186GT	6V	77 x 64	298	1788.1
237	318W	18W	65 x 50	165.9	2986.2

CARS BUILT FOR SPECIAL PURPOSES OR TO CUSTOMERS' SPECIAL ORDER

The most important group in this section is naturally the story of the various attempts made by Ferrari to win the Indianapolis classic.

The success of the 4.5-litre Ferrari in European competition was indisputable and Luigi Chinetti, Ferrari's American Distributor, was responsible for some high pressure promotion to show the car's capabilities at Indianapolis. For the 1952 event three cars were sold to private owners and Ferrari decided to enter one car sponsored by the factory. Work began on the Indianapolis model during the winter of 1951 — 2. A new chassis was produced with a wheelbase of 7 ft 8 in. and a front and rear track of 4 ft 3½ in. and 4 ft 3 in. respectively. The frame was strengthened by welding a triangulated system

(Top) The streamlined V8 Ferrari. Reims 1956. Normal bodywork was used for the race

(Middle) The experimental Bardahl-Ferrari using a 6 cyl Ferrari engine in a Kurtis chassis. Nino Farina was entered in this car for the Indianapolis 500 of 1956

(Bottom) The Kurtis chassis with the 4.4 litre 6 cyl engine installed

(*Top*) The 4.4 litre 6 cyl engine in the Bardahl car
(*Middle*) The 4.1 4 cam 412 was built for Monza's 'Race of Two Worlds'
(*Bottom*) The Type 296 MI Monza 3 litre V6 was qualified by Phil Hill at an average of 161 mph for the 'Race of Two Worlds'

(Top) John von Neumann in one of the two Type 412 sports cars. This is car No. 6674. The 4.1 engine was the same as the factory Type 335 Sports

(Bottom) Phil Hill in the 412 MI at Riverside. Although it retired through minor trouble it was more than a match for the opposition

(Top) The 410 MI twin cam per bank. This car was
formerly raced by Hill and Ginther for the Von Neumann
Team

(Middle) The ex Whitehead/Clark 3.5 litre Super Squalo
Ferrari being raced in GP guise for the last time by Bob
Smith at Levin in New Zealand in 1962

(Bottom) New Zealand Special Ferrari. Originally built
for Pat Hoare with a 2.5 litre four cylinder engine it is
now running with a 2 litre 4 cyl

(Top) Von Trips in a Special New Zealand bound Formula Libre Ferrari PTO (1) in 1960
(Bottom Left) The two cylinder Type 116 F1 GP Ferrari engine designed by Lampredi just before he left Ferrari. It has a displacement of 2493-cc with a bore and stroke of 118 x 114 mm giving 174 bhp at 4800 rpm. For a long time it was thought that this was an unknown four cylinder prototype and no one investigated but it has been confirmed by Ing. Florini that this was the 2 cylinder with twin ignition, twin intake ports per cylinder and twin exhaust ports per cylinder. The engine is now owned by Anthony Bamford
(Bottom Right) Sohc V6 Dino engine

(*Top Left*) The Cegga-Ferrari showing the installation of the 3 litre V12 Ferrari engine

(*Top Right*) Enzo Ferrari (far right) shows Raymond C Firestone (2nd from left) an experimental 12 cyl Ferrari engine details of which are still unknown at date of publication

(*Bottom*) The exciting experimental P5 Ferrari executed by Pinin Farina. It uses a 3 litre 4 ohc engine

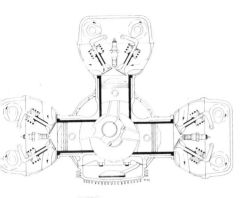

(Top Left) The W18 concept was developed in 1969. A three cylinder test version only was actually built
(Top Right) Pinin Farina's Ferrari P6 Berlinetta Speciale at Turin 1969
(Middle) The Cegga-Ferrari with coachbuilder Piero Drogo. This was an attempt to graft a Ferrari engine into another maker's chassis. The Swiss inspired Cegga was made by Drogo at Modena
(Bottom) Pinin Farina's Modulo Ferrari, 1970

(*Top*) Pinin Farina's Ferrari 512S at the 1970 Turin Show
(*Bottom Left*) This 1953 built 2.5 litre 4 cylinder Vignale bodied car was a one-off
(*Bottom Right*) The four cylinder 850-cc engine of the Ferrarina

(*Top*) The Ferrarina. An 850-cc 4 cyl experimental saloon of 1960
(*Middle*) ASA-Mille prototype used a 4 cylinder Ferrari engine
(*Bottom*) Peter Whitehead driving the 1.5 litre supercharged Thinwall
Special in the International Trophy 1950

(Top) Alberto Ascari driving the Thinwall Special 1.5
litre two stage blown Ferrari at Silverstone in the BRDC
meeting 1950. He spun off in the wet
(Middle) Peter Schetty at Modena May 1969 in the
Ferrari 212E, 2 litre 180 degree engine
(Bottom Left) Reg Parnell in the modified 4.5 litre
Thinwall Special with long carburetter air intake
(Bottom Right) Taruffi in the Thinwall Special Ferrari

(*Top*) Chris Amon at Las Vegas 1967 in the 4.2 litre Can Am car
(*Bottom*) Chris Amon in the Type 612P Can Am car at Elkhart Lake 1969

(Top) The 6.9 litre Can Am engine that was used for practice only at Riverside 1969
(Bottom) The original Breadvan. Carlo Abate driving the SSS Venezia 3 litre at Brands Hatch

(Top) Another of Drogo's special bodied 'breadvan' 3 litre Ferraris. This one is driven by Chris Kerrison

(Bottom Left) The Auto-Avio Costruzioni Type 815 built for the 1940 GP of Brescia (Mille Miglia 1940). Photographed at the entrance to the Milano-Torino Autostrada

(Bottom Right) Drogo specialised in special bodied 3 litre GT Ferraris. Each body was different, this is the Ecurie National Belge car

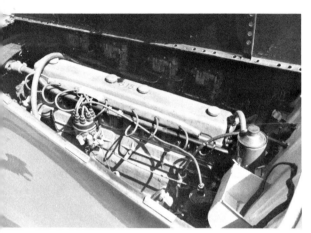

(Top Left) 1940. The Auto-Avio Costruzioni Type 815 designed by Alberto Massimino has two FIAT 508 blocks with one cast sump and head (ohv)
(Top Right) 1940 Auto-Avio Costruzioni (Ferrari) Type 815. Two were built for the 1940 Mille Miglia. This is the Rangoni car. The other was scrapped
(Bottom) Pescara August 1948. Coteses's Ferrari on the left of the starting grid. But most important is the Type 815 of Beltracchini on the right. This proves that these cars were not just used to race in the 1940 Mille Miglia

(Top Left) Sommer at Turin with the Type 159, 12 October 1947. He took the lead and held it to the end. Ferrari wrote in his memoirs that when he heard of Sommer's victory, he (Ferrari) burst into tears with emotion

(Top Right) Franco Cortese with the first 1500-cc Type 125 at Piacenza May 1947. It was his first appearance in the car

(Middle) 1951 Madame Simon at Reims with the Zagato bodied 2 litre Type 166

(Bottom Left) Ferrari Type 166-Inter No. 0161

(Bottom Right) This was the next Ferrari to appear, this time with cycle wings. It won at the Roman Caracalla Circuit in 1947 driven by Cortese. This was Ferrari's first win. Nuvolari drove this car to a class win at Forli on 6 July 1947, its last appearance in this guise and it is possible that this car was rebodied to become the Type 159 which Sommer drove to victory at Turin on 12 October 1947

(Top) Soave Besana in either car No. 002C or 004C at Pescara 1948
(Bottom Left) Romano's Type 166 at the Eifel Cup meeting on the Nurburgring June 1951
(Bottom Right) Ferrari Type 166 Mille Miglia by Touring Superleggera

of small tubes on top of the normal side members. The bonnet line of the car was lowered with the provision of a large air scoop intended to give some ram effect to the ingoing air. Much work was done on the engine and the final power reading on the bench was 430 b h p.

The Indianapolis cars were given a preliminary outing in the Turin Grand Prix which was held under the original Formula 1 rules. Farina and Ascari drove two Indianapolis models while Villoresi had a car that had the Indianapolis chassis with an earlier type engine. The three Ferraris went into line ahead formation at the start of the race. Ascari was leading with three laps to go when his fuel tank split and he was forced to retire. Farina had trouble with his gearbox and went off the road but Villoresi saved the day and won.

The Villoresi car was then fitted with a new engine and the other two cars were overhauled. A fourth car with several modifications was also prepared and the cars were shipped to the USA for the Indianapolis event. The first three cars were for the Grant Piston Ring Corporation, Howard Keck and Johnny Mauro. The fourth car was the factory entry for Alberto Ascari. Ascari qualified at 134.308 m p h and the Keck car fitted with fuel injection recorded 134.2 m p h and the others being non-qualifiers. Ascari found his car totally unsuited to the Indianapolis track and was the only driver in the race that had to change gears. Only by sheer driving ability was he able to place the unsuitable car anything but last before hub failure finally put him out of the running.

As a result of these experiences, Luigi Chinetti decided to have a special car built for the 1953 season. During the winter several components used on the Indianapolis Offenhauser-engined cars were studied at the Ferrari factory. A new gearbox with only two speeds was also investigated. Despite the intensive studies the car that resulted was not very exciting. A shorter chassis was employed with a wheelbase of 7 ft 2 in. The chassis construction was only slightly altered from that used on the unsuccessful Ascari car. The new model had an additional superstructure in the centre of the car and bracing struts running from the superstructure to the front built-up crossmembers. No

alterations were made to the V12 engine except for the fitting of three four-choke carburetters. The only other differences between this special and the earlier type was that the rear hubs were increased in size to 54 mm and additional bump stops were provided by a light coil spring with central rubber inserts mounted at the rear.

The car went to Indianapolis without a driver being nominated. The local drivers who tried the car pronounced a definite dislike for it and the car did not qualify. It was next seen at Daytona Beach where it was tried by various people over the measured mile. The car did not achieve very much over 150 m p h until Bob Said was offered the drive. Said's one-way run of 174 m p h and a two-way average of 170 m p h was more due to the driver's courage than the car's stability and the Special went under dust sheets. It was hauled out again the following season for the Daytona event, this time with Indianapolis veteran Bill Holland at the wheel. Chinetti had carried out various modifications on the car including a new nose to improve penetration. The car turned in a speed of 155 m p h but Holland could do no better due to the poor condition of the beach.

Chinetti engaged Carroll Shelby to drive it in two hill climbs which he won with ease, the car then disappeared again under wraps. The next outing for the Special was when Farina used it for practice at Indianapolis prior to his unsuccessful attempt at qualifying with the Bardahl Ferrari.

Chinetti then sent the car back to Italy for modification. The engine capacity was reduced to 4.2-litres so that it could run in the 500 miles of Monza. The bodywork was cleaned up and, complete with a new paint job, it went to Monza for Harry Schell to drive. During practice the car suffered from magneto trouble and Schell was only able to qualify at the last moment at a speed considerably slower than the American cars. In the event it was plagued with the same magneto trouble as in practice and it was never in the picture. The car was then kept under wraps for some time until Chinetti decided to have it rebodied by Scaglietti with much smoother lines and the exhaust pipes on either side running upwards and along the side of the body instead of underneath as previously. It remained in Chinetti's showroom on 11th Avenue in New York for some time as a showpiece and then passed into private hands. With some more body restoration and an engine overhaul by Chinetti, the car now runs in vintage car events. In the first of such events, none other than Bob Said returned to the wheel to give the racing enthusiasts a taste of what the old V12 sounded like.

The Bardahl Special

These poor performances at Indianapolis discouraged Ferrari from any further attempts but Chinetti maintained his interest. When Nino Farina announced his retirement from racing he also stated that he would have a go at the great American race as his swansong. Chinetti suggested that an American chassis be used and mated with a Ferrari engine. Farina had the support of the Italian Bardahl company and Ferrari himself took an interest and began the preparation of a 4.4-litre 6-cylinder engine. The car was assembled in Ferrari's experimental department but when it became apparent from sports car experience that the 6-cylinder engines were a failure, Ferrari lost all his interest in the project and the car was shipped to the OSCA factory in Bologna for completion. Farina failed to qualify the car for the Indianapolis race and retired the following year to make another try at getting into the lineup. The car was completely wrecked when an American driver hit the wall with it, losing his life in the process. The wreck was returned to Italy and was last seen in a customs shed rusting away under sheets.

The 500 miles Monza race of 1957 should have been an opportunity for Ferrari to show what he could do against the Indianapolis cars but the U P P I banned their drivers from taking part in the event and no entry was seen from Ferrari. The following year there was no ban by the drivers and Ferrari decided to show what could be done on home ground. Two cars were prepared a V12-cylinder 4.1-litre and a V6-cylinder 3-litre. The 4.1-litre was intended as an out and out challenge to the Indianapolis cars on the fast Monza circuit. The 3-litre was in the nature of an experiment. Despite his lack of success at Indianapolis, Ferrari had still kept a certain interest. In a discussion with Bob Estes, then the president of the Indianapolis Car

Owners Association, Ferrari mentioned that he would like to supply some of his 4.1-litre engines for Indianapolis car owners and that his 3-litre V6 was an experiment which, if successful, might be seen at Indianapolis in the future.

The Type 412 M1

The 4.1-litre type 412 M1 had a chassis built on the lines of the successful 4.5-litre Formula 1 cars of the 1950 — 51 era and the engine was derived from the 1957 world-championship-winning sports car. The engine had twin overhead camshafts per bank of cylinders and the power was quoted as being 447 b h p at 7,700 r p m which seemed adequate enough to deal with the Offenhauser-engined opposition. A gearbox similar externally to the old type used on the 4.5-litre was employed but it had only three forward speeds. The De Dion layout with a leaf spring was used at the rear and at the front a layout similar to that on the 555 Supersqualo was used although larger coil springs were fitted.

The engine of this single seater was actually the engine extracted from the de Portago wreck in the 1957 Mille Miglia.

While the racing history of the sports cars is discussed in Chapter 11 these particular four-cam engines can really be included among Special and Experimental types. The first of this model was No. 0656 labelled 315 MM, it was followed by No. 0674 a 412 MI later sold to John Von Neumann with a Testa Rossa pontoon-type body.

No. 0676 was labelled 335SP and was the 4.1 litre in which de Portago was killed, the engine eventually being transferred to Chassis No. 0744.

No. 0684 was also labelled 335SP and is believed to be the car with which Taruffi won the Mille Miglia in 1957. No. 0744 was the 412 MI which had the de Portago engine installed after it was taken out of the single seater Monza car. Its various owners were Von Neumann for Phil Hill and Richie Ginther to drive in opposition to the Reventlow Scarabs. It then passed on to Harrah's collection from there to Pinkham who restored the car to win the Ferrari class at Pebble Beach Concours d'Elegance in 1973.

After Pinkham's death it was acquired by Steve Earle of Los Angeles to race in vintage car events.

The Type 296 M1

The 3-litre type 296 M1, Ferrari's second car for the Monza race, was based on the 246 Dino. The chassis had the steering arms and wishbones much strengthened and double shockabsorbers fitted front and rear. The rear end layout was De Dion with a coil spring setup which was later also used experimentally on the 246 Dino. During practice Ferrari experimented with a new type of cast rubber coil spring, the rubber acting as a boot round the metal coils. This arrangement was found to be totally unsuited for the banked track and the original coil spring layout replaced it. The V6 engine had a bore and stroke of 85 x 87 mm giving 2962-cc and had a power output of 316 b h p at 7,800 r p m.

The type 412 M1 caused a sensation, Musso drove a practice lap at 171.9 m p h which was only a fraction slower than fastest time of day set by Fangio in an American car. During qualification, Musso was even more impressive and the Ferrari sat on the pole position with three laps at 174.5 m p h. The smaller type 296 M1 also qualified, Phil Hill completing his three laps at 161 m p h.

Musso went straight into the lead but both cars had their troubles. The 3-litre finally retired with magneto trouble and the big 4.1-litre was filling the driver's cockpit with fumes, wearing out tyres at a tremendous rate and breaking spokes in the rear wheels. Musso had to come into the pits because of the fumes and Hawthorn took over. When Hawthorn stopped Phil Hill took his place and the car was finally classified 3rd overall after a rousing performance that kept the crowd on its toes.

The engine of the 412 M1 was then taken out of the single seater and was used for a special sports car; the 296 M1 engine met the same fate.

Ferrari had several enquiries for the 4.1-litre engines to be fitted into an American chassis and several of the Indianapolis owners made trips to Maranello for discussions. However, nothing ever came to these talks and Ferrari is still as far away as ever from a victory in the American classic.

In an interview with the French Magazine *Sport Auto* Enzo Ferrari was asked 'What is your greatest disappointment in competition racing' to which he replied 'To not have won the 500 Miles of Indianapolis'.

That is the extent of the special cars prepared for the factory's own use. Apart from these Indianapolis and Monza specials Ferrari built a few cars to customers' special order. The Australian and New Zealand races were too far away for Ferrari to participate and the dates interfered with his winter preparation. He nevertheless felt that something should be done about these particular races and expressed a willingness to supply special cars to selected customers.

The first of these cars were the result of a trial made in Argentina. In 1953 Ferrari had successfully sent three 2.5-litre engines to be mounted in the type 500 2-litre chassis for the Formula libre Grand Prix of Buenos Aires. In 1955 he decided to repeat this plan and sent three modified 3-litre type 750 Monza engines to Argentina to be mounted in the type 625 chassis. This time the opposition was a little stiffer due to the presence of Mercedes Benz with 3-litre engined cars. Farina however, won the first heat from the German cars and was all set to win the final when he was forced off the road by an Argentine driver.

The Australasian Specials

After the Argentine races one of the type 750/625 cars was supplied to Peter Whitehead and a 750/500 to Tony Gaze who took them to Australia and New Zealand where they were raced with great success, the cars eventually being sold to private owners in Australia.

Peter Whitehead once again requested a special car for the New Zealand races in the winter of 1955 – 56. This time he was partnered by Reg Parnell. Ferrari having no more use for his type 555 Supersqualo decided that this was an opportunity to get rid of them and had them modified to take the type 860 4-cylinder engine. This engine was derived from the sports car unit and had a bore and stroke of 102 x 105 mm giving a capacity of 3431-cc. The two drivers had no difficulty whatsoever in making a clean sweep of all the races. The cars were then sold locally at the end of the season and are still sometimes seen in competition to this day.

Ferrari maintained his interest in the New Zealand races but, despite lengthy negotiations with the organizers of these events, he decided that he could not participate. To make up for this he agreed to supply a special car to New Zealand driver, Pat Hoare, so that the name of Ferrari would be represented.

The Special was typical of Ferrari's policy with customers' cars. Nothing exceptional was designed and he settled on using up components that were available and not much use to the factory. The basis of the car was a type 500 chassis fitted with a specially tuned version of the type 625 4-cylinder Le Mans sports car engine which had been bored out from 2.5 to 2.8-litres. A Supersqualo transmission was used to give a lower seating position and a neat body, incorporating a Lancia fuel tank, completed the car. With this car Pat Hoare ran in most of the races in New Zealand where the car performed with a certain amount of success.

The 4-cylinder engine was inclined to be troublesome and Hoare tried to find a 12-cylinder as a substitute. An appeal to the factory brought forward the suggestion that a completely new car be provided and the New Zealander agreed to this. This time the simple expedient of using a chassis from a 256 Dino was made, mating it with the highly successful and reliable 250 Testa Rossa sports car engine. Again the combination proved satisfactory and Hoare had considerable success with the car in local events. He scored 1st places with it at Blenheim, Dunedin and Ohakea, a 2nd at Waimate and a 4th at Ardmore in the New Zealand Grand Prix, thus becoming New Zealand champion driver for the 1961 – 62 season.

For the 1960 Argentine races Ferrari prepared another special car. It was intended that the car be sold to Ferrari of California but this company decided against purchasing the car as there would be no races for it after the Buenos Aires event. This car was simply a 246 Dino chassis with the 296 Dino engine that had been used at different times for the Monza special and the 3-litre sports car. The car was to have been driven by Ginther at Buenos Aires but when the deal fell through with the California representatives the 3-litre engine was replaced by the spare 2.5-litre unit and the car given to Gonzales to drive in the Argentine Grand Prix.

EXPERIMENTAL DESIGNS THAT WERE SHELVED

In the early days of his tests for an Indianapolis challenger Ferrari had considered a supercharged version of his 12-cylinder type 250 engine. The project was put off for some time but every now and again would be pulled out from under the dust sheets to be given some further study. Eventually a design based on experiences with the 1500-cc two stage supercharged engine was produced.

A twin overhead camshaft head was fitted on a type 250 block; with a bore and stroke of 68 x 68 mm. The engine had a capacity of 2963-cc. In its two stage supercharged version it gave 510 b h p at 7,000 r p m on the bench.

Despite this excellent performance during tests Ferrari decided that it was not worth while to continue its development. He claimed that the solution to the Indianapolis problem lay in the chassis design and that his available engines were already powerful enough to win without his having to embark on the expensive development of an extra design. With this decision all further work on the 3-litre supercharged engine was abandoned.

Disc brake experiments

Jaguar created a stir in the racing world when they came out with disc brakes on their Le Mans models. Ferrari at that time was unwilling to use British components on his cars but he thought that the idea of disc brakes merited further investigation. He consequently set about designing his own and fitted them on a type 500 2-litre car for testing. The brakes were larger than those used on the Jaguar and relied on multiple pads fitted round the circumference of a flange on the disc. Mike Hawthorn tested these brakes on the centre strip of the Modena airport but after two runs the brakes caught fire. Ferrari junked his design in disgust and it was a long time before disc brakes were seen again on a Ferrari.

A set of Messier disc brakes were fitted with Ferrari's approval to a type 750 Monza sports car but Ferrari was not impressed. Ferrari's resistance to foreign ideas was finally overcome and Dunlop disc brakes were fitted to Hawthorn's 246 Dino in time for the Monza and Casablanca races in 1958.

The Streamlined Lancia/Ferrari

When Ferrari received the Lancia material he found amongst the consignment a fully streamlined body intended to be fitted on the V8 cars for Rheims and Monza. He carried out several experiments with this body and finally cut off the front section which he fitted to an otherwise normal car for tests at Monza. After these tests he arrived at Rheims with a still further modified streamliner. The body was entirely new having been totally built by Ferrari's coachbuilder. It retained the same air intake shape as the original Lancia streamliner and the front piece bolted on in place of the normal Ferrari cowling. It had wheel arches cut away to give the driver a view of the wheels. At the rear the body was cut to produce two large mudguards which enclosed the rear wheels and bolted on to a normal Ferrari tail unit. The car was extensively tested during practice at Rheims but for the race the car appeared with the streamlined sections replaced by the normal Ferrari nose and tail.

During 1955 Ferrari found himself in real trouble with the Mercedes Benz and Maserati opposition. His 625 was outdated and the 555 was giving him nothing but trouble. Chief designer Lampredi was called into the office of the *Commendatore* and told to do something drastic about the situation. Lampredi came up with an idea to produce two different designs: one that would serve for short and twisty circuits and the other for fast circuits like Monza and Rheims. The two cars would be totally different in concept; the type 116 for twisty circuits would have a small and light chassis and the type 115 for the fast circuits would have a more conventional chassis.

The 2-cylinder engine

The type 116 engine was designed as a 2-cylinder with the enormous bore and stroke of 118 x 114 mm giving a capacity of 2493-cc. The engine was given considerable testing on the bench and eventually gave 175 b h p at 4,800 r p m. Many problems were experienced with it and eventually the whole idea was scrapped.

At the same time, as the tests were being conducted with the 2-cylinder, Lampredi put his experimental 6-cylinder type 115 engine on test. This engine was derived from the type 114 which was an experimental 3-litre sports car engine. The type 115 had a bore and stroke of 82.4 x 78 mm which gave a displacement of 2495-cc. Its power output was a satisfactory 250 b h p at 6,500 r p m but the problems of overheating and subsequent distortion that plagued the bigger 6-cylinder engines were also encountered in this new design so it also had to be scrapped.

The book on all these projects was closed when Ferrari was given the Lancia material and Lampredi left to join Fiat.

It just remains to mention a few odd projects which Ferrari undertook over the various years.

One was a final attempt to turn the Supersqualo into a race winner by fitting a Lancia D50 engine into a type 555 chassis. This car was run experimentally at Buenos Aires but was a complete failure.

An experimental 4-cylinder engine for a racing boat was produced with a bore and stroke of 99 x 99 mm and a capacity of 2.7-litres but nothing further came of this.

Another little project of Ferrari was a lightweight diesel of 1500-cc. This idea was given up after one engine and parts for about twenty others had been completed. The whole project was handed over to the Maserati brothers at Bologna where the labels identifying the design with Ferrari were removed and replaced with OSCA identification.

A further project that came to nothing was the fitting of a single-cam-per-bank V6 engine into a 246 Dino chassis. It was hoped that the single cam engine would give the car better performance low down so that it could be used for racing on twisty circuits. The car was tested by Richie Ginther at the Modena autodrome but results were not conclusive and the project was abandoned.

THE THINWALL SPECIAL FERRARIS

Although these cars were in no way connected with the factory's activities the story of Mr Vandervell's Thinwall Special Ferrari deserves mention in detail. Vandervell's progressive development of the 4.5-litre Ferrari was an interesting exercise. It showed the full potential of Aurelio Lampredi's design which had made itself famous by ending the supremacy of the 158/159 Alfa Romeo.

With the defeat of the Alfa Romeo team the 1.5-litre supercharged and 4.5-litre unsupercharged formula died prematurely at the end of 1951. Alfa Romeo was smart enough to realize that their design had already overstepped the development limits whilst Ferrari still had the potential of improving their unsupercharged design. The result of this was that Alfa Romeo withdrew from racing permanently while they were still ahead in the game.

Alfa's withdrawal left Ferrari with the dubious opposition of BRM. Race organizers were well aware of BRM's no show and low reliability record and were not willing to run the risk of organizing Ferrari benefits. The old formula still remained technically in effect but all the organizers switched over to the 2-litre Formula 2 for World Championship events. The races turned out to be just as much Ferrari benefits as the original Formula would have been but it had the effect of introducing many new marques to make up the field.

Vandervell had by this time decided to manufacture a team of his own Formula 1 cars and looked upon the further development of the Thinwall Ferrari as an exercise to give the mechanics experience and to get his team management into shape for the day when the Vanwall cars would take to the track. Although the 4.5-Thinwall was the car that made the name famous, it was not the first to bear the name. Tony Vandervell had gone through less favourable experiences with two other cars before he finally hit on the winning combination.

The first Thinwall Special

It all began when Vandervell supplied his 'Thinwall' bearings to Ferrari for use in the V12 racing engines. Vandervell decided to get some information first hand and talked Ferrari into selling him one of the 1.5-litre single stage supercharged Grand Prix cars. This car was duly entered in the 1949 British Grand Prix with Raymond Mays driving.

It did not take long for Vandervell and Mays to regret their acquisition. The car had the old type rear suspension and was notoriously difficult to drive. After a few laps the driver commented 'its like riding a greased pig on ice'. It was tricky through the corners and it would crab on the straight. Mays circulated unhappily in 9th place, by the time three-quarters of the race had been run he had had enough and pulled into the pits to hand over to Ken Richardson. Richardson went one lap and lost it in a big way. That was the end of Thinwall Special No. 1.

The following year at Silverstone the next Thinwall Special made its appearance. Vandervell had obtained the car with which Ascari had won the Grand Prix of Italy, this being the much more powerful twin-cam two stage supercharged Ferrari. The car not only had more power but handled very much better due to a long chassis and many suspension changes.

Vandervell had special cambox covers cast up with the name 'Thinwall Special' on them but some one slipped up and the name came out 'Thinwell Special'. Mr Vandervell's ill humour about this was not improved when the Italians started to call him 'Mr Wonderweld and his Tinwall Special'. The Italians have always been good at messing up English names.

Alberto Ascari had been signed up to drive the car but Vandervell had no better luck with the new car than with the old. The Special ran badly and Ascari could do nothing with it. In the pouring rain he spun off on a corner and decided that he had had enough, parked the car on the grass and walked back to the pits.

So back to the factory. Vandervell traded the supercharged car for one of the 1950 type 4.5-litre cars with a single ignition engine mounted in a De Dion chassis. It was given a coat of green paint with the name 'Thinwall Special' inscribed on either side.

Silverstone 1950

Reg Parnell was engaged to drive it in the Daily Express Trophy meeting at Silverstone where he faced the full might of Alfa Romeo. The choice of Parnell proved a wise one. In heat one he was matched against Fangio and Bonetto for second place. When he finally got by the Italian he set out after Fangio who was 12 seconds ahead. Parnell closed to 6 seconds on Fangio and the Alfa pits hung out the faster signals; the maestro replied with a new lap record followed by another. When Parnell's pit gave him the news, he had already lost 4 seconds by Fangio's spurt, but that day Parnell ranked with the greatest. He really set about motoring his new mount and it was a very startled Fangio that sneaked home by 3 seconds.

In the final Parnell was faced not only with his two previous adversaries but also the formidable Dr Farina and Sanesi. As the cars lined up there was a torrential cloudburst, water flooded over the circuit and some of the cars had difficulty in starting. As the flag dropped Parnell was off into the lead. It was almost too dark to see and there was such a downpour that the spectators saw blobs of spray running past them instead of cars. Parnell pressed on while the Alfas frantically tried to catch up. By the third lap a hailstorm started, stones as big as walnuts bouncing off the cars and driver. The track looked as if it were a cobblestoned street. The organizers decided that things were getting too rough and the race was called off after six laps. Reg Parnell was first with the whole Alfa team behind him. Technically it was the first postwar defeat of the invincible Alfa team but due to the freak conditions the motor racing world had to wait for confirmation of the Ferrari superiority until Gonzales did the job properly at a later date.

A Goodwood lap record

Mr Vandervell was very satisfied with Parnell's performance and engaged him to drive the Special again at Goodwood. Here the Thinwall and Parnell caused another sensation. From a standing start Parnell broke the lap record and went on to an easy win in the first heat. In the final he was up against Farina and De Graffenried on 4CLT48 Maseratis. Farina's car was the hottest 4CLT ever built and it was the factory's last ditch attempt to equal the Alfas and Ferraris. Parnell again went straight into the lead but found that Farina, once he had passed De Graffenried was catching up 2 seconds per lap. Down went the foot and nearly 2 seconds came off the lap record, Parnell pulling away to win again.

Farina had his revenge on Parnell at the Ulster Trophy; he put away his Maserati and coaxed Alfa Romeo to lend him one of the 158s. Parnell

was first with a new lap record for the Thinwall, but Farina bettered it. In the race Farina drove as only he could, flinging the Alfa round as if it were a toy in the attempt to gain as much time as possible before the refuelling stop that he would have to make. Parnell was unable to keep up and had to rely on the hope that he could pass the Alfa while it was refuelling, the Thinwall being able to run through non-stop. Farina timed the whole thing nicely; when he pulled out after taking on fuel Parnell had a lead of only 3 seconds an advantage which Farina wiped out on the same lap and then cruised on to win.

A Thinwall goes to Europe

The first appearance of the Vandervell organization on the Continent was for the French Grand Prix at Rheims. Here the Thinwall faced full teams of Alfa Romeo and Ferrari. Parnell had been signed on to drive for BRM so Brian Shawe Taylor was entered in the Vandervell car. At the last minute no show of the BRMs, Parnell switched to the Thinwall. On the fast French circuit the Thinwall had no real hope of competing with the factory entries. Fangio set the fastest practice lap at 2 min. 25 secs., Parnell's best was 2 min. 44 secs. At least it was the fastest time behind the factory's two cars. Parnell improved his time to 2 min. 40.5 secs. during the race and cruised around steadily behind the tremendous battle that involved the two works teams; as the cars ahead of him broke down he moved up. On the last lap, just a short way from the finishing line, the Thinwall's rear axle broke and Parnell had to coast home in 4th place. It had certainly been his lucky day and he had the laugh on Farina whose Alfa was hardly running, with the ignition completely haywire. As Farina puttered towards the finishing line, Parnell coasted by him and robbed him of 4th, much to the good doctor's chagrin.

Vandervell was without Parnell for the British Grand Prix as Alfa Romeo had decided that the lead-footed Derbyshire farmer would be safer on their side so he was given the fourth works 158. Vandervell engaged Peter Whitehead to drive the car. Whitehead was the only other Englishman with extensive experience on Ferraris. Whitehead was fastest, after the works cars, during practice but during the race he was plagued with brake trouble and could do no better than 9th place, the worst performance that the Thinwall had during its whole career.

The Thinwall now began to undergo the first of a long series of modifications: Vandervell had become very interested in improving its performance as the car was clearly not up to the factory standard. The first modification was an extension forwards of the air intake so that it jutted out of the bonnet to give some ram effect to the incoming air. The original Ferrari brakes were removed and BRM type Girling three shoe brakes fitted. The Y-shaped carriers for the three shoes were turned through 90 degrees at the front and 180 degrees at the rear in order to allow for the fitting of the Ferrari hubs and brake lines.

In this new shape Parnell took the car to Winfield for the final event of the season. Needless to say he walked away with the race.

During the winter of 1951 — 52 the car underwent further modification as Vandervell had decided that he wanted a really competitive car for the following season. All hopes of a full Grand Prix season were squashed when Alfa Romeo retired from racing and the World Championship was switched over to the 2-litre formula. The British organizers however assured Vandervell of adequate racing by organizing a number of Formula Libre events in which the Thinwall and its chief opponent the BRM could run. The Argentine driver, Froilan Gonzales was engaged to drive the car for the event. He finished some 26 seconds ahead of second man, Mike Hawthorn. Ken Richardson was given the car to drive in the second event but repeated his performance with Thinwall No. 1 and spun off to retire on the first lap.

Ulster victory

For the Ulster Trophy, Vandervell took on Piero Taruffi as chauffeur for the green Special. The car was once again modified and had a new twin ignition cylinder head fitted. A completely new body was built on the car making it look monstrous. It had a large round air intake in the nose and a box like air scoop for the carburetters. A staggered exhaust system was fitted to give access to the twenty-four plugs. Taruffi was pitted against Moss and Fangio with the re-

vamped BRMs. With this strong team the BRM equipe had high hopes of victory. These hopes were raised when Taruffi had difficulty in getting the Thinwall off the line. On the first lap Taruffi was nowhere but by the fifth lap he was already in 2nd place. His time over the measured mile was 144.9 m p h to Fangio's best with the BRM of 141.8 m p h. By quarter distance Taruffi was in the lead and pulled out enough time for a stop to change tyres. After his stop he regained the lead and slowed down for a comfortable win.

Taruffi again drove the car in the Formula Libre race at Silverstone. Unfortunately he jumped the start and was penalized 30 seconds. The opposition was tough, with Gonzales and Wharton on BRMs, Villoresi on the factory Indianapolis-type Ferrari and Landi and Rosier with privately entered 4.5-litre Ferraris. The Vandervell pit crew had a somewhat difficult time in trying to communicate to Taruffi that, despite the fact that he was circulating a healthy distance ahead of all the other cars, his penalization had dropped him to 5th place. When Taruffi caught on he quickly increased his speed and began making up 2 seconds a lap on the actual leaders. He moved up to second place behind Villoresi when Gonzales crashed the BRM and, despite a frantic chase by the portly Argentine driver who then took over Wharton's BRM, Taruffi overcame the works Ferrari, BRM and penalization all in one to win with time in hand. The Thinwall was really on good form and Vandervell's development work was paying off.

Vandervell had been noticing young Mike Hawthorn. When Mike gave Villoresi and the factory 4.5-Ferrari such a fright at Boreham, Tony Vandervell decided to give Hawthorn a try on the big car. Hawthorn was sent to a small meeting at Turnberry where he took the lead only to retire when the gearbox gave trouble. Vandervell decided that he was going back to more experienced drivers and contracted Farina to drive the car at Goodwood. With the rapid doctor at the wheel, fireworks were expected as he was pitted against the equally fiery Gonzales and Parnell, with Wharton making up the BRM team. Farina made a poor start when his back axle began to break up and he had to work hard to finish 2nd.

Too much power

Farina again drove the car at Charterhall but once again the back axle broke causing his retirement. The power that Vandervell was getting out of the Ferrari engine was beginning to tell in the strain on the transmission components.

When the car appeared for the 1953 season it was once again modified. It was beginning to be difficult to tell its Ferrari ancestry. The body shape was altered but the car still looked monstrous. The exhaust layout was changed with the removal of the original Ferrari pipes which extended to the tail of the car and substituted by short stub exhausts, six protruding out of the body on either side. Transmission parts were specially manufactured to take the much increased horsepower of the engine which had been pushed to over 400 by Vandervell and his team. The Girling three-shoe brakes were removed and replaced by special Goodyear disc types. Alloy radiators and tanks replaced the original Ferrari components and served to lighten the car.

Taruffi was once again engaged to drive the car at the opening Goodwood meeting but the Italian was unfamiliar with the new disc brakes and did not put up his best performance. He was placed 2nd a long way behind Wharton's BRM. It was the only occasion when the Thinwall was well and truly beaten by BRM in their many encounters.

For the Grand Prix of Albi, Farina returned to the Vandervell team. Opposition was strong in the shape of three BRMs with Fangio, Gonzales and Wharton, a factory Ferrari driven by Ascari and the two private 4.5-litre Ferraris of Rosier and Landi. During the practice Farina had problems with carburetter settings and the gearbox. A set of four-choke carburetters was fitted in place of the twin choke type to try for extra speed on the very fast French circuit. The four choke carburetters made it almost impossible to change the twenty-four plugs so practice went by without Farina being able to do much circulating. When he finally did get out his car's bonnet flew off at full speed down the straight and then the car ran out of fuel. Farina had a habit of getting very temperamental about such things and it was lucky that most of the Vandervell team did not understand Italian when he came stamping in on foot.

Farina's ill humour put him in the right mood to tackle the number ones of the BRM and Ferrari teams. The first lap of the Albi Grand Prix was a sight never to be forgotten by anyone who was there. The order was Fangio, Ascari, Farina, the V16 howling its head off and the V12s shrieking in close pursuit. The pace was fantastic, Fangio had beaten the lap record by several miles per hour on his standing lap as had Ascari and Farina. It was motor racing at its very best with cut and thrust that only these great champions could indulge in with impunity. On taking the corner out of the pits, the tail of Fangio's BRM was actually inside the nose air intake of Ascari's Ferrari. Just when it looked as if the Thinwall was really going to give the Ferrari and BRM a run for their money, Farina came sliding into the pits covered from head to foot in hot oil. He was furious, not about the oil, but that his fun had been cut short, apparently he had been practising rubbing off green paint on to the red tail of Ascari's Ferrari down the straight where the cars were approaching 190 m p h.

The first 100 mph Silverstone lap

Farina was back in the Thinwall for the Silverstone meeting. He wasted no time with the BRMs and led from start to finish, setting a new lap record, the first over 100 m p h lap on the circuit.

Again Farina met the BRMs at Charterhall, it was the same story, straight into the lead. This time he did not finish, the engine began to misfire and Farina pulled into the pits.

Mike Hawthorn was given another tryout for the Vandervell team for the final Goodwood meeting. The car had trouble in practice, the strain of giving over 400 b h p regularly was beginning to tell. Hawthorn got the car to the line just in time for the start. Despite strong BRM opposition, the green monster flew straight into the lead; Hawthorn set a new lap record and won with ease. Later in the day Hawthorn drove the car in another event, it was a repeat of his earlier performance.

The Thinwall's Last Season

The following year Peter Collins was signed on to the Vandervell team to drive the long awaited Formula 1 Vanwall. While Hawthorn drove the Formula 1 prototype as No. 1 driver, Collins was given the Thinwall Special to keep his hand in. Collins ran the car at Aintree where he had an easy time against some strong opposition from Moss, Parnell, Behra and Flockhart. While in the lead he set a new lap record of 2 min. 12 secs. but a misfire in the engine slowed him and he eventually retired.

Collins met the BRMs again at Goodwood. One of the BRMs held the lead for four laps when Collins pushed the Thinwall by to score yet another win for the fantastic car. He thoroughly trounced the BRM the following week at Snetterton and took up the challenge again at the late season Goodwood meeting. Practice was not too promising, Collins managed 1 min. 34.8 secs. but Moss with the new 250F Maserati turned in 1 min. 32.6 secs. and Wharton's BRM 1 min. 32.8 secs. The race turned out differently: Wharton held the lead for just one lap before the screaming green car swept by. Collins pulled out 2 seconds a lap on his opposition and once again the Thinwall went on to an easy win.

The car's final appearance was at the second Aintree meeting. Collins knocked almost 8 seconds off his lap record, the Thinwall sounding great. At half distance the engine started to go rough and a few laps later Collins pulled in to retire. The old faithful car had run its last race, the engine had finally given up and Tony Vandervell was too busy with his Formula 1 project to take care of the old monster.

In his development of the original 4.5-litre Ferrari design, Tony Vandervell had shown the true potential of Enzo Ferrari's ideas. Ferrari had broken the supremacy of the supercharged Alfa Romeos with an unsupercharged design, an idea considered unthinkable at one time. The BRM with its tremendous power and development potential should have inherited the crown of the racing world from Alfa Romeo but Vandervell with his Thinwall had beaten them even more convincingly than Ferrari had done with Alfa Romeo. In all, the 4.5-litre Thinwall Special raced in 30 events in which it broke down 7 times and scored eleven 1sts and eight 2nds, a truly remarkable record for any racing car.

The Can-Am cars

The Type 212E was a 2-litre sports car intended for the 1969 European Hill Climb Championship. While not fitting truly into any of the categories listed at the beginning of this chapter, it can nevertheless be included in a Special and Experimental category. The engine was a flat 12 developed from the flat 12 Grand Prix car run by Bandini and Surtees in the 1965 World Championship. The model was No. 229 in the Ferrari Type list and was also listed as the 212E - Experimental. The engine had horizontally opposed cylinders with a bore and stroke of 65 x 50 mm, a unit capacity of 165.9 cc and a total displacement of 1990.8 cc. Compression ratio was 11 : 1 and it gave 280 bhp at 11,000 r p m. Lucas fuel injection was fitted. No chassis details or dimensions are given in the Ferrari Type list.

The car was driven by the Swiss Peter Schetty who was later to become Ferrari team Manager. The car was outstandingly successful beginning with a victory at Montseny followed by Rossfeld, Mont Ventoux, Trento-Bondone, Cesana-Sestriere, Friburg and Ollon-Villars. It easily won the European title and was later sold to Edoardo Lualdi Gabardi who already had a reputation in Italy as a successful private owner of Ferraris.

A further group of special cars were those prepared for the Canadian-American Challenge races. I am indebted to Geoff Willoughby and Steve Earle for the majority of the following details.

The Can-Am race series was begun in 1966. Originally the CSI had suggested an international challenge race as a championship for constructors of Group 7 cars the events to be held in Europe, Canada and the USA. Nothing came of this venture and the Canadians and Americans worked together to launch the Can-Am series.

Ferrari took no part in this series until September of 1967 when on the 17th of that month NART (North American Racing Team) of Luigi Chinetti entered a car for the Bridgehampton 200. In 1967 Ferrari had won the prototype championship with his 330P4 with support from the concessionaires using 330P3/4 cars. The factory cars had the 36 valve 24 plug twin-cam fuel injected engines and the concessionaires having the twin-cam 24 valve carburetted engines. Chinetti sent the NART P3/4 to Modena where the standard body was replaced with one of a much lighter type. The front end was much lower and smoother with single headlights. A roll bar was fitted behind the driver's head. The windshield was lowered with an aerodynamically shaped rear view mirror mounted on top of it. An air intake for the carburetters was offset to the left behind the driver. The specific nomenclature of this car has not yet been established.

Ludovico Scarfiotti was nominated as driver for the second and third races of the series held at Bridgehampton and Mosport respectively. The Ferrari was not up to the performance of the top class Can-Am cars and Scarfiotti recorded 1 min. 34.8 secs. at Bridgehampton compared to the McLaren time of 1 min. 29.85 secs.

At Mosport the Ferrari time was 1 min. 25.2 secs. compared to the McLaren at 1 min. 20.8 secs. At Bridgehampton Scarfiotti finished 7th and at Mosport retired with a flat tyre.

Project No. 218

For the final races of the 1967 season two specifically prepared cars were sent by the factory for Chris Amon and Johnathan Williams to drive. They were based on the 330P4 with an increase in displacement to 4.2-litres and with a saving of 365 pounds in weight. At 480 b h p the new cars gave 60 h p more than the NART Ferrari and differed otherwise from the Chinetti Ferrari by the use of a monocoque centre section made of fibreglass with frame extensions for the engine and body instead of the same section being in aluminium as on the NART car. The factory cars differed in appearance as they had no headlight. Two large intake scoops were fitted to the rear deck and a spoiler was fitted at the rear.

The official factory record has these cars as project No. 218 type Can-Am V12 bore and stroke 79 x 71 S/B ratio 0.9, unit capacity 348.04-cc, total capacity 4176.5-cc, compression ratio 11 : 1, 480 b h p at 8,500 r p m, Lucas fuel injection.

The cars were driven at the Monterey GP held at Laguna Seca on October 15th by Amon (No. 23) and Williams (No. 27). Amon recorded 1 min. 5.77 secs. and Williams 1 min. 7.35 secs. compared to the fastest time of 1 min. 2.68 secs. Amon started in 16th position and Williams in 20th position. Amon finished 5th and Williams 8th.

On October 29th the Times Grand Prix was held at Riverside. Again Amon (No. 23) and Williams (No. 27) were entered. Amon recorded 1 min. 44.4 secs. and Williams 1 min. 45.7 secs. compared to the fastest time of 1 min. 39.3 secs. Amon started in 15th and Williams in 21st position on the starting grid. Amon finished 8th and Williams retired.

The final race of the 1967 season was the Stardust Grand Prix at Las Vegas, this race was held on the 12th November. Amon qualified for 13th place in practice at 1 min. 35.0 secs. and Williams for 19th place on the grid at 1 min. 36.3 secs. compared to the fastest lap of 1 min. 30.8 secs. Amon was forced to retire on lap 66, four laps from the end of the race while lying 5th while Williams was forced out on the opening laps when he was involved in someone else's accident.

It is assumed that chassis No. 0858 was the car that Williams had driven and was the one sold at the end of the season to the Australian Scuderia Veloce of David McKay and later purchased by Paul Hawkins.

For 1968 the Ferrari factory decided to make an all out effort in the Can-Am series but it did not work out that way and the new car did not appear until the final race of the season at Las Vegas.

In the meantime NART fielded a 'mystery' car that apparently Ferrari had sent to Chinetti without the latter's knowledge. It was one of the modified P4s and was apparently the spare built as a backup for the previous season. The NART car appeared at Elkhart Lake on 1st September 1968 and was driven by Pedro Rodriguez. It set a time in practice of 2 min. 15.8 secs. compared to the fastest time of 2 min. 9.8 secs. and qualified 10th fastest. Rodriguez finished 13th.

At Bridgehampton on September 15th Rodriguez recorded 1 min. 32. 10 secs. compared to the fastest time of 1 min. 27. 69

secs. this gave him 11th fastest time. During the race Rodriguez clashed with Posey's Lola and retired with a broken suspension.

Project No. 228

On November 10th the Stardust Grand Prix was held at Las Vegas. The new Ferrari factory car was known as the 612 Can-Am and was recorded in the official Ferrari register as Project No. 228, Can-Am 612, V12, bore and stroke 92 x 78, S/B ratio 0.85, unit capacity 518.46, total capacity 6221.6, compression ration 10.5 : 1, 620 b h p at 7,000 r p m, Lucas fuel injection, Dinoplex ignition system. Other specifications were 4-speed gearbox in unit with differential. Front suspension independent with upper wishbones and single lower arms and radius rods, coil springs, telescopic shockabsorbers and anti-roll bar. Rear suspension independent by single upper and lower arms, radius rods, coil springs with telescopic shockabsorbers and anti-roll bar. Girling disc brakes outboard mounted on all wheels. Cast magnesium 15 in. wheels. Tyres Firestone 6.00/13.50 front, 6.00/15.50 rear. Weight 1750 lb. Wheelbase 96.4 in., front track 59.8 in., rear track 61.1 in. Overall length 160.5 ins., width 82.6 in., height to roll bar 35.0 in., to wing 48.4 in. At 1750 lb it was heavier than the McLarens which scaled 1480 lb. Chassis No. was 0866.

Two intakes between the front wings collected air from oil coolers mounted behind the doors on either side the air exhausting from shaped outlets in the top of each of the rear wings. The centrally mounted airfoil contained brake flaps and the angle was adjustable through hydraulic pressure generated from the engine and controlled by the driver who had a button for this purpose on the steering wheel. A separate hydraulic circuit was used to operate the brake flaps on the wings together with a third on the nose section of the body between the wheel arches.

The chassis was of tubular steel space-frame type with stiffening by means of riveted-on aluminium sheeting around the cockpit area.

The car was briefly tested before the race having run about 200 miles during which it became obvious that there were some problems with braking and handling.

At Las Vegas, Amon qualified 9th fastest with a time of 1 min. 32.20 secs. There was mass confusion at the start and when the dust settled, one of the stationary cars was the new Ferrari. It was out of the race with its throttle slides jammed with debris.

There was nothing left to do but wait for the 1969 season.

In the one event of 1968 the car had been attended by Franco Gozzi as team manager, Mauro Forghieri to supervise the technical end and Giulio Borsari with three factory mechanics plus some American assistance to take care of the hard work.

For 1969 the situation changed and it became a more private enterprise. Chris Amon was still nominated to drive, Bill Gavin acted as team manager and Roger Bailey was in charge of the mechanical end. The car was based in Detroit a long way from home.

Watkins Glen 1969

The car made its first appearance in the 1969 series at the third race of the series at Watkins Glen on July 13th. For this race the airfoil had been removed and there was no provision for an air brake between the forward wheel arches. At the tail the bodywork did not curve down behind the rear wheels, instead it ran at a tangent from the top of the wheels and flared out slightly to run into a spoiler running across the full width of the back. The vents for air spilling out from the oil coolers were no longer visible in the top of the rear wheel arches. Both the chassis frame and the body had been lightened so that the weight was down to 1640 lb.

At Watkins Glen, Amon recorded 1 min. 3.7 secs. compared to the fastest lap of 1 min. 2.21 secs., this gave him third place on the starting grid. The Ferrari ran well and finished 3rd overall.

At the Edmonton, Alberta race, Amon qualified 3rd fastest again with a time of 1 min. 24.9 secs. compared to the fastest at 1 min. 22.9 secs. in this race the Ferrari finished 2nd. A wing was first tried on the car but wobbled from side to side. Bruce McLaren tested the car and was of the opinion that the wing would fall off during the race and as a result it was removed.

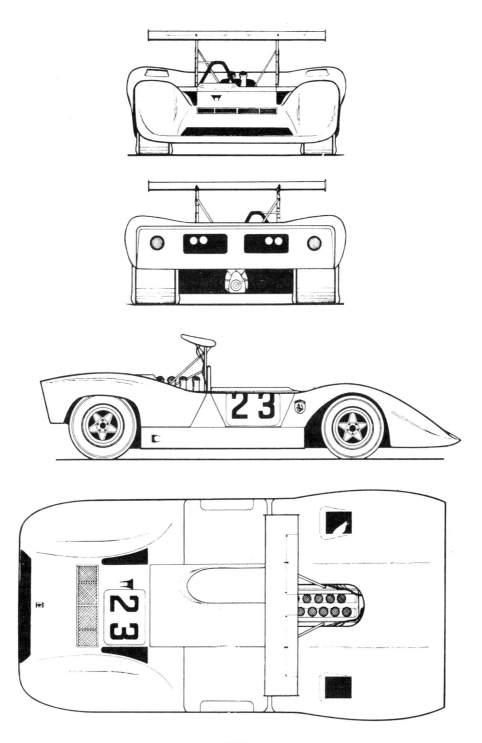

Type 612 CanAm

At Lexington, Ohio, Amon recorded a time of 1 min. 36.0 secs. compared to the fastest at 1 min. 25.9 secs. this qualified him in 12th position. However, the Ferrari again ran well and he finished 3rd. At this race, the car was fitted with a suspension mounted wing designed by Paul Lamar; as it had no bracing, the wing persisted in lurching back and forth and had to be removed for the race. The factory had sent a new engine but it blew up in practice; as a result Amon had to qualify during a wet period. At the next race at Elkhart Lake the wing reappeared this time with lateral bracing running from the supporting struts to the roll bar.

At Elkhart Lake, Amon turned a time of 2 min. 13.0 secs. compared to the fastest time of 2 min. 6.3 secs. qualifying him 7th for the start; The wing was installed and used for the race. It helped handling but the car was not as fast as before. The oil cooler was moved up into the airstream as the oil temperature had been running very high at all the races. The car was running third near the end of the race when it ran out of fuel, no one having calculated that the extra downforce of the wing would have on fuel consumption.

At Bridgehampton the car ran a time of 1 min. 26.31 secs. compared to the fastest at 1 min. 24.62 secs. which qualified Amon in 3rd fastest position. The car made three laps before the belt snapped off the oil-pump drive and the car retired with no oil pressure.

At Michigan, Amon recorded 1 min. 34.0 secs. compared to the fastest time of 1 min. 32.5 secs. but the engine blew shortly after and the car was a non-starter.

At Laguna Seca, Amon lapped in 1 min. 01.8 secs. to qualify but the engine blew and could not be repaired in time. Fastest lap at Laguna Seca was 59.53 secs.

At Riverside, the factory sent over a larger capacity engine reputely a 6.9-litre. However, I cannot find any reference to this engine in the Ferrari register. It seems strange that this new version of the Can-Am engine should not have been assigned a project number by the factory. A piston collapsed in practice and the regular 6.2-litre engine was substituted; Amon practised at 1 min. 35.09 secs. compared to the fastest at 1 min. 34.03 secs. but the car did not finish as it

was disqualified. The engine problem centred around the sump detail. Oil would wash up to the front, away from the oil pump, on braking; the surge back on acceleration loaded up the pump and resulted in the snapping of the drive belt.

The 6.9 suffered from the same trouble, resulting in a broken oil pump drive. Keith Duckworth examined the sump and some changes were made.

For the final race in Texas, Amon qualified at 1 min. 34.5 secs., compared to the fastest at 1 min. 31.6 secs; The 6.9 was reinstalled but it blew a piston and the smaller engine was once again fitted. After 10 laps the oil pump drive again broke.

The car was again revised in body and engine. The oil coolers were moved to the rear centre, the wing removed and a 512M engine fitted. By comparison, the 1969 612 lapped Modena in 48.8 secs. (Amon), the 1970 version 50.6 (Merzario). The car was shipped to Steve Earle and Chris Cord who retained Jim Adams to drive it.

The car first appeared at Donnybrooke. Adams qualified in 6th place at 1 min. 33.1 secs., fastest lap being 1 min. 30.8 secs. He finished in 4th place but was suffering from fuel starvation towards the end of the race.

At Laguna Seca, Adams qualified 11th in 1 min. 04.2 secs. with the pole time being 1 min. 00.6 secs. It retired on the 27th lap with fuel starvation.

At Riverside, the car also qualified 11th at 1 min. 39.78 secs., compared to fastest lap of 1 min. 32.49. The car again did not finish as it was involved in a crash with Peter Gregg on the 15th lap.

At Mosport, the car qualified 8th in 1 min. 22.0 secs. compared to the fastest 1 min. 17.3. It completed the race to finish 8th.

At St Jovite, the car qualified 9th at 1 min. 33.7 secs., fastest lap was 1 min. 32.9. This time the car did not start as the fuel metering unit failed.

At Road Atlanta, the car qualified 10th at 1 min. 22.2 secs. compared to the pole time of 1 min. 17.7. It did not finish as the engine threw a connecting rod while running in 5th place. However, it was listed to have finished in 10th place.

At Watkins Glen, a new factory engine was installed but had problems early in practice and the car did not qualify.

At Edmonton, the car had been given a complete overhaul. Traco rebuilt the engine and body changes were made to the rear spoiler. The car qualified 6th at 1 min. 25.1 secs. the pole time being 1 min. 20.3. The car did not finish, going out with a broken axle.

At Laguna Seca, it qualified 10th at 1 min. 02.45 with pole time 58.78 secs. this time it finished 7th.

At Riverside, it qualified 14th at 1 min. 39.29 secs. compared to pole time of 1 min. 31.96. Once more it did not finish, going out with a split brake line.

The Type 330 LMB

Another group of cars that can be classified as special and experimental cars are the 330 LMBs. I am much indebted to Gerald Roush who was responsible for the following piece of research.

At the Nurburgring 1,000 km race on 27th May 1962, Ferrari had, among other entries, a four-litre prototype coupe to be driven by Michael Parkes and Willy Mairesse. This car was a GTO fitted with a four-litre 400 SA engine with three 46 DCF3 Weber carburetters which necessitated a larger hood bulge. Some authorities credit this car with four wheel independent suspension, but it apparently was standard GTO in nearly all respects except the engine. It finished second in the race behind a Ferrari 246 SP.

For the Le Mans 24-Hour Race on 23rd and 24th June 1962, Parkes and Lorenzo Bandini were entered in a four-litre GTO now fitted with six carburetters. Some sources say this was the Nurburgring car with modifications while others claim it was a second version. Yet another four-litre GTO was built in 1963 for Paul Michael Cavallier of France. At Le Mans Parkes and Bandini were forced to retire their car due to overheating but they had never been in contention after Parkes had parked it in a sand bank while leading the first lap.

There was considerable speculation as the 1962 season drew to a close that the FIA was going to tighten its regulations on GT prototypes for the 1963 season. Consequently

Ferrari's press conference in late 1962 was notable for the absence of the new cars Ferrari intended to use in 1963. Ferrari did, however, state the opinion that the sports/racing cars were now 'dead' and that he was concentrating on the GTs and prototypes, but that on the latter he was awaiting clarification of the rules. Speculation on what Ferrari was eventually going to produce centred on two different attacks on the prototype classification. He was known to be developing a new rear-engined machine with the 12-cylinder three-litre engine but it was surmised that should the regulations get too stiff or complicated he would follow the precedent of 1962 and put four or even five-litre V12 engines into GTO chassis.

When Ferrari finally showed his 1963 cars to the press at a special Monza press conference in early March, it was obvious that he was considering both possibilities. One of the prototypes was an open, rear engined, three-litre V12 engined car designated the 250P while the other was a berlinetta with a front engine, four-litre V12, designated the 330LM -- subsequently known as the LMB to distinguish it from the later rear engined LM. Usually described as a GTO nose on a 250 GT Berlinetta Lusso body, the 330 LMB was in many ways unique. The front fenders from the headlights back followed the Lusso's more straight line rather than the GTO's slightly curved line. Also, there was no sign of either the GTO or Lusso hood bulge. Retained were the GTO's characteristic low, elliptical air intake with three supplementary intakes above. Flanking the intake was a pair of round, recessed driving lights.

There were three side vents on the front fenders, reflecting late GTO practice, and behind the rear wheel arch there were three vents. Above the rear wheels raised sheet metal covers slotted fore and aft were fitted. The purpose of these appendages has been variously reported as allowing more tyre clearance and assisting in rear tyre cooling. Probably both functions were intended. Although there were small detail variations such as recessed door handles, the remainder of the body generally followed regular Lusso lines, even to a spoiler-less rear end.

It has been generally believed that the LMB

body was a hybrid, resulting from the mating of GTO elements with elements from the Berlinetta Lusso which had been introduced in October 1962. But the late Warren Fitzgerald was working on the theory that the LMB was part of a straight-line progression from GTO to Lusso styles and came between the GTO and Lusso. Also, that the basic shape of the LMB/Lusso lines were developed at the Ferrari factory and not by Pininfarina.

Powering the 330 LMB was a further development of the unit used in the 1962 four-litre prototypes. Based on the 400 SA engine it was a V12 with a single overhead camshaft per bank. Bore and stroke was 77 x 71 mm giving 3,967-cc displacement. Induction was by six Weber 42 DCN carburetters and there was a single spark plug per cylinder. The compression ratio was 9.0 to 1 and the output was 400 b h p at 7,500 r p m.

The chassis followed GTO practice and was a multi-tubular affair. Independent suspension was fitted at front using double A-arms and coil springs. At the rear there was a live rear axle with alloy centre-section and leaf springs assisted by coil springs on the shockabsorbers. Although this rear suspension followed established GTO practice, it was apparently the cause of some confusion as several sources mistook the coil spring 'compensators' for evidence of an independently sprung rear suspension and the car is so listed in several references. Dunlop disc brakes and Borrani wire wheels with triple-eared knock-offs were used all around. The transmission was a four-speed/reverse unit mounted with the engine. Wheelbase was 2,500 mm, front track 1422 mm and rear track 1414 mm.

The first competition appearance of the 330 LMB was at the Sebring 12-Hour Race on 23rd March 1963. Only one was entered, driven by Parkes and Bandini. Running steadily around sixth place through the first four hours the car was retired after 72 laps with a split fuel tank. Parkes had lost control on a slippery spot and hit one of the course's infrequent trees. He was able to get the car back to the pits but the race was finished. As this was not the first off-course excursion for the car there was apparently some problem with either the handling or the brakes, or both.

Le Mans 1963

The 330 LMB was next seen at the Le Mans practice session held in early April. Parkes turned the fifth fastest practice lap of the session in the LMB, the four faster times being set in the 250P. Parkes' time was 3 min. 51.4 secs., well under the lap record of 3 min. 57.3 secs. set by Phil Hill in the 1962 winning car. Also bettering the lap record in the LMB were Mairesse, with a time of 3 min. 53.3 secs. and Bandini, with 3 min. 55.8 secs.

The 330 LMB did not appear at either the Targa Florio or the Nurburgring, but for Le Mans in mid-June no less than three of the four-litre Berlinetta and one similarly bodied three-litre car were entered. The serial number on the 330 LMBs were 4381, 4453 and 4725 and the 250 LMB was 4713.

In the Ferrari Owner's Newsletter Nos. 4383 and 4385 were also listed as newly discovered LMBs. Research by Gerald Roush and Chuck Queener, however, comes up with the theory that these two were not LMBs but customized Lussos. No. 4561 was also included in the Newsletter but again research by Roush indicated that this car was originally a 4-litre GTO built for Paul Michael Cavallier. However 4619 was an LMB delivered to the famous shipbuilding yard, Cantiere del Timavo, S.p.A. Trieste on 11th November 1963, and subsequently imported to Paris on 9th September 1963.

No. 4381 was the Parkes/Bandini car from Sebring, and was also apparently the press conference car and the Le Mans trials car. At Le Mans it wore race No. 9, and was driven by Pierre Noblet and Jean Guichet, entered by Noblet. For the first time the car had a bolted-on tail spoiler, reminiscent of early GTOs. The lightest LMB entered, at 1211 kg or 2680 lb, it was also the fastest during the race. It led the LMBs and ran as high as fifth overall, turning a lap in 3 min. 58.6 secs. before retiring after 75 laps with no oil after the oil filter came loose. This car carries engine No. 4619GT.

The retirement of Noblet/Guichet allowed another 330 LMB to take over fifth place, No. 4453, entered by Chinetti's North American Racing Team and driven by Dan Gurney and Jim Hall. During practice before the race this car, with Dan Gurney driving, had been seventh fastest of all the entrants with a time of 3 min. 59.5 secs. Bearing race No. 11 the car was placed as high as third and was running in fourth place when forced to retire after 126 laps with rear axle problems. This performance was managed despite problems with the tyres on the car -- N A R T using a different brand than the rest of the Ferrari entries. The fastest lap turned by No. 11 before retiring was 4 min. 1.1 secs.

No. 12 was the 330 LMB No. 4725 driven by Jack Sears and Mike Salmon, entered by Maranello Concessionaires. As befits an English entry it was equipped with right hand steering. It was also the heaviest car in the race at 1258 kg or 2770 lb, and all three 330 LMBs outweighed the other cars in the race. Bothered by clutch problems and water losses, the Sears/Salmon car survived the 24 hours to finish fifth, its fastest lap being 4 min. 4.2 secs.

Finishing in sixth place, behind two 250Ps, two 250 GTOs and the 330 LMB was car No. 26, the three-litre LMB driven by Masten Gregory and David Piper and entered by N A R T. Although visually similar to the four-litre cars the 250 LMB was built on a standard GTO chassis with 2400 mm wheelbase and was considerably lighter at 1147 kg or 2520 lb. It had a type 168 GTO engine with six twin-choke Weber 38 DCN carburetters, and was serial No. 4713. In the early morning hours of the second day of the race, the car was running third, ten laps behind the leading 250Ps. Then time was lost with electrical problems and attempting to make it up, Gregory stuffed it into one of Le Man's infamous sand banks. This was to cost them the GT class win and dropped them back as far as tenth before finally finishing sixth. Its fastest lap was 4 min. 5.6 secs., faster than either of the GTOs that finished ahead of it but during the race it had been no match for the GTO of Abate/Tavano (No. 4757) which crashed after 105 laps. This despite the fact that the LMB was heavier than the GTOs.

In August, 1963 one of the 330 LMBs was entered in the 50 lap Guards International Trophy Race at Brands Hatch, England. Finishing three laps behind the winning sports car, and one lap behind the GT winning GTO, the LMB driven by Bandini won the Sports and Prototype

Over 3,000-cc class ahead of a D-Jaguar and a Maserati Tipo 151. The Ferrari was No. 4725.

The history of 4381 following Le Mans is not very clear. Somewhere along the way it received a bit of what Warren Fitzgerald called Tom Mead 'street-izing' and has been reported as passing through the hands of an owner in Africa, another in Connecticut and is now in California, owned by Steven Fry. Also somewhere along the way it picked up a new engine, No. 4619. It has the proper racing instruments - 10,000 r p m tach, no speedometer, tank and fuel pressure, oil pressure and temperature, and water temperature but no exposed gear shift gate. It is left hand drive.

No. 4453 is also now in the United States, owned by John W. Carmack of Indiana. After Le Mans it was shipped to Chinetti in the United States and title was transferred to Donald Fong of Atlanta. Fong arranged to have Dan Gurney drive the car in the Bridgehampton Double 500 on 15th September 1963. At this time a hood scoop was added to the car and a brace added on the passenger side to give more lateral strength between the frame and the transmission. This cut-off brace was later to give rise to the speculation that the car was at one time right hand drive. It has always been LHD. The car was at this time painted a metallic gold/brown.

In the race Gurney was no match for Hansgen in a Cooper-Buick or Rodriguez in a 250P Ferrari, but managed to survive the close racing and attrition rate of the also-rans to finish third, one lap behind the leaders.

After Bridgehampton Carl Bross acquired the car, and then Joel Martino of Chicago. Mr Martino had the car painted its present yellow, formed in the bolt-on rear spoiler, and did some other modifications including an interior the present owner describes as one 'that you wouldn't believe.' Mr Carmack acquired the car in the fall of 1969 and among other items of restoration he has redone the interior in the original black. The car has a porcelain enamel N A R T badge on the rear panel and an engine hour meter that never worked very well. Mr Carmack has measured his car as well as a Berlinetta Lusso which he also owns and found that above the cowl line, and except for the slightly longer and flatter rear window, the two bodies and windows are exactly the same.

The third 330 LMB, No. 4725, is now owned by Pierre Bardinon of France. It was if anything more like a Lusso than the other LMBs in that it had the interior done even before Le Mans as a touring car with all the bright work, nice upholstery, insulation and glass windows. This probably accounts for the heavier weight at Le Mans which later led to speculation that the car was steel bodied, which in part it was.

Before Le Mans Pete Coltrin experienced a ride with Mike Parkes in a shake-down test run of this car on the Autostrada, and his impressions were recorded in *Car and Driver,* November 1963. After Le Mans Maranello Concessionaires tamed it down a bit to make it more suitable for road use and at this time the original six carburetters were replaced by three. The car later passed through the hands of Ferrari France where Jess Pourret had the opportunity of driving it and contemplated buying it. While he liked the RHD, the crash gearbox, power and top speed, he found the brakes marginal and the handling not as light and easy as a GTO. He decided against it and the car wound up in Bardinon's collection.

Among the many side excursions taken by Ferrari history is the case of GTO No. 3451 which for some time was rumoured to be the 250 LMB. It seems, the story went, that the 250 LMB was merely a rebodied GTO and after Le Mans it was restored to its original configuration. When the car was in France 1963 Le Mans race sheets were found in it giving its 3451 GT number and calling the car a 250 LMB with Gregory and Piper as drivers and what happened each lap. How this came to be is a mystery, for the car was in all probability always a Series 1 GTO.

The real 250 LMB was No. 4713, and is currently owned by Mr William Reardon of Villanova, Pennsylvania. After Le Mans it was entered in the Tourist Trophy race at Goodwood, England, on 24th August 1963, driven by Roger Penske and entered by N A R T. Penske was at a disadvantage with the other 3-litre Ferraris in the race because of the extra weight of the LMB as compared to the GTO and he never seriously challenged the leaders, running in fifth and sixth position and

carrying on a running fight with Sears in a Jaguar. Late in the race he faded back and finally finished eighth.

Next N A R T entered the car in the Tour de France to be run 14-22nd September 1963. Drivers were Jo Schlesser and Claude Leguezec, rally No. 170. Following the start at Strasbourg, the first timed event was a night hill climb from Turkheim to Trois Eois and Schlesser made fastest time of the night. This was followed by a fourth fastest in the one-hour race at the Nurburgring the next morning and a first place in the one and one-half hour race at Spa. This put the car first in 'le classement general' at the end of the first stage, ahead of three GTOs.

The second stage took the cars to the circuit at Rheims for a two-hour race. Guichet, in a GTO, was Schlesser's close rival and while Schlesser got off to a good start, Guichet soon made it apparent that his GTO was faster. Guichet was content, however, to stay in second place behind Schlesser and slipstream the LMB and conserve fuel. Guichet was able to finish the race without stopping but Schlesser had trouble on his refueling stop and overshot his pit requiring him to go back out and complete another lap before stopping for gas. Schlesser returned to the fray quite upset and over-revved his engine [9,400 r p m was seen on the tell-tale — Ed.] and lost a valve. Schlesser finished third in the race and made fastest lap at 2 min. 32.9 secs. It took the Ferrari mehanics one hour and twenty-three minutes to change the valve spring so when Schlesser left the control at Rheims he had to make up the lost time. When he arrived at the Hirson control it was discovered that he had missed getting two signatures at the checkpoints along the way and this disqualified him.

The car was next entered by N A R T in the Daytona Continental 2,000 km race on 16th February 1964, driven by Walt Hansgen and Bob Grossman. They ran as high as second before finally finishing third behind two GTOs. Next the car was entered in the Sebring 12-hour race on 21st March 1964, driven by Bob Grossman and Dick Thompson but they were never in contention and finished 15th overall, 11th in GT class. The car's last appearance in International competition was at the Player's 200, Mosport, Canada on 6th June 1964. The race was run in two heats and when the final placings were tallied Bob Grossman was tenth overall and second in the GT class in the LMB.

Grossman, who now owned the car, raced it quite a bit in S C C A regional and national events in the north-eastern United States. Trying to track down all the appearances of the car is made difficult by the constant reference to it as a GTO.

In June, 1964 Bob advertised the car for sale and in September it was purchased by H. F. Hanscom of Barrington, Rhode Island, and he was the first owner to register the car. He changed the rear axle ratio to improve street driving and gasoline mileage, replaced the plastic windows with roll-up windows exactly like the Lusso's using Lusso parts, and added a heater. In several details the car differs from the 4-litre LMBs. It is, as already mentioned, built on the standard GTO wheelbase, a factor which allowed it to be campaigned as a GT and not a prototype although it was in appearance a one-off. Its engine is a type 168 GTO engine with six Weber 38 DCN carburetters and it has side instead of rear exhaust, and a five-speed transmission.

Mr Reardon acquired the car early in 1969, and with the car came a legendary victory of the 24 Hours of Spa in 1963. No such race was held and the reference must be to Schlesser's first place finish in the Spa event on the Tour de France. The engine has been rebuilt and the car remains in racing trim.

During 1963 Ferrari also produced another four-litre prototype which consisted of a 250P fitted with the larger displacement engine. With Parkes as driver this car was seen at the Prototype and Sports Car race which preceded the French Grand Prix in June and the Sports and Grand Touring race following the British Grand Prix in July. Development of this prototype continued in 1964 when Ferrari introduced the successors to the 250P -- the 275P and the 330P. From there development proceeded through the P2, P3, and P4 series.

The 330 LMB however appears to have been a dead-end. At the Paris Auto Show in October, 1963 Ferrari's new Berlinetta, the rear engined 250 LM, was introduced. When the new Berlinetta failed to be homologated for 1964 Ferrari produced a new version of the 250 GTO, the 250 GTO 64. But in the prototype field he stayed with rear engined cars and no further experiments were carried out with front engined prototypes. Even when Ferrari began his series of production four-litre automobiles in 1964, he used a new version of the V12 with wider bore centres. Only the very first 330 GTs - 250 GTE 2 + 2s with four-litre engines - used the four-litre from the 400 SA.

The 250 GT Breadvans

Once again I am indebted to Chuck Queener and Jess Pourret for the research on the Breadvan 250 GT Ferrari variations. Due to the nature of these cars they have been included in the 'Special and Experimental' group.

The first question arises with how many of these cars were actually built? With minor differences to each one, three such cars were constructed. The bodies in all cases were built by the late Piero Drogo, while the mechanical work was done by Giorgio Neri and Luciano Bonacini.

Dealing with these cars now is best done chronologically as they were not built in numerical order. It seems likely that chassis No. 2819 was the first one as it was the first to appear in competition. Giotto Bizzarrini, the man responsible for the GTO, helped as an advisor for the car's construction. Going back to its origin No. 2819 was an alloy-bodied (Scaglietti), 280 b h p Competition SWB sold to Oliver Gendebien on 11th September 1961. Gendebien took delivery in Modena after which he entered the Tour de France with Lucien Bianchi as co-driver. On Race No. 145, they finished 2nd overall and 2nd in class. Somewhere between the end of September 1961 and 18 May 1962, the new body was added and the car was sold to Count Volpi of Scuderia Republica de Venezia. It was entered at Le Mans where it failed to finish. Neither of the next two cars were as striking as No. 2819.

The second car is a real disaster in terms of destroying its original character. Chassis No. 2735 was also a Competition SWB berlinetta and it was sold new to Stirling Moss on 30 May 1961. This car was one of the two SWBs run by Rob Walker/S. Moss and was responsible for five first place victories in GT events in 1961. The car was later sold to Chris Kerrison and was entered in the Tourist Trophy at Goodwood in 1962. It became involved in a crash with John Surtees and Jim Clark which badly damaged Surtees' GTO and Clark's Aston Martin. Kerrison then sent the SWB berlinetta to Drogo's for its current body.

After the usual shunts, the car was last reported to be in England and its original engine is now resting in No. 3729 GTO while a 2+2 engine, No. 3635, is pulling it around.

The third car was No. 2053. Another SWB, it was purchased in Torino by C Toselli on 2 August 1962. Toselli ran it in a few races after which the car was returned to SEFAC where it sat until 1962, when it was sold to Francorchamps. Entered at Le Mans for Berger/Darville, the car crashed heavily. It then went to Equipe National Belge whose headquarters are located at Jacques Swaters where it was transformed into the last of the 'Breadvans'. Its last competition for ENB was at the Le Mans trials after which the car was sold to Mr Remordu who managed to win several races during the later half of 1963. No. 2053 continued to run club events and in 1964 at one such meeting at Spa the car was destroyed. It has been rumoured that the car was later rebuilt by Willy Mairesse's brother for a Mr De Feierland. This has never been substantiated.

Described as 'counterfeit' GTOs, it was not formerly known how many of these specials had been completed.

The ASA 'Mille' story

In 1959 Ferrari also built a brand new engine which was scheduled for a small capacity touring car. This engine was first installed in a Fiat 1100-cc chassis and was thoroughly developed by Ferrari. At one time there were plans to develop this car for Ferrari production but it would have required a greater layout than Ferrari and his newly formed SEFAC company were willing to put out.

Finally the engine design was sold for production to the De Nora family who began construction of the small four cylinder Ferrari under the name of ASA 'Mille'. Several of the ASA 'Mille's were built and imported into the USA to compete with the then current Porsche in its price range. It was quickly discovered that the ASA was not competitive and although several were sold in the USA, the project was abandoned.

Ferrari records two types of engines for this car No. 125 which was also labelled (164) 950, it was a 4 cylinder in-line with a bore and stroke of 67 x 69 giving a displacement of 973-cc and with two 32DCN carburetters gave 80 b h p at 7,000 r p m. The other was No. 126 also known as the 850 Coupe'; this also was a 4-cylinder in-line with a bore and stroke of 65 x 64 giving a displacement of 849.5-cc, this gave 86 b h p at 7,000 r p m.

CHAPTER ELEVEN
The sports cars

WHEN Alfa Romeo decided to re-enter racing and run their own team in 1938 under the name 'Alfa Corse', the Scuderia Ferrari was absorbed by the Alfa Corse team and the 158 Alfas, spares and necessary material were transferred to Milan with Ferrari, Massimino, Bazzi and the others following. However, in short order things failed to work out and the Ferrari crew returned to Modena in less than a year.

To his Scuderia garage in the viale Trento Trieste, Ferrari set up a machine tool manufacturing plant known as Auto Avio Construzioni.

In the latter part of 1939 Ferrari was approached by two young clients who wanted cars for the Mille Miglia, to be held the coming April. The clients were Alberto Ascari (son of Antonio Ascari) making his debut in international motor racing, and the Marchese Lotario Rangoni Machiavelli di Modena (the latter was killed testing a three-engined bomber during the war).

The decision to built two cars was made in December and Enrico Nardi recalled that it was Christmas Eve and Massimino stated, 'Then, as now, Ferrari's passion for racing cars had not abated nor was it on the wane, and it was with the coming Mille Miglia in mind that he entrusted to me the study of a car adapted for participation in that event.'

The Type 815

Thus the Type 815 was born. It should be mentioned here that in the first edition of *The Ferrari* I briefly mentioned the Type 815. Since that edition was published, old friend Pete Coltrin decided to thoroughly research the subject of the 815 and came up with a host of new material which was later published in *Road & Track* magazine. At the time of my writing the original text, I had just gone through a frustrating period of

research on the 815 and a hunt for what was supposed to be the one surviving car. A healthy sum of money was available to purchase the car but it ended up as a fruitless chase as the car had been broken up by a scrap merchant. On consultation with Massimino he proved non commital about the whole subject. However, times have changed and Massimino was more co-operative in Coltrin's researches. It turned out that the second car did not return to Nardi for conversion into the Nardi-Danese as I had originally been told but remained complete to be discovered by Peter Coltrin and Franco Zagari in the little village of San Martino in Rio near Modena.

The two cars were built at the viale Trento Trieste garage where had so many other Ferrari projects. It should be made clear that Nardi had nothing to do with the design of the 815 as has been previously stated. He had left Lancia to join Ferrari as a test driver and was scheduled to be Rangoni's co-driver. After the war he left Ferrari and returned to his native Turin to go into business with Danese building racing cars. The confusion arose from the fact that at this time he acquired, from Ferrari, 815 engine castings and components which he later used, in 2-litre form, in a space frame chassis of his own design. At his Turin plant he still had an 815 block and crankshaft at the time of Coltrin's research effort and stated 'I only tested the 815. Alberto (Massimino) designed them.'

With less than four months to design, build, and test two cars it was deemed necessary to employ the greatest number of production car parts possible.

The popular Fiat 508 C Balilla 1100-cc was chosen as the basis for the chassis and engine. The channel-section cruciform chassis of the 1100, reinforced, was used along with the front and rear suspension, gearbox and differential. The independent front suspension was a Dubonnet system. The rear suspension was a live axle with semi-elliptic leaf springs and an anti-roll bar. The worm and sector steering box was also Fiat 1100. In all the Fiat 508 C was a logical choice; parts were plentiful and the car was a rugged, well proven model. There was also another reason as will be explained.

The straight-eight engine

Massimino's notes (in quotes) are included in the following description of the engine:

'The field of study and realization limited itself to one engine type only. The solution decided upon was to utilize two 1100 (o h v) cylinder heads, this being the most difficult problem with the given time limit.'

An 8-cylinder in-line one-piece cylinder block was designed and cast in aluminium, as was a one-piece valve cover and finned sump. Ferrari not having his own foundry at the time, the castings were done in Bologna by Fonderia Calzoni. (This, and an examination of the engine, lays to rest the previous misconception, that the block was composed of two 1100 units.)

'Iron cylinder barrels were used in direct contact with the coolant water. The steel crankshaft (made by Ferrari) had a 2-4-2 configuration and turned in five bearings of anti-friction material and of Fiat origin. The forged steel connecting rods and their bearings were also of Fiat origin, as were the valves, valve springs, and rocker arms.

'Obviously, the camshaft was a new design with 16 lobes and had two driven gears for the oil pumps; the Fiat distributors were driven by the original Fiat system. A one-piece sump contained the lubrication oil.'

The two Fiat distributors proved difficult to synchronize and were replaced by a single Marelli distributor, mounted where the forward Fiat unit had been. The tachometer was driven by the rear distributor drive gear.

A single water pump was specially made to handle the increased capacity and power of the engine and was located at the front end of the block.

Four Weber Type 30 DR2 single-choke downdraught carburetters were mounted on two intake manifolds, one per head and in between the two 3-branch exhaust manifolds (siamesed centrally).

Massimino does not recall the exact power figures but contemporary reports quoted 72-75 b h p at over 5,500 r p m and he thinks these figures are very close.

An added inducement to using Fiat components was, according to Ferrari, that Fiat was offering cash prizes to Mille Miglia class winners using its products.

The two Ferrari 815 bodies were made by Carrozzeria Touring and the style was very similar to that of various Touring bodied Alfa Romeos of that period. In 1940 they were considered to be quite aerodynamic and handsome. In this respect they were not improved upon for some time by postwar Ferraris.

When Enzo Ferrari left Alfa one of the terms of their agreement to disagree was that he was obliged not to build or race a car under his own name for four years. Thus the first 'Ferrari' was designated simply '815' to indicate the number of cylinders and the engine capacity - and to avoid the confusion a '158' designation would have caused.

Ferrari said he was almost certain that the car found in San Martino was the Ascari car. Checking serial numbers bore this out. Pete Coltrin talked with the late Marchese Rangoni's brother, Marchese Rolando, who produced papers concerning the registry on later sale (to a local junk yard) of his brother's car; the chassis and engine numbers were 020. Those of the surviving car are 021. Ferrari said that the Ascari car was acquired by a Sig. Beltracchini of Milan. This fits in with reports that the other car spent the war years near Modena and undoubtedly was scrapped some time later. Conversation with ex-Ferrari mechanic, Lucchi, indicate that this might have been as late as 1963 — 64.

The 'Brescia' Grand Prix 1940

The 1940 Gran Premio di Brescia was held on April 28th and consisted of nine laps on a closed, triangular, circuit using the public roads between Brescia, Cremona and Mantua. The total distance was 933 miles. This race is almost always referred to as the 1940 Mille Miglia because of the mileage and the same organizing club — the Automobile Club di Brescia. After the 1938 Mille Miglia, during which several spectators had been killed, the government had banned the race. Thus, for 1940 the AC di Brescia chose the triangular course and called it GP di Brescia in order to gain permission to hold the race.

The 1500-cc class was composed of 15 cars. The 815s of Rangoni/Nardi and Ascari/Minozzi (Ascari's nephew) were both privately owned by a Ferrari team.

From the start the 815s took the lead in their class, the Ascari car leading Rangoni at the end of the first lap. On the following lap, Ascari was forced out with a broken exhaust valve, possibly caused by a rocker arm failure. Massimino says that these two Fiat components were usually quite reliable and an unexpected source of trouble in the race. From this point on, the Rangoni 815 led the class until the penultimate lap when, with a 33-minute lead, he was forced to retire. A contemporary report said a small bearing failed. Nardi maintained that it was the timing chain that broke.

Nardi also recalled that the pre-race strategy had been to take it fairly easy in the opening stages but that Ascari began pressing from the start and Rangoni obliged.

Many have considered the cars a failure because of their Mille Miglia showing but they were not; they were another step in Ferrari's goal in life and a very important one. Thankfully, this car 021, the last of the first, will never see another junkyard.

THE 12-CYLINDER SPORTS CARS

'It was small, red and ugly but it went like a rocket' was the Italian newspaper's report when the V12 Ferrari sports car made its first appearance after the war. During the war years, whilst he had been busily producing machine tools, Enzo Ferrari had formulated his racing plans for the post-war period. All his schemes were to be based on a single design of a V12 cylinder engine. From this he would produce sports cars of various sizes and eventually go on to his great ambition, that of a full Grand Prix car.

Maserati had four cylinders, Talbot had six, Alfa Romeo had eight, why not twelve then for Ferrari? It was daring and farsighted. Aside from the number of cylinders, it was a simple design. Here again as with Pete Coltrin's researches on the 815 I am indebted to a good friend, Stan Nowak, for a great deal of new material on the early Ferraris.

At the time of writing the original manuscript, research material on the early cars was limited and there were many uncertainties. Stan's interests were aroused when he found 004C (then the oldest known Ferrari), brought it to the USA and restored it for display in Henry Austin Clark's Long Island Automotive Museum. Since then Stan has discovered and is in process of restoring 002C which is the oldest Ferrari. After many discussions at the 'Chanteclair' in New York both Stan and I felt that the early history of Ferraris could do with some extra research and revision and as a result he plunged into the job with great enthusiasm and gathered enough material for an article for *Road & Track* magazine from which some of the following material has originated. As already stated it was originally conceived as a 1.5-litre sports car engine. While a timetable of development is not available, it is safe to assume that at least two of the sports car engines were on the dynamometer by autumn 1946.

The November/December 1946 issue of *Inter Auto* contained full details of the new Ferraris and two of them appeared for the first time in public for practice in the sports car races at Piacenza on 11th May 1947. Nino Farina crashed one car in practice and Franco Cortese retired in the race with a seized fuel pump (the early Ferrari used an aircraft-type centrifugal fuel pump driven off the front of the left camshaft). The factory advises that they built only three cars during 1947 and all started out as Type 125 1.5-litre sports cars. From the photographic evidence of the time it can be seen that one was a two-seat cycle-winged car (usually driven by Nuvolari) and the other two were roadsters with full width bodywork thought to be by Carrozzeria Touring. Towards the end of the summer of 1947 two of the engines were bored and stroked to 1900-cc and were renamed Type 166.

The 1947 Season

The complete racing record of all Ferraris for 1947 was as follows: May 11th, Piacenza, Farina was a non starter and Cortese failed to finish after leading the race. May 25th, at the Caracalla circuit in Rome, Cortese finished first overall with the Type 125. June 1st at Vercelli, Cortese took the 125 to another first place. The second race at Caracalla on June 5th turned out differently and the 125 of Cortese failed to finish. On June 15th the 125 and Cortese were back in form again and the Ferrari took first overall.

June 21-22nd were the dates of the Mille Miglia but Cortese and the 125 broke down. On June 29th Cortese took the 125 to another win at Varese. On July 6th Nuvolari joined the team and recorded a first in the sports car class at Forli with a 125. On July 13th Nuvolari repeated his performance with the same car at Parma, with Cortese's 125 in second place. On July 20th Nando Righetti joined the team and finished third overall in a 125 at Florence, Cortese failing to finish. On August 15th at Pescara, the Type 159 (the Type 125 bored to 60 mm) made its debut and Cortese finished second overall. On August 24th Nuvolari had a DNF with his 125. On September 28th the annual Modena Grand Prix was held and Cortese made the fastest lap with the 159 but failed to finish and Righetti brought the 125 into fifth place. The final race of the season was on October 12th at Turin where Raymond Sommer took the Type 159 to a first overall.

The Type 125 was the basic design from which all the 12-cylinder cars to the present date originated. It had a 60 degree V12-cylinder engine with a bore and stroke of 55 x 52.5 mm giving a capacity of 1498-cc with a compression ratio of 9 : 1 and a maximum power output of 118 b h p at 6,500 r p m. The crankcase was in Siluminum light alloy and the cast-iron liners were of the forced-in type. The cylinder head was of light alloy with hemispherical combustion chambers. The high resistance steel crankshaft was counterbalanced and supported on seven bearings, one of which also took axial thrust. Inclined overhead valves were actuated through rocker arms from a single overhead camshaft per bank of cylinders. The camshaft drive was by means of a chain with semi-automatic tensioning.

Ignition was by single plug per cylinder and two Marelli magnetos. Three twin-choke 32 DCF Weber carburetters were used in conjunction with one FIMAC mechanical fuel pump.

The clutch was of the single dry-plate type and the gearbox was in unit with the engine. Five forward speeds and reverse were provided, first gear ratio being 2.41, second 1.74, third 1.27, fourth 1.00 and fifth 0.925; an oil pump and filter were incorporated in the gearbox.

The transmission shaft was two pieces with central support. The rear axle was of the rigid type with a central light-alloy casing containing the differential assembly. Semi-elliptic leaf springs and low pressure hydraulic shock-absorbers took care of suspension.

Front suspension was independent with double wishbones and a single transverse leaf spring. Damping was by means of hydraulic shock-absorbers mounted vertically between the upper A-arms at the front. Hydraulic brakes with a single master cylinder were used on all four wheels together with a mechanically operated hand brake on the rear wheels.

The frame was of tubular construction with oval-section steel tubes. Wheelbase was 2.200 m, front track 1.270 m, rear track 1.250 m. Front wheels were 3.50 x 15 fitting 5.00 x 15 tyres. Rear wheels were the same as at the front but fitted 5.50 x 15 tyres.

Type 166

By January, 1948, the three 1947 engines were being bored and stroked again and the engine was up to just under 2 litres or 166-cc per cylinder and the famous Type 166 Ferrari was born. The old 125 chassis were modified or replaced (the factory is not clear on this though one 166 Touring-bodied coupe exists in the USA, that has what is evidently one of the first three frames, but with later engine and suspension) and two were built with new cycle-winged bodywork. The third car with full-width bodywork looked almost identical to the full-width cars that had run in 1947.

These two Type 166 cars were 002C and 004C, with identical cycle-winged bodywork. They were completed in January and March

(*Top Left*) Dr Cacciari in his Type 166 Ferrari with 'Autodromo' body in the 1953 Mille Miglia. This is the body Prototype of Ascari's 4 cyl Monza. The co-driver is Jacques Swaters. The car was later converted to a 'Burano' for the filming of 'The Racers'

(*Top Right*) Ascari driving the Type 166 (triple carburetter model) in the 1950 International Trophy meeting at Silverstone

(*Middle Left*) The Spear/Roberts 2 litre Ferrari which finished 4th in the first Sebring race in 1950. Here being 'chased' by a Morris Minor

(*Middle Right*) Le Mans 1951. This Type 166 was co-driven by Betty Haig and Madam Simon to finish 15th overall

(*Bottom*) Type 166 rebodied by Carrozzeria Fantuzzi of Modena

(Top Left) A late Type 166MM rebodied by Abarth for Franco Cornacchia's Scuderia Guastalla. It was raced in 1953 by Giulio Musitelli. Carlo Abarth stands on the far right
(Top Right) Jim Kimberley in Briggs Cunningham's Type 195-Inter 2.3 litre in Argentina 1951
(Middle Right) Mario Crepaldi's 2.3 litre Type 195-Inter Spyder by Touring
(Bottom) Torrey Pines 1952. Phil Hill scores his first Ferrari victory with the Type 212-Inter 2.5 litre that won the 1951 Tour de France driven by Pagnibon/Barraquet

(*Top Left*) Stagnoli's Vignale bodied Ferrari Type 225 2.7 litre at Monaco 1952

(*Top Right*) The engine of the 212E Ferrari which took 3rd overall at the 1973 Pebble Beach Concours d'Elegance. It is owned by Steve Griswold

(*Middle*) Pagnibon at Monaco 1952 with a Type 225 2.7 litre

(*Bottom Left*) Angel Maiocchi in the Argentine with an unusual Vignale bodied Type 212-Inter

(*Bottom Right*) Villoresi with the Vignale bodied 2.5 litre at the Coppa Intereuropa Monza 1951

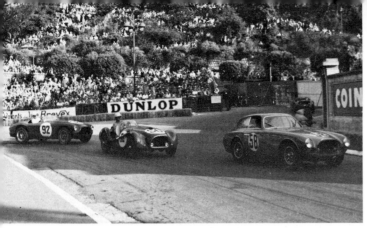

(*Top*) (58) Lucas leads (50) Stagnoli leads (92) Castellotti at Monaco 1952 all three in Type 225s

(*Middle*) 2.7 litre Type 225 being driven by Franco Cornacchia at Monza 1952

(*Bottom*) Appenine Cup 1952, the Marzotto/Marini Type 225 2.7 litre

(*Top*) Bobby Baird in his 2.7 litre Ferrari which he placed first at the Knockagh Hill Climb
(*Middle*) Bracco wins the 1952 Mille Miglia with the 3 litre 250MM (experimental engine)
(*Bottom Left*) Roberto Rossellini in his 250MM at the start of the 1953 Mille Miglia
(*Bottom Right*) Bracco's 1952 Mille Miglia winning 250MM as it is today owned by Ernie Mendici. Factory documents definitely establish that this was a Prototype and numbers coincide with those of the original

(Top Left) 250MM Vignale Spyder. The body is similar to the 4.1 litre Mille Miglia winning car
(Top Right) The ex Phil Hill 250MM now owned by Rick Busenkell
(Bottom Left) Bianca Maria Piazza with a 250MM at Monza 1953
(Bottom Right) Villoresi wins at Monza 1953 in a Type 250MM Coupe

Ferrari 250 M/M
Berlinetta Pinin Farina

(*Top*) Type 250 Mille Miglia Competition Coupe bodied by Pinin Farina
(*Middle*) A 250MM Farina Coupe at the 1973 Virginia City Hillclimb owned by Roger Ellis
(*Bottom*) Bill Spear in the Type 340 America 4.1 litre leading Fred Wacker's Cadillac Allard at Watkins Glen. Spear's car was one of the first large engined cars to be raced in the USA

(*Top Left*) Pan American Road Race 1952. Alberto Ascari's
4.1 litre Type 340 Mexico
(*Top Right*) Taruffi's 4080-cc Ferrari. Mille Miglia 1952
(*Middle*) Mike Hawthorn with the Type 340 Mille Miglia 4.1
litre bodied by Touring of Milan at Silverstone
(*Bottom Left*) Giannino Marzotto wins the 1953 Mille Miglia
in the 4.1 litre 340MM Vignale bodied car
(*Bottom Right*) Marzotto in the 4.1 litre Coupe, Le Mans
1953

1948 and were the first Ferraris ever sold. Number 002C went to Gabriele Besana and 004C to his brother Count Soave Besana. Almost immediately after taking delivery, Gabriele shipped his car to Argentina where he participated in the Temporada series of races. He did not do well but the car attracted much attention as it was the first Ferrari ever seen in South America. *Road & Track's* Southern American correspondent in the early '50s, Dr Vicente Alvarez, remembers the car and its inexperienced driver well, and in going through his files, found two photographs he had taken of 002C in Buenos Aires in February 1948. Shortly afterwards, it was shipped back to Italy.

The first records of 004C, show that the engine was dynamometer tested on 12th February 1948 and the car was then driven by Count Besana and Count Bruno Sterzi into sixth place overall in the circuit of Sicily race on March 4th. Besana must have been well satisfied with the car as he took delivery of it officially on March 14th.

This car retained the V12 engine, but the bore and stroke were altered to 60 x 58.8 mm giving a displacement of 1995-cc and utilized pistons which gave compression ratios between 8.0 : 1 and 10 : 1; it had a maximum power output of 140 b h p at 6,600 r p m. The engine was of exactly the same construction as the Type 125 except that three Weber 36 DCF carburetters were fitted in place of the 32 DCFs on the earlier model. Clutch, gearbox, gearbox ratios and general suspension layout remained the same as did wheelbase and track, the only alterations being to fit 5.50 x 15 tyres on the front instead of the 5.00 x 15 fitted on the earlier model and the fuel tank capacity was increased to 145 litres. This model immediately proved to be superior to its Maserati counterpart and Ferrari registered wins in the Tour of Sicily and Mille Miglia with Biondetti. Luigi Chinetti added to these victories by winning the 12 Hours of Paris and setting new world records in the 2-litre class for 1 hour, 100 miles and 200 kilometers.

The 1948 Season

The 1948 Targa Florio and the Tour of Sicily were held as one event this being one lap around the island, a total distance of 1,080 kilometres.

The race was held in two groups, Sports and Touring and three Ferraris were entered in the sports category. Biondetti drove with his car's owner, Prince Igor Troubetzkoi. Cortese and Besana were the drivers of the other two. Cortese was eliminated because of the use of impure alcohol in his fuel blend and Besana also retired. Biondetti had a difficult win as he was hounded all the way by the little 1100-cc Cisitalia driven by Piero Taruffi. In the early stages Ascari and Villoresi with the new 2-litre Maseratis had led but Villoresi had engine trouble and Ascari ran off the road. Biondetti covered the single lap in 12 hrs. 12 min. averaging 88.86 k p h (54.15 m p h).

The 1948 Mille Miglia was held in April and Ferrari entered the car that had won the Targa Florio/Tour of Sicily for Biondetti/Navone. Other Ferraris were entered by Cortese/Marchetti, Nuvolari/Scapinelli, Righetti/Bruni and G. Besana/S. Besana. The race became a battle between Biondetti and Nuvolari. Between Rome and Livorno the Cortese/Marchetti Ferrari retired as did the Besana/Besana car. Nuvolari made a tremendous effort to win the race; he had lost a mudguard due to an offroad excursion, in another spin he damaged a spring and broke the mechanic's seat loose and then he lost the complete bonnet of the car! On the leg from Bologna to Asti, Nuvolari went through Reggio Emilia with a lead of 29 minutes over Biondetti but the car broke down when the damaged spring shackle finally gave out. Biondetti/Navone went on to win in 15 hrs. 5 min. 44 secs.

The 12 Hours of Paris took place in September. Chinetti entered a cycle-fendered Type 166 for himself and Lord Peter Selsdon to drive. It was ostensibly a sports car race but some of the cars were thinly disguised GP machines.

At the start it was Guy Mairesse substituting for Chiron on the 4.5-litre Talbot that took a tremendous lead over the rapid 1.5-litre Simca of Manzon/Veyron. The Simca was out quickly with engine troubles and the first three places at 3 hours were held by Mairesse/Giraud-Cabantous (Talbot), Pozzi/Chaboud (3.6-litre Delahaye) and the Chinetti Ferrari. Despite several pit stops, one of which was to have his finger disentangled from the horn button, Chinetti took a temporary lead. After 6 hours the Pozzi/ Chaboud Delahaye was leading at 77 m p h but Chinetti was on the same lap. Selsdon resigned himself to being a spectator as Chinetti pressed on with his battle. After 9 hours Chinetti had a firm lead averaging 77.5 m p h having covered 84 laps to the Pozzi/Chaboud Delahaye at 82 laps. The Ferrari took the checkered flag at the 12-hour mark having covered 870.046 miles at an average of 72.5 m p h with the Delage of Louveau/Brunet second some 30 miles behind.

Spyder Corsa

Ferraris 002C and 004C were the first of a series of cycle-winged Ferraris made during 1948 and this model was called the 'Spyder Corsa'. Nine of these were built and only even numbers were used to identify the chassis and engines as these were considered lucky, and the odd numbers were reserved for the touring models which were introduced in the summer of 1948.

After the first three or four Spyder Corsas were completed, the suffix 'C' was dropped and 'I' for 'Inter' was used instead. The car that John Willement owns, which was the original Folland/ Wyer car, bears the number 010-I and Briggs Cunningham's car is 016-I. The 'C' for 'Corsa' was then reserved exclusively for the Grand Prix cars then under development and on 5th September 1948, the Ferrari 1.5-litre supercharged Grand Prix cars were seen and heard for the first time in the Italian Grand Prix at Valentino Park, Turin. The 'Spyder Corsa' era had ended and the 'Corsa' era had begun. No more cycle-winged Ferraris were produced and the first 1949 model Ferrari sports/racing car began a new number series with number 0002-M - a Type 166 'Mille Miglia' with full width 'Barchetta' roadster body by Carrozzeria Touring this car now being in the Harrah collection.

The 1949 Season

The following year, 1949, the power output of the engine was again increased and success followed success. In the USA Ferrari won the Seneca Cup at Watkins Glen and followed up with another clear cut victory in the Mille Miglia. Luigi Chinetti put Ferrari amongst the immortals with a convincing win in the 24-Hours

of Le Mans and the 24-Hours of Spa, and Bracco began to make a name for himself in winning the Biella-Oropa and Vermicino-Rocca di Papa hill climbs at the same time annexing the title of Italian hill climb champion.

The 1949 season began with Biondetti/ Benedetti winning the combined Tour of Sicily/ Targa Florio with a type 166 MM. This was followed with a major effort in the all-important Mille Miglia; 2-litre Ferraris being entered by Bianchetti/Sala, Mosters/Bianchi, Biondetti/ Salani, Bracco/Maglioli, Gabriele Besana/ Cortese, Vallone/Sighinolfi, Vaccari/Mori, Bonetto/Carpani and Taruffi/Nicolini.

The 1949 Mille Miglia was run over a different circuit from that used in 1947 and 1948. The race was shortened from 1134.6 miles to 987.7 miles and the event took place April 24th - 25th.

Bonetto was fastest in all the stages to Rome averaging 168 k p h (104.31 m p h) at Parma and 128 k p h (79.49 m p h) at Livorno. At Livorno he was 2 minutes ahead of Taruffi with Besana/Cortese 3rd at 5 minutes then Biondetti, Rol's Alfa Romeo and Bracco's Ferrari. At Rome, Bonetto averaged 132 k p h (81.97 m p h) leading Taruffi by 4 minutes and Biondetti by 7 minutes. By the time he reached Pescara, Bonetto's brakes were giving trouble and Taruffi took the lead with Biondetti in second place. Taruffi reached Ravenna averaging 130 k p h (80.73 m p h) with a 6 minute lead over Biondetti but the pace had been too hot and Taruffi retired leaving Biondetti in the lead with Franco Rol's Alfa Romeo in second place. After Ravenna, Bonetto was able to speed up again and succeeded in overhauling the Alfa before Brescia which gave Ferrari a well deserved 1st and 2nd place in the classic Italian race, Biondetti won at 81.5 m p h covering the distance in 12 hrs. 07 min. 05 secs. with Bonetto 28 minutes behind and Rol 44 minutes behind. The only other Ferrari to finish was the Vaccari/Mori car in 34th place.

Le Mans

On 25th and 26th June 1949 the famous Le Mans race was run for the first time in post World War 11 years. With Government assistance, the Automobile Club de l'Ouest had constructed an imposing set of pits, grandstands and other related buildings.

Two Ferraris were entered, both Type 166 MM Barchettas. No. 22 driven by Luigi Chinetti and Lord Peter Selsdon and the other No. 23 driven by Jean Lucas/Ferret. Lucas/Ferret only just made the starting line as Lucas had damaged the car during the night practice when he found a child wandering across the road. Chinetti was worried about his oil pressure at the start of the race.

At the start it was the 4.5-litre Delahaye of Chaboud that took the lead followed by Rosier's 4-litre Talbot, Paul Vallee 4.5-litre Talbot, Brunet 3.6-litre Delahaye, Johnson 2.5-litre Aston Martin and Veuillet 3-litre Delage, followed by the Ferraris of Lucas and Chinetti.

After one hour Chaboud still led with Flahault 4.5-litre Delahaye in 2nd place the Lucas/Ferret Ferrari 3rd, Rosier's Talbot 4th and Chinetti 5th. At 8 p.m. after 4 hours of racing, the two Delahayes still led but Chinetti was next up followed by Lucas/Ferret. Half an hour later Chaboud's Delahaye caught fire and Chinetti took the lead. At Chinetti's pit stop for fuel, Ferret took the lead but crashed at White House, the furious but unhurt driver making it back to the pits on foot. At midnight Chinetti still had the lead but was on the same lap as the Vallee/Mairesse Talbot and the Veuillet/Mouche Delage. When the Valee/Mairesse Talbot broke down Chinetti increased his lead to just over 1 lap ahead of the Delage.

At 5 a.m. Chinetti was about 2 laps ahead of the Louveau Delage. Lord Selsdon drove a few laps during the night and by 11 a.m. Chinetti held a three-lap lead. Mouveau began to put on the pressure to try to catch the Ferrari. Chinetti made a routine pit stop but then made another stop shortly afterwards. After this the Ferrari clutch began to slip and the cockpit was drenched in oil. Louveau now began to drive Grand Prix style in his attempt to catch the slowing Ferrari. With 20 minutes to go Louveau was only 9 miles behind but Chinetti was aware of his opponent and went on to win with an advantage of 9.92 miles covering 1,970 miles at an average speed of 82.27 m p h.

Following his victory at Le Mans, Chinetti entered the 166 in the 24-Hour race at Spa in Belgium. This time his co-driver was Jean Lucas. Villoresi and Ascari in another 166 were entered but were non starters. The only other Ferrari was a private entry by Roosdorp and De Ridder.

The race was scheduled to be run by classes only, there being no official overall classification. Nevertheless the centre of interest was naturally the overall leaders. At the start it was the two fast 1500 Simcas of Trintignant and Manzon that took the lead with Chinetti in third place. After the first hour the Trintignant Simca was in the pits and Chinetti moved into second place. With Manzon dropping out and Trintignant slowed by his pit stops Chinetti took the lead by the 3rd hour. With the second Simca out with engine trouble Chinetti's challenge came first from the Johnson/Brackenbury Aston Martin and then from the big 4-litre Delage of Louveau/Mouche.

The race was uneventful with the Delage chasing the Ferrari until there were 25 minutes left to go. Louveau suddenly lost a great deal of oil and slowed down to a crawl in an attempt to finish. Chinetti spun on Louveau's oil and crashed into a house injuring a woman. He stopped to give first aid before driving off with a very battered car at a slow pace. In the meantime Louveau had stopped within sight of the finishing line waiting to cross after the Ferrari but learning that the Ferrari had crashed, his pit crew waved him on. Louveau continued on slowly but the Ferrari although going at a much reduced pace, was faster and Chinetti completed two more laps to win at 78.86 m p h. The Roosdorp/De Ridder Ferrari finished 7th in the 2-litre class 17 laps behind Chinetti.

On August 7th the Grand Prix of the A C F was held at St. Gaudens. The circuit was one of the fastest in Europe at the time, Chiron's Alfa having lapped at 108.9 m p h in 1935 and Le Begue's Talbot holding the fastest sports car lap at 101.4 m p h set in 1939. The 1949 event was restricted to sports cars and Chinetti entered the Le Mans winning Ferrari. The title of 'sports car race' was somewhat of a misnomer, the 4.5-litre Talbot entered by Harry Schell being the 1939 GP car with the latest 4.5-litre Talbot engine provided by Raymond Sommer, who was nominated to drive the car.

Sommer was easily the fastest in practice and in the race took an immediate lead ahead of Chiron's Talbot, Chaboud's Delahaye, Pozzi's

Delahaye and Chinetti's Ferrari.

The three fast 1500-cc Simcas of Trintignant, Scaron, and Manzon gave Chinetti some trouble in the early stages but by 15 laps Chinetti was in 4th place behind Sommer, Pozzi and Chaboud. The heat was tremendous and many pit stops were made just to cool off the drivers. Only Chinetti and Englishman, John Heath seemed unaffected. At 30 laps it was Sommer, Pozzi and Chinetti. Then Harry Schell took over from Sommer and six laps later the Talbot blew up.

Spectators became a problem wandering all over the track. Trintignant crashed his Simca to avoid some of them. Just before the end Chinetti too fell victim to the spectators, he crashed to avoid a group of them and on returning to the track was, without his knowledge, given a couple of pushes by unwanted hands. Officials were made aware of this and the unfortunate Ferrari driver was robbed of his second place and given 8th place in the standings. Chinetti reports that after winning the 12 Hours of Paris, the Le Mans winning Ferrari was sold to T A S O Mathieson.

The Type 195 Sport

The 166 was so successful that, although Ferrari built a larger capacity car, the 2.3-litre Type 195 Sport was built only in a very small quantity and never achieved the fame of its smaller brother. It had a bore and stroke of 65 x 58.8 mm with a displacement of 2340-cc and with a compression ratio of 10 : 1 gave 145 b h p at 6,600 r p m. This car was also fitted with the three twin-choke Weber type 32 DCF carburetters and had different ratios in the five speed box, first being 3.08, second 1.9, third 1.38, fourth 1.0 and fifth 0.925. The wheelbase was increased to 2.500 m with a front track of 1.270 and a rear track of 1.250; 3.50 x 15 wheels were used all round fitting 5.90 x 15 tyres and dry weight increased from 800 kg to 900 kg.

Type 212 Sport

This car was in turn followed by another of increased capacity, the type 212 Sport. A displacement of 2562.51-cc was obtained with a bore and stroke of 68 x 58.8 mm and 150 b h p was achieved at 6,500 r p m with a compression ratio of 8 : 1. The car was to all intents, similar to the earlier models, changes being made in gearbox ratios, first being 3.157, second 1.946, third 1.403, fourth 1.00 and fifth 0.914. Wheelbase was again shortened to 2.250 m with a front track of 1.270 and a rear track of 1.250 m 4.40 x 15 wheels were fitted mounting 6.40 x 15 tyres. Tankage was reduced to 120 litres and weight reduced to 800 kilos.

The 2nd Mexican Road Race was held in 1951 and was won by Ferrari with Taruffi/Chinetti 1st in 21 hrs. 57 min. 52 secs. with a similar Ferrari in 2nd Ascari/Villoresi covering the distance in 22 hr. 5 min. 56 secs.

The race was run in reverse from the previous year and began at Tuxtla Gutierrez to Ciudad Juarez on the USA border a distance of 1,936 miles.

Taruffi/Chinetti averaged over 88 m p h compared to the previous year's record of 72.4 m p h and on the last leg from Chihauhua to Juarez the Ferrari raised the average from 100.5 m p h to 114 m p h.

The cars were 212 Inters having chassis similar to that of the 4.1-litre car that was shown at the Paris Auto Show. They had new rear suspensions with semi elliptic springs on each side and four seater bodies by Vignale. The cars were quite a bit over the weight anticipated, scaling in at 26 cwt, this was blamed on the hasty preparation by the Turin coachbuilders who built bulkier bodies than anticipated.

The two Ferraris had 33-gallon fuel tanks which was just about adequate for the longest run as their mileage averaged about 10 m p g. They had a top gear which yielded 19.5 m p h per 1,000 r p m and gave a maximum speed of 136 m p h at 7,000 r p m which could be attained on the last stages of the race at an altitude of about 4,000 ft above sea level. Before the race Ferrari decided to strengthen the rear suspension with the addition of an extra leaf in the springs.

All the cars were required to use 'Supermexolina' fuel produced by the Mexican National Petroleum Company, its octane rating being 80. The Ferraris ran on 640 x 15 Pirelli 'Super Sport' tyres. During the first stage from Tuxtla to Oaxtaca (329 miles) the Packard of Trevous was in the lead; the two Ferraris suffering from

repeated stripping of their tyre treads. Taruffi/
Chinetti lost 31 minutes and Ascari/Villoresi
lost 53 minutes with these troubles. They
replaced the 'Super Sports' with racing tyres
and eventually had to use the Mexican-manufact-
ured Goodrich-Euzcadi tyres as their supplies
of Pirellis ran out. The Goodrich tyres proved
to be excellent. On the second stage from Oaxaca
to Puebla (256 miles) Ascari/Villoresi were first
in 3 hr. 22 min. 5 secs. with Bracco/Cornacchia
2nd in a Lancia at 3 hr. 23 min. 3 secs. and
Taruffi/Chinetti third at 3 hrs. 27 min. 52 secs.

On the difficult 81-mile run from Puebla to
Mexico City, Taruffi/Chinetti won in 56 min. 29
secs., Bracco/Cornacchia were second in 57 min.
14 secs.

The 4th stage between Mexico City and Leon
(267 miles) was won by Ascari/Villoresi in 2 hrs.
44 min. 36 secs. with Taruffi/Chinetti 2nd in 2
hrs. 48 min. 11 secs. The 5th stage Leon to
Durango (333 miles) was won by Ascari/
Villoresi in 3hrs. 24 min. 21 secs. from Betten-
hausen/Metzler in a Chrysler with Taruffi/
Chinetti 3rd at 3 hrs. 29 min. 11 secs. The 6th
stage Durango to Parral (251 miles) was won by
Ascari/Villoresi in 2 hrs. 37 min. 7 secs. from
the Bettenhausen/Metzler Chrysler with
Taruffi/Chinetti third. The 7th stage Parralto
Chihuahua (186 miles) was won by Betten-
hausen/Metzler at 1 hr. 39 min. 21 secs. from
Ascari/Villoresi at 1 hr. 43 min. 1 sec. and the
8th and last stage from Chihuahua to Juarez it
was the Bettenhausen/Metzler Chrysler again.
However on the overall timing the two Ferraris
came out first and second.

Type 225 Sport

The 212 was followed by the Type 225 Sport
(No. 38 in the Ferrari official register). The car
had a cubic capacity of 2715.4-cc with a bore and
stroke of 70 x 58.8. With a compression ratio of
8.5 : 1 it gave 210 b h p at 7,200 r p m; three 36
DCF Weber carburetters were fitted. It had the
same wheelbase and front and rear track as the
212 Inter at 2,250 mm, and 1,278 mm front and
1,250 mm rear. However, it used 5.25 x 16 tyres
at the front compared to the 212 Inters 5.50 x
16. Rear tyres were identical at 6.50 x 16. Fuel
tankage was upped from 120 litres to 150 litres
but weight remained the same at 850 kg.

The 1952 Mille Miglia saw 225 Sport Ferraris
entered by Biondetti Castelotti, Paolo Marzotto,
Vittorio Marzotto and Scotti, but it will always
be remembered as the Mille Miglia in which the
new 3-litre Ferrari of Bracco beat the Mercedes.

The 250 Mille Miglia

Ferrari undertook development of a three-
litre version of the Lampredi V12 but, when the
car appeared, it was a bored-out variant of the
2.7-litre 225 Sport, incorporating several
improvements to increase horsepower. The car,
built in the early part of 1952, looked identical
to the 225 Sport coupe's with Vignale bodies,
and in fact had been originally slated for that
successful series of 'customer' sports racing cars.

The 3-litre volume was achieved by means of
a three millimetre bore increase to 73 mm. This
resulted in a total displacement of 2953 cc with
the 58.8 mm stroke. Three Weber 36 DCF/3
carburetters were fitted, and with 8.2:1
compression and a new camshaft grind, the
engine probably developed about 220 b h p at
its maximum of 7,000 r p m. The chassis was the
Export Tuboscocca having the Ferrari five-speed
gearbox and 4:1 rear axle.

Strong preparations were being made by the
Mercedes team for the 19th Mille Miglia, to be
run during the first week in May of 1952.
Despite the fact that an excess of 30 Ferraris
were entered by private competitors, Ferrari
rushed the 250 Sport to completion as well as a
Barchetta with a Lampredi V12 engine for
power. Taruffi was chosen to drive the 4.1,
while the prototype 250 Sport, fitted with a
Vignale coupe body similar to the 225's, was
handled by Giovanni Bracco. Bracco, intimately
familiar with the difficult course, replaced
Villoresi who had been injured at Bern, and
Ascari who was at Indianapolis.

The race was held during a wet spell, which
reduced expected speeds but, from the starting
point, Brescia to the first checkpoint, Verona
Bracca held the lead with a 93 m p h average. He
was five minutes ahead of Kling's Mercedes.
However, at Racenna, the fourth checkpoint,
Bracco was forced to reduce his pace, simply
because he had exhausted his supply of tyres. By
the time he reached L'Aquila, he had lost 13

minutes to the 300 SL. Bracco was now driving on tyres that were of unsuitable size for the car.

Kling set the pace into Rome with a total elapsed time of 6 hours, 45 minutes, 55 seconds, with Taruffi 2nd in 6 hours, 52 minutes, 10 seconds. Bracco arrived 3rd at 6 hours, 57 minutes, 53 seconds. On the northward leg of the event, the Ferrari/Mercedes dual became heated. At Siena, Taruffi took over the lead from Kling, only to have transmission failure at Poggibonsi. Taruffi's Barchetta was purportedly equipped not with a 4.1, but a 4.5-litre Grand Prix engine.

At the Siena checkpoint, Bracco had reduced his deficit to eight minutes. By the time Florence was reached, he was lagging only four minutes behind the 300 SL

Then began Bracco's now legendary drive over the Futa Pass, this being over the final leg of the race. Using his knowledge of the treacherous road, he caught up with and passed the Mercedes. When he reached Bolonga, at the foot of the pass, he was four minutes ahead of Kling, a lead which he maintained for the balance of the race through Modena, Reggio, Emilia and Piacenza.

This section, all on good, paved roads, gives further credit to Bracco and his co-pilot Rolfo, who never again allowed the 300 SL to close up with them.

Bracco re-entered Brescia victorious with an elapsed time of 12 hours, 9 minutes, 45 seconds, giving an overall average of 79.9 m p h. Kling was 2nd with a time of 12 hours, 14 minutes, 17 seconds. Several empty bottles of Chianti were seen in the back of the 250, and Bracco could hardly stand unaided. Whether this was due to sheer exhaustion, the Chianti, or both has never been satisfactorily answered. Whatever the case, Bracco remains as one of the most daring amateur drivers ever, a driver who was able to tackle the machine like efficiency of the Mercedes team.

After the Mille Miglia, the 250 prototype was modified, receiving three 4-choke Weber carburetters requiring a larger hood scoop. The rear fender wells were also vented to improve brake cooling.

The car was entered by the factory in the Le Mans race for 1952 with Ascari and Villoresi driving. After setting a new lap record, Ascari pushed things a little too hard and the car went out. Its final appearance in 1952 was at the Mexican Road Race, again with Bracco driving. Bracco again lead the Mercedes team, and appeared the sure winner. But Mercedes had their vengeance when the differential broke.

Final modifications on the prototype included the four-speed gearbox and stronger rear axle, both originally designed for the 342 America. Thus the car became the first of the 250 Mille Miglia series of 1953, about 40 of which were built and raced by private owners. Today, the prototype, No. 0156ET, is in the hands of a California collector.

In the Targa Florio three of the 225 Sport Ferraris were entered. Vittorio Marzotto, however, was a non starter, Marcini retired on the 2nd lap and Tom Cole finished 11th after having been credited with a time over the flying kilometer at 201.117 k p h, faster than anyone except Bracco's 4.1 Ferrari.

At the International Maloja Hill Climb Piotti took his 2.7 to second place in the 2 to 3 litre category.

In the Tour of Sicily, Castelotti brought his 2.7 home 5th in general classification and 2nd in the sports category.

Castelotti won the Portuguese Grand Prix with his 2.7 Type 225 Sport with Stagnoli in 3rd place also with a 2.7.

In the Coppa d'Oro delle Dolomiti, Paolo Marzotto won the event with his 2.7 from his brother Giannino in a 4.1 Ferrari. The other Marzotto brother, Vittorio was 4th in a 2.7. Piotti was 9th and Tom Cole 10th in their 2.7s.

At the 12 hours of Pescara the 3-litre Ferrari of Bracco/Marzotto won but the 2.7s of Biondetti/Cornacchia and Piotti/Mallucci were second and third respectively.

Cornacchia took 9th place in the Stella Alpina with his 2.7.

In the Goodwood *News of the World* 9 hour race two of the 2.7s were entered by Baird/Salvadori and Tom Cole/Graham Whitehead. The Baird/Salvadori car led the race at one time but the battery failed and dropped it behind. Tom Cole and Graham Whitehead came in second behind the winning Aston Martin and the Baird/Salvadori 2.7 was eventually 3rd.

At Le Mans the Scuderia Ferrari officially entered a 2.7 for Tom Cole/Pagnibon as a backup car to the Ascari/Villoresi 3-litre but the car retired by 6 a m with ignition trouble.

At the Craigantlet Hill Climb, Baird took his 2.7 Ferrari to win in his class and also won the overall General Handicap.

At the Grand Prix of Monaco 2.7 Ferraris were entered by Vittorio Marzotto, Eugenio Castelotti, Jean Lucas, Pagnibon and Antonio/ Stagnoli/Clemente Biondetti. It was a complete Ferrari triumph with Marzotti 1st, Castelotti 2nd, Stagnoli 3rd, Lucas 4th and Pagnibon 5th.

Another victory for the 2.7 was with Roberto Bonomi in Buenos Aires.

The following serial numbers have been noted for the 225 Sport type:

0160ED	Vignale Spyder, Bonomi's Buenos Aires winner
0162ED	Vignale Spyder, Biondetti/Cornacchia 2nd place Pescara
0164ED	Vignale Coupe
0166ED	Touring Barchetta, Castelotti 1st Portugal, 5th of Sicily
0168ED	Vignale Coupe
0172ET	Vignale Spyder
0175	Vignale Coupe
0176ED	Vignale Spyder, Stagnoli
0178ED	Vignale Coupe
0182ED	Vignale Spyder, Marzotto
0192ET	Vignale Spyder
0194ET	Vignale Spyder
0198ET	Vignale Spyder
0218ET	
220ED	Vignale Spyder, Alfred Momo
0223EL	Vignale Coupe

The Tom Cole 2.7 Ferrari has recently been restored in England. It differed from the other 2.7s in having a longer wheelbase and chassis similar to type 340 design. The author spent a great deal of time with the Tom Cole 2.7 practising for the 1953 Mille Miglia with Tom Cole during which time four crossings of the Futa Pass were made. One of these was through a hailstorm at Bologna that left the car with a ripple finish on the body.

The 250 Sport

This was followed by the long awaited 3-litre version, the first type being known as the 250 Sport having an engine based on the Colombo V12-cylinder engine described further on in this book; it had a bore and stroke of 73 x 58.8 mm, a displacement of 2963.45-cc and with a compression ratio of 8.5 : 1 it had a power output of 220 b h p at 7,000 r p m. Three Weber type 36 DCF twin-choke carburetters were fitted and a multi-disc metallic clutch used. The five-speed gearbox was retained with a first gear ratio of 3.157, second 1.946, third 1.403, fourth 1.00 and fifth 0.914. Wheelbase was increased to 2.400 m with front track 1.300 m and rear track 1.320 m; 4.00 x 16 wheels were fitted to take 5.50 x 16 tyres at the front and 6.00 x 16 tyres at the rear. The dry weight was maintained at 800 kg.

This car in coupe form (0156 ET) was to gain itself a place in the history of motor racing for the tremendous battle that it put up with Bracco driving against the whole of the Mercedes Benz team in the Mille Miglia. The car was privately entered by Bracco who did not even have enough tyres to finish the race. He had to continue to Pescara with the canvas showing, and there had to mount tyres that were too small; nevertheless despite all these difficulties Bracco, drinking large quantities of brandy and chain smoking all the way, pulled ahead of the Mercedes on the difficult and wet roads of the Futa Pass to come in victorious at Brescia.

The 250 Sport then underwent considerable modifications and was named 250 Mille Miglia in honour of the victory.

The Colombo-type engine underwent considerable revision, receiving individual intake ports, roller cam followers and 9.0 : 1 pistons. With three Weber 36IF/4C carburetters, the 250 MM engine was rated at 240 b h p at 7,200 r p m.

A new type of gearbox with four synchronised gears replaced the well known five-speed type, first gear being 2.536, second 1.701, third 1.256, fourth 1.00. The rigid rear axle with the light alloy central casing containing the differential was retained but a heavier unit as found on the Type 340 chassis was adopted. Semi-elliptic longitudinal leaf springs plus Houdaille shockabsorbers provided front and rear damping. Front suspension was modified to take a heavier transverse leaf spring held by 4 Silentbloc bushings together with wishbones and integral rubber buffers. Brakes were hydraulic, two leading shoe types with twin master cylinders. Wheelbase was 2.400 m with a front track of 1.300 m and a rear track of 1.320 m, 4.00 x 16 wheels were fitted for 5.50 x 16 tyres at the front and 6.00 x 16 tyres at the rear and dry weight crept up to 850 kg with tank capacity increased to 150 litres. Most of these cars found their way into private hands as the factory was concentrating on their larger capacity models. The cars were produced in two forms, a coupe version built by Pinin Farina and an open 'spyder' built by Vignale. Ferrari entered one of these 3-litre cars in the 1953 Mille Miglia to be driven by Mike Hawthorn but before the car left the factory it already had trouble with its brakes, a problem which arose again shortly after the beginning of the race, causing its retirement. When the car was driven back to Modena it broke its rear axle, another problem that was to plague the 250 Mille Miglia throughout its life. Paolo Marzotto driving a privately owned 250 MM coupe was well up in the Mille Miglia classification when the car caught fire with only a short distance left to cover before Brescia.

The 250 Mille Miglia nevertheless showed itself to be a very potent car and Phil Hill scored several victories with one in American competition. It was a unique 1953 Vignale spyder, 0260 MM. Notable results were also achieved in Europe by Portuguese driver Casimiro Olivera but he was constantly plagued with rear axle breakage. The factory entered two cars in the Supercortemaggiore race at Monza which was limited to 3-litres, a coupe for Villoresi and a spyder for Farina. When the 4-cylinder car of Ascari crashed, Farina went on to win the event with the 12-cylinder car. Another notable performance was that of Harry Schell and 'Fon' de Portago who won the 3-litre class and were placed 2nd overall behind the 4.5-litre of Farina/Maglioli in the 1,000 km of Buenos Aires in 1954.

Whilst all this development was going on with the Type 125-based engine, Ferrari had commenced the production of a larger engine to compete with the powerful Cadillac and Chrysler engined Allards that were sweeping the

board in American competition. In producing this larger engine he also had in mind the possibilities of producing a 4.5-litre unsupercharged Grand Prix car to replace his 1500-cc blown types. His first step in this line was to produce an unsupercharged engine of 3.3-litres for his Grand Prix project, but he decided to use it at the same time for his sports car experiments. The Grand Prix engine was known as the 275/F1 whilst the sports car version was known as the 275/S. This engine had a bore and stroke of 72 x 68 mm and gave 220 b h p at 7,000 r p m. The car made its first appearance in the 1950 Mille Miglia driven by Villoresi. The engine was fitted into a 250 MM chassis with a wheelbase of 2.400 m with front track of 1.300 m and a rear track of 1.320 m and was altogether similar to the 250 MM model. Villoresi's car dropped out due to gearbox troubles.

This new Lampredi designed engine was basically similar to the type 125 that had originally been designed by Colombo, a common feature being that a larger bore than stroke was used.

The two cylinder heads are light alloy castings with inserted valve seats and two valves per cylinder, inclined at an included angle of 60 degrees. Each valve was closed by twin hairpin type valve springs having ten effective coils. The crankshaft ran in seven Vandervell Thinwall type bearings and the front of the crankshaft provided a drive for a roller chain which transmitted to the camshafts of which there was one per bank of cylinders. Vandervell bearings were used for the big ends. The Borgo light alloy pistons were steeply domed and gave, by use of different crowns, compression ratios running from 8 : 1 to 11 : 1. Gudgeon pins attached them to H section connecting rods which were connected to the crankpins to lie side by side.

The cylinder axes were at the included angle of 60 degrees and the firing order was 1, 7, 5, 11, 3, 9, 6, 12, 2, 8, 4, 10. On the 3.3-litre the 4.5-litre and the first of the 4.9-litres ignition was by one plug per cylinder. On the single ignition types two Marelli distributors mounted vertically at the back of the block were used but the twin ignition types used various layouts which are described later in this book.

The single ignition Sport 3.3-litre gave about 220 b h p at 7,000 r p m but after the various stages of development of this engine it went up to 400 b h p on the 4.9-litre.

On the 3.3-litre, three downdraught Weber 40 DCF carburetters were used each carburetter being of the twin-choke type thus in effect giving one carburetter for two cylinders. Later on in the larger engines three four-choke Weber Type 40 IF/4C carburetters were fitted giving the effect of one carburetter per cylinder. The tuning of the engines with these was found to be rather complicated and access to the plugs with the twin ignition heads was found extremely difficult, so they were abandoned.

The carburetters received air from an external scoop let into the top of the bonnet and they fed fuel into a water heated manifold. The carburetters themselves were fed by a Fimac mechanical pump and an Autoflux electric pump, the former being driven from the front of the right hand camshaft whilst the latter was situated by the fuel tank.

Lubrication was by wet sump with an external oil radiator, there being an oil pump of the gear type transversely mounted at the nose of the crankcase. Delivery from the pump was partially through the oil radiator with a thermostat preventing delivery to the radiator core until the oil reached a certain temperature and there was also a spring loaded relief valve from the exit so that in fact the oil cooling system was under low pressure. Oil was delivered to the main bearings through a gallery pipe extending the whole length of the engine. From this there were branches to each of the seven main bearings. The crankpins were cross-drilled and the sump contained two gallons of oil. The 3.3-litre was never in fact sold to any of Ferrari's customers and must be regarded as an experimental stage in the development of the large capacity V12s.

Type 342

The first 'big' engine produced by Ferrari for sale to customers was the 342 America Sport. This car in its initial form was intended to be the answer to the Cadillac Allards but the early models with only 200 b h p could not cope. The engine of 4.1-litres was then progressively developed through the 340 Mexico to the 340 Mille Miglia the latter model having a power output of 300 b h p.

The Type 342 had a bore and stroke of 80 x 68 mm with a displacement of 4101.66-cc; with a compression ratio of 8 : 1 it gave a maximum output of 200 b h p at 5000 r p m. Three Weber 40 DCF carburetters were fitted and a single dry plate clutch was used in unit with a four-speed gearbox, first gear ratio being 2.536, second 1.701, third 1.256, fourth 1.00. The rear axle was of the rigid type with the light-alloy central casing containing the differential assembly. Rear suspension was by means of semi-elliptic longitudinal leaf springs and damping by Houdaille shockabsorbers. Front suspension was by the classic Ferrari wishbones and single transverse leaf spring with integral rubber blocks and Houdaille shockabsorbers.

The 2-leading-shoe hydraulic brakes had two master cylinders one serving the front brakes, the other the rears, and a hand operated mechanical brake on the rear wheels.

The frame was welded construction with elliptical section steel tubes. Wheelbase was 2.650 m with a front track of 1.325 m and a rear track of 1.320 m. Wheels were 4.50 x 15 fitting 6.40 x 15 all round and dry weight was 1200 kg with tank capacity 120 litres.

Type 340 Mexico

Interim models of the 342 America had some success in the hands of Jim Kimberly and Bill Spear and it was this type of car that Chinetti, Ascari and Villoresi used in the Pan American road race. The Mexican event was the inspiration for Ferrari's next model, the type 340 Mexico. Only three coupe versions were built of this very much improved car, which were intended to win the Pan American road race; a fourth car with spyder body was then built after the venture to Mexico.

In these models the bore and stroke of 80 x 68 remained the same, as did the displacement of 4101-cc. The power output was however much higher and with a compression ratio of 8 : 1, 280 b h p was obtained at 6,600 r p m. Three Weber 40 DCF twin-choke carburetters were fitted and a five-speed gearbox replaced the four-speed type of the 342 America. First gear ratio was 3.157, second 1.946, third 1.403, fourth 1.000, fifth 0.914. Rear axle remained of the rigid type with location by four radius rods and semi-elliptic longitudinal leaf springs damped by four Houdaille shockabsorbers, two per side being fitted. Front suspension was independent with the usual Ferrari wishbones and single transverse leaf spring with integral rubber blocks and damping by Houdaille shockabsorbers.

The usual system of brakes with two-leading-shoe hydraulics operating on two master cylinders. The frame was a welded construction of elliptical section steel tubes. Wheelbase was 2.600 m with front track 1.278 and rear track 1.250; 4.50 x 16 wheels were used mounting 6.00 x 16 tyres at the front and 6.50 x 16 at the rear, dry weight was 900 kg with tank capacity 150 litres.

After the Mexican event these cars went to the USA where they competed regularly in national events. Phil Hill took one of them to the Mexican race the year following but went off the road. He also took this car to the 1,000 km of Buenos Aires in 1954 but by then the car was already outclassed by the bigger 4.5-litre.

Type 340 MM

For the 1953 Mille Miglia Ferrari produced a new model known as the 340 MM. The engine of this car remained the same with a bore and stroke of 80 x 68 mm and with a displacement of 4101-cc. It retained a compression ratio of 8 : 1 and power output was further increased to 300 b h p at 6,600 r p m, the four-choke Type 40 IF/4C Weber carburetters were fitted on this model and two magnetos replaced the distributors. A multiple disc metallic dry clutch was used and the Mexico's five-speed gearbox was replaced by the four-speed unit. First gear ratio was 2.424, second 1.722, third 1.235, fourth 1.00.

The rigid rear axle was retained but the light-alloy central casing now contained a ZF limited-slip differential. The rear axle used radius rods to absorb acceleration and braking strains and suspension was by means of semi-elliptic longitudinal leaf springs and Houdaille shockabsorbers. Front suspension was as on the Mexico by means of wishbones and single transverse leaf spring with integral rubber blocks. Wheelbase was shortened to 2.500 m with a front track of 1.325 m and a rear track of 1.320 m; 5.00 x 16 front wheels were used mounting 6.00 x 16 tyres whilst at the rear 5.50 x 16 wheels mounted 7.50 x 16 tyres. Dry weight was 900 kg and tank capacity was increased to 180 litres.

Mille Miglia 1953

The 1953 Mille Miglia was held on April 26th and Ferrari had a strong entry made up of factory cars supported by a host of customers' cars. The factory entered two brand new 4.1 spyders with bodies by Touring while the customers' versions of the 4.1s had bodies by Vignale.

Farina/Parenti had the Touring bodied 4.1 No. 615 and Villoresi/Cassani the No. 613 Touring 4.1. Tom Cole/Vandelli had the 4.1 Vignale model with car No. 608 as did Giannino Marzotto/Crosara with car No. 547. Corrado Millanta started the rumour that the Marzotto/Crosara No. 547 had a 4.5-litre engine in it and stated this in his report to *Road & Track*. That this was a possibility is undoubtedly true but the official records have the car listed as a 4.1 throughout and in the absence of any substantiating information the car must be considered to have been a 4.1. Hawthorn/Cappi in No. 625, Cabianca/Roghi in No. 633 and Scotti/Contini had the latest Vignale-bodied 3-litre 250 Mille Miglias and 3-litre Migle Miglia coupe's were in the hands of Paolo Marzotto/Zignago, Bracco/Rolfo and Bruno Sterzi/Rovelli. Other Ferraris of various capacities were driven by Castelotti/Regosa, Orlandi/Fontana, Gerini/Danazzolo, Piazza/Piazza, Gassabini, Testa Gay, De Tornaco/Swaters, Roberto Rossellini/Tonti, Leonardi/Vallone, 'Serano', Bosisio/Ercole, Musitelli/Musitelli, Cacciari/Mason, Arosio/Di Giuseppe, Piotti/Franzoni and E. Sterzi/Rossi.

All the Ferraris including both factory and customers' cars were scheduled to leave the Ferrari customers' department in Modena in a great convoy to rendezvous at one of Marzotto's establishments just outside Brescia. The convoy set out with Farina in the lead and before long the orderly convoy was reduced to a shambles and a glorious free for all race ensued. Villoresi's car needed some work and stayed behind. Tom Cole and the author also remained behind to have a tachometer drive replaced and Hawthorn elected to remain behind to wait for our group.

These three cars left for Brescia some 30 minutes behind the convoy and Villoresi led at a cracking pace, being absolutely determined to catch up with the convoy. Cole followed a few yards behind and Hawthorn was hard pressed to keep up with the two 4.1s. With holiday traffic on the already crowded Via Emilia the three Ferraris nonetheless were driven almost flat out. We caught up with the tail end of the convoy just after the Piacenza to Cremona turn-off. The first Ferrari we passed was that of De Tornaco/Swaters who were quite surprised to have three Ferraris storming by at racing speeds in what was supposed to be a 'leisurely' run to Brescia. There also remained several startled drivers of Fiat Topolinos on the Via Emilia who would long remember the day when they were passed on both sides almost simultaneously by three screaming Ferraris!

Competition for Ferrari came from the new 2.9-litre Lancias of Taruffi, Bonetto, Maglioli and Biondetti as well as the new 6C-3000 Alfa Romeos in the hands of Fangio, Kling and Sanesi.

The Alfas set a great pace at the start and Sanesi passed through Ravenna averaging 113.64 m p h with Farina's Ferrari 2 minutes behind and Giannino Marzotto about 5 minutes behind. On this first section Scotti's and Villoresi's Ferraris dropped out as did a number of the opposition.

At Pescara (the 630 kilometre mark) Sanesi's Alfa was averaging 115.50 m p h with Farina 4 minutes behind, Kling's Alfa 9 minutes 30 secs. behind and Fangio's Alfa 10 minutes behind followed by Giannino Marzotto. Between Ravenna and Pescara Hawthorn retired with a broken rear end and Castelotti's Ferrari also retired. Between Pescara and Rome, Sanesi's Alfa ran out of steam and Kling took the lead followed at only 40 seconds by Fangio with Marzotto now 4 minutes behind and Bracco, now fourth, 7 minutes behind him.

After Rome, Kling dropped out and Fangio led to Siena at an average of just 90 m p h. However, Marzotto had closed up the gap to 2 minutes with younger brother Paolo Marzotto in the three-litre coupe now in third place but some 17 minutes behind. The battle was on and, between Siena and Florence, Gianninio

Marzotto lost only 4 seconds to the Argentine World Champion.

At Bologna, Alfa hopes were dashed, Marzotto arrived after negotiating the difficult Futa Pass 3 minutes ahead of Fangio with Paolo Marzotto still third. The reason for Fangio's slow time was defective steering which cost him the lead in this most critical part of the race.

Giannino Marzotto led into Brescia crossing the line 12 minutes ahead of Fangio. After Paolo Marzotto retired Bonetto took over 3rd and Tom Cole brought the Vignale 4.1 in fourth. Marzotto set a new record of 142.374 k p h breaking the old one set by Biondetti in 1938.

Type 375 Mille Miglia

Despite their great power these cars had very little further success mainly due to their instability which made them very difficult to drive. The factory disposed of them to private individuals but three of them were destroyed when their owners had fatal accidents with them. For Le Mans that year the 4.1-litre appeared in coupe form with wheelbase lengthened to 2.600 m. At the Senigallia race in 1953, at the same time that the new Type 735 4-cylinder Ferrari made its first appearance, another new model also appeared. The first example looked like a Vignale-bodied 340 Mille Miglia but driven by Villoresi it put up times some 14 seconds a lap faster than the 4.1-litre. This car was the new 375 Mille Miglia, with a bore and stroke of 84 x 68 mm it had a displacement of 4522-cc and with a compression ratio of 9 : 1 it gave 340 b h p at 7,000 r p m. Again three of the four-choke 40 IF/4C Weber carburetters were fitted as were two Marelli magnetos. Four forward speeds and reverse were provided with first gear ratio 2.54, second 1.7, third 1.255 and fourth 1.00. Chassis and brake layout remained exactly the same as on the 340 MM model but the wheelbase was increased to 2.600 m the front track was 1.325 m and the rear track 1.320; 5.00 x 16 wheels were used all round fitting 6.00 x 16 tyres at the front and 7.00 x 16 tyres at the rear. Dry weight remained at 900 kg and tank capacity at 180 litres. Although the first car had a body built by Vignale, all subsequent cars had bodies constructed by Pinin Farina. Unlike the 340 MM, the 375 MM model proved a very stable and successful car. It was sold in quantities to customers and recorded large numbers of successes all over the world. The car was so tractable that certain people transformed the racing version into a road car and several are used for this purpose even today. Despite its qualities the car failed to win Le Mans although Ascari and Villoresi with a Pinin Farina built coupe version had a tremendous battle with the Jaguars, they finally had to give up having lost their clutch and brakes. Nevertheless the car made up for this by winning the 24 Hours of Spa and the 12 Hours of Pescara whilst at the 12 Hours of Rheims it was many laps in the lead when it was disqualified in the midst of a controversy that almost resulted in the withdrawal of the works Formula 1 team from the Grand Prix of France.

The car started off 1954 with a win in the 1000 km of Buenos Aires and private owners, Masten Gregory, Jim Kimberly and Bill Spear had considerable success in American events with this type Ferrari.

Type 375 Plus

For the Mille Miglia of 1954 Ferrari appeared with yet another model this time known as the 375 Plus. With a bore and stroke of 84 x 74.5 mm it had a displacement of 4954.342-cc and with a compression ratio of 9.25 : 1 it gave 344 b h p at 6,500 r p m. For this model Ferrari reverted to the twin-choke Type 42 DCF carburetters but retained the magnetos. A dry multiple disc clutch was used with four-speed gearbox in unit with the differential, this being quite unusual for a 12-cylinder sports Ferrari. First gear ratio was 2.20, second 1.753, third 1.252, fourth 1.00. The rear axle was De Dion, again an unusual layout for a sports Ferrari.

Two spur gears were used for the final drive enabling a low entry line for the propeller shaft into the four-speed gearbox. The gearbox/differential unit was split lengthwise at its centre and a wide range of final and indirect gears were provided. Nevertheless with the split housing, a considerable amount of time had to be spent in changing axle ratios. Drive to the wheels was by means of two universally jointed halfshafts. Radius arms were in pairs lying parallel one above the other to take engine torque and brake

reaction, the wheel position being controlled by a De Dion tube which was made in three parts. The location of the De Dion was controlled by a fixture on the front side of the tube running in a slot on the back of the gearbox/differential housing. This was coupled with a roller on the back edge of the tube which engaged with a slot fixed to a tubular arch extending between the rear ends of the side tubes of the frame. The suspension was effected by a single transverse leaf spring.

At the front end there was also a leaf spring which connected to the bottom link of the wishbone layout. Damping all round was by means of twin-mounted Houdaille shockabsorbers. The brake drums were equipped with vents on their surface and were heavily finned on their peripheries. Their mounting was such that they projected into the airstream behind the wheel to ensure maximum cooling effect. They were of the two leading shoe type which had a central guiding member to eliminate servo effect, the front and rear brakes being operated by separate master cylinders.

Wheelbase for this model remained at 2.600 m with a front track of 1.325 m and a rear track of 1.284 m; 5.50 x 16 wheels were used all round fitting 6.50 x 16 tyres the front and 7.50 x 16 tyres at the rear. The dry weight was 1000 kg and tank capacity was 175 litres.

Le Mans 1954

After a discouraging outing in the Mille Miglia, Ferrari entered three of the 4.9-litres in the 24 Hours of Le Mans on June 12th and 13th. These cars were driven by Froilan Gonzales/ Maurice Trintignant (No. 4), Paolo Marzotto/ Umberto Maglioli (No. 3) and Louis Rosier/ Robert Manzon (No. 4). They were backed up by a 4.5-litre coupe entered by Luigi Chinetti for Count Baggio and Porfirio Rubirosa and the 4.5-litre modified open Cunningham-Ferrari driven by John Fitch and Phil Walters, the latter car having liquid-cooled brakes designed by Alfred Momo.

The race was held in bad weather and proved to be a dramatic battle between the 4.9-litre Ferrari and the new D-type Jaguars. The previous practice record was held by Ferrari at 4 min. 27.4 secs. and Moss with the Jaguar set the practice pace with a lap in 4 min. 21 secs. Gonzales took his Ferrari round in 4 min. 23 secs. and during the Friday practice Maglioli's Ferrari lapped at 4 min. 18 secs. a time that was equalled by Peter Walker's Jaguar.

The start saw the three Ferraris of Manzon, Marzotto and Gonzales take an immediate lead. On the first lap Gonzales led from Marzotto and Manzon closely followed by the Jaguars of Moss, Rolt and Wharton with the Cunningham Ferrari next in line. Moss mixed in with the Ferraris and by 4.30 it began to rain a little with a blustery wind blowing. Despite this Marzotto set a new lap record. By 6 pm Gonzales still led from Marzotto with the Jaguars of Moss and Rolt 3rd and 4th. Baggio slid into the sand at Tertre Rouge with the Chinetti coupe. After much effort he was unable to dig himself out and the car was retired.

The Marzotto Ferrari speeded up from its regular 4 min. 21 secs. per lap to 4 min. 19 secs. on lap 26, to 4 min. 16.8 secs. (118.5 m p h) on lap 28 but on lap 29 Gonzales broke the record again with a time just a fraction faster than Marzotto.

After the regulation 30 laps or 250 miles had been covered, pit stops began and driver changes were made. Gonzales and Marzotto continued but Rosier replaced Monzon. An hour later the 4.5-litre Cunningham Ferrari was in the pits for an unscheduled stop.

After 4 hours the positions were 1) Ferrari Gonzales/Trintignant, 2) Ferrari Magiloli/Marzotto, 3) Ferrari Rosier/Manzon, 4) Jaguar Whitehead/Wharton.

At 11.30 the Marzotto/Maglioli Ferrari retired with a broken ball race in the gearbox and it was up to the Gonzales/Trintignant car which by now held 3 laps lead over the Whitehead/Wharton Jaguar.

At 8 hours it was Gonzales/Trintignant having covered 102 laps at an average of 107 m p h. Whitehead and Wharton were second two laps back and the Rosier Ferrari third.

At about the 12 hour mark (4 am) the order was Gonzales/Trintignant 151 laps at 105 m p h average followed by the Rolt/Hamilton Jaguar and the Rosier Ferrari. The Moss/Walker Jaguar had retired with brake trouble.

At 5 am the Fitch/Walters Cunningham

Ferrari retired with a broken rear axle and by 5.30 am a mist of rain began again. After a routine pit stop the Rosier/Manzon Ferrari began to slow and eventually pitted to retire at 6.45 am with gearbox failure. The road dried again and the Rolt Jaguar started making up time on the leading Ferrari. At 7.30 am the Jaguar pulled up to less than 2 laps behind.

At 8 am after 16 hours it was Gonzales/Trintignant 203 laps at an average of 106.4 m p h with the Jaguar just under 2 laps behind. At 8.15 am it began to pour with rain again and this affected the Ferrari more than it did the Jaguar; by 9.05 am the Jaguar's deficit was down to 1 lap and 45 seconds and as the Ferrari slowed for refueling the Jaguar unlapped itself. One minute and 45 seconds later the Ferrari left the pits with Gonzales back at the wheel but at 10.14 Rolt pitted the Jaguar with a damaged front having been baulked by a Talbot. Gonzales profited by this to extend his lead to one lap plus, both the Ferrari and the Jaguar being timed in the rain at 158 and 157 m p h respectively on the measured kilometre. The rain stopped again and at 11.45 the Ferrari was called in for Trintignant to take over. At 20 hours the Ferrari had covered 253 laps at an average of 106 m p h. Then the rain started again with the Ferrari holding a lead of about 10 minutes.

The storm became heavier and when Trintignant came in at 2.21 to hand over to Gonzales there was drama at the Ferrari pits; the car steadfastly refused to start and the Ferrari was in the pits for 7½ minutes before rejoining the race. Gonzales held a lead of only 1 min. 55 secs. over the Jaguar as a result of this delay. Rolt handed over to Hamilton at 3.01 and Hamilton closed the gap to 1 min. 36 secs. A signal was given to Gonzales and the Ferrari began to draw away again. At 4 pm the Gonzales/Trintignant Ferrari took the flag having averaged 105.1 m p h for the 2,524 miles covered.

Gonzales won the sports car race at Silverstone and Maglioli took the last of the Mexican road races setting a new record. Ferrari then sold the cars to private individuals and Saenz Valiente together with Ibanez won the 1,000 km of Buenos Aires with one of them.

Ferrari abandoned the idea of the 4.9-litre as being too heavy and unmanageable and concentrated his effort on the 6-cylinder in-line models for 1955.

Type 410 Sport

After the failure of the 6-cylinder cars to hold off the Mercedes Benz challenge, Ferrari decided to go back to his 12-cylinder design. He built a lighter chassis with a reduced wheelbase of 2.500 m and altered the bore and stroke of the engine to 88 x 68 mm giving a displacement of 4961.576-cc. The new Model was known as the 410 Sport and with a compression ratio of 9 : 1 the engine gave 380 b h p at 6,800 r p m. Ferrari used twin plugs per cylinder similar to the layout used on the 4.5-litre Formula 1 car. Three Weber Type 42 DCZ/4 carburetters were fitted and the same gearbox ratios were used, the gearbox being in unit with the differential casing, De Dion rear axle layout being retained.

Two of these cars made an appearance in the 1,000 km of Buenos Aires race but both of them broke down with rear axle trouble although they had been in the lead. Ferrari immediately disposed of these cars, one going to John Edgar in the USA and the other being sold in Sweden. The John Edgar car was tremendously successful in the hands of Shelby, Gregory and Kessler at different times. But the Swedish owned car was just as conspicuous in its lack of success. Tony Parravano also purchased two of the 4.9-litres (one having a rigid rear axle and a five-inch shorter wheelbase) and another standard model.

Type 290 Mille Miglia

For the 1956 Mille Miglia, Enzo Ferrari had his new 12-cylinder engine ready. The design followed the previous V12s and the long expected twin ignition cylinder head, that originated from the 4.5-litre Grand Prix car, was used. The new car was known as the type 290 Mille Miglia and it was designed to replace the interim model 4-cylinder Type 860 Monza. The engine, with a bore and stroke of 73 x 69.5 mm, had a capacity of 3490-cc and with a compression ratio of 9 : 1 it gave 320 b h p at 7,200 r p m. The new engine weighed 204 kg and had a maximum torque of 32 kgm at 5200 r p m. Inlet valves had a diameter of 35 mm and exhausts 29 mm. Basically, it was a Lampredi-type engine,

but more similar to the Colombo type in bore and stroke, and in fact used the earlier Colombo-type con rods with angled caps. Dry sump lubrication was used and the single overhead camshaft was chain driven. Ignition was by two plugs per cylinder with four rear-mounted distributors and coils. There was a multi-plate aluminium clutch and the four-speed gearbox was in unit with the differential. First gear ratio was 2.2, second 1.565, third 1.25 and fourth 1.00.

Front suspension had wishbones and coil springs and rear suspension incorporated a De Dion with a transverse leaf spring. Brake drums of 360 mm with a shoe dimension of 65 mm were provided at the front with drums of 330 mm and shoes of 60 mm at the rear. 6.00 x 16 tyres were mounted at the front and 7.00 x 16 tyres at the rear; total dry weight was 880 kg with an all-up weight of 1060 kg. An oil tank of 20 litres was fitted together with a fuel tank containing 190 litres; wheelbase was 2.350 m front track, 1.310 m and rear track 1.286 m.

The car was immediately successful and Castelotti won the Mille Miglia with ease from two Type 860 Monza Ferraris driven by Collins and Musso, with Fangio bringing up 4th place in another 290 Mille Miglia.

The Grand Prix of Sweden saw another victory for this type with Phil Hill and Maurice Trintignant driving. Fangio and Castelotti drove one into 2nd place in the 1,000 km of Nurburgring and at the start of the 1958 season, a privately owned 290 Mille Miglia entered by Temple Buell won the 1000 km of Buenos Aires driven by Masten Gregory and Castelotti. For the 1957 Nassau event Temple Buell rented a 290 Mille Miglia from Jan De Vroom for Stirling Moss to drive, and he took the car to an easy victory against much bigger machinery in the main event with Bonnier driving Buell's other 290 MM in 5th place.

Type 130/S56

After the appearance of the twin ignition Lampredi-type heads on the sports car the next step was to produce another model, this time with the heads replaced by one having twin overhead camshafts per bank of cylinders as first used on the two-stage supercharged 1500-cc. Grand Prix cars. This engine was designated the Type

130/S56 which had a bore and stroke of 73 x 69.5 giving a displacement of 3490-cc. This type of car was only used in the 1000 km of Buenos Aires in 1957 but proved to be less reliable than the single-cam 290 Mille Miglia which won the event.

Type 315 MM

By the time Sebring came round Ferrari had already increased the capacity to 3.8-litres, the new model being known as the 315 Mille Miglia. The bore and stroke of this engine was 76 x 69.5 giving a displacement of 3790-cc. The four overhead camshafts were chain driven and at 7,600 r p m the engine gave 380 b h p with a compression ratio of 9 : 1. The engine was a little lighter than the single-cam-per-bank type weighing 195 kg instead of 204 kg. At Sebring the factory sent four cars, two of the 3.8-litres and two of the 290 Mille Miglia single-cam types.

One of the single-cam cars was entered by the factory in the name of Temple Buell, to be driven by Masten Gregory, and Brero had to uphold the Ferrari honours by coming in 4th after all the others had broken down. Unlike Buenos Aires the new 3.8-litres showed themselves to be considerably faster than the 3.5-litres and with more reliability could have shown promise.

Type 335 Sport

In the ill-fated 1957 Mille Miglia yet another model appeared, a 4.1 version driven by De Portago who replaced Musso as the latter was ill. Von Trips, Taruffi and Collins drove the 3.8 litres. Jean Behra's accident two days before the Mille Miglia put out one of the 4.5-litre Maserati's and Stirling Moss broke the brake pedal on his Maserati only 12 km from the start at Brescia, so the Ferraris were set for a field day. Collins was comfortably in the lead when his rear axle broke at Parma with only a short distance to go for the finish. This put Taruffi into the lead with Von Trips second and De Portago, in the 4.1-litre, third. Then came the accident to De Portago, a burst tyre sending him off the road causing his death and that of his co-driver, Gurner Nelson. Taruffi went on to win with Von Trips second. The 4.1-litre appeared again at Le Mans but, although Hawthorn set a

new lap record at over 120 m p h, the cars broke down, Collins having to retire on the first lap with a burnt piston. It was left to Lewis Evans and Severi, driving an experimental 3.1-litre, to take fifth place for Ferrari. The 4.1-litre was known as the 335 Sport and had a bore and stroke of 77 x 72 mm giving a displacement of 4022-cc with a power output of 447 b h p at 7,700 r p m. The other two cars present at the 1957 Le Mans were two experimental types. one a 3-litre version of the 290 Mille Miglia, the Testa Rossa and the other a 3.1-litre version of the 290 Mille Miglia. The Testa Rossa prototype was fitted with a rigid rear axle and the 3.1-litre had a De Dion. The 3-litre prototype surprised everyone by trailing the Moss 4.5 Maserati in close company for a considerable time, but it finally went out with a burnt piston like its larger 4.1 brother. The 3.1-litre, as mentioned before, continued to take 5th place. This latter car turned out to be a prototype chassis for what were to be the factory 250 Testa Rossas for 1958 whilst the other car was the actual prototype of the 250 Testa Rossa that was to be sold to the Ferrari's customers.

For the final event of the 1957 World Championship Ferrari entered two of the 4.1 litres for the 1,000 km of Venezuela together with two of the 250 Testa Rossa prototypes. With all the factory-entered Maseratis having been eliminated by accidents, the Ferraris had a comfortable win, the two 4.1-litres being placed first and second with the two 3-litres running third and fourth. Ferrari thus again won the Manufacturers' world championship.

The 3.8-litre and 4.1-litre four-cam cars were then sold in the USA as the CSI had limited sports car engine capacities to 3-litres. There the 3.8-litres were run by Gene Greenspun and George Arents. Greenspun gave up racing so the car was returned to Chinetti and Arents completely destroyed his car in an accident. The two 4.1-litres were seen again in American racing, the first being sold to George Tilp with which car Phil Hill won the first event at Nassau in 1957. The other car went to the North American Racing Team, an organization set up by Chinetti with Jan De Vroom and George Arents. With this car Stirling Moss won the ill-fated Cuban Grand Prix and Lance Reventlow, together with

Gaston Andrey, won the Elkhart Lake 500 mile race.

Late in 1958 another version of the 4.1-litre 'sports car' was produced for John Von Neuman. This utilized what was in effect the prototype chassis for the 1959 3-litre factory sports car in which the clutch, gearbox, starter motor and differential were in unit at the rear axle, this layout having been copied from the Dino Grand Prix design. The engine came from the car Ferrari built for the 500 Miles of Monza race. The purpose of this car was to meet the challenge from the Scarabs built for American short distance races by Lance Reventlow, but on the two occasions that Phil Hill drove it in competition with the 'all American built' cars the Ferrari came off second best. Due to its engine, the car was called the 412 MI (Monza Indianapolis).

250 Testa Rossa

As mentioned previously Ferrari ran a prototype 3-litre in the 1957 Mille Miglia with the intention of producing a car for sale to his customers. This car was known as the 250 Testa Rossa and was intended as a follow on to the 2-litre 4-cylinder Testa Rossa. The idea was to give the customer, who had competed with the smaller car, an engine of larger capacity which would be fitted into a chassis with similar handling characteristics to the 2-litre model. However, Ferrari also had a good idea that the CSI were very likely to reduce sports car engine capacities to 3 litres for the 1958 season, so he would also have the basis for a world championship car at the same time as satisfying his customers. To this end he decided to use the very reliable 250 Gran Turismo 12-cylinder engine as a basis with modifications to increase the power. These modifications included machined connecting rods, the use of higher-compression-ratio pistons, complete revision of the cylinder heads and the use of six twin-choke carburetters.

The 250 Testa Rossa made its debut at the Nurburgring in May of 1957 when the factory entered the car for Temple Buell's team. Buell had an arrangement with Ferrari to be a sort of tag-on to the factory team; he would finance the cars and the factory mechanics would take care of it.

At the Nurburgring the TR was driven by Gregory and Morolli. Several of the Ferrari team drivers tested the new car during practice and declared their satisfaction with it. During the race Gregory was up with the leaders but his co-driver Morolli was not experienced enough to maintain the pace and the car finished well down in the results.

The next appearance of the 250 TR was at Le Mans where it was driven by Gendebien/Trintignant. This car had a 75 x 58.8 mm bore and stroke with a total capacity of 3117 cc. It was fitted with a live axle instead of the De Dion on the Gregory/Morolli Nurburgring car and had a new style of bodywork with deeply cutaway front fenders and was actually the prototype for the future customers' version of the 250 TR. Gendebien held a most impressive 3rd place at Le Mans before a piston broke.

The engine had a bore and stroke of 73 x 58.8 giving a capacity of 2953-cc and with a compression ratio of 9.0 : 1 the power output was 300 b h p at 7,200 r p m. A four speed gearbox was used in unit with the engine and a rigid rear axle was employed. Front suspension was the usual Ferrari type wishbones and coil springs, whilst rear suspension was by means of coil springs and double size shockabsorbers. The rigid rear axle was located by radius arms and a reaction triangle.

Wheelbase was 2.350 m with a front track of 1.308 m and a rear track of 1.300 m, total dry weight was 800 kg and tank capacity 140-litres; 5.50 x 16 tyres were fitted at the front and 6.00 x 16 tyres at the rear. By the time the 1958 Sebring race came along, the factory cars already had a new chassis developed from the 3.1-litre experimental car used at the previous year's Le Mans. These cars used a De Dion rear axle with a transverse leaf spring. During the race they showed that, although they were not as fast as the Aston Martin opposition, they were more reliable and Collins, driving with Hill, had no difficulty in winning the event. The cars registered another win in the Targa Florio but were beaten by the Aston Martin on the Nurburgring. Their great reliability was once again shown when Hill and Gendebien won the 24 Hours of Le Mans. With the sports cars manufacturer's championship already won, Ferrari did not appear at the Tourist Trophy, the last championship event of 1958.

Type 312 LM

During the season however, Ferrari carried out some experiments with a dohc cylinder head for the factory Testa Rossa models. The type was known as the 312 LM and had a bore and stroke of 73 x 58.8 giving a capacity of 2953-cc and the engine had a power output of 356 b h p at 8,600 r p m. This car was first run by Gendebien at the Spa sports car race but, after showing itself to be very fast, turned out to be unreliable as well. This car was not seen again during the 1958 season being returned to the development department to be saved for a future date.

For the 1959 season Ferrari spent a great deal of time testing the reliability of a new version of the 250 Testa Rossa. A new space-frame chassis was incorporated plus a new cylinder head for the engine, and the car was equipped with disc brakes. Phil Hill together with several Italian drivers put the car through its initial paces at Monza during the autumn of 1958.

THE 4-CYLINDER TYPES

The origins of the 4-cylinder sports Ferrari really began during the 1950 Formula 2 season. Stirling Moss with the 4-cylinder HWM had caused the official Ferrari team a great deal of worry on many of the European tracks and Enzo Ferrari realised that this type of engine had torque and weight characteristics well suited to the twistier types of circuit. He immediately put his newly employed engineer, Aurelio Lampredi, to work on a 4-cylinder design. The prototype engine was quickly completed and first saw the light of day as a 2.5-litre. This engine was first tested in a Grand Prix chassis, the main objective being the production of a 2-litre engine for Formula 2 and a 2.5-litre engine for the future Formula 1.

However, when it was found that this 4-cylinder engine was so successful that it could also be used on fast circuits as well as the twisty ones, Ferrari turned his mind to producing 4-cylinder sports car engines of 2-litres and 3-litres capacity that could eventually be sold to customers who wanted to race in these categories.

During 1953 a 2.5-litre engine was fitted into the chassis of a Type 250 MM and preliminary experiments were conducted.

Senigallia was one of the few races that Enzo Ferrari ever attended personally in the postwar years and there, in 1953, the 3-litre sports car made its first racing appearance. The Type was known as the 735 and was, in effect, a bored out 2.5-litre. Maglioli drove the car which showed tremendous speed until a broken connecting rod put an end to its run. A second car was then built with a new body designed by Lampredi and built by the Autodromo coachwork company in Modena. The original Senigallia car and the new type were both sent to Monza, Ascari driving the new car and Hawthorn in the Senigallia car. During practice Ascari blew up the engine of his car so the 3-litre engine from Hawthorn's car was taken out and put into Ascari's. Hawthorn was given one of the older 2.5-litre experimental engines. During the race Ascari was leading with ease when another competitor, whom he was about to lap, forced him off the road, the car being wrecked but without damage to Ascari. Hawthorn's car, although running perfectly, did not have enough power and Farina won for Ferrari with a 3-litre 12-cylinder 250 MM.

In January of 1954 Bonomi and Menditeguy took the Senigallia car to Buenos Aires in company with Milan who had purchased a new car which had a Vignale body similar to the original Senigallia car.

Bonomi and Menditeguy had a great battle with the 3-litre 12-cylinder of Harry Schell and 'Fon' de Portago. Just as it seemed that they had the upper hand, Bonomi took off from the pits after a fuelling stop and the rear axle spread itself all over the track. Milan continued plodding along with his new car and finished a conservative 5th.

All these cars were still of an experimental nature being of the Type 735 with the engine derived from the 625 2.5-litre engine. At the end of the 1953 season, the Ferrari Supersqualo had appeared with a new version of the

4-cylinder engine, having a different bottom end and a completely altered cylinder head.

Type 750 Monza

Using the Type 555 4-cylinder engine as a basis, Ferrari produced the Type 750 Monza engine.

The first appearance of these new cars was at Monza on 27th June 1954. Hawthorn and Maglioli were involved in a race-long battle with the Fangio/Marimon prototype 2.5-litre Maserati but towards the end of the event the Maserati blew up and the Ferrari had an unchallenged lead; it carried on to win, with Gonzales and Trintignant taking second place with a similar model. Both these cars had new body styles, the Hawthorn car had a body built by Scaglietti similar to the original Autodromo body used on the previous year's Ascari car. The Gonzales car had a body designed by Ferrari's son, Dino, but built by Scaglietti. This was the body that was eventually used on all the Type 750 Monza production chassis. The car also made an appearance at the 12 Hours of Rheims where it showed a tremendous turn of speed being faster than the Jaguars, and Maglioli, after a bad start, went by car after car until he was just about to take the lead when the gearbox gave out.

A team of Hawthorn/Maglioli and Gonzales/Trintignant was sent to the Tourist Trophy. Maglioli had to leave before the race for family reasons and Gonzales crashed in practice injuring his spine, so Trintignant drove with Hawthorn who was at his most brilliant during the race and, despite the strongest possible opposition from a formidable Lancia team, he had no difficulty in winning.

The car that Gonzales crashed was not badly damaged and it was rebuilt and sold to the Marquis De Portago who took it to Mexico for the Pan American Road Race. Portago, who was joined in the race by another 750 Monza driven by Bracco, started in No. 2 position in the race, one minute behind McAfee's 4.9-litre Ferrari. Before the long straight at Tehuantepec, Portago had made up his minute and overtaken McAfee, only to be passed again on the Tehuantepec straight where the bigger car could really use all its power. However a few miles further on Portago's car broke down with a burnt piston due to the inferior quality gasoline that had been provided at the start. Bracco's 750 Monza was also out of the running, his trouble having been a broken oil pump.

The 750 Monza engine

The construction of the Monza engine was highly unusual, but it nevertheless embodied many traditional racing engine features, amongst which was the use of twin overhead camshafts with integral heads and cylinders. This basic Siluminum upper-end casting included the ports, combustion chambers and water jackets, but not the cylinders themselves, which were separately cast of iron and threaded into bosses surrounding the chambers. Complete inspection for casting flaws was thus allowed, and liner thickness and cooling could be precisely controlled.

Intake valves were inclined at 45 degrees to the vertical and were at 85 degrees to the exhaust valves, which had sodium-filled stems. The valves seated in shrunk-in inserts. The combustion chamber was a modified hemisphere, with special contouring around the spark plug holes. Placed at the fore and aft ends of the chamber, the twin spark plugs were close to the exhaust valve and, with a bore over 4 inches, were vital to proper ignition of a widely distributed mixture.

Unusual valve gear

In designing the valve gear Lampredi had some special ideas of his own, twin hairpin valve springs were placed in the fore and aft plane and closed the valves through a collar retained by split keepers. Above this, tappets and camshaft were carried in separately cast light alloy boxes. T-shaped in cross section, the alloy tappets were guided by their stems and carried thin rollers which protruded only slightly from the wide tops. The lower parts of the rollers themselves rode in vertical slots and thus prevented the tappet from rotating.

To ensure that this assembly was held in contact with the cam a pair of very light concentric coil springs acted up against each tappet only, leaving the hairpins to deal solely with the valves. Shim clearance adjustment was provided.

The separate tappet boxes allowed thorough lubrication of cam and followers without forcing leakage down the valve stems, and accounted for the unusually high and wide Monza cam boxes. This somewhat complex valve system had to take the stresses from cams that provided 310 degree of intake duration, and 98 degrees of overlap. Lobes little more than 3/8 of an inch wide did the job, and were carried on large diameter tubular shafts, which in turn rested in five plain white-metal bearings each.

Exhaust porting had been extensively studied, the outer opening being flared considerably from the diameter at the valve. Properly tuned manifolding was used, with the cylinders paired 1-4 and 2-3, all four later joined at a single expansion chamber.

Induction was by Weber carburetters, and the Monza engine used two of the twin-choke type 58 DCOA/3. These were very large and carried 44 mm venturis. Webers are noted for their careful interior streamlining and 'straight through' design, which works well at high r p m. Very short alloy pipes connected these carburetters to the ports and stubby velocity intakes were fitted. A heavy throttle linkage cross shaft was carried in two ball bearings. The Monza produced a fantastic amount of torque and at high revs imposed a high level of stress on the rest of the engine and drive train. Consequently with a slightly overstressed bottom end, the engines had a relatively short racing life; clearances became excessive after several hours of racing making the car more suitable for short races rather than the endurance races like Le Mans.

The crankcase

The short head and cylinder unit bolted directly to the very deep Siluminum crankcase, and rubber rings formed water seals at the bottoms of the individual cylinders.

A very simple solid webbing supported each of the 5 main bearings which were 2.36 inches in diameter and available in four undersizes. The webbing continued down an inch and half or so beyond the crank centreline, to give the deep I sectioned bearing caps some lateral support. There were two retaining studs per cap.

In order that it could carry the oil supply to the crank and big ends, the centre main bearing

was 5/8 of an inch wider than its 1 1/8 inch companions. Completely devoid of elaborate counterbalancing, the forged steel crankshaft had 1.97 inch diameter crankpins and the big ends were fitted with Vandervell Thinwall bearings, similar to the main bearings, there being four undersizes available.

Connecting rods were short and simple, the sides of the I-section centre being perfect tangents to the outer diameter of the gudgeon pin end. Two bolts retained the big end cap, while the fully floating gudgeon pin received its lubrication from splash alone. The pistons were completely skirted and carried two compression and two oil rings, one of which was below the gudgeon pin.

An alloy cover at the engine front concealed the accessory and camshaft drive train of 3/8 of an inch width spur gears. The upper gears dealt with the cams, while the water and oil pumps were placed low down at the front. Dry sump lubrication was used, and two screened pickups scavenged the front and rear of the intricately finned cast-alloy sump.

The scavenge oil pump had two idlers to ensure that it kept up with the demand. It supplied a riveted reservoir on the right hand side.

A single idler pressure pump drew from the tank and replenished the mains through a sump-mounted full-flow filter. Lampredi relied heavily on external and internal piping to carry the oil around, and apparently did not want to mar his crankcase with too many cast or drilled-out oil passages.

The cooling system was extremely simple. It was kept in motion by a twin outlet pump adjacent to the scavenge oil supply. Drawing from the bottom of the finned tube radiator, the pump sent the cooled water to both sides of the crankcase, where it could absorb some heat from the main bearings. From there it rose past the cylinders to outlets directly above each combustion chamber. Thus the water was at its warmest when it reached the exhaust valves, which did not receive any high velocity cooling stream. The use of sodium-filled valve stems was clearly required.

Though it had to be lower than the cylinder head, the header tank was integral with the radiator.

Coil ignition

An extension from the cam gear train bevel drove a cross shaft within a magnesium alloy box at the front, further bevels rotated the central 12-volt generator and the Marelli distributors at each side. Earlier cars used magnetos, and the bottom end was used experimentally on some of the Grand Prix engines with a cover plate in place of the generator. Coil ignition was deemed better for all round 'production car' use. A FIMAC mechanical pump driven from the rear of the exhaust camshaft supplied fuel to the carburetter system. A rear-mounted Autoflux electric pump was used as a booster. Four rubber mountings suspended the riveted alloy fuel tank.

Transmission

The starter motor protruded back from the top of the shallow clutch housing, which enclosed a ten inch dry double-plate clutch with flexible centre. A short extension supported the Hooke-type universal at the forward end of the drive shaft.

Four heavy crankcase brackets mounted the engine on Silentbloc rubber inserts. The torque of the engine was transmitted to the rear-mounted gearbox by a tubular shaft and another universal, there being a splined joint at the forward end of the shaft. Placed just ahead of the final drive gears, the transmission was split vertically in line with the mainshaft and carried the countershaft on the right and the selector mechanism on the left. Dog clutches engaged constant mesh gears in the top four of the 5 speeds, while a sharply-angled jointed shaft transmitted from the centrally placed cast gearshift gate and lever housing. A compact conventional gate was used with a simple reverse stop.

A few of the early Monzas had four-speed gearboxes, but the five-speed version was prepared in time for early 1955 use. The 2-litre Mondial had received a similar arrangement a few months earlier.

A large spiral bevel gear at the back of the mainshaft drove a similar gear on a short cross shaft at a ratio of 1 : 1, and the ZF torque-bias differential was directly driven from the short shaft by helical gears. This final-drive alloy casing was also split vertically down the middle, allowing rapid disassembly and selection of any one of many possible ratios. The use of the cross shaft and the flat layout of the gearbox kept the whole assembly very low, and prevented any interference with the seats. Deep longitudinal fins cooled the sump of the alloy transmission case, while a gear-type pump circulated the lubricant.

Needle-bearing universal joints were carried almost within the final drive case, as a follow through from the old swing axle days, and allowed angular variation in machined halfshafts. Simple splined clamp joints facilitated disassembly, and connected to the hub-mounted pot-type universals.

The chassis frame

The early angled-tube chassis experiments conducted with the 500 Mondial and prototype 750 Monzas were refined into a smoothly-contoured structural base for the 'production' cars. Two oval section tubes constituted the main members, and were cross-linked and integrated into the body by many smaller round steel tubes. It was thus not a true space frame. Rear suspension was by De Dion. The 2½ inch diameter steel axle tube curved behind the differential and connected the fabricated hubs.

At the tube centre a ball carried a square bronze block vertically between steel plates in the back of the rear end casing, and thus located the tube laterally. This point also determined the rear roll centre. Two parallel trailing arms on each side guided the tube and absorbed braking torque. Since each set of arms formed a parallelogram, vertical movement of one end of the tube would produce no twisting moment between hubs, and floating mountings were avoided.

Rubber bushings were used at the chassis connections, while the axle ends of the arms had ball joints.

A transverse leaf spring was frame mounted above the axle casing, and was connected to the hubs by long drop shackles. Houdaille vane type shockabsorbers damped the vertical oscillations, which were limited by rubber buffers acting against the De Dion tube. Most of the Monza leaf springs used on the early types were quite flat while in static position, later models used a more highly arched type which gave more progressive suspension action.

A change to coil springs

Early Monza front suspensions also used transverse leaf springs as it was then current on Grand Prix cars. When Hawthorn found that the coil-spring layout used on his 555 Supersqualo gave excellent results at Barcelona, Ferrari changed over to coil springs on the later 750 Monzas. Basic geometry remained the same with two low and close-placed parallel wishbones to each wheel, the bottom arm being roughly half as long again as the top. The arm components were forged, polished and bolted together. A single wide bronze bushing pivoted the top arm to the boxed front cross member while two bushings were used for the wider bottom arm. The latter carried brackets for the shockabsorber linkage and at the end of the torsion anti-roll bar as well as for the bottom end of the small slightly splay-legged coil spring. The front suspension geometry was such as to give a roll centre very near the ground level, but was raised somethat by the anti-roll bar. As a result more of the overturning couple was resisted by the front wheels, producing a degree of understeer and leaving the rear wheels free to put power on the road. This, plus the semi-solid differential action, frame-mounted drive gears and low rear unspring weight gave the 750 Monza excellent traction on the tricky European road circuits. Tapered steering arms extended forward from the forged stub axles, and were connected by a three-piece track rod. The length of the outer member was so calculated as to be geometrically consistent with the suspension movement. A forward pitman arm transferred movement from the worm-and-wheel steering box, and was balanced by a slave arm on the left hand side. The steering column was carried round the carburetters by means of three universal joints.

Braking

Brakes were mounted at the wheels all round, to simplify installation and cooling. Their mechanical layout employed a central guide for each shoe to balance out the servo effect and wear, and thus avoid the excessive self wrapping effect of the usual two leading shoe brake gear. Two double-acting cylinders per wheel applied force equally to all four shoe ends, and received it from a single-bore master cylinder with separate circuits and reservoirs for front and rear systems.

The usual Ferrari method of deep tapered finning bonded to steel liners for the brake drums was used, these employed four simple screened apertures per wheel. Air circulation was induced by so ducting the face of the brake drum that it acted as a centrifugal fan and rapidly exhausted warm air from the interior of the unit.

These brakes served very well, but when Lucas had Messier disc brakes fitted experimentally to his car at the Monza Circuit he had no difficulty in outbraking the standard cars.

The Borrani wire wheels were set well out from the brakes, leaving the finning of the latter exposed to the best advantage. Wheel rims were light alloy and the hubs the familiar Rudge type, with two-eared locking nuts.

Racing experience was revealed in the disposition of the electrical equipment where it was readily accessible in the event of a small breakdown. The battery rested above the gearbox and between the seats, while all junction boxes, relays, etc. were on a single panel, under the cowl on the passenger's side. Instrumentation was compact and complete, with rev counter, ammeter, oil pressure and water temperatures. The handbrake lever was suspended on the right hand side of the driver's cockpit and applied the rear brakes through a cable system.

Type 500 Mondial

At the same time as he was developing the 3-litre Monza, Ferrari was working on the smaller 2-litre type 500 Mondial. The prototype of this car was similar to the original Type 735 3-litre having a chassis of the same design as the 250 Mille Miglia with a rigid rear axle and the gearbox in unit with the engine. Bodywork was by Scaglietti, and it can be said that this was the true prototype coachwork for the standard 750 Monza and Series 2 500 Mondials.

This car made its first appearance in the sports car race at Casablanca where Ascari and Picard had no difficulty in taking a second place behind the much larger 4.5-litre Ferrari.

Several modifications were made before the Series 1 Mondial went into production for sale to the public. The chassis layout was altered to one similar to the production Monza with a De Dion rear-axle layout and the gearbox in unit with the differential. The majority of the Series 1 Mondials had bodies built by Pinin Farina which bore a close resemblance to the bodies on the big 4.5-litre 12-cylinder cars. Towards the end of the series Farina built a 'one off' car, with a much longer nose, that was eventually exported to America. It was intended to be the prototype of the Series 2 Mondials but Ferrari did not like the design, and by this time his son Dino had finished his layout for the Series 2 body which was also to be used for the 750 Monza. The final car of the Series 1 was sent to Scaglietti and Dino Ferrari's design was built on the chassis which was then delivered to the American, Bob Said. He took the car on an Italian tour and scored second place at Bari and Syracuse and a third at Senigallia before returning to the USA where he raced it with considerable success.

The Series 1 Mondials all used the earlier 4-cylinder engine with a bore and stroke of 90 x 78 mm giving a total displacement of 1984.8-cc and with a compression ratio of 8.5 : 1 it had a power output of 160 b h p at 7,000 r p m. The crankcase was the Lampredi Siluminum light alloy type with screwed in cast iron liners. The light alloy cylinder block had hemispherical combustion chambers and the crankshaft was counterbalanced and supported on five bearings one of which also provided for axial support. Inclined overhead valves were actuated through tappets by two overhead gear-driven camshafts. Dry sump lubrication was used with a double bodied scavenge pump and a separate 16-litre oil tank. There were two plugs per cylinder in conjunction with two Marelli magnetos, and two twin-choke Weber Type 42 DCOA/3 carburetters took care of fuel and air mixture.

The clutch was a dry multiplate and the gearbox was in unit with the differential assembly on the rear axle. An oil pump and filter were incorporated in the gearbox which contained four forward speeds and reverse; first gear ratio was 2.25. second 1.5, third 1.108, fourth 1.00 : 1. Transmission shaft was two piece with a sliding joint, connected to the crankshaft by means of a Fabbri universal joint and to the gear input shaft by a Saga elastic torsional joint.

A De Dion rear axle layout with the light alloy central casing contained a self locking differential. Four radius rods located the hub ends of the De Dion and a centre-pivoted transverse leaf spring was employed together with Houdaille vane type shockabsorbers. Front suspension was independent with double wishbones and a transverse leaf spring, integral rubber blocks and damping by Houdaille shockabsorbers.

Hydraulic two-leading-shoe type brakes acted on all four wheels with twin master cylinders.

Wheelbase was 2.250 m with a front track of 1.278 m and a rear track of 1.284 m, 4.50 x 16 wheels all round were fitted with 5.25 x 16 tyres at the front and 5.50 x 16 tyres at the rear. The chassis was right-hand drive, dry weight was 750 kg and fuel capacity 150 litres.

The Series 2 Mondials

The first of the Series 2 Mondials made its appearance at the Bolzano Mendola hill climb in 1955 driven by Castelotti. The body was different from the prototype and could only be distinguished from the Monza by the fact that the side panels were rolled under to meet the lower chassis tubes instead of coming straight down and completely hiding the frame as on the bigger 3-litre model.

The same bore and stroke of 90 x 78 mm was retained but the Type 553/F2 block replaced the normal type 500. It will be remembered that the Type 553 was the 2-litre prototype of the 'Squalo,' two of the cars making their appearance at Monza for the last of the 2-litre Formula 2 events in the hands of Maglioli and Carini.

The capacity remained at 1984.8-cc as did the 8.5 : 1 compression ratio. Power was increased from 160 b h p to 170 and two twin-choke type 45DCOA/3 Webers replaced the type 42 DCOA/3 models used on the Series 1.

Other changes were the use of a double dry-plate clutch with Raybestos lining and the installation of a five-speed gearbox with first gear ratio 2.592, second 1.929, third 1.445, fourth 1.099 and fifth 1.00 : 1. A similar type of transmission shaft was used as on the Series 1, and the De Dion rear axle layout was retained with the transverse leaf spring and four radius arms.

Front suspension was altered to incorporate wishbones and coil springs in place of the wishbones and transverse leaf spring on the Series 1 cars. Wheelbase remained the same at 2.250 m with front and rear tracks of 1.278 m and 1.284 respectively, ground clearance was reduced from 150 mm to 140 mm and wheel sizes went up to 5.00 x 16 fitting 5.25 x 16 tyres at the front and 6.00 x 16 tyres at the rear, dry weight was also slightly reduced to 720 kg.

It was with the Series 2 model that Della Favera had such consistent success until he had his fatal crash with a 750 Monza at Parma-Poggio di Berceto hillclimb the same day as the 1955 Le Mans crash.

The Testa Rossa

Despite the many improvements on the Series 2 models, the cars were no real match for the new 4-cylinder 2-litre Maseratis, so Ferrari decided to go on with yet another 4-cylinder model to be named the Testa Rossa. This car was so named because the cylinder head was painted red, and this again was produced in two series, the first series having Scaglietti bodies with air intakes on the bonnets, being known as the Type 500 Testa Rossa, and the second series with a much smoother and lower body line known as the Type 500 TRC.

The Testa Rossa retained the 2-litre 4-cylinder engine with the bore and stroke of 90 x 78 mm, thus capacity remained the same as in the Mondial series, 1985-cc. The head was again altered reverting from the Type 553 to one similar to the original Type 500, but employing a different type of cam box cover. Internally the engine underwent strengthening at the bottom end and a new type of connecting rod was produced with strengthening ribs running round the bearing caps. Ing. Massimino, who had previously worked for Maserati, was called in to complete the redesigning of the 2-litre as Lampredi had by this time left Ferrari to work for Fiat.

Twin-choke Weber type 40 DCOA/3 car-buretters replaced the 45 DCOA/3 types and ignition was by Marelli magnetos.

The clutch remained a double dry-plate type but the gearbox reverted to the four speed and was mounted in unit with the engine.

The rear axle was of the rigid type with a light alloy central casing containing the self-locking differential.

Front suspension was independent, with double wishbones and coil springs, damping being by means of Houdaille adjustable vane-type shockabsorbers. Rear suspension was by means of two coil springs and damping again by means of Houdaille shockabsorbers.

The drum-type brakes employed two leading shoe systems operating on two master cylinders plus a mechanical handbrake to the rear wheels. Wheelbase was 2.250 m with a front track of 1.303 m and a rear track of 1.250 m. Dry weight was reduced to 680 kg and fuel capacity reduced to 120 litres. The 2-litre 500 TRC was never run by the factory as a team car, Ferrari having built these simplified models purely to sell to his customers. Nevertheless it turned out to be a most successful car, the customers finding it to be very manageable and easy to maintain, consequently these cars had a great deal of success in competition.

Masten Gregory won the 2-litre Class at Nassau 1956 being placed second overall in the main race, Bob Said repeated this in 1957 also winning the handicap award. Gino Munaron won the 2-litre class in the 1957 Mille Miglia, Julio Pola and Piero Drogo won the 2-litre class in the 1,000 km of Buenos Aires, and Julio Batista and Jan de Vroom won the 2-litre class in the 1,000 km of Venezuela. In the USA, Shelby won at Brynfan Tyddyn and Gregory took the 2-litre class at Thompson whilst in 1958 Markleson with the ex Buell-Gregory car won top place standing in class for the USAC championship.

The production of the 2-litre TRC stopped when Ferrari decided to replace it with the 3-litre 250 Testa Rossa, a design based on the 250 Gran Turismo model.

Type 625 Le Mans

After the 1955 Le Mans accident, the organizers of the race decided that a new set of rules would be issued for the 1956 event. Prototypes would be limited to 2.5-litres capacity, although production cars could remain unlimited. This meant that the race no longer counted for the Manufacturers world championship and for some time it seemed doubtful whether Ferrari would take part. However just in time for the final day of entries, Ferrari announced that he would participate with a new model known as the 625 Le Mans.

This car was a 4-cylinder with a bore and stroke of 94 x 90 mm giving a displacement of 2498-cc. It had a compression ratio of 9 : 1 and gave a maximum output of 225 b h p at 6,200 r p m. The engine followed the usual Ferrari 4-cylinder layout with a Siluminum block, threaded-in cast iron liners, light alloy head with hemispherical combustion chambers, a counter-balanced crankshaft on five bearings, one being for axial support, and dry sump lubrication with a separate 16-litre tank. The engine was in fact a bored-out version of the Testa Rossa 2-litre, but with the carburetters replaced by type 42 DCOA/3 twin-choke Webers, and the ignition by Marelli magnetos.

The chassis layout was also very similar to the Testa Rossa. The gearbox used four forward speeds and reverse all forward being synchromesh. The rigid rear axle had a light alloy central casing to house the ZF differential. Front suspension was by means of double wishbones with coil springs and Houdaille shockabsorbers whilst the rear suspension was by means of coil springs, the axle being located by radius rods and an A bracket under the differential.

Wheelbase was 2.250 m with a front track of 1.308 m and rear track of 1.250 m 5.00 x 16 wheels were fitted, taking 5.50 x 16 tyres at the front and 6.00 x 16 tyres at the rear. The car had a dry weight of 700 kg and a fuel capacity of 130 litres.

For the 1956 Le Mans race Ferrari officially entered three of the 625 models to be driven by Fangio/Castellotti, Musso/Gendebien and Trintignant/Schell. In reality the line-up was completely changed around with Simon/Phil Hill in car No. 10, De Portago/Duncan Hamilton in car No. 11 and Gendebien/Trintignant in car No. 12.

Two-litre Testa Rossas were entered by Ecurie Nationale Belge, for P. Meyrat and Porfirio Rubirosa. The ENB No. 20 was driven by De Changy/Bianchi, the Meyrat No. 21 and Tavano as co-driver and the No. 22 Chinetti entry was assigned to Francois Picard/Bob Tappan instead of Rubirosa.

Le Mans 1956

The race started without any Ferraris among the front runners. On lap 2 the De Portago/Hamilton car was eliminated when Frere's Jaguar spun at the Esses causing Fairman to spin and Portago to collide with Fairman's car splitting his oil tank.

By 5 pm the Ecurie Ecosse Jaguar of Flockhart held the lead with the Moss Aston Martin next up. Simon's Ferrari was 5th and Gendebien's car 7th.

The Manzon Gordini led on the index of performance with Gendebien's Ferrari trying to take that lead by moving up through the field.

Gendebien and Simon pulled in at the same time as the leading Jaguar but Simon's Ferrari had more than enough fuel left although the car experienced trouble getting away from the pits. Rain started to fall and after the fuel stops the Hill/Simon car was in 6th place, the No. 21 Ferrari of Mayrat/Tavano spun, moved onto the pit approach and was rammed in the rear by Glockler's Porsche which immediately burst into flames.

At 6 hours the Moss/Collins Aston Martin was in the lead with the Flockhart/Sanderson Jaguar second the Gendebien/Trintignant Ferrari third and the Simon/Hill Ferrari 4th. At 12.45 am the Flockhart Jaguar had the lead from Moss and Collins with the Gendebien/Trintignant Ferrari still third. After the 9th hour the Simon/Hill Ferrari retired with a broken rear axle and at 4 am, after 12 hours the Gendebien/Trintignant car still held third at 142 laps to the leader's 146 laps.

At 7 am the Picard/Tappan Ferrari was disqualified for refueling before the required number of laps.

After 18 hours the Flockhart Jaguar had a two-lap lead over the Aston Martin with Gendebien/Trintignant another three laps down on the Moss/Collins Aston. There was no more change of position and the race ended with the Ferrari third having covered 2,446.71 miles at an average speed of 101.95 m p h compared to the

(*Top Left*) Ascari at the wheel of the Prototype 4.5 litre Ferrari. Together with Farina he won the 1000 Km of the Nurburgring
(*Top Right*) Tom Cole's 4.1 Type 340MM rebuilt by Scaglietti after Cole's fatal crash at Le Mans 1953
(*Middle Left*) 1954 Ferrari Type 375MM
(*Middle Right*) Ferrari Type 375MM Competition Coupe by Pinin Farina
(*Bottom*) The Type 375MM Coupe with which Hawthorn/Maglioli won the 1953 12 Hours of Pescara

(Top Left) Phil Hill and Richie Ginther
came 2nd overall in the 1954 Pan
American Road Race in the 4.5 litre
Type 375MM belonging to Allen
Guiberson
(Top Right) Gonzales with the 4.9
litre Type 375 Plus winning the 1954
Daily Express Trophy Race at Silverstone
(Bottom) Jim Kimberley's special
Type 375MM 4.5 litre Ferrari

(Top Left) Dan Gurney with the Arciero
Type 375 Plus that was originally owned
by Parravano. The car was rebodied by Sutton
in Los Angeles
(Top Right) Peter Collins with the Type 410
Sport at Buenos Aires. This was the only
time the factory raced these cars
(Middle) John Edgar's 410 Sport being driven
by Jo Bonnier at Riverside
(Bottom Left) The ex-Cornacchia 250 Monza in
the colours of Guatemala, driven by Manfredo
Lippman
(Bottom Right) Bob Drake at Bonneville Salt Flat
with the Type 375 Plus ex-Parravano car with
which he has attempted several speed records

(*Top Left*) Franco Cornacchia with the Scuderia Guastalla 250 Monza at the 1954 Pan American Road Race
(*Top Right*) The Type 290 single cam 3.5 litre of Scuderia Buell which won the 1957 1000 Km of Buenos Aires driven by Gregory/Castellotti/Musso
(*Bottom*) 1956 Swedish GP. The winning Hill/Trintignant 3.5 litre V12

(Top) 290MM prior to the 1956 1000 Km race at Nurburgring. This is a Scaglietti built car using the Type 130 V12 of 3.5 litres and de Dion rear suspension
(Bottom) Stuart Lewis Evans during the pre Mille Miglia test of the 3.8 litre 4 cam

(*Top Left*) De Portago in the 1957 Sebring 3.8 litre
Twin Cam 12 cyl
(*Top Right*) Ascari in the 'Autodromo' bodied 3 litre
4 cyl Monza Prototype
(*Middle*) Luigi Musso at the 1957 Swedish GP in the
4.1 litre 4 cam
(*Bottom*) Phil Hill at the 1957 Swedish GP in the 4.1
litre 4 cam

(*Top Left*) The Type 735 Monza, Argentina 1954. This is the original Prototype Monza which first appeared at Senigallia 1953

(*Top Right*) Bob Said at the wheel of a 750 Monza at the Daytona Beach Speed Trials

(*Middle*) A standard customer's 750 Monza 4 cyl 3 litre at Silverstone

(*Bottom Left*) Tourist Trophy 1954. Mike Hawthorn at the Hairpin with the 750 Monza Ferrari. Alone he defeated the might of the Lancia Team which included Fangio and Ascari

(*Bottom Right*) The experimental 2.5 litre Prototype Monza engine used in Mike Hawthorn's car at Monza 1953

(Top Left) The engine of the 4 cyl 3 litre 750 Monza in the Briggs Cunningham Museum

(Top Right) The series 1 Type 500 Mondial 4 cyl

(Middle) Gary Laughlin of Fort Worth, Texas with his Type 750 Monza. He was a consistent winner of SCCA races

(Bottom) Carroll Shelby of Dallis, Texas with his 3 litre 4 cyl Type 750 Monza which he co-drove with Phil Hill at Sebring. They thought they had won but a timekeeping error later found that they were beaten by the Jaguar

(Top Left) The first appearance of the 850 M Ferrari driven at the Tourist Trophy by Taruffi

(Top Right) A one-off 500 Mondial built by Pinin Farina using the same style of the 375 MM of 1953 - 1954

(Middle) 'Ferrari 500 Testa Rossa 1956 - 1957 4 cilindri in linea 2000-cc 190 HP'

(Bottom Left) Bob Said in the 'Trullo d'Oro' race at Bari where he finished second to Bordoni's Gordini. In the background is a 'trullo', a typical peasants house of the Bari region

(Bottom Right) The Testa Rossa 2 litre 4 cyl engine

(*Top Left*) TRC line-up at the 1957 Swedish GP
(*Top Right*) The 1957 TRC entered in the Swedish GP by Julio Batista and Gino Munaron
(*Middle*) With photographer Louis Klementaski as passenger (far right), Peter Collins drove this 860 M in the Mille Miglia
(*Bottom Left*) Castelotti in the Type 860 Monza 4 cyl at the Swedish GP
(*Bottom Right*) Nurburgring 1000 Km 1956. Castelotti in the Type 860

(*Top*) John Edgar owned Type 860 Monza raced successfully (here) by Jack McAfee, Carroll Shelby and others in the USA
(*Bottom Left*) The Parravano 4.4 litre 6 cyl Type 121 LM in construction at the Scaglietti workshops
(*Bottom Right*) Castelotti in the 4.4 litre 6 cyl at Le Mans 1955

(Top) Riverside 1959 for the Times GP - practice. This is the Parravano rebodied car driven by Rodger Ward which was involved in a three car crash at the start line
(Bottom Left) Jim Kimberley with his 'altered' 4.4 litre 6 cyl. The nose has been modified from the original to improve cooling
(Bottom Right) The Type 121 LM with Indianapolis driver Rodger Ward at the wheel in Riverside 1959

(Top Left) The first series of Testa Rossas (V12) was bodied by Scaglietti and were completely cutaway at the front to allow air flow to the finned drum brakes
(Top Right) Loyal Katskee with the ex Kimberley 4.4 litre at Meadowdale
(Bottom Left) The Colombo designed 3 litre V12 in a very high state of tune in the Testa Rossa. This is engine 0750TR
(Bottom Right) The 1958 250 TR of Ecurie National Belge on display in the Brussel's Shell Oil Building

(*Top Left*) The factory team at Sebring 1958. No. 14, Hill/Collins won. No. 16 Musso/Gendebien was 2nd, and No. 15 Hawthorn/Von Trips retired

(*Top Right*) Peter Collins in the winning 1958 Sebring 250 TR. He co-drove with Phil Hill

(*Middle*) 1958. Von Trips, sharing with Gendebien, also in the 250 Testa Rossa

(*Bottom Left*) Pit stop at the 1958 Targa Florio with the 2nd place TR of Hawthorn/Von Trips

(*Bottom Right*) 1958. Hawthorn in the 250 Testa Rossa at Nurburgring

(*Top Left*) The Hill/Gendebien 250 TR at
Le Mans 1959. It retired with cooling
problems
(*Top Right*) Again at Modena, the 250 TR now
painted
(*Middle*) Ferrari won the 1959 Sebring 12
Hours with the Hill/Gendebien team 250 TR
(*Bottom*) The Reventlow/Martin 250 TR
finished 6th in the 1959 Sebring 12 Hours

(*Top Left*) Full size windscreens plus wipers were required for
1960 (FIA)
(*Top Right*) Phil Hill in the 1960 Ferrari 250 Prototype at Monza
(*Middle Left*) Richie Ginther in the 1961 Testa Rossa at Modena
(*Middle Right*) The 2nd series Testa Rossa eliminated the deep
cutaway front wings. Ginther here at Riverside
(*Bottom*) The 250 TR was raced frequently by private
customers. A series was built based on the first 1958 design but
with 'pontoon' front wings. This is an American Le Mans entry of
1959

Jaguar's 2,507.18 miles and 104.46 m p h. The Ferrari finished 7th in the index of performance.

These Type 625 Le Mans cars could only be distinguished from an ordinary Testa Rossa by the fact that their cylinder heads were not painted red and that they had bodies made by Touring of Milan, with cutaway sections behind the wheels.

The cars were never raced again by the factory after Le Mans, but the chassis and bodies were used for receiving the normal 2-litre Testa Rossa engines, in which form they were raced in the Supercortemaggiore race at Monza, Collins and Hawthorn sharing the winning car. The cars were then reconverted to 2.5-litres and sold in the USA. One special version was built for John Von Neumann with a Scaglietti body resembling that of the normal 500 Testa Rossa, the only difference being that there were two bumps in the bonnet to give clearance to the fronts of the cam boxes.

Another engine was prepared and bored out to 2.8-litres, this being mounted in a single seater chassis built to the order of Pat Hoare from New Zealand.

The 129/S 860 Monza

Whilst all this development had been progressing, the Type 750 Monza was becoming outdated. Ferrari intended eventually to replace the Monza with a 3-litre 12-cylinder version, but in the meantime the cubic capacity race had begun once more and his immediate plans were for a 3.5-litre 12-cylinder. As it would take some time to prepare this 12-cylinder car, he decided to increase the capacity of the Monza and use it as a stopgap. This engine was known as the 129 S or the 860 Monza. It had a bore and stroke of 102 x 105 mm which gave a total capacity of 3431-cc. It had a compression ratio of 8.5 : 1 and gave out 280 b h p at 6,000 r p m. It used the same chassis as the 750 Monza and made its first appearance at the Tourist Trophy Race where Taruffi faced a full team of Mercedes Benz, Jaguar and Maserati. The car was disappointing in its performance and was never in the picture.

This car, which could be distinguished from a 750 Monza by two long fairings on the bonnet to allow for the cam boxes, was then sent to the USA where it won the main event at Nassau with Phil Hill driving. A second car fitted with a tailfin was sold to John Edgar who had it driven by Jack McAfee but with no great success. Edgar then had Shelby to drive the car and with it he chalked up several victories in the United States. The Phil Hill car which was owned by George Tilp raced at Sebring with Hill and Gregory driving, but the car broke down early in the race which was won by Fangio and Castelotti driving a much improved version that featured coil spring front suspension instead of the transverse leaf spring.

The new model had quite a successful career. Collins took second and Musso third in the Mille Miglia behind Castelotti's 12-cylinder 3.5-litre, Fangio was second to Moss at Caracas and second again in the 1,000 km of the Nurburgring. Collins and Von Trips took second to Phil Hill and Trintignant's 12-cylinder in the Swedish Grand Prix and De Portago was easily leading the Cuban Grand Prix when a minor mechanical breakdown dropped him to third place.

With the obvious success of the 12-cylinder 290 Mille Miglia model, Ferrari abandoned his 4-cylinder design to go all out on his plans for bigger and better 12-cylinder models.

THE 6-CYLINDER IN LINE TYPES

Type 118 LM

In 1955 when Mercedes Benz appeared with the 300SLR sports car, Ferrari knew that he would be hard pressed to win the manufacturers' championship with the 3-litre Monza and his projected 3.5-litre Monza. As usual he had something up his sleeve for he had already been experimenting with a 6-cylinder in line design, based on the successful 2-litre 4-cylinder, in an attempt to produce a new 2.5-litre Formula 1 engine. As a result of this he decided to use the 2.5-litre 625 engine as a basis for a new sports car bringing it up to a larger capacity by adding two cylinders. The new type was known as the 118LM and had a bore and stroke of 94 x 90 mm which gave a displacement of 3747.480-cc. Compression ratio was 8.75 : 1 and maximum power output was 310 b h p at 6,000 r p m. The classic construction used in the 4-cylinder engines was followed with a Siluminum light alloy crankcase. The cast iron liners were threaded into recesses surrounding the combustion chambers. The cylinder block was light alloy with hemispherical combustion chambers and the crankshaft supported on seven bearings, one of which was for axial support. Inclined overhead valves were actuated through tappets by twin overhead gear-driven camshafts. Dry sump lubrication was used with a double-bodied scavenge pump and a separate 16-litre oil tank. There were three Weber 45 DCOA/3 twin-choke carburetters together with a FIMAC mechanical fuel pump and an Autoflux electric pump which was controlled by a switch on the dashboard.

Two plugs per cylinder and Marelli distributors provided ignition. In all other respects the engine was similar in its construction details to that of the 750 Monza described in the 4-cylinder sports car section of this book.

Clutch was a multiple dry plate type with an elastic hub. The gearbox was in unit with the differential assembly having an oil pump and filter incorporated. Five forward speeds and reverse were provided; first gear ratio being 2.78, second 1.96, third 1.4, fourth 1.12 and fifth 1.00. The transmission shaft was two piece with sliding joint incorporating two Fabbri universal joints.

Rear axle was of the De Dion design and the differential was of the ZF limited slip type. Four radius rods provided hub end location for the De Dion and a centre-pivoted transverse leaf spring was employed with Houdaille vane type shock-absorbers.

Four-wheel hydraulic brakes were used with twin master cylinders and two leading shoe action, plus a mechanical handbrake on the rear wheels. The frame was a 'one-piece' construction utilizing elliptical section steel tubes. Wheelbase was 2.400 m with a front track of 1.278 and a rear track of 1.284 m. At the front 5.00 x 16 wheels were fitted, mounting 5.50 x 16 tyres whilst at the rear 5.50 x 16 wheels were used with 7.00 x 16 tyres. Dry weight was 850 kg and fuel capacity 150 litres.

This car made its first appearance in the 1955 Argentine season. Gonzales drove the car which put up a very impressive performance, continually changing the lead of the 1000 km of Buenos Aires with the Ibanez/Saenz Valiente 4.9-litre Ferrari until Gonzales was disqualified for taking a short cut back to the pits. The car ran again in the Formula Libre Buenos Aires Grand Prix but retired early in the event.

Type 121 LM

The next outing for the car was in the Mille Miglia and there it was joined by a larger model known as the 121 LM which was in effect a 3-litre Monza engine with two cylinders added.

The bore and stroke of this engine were 102 x 90 mm giving a displacement of 4412.49-cc. It had a compression ratio of 8.75 : 1 and gave 360 b h p at 6,000 r p m. Again similar construction methods to the 4-cylinder Monza engine were used with the crankshaft on seven bearings. The 45 DCOA/3 Weber carburetters were replaced by Type 50 DCOA/3. It had dry sump lubrication again with a 16 litre separate tank and twin plug ignition also with Marelli distributors and coils.

The gearbox, as on the earlier model, was in unit with the differential, the box having five forward speeds and reverse, first being 2.78, second 1.96, third 1.4, fourth 1.12 and fifth 1.00.

The chassis layout remained the same as on the smaller car, with wishbone and coil spring front suspension, and a De Dion rear axle together with a transverse leaf spring. Wheelbase remained at 2.400 m and front and rear track were 1.278 m and 1.284 respectively; 5.00 x 16 wheels were fitted at the front and 5.50 x 16 at the rear which mounted 5.50 x 16 tyres at the front and 7.50 x 16 at the rear. Dry weight remained at 850 kg and the fuel tank contained 152 litres.

1955 Mille Miglia

Castelotti was entered to drive the 4.4-litre car with Taruffi, Marzotto and Maglioli running the 3.7-litres. Castelotti showed a tremendous turn of speed, averaging over 120 m p h through

Verona and catching up the complete minute that he had started behind Moss with the 300SLR Mercedes Benz that was eventually to win the race.

Castelotti's effort did not last very long when the car went out with blown rear tyres, causing enough damage to force his retirement. Marzotto was out before Ravenna with the same trouble but Taruffi got his 3.7-litre into the lead only to have to retire with oil pump failure before Viterbo. The Mercedes were left with an unassailable lead and Maglioli had to struggle hard to finish in third place behind the two German cars.

The 3.7-litre car next made an appearance at Bari where Taruffi drove it again but, although it led the race again for a time, it eventually went out with the same oil pump trouble that had put it out in the Mille Miglia. Farina then took the 3.7-litre car to the Nurburgring where he trailed the two Mercedes of Fangio and Moss for a time and battled with Kling on the third works Mercedes. However the car began to lose power and the day was saved by Masten Gregory who brought his 3-litre Monza into third position behind the two Mercedes and ahead of Kling's 300SLR and Farina's 3.7-litre 6-cylinder, altogether an exceptional performance.

Le Mans 1955

For the 1955 Le Mans race Ferrari entered three of the 4.4-litre 6-cylinder cars for Taruffi/Marzotto, Maglioli/Farina and Trintignant/Schell. In private hands were two 3-litre 4-cylinder Monza Ferraris driven by Sparken/Picard and Helde/Lucas.

In fact the factory cars were driven in the race by Maglioli/Hill (car No. 3), Castellotti/Marzotto (car No. 4) and Trintignant/Schell (car No. 5).

The lap record stood to Maglioli in the 4.9 Ferrari set during practice in 1954 at a time of 4 mins. 18.4 secs. (116.5 m p h).

The new 6-cylinder Ferraris were unfortunately hastily prepared and in 1955 found a stronger Jaguar team together with a formidable challenge from Mercedes-Benz to face.

During practice Moss in a Mercedes posted fastest lap at 4 mins. 15.1 secs. The Simon/Kling Mercedes lapped in 4 min. 16.4 secs. and the fastest Ferrari was the Castellotti/Marzotto car

at 4 min. 21 secs. with the Rolt/Hamilton Jaguar following at 4 min. 23.3 secs.

During the Friday practice Castellotti took the 4.4 Ferrari round in 4 min. 14.1 secs. (119 m p h) with the Fangio/Moss Mercedes at 4 min. 18.5 secs. and Hawthorn/Bueb Jaguar at 4 min. 20.6 secs.

As the starting flag fell it was Castellotti and Maglioli with the Ferraris that took the lead with Phil Walters in the Cunningham-entered Jaguar in third place. The pace during the first hour was tremendous. Hawthorn moved his Jaguar into second place behind Castellotti and in five laps Fangio had his Mercedes in third place. Castellotti on the second lap set a new lap record at 117.49 m p h but on the fifth lap Fangio beat it by 1 second, being timed over the flying kilometre at 175 m p h.

On lap 16 Hawthorn took the lead from the Ferrari and on lap 17 Fangio recorded 4 min. 9.7 secs. (120.8 m p h) to pass the Ferrari into 2nd place. Hawthorn equalled the Mercedes time and Fangio replied with 4 min. 8.2 secs. The Trintignant/Schell 4.4 Ferrari was already in trouble while Castellotti fell further and further back. At 6 pm Fangio's Mercedes led from Hawthorn's Jaguar with Castellotti 3rd and Maglioli 4th all on the same lap. Sparkens 3-litre Monza Ferrari had already retired. Castellotti was the first to refuel and about this time the disastrous Le Mans accident occurred in which Levegh's Mercedes crashed, causing over 200 casualties of which more than 80 were fatal. The Ferraris fell back and at 8 pm the Maglioli/Hill car held third place averaging 113.5 m p h to the first place Mercedes averaging 115.8 m p h while the Castelotti/Marzotto car dropped to 7th before retiring during the 5th hour. The Maglioli/Hill car continued to hold 3rd place through the 5th hour dropping to 10th at the 6th hour before retiring.

The Trintignant/Schell Ferrari was never in contention although it moved up from 54th position during the 1st hour to 9th by the 7th hour and dropping again to 10th before retiring.

The Lucas/Helde 3-litre Ferrari moved up to 11th at the 7th hour but dropped to 18th before retiring. All three factory cars retired from over-heating trouble. This car serial number 0484 LM, remains in Southern California.

Swedish Grand Prix

Castellotti took a lone 4.4 litre to the Swedish Grand Prix but on the bumpy circuit could not hold on to the Mercedes of Fangio and Moss and had to be content with third place. In the meantime several of the 4.4-litre cars had been sold, one to Ernie McAfee who raced it in Californian events and two special bodied ones delivered to Jim Kimberley and Tony Parravano. Kimberly had no luck at all with his car and broke the crankshaft before disposing of it. Parravano sent his car to the small and twisty circuit of Oulton Park where Shelby, who was driving, had no hope at all of getting round the track even as quickly as a much older Monza was doing. The car returned to Italy for modification before being sent to Venezuela where Maglioli drove it only to retire almost at once with the same overheating trouble.

A similar car had been ordered by Von Neumann for Phil Hill to drive at the Venezuelan Grand Prix, but it too retired from overheating.

Ernie McAfee crashed to his death in his 4.4-litre and Luigi Chinetti prepared one of the cars for Caroll Shelby to drive. With this car Shelby set a lap record at Elkhart Lake and won the only two events in the car's history until Katskee, who had purchased the ex-Kimberly car, won one of the first of the American professional sports car races in 1958.

The 4.4 thus disappeared from the scene as the Ferrari trend went back to the 12-cylinder engine and it became obvious that more power could be extracted from the new four-cam versions of the V12.

THE V 6-CYLINDER TYPES
The Dino 206

When it became obvious that the 2-litre 4-cylinder Testa Rossa Ferraris were no longer a match for the 1600-cc Porsches, something new was expected from Ferrari. For a long time it was rumoured that a 1500-cc sports car based on the V6 Dino Formula 2 car would be produced. Rumour had it that the car would appear at the 1957 Nassau event and then at the 1958 Sebring race. However when it appeared it did so in 2-litre Form, the new model being known as the Dino 206. The V 6-cylinder engine was based on

the Dino 246 Formula 1 engine, and had a bore and stroke of 77 x 71 mm giving a displacement of 1983.724-cc, and with a compression ratio of 9 : 1 it had a power output of 225 b h p at 9000 r p m. Two Marelli magnetos took care of ignition and three twin-choke Weber carburetters were used. The weight of the engine was 130 kg. The wheelbase was 2.220 m with a front track of 1,240 mm and a rear track of 1,200 mm; 5.50 x 16 tyres were used at the front and 6.00 x 16 tyres were mounted at the rear.

A new lightweight chassis, basically of twin-tube construction with a trussed superstructure was introduced, and front suspension was by means of the usual Ferrari wishbones and coil springs with rear suspension the same as the 2-litre Testa Rossa with the rigid axle and coil springs, the four-speed gearbox being in unit with the engine.

This car made its first appearance at Goodwood with Peter Collins taking it to a first place. It then appeared at Naples with Musso and at Monza was driven by Munaron. During the latter part of 1958 a great deal of testing was done by various Italian drivers on this car with a view to getting it into production for delivery to customers in August 1959.

The Dino 296

Another V 6-cylinder engined car made a brief appearance during 1958. This was the Dino 296 or the 296 MI. With a bore and stroke of 85 x 87 mm it had a power output of 316 b h p at 7,800 r p m, the capacity being 2962-cc. This car was fitted into a chassis that was basically the prototype for the 1959 Testa Rossa factory cars, with clutch, gearbox and differential on the rear axle which was De Dion. The starter was mounted on the gearbox above the clutch and a spring loaded lever above it was arranged to engage the starter pinion and actuate the switch in one motion. This car made its one and only appearance in 1958 at the Silverstone event where it finished 3rd with Hawthorn driving it against bigger machinery. The engine was removed after the race and used for the single seater prepared for the Monza 500 miles and the chassis was used for the 12-cylinder 3-litre 4-cam engine to conduct some experiments.

The 250 Testa Rossa

For the 1958 season Ferrari decided to concentrate on his very fast 3-litre 12-cylinder Testa Rossa model for the manufacturers' world championship events. A number of 250 Testa Rossa models were produced for customers to drive, Ferrari maintaining that the 250TR was a logical development of the 200 Testa Rossa two-litre.

With the 2-litre he had planned to give the customers a car with which they could drive well and still win races. It was a car without any of the vices of Ferrari's more exotic machinery and was easy for the amateur to master. Ferrari claimed that the 3-litre 12-cylinder Testa Rossa was built with the same plan in mind and any customer who had experience with the smaller car would be able to handle the 3-litre just as well. The customer's version of the Testa Rossa kept the cutaway body style which had been used for the 1957 Le Mans prototype and had a live rear axle. The factory cars differed in having a new body without the front fender cutouts. The factory cars too were tested with De Dion axles and later in the season this became standard for the team cars.

The 1958 Season

For the first race of the championship season at Buenos Aires, Ferrari sent three cars, for Collins and Phil Hill, Musso and Gendebien and for Hawthorn and Von Trips. Two of the cars had the De Dion rear axle and the third, a live axle similar to that used on the customers' cars of which one was entered by Seidel and Von Neumann and another by Drogo and Gonzales.

Collins went straight into the lead followed closely by Von Trips, Musso led the second bunch of cars but was out on the second lap after steering failure due to a collision with Trintignant. This allowed his co-driver to substitute for Hawthorn as co-driver on Von Trips' car, as he was suffering from a bad case of sunburn and was not really fit to drive. Fangio driving for Maserati passed Von Trips for second place but in the attempt to challenge Collins for the lead, overdid things and badly bent the front of his car. From then on it was a procession with the Collins/Hill car leading easily and lapping all the field except the Von Trips/Gendebien car. The latter team had quite a bit of difficulty with the Moss/Behra Porsche, finally taking second place only 9 seconds ahead of the German entry. It was a satisfactory start for Ferrari with a first and second place, the fastest lap going to Phil Hill at an average of 102.937 m p h. The privately entered 250 Testa Rossa of Drogo/Gonzales finished fourth, the Von Neumann/Seidel car having retired on the 9th lap with a broken rear axle.

Sebring

The next manufacturers' championship race for Hawthorn/Von Trips, Collins/Phil Hill and Musso/Gendebien. Private entries of Testa Rossas were Ginther/Von Neumann, Fitch/Hugus and Chet Flynn/Martin all in the 3-litre models. The earlier 2-litre 4-cylinder Testa Rossas were in the hands of Bob Said/Mike Rivera from El Salvador, Gomez Mena/De Vroom Carreras from Cuba, Gonzales/Galtes Carreras also from Cuba and Rubirosa, Helburn and Malle a joint Dominican Republic, USA and France entry.

At the start it was Stirling Moss in an Aston Martin who took the lead followed by Mike Hawthorn in the 3-litre Testa Rossa with Phil Hill fourth and John Fitch, in the first of the private entries, 6th. By lap four Moss had a 12-second lead on Hawthorn. Gendebien was held up due to an accident with Scott Brown's Lister Jaguar but was able to continue. After the first hour Moss was a long way ahead of Hawthorn, Phil Hill and Salvadori in the second Aston who were fighting it out for second place. Moss blew a tyre but his lead was so long that he still had a 50 second lead over the Ferraris after his pit stop. The Collins/Hill Ferrari was firmly established in 2nd place followed by Von Trips/Hawthorn, Ginther/Von Neumann and Musso/Gendebien, the latter team having made up considerable ground after the accident. When Brooks took over from Moss, Collins was able to make up time until Brooks was forced into the pits. The Ferrari then took the lead; after repairs Moss put up a magnificent show reducing Collins' lead from 3½ minutes to only 7 seconds before trouble struck again and the Aston Martin was eliminated. The Ferraris then had it their own way, although both the Collins/Hill car and the Hawthorn/Von Trips car were suffering from lack of brakes. The order became set with Collins/Hill in first place. The Hawthorn/Von Trips car retired with a broken gearbox and after the 10th hour the Ginther/Von Neumann car broke down with rear axle failure. Collins and Hill won, setting a new race distance record of 1,040 miles in 12 hours. Of the privately owned 3-litres, Fitch/Hugus broke a valve spring and the Flynn/Martin car crashed. In the 2-litre class the Rubirosa/Helburn/Malle car won the class after the El Salvador and one of the Cuban cars retired.

Targa Florio

For the Targa Florio, run over 15 laps of the 'Little Madonie Circuit' Ferrari entered three cars for Musso/Gendebien, Hawthorn/Von Trips and Collins/Hill. The Musso/Gendebien car had a neat new body which was all enveloping with two slots cut in the body for brake cooling. The Von Trips/Hawthorn car still retained the cutaway front fenders which had been first used on the prototype and customer cars. The Ferraris seemed to have things set when Moss had trouble with the Aston Martin. Gendebien/Musso were then first, Hill/Collins second and Hawthorn/Von Trips third. At this point Behra driving a Porsche overtook Hawthorn and later managed to pass Hill for 2nd place. In trying to catch up, Hill spun off and dropped to 5th place. Musso/Gendebien went on to win, followed by the Porsche, with Hawthorn/Von Trips third and the Collins/Hill car moving up one place to 4th in the last stages of the race.

The results of this race together with those of the Sebring and Buenos Aires gave Ferrari a large lead in the championship.

The ADAC 1000 Km

The next race was the 1000 km of the Nurburgring and Ferrari this time entered 4 cars, for Hawthorn/Collins, Von Trips/Gendebien, Musso/Hill and Munaron/Seidel. Musso and Phil Hill used the Targa Florio winning car and the others had the cutaway versions. On the first lap it was the Aston Martin of Moss that led by 12 seconds from Hawthorn's Ferrari. Moss increased his lead to 21 secs. by the third but when Brabham took over from Moss, Hawthorn

quickly made up ground and overhauled the Aston Martin. Hawthorn lost his lead when a tyre blew and the Moss car once again was out in front. Hawthorn returned to the race and quickly regained second place with the Von Trips car safely in third but the Porsche of Behra holding off the Hill/Musso Ferrari for 4th place. Phil Hill blew a tyre on the circuit and had to change it himself which lost him some time while Collins began to make up 30 seconds a lap on the Aston Martin which was once again being driven by Brabham. When Moss took back the Aston, the race was set as he pulled out to 72 seconds over the second place Ferrari. The Ferrari hopes of a win were completely squashed when Hawthorn spun and had to manhandle the car back on the road leaving Moss with a lead of over 4 minutes. However, the Ferraris showed fine dependability with Hawthorn/Collins 2nd, Von Trips/Gendebien 3rd, Musso/Hill 4th and Seidel/Munaron 5th. The first of the private Ferraris was the Kochert/Bauer entry from Austria in 10th place. Bauer had the misfortune to crash on the slowing up lap, after the race was over, losing his life in the process. Another 250 Testa Rossa finished 12th driven by the Finnish team of Lincoln/Keinanen.

Le Mans

For Le Mans, Ferrari entered three cars, all being without the cutaway front and all three being fitted with De Dion rear axles. The teams were made up of Hawthorn/Collins, Gendebien/Hill, and Von Trips/Seidel. There was also a host of privately entered 250 Testa Rossas to back up the factory team. These cars were driven by Gurney and Kessler for the North American Racing Team, Hugus/Erikson from the United States, Beurlys/De Changy from Belgium, Martin/Tavano from France, Gomez Mena/Drogo, a joint Cuban-Venezuelan entry, and Picard/Juhan a joint French and Guatemalan entry.

Stirling Moss in the Aston Martin took an immediate lead with a tremendous battle going on right behind him between Hawthorn's Ferrari, Brooks' Aston Martin and Von Trips' Ferrari. The two Ferraris had been given instructions to go after the Aston Martins to try and get them to break and it was up to the Gendebien/Hill car to try and win the race. The tactics paid off and

Moss was out two hours from the start. A tremendous rain storm slowed the pace and Phil Hill pushed his Ferrari into the lead. Hawthorn registered the fastest lap of 4 min. 8 secs. a speed of 121.3 m p h and then the car retired with a burnt out clutch. Seidel put the car he was sharing with Von Trips into the ditch. The private owners were also having their problems.

The Picard/Juhan Ferrari ran into Chamberlain's Lotus when the latter spun and Kessler crashed the Chinetti entered car into the wreck of Mary's Jaguar. When the leading Ferrari of Hill/Gendebien stopped for fuel the Bueb/Hamilton Jaguar took the lead but shortly afterwards the Ferrari was back out in front and stayed there for the rest of the race. The Gomez Mena/Drogo Ferrari retired with a broken clutch as did the Martin/Tavano car. De Changy and Beurlys brought their 250 Testa Rossa home in 6th place with the Erikson/Hugus car right behind them in 7th place. Ferrari's win at Le Mans gave the Maranello team a total of 38 points in the manufacturers' championship so no one could challenge them. As a result of this, Ferrari did not enter the last race of the season, the Tourist Trophy.

The 1959 Season

The beginning of the 1959 season saw very little change in the 250 Testa Rossa but a big change in the driving team. The cars now had the all-enveloping body as standard, the new bodies being made by Fantuzzi, who had left Maserati, instead of Scaglietti. The only major change was that the cars were now fitted with Dunlop disc brakes in place of the outdated drum brakes.

Sebring

The first race of the championship season was the 12 hours of Sebring. Ferrari entered cars for Jean Behra and Cliff Allison, Dan Gurney and Chuck Daigh, all newcomers, and one car for Gendebien/Hill. Salvadori's Aston Martin took the lead but was soon passed by Gurney's Ferrari, Behra followed suit and set the fastest lap at 92.857 m p h which took him into the lead. Gendebien in the meantime sat behind the Lister Jaguars but moved up into the lead by the time the first of the pit stops came along. The

new disc brakes were giving some trouble and the Behra/Allison car lost a lap in the pits. After 4½ hours the Hill/Gendebien car came to a halt with a broken rear axle and the Gurney/Daigh car inherited the lead. The car driven by the two Americans was called in to hand over to the more experienced team of Gendebien/Hill but repairs to the electrical system dropped the car to second place behind Behra and Allison. As rain began to fall Phil Hill began to gain ground on his team mates and worked his way into the lead. The second Ferrari had trouble from the works Porsche but when the road dried out, the greater horsepower told and the Ferrari established itself firmly in second place. Again Ferrari was off to a good start to the season with a first and second place with private owners Martin and Reventlow 6th and Lunken/Pabst and Andrey 7th.

The Targa Florio

For the Targa Florio Ferrari entered four cars, two normal Testa Rossas for Behra/Brooks and Gendebien/Hill, a special Testa Rossa with larger carburetters and giving several b h p more than the others for Gurney/Allison and a semi-official works entry for Scarlatti and Cabianca. Ferrari had been criticized for not engaging any Italian drivers. He had countered by making the semi-official entry for the two Italians who could not be called first-flight drivers. The car they used was an experimental type having a chassis similar to the old 2-litre 4-cylinder Testa Rossa but with a V6 Dino engine of 2-litres capacity fitted.

Behra fought for the lead with Bonnier's Porsche with Gurney and Gendebien close behind. Gurney's extra b h p told and he moved the Testa Rossa special into the lead. The first Ferrari casualty was Gendebien when the rear axle broke on the first lap. This was followed by the retirement of the Cabianca/Scarlatti 206 Dino. In his attempt to make up time on the Porsche, Behra rolled the Ferrari in a field but managed to continue and delivered a very bent car to Brooks. Brooks damaged the car even further and then fell out with rear axle failure. The whole of the Ferrari team was eliminated and the only Ferrari to finish the race was the old 2-litre Testa Rossa privately entered by Cammarotta and Tramontana who finished 8th.

The ADAC 1000 Km

For the 1000 km of the Nurburgring, Ferrari again entered four cars. The V6 Dino 2-litre was again driven by Scarlatti and Cabianca and the factory Testa Rossas were driven by Gendebien/Hill, Brooks/Behra and Gurney/Allison.

Stirling Moss in the Aston Martin was once again Ferrari's No. 1 enemy. He took the lead on the first lap coming up with 18 seconds in hand on the first, which he had increased to 5½ minutes by the 17th lap. The Gendebien/Hill car was in second place, Allison and Gurney third, and Behra/Brooks fourth. When Fairman took over the Aston Martin, the Ferrari team began to make up time rapidly. When Fairman spun into the ditch and had to dig himself out, the Gendebien/Hill Ferrari took over the lead with Behra/Brooks second. It took Moss four laps to regain the lead with the Aston Martin. Allison handed his car over to Gurney with a slipping clutch and Moss pulled out a lead of 1 min. 43 secs. over the closest Ferrari before handing over again to Fairman. Phil Hill had taken over the Ferrari from Gendebien and proceeded to polish off the Aston's lead at a great pace, two laps later the Ferrari was back in first place. Moss had the Aston called in and took over for the rest of the race. Phil Hill tried his best to hold off the flying Moss but it was one of the Englishman's great days, on the 39th lap the Aston swept by the Ferrari at the Flugplatz and was never again challenged for the lead. Gendebien/Hill finished 2nd, Brooks/Behra 3rd and Gurney/Allison, still plagued with clutch trouble, 5th. The Cabianca/Scarlatti V6 Dino went out on its 10th lap with engine failure.

Le Mans

For the 24-Hours of Le Mans, Ferrari entered three Testa Rossas and the V6 Dino 2-litre for Cabianca/Scarlatti. The Testa Rossa team was made up of Behra/Gurney, Gendebien/Hill and Cliff Allison with Brazilian driver Da Silva Ramos.

The Ferraris were faster than anyone in practice but once again it was Moss with the Aston Martin who took the lead. The first time round Moss still led but the Ferraris of Da Silva Ramos and Gendebien were not far behind. Jean Behra in the third Ferrari took on the task of trying to get the Aston to break and after a lap at 124.99 m p h he passed into the lead. The Phil Hill/Gendebien car moved into third and began to threaten the Aston Martin. The Allison/Da Silva Ramos car was already in trouble with a faulty gearbox and dropped out on the 41st lap with a blown engine. The Hill/Gendebien car stopped briefly for carburetter adjustment and, as night wore on, the second Aston Martin of Salvadori/Shelby took the lead from the Behra/Gurney car which had been in the pits to fix a broken gear lever plus carburetter and electrical problems. Behra finally pulled into the pits with a broken engine. Gendebien/Hill made up for the loss of the Frenchman's Ferrari and passed the Aston into the lead and began to settle down to try and last out the race. This year however, Ferrari was out of luck and at about 11 am the leading Ferrari pulled into the pits with overheating. The car continued for a few more laps and was then retired with a water leak. The Cabianca/Scarlatti 2-litre once again failed to finish, retiring on the 63rd lap with fuel feed troubles.

Goodwood

All was not well for Ferrari and despite his strong team he was having difficulty in the world championship. The last event of the season was the Tourist Trophy held at Goodwood, a circuit not completely suited to the large Ferraris. Ferrari had to win the T T to gain the championship as a second place would only tie the score. The 2-litre Dino was entered again this time with Scarlatti and Scarfiotti driving. The three Testa Rossas were handled by Hill/Allison, Gendebien/Brooks and Brooks/Gurney.

Things went badly at the start of the race, the Ferraris not running in the first three places. On the first lap the Hill/Allison car broke down with a cracked rocker arm but Gurney piled on the pressure and was soon breathing down the neck of Shelby who held second place a long way behind Moss. Brooks found himself with faulty brakes which gave him a great deal of trouble and Phil Hill took over Gendebien's car as the Belgian was not too happy on the Goodwood circuit. Hill handed over in turn to Allison who had a great deal of local experience.

He moved the car up to third place. Gendebien was once more flagged in to have his place taken by Brooks who was also more familiar with the course and Brooks started to make up time setting a new lap record of 1 min. 31.8 secs. an average speed of 94.12 m p h. At this stage the Ferrari pit management made an error by showing Brooks signals that he was ahead of the Porsche when in fact he was behind. If the Ferrari could move up to second place the score would be tied. When Ferrari discovered the error Brooks tried his best but was held back by Moss who had just lapped him. The Aston Martin pits knew they had to keep the Ferrari out of second place and Moss did a good job of slowing Brooks. Porsche finished 2nd but only 5 seconds ahead of the Ferrari. Aston Martin had de-throned Ferrari for the first time winning the Manufacturers' Championship by 24 points to Ferrari's 22.

The 1960 Season

The first race for the 1960 Manufacturers' Championship was held at Buenos Aires. Ferrari sent three cars, two 250 Testa Rossas for Phil Hill/Cliff Allison and Ginther/Von Trips. The third car entrusted to Scarfiotti and old-time Ferrari driver, Froilan Gonzales was in a new prototype model with a 246 Dino V6 engine of 2.5-litres capacity mounted in a chassis similar to that used on the 2-litre 4-cylinder Testa Rossa and the V6 2-litre Dino of the 1959 season.

The 'Birdcage' Maserati of Dan Gurney and Masten Gregory led the race from the start but was passed by both the Hill/Allison and the Ginther/Von Trips Ferraris. Scarfiotti had a difficult time with the 246 Dino and it was retired with distributor trouble in the 39th lap.

Sebring

After the Maserati retired, the two Ferraris were unchallenged and once again opened the season with a convincing win for Maranello. For the 12-hour race at Sebring there was a dispute about fuel. The organizers of the race tried to force Ferrari and others to use one particular type of fuel, but as Ferrari already had a commit-ment with the Shell company, he refused to enter his cars under the organizers conditions. Consequently it was left for the private owners to uphold the Ferrari name in the Florida race. Two private 3-litre Testa Rossas were entered for Daigh and Ginther and Nethercutt/Lovely and a 2-litre V6 Dino was entered for the Rodriguez brothers. The Nethercutt/Lovely car led for the first two laps but was passed by the Moss Maserati. Ginther and Daigh then took over second place but lost a lot of ground to the Maserati. At half distance the Maserati had a five-lap lead and the Daigh/Ginther car blew a head gasket in the attempt to catch the rival marque from Modena. The V6 Dino failed once again when the Rodriguez brothers retired with a defective clutch. Nethercutt and Lovely were unable to catch the two Porsches ahead of them when the Maserati went out and had to be content with third place.

The Targa Florio

At the Targa Florio, Ferrari turned out with a host of cars. There was one 246 Dino 2.5-litre with independent rear suspension, the second 246 Dino was the same car that had been run by Scarfiotti and Gonzales in Argentina. The Rodriguez brothers had the 206 Dino 2-litre in the live-rear-axle chassis which they had run at Sebring, the car being entered semi-officially by Chinetti's North American Racing Team. Ferrari also brought along two 250 Testa Rossa 3-litres but with the De Dion rear axles substituted by an independent layout of wishbones and coil springs.

In practice the Rodriguez brothers damaged their car but were able to get it fixed in time for the race. Allison practising with a V12 Testa Rossa completely wrote the car off when a tyre burst. Paul Frere also crashed during practice with a Testa Rossa. As a result of these accidents there was a great deal of shuffling around of the team. Hill/Von Trips were given the 246 Dino with the independent suspension, Scarfiotti/Cabianca and Mairesse shared the 246 Dino with the live rear axle and Allison and Ginther shared a repaired Testa Rossa. Bonnier's Porsche led at the start followed by Maglioli's Maserati. Von Trips hit a rock with his Ferrari and was de-layed. On the second lap the Porsche still led, followed by the Maserati and Gendebien's Porsche. The Ferraris were next in the order Allison, Mairesse, Von Trips and Rodriguez.

Ricardo Rodriguez crashed the 206 Dino but was able to continue. The Von Trips car moved up to 3rd with Mairesse 5th and Allison 6th. Ginther then crashed the V12 Testa Rossa and Pedro Rodriguez crashed the 206 Dino again, once more being able to resume. Phil Hill moved up to second place and the Maglioli Maserati broke down. Pedro Rodriguez once again crashed the poor Dino, this time rolling it over twice and having to replace two wheels before he could continue. Von Trips took over Phil Hill's car and tried to catch Bonnier's Porsche. He completed his last lap in 43 min. 38 secs. but Bonnier was faster so Porsche won their second race of the championship. Von Trips and Hill were second, Scarfiotti, Mairesse and Cabianca 4th and the Dino 206 finally finished a race despite the efforts of the Rodriguez brothers to eliminate it, the two Mexicans coming in 7th.

The Nurburgring 1,000 Km

For the 1000 km of the Nurburgring Ferrari sent one of the Targa Florio independent rear suspension Testa Rossas for Phil Hill and Von Trips. A second Testa Rossa with a De Dion rear axle was driven by Allison and Mairesse. Scarlatti and Cabianca were given a 246 Dino and the Rodriguez brothers were present with the 206 Dino. Moss made his usual fast start with the Maserati and was followed by Jim Clark's Aston Martin with the two Ferraris of Von Trips and Allison close behind. Bonnier's Porsche moved up into second place but by ten laps the Maserati was still first and Von Trips Ferrari in second place with the Porsche behind him.

Scarlatti, lying in 8th place, stopped to hand over to his co-driver and as the car was being fuelled it caught fire and was totally destroyed, Scarlatti escaping with a badly burnt hand. The 206 Dino of the Rodriguez brothers broke its engine. At 20 laps the Maserati was in the pits and the Hill/Von Trips Ferrari took the lead with the Allison/Mairesse car fourth. Gurney was able to get the Maserati going again and closed to within 42 seconds of the leading Ferrari. Just at this time the Ferrari engine gave out and it was left to the Allison/Mairesse Ferrari, the sole surviving works car, to try and

save the day and it was called in for Phil Hill to take over. The American drove superbly but could not make up all the deficit and had to be content with a third place.

Once again Ferrari was badly placed in the championship and it was absolutely necessary for him to put up a good performance at Le Mans if he was to have any hope of clinching the title. Consequently he decided to rely on the well tried 12-cylinder Testa Rossa 3-litre. He sent three De Dion axled cars for Gendebien/Frere, Von Trips/Phil Hill and the NART entry of Ricardo Rodriguez/Andre Pilette. Added to these were the two wishbone irs cars of Mairesse/Ginther and Scarfiotti/Pedro Rodriguez.

Le Mans

The Le Mans race turned out to be quite dull. The Maserati of Masten Gregory took the lead early on with Frere/Gendebien 2nd and Hill/Von Trips 3rd. The Ferrari team management however had made a mistake in their fuel consumption calculations. During the second hour the Hill/Von Trips car ran out of fuel and was abandoned on the circuit. Frere and Gendebien moved into the lead when the Maserati broke down during the second hour and the Mairesse/Ginther car took over second place. Scarfiotti and Pedro Rodriguez also ran out of fuel during the second hour while Ricardo Rodriguez and Pilette became involved in a battle for second place with the Ginther/Mairesse car. The Rodriguez/Pilette car moved into a permanent 2nd place during the 14th hour and Gendebien/Frere were running like clockwork in the leading Ferrari holding the first place from the 2nd to the 24th hour. Ferrari scored a 1, 2 victory which gave them a win in the world championship with 30 points to Porsche's 26 points.

The 1961 Season

For 1961, the first race of the championship was held at Sebring. The 3-litre Testa Rossa cars had been altered considerably with the new Fantuzzi bodies which were the result of some aerodynamic studies. The team for the Florida event was made up of Hill/Gendebien, Baghetti/

Mairesse with the 250 TR/6IS, as they were known, Pedro and Ricardo Rodriguez with NART's TR/60 and Von Trips/Ginther in a brand new rear-engined car with a V6 Dino 2.5-litre engine known as the 246/SP. Hall and Constantine and Hugus/Connell had the previous year's front engined 246 Dinos and the teams of Sharp/Hissom and Reed/Sturgis had 1960 models of the 12-cylinder Testa Rossa.

Type 246/SP

The 246/SP was a big departure for Ferrari, and owed a great deal to the rear-engined Formula 2 cars that were introduced in 1960. A multi-tube chassis was used and the same front and rear suspension by means of double wishbones and coil-spring/damper units, as employed on the 1961 1500-cc Formula 1 car, was deemed the correct thing for the new sports model.

Sebring

At the end of the first hour Ferrari were already established in a commanding position. The Rodriguez brothers' 250 Testa Rossa led a short distance ahead of the new 246/SP of Von Trips/Ginther, who were in turn followed by the Gendebien/Phil Hill V12. Von Trips moved the V6 into the lead and then went off the road with broken steering. Von Trips made his way back to the pits on foot and took over the V12 car of Mairesse/Baghetti. The Rodriguez brothers were back in the lead after the accident to the V6 and setting a hot pace, stayed in front from the 4th to the 9th hour, during which time they pulled out to a lead of over two laps on the Hill/Gendebien car. When the NART car came into the pits with dynamo trouble and to replace the brake pads, the Rodriguez brothers lost 17 minutes and the fight for the lead was between the Ferraris of Hill/Gendebien and Von Trips/Ginther which they had taken over from Mairesse/Baghetti. Ricardo Rodriguez then put up a brilliant display of driving and began to catch up on the 1st and 2nd place Ferraris. He got back onto the same lap as the Ginther/Von Trips car but had no hope of catching the No. 1 Ferrari. When the race ended it was the old faithful team of Gendebien/Hill that won, with Ginther/Von Trips in second place and with the incredible Rodriguez brothers finishing third,

only a few seconds behind the second works Ferrari. The Sharp/Hissom 250 TR/60 finished 4th and the 246 front engined car of Hall/Constantine finished 6th. The other V6 of Hugus/Connell broke at 7.15 pm and the Nethercutt/Lovely 250 Testa Rossa broke down with a defective oil pump after only 18 minutes of the race had taken place.

Targa Florio

The next event for the championship was the Targa Florio. Ferrari entered three official cars, two of the new 246/SP rear-engined V6 types for Gendebien/Hill and Von Trips/Ginther and a V12 Testa Rossa 61 for Mairesse and Pedro Rodriguez. There were no other Ferraris entered. During practice the fastest times were put up by Moss and Bonnier with the factory Porsches. Von Trips with a 246/SP put up third fastest time.

Before the start there was a big mixup in the Ferrari team which did nothing to boost the morale of the drivers. Gendebien was switched to drive with Von Trips and Phil Hill ended up with Ginther. Phil Hill was furious at this setup and as he started after Von Trips, tried his best to overtake the German driver. He overdid things and crashed only a few minutes after the start of the race. Hill managed to continue but went off again three miles further on, and one of the 246/SPs was eliminated. By the fourth lap Moss in the Porsche was 1 minute and 40 seconds ahead of Bonnier in the second place Porsche. Bonnier held a precarious five-second lead over the Ferrari of Von Trips. In the meantime another Ferrari was eliminated when Pedro Rodriguez went off the road with the 12-cylinder Testa Rossa and smashed his fuel tank too badly to continue. Graham Hill, who was Moss' co-driver on the Porsche, lost considerable ground to Gendebien and when he came in the Ferrari was in the lead by 36 seconds. Moss lost more time in a bad fuel stop and Gendebien came round with over 60 seconds lead. But once again Moss showed his class and turned a new lap record of 40 min. 41 secs. which put him 19 seconds ahead of Gendebien. Gendebien handed over to Von Trips who had proved to be the fastest of the Ferrari drivers on the Madonie circuit. Von Trips pulled out a brilliant 40 minute and 3 second lap but the effort was not necessary as Moss, with 15 seconds lead and four miles to go broke his transmission, and Ferrari had a victory for the 246/SP on its second appearance.

The ADAC 1,000 Km

The next event for the world championship was held at the Nurburgring. Ferrari again entered three cars with the 246/SP V6 models for Von Trips/Phil Hill and Ginther/Gendebien. The one V12 Testa Rossa/61 was in the hands of the Rodriguez brothers.

On the first lap it was the incredible Stirling Moss in a 1.7-litre factory Porsche that came by in the lead. Five seconds behind him came the 246/SP Ferrari of Hill/Von Trips followed by the Ginther/Gendebien Ferrari with a group made up of Jim Clark in an Aston Martin, Rodriguez with the 250 Testa Rossa Ferrari, and Mairesse in a Gran Turismo Ferrari.

At the end of the 2nd lap Phil Hill took the lead from Moss but the second Ferrari was already 6 min. 7 secs. behind the Porsche which held second place. On the fourth lap the Ginther/Gendebien Ferrari moved up into second place. On the 14th lap the Rodriguez brothers' Testa Rossa displaced the Ginther/Gendebien car from second place but on the following lap the Belgian/American combination was ahead again.

Phil Hill broke the lap record with a 9 min. 15.8 secs. on his 8th lap and the car led the race until the middle of the 24th lap at which time he made a fuel stop which let the Gregory/Casner Maserati into the lead. The Ginther/Gendebien car dropped back until it was 9th and the Rodriguez brothers fell back to 4th on the 20th lap with rain and snow slowing all the competitors. The Rodriguez brothers with some of their usual exciting driving moved their car up to third on the 22nd lap and second on the 25th lap where they stayed for the rest of the race. Von Trips took over the Ginther/Gendebien car and immediately began to make up ground; from 9th on the 32nd lap he moved up to 8th on the 33rd and 7th on the 37th lap, 6th on lap 38, 5th on lap 39, 4th on lap 40 and 3rd on lap 41 in which position he remained till the end of the race. The Gregory/Casner Maserati won but

the Ferrari of the Rodriguez brothers finished 2nd with the Von Trips/Hill/Gendebien/Ginther car 3rd with the fastest lap standing to Phil Hill at 91.780 m p h.

Le Mans

The next race for the championship was Le Mans in France. Ferrari sent a Testa Rossa 61 for Phil Hill and Gendebien having a cubic capacity of 2961-cc. Mairesse and Parkes and the Rodriguez brothers had Testa Rossa 61s with a cubic capacity of 2953-cc and Ginther/Von Trips had a 246/SP V6 of 2.5-litres.

Although Jim Clark with the Aston Martin was first off he was passed by the whole of the Ferrari horde on the first lap. The Ferraris were led by the Rodriguez brothers, followed by Phil Hill/Gendebien and Von Trips/Ginther. At the fourth hour the Gendebien/Hill car was in the lead with the Rodriguez brothers 2nd, the Ginther/Von Trips car third and the Mairesse/Parkes car fourth. By the 5th hour the two young Mexicans had taken the lead but by the 6th the famous team of the American and Belgian were again out in front. At the 7th hour the Rodriguez's were back out front only to lose their position by the 8th and regain it on the 9th. In the 11th hour the Mexicans dropped to 2nd again but reasserted themselves from the 12th to the 13th hour after which they were in the pits with condenser trouble which dropped them to 4th and let the Ginther/Von Trips up into second. Just as they had secured 2nd place the 246/Dino ran out of fuel and once again the lack of adequate calculation by the Ferrari team management resulted in the retirement of a car that was still in perfect running condition. The Mairesse/Parkes car took over second place to Phil Hill/Gendebien on the 17th hour but the Rodriguez brothers with their fiery driving passed the factory entry into 2nd place at the 20th hour, holding this position until the 22nd hour, when their car finally gave up with a broken piston. From then on the scene was set. The two works Ferraris of Hill/Gendebien and Parkes/Mairesse toured round to take 1st and 2nd places. Hill and Gendebien set a new distance record for the 24 hours, covering 2,781.7 miles at an average speed of 115.904 m p h.

Pescara

The last event of the 1961 championship season was held at Pescara in the form of a 4-hour race.

Ferrari already had the championship tied up, so he sent just one car, a 246/SP for Ginther and Baghetti to drive. He lent one of the old faithful 250/TR/61 V12-cylinder cars to the Scuderia Centro Sud of Mimmo Dei for Bandini and Scarlatti to drive.

Ginther took the 246/SP into the lead at the start and handed over to Baghetti who was forced to retire almost at once with a fractured steering arm. The Casner Maserati then took the lead but when he was forced off the road by a slower competitor the Scarlatti/Bandini car installed itself in first place where it remained until the end of the race. Ginther had the consolation of setting the fastest lap with a 9 min. 55.5 secs., an average of 96.107 m p h.

Once again Ferrari took the World Championship of sports car constructors with a total of 30 points to Maserati's 16 points and Porsche with 13 points.

The 250 GTO

It is at this point that the 250 GTO should be discussed, for it is during 1962 that the Manufacturers' Championship was changed to 'cover' GT cars, although prototypes (sports cars) were permitted to run.

I am very much indebted to Chuck Queener and Jess Pourret for the following information on the 250 GTO.

There is a problem with historic trivia that has me questioning the sanity of us all. Where do we stop? Is anyone really interested? Of course finding all the engine numbers is the first step. After that its physical indentification *i.e.* 'Built-in blinkers, small spoiler, no brake holes, L.H.D.' The racing history becomes hectic and in several cases Jess went directly to organizers responsible for each event. During the GTOs racing activities serial numbers were not considered good copy, maybe they tried to tell us something, but this made it difficult to trace many of the cars.

It is now certain that the total production run during 1962, 1963 and 1964 is 40 units; thirty-three 3-litre cars with Series I bodies, three 4-litre cars with Series I bodies, three 3-litre cars with Series II bodies and one 3-litre car with LMB body work. The curiosity of the 3-litre with an LMB body comes from factory records listing chassis number 4713 as a GTO! In light of past discussions regarding the LMBs, this comes as a real surprise. To say that it is in fact a GTO can be argued on both sides, however, it is the only such bodied car with a 5-speed gearbox and a 94.5 in. wheelbase, both traits of the GTO.

As for the other cars, we thought we would deal with each of them one by one beginning with the earliest Pininfarina 400 Super America lightweights.

Three of these experimental vehicles were built, one No. 1737GT as a roadster. It was an aluminium bodied, short wheel-base chassis with a type 168F 3-litre engine with 3 Weber 36DCs and TR headers. The car is in France at this time. The second, No. 2429GT, in coupe form, carried the same 250 type engine but this time three 46DCL Webers were mounted. The car was first sold 16th May 1961 to M. Villard of Paris. The third 400SA is the one raced in America by S. Moss. This car, No. 2649, was sold to Luigi Chinetti on 26th January 1962 just before the Daytona 3 Hours where Moss finished 4th overall and 1st in GT. The car was built in the early part of 1961 and was a SEFAC entry at Le Mans that year, driven by Tavano and Baghetti. It failed to finish. All three cars had 4-speed gearboxes as did chassis No. 3175, the SEFAC prototype GTO. Described as the 'ant eater' because of its unusual snout, this car carried out most of Bizzarinis' pre-production tests with Willy Mairesse. It seems likely that this car was broken up and destroyed as it certainly would have shown up by now.

The Press Conference car, No. 3223, went to Sebring in March of 1962 as a SEFAC entry finishing second overall and first in GT. Luigi Chinetti was the first owner and Bob Grossman did most of the driving during its stay with NART. After many races, owners and years, Grossman swapped the heads for some twit who was frightened by the GTOs power! The GTO heads now rest on some 2+2.

Chinetti was Ferraris' biggest customer where the GTO was concerned taking delivery of 7 cars in 3 years. The second one, No. 3387, went to him in March of 1962. It was driven by member Charlie Hayes and Doug Thiem but never achieved success.

FERRARI CHAPTER 11

On page 105 (fold out) of the Fitzgerald-Merritt book,* you will find a photo of chassis No. 3413 in its original body. It finished 4th overall in that particular Targa and 2nd in class.

A car that we always felt was particularly well done for a special was the one Piero Drogo did for Ulf Norinder. It was originally purchased in GTO guise by Luciano Conti of Bologna for Scuderia Venezia (SSS). It was sold to Norinder some time in 1963 and was sent to Drogos' in 1964.

One of several GTOs living in France, No. 3451, has had a scattered history having been wrecked several times. In 1964 the engine was replaced with that of No. 3769 GTO and it then participated in a variety of minor races. It was again badly crashed in 1970 but has since been straightened. Its original engine is with No. 3769.

Stirling Moss was a director of the UDT-Laystall team in 1962, which purchased No. 3505 with which Innes Ireland won the 1962 Tourist Trophy.

With only 34 more cars to describe we suggest you take a break. Pick up a copy of *Penthouse* and look at Coco Chinetti standing next to his 4-passenger Daytona.

At any rate, chassis No. 3527 ran a few races in 1962 and was sold back to SEFAC. On 10th September it was sold to Lucien Bianchi. Bianchi entered the Tour de France and was leading that event when he struck a truck. The car was repaired but later disqualified for lack of hood fenders.

As yet we have absolutely nothing on No. 3539.

The next car has an interesting history. Ronnie Hoare purchased No. 3589 in April 1962 and Mike Parkes drove it to many victories for Equipe Endeavour. It was then sold to Tom O'Conner of Team Rosebud in time for the Nassau Speed weeks. Innes Ireland was O'Conners driver and then were never particularly successful. The interesting part of this car's history is that when O'Conner was through with the car he gave it to the Victoria High School shop class in Victoria, Texas where it stayed for 7 years. After hundreds of students learned all about Ferraris the car was put up for sale. Advertised as nothing more exciting than a 250GT, the car was purchased sight unseen by a chap in Cleveland, Ohio. When the fellow from Cleveland tried to sell the car in Hershey, Penn., he couldn't get a buyer because people felt it was not a legitimate GTO. He wasn't too pleased with the situation. Since our 1971 trip to Europe, we discovered the car and gave its present owner the reassurance he needed. The car later sold for $28,000.

Jess Pourret's GTO No. 3607 ran many races in France and in February 1968 Pourret bought the car from Pierre Bardinon.

Many GTOs received heavy damage during their fabulous careers and our next car, No. 3647, tops the list. Its first crash was at the hands of John Surtees in the 1962 Tourist Trophy. As it lay wounded away from battle, helplessly uninvolved, it was attacked by the Aston Martin of Jim Clark and the Ferrari of Chris Kerrison. Kerrison started the scrap ending in an expensive junk pile. The car was then sold to Prince Tcho Kotoua who hired Tommy Hitchcock, why I don't know, because Hitchcock managed to flip the thing at the Nurburgring in 1963.

As I have said, three 4-litre cars were built and No. 3673 seems to have disappeared. This was the second place Nurburgring car of 1962. Little else is known at this point.

The 1962 GT winner at Le Mans in No. 3507. It is now in Switzerland.

Roy Salvadori took delivery of No. 3729 in July of 1962. It never distinguished itself and now carries engine No. 2735 from the ex-Kerrison Breadvan.

The next car, No. 3757, has the distinction of having been crashed by Stirling Moss. It was also driven by Charlie Hayes several times.

The second 4-litre GTO is No. 3765. It was crashed at Le Mans on the first lap by Mike Parkes. The car later retired with a blown engine from overheating. It went back to the factory where the Super America block was repaired and then the car was sold to Cantieri Del Timavo in Trieste. Some where along the line a Testa Rossa engine No. 0796 was installed and the front end modified. It was the Sicilian Hillclimb champion in 1965.

Ronnie Hoare gets close to Chinetti in numbers of GTOs purchased. No less than 5 cars

230

went to him. David Piper drive No. 3767 many times, winning only one race at Kyalami in South Africa.

Number 3769 was involved in that engine swap with No. 3451.

There is some question as to the history of No. 3809 but it will sort itself out.

Only one person was ever killed driving a GTO, a remarkable record that says a great deal for its balance. The unfortunate soul was Oreillier who impaled himself on the gear lever, of all things, in October 1962 at Montlhery. It, No. 3851, was sold to someone in England, but for how much, we don't know.

David Clarke owns No. 3869 which was the London Show car in 1962. Little is known of No. 3909 other than 6 races it ran, none too successfully. Another French car is No. 3943.

The 1962 Nassau TT winner with R. Penske is No. 3987. This car also won the 1000 kms of Paris with P. Rodriguez. Driven by Roger Penske and Augie Pabst in several races, the car eventually wound up in Southern California. A horse once attacked it in Griffith Park. What could he have been thinking?

Four Series I GTOs were rebodied as 1964 types and No. 4091 is such a car. Shown on page 103 of the Fitzgerald-Merritt book,* the car now resides in Ann Arbor, Michigan.

Another car with little history is No. 4115. The 1964 Tour de France winner is No. 4153.

Sports Car Graphic once did a driving impression of No. 4219 which was also the 1963 Daytona Continental winner with P. Rodriguez.

Steve Earles' No. 4293 did 3 other races after its 2nd overall at Le Mans in 1963 before coming to America. It was 6th overall and 2nd GT at the Targa Florio that year.

Anthony Bamford has probably the winningest GTO of the lot with No. 4399. Graham Hill and Mile Parkes won 7 races between them with both body styles.

One of David Piper's cars which he owns is No. 4491. He was its original owner and it's nice to see him reunited with a car that gave him many exciting races.

The third 4-litre GTO was more of a special as it was built for Paul Cavalier, then a SEFAC

Director. No. 4561SA is now in England.

Another rebodied 1962-1963 GTO is No. 4675. This car won its class in 1964 at the Targa finishing 5th overall.

The next car, No. 4713, we mentioned earlier so anything else we could say would be academic.

The subject of an article in the June 1973 issue of *Car* is No. 4757. It has won many minor races and hillclimbs but was involved in a bad crash during the Tour de France with Bandini. His co-driver, Tavano, wound up in the hospital.

Finishing 2nd in the 1963 Tour de France was No. 5095. This car was later used by the ACO for their drivers school on the Bugatti circuit at Le Mans.

The first place finisher in the 1963 Tour de France was No. 5111. It finished 2nd the following year.

The only major success for No. 5571, the first of the true Series II bodied cars, was winning Daytona in 1964. Another misused GTO was No. 5573. This poor car has been the victim of several crashes both on and off the race track.

The last GTO manufactured was No. 5575. It won its class in the Paris GP of May of 1965 and was 2nd overall and 1st GT at the 1964 Tour de Belgique.

THE END. Not quite. This describes a lot of cars, but still 60 short of the 100 needed for homologation. There were not as many phonies built as we had originally suspected. One did turn up in Spain, offered for sale by a not-so-honest person. I suppose the value of this type of research does tend to thwart the chap interested in falsifying records in order to make a killing on an unsuspecting buyer.

*The 'Fitzgerald/Merritt' book is published by Bond/Parkhurst Publishing of California. It is entitled *Ferrari: The Sports and Gran Turismo Cars* by W. W. Fitzgerald and R. F. Merritt

The 1962 Season

In 1962 the World Championship of Manufacturers was changed and based on the points obtained by each manufacturer in the various Gran Turismo categories. Because of the spectator appeal the sports car categories were still retained but the capacity of the Prototype Sports cars, as they were called, was raised to 4-litres. These prototypes however, were unable to compete in the World Championship event for points. All the races of the 1962 season were in fact won by the prototype or experimental sports cars but it was the Gran Turismos that decided the championship.

Sebring

At Sebring Moss and Ireland were originally entered to drive the brand new V8 Ferrari, known as the 248/SP, but due to the long distance of the race elected to drive the well-tried 250 Testa Rossa/61 instead. The new V8 was turned over to the American/Canadian team of Bob Fulp and Peter Ryan and the Rodriguez brothers had a 246/SP V6 Dino. The famous Ferrari team of Gendebien/Phil Hill was entered with a 250 Gran Turismo car.

Type 248/SP

The new Type 248/SP had a sohc V8 engine of 77 x 66 mm bore and stroke giving a capacity of 2458-cc. The engine gave 250 b h p at 7,400 r p m and carburation was by means of 4 twin-choke Webers. The chassis was multi-tubular in construction and suspension was independent on all four wheels by means of coil-spring/damper units and wishbones. A four-speed and reverse gearbox was fitted in unit with the differential and Dunlop discs provided the braking. The front and rear track of the new car were 4 ft 0½ in. and 3 ft 11¼ in. respectively while the wheelbase was 7 ft 7¾ in. Bodywork was identical to the 246/SP.

Private entries were from the Scuderia Serenissima who entered Bonnier and Graham Hill in a 250 Testa Rossa. However, Hill had spinal trouble and was replaced by Bianchi at the last moment.

The Moss/Ireland car went into the lead and by half distance was over two laps ahead of all other competitors. Unfortunately, while this car had been pressing on, the officials had been debating the disqualification of the entry as the car had been illegally refuelled. The car was finally disqualified and the 246/SP of the Rodriguez brothers held the lead after a bad start.

The Fulp/Ryan V8 was out after the first hour and after the 7th hour the Bianchi/Bonnier Testa Rossa was in the lead which it held until the end of the race. The privately entered Ferrari of Grossman and Connell was taken over by the Rodriguez brothers, after their own car had broken down, and at the 8th hour the two Mexicans pushed it into second place which they held until halfway through the 10th hour when that car too retired, with failing oil pressure. The next event for prototype and experimental cars was in Sicily for the Targa Florio. Ferrari entered three cars, the new V8 Type 248/SP was down to be driven by Phil Hill and Gendebien, Rodriguez, Mairesse had a Type 246/SP V6 and Baghetti/Bandini were entered on a 2-litre Type 206/SP V6.

Targa Florio

Phil Hill took the V8 out in practice only to have the throttle jam in the open position. The car ran over the banking, slamming to a landing on its wheels despite Hill's efforts to bring it to a halt. It was completely written off, fortunately without damage to the driver. Hill was extremely annoyed with Ferraris preparation of the car and told team manager Dragoni so. The result was that the team manager decided that Hill would be a non-starter and put Gendebien with the Rodriguez/Mairesse car.

Mairesse put the 246/SP into the lead on the first lap with a time of 40 min. 43.2 secs. Gurney with the Porsche was second and the Baghetti/Bandini 2-litre Ferrari third. Mairesse set another lap record when he turned a 40 min. 2.9 secs. time before handing over to Rodriguez who kept the car in first place and until he handed over to Gendebien to finish the race. Baghetti hit a wall with the 2-litre and fell way back in classification but after a pit stop Bandini climbed back from 7th to 3rd place. Baghetti in his final stint in this car made up for his accident and overtook the factory Porsche for the 2-litre Ferrari to install itself in 2nd place, which it held until the end of the race, finishing 12 minutes behind the winning 246/SP Ferrari.

Nurburgring - the 330/LMB

The Nurburgring was the next event for the championship and Ferrari sent three assorted cars. Hill/Gendebien had the 246/SP that had won the Targa Florio. The Rodriguez brothers were given the Targa Florio 2nd place car the V6 type 206 Dino, and the team of Mairesse/Parkes had the brand new 4-litre V12 prototype coupe. This new car was known as the 330 GT or 330/LMB, its V12-cylinder engine had a bore and stroke of 77 x 71 mm giving a capacity of 3967-cc, the power output was 390 b h p at 7,500 r p m. Six Weber twin-choke carburetters were fitted and suspension was by double wishbones and coil-spring/damper units all round. Dunlop disc brakes provided stopping power and the car was fitted with a 4-speed and reverse gearbox. Front track was 4 ft 8 in., rear track 4 ft 7¾ in. and wheelbase 7 ft 9½ in.

Much to the surprise of everyone it was the 1500-cc Lotus prototype that led the race from the start, driven by Jim Clark. At the end of the 3rd lap the Lotus was more than 1 minute ahead but when the Lotus broke down it was Phil Hill in the Ferrari who took over the lead. Before long the Mairesse/Parkes coupe was in second place. The third place Porsche made a tremendous effort to catch the second place Ferrari but broke its transmission on the last lap. So for the first time since 1953 Ferrari won a sports car race on the Nurburgring with the prototype 4-litre in second place.

Le Mans

For Le Mans, Ferrari entered the team of Gendebien/Hill with an experimental car having a 4-litre engine in a body similar to the 3-litre Testa Rossa/61. The car also had independent rear suspension by means of double wishbones and coil-spring/damper units. Baghetti and Scarfiotti were entered in an experimental V8 Ferrari with a capacity of 2645-cc. The Rodriguez brothers had a 246/SP with the V6 2.4-litre engine. Parkes and Bandini had the Nurburgring 4-litre coupe which had been modified for Le Mans and the teams of Grossman/Roberts, Abate/Davis, Bonnier and Gurney had experimental Gran Turismo cars.

After only one hour of the race had been run

the Hill/Gendebien car was already in the lead with the Rodriguez brothers running second. As Hill and Gendebien stopped for fuel the lead switched to the two Mexican brothers and at four o'clock in the morning Ferraris occupied the first five places. In the early morning the Rodriguez's were still in the lead by some 31 seconds and also led on index of performance. In the meantime the Bonnier/Gurney experimental G T had retired with transmission failure, the Parkes/Bandini car was out with overheating after Parkes had put it in the sand at Tertre Rouge. The V8 was doing quite well and Baghetti/Scarfiotti were running in 5th place.

The Rodriguez brothers' Ferrari retired as dawn came and the Fulp/Ryan car was also out, the Americans having crashed the 2.5-litre. Before noon the V8 was in second place but at noon the car was out with a broken gearbox. The Grossman/Roberts experimental G T dropped out during the 24th hour when the car refused to start after a pit stop for fuel. Hill and Gendebien made it three years in a row when they took the 4-litre experimental Ferrari over the line in first place. Noblet and Guichet made certain that Ferrari took the points in the manufacturers championship by taking second overall in their Gran Turismo Ferrari with Elde and Beurlys third in a similar car.

With this result Ferrari took the Manufacturers World Championship for Gran Turismo cars in Class Three (over 2000-cc) with 45 points to Jaguars 16 points, Chevrolet 9 points, Lancia 4 and Aston Martin 1.

The 1963 Season

At the end of the 1962 season Ferrari carried out a series of tests on his 1963 cars at Monza. Two completely new models were produced, the 250/P a rear-engined V12 3-litre, and the 330/LMB, an experimental 4-litre V12 Gran Turismo prototype which was based on the Le Mans winning V12 4-litre of 1962.

Type 250/P

The 250/P was an extremely clean little car with an aerofoil section on the body behind the driver's seat to give better stability. The V12 engine was basically the same as the well known Testa Rossa power plant. It had a bore and stroke of 73 x 58.8 mm giving a cubic capacity of 2953-cc with a power output of 310 b h p at 7,500 r p m. Six Weber twin-choke carburetters were fitted and the chassis frame was a multi-tubular construction with coil-spring/damper and double wishbone independent suspension all round. A five-speed and reverse gearbox was in unit with the rear axle and Dunlop disc brakes provided the stopping power, the rear brakes being inboard adjacent to the differential unit at the rear. Wheelbase was 7 ft 11 in., front and rear tracks were 4 ft 5¼ in. and 4 ft 4¾ in. respectively.

Type 330/LMB

The 330/LMB was a coupe version of the Le Mans winning roadster and had a bore and stroke of 77 x 71 mm giving a capacity of 3967-cc with a power output of 400 b h p at 7,500 r p m. The engine was based on the Type 209 400 SA. Six Weber twin-choke carburetters gave the effect of one carburetter per cylinder.

The multi-tube chassis had double wishbone and coil-spring/damper independent suspension on all four wheels, brakes were of the disc type manufactured by Dunlop and the wheels were the normal Borrani wire types with knock-off hub caps, a four-speed and reverse gearbox was used and the wheelbase was 8 ft 2¾ in. with front and rear tracks 4 ft 8 in. and 4 ft 7¾ in. respectively.

Sebring

The 1963 season opened at Sebring, Florida. Ferrari entered one of the 4-litre 330/LMBs to be driven by Mike Parkes and Lorenzo Bandini another 4-litre, the Le Mans winning car was entered by the semi-official North American Racing Team of Luigi Chinetti with Pedro Rodriguez and World Champion Graham Hill driving.

The brand new 250/P prototype Ferraris were entered for John Surtees/Ludovico Scarfiotti and Willy Mairesse/Nino Vacarella to drive. A 2.4-litre V8 was also entered for Buck and Fulp to drive as a standby. Phil Hill with a Ford-Cobra took the lead at the start but Pedro Rodriguez put the 4-litre Ferrari of NART into first place on the second lap. The new 250/Ps

were in trouble almost at once with Surtees pulling into the pits first, after only two laps, to have the spark plug terminals replaced. After half an hour the Mairesse/Vacarella car was in the pits with the same problem and dropped to 28th place by the end of the first hour.

In the meantime the leading Ferrari of Pedro Rodriguez was passed by Jim Hall's Chapparal which took over first on the 13th lap. This Chevrolet-based car held on to the lead for another hour and a half before retiring and letting the Ferrari back into the lead. During the 2nd hour the 250/P of Surtees and Scarfiotti began to challenge the leaders as did the second car of this type driven by Mairesse/Vacarella. John Surtees moved into second place and set a new lap record of 3 min. 11.4 secs., a speed of 97.805 m p h. The Ferraris were now running 1st, 2nd and 3rd with the Rodriguez/Graham Hill 4-litre in front, the Surtees/Scarfiotti close behind and the Mairesse/Vacarella car third. A Ford-Cobra separated the three leading Ferraris from the first of the Gran Turismo Ferraris of Penske and Pabst and there were seven Ferraris in the first ten.

As the race wore on the Rodriguez/Hill car was in the lead, occasionally losing first place through pit stops to the Surtees/Scarfiotti 3-litre. The Ford-Cobra fell back allowing the Penske/Pabst Gran Turismo Ferrari into 4th place. The lightweight Jaguar of McLaren/Hansgen was just ahead of the experimental V8 Ferrari of Buck Fulp. After the sixth hour, Graham Hill/Rodriguez were still in first place followed by Surtees/Scarfiotti and Mairesse/Vacarella on the 250/Ps. All these three cars were on the same lap although all of them were having troubles of one sort or another. The leading car had headlight and tail-light problems, the third place Ferrari suffered from overheating and Surtees and Scarfiotti were having a great deal of trouble with fumes in the cockpit which forced them to change drivers every hour. At the 10th hour the Rodriguez/Graham Hill car had electrical problems again, they had to replace a headlight and then a tailpipe came adrift, the total repairs dropping them two laps. All the three leading Ferraris made a stop with Mairesse/Vacarella having to stop for fuel, which cost them any possibility of catching the Surtees/

Scarfiotti car. The race finished with Surtees/Scarfiotti in first place, Mairesse/Vacarella in second spot and the ailing Rodriguez/Graham Hill 4-litre in third. The Ferrari supremacy was accentuated by the GTO Ferraris taking 4th, 5th and 6th places. The winning team covered 209 laps but failed to equal the record set by Phil Hill/Gendebien in 1961 by a mere fraction.

Targa Florio

The next race for the championship was the Targa Florio. Ferrari entered two of the Sebring 250/P 3-litres which were the same as the originals except for the single-curvature glass windscreens and modifications to reduce the problems of fumes in the cockpit. Added to the 3-litre works car were two 2-litre rear-engined V6 cars. Vacarella, one of the nominated team drivers, had trouble with the sporting commission and found himself without a licence so the team line up was Scarfiotti/Mairesse and Parkes/Surtees on the 250/Ps and Bandini/Scarfiotti on the 2-litre V6 with the private team of Lualdi and Bini on another V6 2-litre.

Scarfiotti led the race with a standing lap of 40 min. 48 secs. Mike Parkes was 3 seconds behind, followed by Bonnier's Porsche and Bandini's 2-litre Ferrari. Scarfiotti unfortunately ran over a rock and squashed his tail pipes flat which caused fuel starvation. When he pulled in to the pits a lot of work had to be done on the car and Mairesse took over but after two more laps the fuel pumps packed up and the 250/P was retired. This let the Parkes/Surtees car into the lead and Surtees took over the car, still in the lead. He had problems with the car bottoming in various places on the circuit but finally went off the road when the front tank burst and he spun just before Polizzi. This left Ferrari with just one 2-litre which lost its lead when Bandini came in to hand over to Scarfiotti. When Bonnier made his pit stop the Scarfiotti Ferrari took the lead again. At the Bivio Polizzi, Scarfiotti's lead was just under one minute and things looked set for a win by the Maranello entry. As rain threatened and Scarfiotti had driven some seven laps, Dragoni, the Ferrari team manager decided to call him in and substitute Mairesse for the final driving stint. Mairesse set off with still about one minute advantage over the Porsche. On the last

lap Mairesse spun in the esses after the final straight and badly damaged the car. The whole of the rear part of the body was smashed and the gearshift linkage was bent. Mairesse was able to continue slowly but his minute advantage began to dwindle fast. Mairesse crossed the line with the rear bodywork trailing behind him to learn that he had just lost first place to Bonnier by 12 seconds.

The ADAC 1,000 Km

The championship trail moved to the Nurburgring for the next event. Ferrari sent three of the 250/P 12-cylinder models, one for Surtees and Mairesse, another for Scarfiotti and Parkes and a third for Vacarella and Bandini. Vacarella crashed near the Flugplatz in practice and wrote the car off, the driver breaking his arm, so Ferrari was reduced to two cars for the race. A front-engined V12 was entered by the Argentine Juan Manuel Bordeu for Abate and Maglioli to drive. John Surtees set fastest practice lap with a time of 9 min. 13.1 secs. which broke Phil Hill's old record of 9 min. 15.8 secs. The Parkes/Scarfiotti car was second fastest in 9 min. 21.1 secs.

As the cars came round on the first lap it was Peter Lindner's Jaguar that came by in first place with the two works Ferraris close behind. The two Ferraris swept by the British car as they entered the south turn and from then on Surtees and Scarfiotti were not challenged. On lap 14 Surtees came into the pits to hand over to Mairesse and on lap 15 Scarfiotti was in to hand over to Parkes, the two cars still maintaining their 1st and 2nd places. All looked set for a walkaway win but as Parkes rounded Ahremberg he lost control of his car on a slippery patch and hit a stone bridge. The car practically disintegrated and pieces of it flew all over the road. Willy Mairesse who was just behind managed to avoid the wreck but burst a tyre on the debris as he ran over it. Mairesse set to work to change the wheel and substitute the spare but Phil Hill on the works Porsche went into the lead and gained half a lap before Mairesse could get going again. Mairesse stopped at the pits and had the spare changed for safety and set off again, in 4th place.

With 26 laps to go he had time to improve his

position. Five laps later he was back in 2nd place and moved into first when Phil Hill missed a gear and crashed at the same spot that had eliminated Parkes.

From then on the pattern of the race was set. Surtees and Mairesse cruised around to win at an average speed of 82.703 m p h finishing eight minutes ahead of the second place car, a Gran Turismo Ferrari.

Le Mans

The next championship event was at Le Mans. Ferrari was out in force with three of the 250/P 3-litre V12s. A 4-litre front-engined V12 was entered by Luigi Chinetti's North American Racing Team and three of the 4-litre prototype coupe's plus a hose of 250 GT Ferraris made up the Maranello effort.

Rodriguez with the NART 4-litre set up fastest practice lap with a time of 3 min. 50.9 secs. which was well below the previous best set by Phil Hill in a similar car of 3 min. 57.3 secs., both Scarfiotti and Parkes turned 3 min. 51 secs. which rather shook everyone.

At the start it was the Aston Martins of Phil Hill and Bruce McLaren that were off first, just ahead of Pedro Rodriguez in the NART Ferrari. Phil Hill's lead lasted until Mulsanne and then the enormously powerful 5-litre Maserati of Andre Simon took over first.

As the cars passed the pits Simon was well in the lead with the rival Modena marque's production. Rodriguez was second followed by Surtees and Parkes. The 4-litre of Pedro Rodriguez, although being driven extremely well, was unable to deal with the big Maserati and in the background the two 250/Ps were waiting for both Simon and Rodriguez to break their cars. Surtees and Rodriguez took turns in breaking the lap record and finally the fastest time went to Surtees at 3 min. 53.3 secs. a speed of 129.071 m p h. The 250/Ps had been geared specially to last out the race. A conversation with Surtees later revealed that the 250/Ps could have gone some 5 seconds a lap faster if they had been specially geared for setting fast laps at Le Mans, which is pretty incredible for 3-litre cars. When Casner took over from Simon the big Maserati began to slow, Penske took over from Pedro Rodriguez and immediately began to lose

between two to four seconds to the 250/Ps. Parkes went into the lead before he handed over to Maglioli and Surtees came in to hand over to Mairesse. Parkes was lapping at around 3 min. 57.5 secs., almost the same time as Phil Hill's old lap record, Surtees and Mairesse were lapping at 3 min. 58 secs. and Penske in the 4-litre NART car was lapping in 4 minutes. Soon after midnight Penske blew up the 4-litre front-engined Ferrari and by 4 am Surtees and Mairesse led by a lap from the Bandini/Scarfiotti 250/P. With Willy Mairesse at the wheel, and with almost two laps lead over the second-place Ferrari, the red car on entering the esses burst into flames through overfilling of the tank. The car crashed into the bank and Mairesse escaped with some bad burns that put him out for the rest of the season. With the No. 1 Ferrari eliminated, the Bandini/Scarfiotti car inherited the lead and by dint of cautious driving the car carried on to win yet another 24 Hours of Le Mans for Ferrari. A Ferrari Gran Turismo finished second and one of the 4-litre prototype coupes finished 5th. It was a complete Ferrari triumph as his cars occupied all the first 6 places.

The 1964 Season

Towards the end of the season Ferrari introduced a new version of the 250/P at the Paris Automobile Show. The new model was known as the 250/Le Mans or 250/LM and it was ostensibly a 250/P with a roof on it. Ferrari had said that his rear-engined prototypes were destined to become actual production cars and the unveiling of the 250/LM seemed to be the first step of this policy. However the 250/LM was to have a chequered career.

Power was by the single-cam Ferrari V12-cylinder engine, with Testa Rossa cylinder heads and six twin-choke Weber carburetters. Power was reputed to be 300 b h p at 7,500 r p m. The engine followed GT procedure with a chain-driven overhead cams and a pulley on the crank nose to drive an AC generator, mounted on the frame off to one side to save space. Inside the front cover was the pressure pump of the lubricating system which was of the dry sump type. This system was adopted partially to enable the lowest possible engine placement and the consequent lowering of the centre of gravity of the whole car. Far more diagonal trussing was used than in the 250/P, which obtained its stiffness with stressed aluminium sheet pop-riveted to the frame sections where access was not needed. Considerably more robust tubing was used in the 250/LM's lower sill framework which was lowered to improve the cockpit accessibility. Another point of difference was the wider, heavier cowl structure to support the more complex doors required by the coupe configuration. The fuel tanks were placed between the firewall and the rear wheels; this gave additional room for cockpit access.

The suspension was a direct follow-on from the 250/P with fabricated tubular wishbones and coil-spring/shockabsorbers at all four wheels. At the rear, the same pigeon-toed axes were used to give the effect of placing the suspension under compression during acceleration, which reduced deflection of the members under such conditions and prevented unwanted rear-end steering effects. Anti-roll bars were used back and front.

In May of 1964 the definitive version of the car was shown and it turned out to have a displacement of 3286-cc with a bore of 77 mm instead of the 2953-cc's 73 mm. The car in this state should by all rights have been called the 275/LM and in several instances it was referred to by this name. However, Ferrari insisted that it be called a 250/LM as he had experienced a great deal of trouble in getting the FIA to homologate the car. The reason why this GT car is included in the Sports Car section is that for a long time, because of lack of homologation, it was forced to race in the sports car class.

Types 275/P and 330/P

For 1964, Ferrari announced that his prototypes would be the 330/P four litres and the 275/P, a 3.3 litre V12 destined to replace the 250/P 3 litre. In this way he would not compete with his customers driving the 250/LM, the car based on the 250/P.

An interim version of the 250 GTO was produced when the 250/LM could not be homologated in time for the 2,000 kilometres of

Daytona and it won the event first time out.

Sebring

The first race of the manufacturers' championship for GT and Prototype cars in 1964 was held at Sebring on March 21st. The factory was out in force with Parkes/Maglioli, Scarfiotti/Vaccarella and Surtees/Bandini all in 330 Ps. In the GT category, Shelby had a formidable array of Cobras to attempt to wrest the GT championship from Ferrari. At Sebring, the American effort met with great success, although the Ferrari opposition in the class was light with the best of the Ferrari GT cars in the hands of Rodriguez/Piper/Gammino finishing 7th, the Grossman/Thompson GT finishing 15th and the Abate/Guichet team retiring at the seventh hour with a broken valve. This left the Cobras with a 1st, 2nd and 3rd in the class.

In the prototype category, it was Ferrari all the way. On the first lap, Roger Penske had one of the lightweight Chevrolet Stingrays in the lead but then it was all over. The Surtees/Bandini Ferrari was firmly in the lead and with it Surtees set the fastest lap in 3 mins. 06.2 secs., an average speed of 100.54 m p h. In 2nd place was Graham Hill/Bonnier entry by Maranello Concessionaires with the factory 330/P of Parkes/Maglioli following in 3rd place and the Scarfiotti/Vaccarella car in 4th. Between the 2nd and 3rd hour of the race, the Scarfiotti/Vaccarella car moved ahead of the Parkes/Maglioli entry but the order was reversed between the 3rd and 4th hours before the all Italian entry once again got ahead of the English/Italian team. Chinese Firedrill pit stops cost the Surtees/Bandini car valuable time and between the 6th and 7th hour the G. Hill/Bonnier Ferrari took the lead only to lose it again to the factory car between the 7th and 8th hours when transmission trouble slowed the British entered car and finally caused its retirement. After another hour in the lead, further pit stops dropped the Surtees/Bandini combination to 3rd place while the Parkes/Maglioli entry jumped up from 3rd to 1st place, between the 10th and 11th hours, and remained there until the end of the race, covering 1112.8 miles and averaging 92.36 m p h. Scarfiotti and Vaccarella finished 2nd and Surtees/Bandini 3rd.

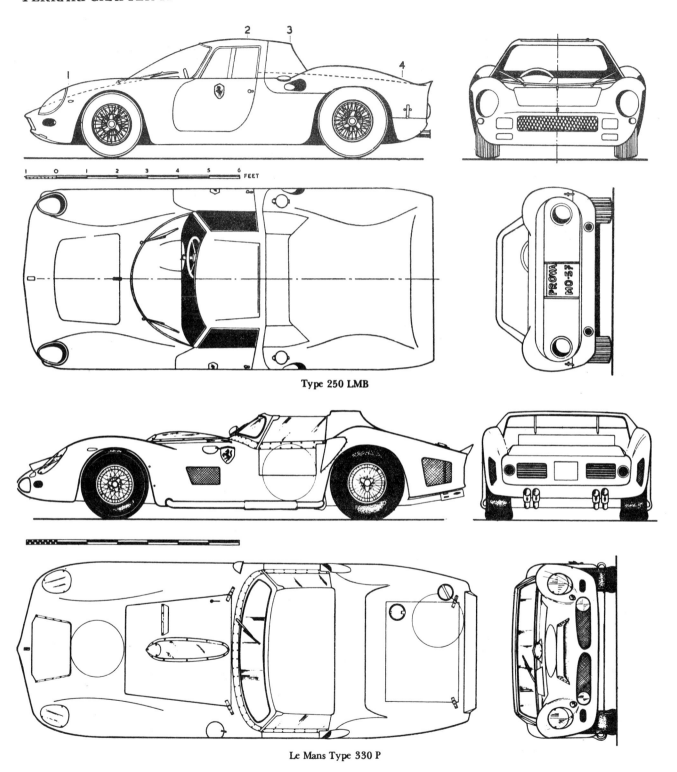

Type 250 LMB

Le Mans Type 330 P

Targa Florio

The 1964 Targa Florio was held on April 12th but there were no official Ferrari entries. Anything bearing the name Ferrari was in private hands and, in the GT class, the private owners were left alone to face the full team of factory Cobras. In the absence of the factory Ferraris, Porsche had a field day and took the first two places. A GT Ferrari came in 5th driven by Ferlaino and Taramazzo, winning the class, and the GT Ferraris of Norinder/Troberg from Sweden came in 9th followed by the Spanish/French team of De Bourbon Parma/Bourillot with another GT in 10th.

Nurburgring

The next championship event was at the Nurburgring on May 31st for the ADAC 1,000 kilometre race. The race was marked by the debut of the new Ford challenger to the Ferrari supremacy in the hands of none other than ex-Ferrari driver Phil Hill.

The Ferrari factory entered two of the 3.3-litre 275/Ps for Surtees/Bandini and Scarfiotti/Vaccarella and a GTO for Parks/Guichet. The factory team was supported by a third 275/P entered by Maranello Concessionaires and driven by Graham Hill and Innes Ireland.

John Surtees impressed everyone suitably when he set the fastest lap in practice with a time of 8 min. 57.9 secs., but old master Phil Hill took the Ford around in 9 min. 4.7 secs. to take second fastest time. For once the weather at the Nurburgring was warm and sunny and from the drop of the flag Surtees spurted away from the rest. He was followed closely by Scarfiotti, Phil Hill and the flat eight Porsche of Bonnier. Surtees' first lap was covered in 9 min. 17.7 secs. only 1.7 seconds slower than the sports car record. After five laps, Surtees had increased his lead to 50 seconds with Graham Hill in the Maranello Concessionaires entry in 2nd place, Scarfiotti 3rd and Phil Hill 4th.

Surtees set a new record in 9 min. 9.0 secs. which was not broken again during the race.

On lap 14, Surtees made a fuelling stop which let Graham Hill into the lead and Scarfiotti into 2nd place, a situation which lasted two more laps when these cars had to make their stops. On lap 16, the Surtees car was back into the lead with Bandini at the wheel and Vaccarella had brought the second works car into 2nd place, the Maranello Concessionaires car being 3rd with Innes Ireland driving. The Ford challenge came to an end when the car dropped out with a broken rear suspension radius rod.

This allowed Parkes and Guichet to move the GTO into 4th place, the Ferraris now holding the first four positions. Instead of things settling down, Ireland started to put pressure on to Vaccarella and in turn spurred the Sicilian to start challenging his team mate Bandini. This did not make team manager Dragoni at all happy. His degree of amusement took an even further dive on the next lap when Ireland's privately entered car came round ahead of the factory cars. Dragoni brought Bandini in on lap 27 and Surtees took off in 3rd place. Ireland was due to make a stop and hand over to Graham Hill but the Ferrari never completed the lap as the fuel tank split and it ran out of fuel on the circuit. Graham Hill requested permission to carry fuel with him to bring the car in but when he did so the car was disqualified on arrival at the pits. Ferrari's troubles were not over. Surtees making up time fast and as he came through Quidelbach - his right hub sheared and he lost a wheel. The Ferrari buried itself in the hedge fortunately without damage to Surtees. This left the Scarfiotti/Vaccarella Ferrari in the lead with the Parkes/Guichet GTO in 2nd place, positions which they held until the finish. They were supported in 4th place with the Bianchi/Van Ophem GT and in 7th by the Piper/Maggs GT. Surtees set the fastest lap at 9 min. 09.0 secs., an average of 92.95 m p h and the winning car took 7 hrs., 08 min. 27.0 secs. to complete the 1,000 km.

Le Mans

The final championship event was the Le Mans classic held on the 20th and 21st June. The Ferraris were out in force, Surtees/Bandini, Bonnier/Graham Hill and Rodriguez/Hudson all had 4-litre cars while Guichet/Vaccarella, Parkes/Scarfiotti, Baghetti/Maglioli, Dumay/Langlois and Piper/Rindt all had 3.3-litres.

In the GT category the private owners of GTs

faced the Cobra team without factory support. The key GT drivers with Ferraris being 'Beurlys'/Bianchi, Ireland/Maggs and Grossman/Tavano.

Again the Ferraris were challenged by the Ford team but this time in force instead of the single Nurburgring entry. The Fords made a poor start and the Ferraris were quickly into the lead. As they came round the first time, it was Rodriguez leading Graham Hill and John Surtees. Ginther had moved up from 6th place to 4th in the speedy Ford and was setting such a fantastic pace that he was past the three Ferraris on the second lap and continued to lap at over 127 m p h. For an hour and a half, the Ford sped on, before coming in to refuel. Surtees stopped the Ferrari at the same time and, in the battle of the pits, the Ferrari team came out ahead with a stop of 1 min. 28.0 secs., while the Ford team took 2 min. 07.0 secs. This let the Bandini/Surtees Ferrari into the lead where it remained to dominate a greater part of the race. The Ford stayed in 2nd place until the end of the 4th hour and then slipped to 26th during the 5th hour, finally retiring with gearbox trouble. At the halfway distance the Surtees/Bandini Ferrari lost its first place to the smaller engined team car of Vaccarella/Guichet with the Graham Hill/Bonnier car firmly in 3rd place. At the 15th hour the G. Hill/Bonnier car moved ahead of the Surtees/Bandini car and the positions remained unaltered until the end of the race. Guichet/Vaccarella covered 2917.7 miles in the 24 hours and averaged 121.6 m p h. Although the Ferrari prototypes swept the first three places, the Cobra finished ahead of the GTs which came in 5th with 'Beurlys'/Bianchi who won the up to 3-litre GT class, 6th Ireland/Maggs, and 9th Grossman/Tavano.

The 1965 Season - Daytona

The 1965 season opened with the Daytona 'Continental' race. Ferrari did not enter officially, their car being under the wing of Chinetti's North American Racing Team. Nevertheless, the new 330/P2 with the new four cam engine, driven by Surtees and Rodriguez, was serviced by factory mechanics under the supervision of Ferrari chief engineer, Mauro Forghieri. A second NART car was entered for Hansgen and Piper but this had the single-cam engine.

The Daytona race marked the first clash between the Ferrari and the Fords in 1965 and in practice the Surtees/Rodriguez car lapped at 2 min. 0.6 secs. (113.731 m p h). The closest the Fords could come to this was Bondurant's time of 2 min. 01.8 secs. (112.610 m p h) which placed the American car on the front row with the Ferrari. The fourth fastest time behind the Miles/Ruby Ford was set by the blue and white NART Ferrari of Hansgen/Piper.

Surtees took the lead at the start but Bondurant dived past him coming off the banking. The Ford lead was shortlived as Bondurant missed the first corner and Surtees was back in front. However, the Ferrari's lead was just as shortlived. Gurney had stormed through from 10th starting place in his 5.3-litre Ford-engined Lotus 19 and dislodged the Ferrari from 1st place. Surtees again led briefly on the 23rd lap but it was Gurney and the Lotus Ford that set the pace. Hansgen was running well in 3rd place, setting a new lap record of 2 min. 01.8 secs., but his run ended when a con rod broke and was ejected with such violence that it burst one of the rear tyres. Hansgen was lucky to escape unhurt. When Rodriguez took over from Surtees he held on to a solid 2nd place until the Ferrari blew a tyre, the tread smashed the battery and Rodriguez had to return to the pits on foot to get another battery. After changing the tyres, Surtees set off determinedly to make up the large amount of distance lost but because of increased pressure he began to have troubles with tyres 'chunking' and the resultant vibration broke the suspension giving round one of the season to Ford.

Sebring

The 1965 Sebring 12-hour race was held on March 27th. Alec Ulmann, the organizer had obtained permission from the CSI to allow unlimited sports cars to run against the prototypes. This did not please Enzo Ferrari in the least as the prototype category, because of the regulations, had several characteristics which put them at a definite disadvantage compared to the unlimited rules for the out and out sports cars. The Sebring organizers wanted the spectators to see the spectacular sports cars and Ferrari wanted to win with his prototypes, the impasse

(*Top Left*) Scarlatti driving the 1959 Type 196S Dino
(*Top Right*) Dino 196 V6 2 litre test car at Modena 1959
(*Middle*) Gonzales in the Type 246 S in the Buenos Aires 1000 Km 1960
(*Bottom Left*) Le Mans 1959. Ferrari Dino 196
(*Bottom Right*) Dino 296 V6 3 litre Ferrari at Silverstone May 1958. Hawthorn drove this car to 3rd place. It was the only time it raced, for the engine was taken out and then used in a single seater

(Top) Type 196 S Dino with Cabianca at the
wheel of the car he shared with Scarlatti in the
Nurburgring 1000 Km 1959. The car later caught
fire
(Middle Left) Targa Florio 1960, Mairesse at the
wheel of the 2.4 litre
(Middle Right) Targa Florio 1962, the 248 SP
V8 Ferrari
(Bottom) The prototype rear engined 246 S,
March 1961

(*Top Left*) Targa Florio 1962, the 246 SP
Ferrari with Mairesse at the wheel
(*Top Right*) Targa Florio 1966, the Baghetti/
Guichet Dino which finished 2nd
(*Middle*) Ferrari TRI (Testa Rossa indepen-
dent rear suspension) 2.4 sohc Dino V6
front engined car with Ginther at the wheel
in Modena February 1961
(*Bottom*) Ferrari Dino 246 GT, a Group 4
car at Modena

(Top) Surtees in the 206/SP Dino at Modena, August 1965
(Middle) Mairesse in the 275 LM ahead of Bandini in the 166 Dino at Nurburgring 1965
(Bottom Left) Scarfiotti in the 3.3 litre 275P LM made fastest practice time for the Le Mans 24 Hour Race in 1964
(Bottom Right) The NART private entry 3.3 litre LM won the 1965 Le Mans driven by Gregory/Rindt

(Top) Surtees testing the V12 rear engined 250 P prototype
(Bottom) The NART entered 275 LM driven by Young/Chinetti Jnr at Daytona 1970

(Top) The Type 250 P at Monza in 1963. Mike Parkes is the driver
(Middle) 4 litre 330 P2 driven by Surtees/Scarfiotti to win the 1965 Nurburgring 1000 Km
(Bottom Left) 11 December 1964. Surtees in the Ferrari P2 at Modena
(Bottom Right) 1963 Monza Ferrari 250 P

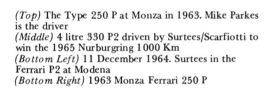

(*Top*) The NART P2 Ferrari rebodied by
Drogo, June 1966. The man with braces is
Luigi Chinetti whilst Piero Drogo has his
left arm on the tail of the car
(*Middle Left*) The NART Drogo bodied P2/3
Berlinetta, Modena 11 November 1967
(*Middle Right*) Mike Parkes with the 375
P2 Ferrari converted from a prototype to a
sports car, Guards Trophy, Brands Hatch
1965
(*Bottom*) Spa 1966. Parkes/Scarfiotti's
winning P3. Parkes set a new lap record at
3m. 46.4s. (139.19 mph)

(Top) The 1967 330 P4 Ferrari
(Middle) Scarfiotti/Parkes finished 2nd to Ford in their P4 1967 Le Mans
(Bottom Left) The 4 litre 330 P4 had a slightly wider track, an inch shorter wheelbase and produced another 40 bhp
(Bottom Right) The 4 litre V12 330 P3 Ferrari, 1966

was resolved when Ferrari decided to give Sebring a miss. As a result of this the only Ferraris entered at Sebring were in the hands of private owners. Maglioli/Baghetti, O'Brien/Hugus/Richards, Mairesse/Bianchi and Graham Hill/Rodriguez with Ferrari 275/Ps, Fulp/McCluskey and Grossman/Hudson with 330/Ps and Piper/Maggs with a Ferrari 275/LM. The two 330/Ps both went out with transmission trouble, Fulp/McCluskey during the 7th hour after running in 4th position and the Grossman/Hudson entry after ten hours.

The 275/P of Graham Hill/Rodriguez held steadily on to 2nd place behind the leading Chaparral and succeeded in gaining some time on the leader when the heat-wave weather changed suddenly into a torrential downpour that left the pits six inches deep in water. The Ferrari was running without second gear and finally succumbed to clutch troubles during the 8th hour being classified in 37th position. Piper/Maggs in the LM came in 3rd behind the winning Chaparral and 2nd place Ford, Maglioli/Baghetti came in 8th, Hansgen/Donohue 11th and O'Brien/Hugus/Richards 12th.

Targa Florio

The 49th Targa Florio was held on 9th May 1965 over the 'Little Madonie' circuit. For the first time of the season it was Ferrari that was out in force and Ford at a definite disadvantage on the twisty Sicilian circuit. The Ferrari line-up comprised two 275/Ps and a front engined 275/GTB entered as a prototype because of homologation troubles. The cars were in the hands of Vaccarella/Bandini. Scarfiotti/Parkes and the GTB driven by Biscaldi/Deserti. Sundry Ferrari LMs and GTOs were entered by private owners plus a lone 206/SP which however finished outside the time limit.

Vaccarella set an unofficial practice record of 39 min. 29 secs. and the best that the lone Ford entry in the hands of Bondurant could do was 41 min. 46 secs. Vaccarella started off for the first stint in the Ferrari as it had been agreed by Dragoni, the team manager, that Vaccarella would make his pit stop after four laps and Scarfiotti after three to avoid crowding of the pits.

Vaccarella set off at a tremendous pace despite orders from Dragoni to take it easy. On his first lap he covered the distance in 40 min. 05 secs., a new record. On his second lap he knocked off 39.3 seconds from the official record set the previous year by Mairesse. Parkes waited in the pits to take over from Scarfiotti but the latter banged against something solid and had to change a wheel. Vaccarella was suitably chastised when he handed over to Bandini and when the impetuous Sicilian took the car over again he obeyed orders coming in to win in 7 hr. 01 min. 12.2 secs., an average speed of 63.73 m p h. Vaccarella also set the fastest lap at 39 min. 21.0 secs., an average of 68.22 m p h. The Scarfiotti/Parkes car retired after it was found that the steering was damaged.

The 1965 24-Hours of Le Mans was held on June 19th-20th. Ferrari officially entered three cars but was supported by a host of private owners. The factory cars were two 330/P2s with 4-litre 4-o h c engines, drivers nominated were Surtees/Scarfiotti and Parkes/Guichet, a back-up car was entered for Bandini/Biscaldi but this also had a 3.3-litre 4-o h c engine.

Both North American Racing Team and Maranello Concessionaires had a 365/P Ferrari apiece, these cars had 4.4-litre GT-based engines, the NART car being driven by Rodriguez/Vaccarella and the Maranello car by Bonnier/Piper. Both NART and Maranello had back-up cars in the shape of 3.3-litre 2-o h c LM coupes, the American entry being in the hands of Gregory/Rindt and the British driven by Bianchi/Salmon. Ecurie Francorchamps had a GTB for Mairesse/'Beurlys' and an LM for Langlois/'Elde'. Scuderia Filipinetti had another LM for Bolle/Spoerry and Dumay entered another 275/LM for himself and Gosselin. Baghetti was in the 2-litre class with a 206 Dino.

Against this selection of Ferraris were 11 Fords ranging from the two 7-litre prototypes to the 4.7-litre Cobra coupes.

The race started in perfect weather. The McLaren/Miles and Amon/Phil Hill 7-litre coupes were more than a match for the Ferraris and at the start dominated the race while the Ferraris in turn were more than a match for the 4.7-litre GT-40 Fords. Baghetti blew the engine on the 166/P Dino early in the race and the Fords lost their lead when they had to refuel after just one hour. However, the Fords had no difficulty in regaining the lead but from then on the American effort began to fall apart. After three hours Ferraris occupied the first five places. As darkness began to fall, the Surtees/Scarfiotti 4-litre was in the lead from Bonnier and Piper's 4.4-litre, Bandini/Biscaldi in the factory 3.3-litre. At quarter distance the only Ford running was so far behind that it could not regain the lost distance and Ferraris occupied the first six places.

Just before midnight, it was Ferrari's turn to start having troubles. Surtees spent a long time in the pits to replace a broken spring. The Bonnier/Piper 4.4-litre was in to fix a broken manifold and the Bianchi/Salmon LM was in with a broken gearbox. One hour after midnight the situation for the Ferraris worsened, the 365/P and 330/P2 models were running into serious trouble with cracked brake discs. They were using a new type of disc with radial ventilation and the problem was too great a temperature variation. The discs were doing their job too well in dissipating the heat and were overcooling which caused cracking. As the leading Ferraris pitted one by one with this trouble, the Dumay/Gosselin private entry found itself in the lead. The Maranello car was definitely out, as the brake failure continued. Every effort was being made to keep the factory cars and one NART car running, and a certain amount of lashing-up had to be done.

At 4 am or half distance, the Dumay/Gosselin LM led the Gregory/Rindt LM with the GTB of Mairesse/'Beurlys' in 3rd place. The factory cars were still in the race but had a lot of distance to make up on the leaders. Problems for the Ferrari team were not over. First the 3.3-litre factory car went out with engine trouble, then the 4-litre of Surtees/Scarfiotti broke a gearbox bearing and leaked oil on the exposed clutch. The resulting pit stop to replace the bearing and clean up the clutch caused such a delay that there was virtually no hope. Surtees rejoined the race but after only a few laps a shaft in the gearbox gave way. No sooner had the factory 4-litre left the pits than the NART 4.4-litre came in with the same problem. As the mechanics worked feverishly, the other factory 4-litre of Parkes/Guichet was running into gearbox trouble. The order remained the same with Dumay/Gosselin leading, the NART LM 2nd and the Belgian GTB 3rd. The factory car managed to displace the GTB from 3rd place but it was only a matter of time before the varied mechanical bothers would force it to retire. The battle between the two LMs for the lead continued. The Dumay/Gosselin car blew a tyre after hitting something on the straight. Gregory and Rindt swept into the lead and held it to the finish to give Luigi Chinetti's North American Racing Team its first victory at Le Mans and to save the day for Ferrari. The last factory Ferrari expired at 3 pm, one hour before the finish of the race. Gregory afterwards said that he did not see how they could have finished the race as both he and Rindt had driven flat out all the time.

Nurburgring

The ADAC 1,000-kilometre race was held on the Nurburgring on 1st August 1965. Ferrari entered a 4-litre for Surtees and Scarfiotti, a 275/P of 3.3-litres for Parkes/Guichet and a 166 Dino for Bandini/Vaccarella. The factory team was backed up by the Maranello Concessionaires 275/P driven by Graham Hill and Jackie Stewart. Sundry other Ferraris were entered by private owners including a pair of LMs by the Belgian Ecurie Francorchamps. Ferrari entered no GT cars as he was still having troubles with homologation. In this race, the Ferrari team faced a full team of Fords of which one was the 5.3-litre version in the hands of Phil Hill.

During practice Surtees showed that Ferrari still had the upper hand and unofficially broke the lap record with a time of 8 min. 53.1 secs. The Graham Hill/Stewart Ferrari was next fastest followed by the Parkes/Guichet Ferrari. The little Dino surprised everyone when it went round in 9 min. 11.1 secs.

At 9 am the field was off to a Le Mans start; Surtees took the lead at once with Graham Hill 2nd and Phil Hill in the Ford 3rd, Bondurant's Cobra 4th, Amon's Ford 5th and Parkes' Ferrari 6th.

Surtees led by 18 seconds on the first lap with Phil Hill forcing the big Ford past Graham Hill.

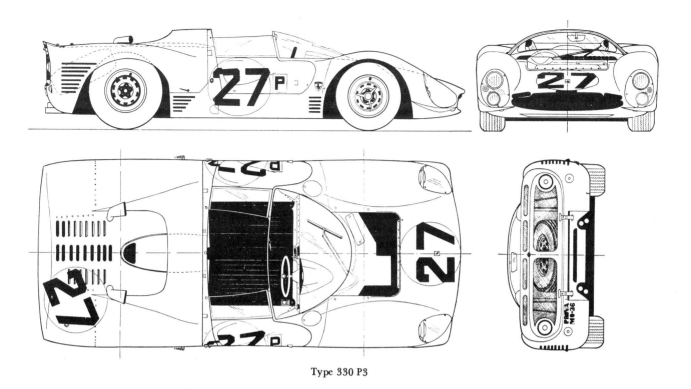

Type 330 P3

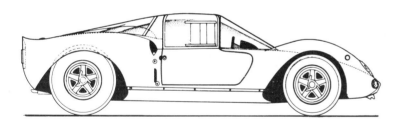

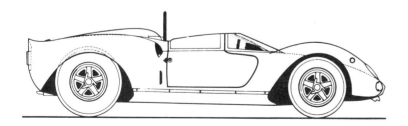
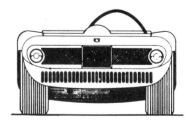

Dino 166 P and 206 P

On the third lap Surtees set a new record of 8 min. 50.5 secs., while Parkes pushed his works Ferrari past Amon's Ford. The little Dino was chasing the lead group and thrust its way ahead of the Bondurant Cobra. At the end of the third lap it was Surtees, Phil Hill, Graham Hill and Parkes; Phil Hill started catching up on the Ferrari much to the delight of the crowd but his efforts proved fruitless when the Ford's transmission gave out after one hour's racing. Parkes displaced Graham Hill from 2nd place, Amon held 4th with a 4.7-litre Ford and the Dino was hurrying along in 5th place. Graham Hill's Ferrari retired with a burnt-out regulator on the 10th lap which moved the Ford and the Dino up into 3rd and 4th places respectively. After 2 hrs. 20 min. of driving, Surtees handed over to Scarfiotti, the team losing the lead as Parkes went by, regaining it when Parkes made his stop to hand over to Guichet. Scarfiotti pulled out a lead of 1 min. 37.0 secs. over Guichet and Bandini handed the Dino over to Vaccarella who was then pursued by Sir John Whitmore in one of the Fords. Amon ran out of gas before he could reach the pits and thus lost a great deal of time which the Ford would be hard put to make up. At about one third distance the order had settled down, Scarfiotti, Guichet, Vaccarella and Whitmore. Whitmore, however, was catching the Dino as was the Bonnier/Rindt Porsche. After nearly five hours, Surtees took over again from Scarfiotti and Parkes relieved Guichet. On lap 35 the Whitmore Ford went out with a broken engine bracket but the Porsche had passed the Dino. The remainder of the race went according to schedule with Surtees stopping at the pits so that Scarfiotti could take the chequered flag, having covered the distance in 6 hrs. 53 min. 05.4 secs. with Parkes/Guichet 2nd some 45 secs. behind and the amazing Dino finishing 4th. Cobra once again took the GT points.

The Ford challenge had not matured and Ferrari remained ahead in the prototype class although he lost the GT title to the Ford-engined Cobras.

The 1966 Season - Type 330/P3

For the 1966 season Ferrari introduced two new cars the 330/P3 and the 206/S. Despite the rumours that he would be out with a 5-litre version of the famous V12 to combat the 7-litre Fords, Ferrari stuck to the concept of a smaller engined car that would also be lighter and would be competitive because of this. He retained the 3967-cc V12 engine which was rated at 420 b h p at 8,000 r p m, no higher than the previous year's figure. Over 65 lb were saved on engine weight by the redesign of the cylinder heads and the use of Lucas fuel injection instead of Weber carburetters. Twin ignition was also used with four Marelli coils, two Marelli distributors and 24 Champion spark plugs; Ferrari having decided to switch from the Marchal plugs used previously. The engine remained a 60 degree V12 with a bore and stroke of 77 x 71 mm and had a compression ratio of 11.4 : 1. The clutch was a dry, 3-plate Borg and Beck and the gearbox a 5-speed and reverse in unit with the differential. The most interesting part of the new car was its chassis made up of a multi-tubular frame with a bonded fibreglass underbody moulded round it, the engine and gearbox also contributing to the strength of the structure. The cellular compartmented structure consisted of small-diameter steel tubes with stressed alloy panels riveted on; the fibreglass underpan bonded underneath to extend into the sides forming fuel tanks.

Suspension was independent by A arms, coil springs, anti-roll bars and tubular shock-absorbers. Girling disc brakes were used, outboard at the front and inboard at the rear, while deeply dished cast-alloy wheels were fitted with three-eared knockoff hubcaps. The total weight saving on the new car was some 220 lb.

The body was built to Appendix J specifications by Piero Drogo's Carozzeria Sports Cars. The new Appendix J height requirement for open cars was altered to 90 cm or 35.4 inches which permitted a reduction from the P2s 41.1 inch height to 37.4 inches for the P3. The extreme inward curvature of the windshield and side windows resulted in a near-coupe' configuration but frontal area was not substantially reduced as the use of larger section tyres increased the width by 4 inches.

The front of the car was considerably different from the P2s, with four headlights in vertical pairs behind large plastic fairings; the front also had separate air intakes for the front brakes above the main radiator entry. Air for the engine and for the rear brakes was taken in through large scoops shaped into the doors. The duct for the injectors separating from the right hand passage running laterally up to the cold air box. With a total weight of 1584 lb, Ferrari gave the top speed as 192 m p h.

Type 206/S

The 206/S with its 65-degree V6 twin overhead camshaft engine was a scaled-down version of the P3. Weight reduction was 105 lb over the previous year's hillclimb champion car the 206/SP. The engine remained much the same with a bore and stroke of 86 x 57 mm giving a displacement of 1987 cc. The only alteration was that it had single ignition instead of the twin plug layout of the earlier model and had the compression ratio lowered to 10.8 : 1 from 12.5 : 1. The power output remained the same at 218 b h p at 9,000 r p m. Carburetters were three Weber 40DCN1 and porting and combustion chamber design alterations were affected by Formula 1 practice. A dry, three-plate Borg and Beck clutch was used with a five-speed and reverse gearbox in unit with the differential. Girling disc brakes were fitted outboard at the front and inboard at the rear. Total weight was given at 1,276 lb.

Sebring

As there had been no factory Ferraris at Daytona Beach, Sebring marked the first clash with Ford in the 1966 season. The Sebring 12 Hours was held at the famous airfield circuit in central Florida on March 26th. Sebring marked the first appearance of the 330 P3 Ferrari with its four overhead camshaft 4-litre engine which the factory entered for Parkes and Bondurant. The factory entry was backed up by Chinetti's North American Racing Team who fielded a 330 P2 driven by Mario Andretti and Pedro Rodriguez.

There was a factory entry in the 2-litre class, Bandini and Scarfiotti sharing the lone Dino 206 to face the Porsche horde. Three practice periods were held on Wednesday, Thursday and Friday before the race. The Ferrari P3 was consistently faster on the first two days but on the third day Gurney showed the potential of the

Mark II Ford when he knocked 5 seconds off the previous year's lap record averaging 107.22 m p h for one lap.

Overcast, cooler weather prevailed on Saturday as the contestants lined up for a Le Mans type start.

First lap leader was Graham Hill in the Alan Mann Ford GT 40 immediately followed by the P3 and the 206 Dino. The Ferrari P3 in the hands of Parkes then took the lead, lapping consistently. The Mark II Ford with Gurney at the wheel had made a bad start and was 63rd on the first lap but started to catch up very fast, moving into 10th place by lap 8. He lowered the lap record to 2 min. 54.8 secs., averaging 107.09 m p h and after 1½ hours he took the lead from the Parkes/Bondurant Ferrari. Parkes made no attempt to match the Ford's furious pace as he had no team car to back him up should he overstrain his car in the chase. When he was challenged by Ken Miles, in the Miles/Ruby Ford, he also allowed the American car to pass.

As the pit stops took place, the Ferrari drivers switched places and the Italian entry remained on the same lap as the leading Ford although unable to make any impression on the Ford's two minute lead. Andretti in the NART car had brushed with a Porsche, smashing in the front of the Ferrari. He was totally oblivious of the fact that as a result of the collision the Porsche had gone off the road and killed several spectators.

About this time the 206 Dino, which easily led the 2-litre class, came into the pits with the linkage frozen in gear. When it was freed, Bandini did one more lap then came in to have the linkage adjusted. This delay erased the Dino's three lap lead over the Porsche and put it, instead, three laps behind.

After Andretti's car had had the nose unbent at the pits, he restarted and fuel vapour drifted out of the exhausts. Someone panicked and a Ferrari mechanic grabbed a bucket of water and threw its contents under the car, unfortunately, as the bucket touched the ground it threw up a shower of sparks and immediately the vapour caught fire. It might have been out in seconds, as the car itself was not on fire, but over-enthusiastic pit work resulted in the car being drowned with the contents of fire extinguishers. This put a swift end to the chances of the P2 returning to the race.

On the last pit stop of the P3, Parkes warned Bondurant that the gearbox needed nursing but a few laps later the car was out with a broken selector. The Dino finished 5th, three laps behind the Porsche.

The Le Mans test weekend was held on April 2nd and 3rd. Ferrari announced that he could do all the high speed testing he needed at Monza and therefore sent no cars. The Ecurie Francorchamps sent along a 375 P2 Ferrari, it had a 1965 chassis with a 1966 body and was powered by the single-cam-per-bank 4.4-litre engine. 'Beurlys' put up some good times with it although he could not match those of the 7-litre Fords. The only other Ferrari present was a private French entry, this being a standard GTO.

Monza 1,000 Km

The 1,000 kilometres of Monza 1966 was held on April 25th but the Ford challenge to Ferrari did not materialize. The only Fords present were the 4.7-litre GT-40s and they were no match for the new Ferrari 330/P3 coupe which was in the hands of Surtees and Parkes. It was Surtees' first race since his accident in Canada the previous year. He showed he was on top form, driving 500 of the 1000 kilometres and setting a new lap record. There were four Dino 206 Ferraris entered. The factory car of Bandini/Scarfiotti had a fuel injected engine and coupe bodywork, the remaining Dinos had carburetted engines. Bondurant wrecked the Dino he should have driven with Vaccarella. The other two were entered by Maranello Concessionaires and Scuderia Sant Ambroeus, driven respectively by Piper/Attwood and Biscaldi/Casoni. There were sundry privately entered 275 LM and 275 GTB Ferraris. Surtees led from the start and pulled away with ease, he refuelled at 25 laps and Parkes took over. The only real trouble with the car was that, on the 30th lap, the windshield wiper broke and the car had to run in the pouring rain without a wiper for the rest of the race. During Surtees' second spell, the engine lost some of its crispness due to the wet conditions but when conditions cleared up the healthy note of the V12 returned. The Surtees/Parkes car won, averaging 103.06 and Surtees set a new lap record of 108.67 mph. The Siebenthal/Peixhino LM Ferrari finished 8th. The Bandini/

Scarfiotti Dino 10th, the Attwood/Piper Dino 13th, the Zwimper/Illert 275 GTB 17th and the Pessina/Botalla 275 GTB 19th.

Targa Florio

The 50th Targa Florio was held on 8th May 1966. The Ferrari factory entered an assortment of cars, Vaccarella/Bandini had a 330/P3 open cockpit version with a fuel-injected engine, Parkes/Scarfiotti and Guichet/Baghetti had 206 Dinos, the No. 1 team having a fuel-injected engine and the backup car a normally carburetted engine. Two experimental cars were entered in the prototype category, one a GTB and the other an LM, with 4-litre single-cam-per-bank production type engines in place of the normal 3.3-litres. Supporting the factory were the private entries of Ravetto and the rapid but erratic Prince Starraba, Epstein/Hawkins and Swanson/Ennis, all on 275/LMs, and Biscaldi/Casoni in the Scuderia Sant Ambroeus Dino. Official practice was not too happy a time for the Ferrari contingent as Parkes went off the road in the Dino and work had to be done on the body and suspension to get it ready for the race. When the official times were announced, the Ferrari team discovered that Klass in the 8-cylinder Porsche was faster than the Sicilian crowd's hometown hero, Vaccarella, in the 4-litre Ferrari. The experimental cars were given to Nicodemi/Lessona and Conti/Ventura to drive.

The start took place in good weather but rain threatened on various parts of the circuit. Halfway through the first lap Vaccarella was leading with the P3 Ferrari, Scarfiotti had the Dino in 2nd place but was being harried by Mitter's Porsche. At the end of the first lap, Vaccarella was still first but the Porsche had passed Scarfiotti's Dino into 2nd place, Vaccarella found the going tricky as it was raining on some parts of the circuit and the Porsche displaced the Ferrari from first place. Further back the Porsche of Klass pushed ahead of Scarfiotti to take 3rd place.

Nurburgring

The 1966 1,000 kilometres ADAC race on the Nurburgring was held on June 7th. Ferrari sent two cars for Surtees/Parkes to choose from; one being a 330/P3 4-o h c 4-litre coupe, the other a similar car but with an open cockpit. After practice they settled for the open car for the race. The factory also entered a Dino for Scarfiotti/Bandini and two other Dinos were in the hands of Rodriguez/Ginther of the North American Racing Team and Piper/Attwood of the Maranello Concessionaires. Scuderia Filipinetti entered a 275/LM for Mairesse and Muller and there were several other sundry LMs and GT Ferraris in private hands.

In practice, Surtees set the fastest lap with 8 min. 31.9 secs., with the nearest opposition from Phil Hill's Chaparral at 8 min. 35.4 secs.

For once, the 1,000 km race was held in good weather and, as the cars were prepared to line up for the Le Mans start, there was a scene in the Ferrari pits as a defective fuel pump was suspected on the factory Dino and a new one was fitted with only minutes to go. Surtees, Scarfiotti, Rodriguez and Attwood were the Ferrari starting drivers and, at the drop of the flag, it was Scarfiotti's Dino that led. On the first lap, Surtees came storming in by 8 min. 48 secs., with a lead of 17 seconds over Scarfiotti's fuel injected Dino. On the second lap, Surtees set a new lap record of 8 min. 37 secs. On lap 3, Bonnier finally forced the Chaparral past the smaller Dino but was already 50 seconds behind the Surtees P3. Scarfiotti was able to keep pace with the big American car, never losing more than a few yards and, in the process, running away from the 2-litre Porsche opposition. Attwood and Rodriguez in the Dinos were running 7th and 8th and Muller was 12th.

As Surtees was about to complete his sixth lap, the P3 came into the pits; a large patch of paint, burned off the right rear wheel arch where the wheel was rubbing, indicated serious trouble. It was found that the eyebolt fixture of the shockabsorber had broken off and caused the collapsing of the suspension. A replacement damper spring unit was quickly found but the Ferrari's lead was lost. The Chaparral now led the race with Scarfiotti's Dino a length or two behind it. After 7 minutes, the P3 was repaired and Parkes took over after refuelling to rejoin the race in 21st place. The NART and Maranello Concessionaires were not too far behind in 5th and 6th places.

When the Chaparral pitted on lap 11,

Scarfiotti took the lead but on the next lap the Dino refuelled and Bandini took over pulling out of the pits just after the Chaparral, now driven by Phil Hill, went back into the lead. With Phil Hill in the car, the situation changed; he pulled out a lead of more than 60 seconds over the Dino by lap 15 and on lap 16 had increased it to over 90 seconds. Ginther was now 3rd in the NART Dino and Parkes had stormed through the field from 21st to 7th, right behind the Attwood/Piper Dino.

Parkes stopped on lap 17 for fuel and Surtees took over but, after one more lap, the same problem that had halted them previously occurred again. A long stop to fit another unit dropped them a lap behind the Chaparral.

At half distance, the Chaparral drivers changed places once more but Bandini was unable to make up the time, and Bonnier was comfortably away before the Dino appeared. On lap 23, the Dino pitted for fuel and front tyres and Scarfiotti stalled the car on take-off having forgotten to switch on all the booster fuel pumps. In the meantime the NART Dino went into 2nd place driven by Ginther. Two laps later it was Ginther who pitted for a driver change and to take on fuel. Rodriguez left the pits still in 2nd place but Scarfiotti put on the pressure and quickly overhauled Rodriguez. The Attwood/Piper Dino had trouble with the tyre rubbing the body and, on the 27th lap, Surtees was in with a very sick P3; there was a strong clutch odour when it stopped in the pits and after repairs Parkes took over. The Maranello Concessionaires' Dino stopped with a damaged gearbox.

As rain threatened, Bandini took over the Dino and the factory P3 crawled into the pits; after some work Parkes restarted, stopped again, on the return road from the south curve, and continued to complete another lap with the transmission and clutch in bad shape. By the time Rodriguez pitted the NART car for Ginther to take over, the rainstorm had started. Bandini stopped briefly to have paper cleared from his radiator but still held on to 2nd place with Ginther 3rd; the Filipinetti car was 11th, having been slowed by a broken seat mount. The Chaparral had to stop for rain tyres, as the car was very difficult to manage in the wet, and the long process of changing the bolt-on wheels caused the Chaparral's lead to dwindle to 60 seconds over the 2nd place Dino. There were high hopes that the Ferrari could catch the American car but Phil Hill left no doubt about his class when in two laps he extended his lead to 96 seconds. The Scarfiotti/Bandini Dino thus had to be content with 2nd place and winning the 2-litre class with the NART Dino of Rodriguez/Ginther 3rd. John Surtees in the P3 was credited with the fastest lap in 8 min. 37.0 secs., 158.8 k p h.

Le Mans

The 24-Hours of Le Mans was held on the 18th and 19th June 1966. It marked the key battle between Ford and Ferrari, a battle in which the Italian team came out second best. It also marked the eruption of personality clashes that had been brewing in the Ferrari team for some time.

Ferrari entered two twin-overhead cam-per-bank 4-litre P3s for Surtees/Parkes and Bandini/Guichet with a third car of this type entered by North American Racing Team for Rodriguez/Ginther. During the pre-race practice, Surtees discovered that team manager Dragoni had Scarfiotti down as reserve driver on the Surtees/Parkes car. The explanation was that it was in case Surtees became tired, harping back to the bad accident he had had at Mosport but from which he had fully recovered. Surtees felt he had not been properly consulted and there was a showdown. An attempt was made to discuss it by phone with Enzo Ferrari in Modena, but Ferrari refused to discuss it and Surtees walked out of the Ferrari team. The parting of the ways had a marked effect on both Ferrari and Surtees, hindsight has shown that the combination would have been strong contenders in 1967 but the situation left Surtees with inadequate cars and Ferrari without top drivers.

Several other Ferraris of various vintages were also in the hands of private owners including three Dinos in the hands of Kolb/Follmer, Salmon/Hobbs and Vaccarella/Casoni. Vaccarella was ready to pack up and return to Sicily, when he heard he had been assigned one of the Dinos, as he thought he should have a place on one of the big Ferraris. The three Dinos were out before the third hour was over, with clutch, final drive and water leak problems. After 9 hours, the Parkes/Scarfiotti car crashed and the privately entered Gregory/Bondurant Ferrari was out with gearbox trouble; the Rodriguez/Ginther car followed at 11 hours with a broken gearbox; the Mairesse/Muller car of the Scuderia Filipinetti was out with the same problem after 12 hours. At 17 hours, the Bandini/Guichet Ferrari was out with a blown head gasket and the story of the Ford domination was almost complete. Rodriguez/Ginther had their car in first place for a brief time at the sixth hour; Parkes/Scarfiotti was 2nd at the sixth hour and Bandini/Guichet were 5th at the fifth hour; these being the best positions that Ferrari held during the race.

When the 24 hours were over, the results showed a Ferrari 275 GTB in 8th place, winning its category, with Pike/Courage and another 275 GTB of Noblet/Dubois in 10th place. It was a disastrous race for Ferrari.

The 1967 Season - Type 330/P4

For the 1967 season, Ferrari produced a new car bearing the designation 330/P4. It was an almost totally new design although in most respects it looked very much like the 1966 P3s. The 330/P4 engine was a modified version of the familiar 60 degree V12. Modifications included two intake valves and one exhaust valve per cylinder, operated by twin overhead camshafts per bank of cylinders. Bore and stroke remained at 77 x 71 mm giving 330-cc displacement per cylinder for a grand total of 3967-cc. With a compression ratio of 11 : 1, a maximum output of 450 b h p at 8,000 r p m was quoted. Marelli twin distributor ignition supplied two 10 mm Champion spark plugs per cylinder and the factory cars used Lucas metered fuel injection with Grand Prix-type, sliding throttle plates. The five-speed constant mesh gearbox was redesigned for 1967 and transmitted the power to the cast light alloy wheels, through sliding spline half-shafts. Wheels were cast in aluminium/magnesium alloy, shod with Firestone 10.15-15 tyres at the front and 12.15-15 tyres at the rear. Knock-off hubs and outboard mounted, quick change ventilated brake rotors were used on all wheels, to facilitate disc replacement during pit stops.

The suspension of the P4 was similar to the P3, with fully independent four-bar linkages front and rear. Concentric coil spring/shock-absorber units, threaded suspension arms and adjustable anti-roll bars were used at both ends, together with very light cast-magnesium hub carriers.

The chassis was of mixed construction with a multi-tube space frame with aluminium and fibreglass panels in the centre section forming a semi-monocoque area to contain fuel along both sides of the cockpit. The wheelbase was decreased by one inch to 93.5 inches with a 58.5 in. front track and a 57.0 in. rear track, these figures being increased by one inch and 0.6-inch over the previous year's car. Overall the P4 was 164.8 inches long, 71.3 inches wide, and 39.4 inches high. The turning circle was 44 feet kerb to kerb. The cars weighed 1950 lb with water and oil but without fuel and driver. The factory quoted the maximum speed as 198 m p h.

Daytona

The 1967 Manufacturers' Championship got underway at Daytona Beach on the 5th February. Ferrari took the Ford challenge very seriously and before the end of the 1966 season he sent a brand new 330/P4 to Daytona for a long series of tests on the 3.81 mile circuit.

For the actual race Ferrari sent two new P4s for Amon/Bandini and Parkes/Scarfiotti. The factory entries were backed up by Chinetti's North American Racing Team with a P3/4 for Rodriguez/Guichet, Ecurie National Belge with a P3/4 for Mairesse/'Beurlys', Piper/Attwood with an older P2/3 and the even older NART P2.

Official practice started on the Tuesday before the race with the Thursday set aside for official qualifying. To the dismay of the Ford group, they found that the Ferraris were consistently faster. The decision was made to set up Gurney's Ford Mark II as a sprint car so that the Fords could, at least, qualify faster than the Italian opposition. The scheme worked well and Gurney sat on the pole position for the start with a time of 1 min. 55.10 secs., a speed of 119.165 m p h. Jim Hall's Chaparral was next fastest, only a fraction faster than Pedro Rodriguez who recorded 1 min. 55.4 secs.

(118.856 m p h), Amon was next with 1 min. 55.6 secs., followed by Andretti's Ford and Scarfiotti's Ferrari in 1 min. 56.4 secs.

One of the cars was an open version, the other a coupe. The open car was the one that had taken part in the pre-Christmas tests and was driven in the race by Amon/Bandini. The cars weighed in at 792 kg dry and 980 kg in race trim.

The P3/4s were 1966 model P3s which had been modified by the installation of P4 suspension and the replacement of the gearbox with the new 5-speed ZF; the two P3/4s used the 1966 carburetted engine.

Franco Lini, who replaced Eugenio Dragoni as Ferrari team manager handled his team extremely well and the Ferraris were not drawn into the Chaparral-Ford battle. Fords fell by the wayside one after another and after three hours the Chaparral was out, leaving the Amon/Bandini P4 in a lead which they never lost. Parkes and Scarfiotti had some trouble during the night with a brake pad change but were never challenged for 2nd place as the 3rd place Ferrari P3/4 of Rodriguez/Guichet was some 26 laps behind. The three Ferraris, although on different laps, crossed the finishing line together. The season had begun well and Ferrari had reason to be optimistic about his chances in the championship.

Sebring

The Sebring 12 Hour race was held on 1st April 1967. Everyone had hoped that there would be a renewal of the Ford/Ferrari battle, started at Daytona. However, Ferrari decided not to enter the race and various reasons were given, the most likely was the closeness of the Le Mans test days.

Also absent was Chinetti's North American Racing Team who were not entered to avoid a writ of attachment on their cars after the involvement in the accident of the previous year.

Therefore, it was only in the 2-litre class that Ferrari had any representation that could be classed as competitive. Results here too were negative, two of the Dinos were out early in the race with engine trouble and the third was damaged when it went off the road.

Monza

The 1,000 kilometres of Monza 1967 was held on the combined road and banked track on April 25th. Ferrari hoped for an easy win as the Ford factory cars were not entered but the late entry of the Chaparral made the event a little more interesting.

Ferrari entered two 330/P4 coupes for Parkes/Scarfiotti and Bandini/Amon. Two 330 P3/4s were entered, one by the North American Racing Team for Rodriguez and Guichet, the other by Scuderia Filipinetti for Muller and Vaccarella. Besides the Chaparral, the only opposition to Ferrari was from the Ford Mirages entered by the Gulf Team, these having their engines enlarged from 4.7 to 5-litres.

In the 2-litre class, the factory entered the 206 Dino with fuel injection and three valves per cylinder. Drivers of this car were Jonathan Williams and Gunther Klass. There were several other Dinos in the race but they were all of the two-valve per cylinder type.

Bandini lapped the P4 in 2 min. 54.1 secs. but the Chaparral was faster, with Phil Hill turning a lap in 2 min. 53.8 secs. Parkes in the second P4 was close behind with 2 min. 54.5 secs., the two Ferraris and the Chaparral being the only ones to break the 3 minute mark in practice. In the Sports class, the battle was to be between the GT 40 Fords and the Ferrari LMs.

Spence in the Chaparral took a slight lead at the start, and Bandini began a wheel-to-wheel and side-by-side battle with the big American car. Parkes positioned his Ferrari just behind the duelling pair and further back with Rodriguez, in the NART Ferrari, the two Mirage Fords of Piper and Ickx, and Vaccarella in the Filipinetti Ferrari. In the 2-litre class, the Dino of Williams was easily leading all the Porsches.

Rodriguez ran into one of the chicanes, having to come into the pits to check for damage before returning to the battle in 6th place. At this stage Bandini was in the lead but the Chaparral remained close by, although Parkes was now beginning to press the Texan car. In the 2-litre class, things were beginning to go wrong for Ferrari, as the Dino began to overheat badly. At just about the one-hour mark, Parkes pushed the Ferrari ahead of the Chaparral, the Chaparral eventually pitting to change a wheel and shortly after to retire with a driveshaft fault. This left Bandini first, Scarfiotti in Parkes' car 2nd, Rodriguez 3rd, and Vaccarella 4th.

Scarfiotti came into the pits early as he was running out of fuel, the pump refusing to pick up the last quarter of a tankful. A wheel was also changed and Parkes took over. This stop let Rodriguez catch up. Amon took over from Bandini and rejoined the race without losing the lead. Rodriguez was seriously challenging Parkes but, in trying to outbrake the factory car, hit the barriers bending the Ferrari seriously and letting the Vaccarella/Muller Ferrari into 3rd place.

In the GT class, the Vestey/Gaspar GTB was leading easily. Vaccarella spoiled a chance for third when he spun and damaged a wheel and dropped to 6th place. After a pit stop to repair the damage, the Filipinetti Ferrari began to gain ground rapidly, finally passing the 4th-place Porsche of Siffert coming off the banking on the last lap. The Bandini/Amon car won in 5 hrs. 07 min. 43.0 secs. at an average of 196.934 k p h with Parkes/Scarfiotti 2nd, Vaccarella/Muller 4th and Gaspar/Vestey 15th overall but winning the GT class. Bandini set a new lap record of 2 min. 55.8 secs., 206.825 k p h.

Francorchamps

The 1,000 kilometres of Francorchamps 1967 was held on May 1st and Ferrari sent only one car, a coupe 330 P4, to be driven by Mike Parkes and Ludovico Scarfiotti. They were supported by entries of two P3/4 models by Equipe National Belge and Maranello Concessionaires, one driven by Mairesse and 'Beurlys' and the other by Attwood and Lucien Bianchi. Another Ferrari was entered in the GT class by Vestey/Gasper who drove a GTB. Only Phil Hill in the Chaparral and Jacky Ickx in the 5.7-litre Ford Mirage broke the 4-minute barrier and Hill was the only one to surpass John Surtees' Grand Prix Ferrari time of the previous year of 3 min. 38 secs. Both the works Ferrari and the yellow Belgian car were close behind the two big V8s. The GTB Ferrari was withdrawn after the chassis was found to be extensively cracked.

Race day turned out to be miserably wet and at 1 pm the cars lined up on the grid with Parkes in the front row with Ickx and Hill. Mairesse in the Belgian car was in the second row, alongside Paul Hawkins' Lola.

As the flag dropped, it was the Ford Mirage that jumped into the lead with the Mairesse Ferrari right behind. The Attwood Ferrari had stalled just before the flag and would not restart.

Attwood waited until everyone was off and then let the car roll towards the bottom of Eau Rouge and finally got started some three quarters of a lap behind the others. The two Belgian drivers were masters of their national circuit and the Ford Mirage and ENB Ferrari left even the works Ferrari behind. However, Parkes held on to 3rd place. As the bad weather continued Parkes came in to refuel and Scarfiotti took over. As the Mirage pitted, the yellow Ferrari went into the lead. The next lap Mairesse was in for a rapid stop and 'Beurlys' took over the Ferrari, still maintaining the lead.

The Ferrari's lead did not last very long as the ENB team had been out-manoeuvred by the Mirage team manager. While 'Beurlys' was trying to get used to the wet, Ickx was kept in the Mirage for a second spell with the result that the Ford-engined car easily took the lead from the Ferrari and continued to build up a great lead; by 38 laps Ickx had a complete lap advantage over the Ferrari. The Ferrari stopped before the Mirage and Mairesse was back in the race. David Yorke, the Mirage manager, did some more manoeuvering and Dick Thompson replaced Rees as Ickx's co-driver which meant that the car would be motoring faster than the opposition expected and, after the mandatory rest, Ickx could take over again to finish the race.

The manoeuvering proved unnecessary as Mairesse, in his hurry to make up time, lost control and went off the road. Behind this scene, Siffert's Porsche was in 2nd place followed by Attwood, who had brought his Ferrari through the field, and in 4th place was the works Ferrari. Parkes was duelling with the Hawkins Lola despite gear linkage trouble which caused a pit stop. Attwood was unable to catch the Porsche and finished 3rd while on the last lap Hawkins' Lola swept by Scarfiotti in the P4, pushing the Ferrari back into 5th place.

Targa Florio

The 1967 Targa Florio was held on May 14th and Ferrari sent only two factory cars. A spyder version of the 330 P4 was provided for Vaccarella and Scarfiotti, and a 206 Dino with three valves per cylinder and fuel injection for Klass and Casoni. Williams was on loan to share Venturi's older 206 Dino, this having the carburetted two valves per cylinder engine.

For the first time on the present Targa Florio circuit, official obligatory practice was held on the Friday before the race. Vaccarella was fastest, without too much trouble recording 37 min. 12.4 secs. Scarfiotti in the same car recorded 37 min. 53.6 secs. and Klass on the Dino third fastest with 38 min. 13 secs.

Supporting the factory team was the Scuderia Filipinetti P3/4 Ferrari driven by Muller and Guichet.

Vaccarella led on the opening lap followed by Mitter's 8-cylinder Porsche and Muller in the P3/4 Ferrari. However, in the centre of the village of Collesano, Vaccarella overdid things and slid into a stone wall breaking his wheels and front suspension. On lap 2 Herbert Muller took the lead, the Porsche having retired, and set a lap record of 37 min. 09 secs. Klass led the 2-litre class but ran the Dino into a bridge on lap 2.

As Guichet took over the Ferrari, he was unable to maintain the times set by Muller and when Muller took over the car once more it was behind a factory Porsche. Muller set off at a great pace to make up the lost ground but the gearbox gave up on lap 7. The Williams/Venturi Dino was the last of Ferrari's hopes, the car eventually finishing 4th behind the three Porsches.

Nurburgring

The ADAC 1967 1,000 kilometre race was held on the Nurburgring on May 28th. Ferrari sent only a token entry in the shape of an experimental car. This was a Dino 206 with the 2.4-litre V6 Grand Prix engine used at the beginning of the 1966 Grand Prix season. The car was entered for Scarfiotti and Gunther Klass but the engine was blown up in a big way during practice and as no spare was available the car was withdrawn. The other Ferrari was the Scuderia Filipinetti entry for Muller/Guichet. Filipinetti had obtained the use of the factory 18-valve Dino but during practice, while Guichet was driving, the car caught fire. Guichet managed to escape unharmed but the car was totally burnt out.

The Le Mans test weekend was held on the 8th/9th June 1967, with the circuit open for practice from 8 am to 4.45 pm on the Saturday, 9 am to 12.30 pm on Sunday morning and 2.30 pm to 4.30 pm on Sunday afternoon.

Ferrari sent two of the 330 P4s which had been seen at Daytona, one being a coupe, the other an open cockpit version. Both cars had the hub-mounted rear disc brakes in place of the earlier inboard mounted type. Bandini, Amon, Parkes and Scarfiotti were brought along to do the driving and before long the 1966 lap record of 3 min. 30.6 secs. was broken repeatedly; at the end of the Saturday practice, Bandini had the fastest time of the day in 3 min. 25.5 secs. (146.5 m p h) with speeds of 198 m p h on the Mulsanne straight. The overall lap speed was greater than that of the Ford opposition but the speed down the straight was some 8 m p h slower than the 7-litre American cars. Ford were hoping for a demonstration of superiority on the Sunday but it rained and the Ford people were not willing to take the chance and left Ferrari with the laurels of the test weekend.

Le Mans

The 35th Le Mans race was run on 10th/11th June 1967 on the classic 8.14 mile circuit. Ferrari faced strong opposition in the shape of four of the new Mark IV Fords, three mark IIB Fords and the new Ford-Mirages sponsored by the Gulf Oil Co. Ferrari entered three factory 330 P4s and had another of the latest P4 models in the hands of the Equipe National Belge for Mairesse and 'Beurlys' to drive. The factory cars were driven by Parkes/Scarfiotti, Amon/Vaccarella and Klass/Sutcliffe.

Supporting this group of P4s were the P3/4 models of Maranello Concessionaires, Scuderia Filipinetti and North American Racing Team, the latter team also fielding an older 330 P2. The NART car was driven by Pedro Rodriguez and Giancarlo Baghetti. Jean Guichet and

Herbert Muller ran the Filipinetti car and the Maranello car was driven by Piers Courage and Richard Attwood. A team of factory Dino Ferraris was also entered but was withdrawn at the last minute to concentrate all effort on an overall win.

On the first practice session on the Wednesday before the race, the Chaparral of Phil Hill was the fastest at 3 min. 27.4 secs., with Mairesse in the P4 second fastest at 3 min. 30.9 secs. The next day the Chaparral was even faster, beating both the lap record set by Gurney in 1966 of 3 min. 30.6 secs. and Bandini's test weekend record of 3 min. 25.5 secs., the Chaparral figure being 3 min. 24.7 secs. Then the 7-litre Fords began to show what they could do and McLaren went round in the dark at 3 min. 24.4 secs. (147.316 m p h). Other Fords held third, fourth, fifth and sixth fastest times with Scarfiotti seventh fastest in 3 min. 28.9 secs.

As the flag fell, it was Pedro Rodriguez' blue and white NART Ferrari that took the lead with the Fords of Bianchi and Gardner close behind. But when the cars came round on the first lap, it was the blue Ford of Paul Hawkins that led by a considerable margin from Gardner's Ford and the Ferrari of Rodriguez who in turn had Schlesser in the Mark IIB Ford and Dan Gurney in the red Mark IV Ford behind him.

By the end of the first hour, the Hawkins/ Bucknum Mark IIB Ford still led with Gurney/ Foyt in the Mark IV 2nd and the McLaren/ Donohue Mark IV 3rd. The Ferraris were running 5th and 6th with Vaccarella/Amon leading Rodriguez/Baghetti.

The Fords had to refuel every hour and the Ferraris only every hour and fifteen minutes; this meant that the Ferraris had an advantage, if not in sheer speed, in pit stop time. Ford would have to make 24 pit stops compared with Ferrari's 19.

By the 4th hour, Parkes and Scarfiotti had moved their P4 up into 5th place with the Amon/Vaccarella car in 6th. At this time, the leading Fords, the Chaparral and the two P4 Ferraris were all on the same lap.

As the 7th hour came round, the Parkes/ Scarfiotti P4 moved into 2nd place when the Fords pitted again, but the Ford had the upper hand in short order, lapping regularly at about the 3.30 mark. The pace was too much for the NART P3/4 and a piston gave way. At the 8th hour, Parkes/Scarfiotti held on to 3rd place with the Mairesse/'Beurlys' P4 now in 6th place; at the 10th hour the Parkes/Scarfiotti Ferrari dropped to 4th.

An accident, involving three of the Fords, Vaccarella/Amon car was eliminated when, on attempting to return to the pits on a flat tyre, a spark set the car on fire and it was burnt out. The Guichet/Muller P3/4 entered by the Scuderia Filipinetti also retired at this period due to a lack of oil.

By the 16th hour, the Gurney/Foyt Mark IV Ford was averaging 137.15 m p h and was seven laps ahead of the Parkes/Scarfiotti Ferrari in 2nd place. The Mairesse/'Beurlys' P4 was two laps behind the Belgian car in 4th. The Attwood/Courage P3/4 was desperately trying to make the distance for an oil stop but when the stop was made it was too late and the engine damage was done. The old P2 of the North American Racing Team was eliminated at this period when it was involved in an accident.

On Sunday morning, Ferrari lost another car when the Klass/Sutcliffe P4 retired with a broken gearbox.

At the 20th hour, the Parkes/Scarfiotti car was still 2nd and held 2nd place in the index of performance. Mairesse and 'Beurlys' hung on to 3rd place, five laps ahead of the McLaren/Donohue Ford. The leading Ford was now lapping in 3 min. 45 secs., while the Ferrari was catching up fast lapping at 3 min. 35 secs., but after the 2.30 pm pit stop both teams evened out their times to the 3.40 mark. Ferrari had conceded victory and were running to finish a secure 2nd. The Parkes/Scarfiotti car was the first to receive the chequered flag at the end of the 24 hours but the all-American team of Gurney/Foyt had won the race. The Ferrari was 2nd, having covered a distance of 3,249.630 miles at an average speed of 134.128 m p h with Mairesse/'Beurlys' 3rd covering 3,217.146 miles at an average of 131.128 m p h.

The BOAC 500

Ferrari were one point behind Porsche for the Manufacturers' Trophy as they prepared for the BOAC 500 race at Brands Hatch. Ferrari planned to make an all out effort and, because the race was run on a tricky British circuit, he set about recruiting some local help. Ferrari drivers nominated were Chris Amon, Ludovico Scarfiotti and Jonathan Williams and to these were added Jackie Stewart, Paul Hawkins and Peter Sutcliffe, all three cars being 3-valve-per-cylinder fuel-injected open-cockpit 330 P4s. The factory team was supported by the Maranello Concessionaires P3/4 with the carburetter, 2-valve-per-cylinder engine. Sundry other Ferraris were entered including the 3.3-litre 250 LM of Dibley/Pierpoint.

Race day was cloudy and overcast with a threat of rain. The front row consisted of the two Lola T70 GTs of Surtees and Hulme and the Chaparral of Spence with the Ferraris right behind them. Surtees, in the red Lola, immediately took the lead followed by two of the P4 Ferraris and the Chaparral. At the end of the first lap, Surtees had already pulled out a large margin over the Ferraris of Scarfiotti and Hawkins. On lap two the scene changed completely, Hawkins came by in the lead with the Ferrari tailed by the Chaparral and Hulme in the second Lola; Surtees headed for the pits.

After one hour of racing, the picture had changed again. The Chaparral led by 4.6 seconds from the Stewart/Amon Ferrari, the Scarfiotti/Sutcliffe P4 was 3rd. Hulme, in the second Lola, had taken the lead but before the hour was out he was in the pits to replace a broken rocker arm.

Scarfiotti fell right back in the field when he spun at Bottom bend, the spin being caused by a tyre going flat. After a pit stop the Ferrari rejoined the race.

As the first stops for refuelling and driver change took place, it became evident that the Porsches were able to go a longer distance without refuelling and Ferrari would have to win the race of the pit stops. With the leading cars in the pits, the Ford-Mirage took the lead holding it until almost the end of the second hour at which time it also had to refuel; at this stage, the Siffert/McLaren Porsche took the lead with the Chaparral 2nd, the Stewart/Amon Ferrari 3rd and the Scarfiotti/Sutcliffe Ferrari 4th. When the Porsche finally stopped, the Chaparral regained the lead briefly before pitting to replace a flat tyre. This allowed the P4 of Stewart and Amon into the lead which they held until the third hour with the Porsche 2nd, the Chaparral 3rd and the Williams/Hawkins Ferrari 4th; both the 1st and 2nd place cars being on the same laps.

At the four-hour mark, the Chaparral was back in the lead, with a margin of 23.6 seconds over the Porsche, and with the Stewart/Amon car now one lap behind the leaders. When the Porsche once again stopped, the Ferrari went by into 2nd place but with no hope of making up the lap on the Chaparral. The problem, for the Ferrari team, was could they stay in 2nd place with another fuel stop coming up and with the Porsche running through? The drivers made every effort to extend their lead over the 3rd place car. A frantic pit stop took place, 20 minutes from the end of the race, 10 gallons were poured in and the Ferrari was off before the Porsche came round. The Ferrari team was given a tremendous ovation when it was announced that the 6 points for 2nd place had won them the championship by one point.

The 1968 Season - A lean year

The 1968 Manufacturer's Championship turned out to be an altogether poor season for Ferrari with no first places in any of the important races.

At the first race of the season at Daytona Beach, Ferraris entered were No. 34 a 275 LM for Ortega Merello/Gunn, a 250 LM (No. 81) for Gregory/Piper, a 275 LM (No. 12) for Vesteley/Pike/Ridgeway and a Ferrari Dino for Kolb/Rodriguez (No. 80).

The Kolb/Rodriguez Dino was out in the 2nd hour with a cracked head. Gregory/Piper crashed in the 4th hour and the Vesteley/Pike/Ridgeway car was retired at the 11th hour with faulty roadholding. The Ortega/Merello/Gunn Ferrari finished in 8th place some 81 laps behind the winning Porsche 907.

For the 12 Hours of Sebring, the Ortega/Merello/Gunn Ferrari was again entered but retired during the 2nd hour with clutch failure. There were no Ferraris at the finish.

At the Brands Hatch 500 miles, the Rodriguez/Pierpoint 275 LM Ferrari finished 5th and the Vesteley/Pike 275 LM 15th.

At the Watkins Glen 6 hours the best placed Ferrari was the Dino of Kolb/Rodriguez in 7th place winning their class; it was followed by the Grossman/Bucknum GTB4 in 9th place.

At the 1000 km of the Nurburgring, there were no Ferrari finishers, Skailes/Liddell retiring their 250 LM (No. 63) with loss of oil pressure. Christofferson/Wagstre had a fire in the carburetter of their Dino (No. 30).

In the Targa Florio, the only Ferrari to finish was No. 206 of Wangstre/Christofferson in 22nd place.

At the Monza 1000 km, the Ferrari of Vesteley/Ridgeway finished 20th and last.

There were no Ferraris listed at the finish of the 1000 km of Spa Francorchamps and the best effort by Ferrari at Le Mans during this lean year was the Piper/Attwood 275 LM (No. 21) which finished 7th. Chevalier/Lagier (No. 36) retired with a lack of oil, Ray/Haldi in the GTB (No. 17) retired with suspension problems, Vesteley/Pike in the 275 LM (No. 19) with gearbox trouble, Gregory/Kolb 275 LM (No. 14) crashed and Muller/Williams 275 LM went out with bearing troubles.

The 1969 Season - Daytona

The 24 Hours of Daytona was held on 2nd February 1969. The Ferrari factory was absent and NART fielded a Dino for Biscaldi/Kolb (No. 40) and other Ferraris entered were a GTB for Posey/Rodriguez (No. 41) and a 275 LM for Merello/Maglioli (No. 38). The Ferraris were never in contention; the Posey/Rodriguez GTB finished 23rd, the Merello/Maglioli 275 LM retired on lap 68 with transmission trouble and the Biscaldi/Kolb Dino retired on lap 152 with a broken cylinder head gasket.

Sebring

The 12 Hours of Sebring was held on 22nd March 1969. The Ferrari factory sent one 312 P based on the Formula 1 V12 car for Amon and Andretti (No. 25). Chinetti had been promised a second car but it did not materialize, so Chinetti entered a modified P3 under the NART banner, this was driven by Rodriguez and Parsons (No. 26). A 2-litre Dino was also entered for Rodriguez/Kolb (No. 37).

At the start the 312 P came round in 7th

place. Attrition to the front runners let the Ferrari up into 1st place at about quarter distance but Amon spun passing a slower car.

At half distance the Mitter/Schutz 908 Porsche led with Amon's Ferrari 2nd but Amon ran into some debris on the track and had to pit for two minutes to make repairs.

The Ferrari regained the lead but pitted again for further repair because of overheating. As a result of this the Ickx/Oliver Ford GT 40 took the lead and won with Amon/Andretti in 2nd place one lap behind. Rodriguez/Kolb in the Dino finished 9th and the Rodriguez/Parsons Ferrari retired at the 10th hour with gearshift failure.

The Targa Florio was held on 4th May 1969 but it was without any entries from Ferrari.

Nurburgring

The ADAC 1000 km race at the Nurburgring was held on 1st June 1969. The Ferrari factory entered Amon and Rodriguez with a Ferrari 312 P (No. 7) with Walton/deCardanet (No. 30) and Wangstre/Christofferson (No. 28) in Dinos.

During practice it was a battle between Amon's Ferrari and the Porsche of Siffert, the latter coming out on top by 0.1 sec.

During the race Amon set a new lap record at 105,69 m p h but retired on lap 28 with electrical trouble. The Wangstre/Christofferson Dino was out on lap 3 with engine trouble and the Walton/deCardanet car out on lap 12 with differential problems.

BOAC 500

Ferrari entered a single 312 P for the BOAC 500 at Brands Hatch for Amon/Rodriguez (No. 60).

During the first practice session Amon set the fastest lap at 1 min. 30.0 secs. but on the Saturday practice Siffert set a time of 1 min. 28.8 secs. with the Porsche.

The race was held under cold and windy conditions and Amon took the lead from the Porsche. After 4 laps Siffert pulled ahead with his Porsche and increased his lead. After 40 minutes Amon's Ferrari had a flat tyre which left the Porsches 1, 2, 3 and the lead Porsche with 2 laps advantage over the Ferrari, at half distance after the sun had come out.

During the 4th hour the Ferrari was back up in 2nd place but over three laps behind the leader.

With one hour left Amon had problems getting full throttle and the Schutz Porsche gained on the Ferrari to pass the Maranello car with 20 minutes left to go. The Ferrari finished in 4th place.

Poor luck at Le Mans

The 1969 Le Mans 24 Hour race was held on June 15th. Two Group 6 type 312 P Coupes were entered by Ferrari for Amon/Schetty (No. 19) and Rodriguez/Piper (No. 18). A privately owned 250 LM (No. 17) was entered for Zeccoli/Rodriguez (no relation of Pedro) and a private 275 GTB (No. 59) was entered for Rey/Haldi.

The Porsches were fastest in practice with the two factory Ferraris 5th and 6th fastest.

On the first lap a privately owned Porsche crashed at White House and caught fire, the burning fuel tank of this car became wedged under Amon's Ferrari. The Ferrari in turn caught fire and Amon was forced to bail out.

Rodriguez/Piper retired the 2nd 312 P during the 16th hour with a broken gearbox after being no higher than 8th. The Rey/Haldi 275 GTB was disqualified during the 6th hour. The only Ferrari to finish was the 250 LM of Zeccoli/Rodriguez which ended up in 8th place.

Tyre trouble at Monza

At Monza for the 1000 km, Ferrari sent two 312 Ps for Amon/Andretti and Rodriguez/Schetty.

Amon set the fastest practice lap at 2 min. 48.2 secs. with Siffert's Porsche at 2 min. 48.7 secs. and Rodriguez/Schetty 3rd fastest at 2 min. 50.6 secs.

The Porsche/Ferrari battle began at the start. Andretti led with Siffert 2nd and Rodriguez 3rd, the trio pulling away from the rest of the field. Siffert used slipstreaming tactics to pass Andretti but Rodriguez set a new lap record of 2 min. 48.1 secs. to take the lead. Andretti hounded the 2nd place Porsche. Then Andretti headed for the pits with a flat tyre.

At quarter distance the regular pit stops began and Rodriguez turned his Ferrari over to

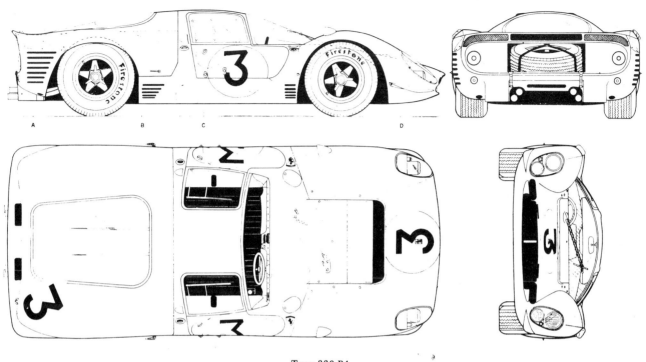

Type 330 P4

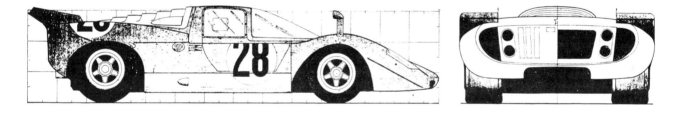

Ferrari 512 S

Type 512 S

Schetty. Schetty led the Porsche with Andretti again coming up fast but, 10 laps after taking over, Schetty pitted with a damaged tyre. This was reportedly due to a faulty set of tyres. The Schetty Ferrari fell to 4th but Andretti took over the lead. Andretti pitted to have Amon take over and immediately left for the USAC race in America.

Amon lasted only 1½ laps more before the Ferrari engine broke.

At half distance the Rodriguez/Schetti Ferrari was falling behind the leading Porsche and on lap 60 it was all over for Maranello when Rodriguez had a flat tyre and spun at the Parabolica. Repairs were made and the car continued but the damage allowed air into the tail section which blew off causing an accident that destroyed the car, fortunately without damage to the driver.

A 2nd place at Spa

The Spa 1000 km was held a week after the Targa Florio. Ferrari entered only one 312 P and, as Amon was ill, the drivers were Rodriguez/Piper.

It rained all during practice and the Ferrari recorded 5th fastest practice time at 3 min. 56.3 secs. compared to Siffert's 917 Porsche time of 3 min. 41.9 secs.

Siffert led from the start using a 908 Porsche instead of the 917, Rodriguez followed in 2nd place. On lap 8 Rodriguez was involved in a collision with a slower car forcing the Ferrari to pit and inspect the damage. When the Ferrari returned to the race it was in 3rd place. Unfortunately Piper was not as fast as Rodriguez and the Ferrari fell behind.

With only 8 laps left of the 71, Siffert held almost a lap lead over the Ferrari. The Ferrari had to be content with 2nd place. A 275 GTB entered by Rey/Berney was the only other Ferrari in the race and finished 14th.

The Austrian Grand Prix was held without any Ferrari entries. The same situation took place at Watkins Glen for the 6 hour race. It was altogether a poor season for Ferrari both in Formula 1 and the Manufacturer's Championship.

The 1969 312 P Ferraris were nothing more than Formula 1 cars with sports car bodywork.

The engines were the same as in the Formula 1 car with Lucas fuel injection in the V of the block and the exhaust piping on the outside of the block. The heads had four valves per cylinder. Power output was quoted at 420 b h p at 9,800 r p m with a bore and stroke of 77 x 53.5 mm and a cubic capacity of 2989.6-cc. cubic capacity of 2989.6-cc.

The chassis was of welded steel tubing enclosed in stressed panels with fuel being carried in side sponsons. The suspension was the same as the Formula 1 car except that the front springs were outboard because of the fully enclosed body.

The 1970 Season - The 512S at Daytona

The 24 Hours of Daytona was held on 31st January 1970. Ferrari entered their 512S types for Giunti/Vaccarella (No. 26), Ickx/Schetty (No. 27) and Andretti/Merzario (No. 28). The Squadra Picchio Rosso entered Manfredini/Moretti with a 512S (No. 30).

The Ferraris were new and were barely finished in time due to labour problems. The FIA had homologated the 512 to compete, having seen enough at the Ferrari factory to convince them despite the fact that 25 cars had not been completed at that time.

The 512 engine differed considerably from the previous 330 series of sports prototypes. However, the 60 degree V12 layout was retained, having a bore and stroke of 87 x 70 mm (3.42 x 2.75 in.), giving a total displacement 4993.5cc. The cylinder heads retained a four-valve per cylinder arrangement and Lucas high-pressure fuel injection. Rated output of the 512S engine was 550 b h p at 8,500 r p m, with a maximum torque 371 lb ft at 5,500 r p m. Unlike the 330s, only one distributor was fitted, a Marelli with the 'Dinoplex' transistor pack, now familiar because of its application to Ferrari and Dino GT cars.

Lubrication of the 512 powerplant was dry sump, and two cooling circuits for each cylinder bank coupled to side radiators. The coolant systems were pressurized to between 28 and 31 lb in². A triple-plate Borg and Beck clutch was coupled to a 5-speed ZF gearbox.

Suspension was conventional independent all around, with outboard Girling disc brakes on all wheels. Springing was provided for by Koni spring/shock units.

Practice showed that the aerodynamics of the cars was not right and it caused many problems.

Luigi Chinetti's NART team had a 512S for Gurney/Parsons (No. 25) and had the two 312 Ps for Posey/Perkins (No. 24) and Adamowicz/Piper (No. 23).

Other Ferraris entered were Young/Luigi Chinetti Jr. by NART in a 275 LM (No. 21) Cluxton/Tatum in a GTB/4 by NART and Bucknum/Pickett in a 365 GTB.

At the start, Andretti in the Ferrari and Siffert's Porsche were side by side but the Porsche led into the first corner followed by Rodriguez and Andretti in 3rd place with Gurney's Ferrari following in 4th.

After the 2nd stops for driver changes, Giunti's 512A hit the wall and broke a rear suspension. The car was worked on for over two hours in the pits but it was found to be impossible to repair.

After darkness fell Andretti was black flagged as his rear lights were not working. Ickx had a tyre deflate. His car hit the wall and was forced to retire. Ickx was then put in the No. 28 car with Andretti in place of Merzario.

At midnight, Gurney's 512S lost his 4th place to Brabham's Matra and Andretti lost 16 minutes in the pits to have the front brake discs replaced. The Gurney/Parsons Ferrari collided with the Squadra Picchio Rosso 512S, repairs were made but the car fell further back. In the morning, the Porsche had a lead of 13 laps over the Andretti/Ickx Ferrari but the 3rd place Porsche was then 39 laps behind the 2nd place Ferrari. Because of this the Ferrari was able to make a 45 minute stop to weld a rear chassis member and make another stop and still retain its 2nd place.

The Rodriguez Porsche in the meantime built up a lead of 51 laps over the Ferrari. Siffert's Porsche was beginning to catch the Ferrari and swept by it to unlap itself. When the Ferrari made its last pit stop it held only 55 seconds lead over the Porsche with 34 minutes remaining to go in the race. Siffert was throwing the Porsche around with great verve, turning a lap in 1 min. 48.7 secs. He closed the gap and with two laps to go passed the Ferrari.

Andretti/Ickx were 3rd, Posey/Perkins were 4th winning the Group 6 prototype category, Adamowicz/Piper were 5th in the second 312 P and Young/Chinetti took 7th in the 275 LM. Bucknum/Pickett retired on lap 142 with cooling system problems and Cluxtun/Tatum retired on lap 308 with the same problem.

Sebring

The Sebring 12 Hours was held on 21st March 1970. Ferrari entered four cars, one of which was reserved for NART. The factory 512Ss were to be driven by Andretti/Merzario (No. 19) Ickx/Schetty (No. 20) and Giunti/Vaccarella (No. 21). The NART car was driven by Posey/Bucknum (No. 24).

All four Ferraris had been modified in respect to the Daytona configurations with a stronger chassis, different aerodynamics and lightened by about 80 lb. The engines with an updated fuel injection system were reputed to give 40 more b h p.

NART also entered their two 312 Ps for Parkes/Parsons (No. 22) and Adamowicz/Luigi Chinetti Jr. (No. 23).

On the first day of practice Siffert's Porsche was fastest at 2 min. 34.47 secs. but on the Friday's practice Andretti took the pole position at 2 min. 33.5 secs.

At the start it was Andretti who took the lead from Siffert the two of them setting a fast pace.

Despite the fact that Siffert set a new lap record, Andretti stayed ahead. After 47 minutes Andretti pitted for fuel and when Siffert also pitted for fuel, some seven minutes later, his crew proved to be much faster than the Ferrari crew. After this Porsches were in 1st, 2nd and 3rd places with the Ickx/Schetty Ferrari 4th but the lead Porsche pitted and another Porsche had a flat tyre. Ickx/Schetty held 2nd place as a result of this with Andretti charging from behind.

At quarter distance the Giunti/Vaccarella car moved up to 3rd and as the leading Porsche limped into the pits a wheel fell off.

At half distance the Ferraris were in fine shape, Andretti/Merzario led, followed by Vaccarella/Giunti and Ickx/Schetty. The Adamowicz/Chinetti car was out on lap 56 while the Parkes/Parsons prototype held 5th. Luigi Chinetti Sr retired the NART 512S as it had been damaged in a crash and had fuel feed troubles.

With Ferraris seeming invinciple, the troubles began. The engine in the Ickx/Schetty car gave out on lap 151 and with 4 hours left in the race, the Giunti/Vaccarella car blew a tyre and the run to the pits on the rim damaged the suspension causing a 24 minute pit stop for repairs.

With just 1 hour and 20 minutes to go, the Andretti/Merzario Ferrari slowed with the gearbox locked in one gear. The gearbox then seized and that was it for the lead Ferrari. Ing. Forghieri put Andretti in the Giunti/Vaccarella car when it came in to refuel but it seemed a hopeless task. However, Andretti was on tremendous form and began to cut 5 seconds a lap off the 2nd place Porsche to pass it with 22 minutes left in the race.

The lead Porsche lost 8 minutes in the pits with a broken hub stud and Andretti sailed into the lead winning by 23.8 seconds from the Porsche 908. Andretti/Vaccarella and Giunti had covered 1,289.6 miles at an average of 107.029 m p h. Parkes/Parsons brought the 312 P home in 6th place eight laps behind the winner.

Brands Hatch

The BOAC 1000 kilometres was held at Brands Hatch on 12th April 1970. The factory Ferraris were 512Ss entered for Ickx/Oliver and Amon/Merzario. The Filipinetti 512S was entered for Parkes/Muller and a fourth car was entered for Williams/Loos but it was a non starter.

Amon set the fastest lap in practice of 1 min. 28.6 secs., Siffert's Porsche was next and Ickx Ferrari and Elford's Porsche with equal time at 1 min. 28.8 secs. The Muller/Parkes Ferrari recorded 1 min. 33.8 secs.

At the start, Elford's Porsche took the lead from Ickx' Ferrari with Amon 4th. After 2 laps Ickx pushed the Ferrari into the lead but because of the rain Ickx had to pit to have his windshield wipers adjusted. The Elford Porsche thus regained the lead but was in turn passed by Amon's Ferrari on lap 17. On lap 20 Rodriguez pushed his Porsche by Amon. Amon touched a slower car and had a flat tyre. Ickx had to stop twice more to attend to his windshield wipers, followed by two more stops with his ignition misbehaving because of the rain.

After the first hour, the best placed Ferrari was Amon in 6th place. The rain stopped but the track remained wet and the lead Porsche had a six-lap lead over the Amon/Merzario Ferrari. Amon/Merzario moved up to 3rd place but due to a defective fuel pump the Ferrari pitted three times in the last hour finally finishing 5th with Ickx/Oliver 8th and Muller/Parkes 13th.

Monza

The 1000 km of Monza was held on 25th April 1970. Ferrari entered three factory 512Ss for Giunti/Vaccarella, Amon/Merzario and Surtees/Schetty, Surtees replacing the injured Ickx.

In practice the Siffert Porsche was fastest at 1 min. 25.31 secs., with Amon/Merzario 2nd fastest at 1 min. 25.78 secs., Giunti/Vaccarella were 4th fastest at 1 min. 26.19 secs. and Surtees/Schetty 6th fastest at 1 min. 26.69 secs.

Scuderia Filipinetti entered a 512S for Parkes/Muller and the Scuderia Picchio Rosso entered a 512S for Moretti/Manfredini.

Giunti took the lead at the start from the Porsches of Rodriguez, Siffert and Elford. Amon was 5th and Surtees 6th. There was a continuous changing of places amongst the first group with Amon and Surtees following up. Elford's Porsche began to pull away while Giunti and Rodriguez duelled for second place with Amon in 4th and Surtees 5th.

After the pit stops, the Elford Porsche led the Rodriguez Porsche with Vaccarella 3rd having taken over from Giunti. Schetty was in 5th after taking over from Surtees and Merzario who took over from Amon in 6th place.

When the second driver switch took place Giunti was 3rd, about 20 seconds behind the No. 2 Porsche and as one of the Porsches retired the Ferrari moved into second place and began to chase the leader.

With just over one hour to go, the Ferrari was 10 seconds behind the leader but then there was another series of pit stops coming up.

As Amon stopped to hand over to Merzario he was asked to take over the Giunti car in a last ditch effort to beat the Porsches but when

Cutaway of the Type 512 S

Amon pressed the starter the car burst into flames. A lap was lost in the confusion while the flames were put out and the car cleaned up.

Amon rejoined the race and fought a neck-and-neck battle with Rodriguez but it was impossible to make up the lost lap. The Giunti/Vaccarella/Amon Ferrari finished 2nd, Surtees/Schetty were 3rd, Amon/Merzario 4th and the private entry of Parkes/Muller 8th and the Moretti/Manfredini Ferrari 9th.

Francorchamps

The Spa 1000 km was held at Francorchamps on 17th May 1970. Ferrari entered three factory 512Ss for Ickx/Surtees, Giunti/Vaccarella and Merzario/Schetty. The Belgian Ecurie Francorchamps entered a new 512S for de Fierlant/Bell.

Despite the fact that the race was started on a wet track it was the fastest road race in the history of European racing with the winning Siffert/Redman Porsche averaging 149.42 m p h and the Rodriguez Porsche setting the fastest lap at 160.53 m p h.

In practice Rodriguez was fastest at 3 min. 19.8 secs., Ickx/Surtees were 3rd fastest at 3 min. 24.4 secs., Giunti/Vaccarella were 5th fastest at 3 min. 30.2 secs., de Fierlant/Bell 7th at 3 min. 31.6 secs., and Merzario/Schetty 9th at 3 min. 35.4 secs.

At the start Siffert and Rodriguez led from Ickx' Ferrari and after a gap Giunti followed. The lead three opened up a 30 second lead over the rest in three laps. Rodriguez passed Siffert but the Ferrari was constantly between them. After an hour the pit stop was made and after the stops Rodriguez held a 10 second lead over Ickx. Rodriguez increased this to 20 seconds but had trouble and Ickx was left in the lead with a 20 second advantage over Siffert.

With the driver change Surtees took over from Ickx and maintained the lead but fluctuating oil pressure caused him to slow and he lost the lead to the Siffert/Redman Porsche.

Bell's Ferrari caught fire when he pressed the starter and the driver was trapped inside for a while. Despite some burns Bell continued to race.

The lead Porsche was now 3 minutes ahead and it began to rain again so Ferrari's hopes were ended. Ickx/Surtees finished 2nd, Giunti/

Vacarella 4th, Merzario/Schetty 7th and Bell/de Fierlant 8th.

Nurburgring

The ADAC 1000 km race was held on 31st May 1970 at the Nurburgring. Only three Ferrari 512S were entered. No. 55 for Surtees/Vaccarella, No. 57 for Giunti/Merzario and No. 58 for Muller/Parkes. The latter car was entered by Scuderia Filipinetti.

Ickx and Schetty were supposed to drive but Ickx damaged his wrist slipping on some stairs and Schetty crashed their car in practice when it aquaplaned. The car was beyond repair for the race.

Fastest lap in practice was by Siffert's Porsche at 7 min. 43.3 secs. and Surtees was fastest Ferrari at 7 min. 57.1 secs. Rodriguez' Porsche jumped into the lead at the flag with Giunti moving up fast into 2nd place on the first lap. Rodriguez led the Ferrari by 14 seconds the first time round with Surtees 4th.

On the second lap the Porsche led by 19 seconds with Siffert's Porsche now second, ahead of Giunti and Surtees. The Giunti/Merzario Ferrari retired almost immediately with fuel injection problems.

With the pit stops, the Ferrari fell behind and at 17 laps the highest placed Maranello car was Parkes/Muller in 4th. The Surtees/Vaccarella Ferrari regained 4th place but lost it again at a fuel stop. With Surtees back at the wheel the car moved up and regained 4th and then passed the Filipinetti Ferrari to take 3rd place where they finished one lap behind the winning Porsche with Parkes/Muller in 4th place.

Targa Florio

The Targa Florio was held on 3rd May 1970. Ferrari sent a 512S for Vaccarella/Giunti (No. 6) and Scuderia Filipinetti entered another 512 for Muller/Parkes (No. 4). Dinos were entered by private owners LoPiccolo/Calascibetta (No. 58) and 'Cinno'/Barbuscia (No. 64).

Because of the rain, the start was delayed from 8.30 am to 9.15 am and the leaders were Muller and Vaccarella who found the road strewn with mud.

On the first lap, Siffert's Porsche led from Vaccarella but in time Larrousse led in a Porsche with Vaccarella's Ferrari in 7th place.

On lap 2 Vaccarella handed over to Giunti still

in 7th place after refuelling. Giunti took the lead during the multiple stops by the opposition to refuel. During the 2nd refuelling stop Vaccarella was out of the pits 4 seconds faster than the Porsche of Siffert to hold 3rd place on actual time, by lap 5 Vaccarella had the overall lead on the road about 41 seconds behind Rodriguez who was leading on time.

By the time Vaccarella pulled into the pits to hand over to Giunti he was in the lead both on the road and on time with a 33-second lead.

Parkes and Muller were running in 8th with the Filipinetti 512. Redman with the Porsche put the German car back into the lead but Giunti's Ferrari was close behind. When Vaccarella took over the car he remained in close contact with the Porsche until he hit a rock and bent the Ferrari's front suspension. Giunti did his best on the last lap with the crippled Ferrari and finished 3rd behind the Porsches.

Le Mans

The 1970 24 Hours of Le Mans was held on June 14th. A host of Ferraris were entered, four factory 512S coupes, three Scuderia Filipinetti 512S and a 512S from the Spanish Escuderia Montjuich as well as a 312 P from NART for Adamowicz/Parsons (No. 57).

The factory cars were driven by Ickx/Schetty (No. 5), Vaccarella/Giunti (No. 6), Regazzoni/ Merzario (No. 8), Bell/Peterson (No. 7). The Filipinetti entries were Parkes/Muller (No. 15), Bonnier/Wisell (No. 14) and Manfredini/Moretti (No. 16). The first two were true Filipinetti cars with long tails and the 3rd was the Squadra Picchio Rosso car entered under the Swiss colours of Filipinetti.

The Ecurie National Belge car (No. 12) was driven by de Fierlant/Walker and the NART cars (No. 11) by Posey/Bucknum and (No. 10) by Kelleners/Loos. The Spanish 512S was in the hands of Juncadella/Fernandez (No. 9).

The Ferraris were fastest in practice. Vaccarella lapped in 3 min. 20 secs. on the first day of practice and 3 min. 20.6 secs. on the second day.

At the start, the Porsches of Elford, Siffert and Rodriguez held the first three places but Merzario and Vaccarella were 4th and 5th for Ferrari.

After 27 minutes of racing, Vaccarella came into the pits with a connecting rod bearing seized. Merzario moved up into 3rd place but the going was tricky with a drizzle wetting the track.

During the third hour the Ferrari challenge was greatly diminished with a multiple accident happening at the Indianapolis corner. Wisell had slowed up as oil covered his windshield. Bell swerved to avoid him, Regazzoni tried to dodge between but he hit Wisell and the Parkes Ferrari ran into the horde of spinning Ferraris. Parkes made it to the pits to retire but the other three Ferraris remained where they were, out of action. The rain continued, but started to diminish after four hours.

Five Porsches now held the first five positions followed by the Ickx/Schetty 512S in 6th and the Manfredini/Moretti 512S in 9th.

The Ickx/Schetty car moved up to third after 6 hours of racing but the Kelleners/Loos 512S was retired because it would not handle properly on the wet track.

Ickx/Schetty moved up to 2nd place. At 1.45 am Ickx spun at the Ford chicane and killed a marshal. The Ferrari caught fire but Ickx was not injured; nevertheless the Ferrari challenge was over. The Spanish Ferrari retired at the 10th hour with a split gearbox and at the 12th hour the Manfredini/Moretti 512S was out with a broken gearbox.

With four hours left Porsches were in the first three places with Posey/Bucknum in the NART Ferrari in 4th place and the Belgian Ferrari in 5th place. The Ferraris held their places until the end of the race. The Parsons/Adamowicz 312 P was actually 10th but was not classified as it had not completed the minimum allotted distance.

Watkins Glen

The Watkins Glen 6 Hours was held on 11th July 1970. There were four Ferrari 512Ss entered, two factory cars and two private entries. The factory cars were allocated to Andretti/Giunti and Ickx/Schetty.

At the start Andretti in the Ferrari and Siffert in the Porsche were side by side with the Ferrari pulling away from the rest of the field. Ickx'

Ferrari battled with the Porsches in the second group.

The Andretti Ferrari began to suffer from vapour lock and before long the Porsches were in command. The Ferrari lost two laps trying to cure the trouble and Schetty in the second factory Ferrari spun during a brief rainstorm. As a result of this the Andretti/Giunti Ferrari finished 3rd and the Ickx/Schetty car 5th.

Kyalami

The last race that Ferrari participated in during the 1970 season was the 9 Hours of Kyalami. It was a non championship event but it gave Ferrari a significant victory. Ferrari sent one of the modified 512s for Ickx/Giunti (No. 4) and the only other Ferrari to race was the Bell/de Fierlant 512S (No. 3).

In practice Ickx set fastest lap at 1 min. 22.4 secs. with Giunti only fractions slower. The Bell/de Fierlant Ferrari recorded 1 min. 24.8 secs. Major opposition was from two 917 Porsches.

Ickx jumped the flag and was off into the lead on the road although he was penalized. By the second lap he had a 5 second lead over Siffert's Porsche with the private Ferrari in 4th place.

After half an hour of racing Ickx' lead extended to 18 seconds but on the first pit stop the Porsche took the lead. Giunti took over and by 4 pm had increased the Ferrari's lead on the road by over one lap, this meant that he had recovered the time lost by the penalty and he was actually in the lead of the race. Giunti was timed at 189.39 m p h down the straight, this being the fastest time of day. The Ferrari was having no difficulty at all in handling the Porsches. With 90 minutes left, Ickx extended the Ferrari's lead to two laps and he won the event covering 370 laps (943.5 miles) at an average of 104.833 m p h. Bell/de Fierlant finished 6th after experiencing some trouble.

So ended the season with Ferrari having been soundly beaten for the Manufacturer's Championship by Porsche only to show a marked superiority over the Porsches in the last event of the season.

The last Championship event of 1970

The Osterreichring 1000 km was held on 11th October 1970, it was the last of the 1970 championship events. Ferrari sent just one factory 512 for Ickx/Giunti. This was a new car that had been seen on test at Imola and Modena. It had a completely revised body shape which improved aerodynamics considerably and was the first of the 512Ms. At Imola it had shown itself to be about 2 seconds faster than the 512S. The only other Ferrari entered in the Austrian event was the 512S for Loos/Pesch.

In practice the Ferrari had fuel feed problems and only completed two or three laps intermittently. Nevertheless, Ickx was able to record 1 min. 40.75 secs. until being fractionally beaten for the pole by the Rodriguez Porsche.

At the start Ickx led the Porsches with the privately entered Ferrari in 11th place.

Ickx was in great form with the new Ferrari and completely ran away from the Porsches, setting a new lap record in the process at 1 min. 40.0 secs. When he pitted for fuel he was 25 seconds ahead of the 2nd-place Porsche. Loos/Pesch were suffering from fuel feed problems while Ickx continued to increase his lead. Suddenly the Ferrari stopped and Ickx came in on foot for a new battery. He took one back with him to the car and restarted with a nine-lap deficit and pitted for Giunti to take over but the latter retired shortly afterwards with a defective alternator.

The Loos/Pesch Ferrari struggled on to finish 7th.

The 1971 Season - Type 312P at Buenos Aires

The first race of the 1971 Manufacturer's Championship series was held at Buenos Aires on January 10th. Ferrari debuted the new 312 P with the flat 12 cylinder engine. It had been tested extensively at Modena, Paul Ricard and Kyalami and had a 2,000 kilometre testing mileage. Peter Schetty, the new Ferrari team manager, however, stated that the car was not yet perfect. The 312 P was driven by Giunti/Merzario (No. 24). Other Ferraris entered were Scuderia Filipinetti with a 512M for Parkes/Bonnier but this car was crashed in un-

263

official practice by Peterson and required a great deal of work to make it raceworthy.

Other Ferraris were the 512S for Juncadella/Pairetti from the Escuderia Montjuich, the NART 512S for Posey/Veiga/di Palma and the Belgian entry of de Fierlant/Gosselin.

Giunti recorded 1 min. 52.74 secs. which stood as fastest lap for a long time in practice but was bettered by Rodriguez' Porsche at the last minute with a time of 1 min. 52.70 secs.

At the fall of the flag, Giunti was off first in the 312 P and only the Porsche's superior power allowed it to get by on the straight. Siffert, in the 2nd Porsche, took six laps to get by the flying Ferrari. Finally, the greater capacity of the Porsches told and Giunti held 3rd, 10 seconds behind.

On the 30th lap Giunti moved over to lap Parkes' Ferrari and crashed into the back end of the out-of-fuel Matra that was being pushed by Beltoise along the track. The Ferrari caught fire and Giunti was fatally injured. This cast a pall over the event. Parkes' was the only other Ferrari in contention but he lost two laps in the pits when troubled by wheel vibration. Juncadella/Pairetti were 5th, De Fierlant/Gosselin 6th, Bonnier/Parkes 7th, and Posey/di Palma/Veiga 8th.

Daytona

The 1971 24 Hours of Daytona was held on January 31st; cars entered were 512Ms for Donohue/Hobbs by the Penske team (No. 6), Posey/Revson by NART (No. 22) and Young/Gregory by Young American (No. 20). 512Ss were entered for Bucknum/Adamowicz (No. 23), the Belgian Swaters entered a 512S (No. 26) for De Fierlant/Gosselin and the Spaniard Juncadella entered a car for himself and Merzario (No. 28). NART also entered their modified 312 P for Luigi Chinetti Jr/Veiga.

During practice the Donohue/Hobbs Ferrari set fastest lap at 1 min. 42.42 secs., 1.26 seconds faster than the Rodriguez/Oliver Gulf Porsche. Posey and Revson were in the second row of the grid with 1 min. 43.95 secs.

Donohue jumped away from the rolling start and led the Rodriguez Porsche by two seconds on the 1st lap. On the 13th lap Rodriguez passed the Ferrari only to be repassed by Donohue who

then moved into a 1.5 second lead. Revson's Ferrari was black flagged for lack of brake lights. Gregory's Ferrari broke a connecting rod and Merzario pulled in with low oil pressure.

After 30 laps both Donohue and Rodriguez pitted for fuel and the Ferrari regained the race 8 seconds ahead of the Porsche. Siffert's Porsche in the meantime had taken over the lead. When the Swiss driver pitted, Donohue regained his lead. Donohue pitted again for a change of both rear wheels and had trouble restarting; this cost the Ferrari 44 seconds which resulted in the two Porsches running 1st and 2nd. Donohue closed the gap and regained 2nd place and when Siffert pitted again he retook the lead.

Donohue was then forced into the pits with electrical problems and it took 5 minutes to trace and attempt to fix a faulty alternator. It was not permitted to change alternators and the Ferrari was forced to stop a second time with the same problem this time losing 8 minutes. After three hours the Donohue/Hobbs car held 3rd place, four laps down on the leading Porsche with the Gosselin/De Fierlant Ferrari 4th.

Just before midnight Elford's Porsche burst a tyre and as Donohue slowed for him, a Porsche ran into the Ferrari. The repairs took until 3 am when the Ferrari rejoined the race, incredibly, still in 4th place but some 53 laps behind.

At three-quarters distance the NART Ferrari of Bucknum/Revson was second but also some 43 laps behind the leading Porsche having lost some of its rear bodywork. The Rodriguez Porsche had to pit with a jammed gearbox, the gearbox having to be rebuilt. It took the 2nd place Ferrari almost an hour to take the lead.

However, the Porsche was back in and 45 minutes later overhauled the Ferrari. With 25 minutes to go Donohue/Hobbs had to stop for a fuel pump change dropping it to third. The Porsche won by 13 laps over the Bucknum Ferrari. Hobbs and Donohue were third, Chinetti/Veiga 4th and Donohue/Hobbs were credited with fastest lap at 1 min. 41.25 secs.

Sebring

The 1971 12 Hours of Sebring was held on March 20th and Ferraris 512s were entered for Donohue/Hobbs (No. 6); Young/Gregory (No.

(Top) The prototype 312 P of 1969. It was fitted with a V12 engine derived from the Formula 1 car of that period
(Middle) The V12 engine of the prototype 312 P
(Bottom) The Adamowicz/Piper 312 P coupe entered by NART for the 1970 Daytona 24 Hours. The car was placed 5th. It was fitted with the V12 engine being a version of the 1969 312 P

(Top) NART rebodied version of the V12 Type 312 P at Daytona 1971
(Middle) Squadra Picchio Rosso's 512 S at Daytona 1970. This was an early car driven by Manfredini/Moretti. It crashed
(Bottom Left) Chuck Parsons watched Dan Gurney as he prepares to practice for the 1970 Daytona race in the NART 512 S
(Bottom Right) The Ferrari Type 312 P at Buenos Aires 1971

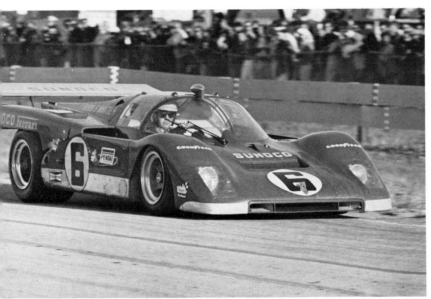

(*Top*) Mike Parkes driving the 512 S at Buenos Aires 1971
(*Middle*) Mark Donohue at Sebring 1971, in the Penske/
White Ferrari 512 M. This car was deemed the best prepared 512 by Ing. Forghieri. When running it was the equal
of the 917 Porsches
(*Bottom Left*) The Scuderia Filipinetti 512 M, Le Mans
1971
(*Bottom Right*) 1971 Sebring. The Ickx/Andretti 312 P
retired with transmission trouble after enjoying a four lap
lead

(*Top*) 1971 1000 Kms Nurburgring. The Ickx/Regazzoni 312 P. Here, in the lead
(*Middle*) Le Mans 1973. The Merzario/ Pace Ferrari 312 P finished 2nd, six laps down to the winning Matra
(*Bottom Left*) Ferrari 312 P ready for the Monza 1000 Km. 24 April 1972
(*Bottom Right*) 1973 Ferrari 312 P

(*Top Left*) 'Ferrari 212 Inter - Coupe Vignale'
(*Top Right*) Type 195 Inter 2.3 litre with Sperleggera body
(*Middle*) Type 166 Inter convertible touring car with body by Stabilimenti Farina
(*Bottom Left*) Ferrari 166 (Inter chassis) with the body by Carrozzeria Touring
(*Bottom Right*) A Type 166 MM with a special body by Franco Reggiani built for the Marzotto Brothers

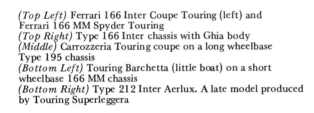

(Top Left) Ferrari 166 Inter Coupe Touring (left) and
Ferrari 166 MM Spyder Touring
(Top Right) Type 166 Inter chassis with Ghia body
(Middle) Carrozzeria Touring coupe on a long wheelbase
Type 195 chassis
(Bottom Left) Touring Barchetta (little boat) on a short
wheelbase 166 MM chassis
(Bottom Right) Type 212 Inter Aerlux. A late model produced
by Touring Superleggera

(Top Left) A very early Vignale bodied 340 America
(Top Right) The 2.5 litre 212 Inter chassis
(Middle Left) The 2.5 litre 212 Inter engine
(Middle Right) An early Vignale coupe on an Inter chassis
(Bottom) The ex Umberto Marzotto 212 Export of 1951.
Chassis No. 0090E

(Top Left) 1951 Ghia bodied 212 Inter
(Middle) Tony Parravano's 340 America coupe
(Bottom Left) A Type 195 with Vignale body
(Bottom Right) Giovanni Michelotti designed Vignale built coupe
on an early 340 America chassis No. 0132A

(Top Left) 1952 Type 212 Export Vignale
(Top Right) 1952 Type 212 Inter Vignale
(Middle) 1951 Vignale bodied 212 Export No. 0106E
(Bottom) Gianni Agnelli purchased this Type 195 Inter bodied by Vignale

(*Top Left*) Carrozzeria Ghia built Type 212 Europa displayed
at the Paris Show 1952
(*Top Right*) Vignale 1952 225 Inter
(*Middle*) The unfamiliar front of the 212 Inter Vignale 1952
(*Bottom*) A 1952 Vignale effort showing the familiar
Michelotti intake ducts either side of the grille

(Top Left) A 2 + 2 design by Michelotti for Vignale
(Top Right) Pininfarina Ferrari 250 MM coupe 1953
(Upper Middle Left) Michelotti's design for Vignale to be called the 'Geneva Coupe'
(Lower Middle Left) Michelotti design for another Vignale Ferrari
(Bottom Left) 1952 Vignale Type 225 Sport
(Bottom Right) A special Vignale design for the proprietor of the famous Lily Ann Store in San Francisco

(*Top Left*) 1953 Pininfarina Type 342 America
(*Top Right*) 1953 Pininfarina Type 342 America drophead
(*Middle*) Pininfarina Type 375 MM Competition coupe 1953
(*Bottom*) 1954 Vignale Type 410 Superamerica

(Top) Displayed at Paris in 1954 was this Pininfarina design for a Type 375 America, No. 0456AM

(Middle) Ghia's unique creation on a Type 410 Superamerica chassis. It was itself incluenced by Chrysler's two styling projects, the Gilda and the Dart but had no influence on any subsequent Ferrari design

(Bottom Left) The predecessor of the GT Ferraris was the 250 Europa. This was powered by the Lampredi V12

(Bottom Right) 'Superfast 1'. Pininfarina's first luxury GT car based in the Type 410 SA chassis

(Top Left) Type 375 AM 1959 built for ex King Leopold of Belgium
(Top Right) 1955 Type 250 Europa Pininfarina
(Middle) The Pininfarina 375 AM built for Agnelli
(Bottom Left) 1955. The Vignale coupe for Princess Liliana de Rethy
(Bottom Right) 250 GT Pininfarina 1955

(Top Left) No. 0515GT Zagato bodied 250 GT 1956
(Top Right) 1957 250 GT Boano
(Middle) 250 GT 1956 Pininfarina shown at the Geneva Show
(Bottom) 1955 Type 375 America Pininfarina shown at the Turin Show

(Top Left) 250 GT Competition Berlinetta by Pininfarina 1955, Geneva Show
(Top Right) 1955 250 GT Pininfarina shown at the Paris Show
(Middle) Gendebien leads on the Rouen circuit during the 1958 Tour de France in the 250 GT. He built much of his and Ferrari's reputation in this event
(Bottom Left) Scaglietti lightweight 250 GT on the 1957 Tour de France, this is the Gendebien (right) and Bianchi car
(Bottom Right) Pininfarina designed, Scaglietti built, the 250 GT Tour de France

20); Revson/Savage (No. 22); Bucknum/Posey (No. 23) and Parsons/Weir (No. 26).

Luigi Chinetti Jr. and George Eaton shared the NART 312 P (No. 21) and Ickx and Andretti had the factory prototype 312 P (No. 25). Grossman and Cluxton entered a GTB/4 (No. 24).

The Penske 512 was of the M configuration and recorded fastest lap in practice, leading the race at the early stages. The Revson/Savage car was an M, the Bucknum/Posey and Parsons/Weir cars were of the S confirguration. The Gregory/Young 512 had M bodywork with an S engine.

The factory 312 P was brand new and led the race on several occasions before retiring with transmission trouble.

Donohue, despite a sprained and bandaged ankle, set fastest practice time at 2 min. 31.65 secs. (123.44 m p h) and second fastest was Andretti in the 312 P at 2 min. 32.47 secs.

Donohue took an immediate lead and by 50 miles had nearly five seconds lead over Siffert's Porsche with two more Porsches in 3rd and 4th, then the Andretti 312 P and Revson in the 512. Young crashed into the sandbank at the hairpin and the car overturned. Young was rescued by the course marshals and just as he got out, the car burst into flames. The 312 P took the lead while the Donohue Ferrari and the Rodriguez Porsche refuelled.

After 3 hours the 312 P led by 64.5 secs. over the Donohue Ferrari and the Rodriguez Porsche. After 4 hours the 312 P was a full lap ahead. Donohue and Rodriguez made contact through the hairpin, the Ferrari having its special refuelling system damaged in the process which cost the car 19 laps in the pits to have repaired.

By the time Donohue was back in the race the 312 P had retired with a broken transmission while holding a four-lap lead. The Bucknum/Posey Ferrari blew a tyre while passing the pits. Bucknum attempted to make for a full lap on the rim but the wheel collapsed and a hole was scraped in the engine which shed all of its oil.

Parsons/Weir retired with a damaged radiator and Revson/Savage with a broken transmission.

The Elford/Larousse Porsche won, Donohue/Hobbs finished 6th, Eaton/Chinetti 8th and the Grossman/Cluxton GTB/4 in 12th place.

The 1971 Targa Florio was held on May 16th but only one Ferrari was entered. This was a private entry for Verna/Cosentino with a V6 Dino (No. 38). It finished in 30th place covering 8 out of the 11 laps.

Brands Hatch

The BOAC 1000 km was held at Brands Hatch on 4th April 1971. Ferrari entered a 312 P for Ickx/Regazzoni. Two privately entered 512s modified to M specifications were entered by Herbert Muller Racing, for Muller/Herzog and the other by Escuderia Monjuich for Juncadella/Hobbs.

The standard to beat in practice was Amon's 1 min. 28.6 secs. set the previous year in a 512S.

On the Friday, the 312 P had fuel injection problems but on Saturday Regazzoni recorded 1 min. 27.4 secs. and Ickx 1 min. 28.0 secs. The Spanish Ferrari recorded 1 min. 31.6 secs. but was then crashed by Juncadella and much work had to be done to make it raceworthy.

Ickx took an immediate lead after the pace lap but on the opening laps the Ferrari was forced off the road by a spinning tail ender. Ickx pitted to have new body sections fitted which cost the car 6 laps in the pits. The 512Ms were running in the middle of the field and Ickx was back in 18th place. Muller moved the 512M from 11th to 4th after 50 laps and Regazzoni by dint of hard driving had the 312 P back up in 5th place right behind Muller. Ickx took over from Regazzoni and lapping at 1 min. 28 secs. moved the 312 P into 4th but the throttle began to jam and Ickx lost two more laps in the pits.

By lap 200, the 312 P was going strong again in 2nd place but the lead Alfa Romeo had four laps over the Ferrari. The Alfa Romeo won with Ickx/Regazzoni 2nd, Muller/Herzog were 4th and Juncadella/Hobbs 5th.

Monza

The Monza 1000 kilometre race was held on 15th April 1971. Ferrari tried to have the organizers build in chicanes as he thought the 312 P could not keep pace with the Porsches. However, when Regazzoni lapped the 312 P as fast as Elford's lap record with the Porsche, the original circuit was maintained.

Ferrari entered a lone 312 P for Ickx/Regazzoni, Herbert Muller had a 512 M for

Zeccoli/Moretti and another similar car for Muller/Herzog. The Escuderia Montjuich had their 512 M for Juncadella/Merzario. The Scuderia Filipinetti a 512 M for Manfredini/Gagliardi and a 512 S for Parkes/Bonnier.

Despite the rain in practice, Ickx was second fastest qualifier and Regazzoni third fastest.

Parkes jumped into the lead at the start. Muller was left behind when his battery refused to function.

After 4 laps, the Porsches established themselves in the lead. On the eighth lap a privately owned Porsche moved into the way of the Spanish Ferrari and in the resultant collision Ickx was involved and damaged the body of the 312 P as well as tearing off the left rear wheel. Parkes/Bonnier went out with a broken engine.

By 60 laps, the Moretti/Zeccoli Ferrari held 3rd place but suffered from clutch trouble and finished 8th while Muller/Herzog finished 6th.

Francorchamps

The Francorchamps 1000 kilometre was held at Spa on May 9th. The factory 312 P was entered for Ickx/Regazzoni while Filipinetti entered a 512 M for Manfredini/Gagliardi; Herbert Muller had a 512 M for himself and Herzog and a 512 S for Kocher/Wiesendanger.

The 312 P could not match the tremendous speeds of the Porsches on the Spa circuit. Ickx recorded 3 min. 22.2 secs. compared to the Porsche's best time of 3 min. 16.0 secs.

Rain threatened at the start and most of the cars were equipped with 'wet' tyres. However, just before the start the weather stabilized and there was a rush to change to 'dry' tyres. In the process of doing this, the Kocher/Wiesendanger Ferrari had its front hub threads damaged and the car was out of the race.

The Porsches leapt ahead and Ickx chased them from a hopeless 3rd place. Muller was 6th and Gagliardi 7th. The pit stops showed that the Ferrari would not have a fuel advantage over the Porsche and the race was set.

On lap 51 the Filipinetti 512 M broke a connecting rod and shortly thereafter Muller's car did the same. Regazzoni with the 312 P had a much slower competitor pull in front of him and in the resultant crash the right rear of the Ferrari was demolished. The 312 P was classified in 8th place although it was not running at the end.

Manfredini/Gagliardi were classified 13th and Muller/Herzog 15th neither of these teams being running at the finish.

Nurburgring

The ADAC 1000 km race was held at the Nurburgring on 29th-30th May 1971. Ferrari 512 Ms were entered for Loos/Pesch (No. 59); Muller/Herzog (No. 60) a 512S for Wiesendanger/Kocher (No. 61) and the Ickx/Regazzoni 312 P (No. 15).

Ickx astounded everyone with the 312 P by turning a time of 7 min. 36.1 secs. (111.976 m p h) during the Saturday practice. This was more than 3 m p h faster than Rodriguez 1970 lap record of 7 min. 40.8 secs. (111.85 m p h).

The 512s were unimpressive during practice.

Ickx took an immediate lead and set a new lap record of 7 min. 40.8 secs. (111.85 m p h) and at the end of five laps was 41 seconds ahead of his nearest opponent.

The 312 P dropped to 4th place while refuelling and then pitted again to take on water for its steaming radiator. This dropped Ickx to 6th place. However, Ickx worked his way back up to third and retook the lead when the others stopped to refuel. Regazzoni took over and the Ferrari began to smoke slightly. Regazzoni lost his lead to the Porsche of Elford/Larousse and came in for more water. As he pressed the starter button water poured out of the exhaust.

Larousse and Elford went on to win for Porsche, the 512 M of Loos/Pesch finished 9th, the Muller/Herzog Ferrari crashed and the Wiesendanger/Kocher Ferrari went out with lack of fuel pressure.

Le Mans

The 1971 Le Mans 24 Hour race was held on June 12-13th, Ferrari 512 Ms were entered Posey/Adamowicz (No. 12); Gregory/Eaton (No. 14); Craft/Weir (No. 16); Loos/Pesch (No. 10); Parkes/Pescarolo/Westbury (No. 7); Juncadella/Vaccarella (No. 15); Manfredini/Gagliardi (No. 6) and de Fierlant/de Cardanet (No. 9). Bob Grossman and Luigi Chinetti Jr. entered a 365 GTB/4 Daytona.

The Ferraris were outclassed by the Porsche contingent and the best placed Ferrari was the

Hobbs/Donohue Penske entered car with a time of 3 min. 18.5 secs. compared to the fastest time by Oliver's Porsche of 3 min. 13.6 secs. This placed the Ferrari in the second row of the rolling start with Juncadella/Vaccarella in row three.

Chris Craft's Ferrari had a fuel pressure release valve seize before the start but was able to set out after the field had taken off for its rolling start.

At the start Donohue came round in 4th place but on the first lap Vaccarella came round in 4th ahead of Donohue. After three hours the Donohue/Hobbs Ferrari was in third place but as darkness began to fall Donohue pitted and the Ferrari was wheeled away.

The Vaccarella/Juncadella Ferrari ran in 4th place and the Loos/Pesch Ferrari broke a piston.

Just before 10 pm Vaccarella maintained his fourth place and moved to 3rd at the 9th hour mark. Mike Parkes crashed the Filipinetti Ferrari at White House and lost 2 hours in the pits having it repaired. The car did not run well from then on and it was pulled in by Pescarolo and retired at about 3 am. The Juncadella/Vaccarella Ferrari took the lead but at 4 am the Spanish entered Ferrari pitted with clutch slip only to have the clutch fail completely when it regained the race.

Posey and Adamowicz moved up into 4th place by 9 am.

The NART Daytona had been leading the GT class finishing 5th overall only to find that they were not in the GT class at all but listed as sports.

The Marko/Van Lennep Porsche won with Posey/Adamowicz 3rd; Craft/Weir 4th and Chinetti/Grossman 5th.

Gregory/Eaton retired during the 4th hour with fuel feed problems; Manfredini/Gagliardi with gearbox trouble during the 16th hour; de Fierlant/de Cardanet also retired with gearbox trouble during the 17th hour.

Osterreichring

The Austrian 1000 kilometres was held at the Osterreichring at Zeltweg on 27th June 1971. Ferrari sent a 312 P for Ickx and Regazzoni. Other Ferraris were a 512S for Muller/Herzog and a 512 M for Masten Gregory both from the

Herbert Muller racing team. The Escuderia Montjuich 512 S was entered for Juncadella/Soler Roig and the Scuderia Brescia Corse 512 S for Pasotti/Casoni.

Ickx qualified the 312 P for the first row at 1 min. 40.10 secs. alongside Rodriguez pole Porsche 917. In the second row was Muller alongside Siffert's Porsche. Juncadella was in the 4th row. The Gregory 512 M would have been in the 4th row but the engine of the car broke at the last moment and it was withdrawn.

Rodriguez led at the start and began to pull away at about 2 seconds a lap from the Ferrari. Siffert's Porsche battled with Muller's Ferrari, 3 Alfa Romeos followed and then Pasotti in the 512 S.

At 10 laps Rodriguez had a 14 second lead and at 20 laps this was increased to 19 seconds. Muller had a vibration in the steering and the front suspension collapsed causing him to crash into a Porsche and be eliminated from the race. The 312 P Ferrari took the lead while Rodriguez refuelled. Rodriguez rejoined the race in 7th place. The Ferrari now had a 45 second advantage over Marko's Porsche.

On lap 44 Ickx pitted to refuel and hand over to Regazzoni, the Porsche closed up finally passing the Ferrari for 1st place on lap 50. As the Ferrari's fuel load decreased, Regazzoni regained the lead on lap 61 and when the Porsche pitted for a driver change, the Ferrari's lead extended to a minute and a half. With the rain falling, the Ferrari continued to extend its lead. Ickx took over and continued to increase the lead considerably. With Rodriguez back at the wheel of the Porsche he began to reduce the Ferrari's lead. At 120 laps he passed the Maranello car and reduced his deficit to 2 laps. Rodriguez then moved the Porsche up into 2nd place and had only a 91 second deficit on the Ferrari.

The Ferrari pit stop took 53 seconds and Regazzoni took over. The Porsche pit stop took only 15 seconds and on lap 145 Rodriguez passed the Ferrari again to unlap himself. On lap 147 Rodriguez set a new lap record of 1 min. 39.35 secs. in the attempt to catch up a whole lap on the Ferrari. However, on lap 148 the Ferrari was out, something broke in the suspension and the Ferrari crashed into the guardrail.

267

Pasotti in the 512 M finished 4th. Juncadella/ Soler Roig had crashed and the Porsches won once again.

Watkins Glen

The Watkins Glen 6 Hours was held on 24th July 1971. Ferrari entered the 312 P for Ickx/ Andretti. Roger Penske had a 512 M for Donohue/Hobbs, NART had a 512 M for Bucknum/Posey, Ecurie Francorchamps entered a 512 M for de Cardenet/Motschenbacher, Herbert Muller entered his 512 M for himself and George Eaton, and a further 512 was entered for Young/Adams.

Donohue's Ferrari qualified fastest at 1 min. 07.74 secs. Ickx was third fastest at 1 min. 08.64 secs. and the NART Ferrari qualified at 1 min. 09.22 secs.

At the start Donohue's Ferrari pulled away with Ickx in fourth place. By lap 13 Ickx had pulled up to 2nd place but Donohue was 9 seconds ahead of the 312 P. On lap 18 Muller was eliminated when he collided with a slower driver and the Swiss Ferrari was out of the race.

On lap 54 Donohue retired with a broken tie rod ball and Andretti in the 312 P took the lead. Peterson's Alfa Romeo pushed ahead of Andretti and, after pitting, the 312 P refused to start with a broken starter. Posey/Bucknum were withdrawn and the de Cardenet/ Motschenbacher Ferrari finished 4th.

The 1972 Season

With a somewhat unsuccessful 1971 season behind him in which he had used the time to experiment and develop his 312 P, Ferrari set about the 1972 season.

The first of the new 312 Ps conforming to the new FIA regulations was unveiled at the Kyalami 9 Hours on 6th November 1971.

For the 1972 season Ferrari decided to build six of the 312 Ps to run in the Manufacturer's Championship races. Ing. Forghieri, who had attended most of the races in 1971 while the cars were being developed, stayed home and the new programme was in the hands of team manager, Peter Schetty.

The plan was to use three cars in each race in such a manner that the team that raced one weekend would be replaced by three fresh ones for the next event while the original three were being completely overhauled by the factory.

For drivers, Ferrari chose to use his three Grand Prix drivers, Ickx, Regazzoni and Andretti and relying on Peterson, Schenken and Redman to share the driving chores for the long races. Ferrari also added Merzario and Munari to the team as it is always good politics to include an Italian driver.

The cars were numbered in even numbers from 0880 beginning with the 1971 prototypes. Giunti was killed in 0882 and the car was never rebuilt. 0884 was built late in 1971 for the Kyalami race and included the experience gained throughout the major part of the 1971 season with 0880. Nos. 0886, 0888, 0890, 0892, 0894 and 0896 were built for the 1972 season.

Type 312 P

The 312 P used the Grand Prix car's horizontally opposed 12-cylinder engine in a detuned form. Each opposed bank had twin overhead camshafts actuating four valves per cylinder. The inlet ports were located between the camshafts and the exhaust ports on the underside of the engine. With a bore and stroke of 78.5 x 51.5 mm and a capacity of 2993-cc, the power output was 440 b h p at 10,800 r p m as compared to the 12,600 of the Grand Prix engine at that time.

A tubular space frame was used with aluminium sheet riveted to the frame giving a semi monocoque effect that was nothing new to Ferrari design. As in the Grand Prix car, the tubes running rearward from the cockpit formed a structure from which the engine was 'hung'. The engine was attached at the front to the main frame and thus became the backbone of the car. Double wishbones formed the front suspension with a wide-based lower member and coil-spring/damper units interspersed. The hub carriers were of cast alloy and extended rearwards to form steering arms. The rack-and-pinion steering assembly was located above the driver's knees and an anti-roll bar, fitted forward of the suspension, mounted on the front bulkhead. The rear hub carriers were located by a lower wishbone together with a cast bracket under the clutch housing and topside by a single transverse link and two radius arms running forward to the bulkhead behind the cockpit.

At Watkins Glen, for the final championship event of the season, a new system was used on two cars with a parallel bottom link layout to decrease the bump steering of the rear wheels.

At the front, the disc brake calipers were fitted on the hub carriers. At the rear, the disc calipers were incorporated in the hub carriers.

Quick-change gear ratios

The gearbox, a five-speed unit, was located at the rear in a manner similar to the layout on the Grand Prix car. During the first part of the season it underwent redesign to facilitate gear ratio changes at race circuits.

The gearbox was actuated by a short gear lever located at the right-hand side of the cockpit. The lever moved in a small gate. Gear selection was conventional, with bottom to the left rear.

Second was in the middle of the gate, forward, with third in the same position but to the rear. Fourth was forward to the right and fifth in the same position to the rear.

The gear lever actuated a control rod leading along the frame to a pivoting link just to the rear of the driver's seat transferring the motion towards the centre of the car. A further control rod ran over the engine to the selector mechanism situated on top of the gearbox.

Instrumentation was fairly simple with the three major gauges visible through the small leather-bound steering wheel. To the left was a vertically split gauge, the right section of which indicated oil pressure and the left section fuel pressure. To the right was another dual gauge, the red needle indicating oil temperature and a white needle for water temperature. The centre gauge was a tachometer reading 2 to 12 indicating engine r p m multiplied by 1000.

Under the oil gauge there was a red indicator light to warn of low fuel tankage level. A fuel reserve was provided which could be activated by a lever. This opened a cock by means of a cable, the lever having a warning light ahead of it.

Amidships in the cockpit was an ammeter located above a panel of switches. These comprised switches for the headlights, Lucas electrical fuel pump and an ignition key which, when turned, started the engine. Another switch connected current to a button on the right-hand spoke of the steering wheel which was used to flash the headlights.

The 12-volt battery was located left of the gearbox with an oil breather tank to the right.

The water radiators were rear mounted on the sponsons on both sides of the cockpit. Ducting in the bodywork fed air to them. The dry sump lubricating system's oil tank was located behind the left hand side water radiator.

Immediately above the clutch housing was an oil radiator for the engine.

A plug-in filler acting as a non-return valve was provided for the oil tank through which oil from a pressurized cylinder could be forced through. This fitting was positioned in the side of the tank with an access panel in the body. An oil level sight glass tube was located behind the oil tank and was visible through a slot in the car's bodywork.

On the opposite side of the car, a similar non-return device was provided for water. A normal filler cap was also provided in the headrest behind the driver's seat.

Wide sponsons were fitted on either side of the car. The right hand sponson was empty and the left hand one contained the regulation 120-litre fuel tank.

Petrol filler

A large filler cap was located to the front of the right-hand sponson. This had a bayonet-type neck of the Avery/Hardoll type which led to a large diameter pipe running across the cockpit floor under the driver's knees to the left-hand fuel tank from which another such bayonet fitting protruded. To this system the refuelling hose was attached and a vented plastic container attached to the left hand tank. The fuel flowed through the transfer pipe into the tank, expelling air into the plastic container.

When fuel rushed up into the plastic container it indicated a full tank, the removal of the fuel hose and the plastic container then automatically sealed the Avery-Hardoll connectors.

Bodywork

A two-piece body made of fibreglass was used. At the rear, the body was located about the points on the roll-bar immediately to the rear of the cockpit and located by pegs with over-centre mechanical clips and rubber tension clips to the rear light mounting. Three variations existed of the tail sections. An intermediate type was the most commonly used weighing 7 kilos more than the short type but increasing speed by about 6-8 k p h. The short stubby type was designed for tight circuits and the long tails were used only for the Le Mans tests.

At the front, the car's bodywork hinged about points by the lower wishbone mounting. The bodywork included the doors and sides of the cockpit, the doors hinging upwards and containing the ducts guiding air to the water radiators.

A full width nose was provided with a slot that allowed air to pass through to an exit in front of the windshield. This air provided a certain amount of down thrust for the front end. At the races, a complete set of front and rear body sections was kept in reserve in case any of the cars crashed.

The nosepiece and the tail of the bodies were red, the sponsons aluminium and the head fairing together with the rear spoiler and tail fins were coloured either, white, yellow, blue or green for identification purposes.

Front wheels were 13 in. diameter with a 10 in. wide rim and rear wheels were 15 in. diameter with a 15½ in. wide rim.

Ferrari won the championship with Firestone tyres and the all up weight of the 312 P varied from 655 to 670 kilos.

Buenos Aires

The 1972 Sports Car Championship began at Buenos Aires on January 9th. Ferrari sent a team of three cars similar to the 1972 specification car which had appeared at the Kyalami 9 Hours in November of 1971.

The cars had chassis numbers 082, 084 and 086. The drivers nominated were Ickx/Andretti, Regazzoni/Redman and Peterson/Schenken.

Ronnie Peterson was signed as a full time sports car driver for the season, as was Tim Schenken, and the two were paired with a brand new car for Buenos Aires. Ickx and Andretti had the same car that they drove at Kyalami and Regazzoni/Redman had the car that was used for testing at Daytona.

The Buenos Aires track had been completely reworked for the event and during the initial practice period, the Ferraris running on Firestone slicks were the fastest, with Regazzoni and Schenken heading two Alfas, and Andretti 5th fastest. On Friday the practice was later and the cars were able to take advantage of the cooler conditions just before dusk. Peterson recorded fastest time at 1 min. 58.9 secs., Stommelen in an Alfa was next at 1 min. 58.90 secs., Ickx at 1 min. 58.98 secs. and Regazzoni 1 min. 59.15 secs.

The times were not improved on Saturday as the two Ferraris with the older type gearboxes had been fitted with incorrect ratios and they had to be changed. The Ferraris were also running on harder compound Firestones which were slower but were intended to last the race, though they did not.

The opposition to Ferrari came from Carlo Chiti's Autodelta Alfa Romeos and Jo Bonnier's very fast Lolas.

At the start it was Peterson's Ferrari leading Stommelen's Alfa. The Alfa slipped by into the lead on the first lap but on the next lap the Alfa Romeo's throttle jammed and the Ferraris took command with Ickx leading Peterson and Regazzoni. Ickx was pushing for a comfortable lead as he was using the soft compound tyres, Regazzoni and Peterson followed nose to tail some eight seconds back.

Wisell had brought the very fast Lola into 4th place and was catching the 2nd and 3rd place Ferrari by 1 second a lap. Peterson stopped for fuel on lap 34, Ickx on lap 35 and Regazzoni on lap 36. This allowed the Lola to take the lead until lap 38 when it too had to come in to refuel, the closest Alfa Romeo was two laps behind in 5th place.

Ferrari's problems began when Andretti pulled in to have the master switch to the battery changed which dropped him to 14th and at one-third distance Schenken/Peterson led Redman/Regazzoni with Wisell's Lola third. The Lola continued to creep up and when the

Ferrari's' next pit stops were completed the Lola was only four seconds behind the Redman/Regazzoni Ferrari. Schenken turned the lead car over to Peterson who retained the lead but only by a short distance over the Lola. The Lola went by into the lead on lap 76.

On lap 80 Wisell took the Lola to the pits to refuel and Larrousse took over but a front hub jammed and the Lola lost two laps before it could rejoin the race. Regazzoni pitted to replace a flat tyre and in so doing dropped a lap behind Peterson but did not lose his second place.

With 50 laps remaining, the order was Peterson/Schenken one lap ahead of Regazzoni/Redman.

Andretti/Ickx made a normal fuel stop but were detained by a broken starter motor bracket which had also cut the cable. The time required for the repair put the car completely out of contention.

Peterson/Schenken won with Regazzoni/Redman 2nd and Ickx/Andretti 10th. The three cars crossed the finishing line together; the winning car covering 1,002.6 kilometres in 5 hrs. 45 min. 58.22 secs. at an average of 173.886 k p h.

A 6-Hour Daytona

For 1972, the traditional Daytona 24 Hours race was shortened to 6 hours. The event was held on February 6th and Ferrari sent three brand new cars while the entries from Buenos Aires were returned to the factory for overhaul.

Ickx/Andretti had chassis No. 088, Regazzoni/Redman chassis No. 090 and Peterson/Schenken No. 092. The Regazzoni/Redman car had the new type gearbox.

NART entered what was basically the 1969 V12 312 P which had a new chassis constructed by the team itself for George Eaton and Luigi Chinetti Jr.

Opposition was again from the Autodelta Alfa Romeos, two T280 Lolas of the Ecurie Bonnier and 908/3 and 908 Porsches.

The standard for the lap was set the previous year by Mark Donohue with a 5-litre 512 M Ferrari at 1 min. 42.42 secs.

The Thursday practice session was slowed by rain but Andretti nevertheless recorded a lap at 1 min. 49.90 secs; a Lola was not far behind. On Friday, the qualification was limited to two hours during which Andretti recorded 1 min. 44.2 secs., Regazzoni recorded 1 min. 44.96 secs. and Peterson did 1 min. 46.04 secs. The Peterson/Schenken car was having some gearbox trouble.

For the race, all three Ferraris were fitted with new engines. The race started behind a pace car and the three Ferraris ran three abreast across the starting line. Then Regazzoni took the lead with Andretti right behind and Schenken third, followed by Wisell's Lola and Revson's Alfa Romeo.

After six laps Schenken was in the pits to adjust his slipping clutch and the Ferrari restarted one lap behind.

The Chinetti-entered car lasted a few laps, being retired with a hole in the fuel tank after its suspension bottomed.

Andretti who was being hounded by Wisell. On lap 24 the Lola was in second place and then began challenging Regazzoni. Regazzoni had a sudden flat tyre and spun, the rear of the bodywork of his car came off and hit the Lola. The Lola headed for the pits while Regazzoni abandoned the Ferrari to walk back to the pits. Andretti now led, followed by the Alfa Romeos. Peter Schetty, the Ferrari team manager, told Regazzoni to bring the Ferrari in and they would see if it could be repaired. Alfa Romeo protested this move but were rejected by the organizers.

Andretti pitted for Ickx to take over and the Revson Alfa briefly led until it too pitted and Ickx put the Ferrari back into the lead.

The leading Ferrari was only running on 11 cylinders but the Peterson/Schenken car was running very well and was moving up. When the leading Ferrari made its routine pit stop, the Alfa went by again into the lead. As the Alfa pitted it was the Schenken/Peterson Ferrari that moved into first place. Peterson was slowed by a flat tyre but the Alfa challenge was over and Andretti/Ickx retook the lead. When they made their next routine stop on lap 101, Schenken/Peterson were back in front.

At this point there was some disagreement between the official lap charts and those of the Ferrari team. Scuderia Ferrari had Schenken/

Peterson in the lead until almost the end of the race but the official charts had Andretti/Ickx in the lead from lap 120 onwards.

At 140 laps officially it was Ickx/Andretti and Peterson/Schenken although the Ferrari team had the reverse. In third place was an Alfa Romeo two laps behind. Regazzoni/Redman were back in the race with their repaired car.

Peter Schetty was wondering whether to protest the official lap scoring as he was using a more sophisticated timing system than were the organizers. He was convinced that his timing was correct.

However, the problem was solved 15 minutes before the end of the race when Schenken pitted with a flat tyre and this put the Andretti/Ickx car back into the lead on the Ferrari as well as the official chart.

Ickx/Andretti won in 6 hrs. 01 min. 36.40 secs. (186.644 k p h). Peterson/Schenken were second, 2 laps behind. The Regazzoni/Redman car finished 4th, 11 laps behind the third-place Alfa which in turn was 4 laps down on the winner.

Sebring 12 Hours

After Daytona, the team were sent back to Modena to prepare them for the BOAC 1000 while the second set of team cars were sent to Sebring for the 12 hour race on March 25th. These were the same cars as those raced in Buenos Aires, being chassis Nos. 082, 084 and 086. Drivers nominated were Ickx/Andretti, Regazzoni/Redman and Peterson/Schenken.

Their opposition came from the TT 33 Alfa Romeos of which Autodelta had sent six cars, two of them as spares. A Ferrari Daytona GTB/4 was entered for Bob Grossman and Luigi Chinetti Jr. by NART.

In practice, Ickx/Andretti were the fastest at 2 min. 31.44 secs., Regazzoni/Redman were second at 2 min. 33.04 secs. then came the Stommelen/Revson Alfa and 4th, the Ferrari of Peterson/Schenken in 2nd place. The signal

At the start Stommelen's Alfa tried to challenge the Ferraris but already on the first lap the Ferraris were 1, 2, 3 with Andretti leading Regazzoni and Peterson.

Before long the Ferraris had pulled away from all opposition and after 1¼ hours, the first of

the routine stops were made in which the Ferrari team's superb pit work was much in evidence. At the third hour, all three Ferraris were still on the same lap with each other and the same team order was maintained. Ferrari's troubles began at the 4th hour. Peterson ran out of fuel on the circuit and all the cars seemed to be losing oil. Ickx punctured a tyre, the replacement of which let the Regazzoni/Redman car into the lead. Schenken/Peterson lost more time when a brake pipe broke and the position at 6 hours was Regazzoni/Redman leading by two laps from Andretti/Ickx, followed by two Alfas and the Schenken/Peterson Ferrari. Ickx burned out a battery lead and came in to replace it allowing Regazzoni/Redman to further increase their lead.

At the tenth hour, Regazzoni's Ferrari caught fire and he had to abandon it, the car being burnt out. Andretti/Ickx then held the lead with Peterson/Schenken in 2nd place and the signal was put out to slow the two Ferraris which then cruised on to 1st and 2nd places. The NART 365 GTB/4 of Luigi Chinetti Jr. and Bob Grossman finished in 8th place, taking third in Group 4 behind a Corvette and a 911S Porsche. The winning Ferrari completed the 12 hrs. 04 min. 40 secs. at an average speed of 179.45 k p h.

The Le Mans Tests

The Le Mans test weekend took place March 18th-19th. It clashed with the Race of Champions at Brands Hatch but Ferrari chose to miss the British event to send his drivers to Le Mans. It was the first test on the new circuit that by-passed the famous White House bend. 0.112-mile was added to the length of the circuit but times were slowed by 15 to 20 seconds.

Ferrari sent two cars, one a new 312 P and the other a 1971 car. Most of the time was devoted to evaluating various aerodynamic tail sections.

On the first day, a big semi-enclosed rear section was tested with four vertical fins across the rear. Two adjustable wings supported by each pair of fins. Ferrari also tested the normal open type short tail section with central stabilizing fins. A third style was a variation of the normal type, being slightly larger and having the fins at the outside extremities with a full-width wing. This third type proved to be the most suitable. Jacky Ickx used this latter setup to record 3 min. 40.4 secs. and Regazzoni recorded 3 min. 41.1 secs. These were the two fastest times of the weekend. Top speed realized by the Ferraris was 193 m p h.

The 1971 car was also modified to take this type of tail section but on Sunday ignition trouble prevented Ickx from turning too many laps while the other car suffered from oil leaking.

Among the Group 4 cars, Claude Ballot-Lena with a Daytona recorded 4 min. 19.4 secs., about 3 seconds slower than the Muller Pantera in the same class. The Ferrari's speed on the straight was quoted as equalling the 190 m p h of the Pantera.

Monza

The Monza 1000 km race was held on April 25th. Ferrari entered three of his 312 Ps for Ickx/Regazzoni, Peterson/Schenken and Redman/Merzario.

For this race the Alfas were absent as was the Gulf Research Mirage and the only competition to Ferrari came from the Bonnier T280 Lolas together with some Porsches.

The starting grid was the usual Monza two by two and the front row was made up of Peterson and Ickx, Regazzoni's Ferrari was in the second row alongside Wisell's Lola. The race was due to start at 11 am but due to the pouring rain the drivers were given several laps to acquaint themselves with the conditions. On one of these warmup laps Peterson went off the road at the *Parabolica* and badly damaged the nose cowling of his car, managing to get himself stuck in the sand at the same time. Ferrari had a spare nose section and the pole position car was readied in time for the revised start at 11.30. Peterson's crash was an omen of things to come for the Ferrari team in a race that should have been little more than a routine victory.

The rain continued unabated. At the start Ickx and Peterson were off together with Redman just behind. Redman lost it at the *Parabolica* and damaged the tail of his car, losing

a considerable amount of time. Fortunately for Ferrari the opposition was also in trouble and the Wisell Lola retired early.

Ickx had electrical problems and pitted. The remaining Lola took second but this car too went off the road and was too badly damaged to continue.

Peterson's Ferrari was well in the lead when he refuelled on lap 32 and continued.

Ickx pitted to hand over to Regazzoni while a Porsche moved up into second place. On the *Vialone* curve Redman spun again and had to abandon the Ferrari. Peterson did the same but was able to return to the pits to have the left rear suspension replaced and to hand over to Schenken.

The Porsche took the lead and two De Tomaso Panteras running in Group 4 were in 2nd and 3rd places. When the Porsche pitted, one of the Panteras took the lead but this car also crashed.

Despite the fact that the Ickx/Regazzoni Ferrari was not running on all 12 cylinders, they were able to outrun anyone else on the track and by half distance the Ferrari was leading again. The Porsche held 2nd, the Panteras 3rd and 4th and the Peterson/Schenken Ferrari 5th. The Panteras began to fail and the Peterson/Schenken Ferrari moved up into 3rd behind the Porsche.

Ickx/Regazzoni won in 5 hrs. 52 min. 05.6 secs. at 176.496 k p h (109.608 m p h) and the Peterson/Schenken car finished 3rd, nine laps behind the winners.

Targa Florio

The 56th Targa Florio took place on May 21st on the little Madonie circuit.

Ferrari was undecided about sending a car but Alfa Romeo were out in full force making a determined effort to win the Sicilian classic. At the last moment, Ferrari decided to enter one car. He sent none of his big name drivers, leaving the lone entry in the hands of the reserve driver for the sports car team Arturo Merzario teamed with Sandro Munari a Lancia rally team driver for whom it was a first ride in a 3-litre sports car. Ferrari's psychology was rather obvious in this move: If Ferrari won it would be a tremendous blow against Alfa Romeo and if Ferrari did not win it was because he only had a lone car with inexperienced drivers. The race proved to be a complete triumph for Ferrari and complete disillusionment for Alfa Romeo.

In practice Merzario set the fastest lap and during the race the Ferrari led for all but two laps.

Merzario led the first three laps before stopping for fuel and to hand over to Munari. At this point the Marko/Galli Alfa Romeo took the lead but two laps later at the next refuelling stop, when Merzario recommenced driving, the Ferrari was back in the lead. Munari did two more laps before Merzario took over for the rest of the race. There was a lot of excitement as Merzario started his last lap 39 seconds ahead of Marko's Alfa. Marko tried everything to catch the Ferrari and closed the gap to 16.9 secs. but the effort was in vain and Merzario/Munari won in 6 hrs. 27 min. 48.0 secs. at an average of 122.537 k p h.

Brands Hatch

For the BOAC 1000 at Brands Hatch on April 16th, Ferrari sent three cars. Ickx/Andretti had their Daytona car as did Regazzoni/Redman while Peterson/Schenken had a new car bearing chassis No. 0894.

Opposition came from the Autodelta Alfa Romeos, the Gulf Research Mirage and a 908/3 and 908/2 Porsche as well as the Bonnier Lola.

Early practice showed Ferrari to have the situation well in hand and Ickx was fastest at 1 min. 28 secs. with Ferraris recording 2nd and 3rd fastest.

On the first practice session on Saturday, Regazzoni was fastest with 1 min. 27 secs. and in the final session on Saturday Regazzoni recorded 1 min. 26.6 secs., Redman 1 min. 28.0 secs., Ickx 1 min. 26.8 secs., Andretti 1 min. 27.0 secs., Peterson 1 min. 27.4 secs., and Schenken 1 min. 29.2 secs.

At the start, the Ferraris took the lead with Regazzoni leading until lap 41 when Ickx went by with Peterson holding 3rd place some 5 seconds behind.

On lap 50 the first routine stops were made by the Ferraris. Peterson stopped first to switch with Schenken, the stop taking fractionally over 20 seconds, next came Regazzoni to change with

Redman and then came Ickx. Due to these stops, Wisell in the Bonnier Lola took the lead, however, on lap 59 Wisell pitted and the Andretti/Ickx Ferrari retook the lead holding some 30 seconds lead over the Regazzoni/Redman car.

At the 150th lap, Ferrari still held 1st, 2nd and 3rd. Peterson/Schenken moved up to second at the second routine pit stop but lost their position again when they had to refuel.

With 35 laps to go, the Ferraris made their third routine stop. Andretti/Ickx led with Redman/Regazzoni close behind and Schenken/Peterson one lap behind.

In the last hour Regazzoni stopped with an oil leak from the gearbox and a misfire in the engine. This caused him to stop three times and as a result the car dropped to 7th place.

The race ended with Andretti/Ickx winning in 5 hrs. 55 min. 27.5 secs. (169.17 k p h). Schenken/Peterson were 2nd, one lap behind, and Regazzoni/Redman back up in 5th place albeit some 15 laps behind the winner.

Francorchamps

Ferrari sent three cars to the 1000 km of Francorchamps at Spa on May 7th. The cars were those that had run at the BOAC 1000 km at Brands Hatch, Ickx/Regazzoni had No. 1 with yellow stripes to identify it, Peterson/Schenken were in No. 2 with blue stripes and Redman/Merzario in No. 3 with green stripes.

Alfa Romeo withdrew from the race leaving opposition to Ferrari in the hands of the Gulf Research Mirage and the Lola.

Practice was held on Thursday and Friday, fastest lap being set by Ickx in 3 min. 20.4 secs. (253.292 k p h) compared to the previous year's best time by Siffert in a 5-litre Porsche at 3 min. 14.6 secs. Claude Ballot-Lena/D. Rouveyroan had the Charles Pozzi-entered Competition Daytona 365 GTB/4 running against the De Tomaso Panteras and Chevrolet Corvettes in the GT class.

At the start, the Ferrari took the lead, Ickx heading Redman and Schenken. Ickx and Redman kept pace with each other while Schenken fell back. Larrousse in the Lola was beginning to catch the 3rd place Ferrari and on lap 8 the yellow Lola was by in third place, however, he could make no impression on the two leaders. Ickx by now led Redman by 13 seconds.

At 17 laps, the Ferraris pitted in quick succession, Ickx first to hand over to Regazzoni who continued in the lead. Redman was next and took on fuel without changing tyres and Schenken was last in for Peterson to take over.

The Ferrari team manager, Peter Schetty called Regazzoni back into the pits to check a left rear hub nut that had not been sufficiently tightened. This allowed Redman to take the lead and, when the Lola pitted, the Peterson/Schenken Ferrari used the opportunity to regain 3rd place.

On the 35th lap the Ferraris again pitted for fuel, tyres and driver change. At this point Redman still led Regazzoni by 35 seconds but with the driver change Ickx quickly made up the deficit and regained the lead. Ickx pressed on, lapping at over 151 m p h and drawing well away from the other two Ferraris, lapping Schenken's car in the process.

On lap 53 the Ferraris were in for their final routine stops. Regazzoni took over from Ickx and continued in the lead but Redman passed by in first place on lap 55 as Regazzoni headed for the pits with the left rear tyre completely gone. The tyre had damaged the tail section and the oil tank so a new wheel, tyre and rear tail section were fitted while the oil leak in the tank was fixed with plastic metal. Ickx took over to try and regain the lead but the stop had cost the car two laps.

Showers began to moisten the track and Peterson was caught by a wet patch which sent him into the guard rail damaging the car badly enough to force its retirement.

Schetty gave Redman and Ickx the 'go slow' sign and the Redman/Merzario Ferrari won in 4 hrs. 17 min. 19.1 secs. (233.429 k p h). Ickx/Redman were second one lap behind while Peterson/Schenken were classified as 12th. The Ballot-Lena Daytona was classified 18th although not running at the finish.

Nurburgring

For the ADAC 1000 km held at the Nurburgring on May 28th, Ferrari entered three cars, a combination of the chassis numbers entered at Spa and Monza. The cars were entrusted to Ickx/Regazzoni in car No. 1, Peterson/Schenken in car No. 3, and Redman/Merzario in car No. 2. Opposition was from two of the Autodelta Alfa Romeos and the Gulf Research Racing Mirage-Cosworth V8.

The weather was as usual on the Nurburgring, with heavy rain both on the Friday and Saturday practice sessions, interspersed with dry periods all combined to cause everyone a great deal of grief.

The practice times were not really conclusive and the first row was shared by the Peterson Ferrari and Bell's Mirage.

Two Alfas were in the second row and the Ferrari of Merzario in the third row alongside a Porsche. Ickx's Ferrari was in the 4th row.

It was not raining when the race started but the circuit was wet and it became a battle of who could guess the conditions best and use the correct tyres for the expected conditions. Ferrari chose to run on 'wet' tyres and the Mirage on 'intermediate'; as a result of this the Ferrari forged ahead in the order: Peterson, Merzario and Ickx in the first three places.

After two laps, the Ferrari sorted themselves out in team order with Ickx leading Merzario and Peterson. After 8 laps the track began to dry out and Bell with the Mirage began to close on the Ferraris using his 'intermediate' tyres to set the fastest lap, improving on it again on lap 9.

At the beginning of lap 10 Merzario refuelled as did the Mirage. The Mirage continued to gain on the Ferraris and at the beginning of lap 11 Ickx and Peterson stopped to refuel and change drivers.

Bell took the Mirage past the Redman/Merzario Ferrari while the Regazzoni/Ickx and Schenken/Peterson Ferrari continued to circulate in 1st and 2nd places.

The Ferraris were still on 'wet' tyres and the circuit continued to dry. The Mirage pushed by the Schenken/Peterson Ferrari to take 2nd place, at which point Ferrari pulled Schenken into the pits and fitted the car with 'intermediates'. The Mirage closed up to within 26 seconds of the leading Ferrari and before long the Mirage was within sight of Regazzoni. Regazzoni tried hard to keep ahead but with his 'wet' tyres he spun off and damaged his car too badly to continue.

The Mirage now took the lead but the Peterson/Schenken Ferrari on the 'intermediates' was moving up rapidly. As the Mirage pitted, the Ferrari retook the lead and at half distance Ferrari held 1st and 3rd places. Peter Schetty, the Ferrari team manager, decided to keep the lead car on 'intermediates' when it pitted for fuel while the Gulf team gambled and changed all four wheels to dry-weather slicks.

Merzario pitted for Redman to take over, warning his co-driver that the Ferrari clutch had seized and he would have to change gears without it. Despite the clutch problem the Ferrari was back in the race before the Mirages tyres were changed so that the Ferraris were 1, 2 again.

At the beginning of lap 29 Schenken came into the pits with a left front tyre flat; this was exchanged so fast that he still retained the lead.

At 35 laps routine stops were made and Merzario's car was switched to 'dry' slicks and as a result the Ferrari was able to deal with the Mirage effectively. At the beginning of lap 37 the Mirage was again in 2nd place as Merzario brought the Ferrari in with a right front tyre in pieces.

Despite the handicap of no clutch, the Merzario/Redman gained on the Mirage which finally blew its engine on lap 43 leaving the Ferraris to come in 1st and 2nd, covering the 44 laps in 6 hrs. 1 min. 40.2 secs. - 166.683 k p h.

Ferrari withdraw from Le Mans

The 24 Hours of Le Mans was held on 10th/11th June 1972. Ferrari had four cars entered but the entry was withdrawn one week before the event. Ferrari felt that the 312 Ps were not really suitable for a 24-hour race as the Boxer engines in tests had failed to show that they were capable of standing up to long drawn-out high-speed tests.

With the World Manufacturer's Championship already in the bag, a failure at Le Mans could only be an anticlimax. As a result of this, the only Ferraris entered were in the GT category by private owners and those by the Ferrari agents of France, Belgium, Switzerland, England and the USA. Opposition to these came from the De Tomaso Panteras, 911 Porsches and Chevrolet Corvettes.

After the first hour, the Rouveyran/Migault Ferrari Daytona took the lead in the class from the Corvette and the GT Ferraris had no problem in winning the class.

Claude Ballot-Lena and J. C. Andruet won the class and were 5th overall in the Charles Pozzi-entered Daytona, followed in 6th overall by the Sam Posey/Tony Adamowicz Daytona entered by NART; 7th overall were Mike Parkes/J. L. Lafosse in the Daytona entered by Scuderia Filipinetti of Switzerland, 8th overall the Derek Bell/Teddy Pilette Daytona of the Belgian Ecurie Francorchamps, then the Daytona of Buchet/Jarier entered by NART with the Laffeach/Doncieux 246 Dino GT also entered by NART in 17th place.

The Westbury/Hine Daytona entered by the English Maranello Concessionaires broke its engine.

It was a complete triumph for Ferrari in the GT class.

Osterreichring

The Austrian 1000 km race was held at the Osterreichring at Zeltweg on 25th June 1972. Ferrari entered four cars in the anticipation of strong opposition from Alfa Romeo with their new 12-cylinder car, Gulf Mirage also with a new 12-cylinder car and the Matra 12-cylinders fresh from their victory at Le Mans. However none of these threats materialized and Ferrari was again faced by the V8 Gulf Mirage and the similarly engined Bonnier Lolas.

In the Ferrari line up there was a new car, No. 0896 together with two of the Spa cars and the Targa Florio winner.

The car that Ickx was to drive with Regazzoni had been modified by fitting an engine similar to that used on the Formula 1 Ferrari. It had straight intake pipes instead of the usual curved type; it had a rev limit of 11,000 r p m compared to the normal 312 P's 10,600 r p m.

Unfortunately, on the day before practice, Regazzoni tripped in the paddock and broke his wrist and Redman was nominated to replace him.

Merzario and Munari were down to drive the car with which they had won the Targa Florio, No. 0884. Peterson and Schenken had No. 0894 and, after having been tested by Ferrari, Carlos

Pace joined the team together with the Austrian Marko.

The Ferraris spent a lot of time sorting themselves out in the changing weather. As a result the Bell/Van Lennep Gulf Mirage pulled off the fastest practice lap at 1 min. 40.6 secs. with the Larrousse/Elford Lola T280 second fastest. This relegated Ickx in the fastest of the Ferraris to third spot on the front row of the starting grid.

At the start of the race both the Lola and the Mirage were slow off the mark and the Ferraris overwhelmed them. Ickx led Marko, Schenken and Merzario. It had been touch and go for Ferrari as Merzario had to have his fuel injection changed just before the start and, during practice, Schenken and Peterson had some differences of opinion on how to set up their car, as each driver had his own view on how the car should handle. Consequently an oversteer-understeer argument developed and the end result was a compromise.

The Ferraris of Ickx and Marko pulled out a lead while Bell took the Gulf Mirage past Merzario to hold 4th place. The Lola had problems with a sticking throttle and was no longer a challenge.

Just as the Gulf Mirage was threatening the third place Ferrari of Schenken, the engine began to fail and the Mirage pitted. The Ferraris were now in a secure 1st, 2nd, 3rd and 4th place order. On the 40th lap Redman took over Ickx's car after an 18-second stop but the tanks were not filled properly and he had to make an early stop on lap 68 to refuel. The left front wheel was changed at the same time and Ickx rejoined the race.

The other team stops went according to schedule, Schenken and Merzario stopped on lap 40 and Marko on lap 42. Marko led while the others were pitting. Munari who took over from Merzario began to lose ground and he was beginning to be threatened by the 2-litre Chevron/BMW of Stommelen/Hezemans. Despite heavy wear on the left front tyres, the Ferraris were running with Ickx/Redman first, Marko/Pace second, Peterson/Schenken third, one lap behind, and Merzario/Munari fourth two laps behind.

On the 103rd lap Peterson stopped for fuel and to change four tyres but, when Schenken took over, the clutch would not disengage. After adjustment Schenken took off with the clutch slipping at peak r p m.

As the pits prepared to service the Merzario/Munari car, Schenken was back in with a flat tyre. While the tyre was being changed, Merzario pitted for a routine stop, but it was found that his battery was dead and this too had to be changed. Immediately after this hectic action, Pace came in to change front wheels because the car was handling strangely. Then Schenken was in again to readjust the clutch. Pace was back when it was found that it was not the front wheels at all but a rear tyre that was going flat. Then Schenken was in again and had a bad time restarting as he could not depress the clutch and restart in gear. He eventually did manage to get away but it was a traumatic scene.

With all this activity, the 2-litre Chevron/BMW was within 37 seconds of the 4th place Ferrari, and gaining, so Merzario was substituted for Munari and the Ferrari circulated to take 1st, 2nd, 3rd and 4th for the first time of the year.

Ickx/Redman covered the 1000 km in 4 hours 58 min. 46.28 secs., at an average speed of 201.92 k p h. Marko/Pace were second, one lap behind, Peterson/Schenken 3rd, four laps behind, and Merzario/Munari fourth, six laps behind.

Watkins Glen

The Watkins Glen 6 Hours was held on July 22nd and Ferrari entered 3 cars for Mario Andretti/Jacky Ickx, Ronnie Peterson/Tim Schenken and Brian Redman/Arturio Merzario. The Alfa Romeos were absent and opposition was from the two Gulf Research Mirages and a lone T280 Lola from the Ecurie Bonnier.

In the GT class, NART entered two Daytonas for Sam Posey/David Hobbs and Jean Pierre Jarrier/Gregg Young.

The 312 P Ferraris had the new tail section that was first used in the Austrian race.

In practice, Schenken was fastest with 1 min. 47.3 secs., Andretti was next fastest with 1 min. 47.3 secs. and Derek Bell's Mirage third fastest at 1 min. 50.6 secs.

At the start, Peterson took the lead from Andretti with the Mirage 3rd and Redman's Ferrari 4th. Andretti and Peterson had a battle for the lead with the Mirage holding third until it pitted with overheating and the Redman Ferrari moved to make it 1, 2, 3 for Ferrari. Andretti had a problem with his engine losing power under certain conditions and he began to drop behind, on the 20th lap he was 20 seconds behind Peterson.

In the GT class the battle was between the Posey/Hobbs Ferrari and the Kemp/Pickett Corvette. The Mirages were in trouble with brakes and were slowed by pit fires when fuel was spilled on the red hot brake discs.

With just one hour left, the Redman/Merzario Ferrari broke its engine while Peterson/Schenken led Andretti/Ickx. However, Peterson's brakes were giving out and Andretti began to move up despite his ailing engine. Andretti reduced his deficit from 80 seconds to 56 seconds in a period of 15 laps and took the lead on lap 159 when Peterson made a routine pit stop.

Andretti extended his lead to 35 seconds, setting a new lap record of 1 min. 47.4 secs.

When Andretti pitted, Ickx took over the whole operation taking only 25 seconds. However, the extra time lost in slowing for the pits and rejoining the race put Ickx 7.6 seconds behind Peterson. Ickx took a lap to warm the tyres and then set off in pursuit of the Swedish driver, cutting down the lead by one second a lap. Ickx set a new lap record of 1 min. 47.2 secs. and closed on Peterson. In his efforts Ickx went off course twice but on lap 188 the cars were side by side with Ickx forging fractionally ahead.

Ickx took the lead with 8 laps left to go and took the chequered flag having covered 195 laps, 658.515 miles in 6 hrs. 1 min. 11.27 secs., averaging 109.39 m p h. Peterson/Schenken were second also covering 195 laps. The Redman/Merzario Ferrari was classified 14th despite its non finish and the Jean Pierre Jarrier/Gregg Young Daytona finished 6th winning Class 4 while the Posey/Hobbs Daytona was classified 16th being a non finisher with a blown engine.

Imola

The Imola 500 kilometre race was held September 17th. Ferrari entered two cars although it was not a Manufacturers' Championship race. Ferrari chose the event to unveil his 1973 version of the 312 P which differed from the 1972 model by having a longer wheelbase, wider front track and other detail changes. The new car was entered for Jacky Ickx while a normal 1972 car was entered for Arturo Merzario. The event was run in two heats and a final, Merzario won with the 1972 car in 1 hr. 7 min. 56.2 secs., averaging 180.414 k p h and setting the fastest lap at 1 min. 40.1 secs., an average of 187.207 k p h. Ickx was second with the new car in 1 hr. 9 min. 01.1 secs.

Kyalami

The last major race for Ferrari in 1972 was the Kyalami 9 Hours held at the Kyalami circuit near Johannesburg on 4th and 5th November.

Ferrari sent two cars for Ickx and Redman and Regazzoni/Merzario. The two 312 P Ferraris were of the latest type which Ickx had first driven at the 500 kilometres of Imola in September. They had a longer wheelbase and wider front track. Modified engines were used, running at 11,500 r p m instead of 10,800 r p m. Nevertheless, all was not well with the cars and many adjustments were made to suspension and aerodynamics. One of the problems was the switch from Firestone to Goodyear tyres which required a period of adjustment.

Team Manager Peter Schetty was present, for his last engagement with Ferrari, accompanied by his replacement Ing. Calieri. Fortunately for Ferrari, the only other 3-litre present was the Bonnier Lola which was damaged too badly to compete, in a pre-race crash. All the opposition to Ferrari came from 2-litre cars. With all the problems the two Ferraris proved to be slower than the times recorded the previous race but Merzario nevertheless took the pole with a 1 min. 20.3 secs. on the Thursday practice and Ickx recorded a 1 min. 20.7 secs. to take second place on the grid.

After a rain storm on Friday, Saturday proved to be sunny and hot. Regazzoni immediately took his Ferrari into the lead followed by Scheckter in the March BMW and Love with a Chevron. The first time round Ickx had moved his Ferrari up into second place behind Regazzoni and after 30 minutes of racing the

Belgian was ahead of his Swiss teammate.

After the first stops for fuel, Ickx/Redman led by one lap from Regazzoni/Merzario as the latter had to pit with brake trouble, a pad having broken.

After 4 hours, Ickx led by 2 laps from his teammates but shortly after came slowly into the pits, the engine in a cloud of smoke-a valve had broken.

The lead Ferrari of Regazzoni/Merzario was having its share of trouble with brakes. Merzario had to stop to check his clutch and brakes.

A sudden rainstorm forced a tyre change and Ferrari was penalized as it required a push start to get the car going again.

An hour later Merzario slid badly at the end of the straight and killed the engine. Fortunately, the starter worked but the clutch was acting up and Merzario regained the road in 1st gear on the starter.

Merzario/Regazzoni won averaging 166.29 k p h for the 365 laps or 1,497.96 km and Ickx was credited with fastest lap at 1 min. 22.8 secs. 178.435 k p h.

The 1973 Sports Car Season

The first sports car race of the 1973 season was held at Vallelunga near Rome on 25th March.

It was thought that the Ferrari superiority in 1972 would continue but the big surprise was in the tremendous improvement of the Matras who had forgone Formula 1 racing to concentrate on the Manufacturers' sports car series.

Ferrari had apparently sold three of the nine cars he had used during the 1972 season retaining six cars for revision and use during the 1973 season.

The 312/P for 1974 had a longer wheelbase, a new nose, and power output uprated to 460 b h p at 11,000 r p m.

The reason for the Vallelunga event was to replace the Sebring 12 Hours but it was certainly not the best choice for a World Championship Sports Car race, being more suitable for smaller competition cars, the circuit measuring only 3.2 kilometres. The writing on the wall for Ferrari was soon made apparent when Cervert took the Matra around in 1 min. 8.5 secs, breaking the absolute lap record set by Fittipaldi with a

Formula 1 car at 1 min. 11.6 secs.

The best Ferrari could do was Redman's time of 1 min. 10.2 secs. Ickx with the Ferrari muscled his way to the front at the start followed by Cervert's Matra and Merzario's Ferrari in third place. This situation remained for about 12 laps then with the warmed-up tyres the Ferraris began to understeer excessively and Cervert put the Matra ahead of Ickx. Cervert then began to run away from the Ferrari. Ickx had to come in for an unscheduled pit stop with front tyre problems. Harder compound tyres were fitted on the cars and all three Ferraris had the rear body section changed. The rear transverse airfoils were lowered but as a result of this work the Ickx/Redman Ferrari was five laps behind the Matra. Nevertheless with all the problems in the Ferrari team, the opposition also had theirs and Reutemann/Schenken placed their Ferrari 2nd with Ickx/Redman 3rd and Pace/Merzario 4th.

Le Mans test weekend

The LeMans test weekend was held on 31st March to 1st April 1973. As they so often have been, the Italian metal workers were out on strike so that the official Ferraris along with the official Alfa Romeo team and Panteras were not present.

However 4 Ferrari Daytonas of private owners showed up. The opposition to the GT Ferraris were the new 3-litre GT Porsches.

The Ferraris were faster but lacking in braking and handling. While there were no true racing Ferraris present, the record had been set the previous year by Ickx in practice at 3 min. 40.4 secs. Ganley in the 1973 trials went round in 3 min. 40.7 secs. in a Gulf Mirage and the Matra set a time of 3 min. 36.3 secs.

The Porsche RSRs were about 10 seconds a lap faster than the Daytonas and if Ferrari were to have any chance in the GT class of the future then it would have to be with the Berlinetta Boxer as it was clear that the 1973 Competition Daytona was absolutely obsolete.

Dijon

The Dijon 1000 km was held on 15th April 1973 because of the cancellation of the BOAC 1000 km.

Ferrari sent two of his 312/Ps and competition was in the form of two Matras and two cars from Gulf Mirage.

The Ferraris were of the latest updated 312/P type for Ickx/Redman and Merzario/Pace.

Larger intakes had been fitted to provide air for the flat-12 engine, the rear suspension had been revised and the cars fitted with a 'shovel nose' bodywork.

Cervert's Matra was fastest in practice at 59.4 secs and the Matras were clearly faster than the Ferraris which caused some consternation to the Italian team.

The 2 by 2 starting grid saw the Matras on the front row with Pace in the Ferrari and Hailwood's Mirage in the 2nd row and Ickx in the second Ferrari in the third row.

Cervert led from the start but a puncture let the Pescarolo Matra into the lead with the Pace Ferrari right behind, harassed by Hailwood's Gulf Mirage. The Mirage slowed with a split exhaust but the Ferraris were having trouble with too much down force given by the new noses. Handling of the Ferraris was improved by the extra downforce but the bodies were pressing against the tyres under certain circumstances so that at the first stop the old type nose had to be refitted.

Despite this, both Ferraris suffered from damage at the front of the cars caused by contact with other cars and with body panels touching tyres.

The story was that the Matras were faster and handled better and despite their own problems came out ahead with Ickx/Redman finishing 2nd, one lap behind the winners, and Merzario/Pace 4th, four laps behind.

Monza

The Monza 1000 km was held on 25th April 1973. The chicanes that had been required for the GODA were eliminated so the event was a typical Monza flat-out type of affair.

Ferrari entered a team of 312/Ps for Ickx/Redman, Merzario/Pace and Reutemann/Schenken.

Their opposition came from the Matra team and the Gulf Mirages. From the start of practice it was a Ferrari/Matra duel. Cervert in the Matra lapped in 1 min. 21.13 secs. and Ickx in the

Ferrari at 1 min. 21.8 secs. A rolling start was used and Beltoise in the Matra led Ickx' Ferrari with Merzario's Ferrari leading Pescarolo's Matra and Reutemann's Ferrari. Unfortunately for Ferrari, Merzario was out after only seven laps with a broken gearbox.

When Beltoise stopped on lap 33, Ickx took the lead and when the Ferrari stopped at 40 laps the Ferrari pit crew were in top form and Ickx was enabled to retain his lead. Slowly however the Matra worked itself into first place.

At 53 laps the situation remained with the Matra leading the Ickx Ferrari; the Ferrari putting constant pressure on the French car. Pescarolo's Matra cracked a stub axle and Schenken moved his Ferrari into 3rd place although being lapped by both Beltoise and Ickx. As Beltoise stopped on lap 68 and Ickx took the lead, the No. 1 French car was in trouble and Ickx was able to extend his lead to one lap ahead.

The Ferrari remained the full lap lead until the scheduled stop on lap 80 when Redman took over from Ickx. Cervert was now in the No. 1 Matra and he began to pile on the pressure so that by lap 103 he had snatched the lead back from the Ferrari.

The Matra had to refuel on lap 105 which gave Redman a 59 second advantage. Cervert, after his stop, again began to chew away and Redman was still scheduled for a fuel stop. Ickx took over and as he left the pits the Matra passed ahead into the lead. 50 laps were left in the race. The French car was pulling away but at 130 laps headed for the pits stopping again at 134 laps. The gearbox was jammed and Ickx had an unassailable lead with Reutemann's Ferrari 2nd.

Ickx/Redman won in 4 hr 07 min. 34.4 secs., an average speed of 242.473 k p h with Reutemann/Schenken 2nd in the other Ferrari 3 laps behind.

Francorchamps

The Spa 1000 km was held on the Francorchamps circuit on 6th May 1973. Ferrari entered two of the 312Ps for Ickx/Redman (No. 0888) painted in red and yellow and the Pace/Merzario car (No. 0896) painted red and green.

Both cars had the high-speed body with the

full Grand Prix tune engines for the fast Spa-Francorchamps circuit.

Ickx lapped at 3 min. 14.0 secs. on Thursday and improved to 3 min. 12.7 secs. on Friday, his lap average being 163.7 m p h which eclipsed the seemingly unbeatable time set by Siffert's 5 litre Porsche in 1971 of 162.07 m p h.

Pescarolo leading the Matra opposition recorded 3 min. 13.8 secs, and the second Ferrari of Pace recorded 3 min. 15.4. The fastest Gulf-Mirage was at 3 min. 16.2.

Ickx and Pescarolo shared the front row of the grid. Ickx led briefly but the Matra was the better car and Pescarolo just drove away from the Ferrari with Pace holding the 2nd Ferrari in 4th place. Pace pitted to refuel but the Ferrari would not restart and had to be fitted with a new battery. This dropped him a long way behind. When Pescarolo pitted, Ickx led briefly, better fuel mileage allowed the Ferrari to gain time and good pit work when the Ferrari also stopped for fuel allowed Redman to take over the car he shared with Ickx with a 33 second lead over the Matra.

The Matra blew a tyre and left the Ickx/Redman Ferrari with a commanding lead. The second Ferrari was in 3rd place a lap off the Pace. Just as the scene was set for an easy Ferrari victory, Ickx returned to the pits on foot, an oil pipe joint to the gearbox had cracked and without oil the gearbox had seized.

Then on lap 47 Pace's Ferrari pulled into the pits with a broken oil line to the cooler. Things were patched up and Pace rejoined the race but not in very good shape and was eventually passed by the Matra of Amon. The best that the Pace/Merzario Ferrari could do was to finish in 4th place, 4 laps behind the winning Gulf Mirage.

The Targa

The 1973 Targa Florio was held on the 13th May 1973 and after 36 years of the classic race it was stated to be the last with the CSI ruling that it was no longer to be included in the international calendar.

The Targa has always been a major event in Sicily with about 700,000 people attending.

For this final running of the event, Ferrari entered cars for Merzario/Nino Vaccarella and Ickx/Redman.

Alfa Romeo were there with two of their new T33/12s and Porsche with their 2-litre Carrera flat 6.

The Porsche was fastest but Merzario was right behind. It was not to be a Ferrari day, Merzario hit a wall damaging the front and Ickx did the same at Colesano and Ferrari had to leave the final race to Porsche.

Nurburgring

The ADAC 1000 Km was held at the Nurburgring on 27th May. For once the weather was superb. The competition was from Matra with a two-car team also from Alfa Romeo.

Ferrari had the 312Ps for Ickx/Redman (No. 0888), the car being normal in all respects while the Merzario/Pace car (No. 0890) was modified, having a lower, smoother tail section supposedly to give a smoother airflow over the rear spoiler. To achieve this, the engine oil cooler was moved from its position above the clutch to the right-hand side of the water radiator although still receiving air from a top duct. A new engine air box above the roll bar, fed air to the top of the flat 12 engine in place of the two normal air scoops in the body. A new type of rear suspension hub was also fitted. There was no doubt that the Ferraris were faster than the previous years' versions but they also seemed to be more 'twitchy' and by no means dominated practice as they had done previously. The Matras set the pace although Ickx qualified for the first row.

At the start, Cervert's Matra set the pace ahead of Ickx and Merzario.

At 8 laps, when the lead cars refuelled, the Matra of Beltoise retained the lead with Ickx 2nd and Pace in Merzario's car 3rd. On lap 14, the Matra was out and the 2 Ferraris were in 1st and 2nd places. The Ferraris were set to take the race when Merzario decided he wanted to win and set out after Ickx. The team manager settled the matter by pulling Merzario into the pits and replacing him with Pace and suitable instructions.

Ferrari thus had a comfortable win with Ickx/Redman covering the 1000 km in 5 hr 36 min. 53.4 secs. at 178.944 k p h and Merzario/Pace 2nd in 5 hr 36 min. 54.5 secs.

Le Mans

The LeMans 24 Hour race was held on 10/11th June 1973 and was the 50th Anniversary of the event.

For a time it looked as if Ferrari would forgo the event, as he had the previous year, since they had missed the test weekend because of strikes at Maranello. But Maranello rallied and entered three cars to oppose the four Matras of which three were of a brand new type backed up by the previous year's winning Matra.

The Ferrari entry comprised three 312/P models with the drivers teamed Ickx/Redman, Merzario/Pace and Reutemann/Schenken. All the Ferraris were colour coded and had the long tailed bodies for high speed circuits. They also had modified brakes which were fitted outboard to enable the discs to be changed more rapidly.

In Group 4, a host of Ferrari Daytonas were entered with two from the French Importer Charles Pozzi for Elford/Ballot-Lena and Dolhem/Serpaggi. NART has four cars entered for Garcia-Veiga/di Palma; Posey/Minter; 'Coco' Chinetti/Migault; Grossman/Guitteny. Ecurie Francorchamps had a similar car for Bond/ Andruet. The Shark Team a single Daytona for Geurie/Grandet, and the British JCB Team a car for Green/Corner.

At the start, Merzario's Ferrari took the immediate lead having a 4-second advantage over the No. 1 Matra on the 1st lap. Two Matras followed, then Schenken's Ferrari. Redman ran in 10th place playing a waiting game.

Merzario extended his lead considerably but when he pitted for fuel, after only 50 minutes, Cervert's Matra took the lead. The Matra led only briefly as it too had to refuel and Merzario had the Ferrari out in front again with a 41 second lead. Schenken alternated between 3rd and 4th places.

When Pace took over from Merzario, the Ferrari had a lead of 76 seconds over the Matra. However, the Ferrari was quickly back in the pits with a leaking seat tank. The Ferrari lost six laps in the pits and the Matra went into the lead. Merzario rejoined the race and drove as fast as he could to make up, in the process setting a new lap record of 3 min. 40.4 secs. As darkness fell, the Ferraris again gained the advantage. Depailler's Matra pitted with a seized engine,

Cervert tried to make up time with his Matra and lowered the lap record to 3 min. 39.6 secs. just before midnight.

At midnight the Schenken/Reutemann Ferrari led by two laps from the Ickx/Redman Ferrari and Merzario/Pace had moved back up so that they were in 5th place.

At 2.30 a m Reutemann pulled into the pits and the Ferrari was pushed away with a hole in its block.

In the GT class the Green/Corner Daytona was in 11th place leading its class.

At dawn the engine note of the lead Ferrari began to change, the exhaust system was beginning to fall off causing overheating problems and the Matra began to catch up.

By 9 a m the Matra was on the same lap as the Ferrari and at the next pit stop the Ferrari team decided to replace the exhaust system. This let the Matra back into the lead but the next lap it was the Matra's turn to fail with a fractured brake pipe. The Ferrari almost made it back into the lead but the Matra was out of the pits a fraction ahead and continued to increase its lead over the Ferrari to almost 20 seconds.

At 11 a m Ickx was forced into the pits with a fuel tank leak similar to that previously experienced by Merzario. It took six laps to repair the damage. The Merzario/Pace car being driven hard was up in third place and the Posey/Minter NART Daytona retired with a burned piston.

By midday Pescarolo/Larousse led in the Matra from Ickx/Redman with Merzario/Pace in third place.

The leading Matra experienced trouble with its steering and Ickx started making up time. The Matra was in the pits for 25 minutes but the Ferrari was so far behind that the Matra was fixed and restarted still holding the lead, but only by a fraction.

At 2.30 p m the Ferrari challenge was over Ickx pitted — the engine had given out with valve gear failure. The Matra won to the great joy of the French with the Ferrari of Merzario/ Pace second, some six laps behind. 6th, and 1st in the GT class, was the Elford/Ballot-Lena Daytona. The Daytona of Dolhem/Serpaggi was 9th; Migault/'Coco' Chinetti 13th and Andruet/Bond 20th.

Austrian 1000 km 1973

The Osterreichring 1000 kms took place on June 24 soon after the Le Mans 24 Hour race. Ferrari were still ahead in the World Championship but, Matra with their Le Mans victory were closing fast. Ickx and Brian Redman were paired in one 312P and Merzario and Carlos Pace in the other works car. At the start the two Matras drew away at over a second a lap with Pace following in third place. Unfortunately Pace at an inopportune moment understeered into a barrier and his car required a quick nose panel change before it could continue. Neither of the two works Ferraris could make any impression on the Matras and even the Gulf Mirages of Hailwood and Watson and Bell and Ganley were pushing them.

The Ickx Ferrari had to pit 4 laps early and Redman was not ready so Ickx continued. Later the same thing happened when Redman came in 2 laps early and Ickx was not ready so Redman continued. The Ferrari engine was running too rich and were forced to switch to the reserve early and pit orders were to come in regardless of schedule when this situation occurred. The situation also caused one extra stop for fuel than was anticipated.

The Pace/Merzario car ran through to the end but it had its share of problems. The body had to be patched again when the temporary earlier work was coming unglued.

Merzario also managed to have a minor off-road incident with further damage to the front end. The spare front end of the other car was fitted but Merzario found he could not see over the lip of the scuttle and time was lost having a piece of the cowl cut off and an extra seat cushion had to be fitted. As a result, Matra won once again with Ickx/Redman 3rd, one lap behind the Pace/Merzario 6th, six laps behind the winners.

Watkins Glen

The Watkins Glen 6 Hours was held on 31st July 1973. Matra and Gulf Mirage were present in opposition to Ferrari but Alfa Romeo stayed home.

Ferrari sent three cars for Ickx/Redman, Pace/Merzario and Reutemann/Schenken. The Ickx and Reutemann cars were normal P3s but the Merzario/Pace car was one specially prepared by Ing. Forghieri with relocated oil coolers and lower tail section. The drivers of this car found that at Watkins Glen they could pull 400 more r p m than the other two.

The previous year's record had been by Ickx Ferrari at 1 min. 47.2 secs. but Cervert with the Matra had no trouble in turning a lap in 1 min. 42.27.

The Ferraris tried all they could but the best Ferrari time was by Pace at 1 min. 44.2 with Reutemann and Redman being the next two fastest. The 312Ps were supported in the GT class by Monaguzzi/Garcia-Veiga, Posey/Migault and Grossman/Yenko in Competition Daytonas. Merzario jumped into the lead ahead of the Matras and managed to stay ahead of them. Then Cervert's Matra suddenly fell back so that Ickx who was immediately behind had to brake hard and hit the Matra, damaging the Matra enough for a 3-lap pit stop but allowing the Ferrari to continue with only a bent exhaust pipe.

The track, which had been wet, allowed the Matra of Pescarolo/Larousse to exploit its potential to the full and move into the lead. It simply remained to be seen which Ferrari would be second. Merzario and Pace had to stop twice, one to change brake pads and the other to change a punctured tyre. Reutemann and Schenken were second until a fuel pump metering drive belt broke and the car retired.

The final results were Ickx and Redman finishing 2nd, 2 laps behind the Matra, Pace/Merzario in 3rd place 3 laps behind and the Daytonas of Monguzzi/Garcia-Veiga 13th, Posey/Migault 14th, and Grossman/Yenko 15th.

CHAPTER TWELVE
The touring cars

UNTIL the advent of the 250 Gran Turismo, Ferrari showed very little interest in his touring cars which were built in small quantities to satisfy a somewhat limited request by certain customers. Quite often these touring cars were only built in series of five and more often than not there was a great deal of variation even amongst the models of the same series. However, when it was established that there was a definite market for a Ferrari touring car, Enzo embarked on his highly successful 250 GT design which has now been developed to the point of actual assembly line production.

Type 166 Inter

The first touring car produced by Ferrari was the Type 166 Inter developed directly from the 2-litre Type 166 Mille Miglia. The car retained the then already classic Ferrari V12 engine with a bore and stroke of 60 x 58.8 mm having a displacement of 1995-cc, a compression ratio of 7.5 : 1 and a power output of 110 b h p at 6,000 r p m. The engine was basically the same as the sports version but was often fitted with only one 32 DCF twin-choke Weber carburetter. Ignition was by single plug per cylinder and two distributors and coils. A single dry-plate clutch with elastic hub was employed and a front-mounted five-speed gearbox had synchromesh on third and fourth speeds.

Independent front suspension was by means of double wishbones and a single transverse leaf spring, together with damping by Houdaille hydraulic shock absorbers.

The rigid rear axle had a light alloy centre casting for the differential and was suspended by semi-elliptic springs and torsional stablising bars. Hydraulic brakes had a single master cylinder operating single slave cylinders in each drum.

The frame was of welded tubular steel construction with elliptical section tubes. Wheels on the earliest cars were of the Gabo alloy type fitting 5.50 x 15 tyres at the front and the same measurement at the rear. Wheelbase was 2.420 m with front track 1.250 m and rear track 1.200 m. The car had a dry weight of 980 kg and a fuel consumption of 14 litres per 100 km.

Type 195 Inter

This model was followed by the Type 195 Inter which was very similar to the early type. The cubic capacity was increased to 2340-cc with a bore and stroke of 65 x 58.8 mm and the b h p increased to 130 at 6,000 r p m. On the early models the single 32 DCF twin-choke Weber was retained although later models went to three carburetters. Gearbox ratios were the same as on the Type 166 Inter, first being 3.08, second 1.9, third 1.38, fourth 1.00 and fifth 0.925 to 1. Frame, braking system and front and rear suspensions all remained the same but the wheelbase was increased to 2.500 m with a front track of 1.270 m and rear track of 1.250 m; 5.90 x 15 tyres were used all round and total dry weight reduced to 950 kg, but fuel consumption went up to 15 litres per 100 km on the single carburetter models.

Type 212 Inter

For the design that followed, known as the 212 Inter, the capacity was again increased, this time to 2562-cc with a bore and stroke of 68 x 58.8 mm, compression ratio was increased to 8 : 1 and 170 b h p was achieved at 6,500 r p m. Three Weber twin-choke Type 36 DCF carburetters were fitted and the five-speed gearbox retained but with different ratios, first being 3.157, second 1.946, third 1.403, fourth 1.00 and fifth 0.914 to 1.

Front suspension was by means of double

wishbones and single transverse leaf spring with integral rubber blocks and damping by Houdaille shockabsorbers. Rear suspension was by means of semi-elliptic longitudinal leaf springs with four radius rods and Houdaille shockabsorbers. Wheelbase was again increased to 2.600 m with a front track of 1.278 m and rear track of 1.250 m; 6.40 x 15 tyres were fitted all round.

Type 212 Export

At the same time as the 212 Inter was produced, Ferrari had another design named the 212 Export which utilized the same engine but with a much shorter wheelbase. The earliest versions of the 212 Export had only one twin-choke Weber 36 DCF carburetter but the later ones, which were often seen in sporting events, used the three-carburetter layout.

The 150 b h p of the first models was increased to match the 212 Inter's 170 b h p, the car being lighter and shorter. Gearbox ratios were the same as the 212 Inter but the wheel-base was reduced to 2.250 m with a front track of 1.270 m and a rear track of 1.250 m; 4.50 x 15 wheels were used all round fitted with 6.40 x 15 tyres.

Ferrari's next move was again to increase the size of his engine this time to 3 litres with his Type 250 Export and Europa. However, instead of using the original Type 125 Colombo-designed 12-cylinder engine as a basis, he used a linered-down version of the big 4.1-litre engine originally built for his Type 342 America. This engine had its shortcomings and was subsequently abandoned in favour of the Type 125-based version.

Type 250 Export

The 250 Export had a bore and stroke of 68 x 68 mm giving a displacement of 2963.45-cc with a compression ratio of 8.5 : 1 and it had a maximum output of 220 b h p at 7,000 r p m. Three Weber 36 DCF carburetters were fitted and ignition was by means of two distributors with one plug per cylinder. A metallic multi-disc clutch was used and the five-speed gearbox remained the same as in the 212 Inter and Export models.

Wheelbase was again changed to 2.400 m with a front track of 1.300 m and a rear track of 1.320 m. Wheel sizes were altered to 4.00 x 16

which mounted 5.50 x 16 tyres at the front and 6.00 x 16 at the rear.

Total dry weight remained the same as in the earlier 212 Export model being 800 kg.

The 250 Europa

Ferrari's first serious attempt at building a Gran Turismo car that could be built in series came when he produced the 250 Europa, which can be called the true ancestor of the present day series 250 Gran Turismo.

For this model Ferrari still used the Lampredi engine developed from the 4.1-litre. With a bore and stroke of 68 x 68 mm and a displacement of 2963.45-cc it had a compression ratio of 8.5 : 1 but the power output was dropped to 200 at 6,000 r p m. Three Webers of the new type 36 DCZ were fitted whilst single plug ignition with two distributors and coil were retained. The major change in this car was the replacement of the long-used five-speed gearbox by a newer four-speed type originally developed for the sports cars. In this box first gear ratio was 2.54, second 1.7, third 1.255 and fourth 1.00 : 1.

Front suspension followed the usual practice with wishbones and single transverse leaf spring with the rubber block inserts and damping by Houdaille shockabsorbers. Rear suspension also remained semi-elliptic leaf springs with Houdaille shockabsorbers taking charge of the damping.

Another change was in the braking system, two master cylinders instead of one and two-leading-shoe system being employed.

Again there was an alteration in the wheel-base, this time it was lengthened to 2.800 m with a front track 1.325 m and a rear track of 1.320 m; a further change was another alteration in wheel size with 5.00 x 15 wheels all round fitting 7.10 x 15 tyres. Through the fitting of a more luxuriously finished body, the weight of the car crept back up to 1,000 kg.

Type 342 America

At the same time that Enzo Ferrari was building his 212 Inters, he decided to go into production with something larger that would appeal more to the American market and that would serve as a basis for a new competition car capable of taking on the Cadillac-and Chrysler-engined Allards which were giving the smaller-engined Ferraris a difficult time in American competition. The new car was known as the Type 342 America. The new engine followed the basic layout of the smaller Type 125 with 12 cylinders in V form at 60 degrees. A bore and stroke of 80 x 68 mm giving a displacement of 4101.66-cc and a compression ratio of 8 : 1 gave a power output of 220 b h p at 6,000 r p m. As on the Europa engine, there were cast iron threaded-in liners as well as a light alloy cylinder block with hemispherical combustion chambers. A standard type Siluminum crankcase was used and the crankshaft ran in seven bearings. The inclined overhead valves were actuated by single, chain-driven, overhead camshafts, through rocker arms. Ignition was by means of a single plug per cylinder with two distributors and high-tension coils.

The clutch was of the single dry-plate type and the four-speed gearbox was in unit with the engine. First gear ratio was 2.536, second 1.701, third 1.256 and fourth 1.000 to 1. The standard Ferrari front suspension was used, with wishbones and single transverse leaf spring and integral rubber blocks damped by Houdaille shockabsorbers. Rear suspension was by means of semi-elliptic longitudinal leaf springs and damping by Houdailles as at the front. A two-master-cylinder brake system was used, with two-leading-shoe brakes, and chassis frame construction was similar to that of the other touring cars. Wheelbase was 2.650 m, front track 1.325 m, rear track 1.320 m; 4.50 x 15 wheels were fitted all round taking tyres of 6.40 x 15 and total weight was 1200 kg.

Type 375 America

The Type 342 America was not a very successful car and Ferrari set to work to remedy the shortcomings of the design. His new model was known as the Type 375 America and had the engine capacity increased to 4.5-litres. With a bore and stroke of 84 x 68 mm a total displacement of 4522.94 was achieved and, with a compression ratio of 8 : 1, power output was 300 b h p at 6,300 r p m. Three twin-choke Type 42 DCZ Webers replaced the type 40 DCF used on the 342 America. A multi-plate clutch replaced the single disc type but the four-speed gearbox

with synchromesh on all four gears was retained. Front suspension with the wishbones and transverse leaf spring remained the same and trailing links with semi-elliptic leaf springs took care of the rear suspension, whilst Houdailles provided the damping. The two master-cylinder, two-leading-shoe brake layout was also retained but the wheelbase was increased to 2.800 m with a front track of 1.325 m and a rear track of 1.320 m. Wheel sizes too were increased with 5.00 x 15 wheels all round these being fitted with 7.10 x 15 tyres; the weight was reduced to 1000 kg.

Type 410 Superamerica

This model was eventually superseded by the Type 410 Superamerica which utilized the very successful 4.9-litre engine that had won the 24 Hours of Le Mans, the Buenos Aires 1000 km and the Pan American Road Race. With a bore and stroke of 88 x 68 mm displacement was 4961.576-cc and, with a compression ratio of 8.5 : 1, a power output of 340 b h p was achieved at 6,000 r p m. Three twin-choke type 42 DCZ Weber carburetters were fitted and a dry multiplate clutch was used. The fully synchronized (Porsche-type) four speed gearbox was employed but using different gear ratios from those on the 375 America. First was 2.20, second 1.753, third 1.252 and fourth 1.00 to 1. The suspension employed on the 375 America was retained as was the braking system. Wheelbase remained at 2.800 m but the track was widened at the front to 1.455 m and the rear 1.450 m. Wheel sizes went up to 5.50 x 16 fitting 6.50 x 16 tyres all round and dry weight went up to 1100 kg. During 1956 410 SAs were built in a small 'production' series.

The 410 Superfast

A development of this car was the 410 Superfast which was a lightweight version having a dry weight of 950 kg and the wheelbase shortened to 2.700 m. This car was considerably modified in the chassis department, the front suspension having the transverse leaf spring replaced by coil springs and having the rear suspension replaced by a De Dion and transverse leaf spring. Final modifications for the 1959 Type 410 Superfast was the introduction of inboard brakes at the rear, the car also being offered with optional disc brakes.

Type 250 Gran Turismo

Ferrari finally standardized his touring cars with the introduction of the 250 Gran Turismo developed from the 250 Europa. In this model the larger 4.1 based engine was dispensed with and the Type 125-based engine re-introduced; with a bore and stroke of 73 x 58.8 mm, it had a displacement of 2953.211-cc and with a compression ratio of 8.5 : 1, gave 220 b h p at 7,000 r p m. Three twin-choke Weber type 36 DCZ carburetters were fitted; also a twin-disc dry-plate clutch with Raybestos lining. A four-speed gearbox with the Porsche patent synchronization was used, first gear ratio being 2.54, second 1.7, third 1.255 and fourth 1.00 to 1. Wishbone and coil spring front suspension was used with damping by Houdaille shockabsorbers.

Rear suspension was by means of semi-elliptic longitudinal leaf springs and damping by Houdailles. Two-leading-shoe brakes were also employed with twin master cylinders. Wheelbase was 2.600 m with a front track of 1.354 m and rear track of 1.349 m; 5.00 x 16 wheels were used mounting 6.00 x 16 tyres all round. Dry weight was 1050 kg for the full touring version and 900 for the sports/touring version.

The Berlinettas

The 'Berlinettas' history begins in the mid-1950s. Enzo Ferrari had been manufacturing coupe versions of his open sports/racing cars since 1949. These cars were called Berlinettas, which in effect, means 'little sedan' or coupe in Italian. The difference between the coupe and the berlinetta was that the berlinetta was the racing version of the coupe. However, through the years every Ferrari coupe has been called a berlinetta.

The differences between the two were many. Lightness was of great importance in the berlinetta. Glass windows were replaced with plastic, steel bodies became aluminium. Interiors were considered 'gutted' in comparison with the coupe. Bumpers were often discarded. In the interest of streamlining, headlamps became enclosed by faired-in plastic covers. Cold-air scoops were provided on the hood, while livelier cams and elevated compression helped increase

the potency of the berlinetta. However, after all was said and done, these racing cars could still be driven on the street. The noise level in the cockpit was higher, as was the temperature but not totally unbearable. Fans to cool the water in the coupe were often omitted in the berlinetta, but this never upset the engine except in stop-go traffic.

By 1955 the FIA had begun to consider establishing international classes for *Gran Turismo* cars, dividing them into categories based on engine size. Largely because of the tragic accident at Le Mans that year involving a sports/racing Mercedes-Benz capable of 180 m p h and an Austin-Healey only capable of 130 m p h, they decided to return to the classic dual-purpose sports car. Mercedes-Benz had been developing the 300 SL, Jaguar had the XK140 and Ferrari had the 250 GT Europa.

The first year of the new championship was 1956, and Ferrari Berlinettas began winning immediately. They so dominated the 10-day long Tour de France that the long wheelbase (102.5 inches) berlinettas have become affectionately known as TDFs.

The 250 GT

By 1959, Ferrari Ing. Giotto Bizzarrini had been developing a new berlinetta, one whose wheelbase was considerably shorter at 94.5 inches. The solid rear axle was still used, but was located in such a way that an independent rear suspension system was of little value. From 1960 to 1962, this car, now referred to as the SWB berlinetta, continued to dominate the Group III (2000 to 3000 cc) GT class.

The SWB Berlinetta was produced in limited numbers from late 1959 until very early 1963. It followed the 250 GT long wheelbase, or 'Tour de France', Berlinetta in production, though six 'Interim' Berlinettas were built between the long and short wheelbase cars. These 'Interim' Berlinettas (chassis Nos. 1461, 1465, 1509, 1519 and 1521) were built on the long (2600 mm) chassis of the Tour de France Berlinettas but featured the styling for the upcoming short wheelbase model.

The SWB Berlinetta was introduced at the Paris Auto Show in October of 1959. Built on the 94.5 inch (2400 mm) wheelbase chassis, powered by the classic three litre V-12 engine, it was destined for many racing successes. But perhaps more than any Ferrari before or since, here was a car equally at home on a race track or a boulevard. A quick change to cooler plugs, racing tyres and the addition of a roll bar and the SWB Berlinetta could contest its class at Le Mans or Sebring.

Early models were turned out in lightweight alloy bodies for the most part, a Pininfarina design executed by Scaglietti. However, more steel bodied cars were built overall. Pininfarina built certain components for the steel bodied cars while the doors, bonnet and boot lids were aluminium, and were constructed at Scaglietti. An educated guess would be that no more than 250 SWB Berlinettas were built, with probably less than one-fourth being the lightweight competition version. Chassis numbers for the model range from Nos. 1539 to 4057.

By studying the development of the SWB Berlinetta body over its three year lifespan, four stages of evolution can be noted. The first eleven cars built were devoid of the characteristic wing vents (front and rear). The earliest examples also had no amber running lights on the leading edge of each front wing and had no vent windows in the side glass. All the early 1960 cars with lightweight bodies had plastic sliding or wind-up windows. Also, a limited number of cars were turned out in 1961 with sliding plastic windows and no vent windows. All lightweight cars had non-padded dashboards painted matte black instead of being covered in leather or plastic.

Body style number two had vents in the front and rear wings and a round running light for each front wing. It should be noted that some of the early cars without wing vents were later changed to add vents, but either Chassis No. 1905 or 1917 was the first SWB Berlinetta delivered with wing vents and running lights.

Style number three marked the coming of vent windows for the side glass. Otherwise, externally the cars remained the same. Body style number four displayed a relocated fuel filler cap - it was now in the top of the left rear wing instead of the upper left corner of the rear deck - and a more horizontal line to the top of the side windows. Also, horizontally mounted 'tear drop'shaped amber running lights replaced the round running lights on each front wing. A few steel bodied cars were built with the oversized competition fuel filler cap in the left rear wing, a characteristic normally seen only on the lightweight cars and then in the upper left corner of the rear deck.

Other changes appeared both externally and internally throughout the model run (oil pressure gauge, roofvents and spare tyre location, for example), but they apparently did not correspond with the changes from one body style to another. All SWB Berlinettas were equipped with the disc brakes except that the 1959 Paris Show car which was originally built with drum brakes and changed to discs for the show.

The earliest chassis number noted for a 'style four' SWB Berlinetta is No. 2111. The car is steel bodied and does not appear to have been rebodied, which brings up an interesting point: the four body styles do not follow in strict chronological order. For example, SWB Berlinetta No. 2237 is a 'style two' alloy-bodied car (the last such built?) and SWB Berlinettas Nos. 2129, 2177, 2243, 2251 and 2265 are style three cars with steel bodies. However, more style four cars were turned out than any of the other three styles.

Power for the SWB came from the 3-litre single overhead camshaft V12. Output was rated at 260 to 280 b h p at 7,000 r p m, some 20 b h p higher than concurrent 250 GTs. The additional output came from higher compression which was 9.2:1 versus the GTs 8.8:1, and slightly larger carburetters. In this form, the engine was designated Type 128 F by the factory, but we have observed one late SWB whose engine was stamped Type 168, which is the GTO's type number. However, this engine was not equipped with six carburetters, rather three 40 DCZs with short intake stacks.

Alloy-bodied cars weighed just under 2,400 pounds with full tanks. Tyre sizes for the earlier cars were 175 x 400 with a front tread of 53.3 inches and 53.1 inches at the rear. Overall length of the car, 163.5 inches.

Though the vast majority of the cars were equipped with the three litre V-12, stories persist of a few SWB Berlinettas being powered by 400 SA engines. In any event, it seems

(*Top*) Pininfarina 410 Superamerica of 1956 - 1957. This is car No. 0493SA
(*Middle*) 410 SA by Pininfarina
(*Bottom*) 1958 410 Superamerica

(Top) The production 250 GT by Pininfarina 1959
(Middle) 250 GT California Scaglietti
(Bottom Left) 250 GT Pininfarina Spyder
(Bottom Right) 1959 second series of Spyder California

(*Top Left*) An early Scaglietti short wheelbase 250 GT Berlinetta
(*Top Right*) The predecessor of the swb Berlinetta 250 GT of 1960
(*Middle*) This is the 'classic' swb 250 GT Berlinetta by Scaglietti
(*Bottom Left*) The 250 GT swb was the precursor to the 250 GTO. Built in both steel and alloy-bodied versions, they succeeded the 250 GT Tour de France in GT racing. This is Stirling Moss driving Rob Walker's swb to win the 1961 Tourist Trophy at Goodwood
(*Bottom Right*) 1960 swb 250 GT Berlinetta No. 1993GT

(*Top Left*) The 1964 or series 2 250 GTO. Only three of these bodies were built by Scaglietti

(*Top Right*) Innes Ireland at the wheel of UDT Laystall's 250 GTO during the 1963 Tourist Trophy at Goodwood. Rear deck spoilers were rivetted on initially, then built into the main body structure

(*Middle*) This is the first series one 250 GTO Berlinetta No. 3223GT 1962

(*Bottom Left*) Lorenzo Bandini at Brands Hatch in the 4 litre GTO. This car was fitted with round driving lights and vent wings

(*Bottom Right*) One of the SEFAC GTO, at the 46th Targa Florio in 1962

(*Top*) Mike Parkes presses Graham Hill's E-type Jaguar at Silverstone, 12 May 1962. Parkes took the UDT Laystall owned GTO to a win
(*Middle*) 'Superfast II' built on a Type 410 chassis was shown at the Turin Show of 1960
(*Bottom Left*) 1960 400 Superamerica by Pininfarina
(*Bottom Right*) The production version of the 250 GT 2 + 2 by Pininfarina

(Top) 1962 Pininfarina 'Superfast III' on the 400 SA chassis
(Middle) 1963 version of the 400 Superamerica
(Bottom Left) The final series of the 250 GT was the GT/L or Lusso
(Bottom Right) 1965 Ferrari 500 Superfast

(Top) 275 GTS. This is a later version
(Middle) 1962 Bertone bodied 250 GT shown at the Geneva Show
(Bottom) Successor to the 250 GT Lusso was the 275 GTB. It was the first Ferrari to use cast wheels rather than wire. It was first shown at Paris in 1964

(*Top*) The Pininfarina 1966 Paris Show car, the last of the 365 GT based California
(*Middle*) The second series of 330 GT coupes, Pininfarina introduced this in 1966
(*Bottom Left*) 1963 330 GT 2 + 2
(*Bottom Right*) The 330 GTS Spyder

certain that all cars had four-speed synchromesh gearboxes with electric overdrive available on later models. Gear ratios for early cars were 2.54, 1.70, 1.26 and 1.00 with at least seven final drive ratios available (3.44 : 1,3.55 to 1,3.67 : 1,378 : 1,400 : 1,425 : 1 and 4.57 : 1). Front suspension used wishbones and coil springs with an antiroll bar. Rear suspension (rigid axle) was by leaf springs and radius arms.

Competition success was quick to come as would be expected from such a potent car. However, due to the fact that the car was built on a new chassis, it was not immediately homologated and ran in the open class for sports cars in international races until the 1960 Le Mans 24 Hour race. Homologation papers, submitted for chassis No. 1539, were valid on 16 June 1960, and thereafter the car competed in the GT category.

In 1960 SWB Berlinettas won the Tourist Trophy race in England, the Tour de France and the 1000 km of Paris at Montlhery. In 1961 the Tourist Trophy again went to Stirling Moss in a Rob Walker SWB. Many class wins in other important events went to SWB Berlinettas enough so that the GT class in the Constructor's Championship for 1961 went to Ferrari, 40 points to 17 for Porsche. By 1962 the GTO was competing and winning in international races, but many class wins were taken by well prepared cars both in Europe and in SCCA events.

In 1961 Ferrari was preparing what was to become the end statement of the 250 GT Berlinetta. For Le Mans that year, he had prepared what appeared to be a 400 Superamerica. Rather than using the usual 4-litre engine, he had substituted a standard 250 GT unit brought up to Testa Rossa specifications (that is to say, different cams, pistons, dry sump, etc.), which developed 300 hp at 7,500 rpm rather than the berlinetta's 280. It was entered as a '250 GT Special' and was driven by Fernand Tavano and Giancarlo Baghetti. (Of special note concerning Tavano is that, whenever a special Ferrari turned up, he was always a co-driver. He is a car dealer in Le Mans and with the usual amount of French politics year after year he managed to secure the latest GT cars from Ferrari). After having risen as high as 7th place overall, it succumbed to engine difficulties in the 13th hour.

This car is considered to be the prototype of the GTO. Two of these coupe cars were built. It was again driven to 4th overall by Stirling Moss in the Daytona Continental 3-Hour at Daytona beach on 11th February 1962. Two weeks later, on February 24th, at his annual press conference, Enzo Ferrari revealed his plans for 1962 and with them the new 250 GTO.

Preceding the press conference, Ferrari and Pininfarina had been collaborating on a body design, pictures of which appeared in several European newspapers and magazines. It was clumsy in appearance. The nose had been described as 'anteater-like'. Two vertical slats were cut into the side of the body, just in front of the leading edge of the door, to relieve engine compartment heat, while a rear quarter panel window was installed for better cockpit ventilation. The rear wing shape was rather odd; it was tacked on, reminding one of the larger auto manufacturers' attempts to disguise new models. This development was carried out on SWB Chassis No. 3175. However, by the time it reached the press conference it had 'all the lumps, bumps, scoops, slots and rivets that typify Ferrari racing cars.' The car was also without the familiar spoiler but by March of that year one had been riveted on. This gave additional high-speed stability as well as stopping exhaust fumes from flowing back into the cockpit under heavy braking. Eventually these spoilers were replaced by ones that were faired into the tail, blending beautifully with the end of the car. At Sebring that month, the GTO made its competition debut in the hands of Phil Hill and Olivier Gendebien. They finished 2nd overall and first in GT. This type of finishing order was to recur many times in the next three years, the GTOs barely being beaten by their sports/racing brothers.

The bodies were built by Scaglietti to a SEFAC design. All of the Series 1, or GTO '62-63', cars were constructed with two side-vent openings. It is believed that after a car had received sufficient front-end damage, Merdardo Fantuzzi added a third vent.

Basically the GTO was a more refined SWB Berlinetta. The engine was given a dry-sump reservoir of 15 quarts allowing the centre of gravity to be lowered as well as assisting the aerodynamics. With its six twin-throat Weber 38 DCN carburetters and potent camshaft grind, the engine claimed 300 b h p at 7,500 r p m with a redline at 8,400 r p m. A 5-speed all-synchro gearbox replaced the old 4-speed. The fact that these cars were identical in layout allowed for several SWB cars to be converted to GTO specifications. The major difference was that the GTO was 250 pounds lighter. It was also 6.6 inches longer and 3.5 inches lower.

Ferrari had made a point of supplying potential customers with brochures. This not only held true with the GT cars but with the race cars as well. However, for some strange reason, Ferrari did not publish a catalogue for the GTO. Brand new, and delivered to competition-minded clients only, the cars sold for $ 18,000 U.S.

'Omologato'

The prefix GT, of course, stands for Gran Turismo, while the suffix O is the derivative of the Italian word 'omologato', to homologate, hence GTO or homologated GT. The process of homologation for this or any car was the cause of great concern, particularly for this car! For a car to be homologated or accepted by Group III rules as listed under Appendix J of the *Federation Internationale de l'Automobile,* the major requirement was that 100 examples had to be manufactured. Although Ferrari had not yet constructed one-fourth this number, he was granted homologation on the grounds that he had been producing 3-litre GT cars since 1955. While looking over the homologation papers for the GTO, it is interesting to note that he illustrates the new car by showing an SWB Berlinetta, then goes on to list the changes such as 5-speed gearbox and dry sump. The car was homologated without question. Full up to date details are given on page 229.

The car was, for all intents and purposes, 'a Testa Rossa with a roof', but this by no means meant that it was not within the spirit of the rules. This fact so enraged fellow competitors that the FIA was asked to find out how many of these cars had actually been built! The FIA was convinced that the car was legal, but was pressured into this situation. When it was

learned that only a handful had been completed, the FIA asked Ferrari if he intended to build the required 100. Obviously, his answer was 'no.' Ferrari felt that the market for such a car had already been saturated. He also said the car was too fast and there were only a few men in the world who could master its ferocity! Even after these statements, the FIA granted homologation for the next two years, proving the car was indeed quite legal.

The factory tells us that they only produced 25 cars but we have been able to locate 39, of which all have been verified as actual GTOs.

There were three 4-litre cars, the first of which was driven to 2nd overall at the Nurburgring by Mike Parkes and Willy Mairesse. The second car also built in 1962 appeared at Le Mans but was crashed on the first lap by Parkes.

The GTO chassis was of the same tubular construction as the SWB, with, as described by French journalist Jose' Rosinski, 'two strong longitudinal members joined by transverse pieces and a central platform traditional with the 250 GT.' Front suspension was independent with unequal-length A arms, these being forged units. A heavy anti-roll bar was fitted which passed across the front of the engine compartment. At the rear, Bizzarrini wanted to replace the semi-elliptic leaf springs with coil springs for greater flexibility. Rosinski tells us that this measure was 'too radical to pass by extension,' and Bizzarrini was forced to retain the leaf springs. However, he added coil units, baptizing them as 'compensatos'. The usual radius rod accompanied by a Watts link assured the location of the live rear axle.

Type 250 Le Mans

For 1964 Ferrari had developed a new car to supercede the two year old 250 GTO.

This car was quite different in that for the first time Ferrari was building a rear-engined 'GT' car. It was called the 250 Le Mans. This car was the berlinetta version of the 250 P sports/racing car, — a 250 P with a roof. History does have a way of repeating itself. In his attempt to homologate this new car, Ferrari had not prepared the papers in time to meet the FIA deadline. Between that time and the next review, the FIA had learned that the required number had not been produced. The 250 LM was then brought up to 3.3 litres, but not to confuse the issue, he continued to call it the 250 LM. In his second attempt to have it homologated he was turned down. This was to cause quite a fuss which extended over to the Italian Automobile Club, with Ferrari threatening to withdraw from competition in Italy. This meant that the 250 GTO was to continue on in defence of the World Championship.

GTO 1964 modifications

Ferrari changed the outward appearance of the GTO by supplying a new body. Its overall length was shortened from 170 inches for '62-63' to 165.7 inches. Width was increased by three inches and height was brought from 47 inches to 44.8 inches. Rear wheel width was widened to seven inches. Dry weight was 1936 pounds. The car was considerably cleaner in appearance. Of the three that were built, No. 5571 (the first) was set apart from the other two by an airfoil set into the roof. This motif also appeared on the 250 LM prototype. This 1964 GTO came straight off the boat to win the 2,000 Daytona Continental, with Phil Hill and Pedro Rodriguez. They averaged 98.2 m p h despite a blown tyre while Rodriguez was at the wheel.

For the third year running, Ferrari won the World Championship. During those three years, of the 28 championship events held, the GTO won 20, finished 2nd in 15 and 3rd in 9, giving this car a reputation for being virtually indestructible by finishing in approximately 70 per cent of the events in which it was entered.

FERRARI 250 GTO ENGINE AND CHASSIS NUMBERS

3223, 3387, 3909, 3943,
3413, 3445, 3987, 4091,
3451, 3505, 4115, 4153,
3527, 3589, 4219, 4293,
3607, 3647, 4399, 4491,
3673, 3705, 4561, 4675,
3729, 3757, 4713, 4757,
3765, 3767, 5095, 5111,
3769, 3809,

No. 2643 GT one of two SA bodies; SWB chassis prototypes.

(Series II, 1964)
5571, 5573, 5575.

(Series II, Rebodied 1962-1963)
3413, 4091, 4399, 4675.

(Four Litre Cars)
3673, 3765, 4561.

GT bodywork

Ferrari, in producing his Gran Turismos, has used a great variety of body styles. The first GT bodies were built by Carozzeria Touring of Milan whilst the first of the 4.1-litre cars had bodies by Ghia of Turin. During the intermediate stage of Gran Turismo production the majority were the Michelotti designs executed by Vignale which held sway until the Pinin Farina era came with the first 250 Europas. The vast majority of the 250 Gran Turismo victories have been gained with the Scaglietti lightweight coupe cars, and these became a standard production item.

Ferrari in 1958 initiated his production line with an output of approximately one car per day. The line included the competition coupe and the California convertible by Scaglietti, and the standard coupe and 'special order' convertible by Pinin Farina. Intermingled with these were the few 'special order' 4.9-litre Superfasts, usually with bodies by Pinin Farina.

In the period 1957 to 1963, Ferrari established a set pattern for the production of Touring and Gran Turismo cars. Instead of building five to ten of a specific model he began to realize that the production of a larger series of cars, that did not involve great problems of parts and maintenance, could be a commercially successful venture. The 250/Europa Gran Turismo was quickly followed by the 250 Gran Turismo which in its turn led to the Pinin Farina convertible in luxury form and the less expensive Scaglietti California convertible. In the coupe form, the first series of Gran Turismos had a body by Boano but then reverted to a Pinin Farina-bodied car still maintaining the classic layout with the V12 3-litre engine and the ladder-type frame with independent front suspension and the live rear axle. The Farina coupe was the first really successful production car and a small scale production assembly line was set up at Maranello. In the bigger class Ferrari restricted himself to a very limited production of the rather exotic 412 Super-americas with a capacity of 4.9-litres which came in various body forms. This model was later replaced by a 4-litre version, known as the Type 400, which had a cubic capacity of 3967-cc and produced a power output of 320 b h p at 7,000 r p m. This in turn was followed by a coupe version in prototype form which ran in various races during 1962 and 1963 being basically designed to take advantage of the FIA prototype category.

Following on from the Farina bodied 250 GT was a four-seater version known as the 2 plus 2 which could in fact seat four people for the first time since the Ghia 4 seaters of 1949-50. This proved a very popular model and, together with the Farina coupe and the Scaglietti convertible, set Ferrari on the road to complete commercial success.

With the introduction of the 250/P sports car, which was a rear engined 12-cylinder 3-litre developed from the extremely successful 3-litre Testa Rossa, Ferrari was much criticized for producing a car which could not be classified as a serious prototype for an eventual production model of a Gran Turismo car. However Ferrari's critics were very wrong; towards the end of 1963 he announced that the 250/P would be produced in Gran Turismo form known as the 250/Le Mans and the first of these models was shown at the Paris Show late in 1963. Ferrari's intentions being to have at least the minimum quantity built before the 24-Hour Le Mans race of 1964 so that he would finally be able to win that classic with a true touring car.

The 250 GT 2 + 2

When the 250 GT 2 + 2 was introduced it was the only Ferrari designed to carry more than two passengers. (There were some early Ferrari 212s built by Ghia in the 1950s that could carry more than two passengers but these models are extremely rare). This filled a long-standing gap in Ferrari production and the 2 + 2 proved an extremely popular model.

The addition of the two extra seats was achieved without lengthening the standard two-passenger 250 GT wheelbase which remained at 96.5 inches, however, the body was lengthened by 12 inches, the steering gear and driver moved forward 12 inches and the fuel tank relocated. With a full tank of fuel and a driver on board, the difference in weight between the normal GT and the 2 + 2 was only an increase of 170 lb for the latter.

The classic V12 engine layout was used with a single overhead camshaft per bank of cylinders acting through roller rockers to operate the overhead valves. Engine displacement was 2953-cc and with a compression ratio of 8.8 : 1 the engine gave 240 b h p at 7,000 r p m with a torque reading of 181 lb ft at 5,000 r p m. The transmission was fitted with a Laycock de Normanville overdrive which sometimes gave trouble, due to the two being lubricated from a common oil supply which could not meet the specific needs of both components. This left Ferrari in the position of using the wrong oil for either the overdrive or the transmission. First gear ratio was 2.45, second 1.72, third 1.24, fourth 1.00 and overdrive 0.778. The steering was three and a half turns from lock to lock with a turning circle of 39 ft. Suspension was the classic GT with wishbones at the front and a live axle with leaf springs at the rear. Wheelbase was 96.5 inches, front track 4 ft 6.2 in. and rear track 4 ft 6.6 in.

The 275 GTB and GTS

Ever since the introduction of a Ferrari touring car these production models have always been noted for their conservative concept. The most radical change in the touring car philosophy came when Ferrari introduced the 275/GTB and GTS with a rear-mounted gearbox and independent rear suspension. Neither rear mounted gearboxes or independent rear suspension were new to Ferrari as both components had been developed through the sports and racing cars before this major change was undertaken on the touring cars.

The rear-mounted transmission had its origins back in the days of the De Dion rear suspended Formula 1 and 2 cars in the 1950s and was used extensively on the Mondial and Monza sports models, as well as the 553, 555, Squalo and

Supersqualo Formula cars. After a period of live-axle layouts in the Testa Rossa era, the rear-mounted gearboxes again appeared in the factory Testa Rossas in 1958 when these cars reverted to De Dion suspension at the rear. In 1959 the De Dion system was retained on the Testa Rossas but a completely new five-speed transmission was designed to be fitted behind the engine and in unit with it. A dry-sump engine was adopted to lower the centre of gravity and the gearbox was designed as an all-indirect unit to allow the engine to be placed as low as possible. The all-indirect layout meant that it had no direct drive as input was on the lower shaft and output on the upper shaft, so that a pair of gears was involved at all times in transmitting the drive.

This five-speed gearbox was used on the front-engined factory-entered sports cars until the time when the rear-engined sports cars were introduced. It was this unit with new external castings to adapt it to the final drive that was used for the new breed of touring cars.

Larger engines

The two new Models also marked Ferrari's departure from a 3-litre power plant. The well-known dimensions of 73 x 58.8 mm, which first came into being in 1952 with the first of the Ferrari 250 series, for long remained an important element in Ferrari's production. The 275 engine series came into being in 1964 for the sports Ferraris and was created by enlarging the bore from 73 to 77 mm, retaining the same stroke of 58.8 mm; the result was an engine of 3286-cc.

The 275/GTB coupe was directed more towards the Gran Turismo Competition type customer and as a result had a higher output than the 275/GTS. Basically it came with the engine tuned to 280 b h p at 7,500 r p m but could be ordered with a higher state of tune. A number of 275 GTBs were built with alloy bodies, and six-carburetter engines with dry sump lubrication. They were called 275 GTB/C. The GTB featured cast aluminium wheels and the coachwork was by Scaglietti. The GTS built by Pininfarina sported wire wheels and with a compression ratio of 9.2 : 1 had an output of 260 b h p at 7,500 r p m, with a torque of 217 lb ft

at 5,000 r p m. Three twin-choke Weber 40 DCL/6 carburetters were fitted to both models, and range on the 19 gallon tank was 228 to 285 miles.

The clutch was a 10-inch dry single-plate type and the five-speed and reverse gearbox was all synchro. First gear ratio was 3.08, second 2.12, third 1.57, fourth 1.25 and fifth 1.04. First gear gave 6.9 m p h per 1000 r p m, second 10.1, third 13.6, fourth 17.1 and fifth 20.6. The final drive ratio was 3.3 : 1.

In normal cases, the synchromesh in a rear-mounted transmission is worked to a greater degree because it has to change the speed of the driveshaft between the engine and the gearbox as well as the clutch driven disc. In the new design, the Ferrari engineers minimized the synchromesh loading in various ways, one being the use of a solid, small, low-inertia driveshaft supported by a centre bearing. Another was the placement of all gear selection clutches on the lower input shaft of the box, which meant that only the input shaft, and not all the gears in the box, had to be accelerated or slowed down by the synchromesh, this being a carryover from the racing gearbox.

Both front and rear suspension was by means of parallel wishbones with coil-spring/damper units and anti-roll bars. At the front the coil-spring/damper was fitted through the wishbones, being attached to the lower unit of the wishbone. At the rear, the coil spring/damper was fitted above the wishbones and attached to the outer end of the upper wishbone unit. Steering was by means of a ZF worm and roller with 3.5 turns lock to lock.

Disc brakes were used front and rear having a total swept area of 475 sq. in. with 11 in. discs at the front and 10.8 in. discs at the rear. The Borrani wire wheels fitted 185 x 14 Dunlop tyres. Wheelbase was 7 ft 10.5 in., front track 4 ft 6.3 in. and rear track 4 ft 6.7 in.

Types 330/GTC and 330/GTS

The 330/GTC and 330/GTS models were introduced to supplement the 2 + 2. The only difference between the GTC and GTS was that the former was a coupe and the latter a convertible.

The s o h c V12 seven main bearing engine with alloy block and heads was used. Bore and stroke were 77 x 71 mm giving a total displacement of 3967-cc. Three twin-choke Weber 40 DCZ/6 carburetters were fitted and, with a compression ratio of 8.8 : 1, the engine was rated at 300 b h p at 7,000 r p m. Chain driven single overhead camshafts actuated the valves through roller-follower rocker arms. This engine was based on the 400 SA powerplant, having the centre-to-centre spacing between the bores lengthened.

Transmission was five-speed all synchromesh rear mounted with an 8.87 in. clutch and a final drive ratio of 3.44 : 1. First gear ratio was 3.08, second 2.12, third 1.57, fourth 1.25 and fifth 1.04. First gear gave 7.1 m p h per 1000 r p m, second 10.3, third 13.9, fourth 17.5 and fifth 21.0.

Front suspension was independent by means of unequal-length wishbones, coil springs and an anti-roll bar. At the rear a similar independent system also used unequal-length wishbones, coil springs and anti-roll bar.

Worm and gear steering was fitted with 3.0 turns lock-to-lock and a turning circle of 38.4 ft.

Eleven-inch Girling solid-disc brakes were used back and front, the total swept area being 423.6 sq. in. 70 x 14 in. Borrani knock-off wire wheels with alloy rims fitted 205 x 14 Pirelli Cinturato HS radial-ply tyres. Wheelbase was 7 ft 10 in., front track 4 ft 7.2 in. and rear track 4 ft 7.8 in.

Ferrari caused a sensation when he introduced the 275 GTB/4, it made the GTS and GTB version seem somewhat mundane with its four-overhead-camshaft 3.3-litre engine. The output of 300 b h p equalled that of the bigger GTC with its 4-litre engine. Many thought it was more of a racing prototype for GT events but when it was first shown it quickly became clear that this was a dual purpose machine.

The engine of the GTB 4 was, as usual, the Colombo V12 as a base; the heads were adapted to it without modifying the cylinder block, with alloy block and cylinder heads. The crankshaft rode on seven main bearings. Bore and stroke were 77 x 58.8 mm giving a displacement of 3286-cc. Compression ratio was 9.2 : 1 and six twin-choke Weber 40 DCN/17 carburetters

were fitted. Valve actuation was by means of four chain-driven overhead camshafts with thimble type followers.

Power output was quoted at 300 b h p at 8,000 r p m and maximum torque as 202 lb ft at 5,500 r p m. It had a specific power output of 91.3 b h p/litre. The transmission was by means of a five-speed all synchromesh gearbox in unit with the differential.

First gear ratio was 3.08, second, 2.12, third 1.57, fourth 1.25 and fifth 1.04. First gear gave 6.9 m p h per 1000 r p m, second 10.0, third 13.5, fourth 17.0 and fifth 20.8.

Wheelbase was 7 ft 10.4 in., front track 4 ft 7.2 in. and rear track 4 ft 7.8 in. Curb weight was 2663 lb.

Suspension at the front was independent by means of unequal length wishbones, coil springs and anti-roll bar. At the rear a similar layout of unequal length wishbones, coil springs and anti-roll bar was also used.

Worm and roller steering was used with 3.2 turns from lock to lock and a turning circle of 36.0 ft.

Alloy knock-off type cast wheels (Borrani wires were an option) of 14 x 7 in. were used to fit 205-14 HR Dunlop Sports Radial tyres. Front brakes were 12.4 in. Dunlop provided the stopping power, swept area being 493 sq. in.

The Daytona

The Daytona is an evolution of the 275 GTB/4 which was the first production car to break away from the 250 series' traditional mechanical layout. The engine displaces 4.4 litres and is rated at 352 b h p DIN at 7,500 r p m. Combined with its rear-mounted 5-speed transmission (transaxle) and high final gearing of slightly more than 3 : 1, the Daytona is capable of 180 m p h speeds. With a wheelbase of 94.4 in. and front/rear track of 56.6 in., the listed dry weight of the car is only 2650 lb. Naturally, with the addition of fuel, water, oil and most important, someone to drive it, the weight grows to over 3,000 lb.

The 2-seat Berlinetta body is a Pininfarina design which, as originally laid out, recessed its headlights behind a clear plexiglass panel. This arrangement did not conform to US Federal safety laws, and several alternative designs were studied before the final one - a retracting type - was adopted.

Retained on the Daytona is the familiar Ferrari tubular frame, with independent suspension front and rear on coil springs that are mounted with integral shockabsorbers.

The engine has a very wide torque range, allowing easy handling in traffic. The clutch is noticeably lighter and smoother in operation than in earlier cars, and the selection of gears is much easier than with the first transaxle models. Seating is extremely well arranged (for two), and visibility is better than any of the comparable mid-engined cars can offer.

Acceleration, when the power is called on, is tremendous; the relatively high gearing allows use of the engine's wide range of power. Breathing is supplied through six twin-barrel 40 mm Weber DCN-20 carburetters. As mentioned before, flexibility hasn't suffered at all over the conventional 3-Weber setup found on the s o h c Ferrari engines; idling speed when the engine is warm and in top tune can be set to 700 r p m.

The 365 GT 2 + 2

Introduced in 1967 in the 365 series was the GT 2 + 2. Also a Pininfarina design, it is a successor to the earlier 250 GTE, and later 330 GT 2 + 2 cars. It was introduced at the Paris Auto Show and can be called a descendant of the Type 500 Superfast.

Massive, but solid, it was the first Ferrari to incorporate power steering and air conditioning as standard for the US market, as well as two real rear seats and a large trunk — structural features which result in a large tail section. And this is the reason for the 365 GT 2 + 2 - complete breakaway from the existing coupe and berlinetta designs. To this end, the car is a success, and the 'truck' analogy is usually uttered by people who feel that the Ferrari character has been lost and/or who have never driven a 365 GT 2 + 2.

But the characteristics are there: smooth clutch, good steering response (a little lighter than expected with the power assist), and flexibility under all conditions. And the throttle — it's all Ferrari ... tap the pedal and the tach jumps 1000 r p m. No 'comparable' luxury car will do that and return to an easy, almost silent idle. Beneath the bonnet is the familiar s o h c V12.

Mounted in the usual Ferrari tubular frame, the transmission, a 5-speed unit of generous dimensions, is coupled directly to the engine. Front and rear suspensions are independent, the rear suspension consisting of two spring/shock units per side — a setup dictated by the potential increase in aft-end weight with two passengers and luggage aboard. Wheelbase is 104.2 in., both front and rear tracks 56.6 in. Weight (dry) is 3487 lb - not light for a Ferrari - and it's considerably heavier when the car is fueled, watered and oiled. Radial tyres, 200 x 15s, take the weight on alloy or optional Borrani wire wheels.

The 365 GTC/4

The 365 GTC/4 is the replacement for the 365 GT 2 + 2. The latter car was a styling outgrowth of the limited-production 500 Superfast, last edition of a series of super-luxury road-going Ferraris built in very small numbers. The 365 GT 2 + 2 was a large car by Ferrari standards — too large in the eyes of many — but, as just described, it offered many refinements along with flexible performance and comfortable ride and directed to the US market in preference to the 365 GTC, which was practically identical to the earlier 330 GTC, except for a larger engine displacement, after 1968.

The GTC/4 combines coupe dimensions with the addition of two small folding seats in the rear. Externally, the car has to be one of the most strikingly different designs to emerge from the famed Pininfarina design establishment. Not one square centimetre of surface is wasted; from front or rear planes, the car is sharp and angular, a series of flat surfaces junctured in 'fiacre' or razor edges. From the profile, however, a flowing line is seen in a flat 2-dimensional effect. The rear deck bears a resemblance to the 365 2 + 2, but is much more blunt. A modern theme is seen in the impact-resistant front and rear bumpers and retracting headlights.

Since 1946, the hallmark of Ferrari has been a small-displacement, flexible and high-revving V12. The company has built some very successful racing 4s, a few frighteningly powerful inline 6s and now flat 12s, but the V12, 60° layout is the 'standard' for the GT cars. When first designed at 1500-cc it produced about 75 b h p; today, at 4390-cc, well in excess of 300 b h p and it will rev past 7,000 r p m with ease. It starts from cold at a touch, idles smoothly, glides along in traffic without noticeable complaint, and in the new GTC/4, has the ability to wind up to the red-line as though the throttle were a rheostat bringing a big electric motor up to speed.

The engine block, sump, heads and auxiliary housings are all alloy castings. Centrifugally cast steel cylinder liners are now a push fit into the block and incline inward towards the heart of the engine, a 52-pound crankshaft, machined to close tolerances by stages from a 300-pound billet of steel. Externally, the GTC/4 engine, designated Type F 101 by the factory, appears to resemble the GTB/4 unit except for the very different carburetion. Actually, aside from the block, crankshaft, pistons, rods, etc., the new engine shares little with the Daytona. Most obvious, of course, are the heads, which have horizontal intake porting and are fitted with six Weber 38 DCOE twin-choke sidedraft units. In the US version, these are modified slightly for emission control, primarily in the idling circuit. Twin Bendix electric pumps supply fuel.

The d o h c heads utilize two valves per cylinder at 45° included angle. Valve timing is such that it allows excellent torque delivery through a wide r p m range. The cams are directly driven via a roller chain. Another major revision from the GTB/4 is a wet-sump lubrication system the GTB/4 is a wet-sump lubrication system holding 17 quarts of oil. Characteristically, dry sumps are used only on Berlinetta series cars.

Bore and stroke are 81 x 71 mm (3.19 x 2.79 ins.), giving a total displacement of 4390-cc (268 cu. ins.). With 8.8 : 1 compression, the GTC/4 is rated at 320 b h p SAE net at 7,000 r p m, with a maximum of 318 lb ft of torque at 4,000 r p m.

The 5-speed gearbox is mounted directly behind the engine and is built by Ferrari. A 9½ inch Borg and Beck clutch is standard. Ratios are 2.49, 1.67, 1.24, 1.1, 0.80. The rear axle is limited-slip type with a ratio of 4.09 : 1. A short, closed driveline couples the transmission to the alloy differential housing.

It has been said that a Ferrari is an engine; true, it's one of the most fascinating pieces of automotive engineering ever assembled, but a Ferrari is also a frame of oval-section tubular steel members, welded together on fixtures. It is obsolescent perhaps in this era of unitized construction, but Ferrari do not build bodies for their GT cars, and this design forms a tremendously rigid platform for both body and mechanical components. The engine, transmission, and differential are actually one rigid unit, coupled by a torque tube and mounted on four Silentbloc pads into the frame. Two of these are located on either side of the engine block, while the other pair are located on either side of the differential housing. Fore and aft movement is restricted by a longitudinal steady rod bolted to the transmission and frame. Suspension is fully independent and incorporates light, forged A-arms built up in front and rear sections, and coupled by flat plates. Koni spring/shock units provide springing, in conjunction with the usual sway bars and self-leveling units on each side of the rear suspension.

The GTC/4 is fitted with ZF power steering having a 8.8 : 1 ratio. It was quite a surprise to many when the 365 GT 2 + 2 was so equipped back in 1968, but the feel which this unit retains is so good that you tend to forget it's power assisted. Fully fueled, oiled and watered, the 365 GTC/4 weighs 3820 pounds and has a 98.2 inch wheelbase with 58.2 inch front and rear track. Standard tyres are Michelin 215 70 VR 15 X radials.

In the period 1957 to 1963 he also built a brand new engine which was scheduled for a small capacity touring car. This engine was first installed in a Fiat 1100-cc chassis and was thoroughly developed by Ferrari. At one time there were plans to develop this car for Ferrari production but it would have required a greater layout than Ferrari and his newly formed SEFAC company were willing to put out.

Finally the engine design was sold for production to the De Nora family who began construction of the small four cylinder Ferrari under the name of ASA 'Mille'. To date nothing much further has been heard about this venture.

The Berlinetta Boxer

Ferrari followed these models with a radical departure offering for the first time a rear-engined full-sized Ferrari named the Berlinetta Boxer. The Dino had preceeded it as a small capacity car but it seemed that the era of the front engined Ferrari was at an end with the introduction of the BB.

The Berlinetta Boxer when tested at Fiorano gave the following performance figures with 215/70 VR 15X tyres and 13/45 axle at 7,000 r p m: 1st gear gave 54 m p h; 2nd 80 m p h; 3rd 108 m p h; 4th 138 m p h; and 5th 188 m p h. Acceleration from 0-1000 meters was 24 seconds at which point 154 m p h was reached.

The location of the engine was central rather than rear with a 12 cylinder horizontally opposed layout. A bore and stroke of 81 x 71 mm gave a displacement of 4,390 cc, compression ratio was 8.8 : 1 giving 380 b h p at 7,700 r p m.

The crankcase and cylinder block were cast in siluminum alloy. The fully-machined crankshaft ran on seven bearings with connecting rods coupled in pairs and running on thinwall bearings. Inclined overhead valves were fitted with four overhead camshafts and thimble type tappets. The camshafts were driven by toothed belts with a tensioner fitted.

Gear-type oil pump lubrication was used with a wet sump and oil cooler. Electronic ignition was fitted with a Marelli magnetic impulse distributor with automatic advance. It was a 12 volt system with alternator and transistorized regulator. Carburetion was by 4 three-choke Weber type 401F3C carburetters and two electric pumps.

A single plate dry clutch with cushioned centre plate was fitted and cooling was by means of water through a front-mounted radiator and expansion tank and automatic fans.

The chassis frame was tubular with a front track of 59 inches and rear track of 59.8 inches, wheelbase was 98 inches, overall length 171.65 inches, overall width 70 inches and overall height 44 inches with a curb weight of 2,472 lb. The gearbox was rear mounted with five all synchromesh gears operated by a central remote-control gearshift lever.

Both front and rear suspensions were independent, four shock absorbers being used at the rear. A limited-slip differential was incorporated in the final drive unit. Rack and pinion steering was used.

Ventilated disc brakes were fitted on all four wheels, operated by a hydraulic pump and co-axial plungers with two separate circuits with brake booster and vacuum pump. A hand brake was fitted for the rear brakes.

Total capacity of the fuel tank was 24.6 Imperial gallons and fuel consumption was 13/14 miles per Imperial gallon.

Cast light-alloy wheels were fitted, mounting 215/70VR15X tyres and a reducible spare. Special pantograph windshield wipers were fitted and air conditioning, radio and power windows were available.

Dino 206 GT, 246 GT and GTS

1968 saw the announcement of the start of the first 'production' line Ferrari in the form of the 'small' Dino 206 GT. Ferrari wanted to get in on the Porsche 2 litre market and he already had a product under his nose. With a road going 'productionised' 206S Dino he could make it. Hence the 206 GT was announced. This was a very smooth, classically shaped mid-engined car, available as both a coupe and spider. The original cries that it was not a true Ferrari were soon quietened when people saw it and drove it. It did however have a new style of bonnet badge which simply said 'Dino'. The engine for this car was a Rocchi designed, Fiat built V6 specially reworked by Ferrari for the transverse mounting of the mid-engined Dino 206 GT. The same engine was also used in a more conventional front engined Fiat-Dino. The 246 GT was a development of the 206 GT. Its engine was enlarged to 2418-cc (92.5 x 60 mm) and gave in home market guise some 195 b h p. This car first appeared in 1969. In 1972 the 246 GTS, an open version was announced, but this was not put on the 'production' line, the bodies being built by Scaglietti. The sales of the 246 have been very good over a number of years, the car always being a match for the equivalent Porsche in terms of handling but not always in terms of speed. Production was halted in 1973/4 to await the second generation Dino; there are many who are sorry to see it go.

Dino 308 GT4

After the announcement of the Berlinetta Boxer, came another unusual (for Ferrari) car, a version of the Dino named the Dino 308 GT4. Ferrari purists have expressed some doubts about the new model as it was powered by a V8 engine and bore a Bertone body more akin to a lesser competitor's product than a Ferrari. Despite the misgivings, the new Dino showed excellent potential.

The engine was a V8 at 90 degrees with a bore and stroke of 81 x 71 giving a displacement of 2,926 cc. With an 8.8 : 1 compression ratio it gave 255 b h p at 7,700 r p m.

The cylinder block was made of light alloy with cast iron liners. The crankshaft was on five bearings with connecting rods paired on the crankshaft.

There were four valves per cylinder and four overhead camshafts with thimble type tappets. The camshafts were operated by a toothed belt fitted with a tensioner. Oil circulation was by a gear-type pump, a wet sump and oil radiator.

Ignition was by two Marelli distributors to eight spark plugs. The electrical system was 12 volts with alternator and transistorized regulator.

Fuel feed was by an electric pump and four double-choke Weber 40 DCNF carburetters.

Cooling was by water with a front-mounted radiator, expansion tank and automatic fans.

A single plate clutch was fitted with a cushioned centre plate.

Front track was 1,470 mm; rear track 1,460 mm and wheelbase 2,550 mm. Overall length was 4,320 mm; overall width 1,800 mm; overall height 1,180 mm; curb weight was 1150 kg.

The engine was in the mid position with a five-speed gearbox placed alongside the sump with the final-drive take off underneath the rearward bank of cylinders. The mounting of the engine was actually transversal ahead of the rear wheels. A limited slip was incorporated in the final drive. Front and rear suspension was independent and steering by rack and pinion. Servo-assisted disc brakes were fitted on all four wheels with a hand brake on the rear discs.

A light-alloy tank contained 80 litres of fuel and consumption was 18/20 litres per 100 kilometers. Wheels were cast light-alloy fitting 205/70 VR14X tyres with a reduced spare.

The performance figures with the 205/70 VR14X tyres and a 18/63 axle at 7,000 r p m were: 1st gear 70 k p h; 2nd 101 k p h; 3rd 140 k p h; 4th 191 k p h; 5th 250 k p h.

Acceleration from zero to 1000 meters was 26 seconds at which time 210 k p h was reached.

CHAPTER THIRTEEN
The development of the Ferrari engine

UNQUESTIONABLY, the most famous racing and high-performance GT engine of the post-World War II era is the Ferrari V12. Many thousands of words have been written extolling its vices and virtues, as well as its racing successes and failures. Sections of road tests and racing reports have gone so far to attempt, some quite eloquently, to describe the sounds produced by this power-plant in both racing and touring versions. Without doubt, more than one Ferrari GT car has been purchased on the sound of its engine alone! And, more recently, words have been written about another seemingly inherent quality of this engine its tendency to emit smoke-laden exhaust!

To Enzo Ferrari goes the credit for the concept of the V12 engine for his cars, while to Gioacchino Colombo, his first chief engineer must go the credit for placing the concept onto paper. In regard to competition development, one of Ferrari's most loyal co-workers, Luigi Bazzi, must assume a great portion of the credit.

Enzo Ferrari has stated that one V12 engine which influenced him was the American Packard; certainly one of the finest of its type ever built. He evidently was most impressed with the engine's smooth, quiet operation, not its output. Indeed, the Packard was designed for just those qualities, along with high torque to adequately handle the heavy American luxury coachwork of the pre-war era. Many other V12 engines both predated and were current with the Packard, the greater number of which were either aircraft or luxury car designs. A number of notable racing V12s were built prior to World War II; the most famous being the 1938-1939 W163 Mercedes-Benz 3-litre Grand Prix cars. Alfa Romeo, for whom Ferrari worked until shortly before World War II, designed several 12-cylinder engines, none of which ever attained high status however. To what degree the sum total of the various V12s affected Ferrari's thinking we cannot say, but it was during the War years that he initiated the layout of a V12 engine for his own cars.

Auto Avio Construzione

Upon leaving Alfa, Ferrari had been fortunate in bringing with him a number of co-workers, around which he formed his own company, AAC (Auto Avio Construzione). Naturally, there was no time to dwell upon automotive design to any degree after 1940; AAC was occupied with the production of 'machine tools,' as Ferrari had stated in the past. To many Italians, this was a period of tremendous grief and bad memories, and Ferrari, along with many others, simply will not discuss this difficult era in any detail. It was during this time, however, that the initial design work was carried out on what was to become the most notable V12 automobile engine of all time.

The author has examined a photostat of a blueprint depicting a Ferrari 'slipper' type rocker arm. It shows machining details, profiles, hardness requirements, and so forth. It was sent recently by the factory to a California enthusiast who was rebuilding his Type 195 Inter, the accompanying letter stating that the customer service department had 'some difficulty' in locating the original. The drawing states that it is for the 'Type 125'. Of importance to the historian is the date on the blueprint - 29th October 1946. We can thus conclude that the general layout of the engine was completed some time before this, as a rocker arm is a relatively small detail. Most fascinating is the fact that the company logo on the blueprint paper is 'AAC;" thus the drawing predates the actual appearance of the name, 'Ferrari' as a company.

By the winter of 1946, three engines had been completed, and components for at least three more were in the works. This was the first Ferrari engine, the Type 125, so designated because its individual cylinder capacity was 125-cc; a small beginning. Simultaneously, Alfa Romeo was developing their pre-war 1500-cc straight-eight Grand Prix engine to an ultimate of over 400 b h p. Originally designed by the same Colombo before the war to produce about 200 b h p for Voiturette racing, it was on its way to becoming the last supercharged Formula engine to race in recent times. Ferrari's own new V12 was rated in its first form at about 70 to 75 b h p maximum. Few would have believed at the time that by 1951 in redevelopment form, this engine would edge out the Alfa Romeo.

DESIGN AND CONSTRUCTION

Initially, the only exotic feature of the Ferrari V12 was the fact that it had 12 cylinders and made an interesting exhaust note; a feature which captured journalists imagination from the car's first appearances. Its bore and stroke was 55 x 52.5 mm (2.15 x 2.06 inches). This figure is interesting, because it was the first important competition engine in modern times to have an oversquare bore-to-stroke ratio.

Following European practice, Colombo designed an engine whose major components were cast in a non-ferrous material, in this case a compound variously called Silumin or Siluminum. This is a copper-aluminium alloy which was easily cast and light in weight but also very strong and resistant to cracking under temperature changes, stress, etc. Cylinder block, heads, timing case and sump were constructed of this material. The cylinders were in two banks at a 60-degree angle. The cylinder liners themselves were made of a very hard cast iron, the lower third of which was a press fit into the alloy block. Centre-to-centre spacing of the bores was 90 mm (3.56 inches). From the beginning, Ferrari blocks have been generously drilled for oil circulation, the main oil channel running horizontally down the centre of the block between the cylinder banks.

Cooling was taken care of by a centrifugal water pump which drew water from the radiator and passed it to the left cylinder bank via a short external pipe. The water circulated around the liners through passage holes in the cylinder block, causing a metering effect. From the liners, coolant passed into the cylinder heads and thence to the upper tank of the radiator.

The crankshaft

Limited production dictated the use of crankshafts machined out of a solid billet of steel weighing about 300 pounds prior to successive turning and grinding to the finished form of circa 50 pounds. Considered an inferior method of production by modern standards to forging, Ferrari crankshafts have nonetheless always been hardened to a very high Rockwell C figure (circa 60) via nitriding to a depth of about ·040 inch. This overcomes any flaws which might exist near the surface of the billet. The crank rotated in seven main bearings, the first six of which had caps made of duraluminum, the seventh being of Silumin and forming the lower half of the flywheel housing. Main bearing diameters were set at 55 mm (2.16 inches), crankpins at 41.2 mm (1.62 inches).

The original Colombo design utilized alloy four-ring pistons, having two compression rings and two oil control rings, one of which was below the piston pin boss. Connecting rods were forged and featured caps which bolted to the rod proper at a 40-degree offset, rather than directly below the rod's vertical centreline. The caps were attached via two bolts which threaded into the upper rod section. All of this facilitated removal and insertion of the piston/rod assembly through the top of the engine. The piston pins were steel and free-floating in both pistons and connecting rod small ends without benefit of bronze bushings. Alloy tablets in either end of the piston bosses held the pins in position.

Bearings

As originally conceived, the engine was to have babbitted bearings, but the availability of precision insert bearings caused an immediate change in design. Subsequently, the American-designed Clevite bearing was adopted. These were license-produced by the Vandervell Company in England, which is a source to this day of Ferrari bearings. Their design, universal practice today, incorporated a lead-indium running surface, backed by an alloy shell which ensured strength, while the coating of indium incorporated good lubricating surface, and the ability to imbed solid impurities. It is on record that Ferrari credits the existence of these bearings for the ability to further develop the basic engine design to further levels of revs and output.

At the front end of the engine was a large Y-shaped casting which housed a triple row roller chain whose primary purpose was to drive the two overhead camshafts. Mounted to this timing case was the water pump and generator, both of which were driven by the timing chain via sprockets. Mounted at the bottom of the timing case was the oil pump, directly gear driven off the front of the crankshaft. A meshed-gear type, it was designed to deliver a high pressure—as high as 90 psi— to the engine bearings and valve mechanism. The very earliest engines had a rotating meshed plate filter, mounted on the front housing, slanted to the right and facing upward at a 45-degree angle. These devices operated mechanically, a series of meshed plates that rotated each time the clutch pedal was depressed; certainly not complimentary to the remainder of the lubrication system which was very well designed. Later, tubular-shaped, removable screens were fitted inside a revised casing, cast into the front housing, facing forward, beneath the generator, a somewhat better layout. This arrangement lasted into the late 1950s. While running, Ferrari engines are very efficiently lubricated. The oil sumps were thick castings, deeply ribbed for heat dissipation and carefully baffled inside by aluminium plates bolted to the sump walls. Later racing development led to the use of a dry sump system on certain versions.

Cylinder head

Colombo designed a very interesting cylinder head for the V12. The basic design, originating with the Type 125 was perpetuated in all single-overhead camshaft versions through the Type 245 (4.4-litre). The head was cast in Silumin and carried the camshaft in six bearings in which no bearing metal was used; the cams ran directly in

bores machined and finished in the head. The upper half of the cam bearings formed pedestals for the rocker arms, each carrying two arms on steel pivot shafts. Two valve springs were fitted per valve of the so-called 'mousetrap' or 'hairpin' type. Small threaded shafts with locknuts at the ends of the rocker arms provided for lash setting.

Combustion chambers were nearly hemispherical in layout. The two valves were fixed at an included angle of about 60 degrees (this angle varied slightly in later engines) and worked in alloy bronze guides. Six exhaust ports were used on each head, but intake ports were paired, each port serving two adjacent cylinders. This seemingly backward step is explained by the fact that at the time when the Ferrari V12 was initially designed, supercharging was still very much a factor in Grand Prix competition. Double porting allowed maximum benefit from a high-pressure supercharge effect, as manifold pressure near adjacent valves would have less tendency to drop. Under normally aspirated conditions, this imposed a limit to the engine's breathing ability. The two overhead camshafts were driven via a triple-row roller chain and suitable sprockets. This assembly, including a spring-loaded sprocket which acted as a tensioner, was housed in the front casting. The earliest Ferrari engines had two six-cylinder Marelli magnetos mounted horizontally, one at each rear end of the heads. When coil ignition was utilized for certain models, two distributors were mounted at the forward end of the timing case on most early models. Ignition distributor positioning has varied on Ferrari engines over the years.

The induction system

Another point of variation on the Ferrari V12 has been the fuel induction system. A total of four basic carburetion setups have been used plus two supercharging variants. With the termination of supercharging in Formula Racing in 1951, no further development was undertaken along this line. The most widely utilized carburetion layout has been three twin-choke downdraught Weber units of varying choke diameter to suit engine size. Operating synchronously, each choke serves two cylinders. Numerous early touring cars were fitted with a single Weber dual choke downdraught carburetter. This setup was not to be commended fully, since an enrichment valve was fitted to the carburetter for full-throttle operation. If so-equipped engines were run for long periods at about 90 per cent full throttle, the enrichment valve was not operative, and the main jets could not supply a rich enough mixture to all twelve cylinders. Burned valves easily resulted. A number of early cars were refitted with three carburetters. One example with which the author is very familiar was retrofitted at the factory with the triple Weber layout. This was the Type 166 Touring-bodied coupe in which the author and the late Mike Hawthorn practised for the 1952 Mille Miglia.

Racing versions of the Ferrari V12 have been fitted with both six twin-choke Webers and earlier, three Weber four-choke units. The latter are among the most impressive appearing carburetters ever built, but were abandoned in favour of the six twin-choke layout due to cost considerations, plus the fact that the four-choke units sometimes caused cutting out on hard cornering.

Fuel supply was taken care of by a single meshed-gear or diaphragm pump, driven off the forward end of the left hand camshaft. The former units were sensitive, particularly in regard to dirt in the fuel system. Very soon thereafter, Ferrari V12s were equipped with a pair of diaphragm-type pumps, mounted at the front of the engine, and driven by small cams from the main camshaft sprockets. Most competition engines retained the gear-type pump however. Installation of the second diaphragm pump was listed as 'experimental' on the factory assembly sheets of car No. 0185 EL, a long wheelbase 212, though twin pumps had been employed earlier than this.

DESIGN FAULTS AND EVOLUTION OF THE COLOMBO V12

Since its inception and initial construction, the Colombo V12 has been subject to considerable development and improvement. For a period of time, it was relegated to touring cars and lightweight Berlinettas, but was resurrected in the late 1950s to become Ferrari's primary sports competition engine. It has proven itself to be both reliable and, more important, flexible. A relatively small amount of modification gave a large return in power, yet little of the design's inherent smooth operation was lost throughout the entire rev range. The initial design had shortcomings; most of the alterations which eliminated them were a direct result of competition experience, or the preparation therefore. It is interesting to note, that, like any essentially good piece of engineering, the basic layout remained practically unchanged; a number of components from the Type 125 would easily interchange with the last 250 and 275 engines.

The primary development to which the original engine was subjected was increased displacement. Subsequent to the 1.5-litre, engines were built in two-litre form (Type 166), 2.3-litre (Type 195), 2.6-litre (Type 212), and 2.7-litres (Type 225). Each level produced its own group of cars; some purely for touring, others for competition or dual-purpose uses. With the Type 166, the engine's stroke was standardized at 58.8 mm (2.32 inches), where it remained through the Type 275. Displacement increases were thus expedited through the much simpler method of bore diameter.

Both the 195 and 212 models were built primarily as powerplants for the early touring models, however very definite exceptions exist.

The Lampredi version of the V12, discussed elsewhere, proved that a well-designed naturally aspirated engine could be a match for supercharged design under certain rules. When Ferrari subsequently ceased further development of his blown Type 125s, the original s o h c. Colombo cylinder head became self-limiting with its siamesed intake porting (the d o h c heads of the final two-stage blown Type 125 were shelved for some time). The paired port limited the amount of overlap which could be worked into a given cam design. This feature was not fully altered in the Colombo V12 until the advent of the Testa Rossa in 1957, remaining on touring cars until 1960.

Development of the engine in unblown form was directed strongly to two now-famous models, the 'Mille Miglia' in both 2-litre (166 MM) and 3-litre (250 MM). The cylinder heads on these engines are unique to the early Colombo series, in that they have six intake ports, which plugs located adjacent to them instead of next to the exhaust porting. The extra breathing advantages were not fully exploited, however, the valve timing remaining a relatively mild 22-66-67-17. This figure became standard on the 250 GT, though the prototype 3-litre car, 0156ET, had its timing at 27-70-22-73. Late 166 MM cars and the 250 MMs were fitted with conventional coil ignition and diaphragm fuel pumps. Both these late 2-litre engines (designated 166/53) and the 3-litre featured the triple 4-choke Weber car-buretters as well as a much-needed internal feature—roller followers on the valve rocker arms. This, as well as the individual intake ports, were carryovers from the Lampredi V12. Rollers were an important change, because as power output rose, heavier valve springs were neces-sary. A typical 1951 or 212 engine has springs of 3.3 mm wire diameter; a 250 MM, 3.5 mm. The shoe-type followers initially had higher frictional loadings on the cams, and with heavier springs, wear would have been further accelerated. A second weakness in the cylinder head layout was the holdown stud pattern, coupled with the fact that the liners were unsupported radially at the top or 'deck' of the block. Thirteen studs were screwed into both decks of the block, forming a triangular pattern around each cylinder, the apex of which was near the centre of the Vee. A separate L-profile steel ring was located in the gap between the block and liner. Interposed between each cylinder and combustion chamber was a compressible copper sealing ring. A rectangular outer gasket fitted over the studs for water sealing. When assembled carefully, this arrangement worked quite well, but counted on the cylinder liners being absolutely flush with the block decks, and correct tightening of the studs. Otherwise, the copper rings blew out and/or water leaks resulted.

Strengthening the bottom end

At first, each main bearing cap was retained by two studs, but in the mid-1950s, the centre main was adapted for a second pair of smaller outrigger studs. Finally, all six forward mains were retained by four studs each. Main bearings were increased in diameter in the later 250

engines from 55 mm to 60 mm (2.16 inches to 2.36 inches), no doubt as a result of competition development, though Ferrari engines have never been prone to crank train damage. For various reasons, the Colombo engine fell into 'disuse' as a front line engine at Ferrari, except in touring cars, which are now called 'Europa II' to distin-guish them from the 'Europa I' and 'America' series, powered at the time by Lampredi V12s.

While the Colombo engine was never resur-rected as a GP powerplant, the era of the Lampredi family of competition engines drew to a close with the obsolescense of the fours, failure of the sixes, and tremendous expense of further development of the twin-cam Lampredi-based, 315 and 335 Sport engines.

Therefore, in 1957, Ferrari turned back to tuned versions of the 3-litre Type 128 engine (as the 250 engine was designated by the factory).

However, it was due to reappear in competi-tion as the 'Testa Rossa,' a name originating with one of the Lampredi fours. Translating into 'Red Head,' the racing engines were so-called due to the fact that their cam covers were adorned with red wrinkle finish paint. The first major revision of the Colombo engine is there-fore, tied in directly with competition develop-ment.

The Testa Rossas

On the 'TR', the angled Colombo connecting rods were replaced with machined billet rods having horizontally split caps. Cylinder heads were finally extensively modified. As in the 166 MM and 250 MM, each cylinder had its own in-take port, along with larger valves and revised valve springs of a much heavier design. Cam timing was naturally stronger. Spark plugs were re-positioned adjacent to the exhaust manifolds, allowing for the new intake porting to be of larger diameter. Compression ratio was set at 9.0 : 1, three ring pistons finally being standardized in the racing engines.

Ferrari briefly experimented with Solex carburetters, but finally adopted six Weber 38 DCN twin-choke units. These differ from standard in that their throttle butterflies are on common shafts, not individual shafts coupled by gears. Each carburetter had two short air stacks.

Normal valve timing on the Testa Rossa engines was 27-65-74-16.

Photographs of the prototype Testa Rossa show a standard wet sump fitted, but factory team cars used a dry sump which had a much narrower oil collector bolted to the crankcase. A single oil filler pipe ran to the collector which angled forward to the front of the engine. As in all competition 12s, a meshed gear fuel pump was used in conjunction with an electric booster near the tank. Competition engines further benefited from very close assembly tolerances.

Output of the Testa Rossa was 300 b h p at circa 7,000 r p m, this in comparison to 240 b h p at 6,800 for the concurrent 250 GT and 260 b h p for some of the Berlinetta engines. Perhaps of even greater importance was that Ferrari claimed the lowest useful rev limit was 1,500 r p m. The TR engine would run without protest on normal city streets, its 'second nature' appearing at about 4,000 r p m.

Success of the Testa Rossa resulted in many of its components being incorporated into subsequent GT engines. Among these was the connecting rod design, the production version being forged rather than fully machined. Three-ring pistons of lightweight cast construction were also fitted; a bronze bushing was pressed into the small ends of the new rods.

About this time, cambox covers on GT cars began to appear with black wrinkle finish ostensibly to distinguish them from the TR engine. Among other detail changes that appeared in the mid-1950s were a second steel strap clamping the generator in place and on GT cars only, a fan, driven off a pulley on the front of the generator. Distributor location was standardized at the rear of each head, positioned vertically.

Head and block modifications

In 1959, a second major revision was incorporated into the 250 engine. With it, the somewhat problematical 13-stud cylinder head clamping arrangement was eliminated with the addition of a 14th stud. This resulted in a rectangular clamping pattern around each cylinder. Further, the liners were modified to have a machined-in ledge at their upper circumference, where they joined the deck of the block. This change eliminated the separate steel ring at this point. The block casting was revised so that the liners seated much more deeply into the alloy crankcase. For this arrangement, a single-piece head gasket was utilized, having built-in steel sealing rings surrounding the combustion chamber.

The new stud arrangement resulted in the abandoning of mousetrap valve springs, ordinary double coils being employed. Heretofore, tightening the head nuts had been difficult, because at certain points, the mousetrap springs interfered with spanner access.

Clutch weaknesses

By 1960, some 14 years after its first runup, the Colombo engine had reached a very high state of perfection and reliability. The Gran Turismo version was renowned for its easy starting, smooth idle, quiet operation, high power output as well as high cost of the cars into which it was fitted! Over the years, its most consistent weak point has been the clutch. With proper gearing, hard starting easily produced clutch slip, leading to premature wear. Clutch application changed over the years; early competition cars up to the Testa Rossa used interposed pressure plates of alternate steel and aluminium. These permitted very little slipping, or warping would occur from accrued heat. Touring cars were usually fitted with more conventional single-plate clutches. Borg and Beck type clutches were adopted for the Testa Rossa, finding their way into all engines. They eliminated clutch problems to a great degree.

Detail changes during the period 1959 to 1964 were the inclusion of a larger oil sump which had a detachable bottom plate, full-flow cartridge oil filtration and a single mechanical fuel pump positioned on the lower left hand side of the timing case. The generator was repositioned to the side of the engine and belt driven. It is interesting to observe that many components right through the Type 213 engine (3.3-litre for the 275 GTB) carried the designation '125' on their part numbers, indicating that they had remained essentially unchanged from the earliest design drawings. Many of the components which were included in the revisions after 1957 will carry the part prefix '128 LM' (Testa Rossa). The last 250 engines bear serial numbers in the 5000 range. Final

Final competition development of the 3-litre engine was the GTO version (Engine Type 168), essentially the final form of the 250 GT engine revised to Testa Rossa specifications. It immediately followed the Testa Rossa series, but was incorporated into Berlinettas rather than sports racing cars. Specifications followed those of the TR, including the harder valve timing and high compression. Six 38 DCN Weber carburetters continued to be employed, as was dry sump lubrication. Connecting rods were of billet construction, and highly polished.

Return to twin cams

In 1966, the Colombo engine once again received d o h c cylinder heads, this time on the 275 (3.3-litre) GT; subsequently it was designated 275 GTB/4. This engine (Type 226) had dry sump lubrication and six Weber carburetters. Its rating was 300 b h p at 8,000 r p m. Valve timing was set at 45-65-60-41. An interesting minor feature was that its cambox covers closely resembled those of the 315-335 Sport engines of the late 1950s, except for the chain cover domes. The 4-point engine mounting was abandoned in favour of a pair of mounts positioned centrally on either side of the block opposite each other. The single-cam 275 engines are designated Type 213 in factory terminology.

Type 400 Superamerica

The current group of Colombo V12s was ushered in by the Type 209 engine, built to date in five directly related versions. Introduced in 1960 in four-litre capacity, it was intended as a replacement for the 410 Superamerica series of luxury GT cars. The new version was called the 400 Superamerica; not only was the engine of Colombo type, but the car rested on the Type 508 (250 GT) chassis.

The Type 209 engine had a bore and stroke of 77 x 71 mm (3.03 x 2.76 inches) which resulted in a total displacement of 3967-cc (242 cubic inches). Following Colombo design, the engine had detachable heads and pressed-in cylinder liners with centres spaced 90 mm (3.56 inches), but the depth of the cylinder block casting was increased to accommodate the longer crankshaft throws.

Other modifications were incorporated into the Type 209 engines which included a larger water pump and the employment of a twin-row roller cam drive chain in place of the earlier triple row.

In order to retain the level of output offered by the 5-litre 410 Superamerica (Lampredi-type), the initial engines built had close to 10.0 : 1 compression and 46 DCF Weber carburetters, which allowed the factory to rate the engine at 400 b h p at 6,750 r p m. This engine gave tremendously fast road performances, enhanced by the fact that the 400s were frequently delivered with high axle ratios. However, a modified version of this engine with 8.8 : 1 compression, and smaller (40 mm) Weber carburetters, was rated at 340 b h p at 7,000 r p m. More flexible in overall performance, this engine was installed in 400s beginning in 1962.

The second version of the Type 209 engine was incorporated into the 4-seat GT cars beginning in 1963. As built, its output was further reduced to 300 b h p at 6,600 r p m, while the rated torque was 277 lb ft at 5,000 r p m. Standard carburetion was three Weber 40 DCZ/6 units.

Prior experience with a 77 mm bore in the 250 GT block, resulted in respacing of the bore centres by 4 mm (.157 inch) to 94 mm (3.70 inches). This permitted more equalized pressure on the head gasket between the bore rims.

The 500 Superfast

In 1964, the final version of the luxury GT Ferrari appeared. Known as the 500 Superfast, it lived up to its name via a unique engine, what can be termed the third version of the Type 209, though more correctly it was a complete offshoot. This engine utilized Lampredi structural dimensions, though its design was Colombo. Its bore centres were set at 108 mm (4.24 inches) as in the Lampredi engines, while its cylinder dimensions were 88 x 68 mm (3.46 x 2.68 inches) which gives a total displacement of 4963-cc (302.7 cubic inches). With the 'standard' GT compression of 8.8 : 1 and 40 DCZ Webers, this powerplant was rated at 400 b h p at 6,500 r p m. Ferrari designated this engine the Type 208. Aside from the vehicles to which it was fitted, this powerplant can be identified easily by the fact that it uses seven cambox retention studs per row as do the Lampredi engines. This is one of the most powerful Ferrari GT engines ever constructed; only approximately 30 were built in the period 1965 to 1968.

The Type 245 engine

The final version of the Type 209 engine was the 4390-cc (267.8 cubic inch) 365 GT. Designated the Type 245, it featured a revised block casting with heavy vertical ribbing on the outside walls. Bore diameter was increased to 81 mm (3.19 inches) stroke remaining at 71 mm (2.79 inches). The bore increase necessitated a modification in the liners, requiring a flat machined onto their outer circumference for clearance between each other. An important alteration on the Type 245 engine was that the liners were no longer a 'force' fit, but a light push fit at room temperature with sealing compound. Most other major components were in series with the Type 209 engine. Three Weber 40 DCF or 40 DFI carburetters were employed, and with 8.8 : 1 compression, output was rated at 320 b h p at 6,600 r p m. Valve timing was set at 13-59-59-13.

In 1968, the Type 245 engine was fitted with d o h c cylinder heads and dry sump lubrication and designated the Type 251 for the 365 GTB/4 'Daytona' Berlinetta. Intended for homologation, this engine proved very versatile and flexible. In GT cars it was rated at 352 b h p at 7,500 r p m. Fitted with six Weber 40 DCN carburetters, the compression ratio was kept at 8.8 : 1. A competition version of the Type 251 was built in limited numbers for homologation in sports racing events. It did not differ radically from the production version internally except for extremely close assembly tolerances. Valve timing for both engines was 45-46-46-38.

The F101 engine

The Type F101 engine is a variant of the Type 251, having revised cylinder heads with intake ports between the camshaft banks and six twin-choke Weber 38 DCOE carburetters. The dry sump lubrication system was replaced with a wet sump and the cam chain arrangement altered. Bore and stroke are 81 x 71 mm (3.19 x 2.79 inches), identical to the Daytona powerplant. Compression ratio is given as 8.8 : 1, a figure seemingly 'standardized' by Ferrari for GT engines. Rated at 320 b h p at 7,000 r p m, the Type F101 was in a much milder state of tune that the Type 251. Torque output was rated at 318 lb ft at 4,000 r p m, the Daytona having the same rating, but at 5,500 r p m. Valve timing was set at 43-38-38-34. In design and construction, considerable effort was directed toward enhancing known Ferrari GT characteristics such as flexibility and reliability with special attention to mechanical silence though in operation these engines produce a very audible exhaust note! This engine, with five-speed unit gearbox was fitted to the 365 GTC/4 and 365 GT/4 2 + 2.

In this section, we have traced the origin and development of the basic Ferrari engine, the Colombo V12. This powerplant proved itself throughout the 1950s and 1960s to be one of the finest for both touring and competition. Costly to purchase and overhaul, it was nonetheless perfectly straightforward to operate, maintain and repair. These features, coupled with its competition record, have made the name Ferrari a legend.

Latter-day versions of the basic Colombo configuration have carried Ferrari into the early 1970s; however the distinction between the sports racing and production engine have become increasingly marked since the mid-1960s, as the Manufacturer's Championship has been contested in the 'Prototype' categories. Excellent performances turned in by the competition 365 GTB/4 Berlinettas and other true 'Production' type cars has caused considerable hope that sports racing will once again return to this category.

THE LAMPREDI ENGINE DESIGNS

One of Enzo Ferrari's primary goals in the post-war era was to defeat his former employer, Alfa Romeo on the Grand Prix circuits. His one and only engine, the Colombo V12, rapidly established itself as a sports and touring powerplant, but the unit was unable to show a strong effect on the GP circuits. The Alfa Type 158, originally a pre-war Ferrari/Colombo effort for Voiturette races, was now undisputed master of the post-war Formula 1. Under the rules of the time, constructors had the option of running 1500-cc supercharged engines or 4500-cc un-supercharged designs.

Colombo was convinced that his V12, given proper development, could match the Alfa. To this end, the 1500-cc Type 125 engine was fitted with twin-cam cylinder heads and two-stage superchargers. The familiar roller chain was displaced in favour of a train of gears for the blower and camshaft drives. In this form, the engine was rated at circa 305-310 b h p at 7,500 r p m. But the Colombo engine could not attain the rev potential of the Alfa at this stage, which in fact was in excess of 8,000. The Alfa was the most highly developed competition engine at the time, and with the technical backing the team was receiving it seemed a nearly hopeless situation for Ferrari.

Since 1926, the Grand Prix engine had evolved around the supercharger, and few designers were willing to try pitting an undeveloped unblown engine against a 400 b h p 1.5 litre that could sweep the field. However, progress since 1926 had brought about supercharged engines that were highly sensitive to tuning, fuel and even atmospheric conditions. These criteria became even more acute in regard to engines of such small capacity as the 1500-cc Alfa. Progressive tuning yielded tremendous power gains, but not without considerable increases in stress, and worse, fuel consumption. Much of the methanol fuel 'consumed' was simply being poured through the engine as a cooling medium for scorching hot blowers, valves and manifolds. In relation to financial considerations, it does not even require a modicum of understanding to comprehend the implications of caring for a blown GP engine—it is reliably reported that Alfa discarded Type 158 crankshafts after only a few races, replacing them with new ones.

Despite these problems, the Alfa still retained a high degree of reliability, and the design establishment, among whom was Colombo, could see nothing else but fighting fire with fire.

A fresh approach

Aurelio Lampredi, employed by Ferrari as Colombo's assistant saw the situation differently.

Connected with Ferrari twice since 1946, he had been closely associated with the development of the Colombo V12. Lampredi was convinced that a properly designed naturally aspirated powerplant could challenge the Alfa successfully, and he voiced this revolutionally conviction to Enzo Ferrari. Lampredi designed a highly modified version of Colombo's engine, which though totally unproven in practice, was rapidly became untenable. Lampredi designed a highly modified version of Colombo's engine, which though totally unproven in practice was evidently convincing enough to Ferrari that he permitted the foundry and tool room to construct an unspecified number of prototypes.

By 1949, Colombo realized that further development of the blown Type 125 was to be suspended and he returned to Alfa Romeo. This left Lampredi, only slightly past 30 years of age, chief engineer at Scuderia Ferrari.

Lampredi retained the concept and essential layout of the single-overhead cam 60-degree V12, but re-engineered it into a more 'genuine' racing powerplant. Lampredi's V12 had cylinder bore centres spaced at 108 mm (4.24 inches) allowing for larger bore diameters; consequently the engine itself was longer than the Colombo 12. However, the most essential revision carried out on the new engine was the elimination of separate cylinder heads. The water jackets were cast integral with the heads, while the steel liners were threaded at their upper end. Passing up through open bores in the bottom of the water jackets, they screwed into matching threaded bosses which surrounded the valve/combustion chamber areas. Obviously, the somewhat weak head/block seal of the Colombo engine was eliminated.

Projecting below the water jacket casting, the liners were located in corresponding bores in the crankcase. A water seal at this junction was formed by a pair of O-rings in grooves near the base of each cylinder. Bolts passing through the blocks secured them to the crankcase.

The Lampredi engine's crankcase served primarily to support the crankshaft, and was roof-shaped in external appearance, lacking the more conventional appearance of the Colombo block. The starter motor, fitted to GT and Sports versions, was attached to the lower left half of the clutch housing, not to the right rear motormount flange as on the Colombo. The crankshaft was a machined billet, having seven main bearings of 60 mm (2.36 inches) diameter, while the crankpins were 43.5 mm (1.71 inches) diameter; both an increase over the Colombo specification. The main oil gallery, instead of being a cast-in channel, consisted of a tube which ran rearward from the oil pump at the front, being secured to the main bearing caps via hollow bolts.

The oil pump was driven by a gear on the crank nose, similar to the Colombo design. However, the water pump was also driven in series with the oil pump, being attached to an extension of the oil pump shaft. It was mounted to the bottom end of the timing chain case. Two steel pipes exited from the pump body and curved around to the crankcase. From there water passed to the cylinders.

Lampredi specified much heavier connecting rods with horizontally divided caps rather than Colombo's angled design. Usually they were forged, but solid billet rods were used on occasion for racing. Various piston configurations were employed, ranging from 8.0 : 1 compression ratio in touring engines to 14.5 : 1 for GP versions where fuel mixtures were permitted. One particular car with which we are familiar, an early 342 America, was delivered to Switzerland new in 1952 with 7.8 : 1 compression.

Single cams

The valve gear arrangement was similar to the Colombo design, a triple-row roller chain driving the single overhead camshafts. Lampredi was first to employ roller cam followers on the rocker arms, increasing complexity, but reducing friction and permitting greater development of cam lobe profiles. All Lampredi 12s utilized individual intake porting cast into the cylinder blocks. Intake and exhaust valves were inclined at 60 degrees included. Mousetrap type valve springs were retained as on Colombo engines of the time, but were of larger diameter wire and had as many as 10 coils per spring to the usual eight on Colombo designs.

Dual ignition

Lampredi initially retained a single spark plug per cylinder, mounted adjacent to the intake porting. Grand Prix and certain sports racing versions of the engine were fitted with two plugs per cylinder, the second set located next to the exhaust porting. This resulted in a notable power increase.

The timing case was similar in basic design to the original Colombo unit, being Y-shaped and housing the triple-row roller chain which drove the camshafts via sprockets. An oil filter housing was cast integral with the timing case, again similar in arrangement to that found on the small-block V12. Touring and sport versions of the engine featured a cast-in cradle with yoke strap for a generator, to be driven from a centrally positioned sprocket. This, again, followed the original Colombo arrangement; however Grand Prix versions lacked the cradle altogether, as no electrical plant other than magneto ignition was fitted. In similar manner, the starter motor could be dispensed with, due to its location on the lower half of the clutch housing, it in itself being detachable.

Fuel delivery and carburetion systems on the Lampredi engines were identical in arrangement to those on the small-blocks; either twin FISPA mechanical pumps were fitted, or in the case of competition engines, a single meshed-gear FIMAC pump driven off the right front camshaft sprocket. Lampredi engines were never fitted with single carburetter manifolds in touring form, but always three Weber twin-choke units, and in certain cases, the 4-choke Weber instruments.

Lampredi V12 engines were constructed in 3, 3.3, 4.1, 4.5 and 4.9-litre dimensions. The 3.3-litre engine is something of an anachronism, since it was the first sports version of the Lampredi engine to be entered into a competitive event (1950 Mille Miglia), while its bore and stroke of 72 x 68 mm (2.74 x 2.48 inches) was never again to be duplicated. Total displacement of this engine, the Type 275 Sport was 3322-cc (203.5 cubic inches). The first Lampredi GP cars were fitted with the 3.3-litre engine.

The 3-litre engine has the distinction of being the only Ferrari V12 powerplant built to have a 'square' bore and stroke at 68 x 68 mm (2.48 x 2.48 inches). With an 8.5 : 1 compression and three Weber 36 DCF carburetters, it was rated at

220 b h p at 6,000 r p m, a relatively low figure that was reflected in performance. This engine was fitted to the first series of true semi-production GT cars, called 'Europa' to distinguish them from the Colombo-powered 250 GT. The Europa I engine displaced 2963-cc (182.0 cubic inches).

Competition development

Considerable development was directed towards the competition versions of the Lampredi V12, however. The Formula 1 engines, after briefly appearing in 3.3 form in 1950 were increased to 4.1-litres and finally 4.4-litres (actually 4494-cc [275.0 cubic inches]). Output figures on the 4.1 and 4.4 engines were extensive; quotes range from 330 b h p at 6,500 r p m to well in excess of 400 b h p in the 7,500 range. All figures within this range are reasonably valid, as numerous compression ratios were utilized; the addition of a second set of spark plugs also helped to elevate the output. Valve timing and diameters, so far as is possible to ascertain, remained relatively static. Valve timing was set at 24-68-70-20 for most of the 4.4 engines. This figure applied to the sports racing versions of the 4.1-litre engine, while the GT version of the same engine had a milder figure of 25-55-58-14. Pomeroy states that the 4.5 GP car had intake valves of 41.1 mm and exhausts of 37.0 mm (1.62 and 1.46 inches).

A second version of the 4.5-litre engine was built strictly for sports and GT cars. Displacing 4522-cc (278.0 cubic inches), it reverted to the 68 mm (2.48 inch) stroke of the 4.1-litre engines, but had its bore increased to 84 mm (3.31 inches). This powerplant was fitted to the 375 America and 375 Mille Miglia chassis, the former engine rated at 300 b h p at 6,200 r p m, with three Weber 40 DCF carburetters and 8.0 : 1 compression. The competition engine had 9.0 : 1 compression and three 4-choke Weber 40 IF4/C carburetters. Both versions achieved notable success for their intended purpose; some of the most ostentatious bodies were built around the 375 America engine and chassis.

Overhaul problems

Several unique difficulties were eventually encountered with the Lampredi engine. By design, top end overhaul was rendered far more difficult since the entire cylinder block had to be removed from the crankcase for access to the valves and seats. Reinstalling the blocks involved reinserting each piston carefully back into its cylinder; broken piston rings resulted unless care and a proper method of compressing the rings was employed.

Replacing one or more cylinder liners could be very difficult, since the threads tended to 'set' with time into the bosses around the combustion chambers. A special spanner which mated with notches at the base of the liner was designed for removal and replacement by the factory.

Time and untreated water took their toll on both the O-ring seals at the base of the cylinder liners as well as the water seal that surrounded the shaft which drove the water pump impellor. Deterioration at one or both these points allowed water to leak down into the oil sump, resulting in emulsification of the lubricant.

The above mentioned problems became evident to a much greater degree in the touring versions of the Lampredi designs due to extended running periods and neglect. Competition versions which were torn down more frequently and overhauled did not suffer such difficulties. At least partial knowledge of these complexities lead numerous persons to replace Ferrari engines with others, notably the Chevrolet small-block V8, when the original had become 'tired' with age.

Larger engines

Subsequent to the 4494-cc and 4522-cc engines, Ferrari developed two final versions that were close to 5-litres in capacity. The first, called the 375 Plus retained the 84 mm, bore of the 375 models, but had a 74.5 mm (2.94 inches) crankshaft stroke, the only Lampredi V12 to have this long a stroke. This engine, of which only several were built for team sports racing cars, had 9.0 : 1 compression and three Weber 42 DCF carburetters. Several conflicting output figures have been published, one being more conservative than the quote for the 4522-cc engine. The most commonly quoted output is 344 b h p at 6,500 r p m; actually this figure may be conservative in respect of the tremendous performances put up by the 375 Plus cars in competition. In 1954, the Ferrari team took the honours at Le Mans with these cars, but the 4.9-litre engine proved to have excess output for the chassis on tighter courses.

The second 4.9-litre engine type reverted to the 68 mm stroke of other Lampredi V12s, but had a bore increase to 88 mm (3.47 inches). Total displacement was 4961-cc (305.0 cubic inches). A competition version, designated the 410 Sport or 410 Plus was fitted with 24-plug cylinder blocks, 9.0 : 1 compression pistons and three Weber 46 DCZ carburetters. Output was in the vicinity of 380 to 390 b h p at 6,800 r p m. These incredibly fast cars raced only once at Buenos Aires; none finished due to mechanical troubles other than the engines.

This engine also superceded the 375 America in a new series of luxury GT cars called the 410 Superamerica. A revised chassis was designed for the new model, appearing in 1955. The engine in this form was rated at 340 b h p at 6,000 r p m with three Weber 40 DCF carburetters and 8.5 : 1 pistons. The 410 cars were built in small numbers until circa 1960. At this time, they were superceded by the 400 Superamerica which was powered by a 4-litre derivative of the Colombo engine.

Development of the Lampredi-based competition engines ceased after 1957. The final versions of these engines were very powerful, but considerably more complex. Twin-cam versions of their single-overhead-cam ancestors, and thus more costly. Furthermore, they chalked up a checkered racing record, frequently suffering from mechanical problems, which, if they did not cause retirement, at least retarded their otherwise impressive performance.

With the obsolescense of the 4-cylinder powerplants, Ferrari turned back to the Colombo V12 as a source for a less expensive competition engine. Resuming where the 250 Mille Miglia had left off in 1953, the 3-litre Colombo engine proved to have had only the surface of its potential as an unsupercharged sports racing engine developed. The record of the Testa Rossa series and subsequent GTOs bears out this statement.

The 4961-cc Lampredi engine was perpetuated through 1960 in the 410 Superamerica series of luxury GT cars. Subsequent to this, a 4-litre version of the Colombo engine was employed in the Superamericas.

Aurelio Lampredi's designs did not leave a lasting effect on subsequent Ferrari powerplants, though their successes, as well as failures were particularly important in the racing history of the marque. Numerous details of his designs found their way into other engines, an example being the roller rocker followers. Lampredi was revolutionary in his original concept for over-throwing the supercharged GP powerplant, but in execution, he was very conservative. Much like famed British constructor, W. O. Bentley, Lampredi believed that the most basic method for increased output of a given design was to increase displacement. The technology of Lampredi's era demanded far more than this simple expedient, however. On several occasions, his designs easily surpassed the chassis and tyre technology of the time. Notable examples were the early 4.1 sports cars, the 375 Plus sports racing spyders and his 4.4-litre inline 6, a design which fell into rapid and lasting disrepute for everything but its extreme torque and ability to rev up past safe limits with astonishing speed.

During the six years he worked for Ferrari as chief engineer, Lampredi was responsible for some of the best engines to emanate from Maranello. When the tide of progress overcame his designs in the mid-1950s, he departed to Fiat and he was replaced by the brilliant Vittorio Jano for a brief period. Probably his most logical successor would have been Andrea Fraschetti, another young, promising engineer who was unfortunately killed while testing a racing Ferrari at Autodromo Modena in 1957.

APPENDIX IA
PERFORMANCES OF FORMULA 1 FERRARIS
1948 — 1500-cc single stage supercharged
TURIN
Sommer	3rd	
Farina	—	Crashed
Bira	—	Transmission broke, 5th for 66 laps

MONZA
Sommer	—	Retired - Illness when 3rd
Farina	—	Transmission breakage when 4th

BARCELONA
Bira	—	Transmission breakage when leading
Farina	—	Transmission breakage when 4th
Pola	—	Engine blow-up

1949 — 1500-cc single stage and 2 stage supercharged
SAN REMO
Whitehead	—	Engine failure

JERSEY
Whitehead	7th

SILVERSTONE
Whitehead/ Folland	} 8th	
Mays/ Richardson	} —	Crashed. (Thinwall)

BELGIAN GRAND PRIX SPA
Villoresi	2nd
Ascari	3rd
Whitehead	4th

SWISS GRAND PRIX BERNE
Ascari	1st	} Modified rear suspension
Villoresi	2nd	
Whitehead	—	

FRENCH GRAND PRIX
Villoresi	—	Retired — Transmission
Whitehead	3rd	Fastest lap, broke gearbox just before end

ZANDVOORT
Villoresi	1st	
Ascari	—	Broke stub axle — Crash

DAILY EXPRESS MEETING
Ascari	1st	
Villoresi	3rd	
Whitehead	—	Retired — Engine

LAUSANNE
Ascari	2nd
Cortese	4th
Whitehead	9th

GRAND PRIX EUROPE MONZA
Ascari	1st		
Villoresi	—	Gearbox } 2 stage supercharged	
Sommer	5th		
Bonetto	—	Retired — Engine }	Modified cars used
Whitehead	—	Retired — Transmission	previously by
			Ascari/Villoresi

CZECHOSLOVAK GRAND PRIX
Whitehead	1st

1950 — single stage and 2 stage supercharged and u/s models
PAU
Villoresi	2nd	} Both single stage
Sommer	4th	

SAN REMO
Villoresi	2nd	
Ascari	—	Engine seized } Both two stage

MONACO
Ascari	2nd	
Villoresi	—	Rear axle.

SWISS GRAND PRIX BERNE
Villoresi	—	Axle breakage Four speed box and de Dion
Ascari	—	Oil pipe Swing axle normal two stage

BELGIAN GRAND PRIX SPA
Villoresi	6th	Long chassis swing axle two stage
Ascari	5th	3.3-litre unsupercharged

FRENCH GRAND PRIX
Whitehead	3rd	3.3-litre unsupercharged practiced but did not start

JERSEY
Whitehead	1st

ZANDVOORT
Ascari	3rd	Formula 2 car
Villoresi	2nd	Single stage long chassis
Whitehead	4th	Single stage short chassis

GENEVA
Ascari	—	Engine } 3.3-litre u/s De Dio Led race
Villoresi	—	Crashed } 3.3-litre u/s

SILVERSTONE
Ascari	—	Spun off Two stage long swing axle,
Whitehead	3rd	"Thinwall"

ULSTER TROPHY
Whitehead	1st

MONZA
Ascari	—	Engine 4.5-litre unsupercharged
Serafini/ Ascari	} 2nd	

BARCELONA
Ascari	1st	} Both 4.5-litre unsupercharged
Serafini	2nd	
Taruffi	3rd	4.1-litre unsupercharged

1951 — 4.5 litre unsupercharged
SYRACUSE
Ascari	—	Overheating when leading 1950 4.5 model
Villoresi	1st	1950 4.5 model
Serafini	2nd	Works de Dion 2.5-litre
Fischer	3rd	Long chassis swing axle 2.5-litre

PAU
Ascari	—	Transmission after leading 1950 4.5 model
Villoresi	1st	1950 4.5 model
Fischer	6th	Long chassis swing axle 2.5-litre
Serafini	—	Steering de Dion 2.5-litre

The colour photograph shown four pages on, of the Ferrari Daytona Competition, was taken in Nevada not at Daytona

SAN REMO

Ascari	1st	1951 Twin plug 4.5
Villoresi	–	Minor crash 1950 model 4.5
Serafini	2nd	1950 model 4.5
Fischer	3rd	Long chassis swing axle 2.5
Whitehead	10th	Long chassis swing axle 1.5 single stage

SILVERSTONE

Parnell	1st	"Thinwall 4.5". Race abandoned 4th lap

SWISS GRAND PRIX BERNE

Ascari	6th	Off form due to burns 24 plug
Villoresi	–	Left road 12 plug
Taruffi	2nd	24 plug.
Whitehead	–	Crashed Long chassis 1.5 single stage
Fischer	11th	2.5 long chassis

BORDEAUX

Fischer	2nd
Whitehead	3rd

ULSTER TROPHY

Whitehead		Piston collapsed

EUROPEAN GRAND PRIX REIMS

Ascari	–	Gearbox
Villoresi	3rd	
Gonzales/ Ascari	} 2nd	Reshaped bodies 24 plugs
Whitehead	–	Gasket failure Long chassis 1.5 single stage

ZANDVOORT

Fischer	4th	2.5 long chassis

PESCARA

Whitehead	5th	1.5 single stage long chassis

FREIBURG HILL CLIMB

Fischer	1st	2.5 long chassis

BARI

Whitehead	5th	1.5 single stage long chassis

BRITISH GRAND PRIX SILVERSTONE

Gonzales	1st	12 plug
Ascari	–	Gearbox 24 plug
Villoresi	3rd	24 plug
Whitehead	9th	1.5 single stage long chassis

GERMAN GRAND PRIX NURBURGRING

Ascari	1st	
Gonzales	3rd	
Villoresi	4th	
Taruffi	5th	
Fischer	6th	Long chassis swing axle 2.5-litre

PESCARA

Ascari	–	Engine – 1st lap 12 plug
Villoresi/ Ascari	–	Rear axle Ascari driving
Gonzales	1st	
Whitehead	5th	

BARI

Gonzales	2nd	24 plug
Ascari	–	Retired
Villoresi	–	Transmission
Whitehead	5th	

GOODWOOD 3 EVENTS

Parnell	2nd	"Thinwall"

WINFIELD

Parnell	1st	"Thinwall"

ITALIAN GRAND PRIX MONZA

Ascari	1st	
Villoresi	2nd	} 24 plug body redesigned high tail and headrest
Gonzales	4th	
Taruffi	5th	24 plug mid 1951
Landi	–	Transmission 12 plug 1950
Whitehead	–	Piston failure 1.5 single stage long chassis

BARCELONA

Ascari	4th	Held up with tyre trouble
Gonzales	2nd	Held up with tyre trouble
Villoresi	–	Engine
Taruffi	–	Chassis breakage

1952 – 4.5 litre unsupercharged

TURIN

Ascari	–	Split fuel tank on last few laps when leading Indianapolis type lengthened chassis
Villoresi	1st	1951 type
Farina	–	Crashed Indianapolis type lengthened chassis
Taruffi	2nd	2.5-litre 4-cylinder prototype

GOODWOOD

Gonzales	1st	"Thinwall"

ALBI

Rosier	1st	} 1951 type
Landi	2nd	

ULSTER TROPHY

Rosier	4th	1951 type.
Taruffi	1st	"Thinwall"

INDIANAPOLIS

Ascari	–	Retired – Broken hub
Grant		
Mauro	}	Cars did not qualify
Keck		

SILVERSTONE

Villoresi	2nd	Modified body
Taruffi	1st	"Thinwall"
Rosier	12th	1951 type
Landi	3rd	1951 type

BOREHAM

Villoresi	1st	Modified body
Landi	2nd	1951 type
Rosier	4th	1951 type

TURNBERRY

Hawthorn	–	Gearbox "Thinwall"

GOODWOOD

Farina	2nd	"Thinwall"

CHARTERHALL

Farina	–	Rear axle "Thinwall"
Rosier	3rd	1951 type

1953 – 4.5 litre unsupercharged

BUENOS AIRES

Ascari	–	Oiling trouble Body much modified

ALBI

Ascari	–	Gearbox Body much modified
Farina	–	Oil leak "Thinwall"
Rosier	1st	1951 type

GOODWOOD

Taruffi	2nd	"Thinwall"

The ex-Portago Ferrari 250MM

Phil Hill driving a Ferrari Type 412MI (4.1 litre twin cam) at the
Riverside GP meeting of 1958

The Merzario/Pace Ferrari 312P at Le Mans in 1973

The Ferrari 512S of Pierre Bardinon

The Michelotti designed body for Luigi Chinetti on a 1967 Ferrari 330
GT chassis

A Ferrari Type 375MM at Pebble Beach, America in 1973

A Ferrari Daytona Competition at Daytona in 1973

A Ferrari 250 GTO at Virginia City Hill Climb, USA in 1973

A 1951 Vignale bodied 212 Inter Ferrari

A 1969 Ferrari Dino 246GT

The interior of a right hand drive 1974 Ferrari 356 GTB4

A rear view of the four seater Ferrari 365 GT4

(*Top*) The Pininfarina prototype Dino 206 with adjustable front
and rear spoilers
(*Middle*) The production Dino 206 introduced in 1968
(*Bottom*) A predecessor of the mid-engined Dino. Note the carburetter
intakes 'inside' the car

(Top) The production Dino 246 GT
(Middle) 1970 365 GT 2 + 2. This one was available on the American market
(Bottom) The 365 GT 2 + 2 introduced in 1967 replaced the 500 SF

(Top) The Pininfarina 365 P Berlinetta Speciale of 1967
(Middle) Ferrari 365 GTB4 Daytona Coupe
(Bottom Left) Ferrari 365 GTS4 Daytona Convertible
(Bottom Right) Pininfarina special 330 GTC of 1967

(*Top*) 365 GTC4 engine of 1970
(*Middle*) Ferrari Dino 246 GTS
(*Bottom*) 1970 Pininfarina 365 GTC4

(*Top*) The prototype Boxer Berlinetta on the Fiorano test course
(*Bottom Left*) The engine fitted to the Berlinetta Boxer in 1971
(*Bottom Right*) The 1971 Pininfarina Berlinetta Boxer

(Top) The Bertone designed Dino 308 GT, a four seater car with a V8 engine
(Middle) The Pininfarina 365 GT4 2 + 2
(Bottom) The 308 Dino V8 engine of 1974

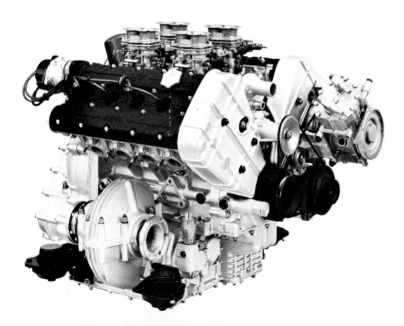

(*Top Left*) Identical engines to the one in the photograph are found in Ferraris 002C and 004C. This picture was published by 'Auto Italiana' in 1947. Unusual features include horizontal magnetos, FIMAC centrifugal fuel pump, ratchet oil filter, valve covers devoid of any name and small flat valve cover knobs

(*Top Right*) Dino Ferrari (left) and his father watch as mechanics Marchetti (centre) and Storchi assemble one of the earliest 1500-cc V12 engines. Note the placement of the magnetos

(*Bottom*) 'Prancing horse' bolt used throughout the engine and chassis of car 004C. This type of bolt has been found on odd and even numbered cars made in 1947, 1948 and 1949

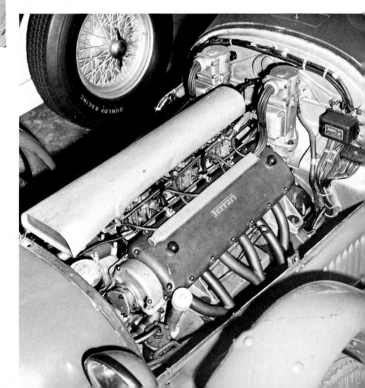

(Top) Ferrari engine serial 004C showing the large air intake over the three Weber 30DCF carburetters, the water and oil filler caps, one of the horizontal Marelli magnetos which goes right through the bulkhead into the cockpit, and one of the nameless valve covers. The last two features are found only on the earliest of Ferraris

(Middle) An early Type 166 MM engine (0018M). Note the vertically positioned Marelli magnetos and the 32 DCF Weber carburetters. By the time this engine was built 'Ferrari' had appeared on the camboxes, but there was still no ribbing. Later 166 MMs were fitted with distributors and 36 IF4/C four choke carburetters along with six inlet port heads and roller cam followers

(Bottom) Briggs Cunningham's 166 Inter engine, No. 016I. This was the first Ferrari in America. Note lack of ribbing on the cam box covers

SILVERSTONE
Farina   1st   "Thinwall"

CHARTERHALL
Farina   Magneto "Thinwall"

GOODWOOD 2 EVENTS
Hawthorn   1st   "Thinwall"

1954 – 4.5 litre unsupercharged
AINTREE
Collins   –   Plugs – after leading   "Thinwall"

GOODWOOD
Collins   1st   "Thinwall"

GOODWOOD
Collins   1st   "Thinwall"

SNETTERTON
Collins   1st   "Thinwall"

AINTREE
Collins   –   Plugs "Thinwall"

FORMULA I 2.5-LITRE UNSUPERCHARGED
1951
BARI
Taruffi   3rd   Prototype 4-cylinder

1952
ALTSTETTEN STOOS HILLCLIMB
Fischer   1st   2.5 engine in 2-litre chassis

1953
BUENOS AIRES
Farina   1st   ⎫
Hawthorn   3rd   ⎬ 2.5-litre engines in 2-litre chassis
Villoresi   2nd   ⎭

ROUEN
Farina   1st
Hawthorn   2nd

SILVERSTONE
Hawthorn   –   Engine

SUSA MOUNT CENIS HILLCLIMB
Maglioli   2nd

1954
ARGENTINE GRAND PRIX
Farina   2nd
Gonzales   3rd
Trintignant   4th
Hawthorn   –   Crash

BUENOS AIRES GRAND PRIX
Farina   3rd   Took over Gonzales' car after brake failure
Trintignant   1st
Hawthorn   –   Engine   Leading until last lap
Gonzales   –   Retired due to heat

SIRACUSA
Hawthorn   –   Crash   Type 625
Farina   1st   Type 625
Trintignant   2nd   Type 625
Gonzales   –   Car burnt   Type 553

PAU
Farina   5th
Gonzales   –   Crankshaft
Trintignant   2nd   After leading most of race

BORDEAUX
Gonzales   1st
Trintignant   3rd

SILVERSTONE
Gonzales   1st   625 after winning heat with 553. 553's engine
                       seized prior to final
Trintignant   6th   Maglioli's 625 handed own car to Gonzales
Maglioli   Handed car to Trintignant for final

BARI
Gonzales   1st
Trintignant   2nd
Maglioli   7th

BELGIAN GRAND PRIX
Hawthorn   4th   Type 625
Trintignant   2nd   Type 625
Farina   –   Engine. Type 553 modified
Gonzales   –   Engine. Type 553 modified

SPANISH GRAND PRIX
Trintignant   –   Gearbox   625 with 553 engine
Hawthorn   1st   553 coil spring model

ITALIAN GRAND PRIX
Ascari   –   Engine   625 with 553 engine
Hawthorn   2nd   625 new engine
Trintignant   5th   625 new engine
Maglioli   3rd   625 old engine.   Gonzales took over
Gonzales   –   553 gearbox
Manzon   –   Engine   625 new engine

SWISS GRAND PRIX
Hawthorn   –   Engine   625 after being 2nd new engine.
Trintignant   –   Engine   625 new engine.
Gonzales   2nd   625 with high tail.
Manzon   –   Crash   553.
Maglioli   7th   553.

GERMAN GRAND PRIX
Gonzales   2nd   625 new engine Hawthorn took over
Hawthorn   –   Rear axle. 625 new engine
Trintignant   3rd   Normal 625
Taruffi   6th   Early 625 (Caen car)

CAEN
Trintignant   1st   Early model 625

SILVERSTONE
Gonzales   1st   625
Hawthorn   2nd   625
Trintignant   5th   625

ROUEN
Hawthorn   –   Crankshaft. New engine in 625
Trintignant   1st   Normal 625

RHEIMS
Trintignant   –   Engine. 625
Hawthorn   –   Engine. 553
Gonzales   –   Engine. 553

1955
ARGENTINE GRAND PRIX
Farina   3rd   Type Argentina 625. Trintignant and Maglioli
                       took over
Gonzales   2nd   Type Argentina 625, Farina and Trintignant
                       took over
Trinitgnant   Engine   Type Argentina 625

TURIN
Farina	—	Gearbox 625
Trintignant	—	Engine 625
Schell	5th	625.

BORDEAUX
| Farina | — | Gearbox 555 |
| Trintignant | — | Brakes 555 |

MONTE CARLO
Farina	4th	625
Trintignant	1st	625
Schell	—	Engine 555
Taruffi	—	Gearbox 555	Drove with Frere

BELGIAN GRAND PRIX
Farina	3rd	555
Trintignant	7th	555
Frere	4th	555

BRITISH GRAND PRIX
Trintignant	—	Engine 625
Hawthorn	6th	625 with Castelotti
Castelotti	—	Transmission 625

ZANDVOORT
Castelotti	5th	555
Hawthorn	7th	555
Trintignant	—	Gearbox 555

ITALIAN GRAND PRIX
Hawthorn	—	Gearbox 555 new gearbox.
Trintignant	7th	555.
Maglioli	6th	555.
Castelotti	3rd	555.

1956 – Type V8 Lancia/Ferrari
ARGENTINE GRAND PRIX
Musso/ Fangio	1st	Fangio took over after his own car broke
Gendebien	5th	Supersqualo Ferrari with Lancia engine
Fangio	—	Engine.
Collins	—	555 Supersqualo rammed by Piotti

MENDOZA
| Fangio | 1st |

SYRACUSE
| Fangio | 1st |

SILVERSTONE DAILY EXPRESS
| Fangio | — | Clutch |
| Collins | — | Clutch |

NAPLES
| Castelotti | — | Engine |
| Musso | — | Engine |

MONACO
Collins/ Fangio	2nd
Fangio/ Castelotti	4th
Castelotti	—	Clutch

SPA
Collins	1st
Frere	2nd
Pilette	6th
Fangio	—	Transmission
Castelotti	—	Transmission

RHEIMS
Collins	1st
Castelotti	2nd
Fangio	4th
De Portago	—	Gearbox
Gendebien	—	Clutch

BRITISH GRAND PRIX
Fangio	1st
De Portago/ Collins	2nd
Castelotti/ De Portago	10th
Collins	—	Engine

NURBURGRING
Fangio	1st
Collins	—	Fuel leak
Castelotti	—	Magneto
Musso/ Castelotti	—	Crash by Castelotti
De Portago/ Collins	—	Carsh by Collins

ITALIAN GRAND PRIX
Collins/ Fangio	2nd
Castelotti	8th
Fangio	—	Broken steering
Musso	—	Broken steering
De Portago	—	Damaged steering.
Von Trips	—	Did not start, crash in practice, broken steering

1957
ARGENTINE GRAND PRIX
Gonzales/ De Portago	5th
Perdisa/ Collins/ Von Trips	6th
Hawthorn	—	Clutch
Collins	—	Clutch
Castelotti	—	Half shaft

BUENOS AIRES GRAND PRIX
Collins/ Gregory	3rd
Hawthorn	4th
Castelotti	5th
Musso	—	Clutch

SYRACUSE
| Collins | 1st |
| Musso | 2nd |

NAPLES
Collins	1st
Hawthorn	2nd
Musso	3rd	V6 Formula 2 car

MONACO
Trintignant	6th
Collins	—	Crash
Hawthorn	—	Crash
Von Trips	—	Crash after engine seizure

ROUEN

Musso	2nd	
Collins	3rd	
Hawthorn	4th	
Trintignant	—	

RHEIMS

Musso	1st	
Hawthorn	—	Engine
Collins	—	Engine
Gendebien	—	Engine

AINTREE

Musso	2nd	
Hawthorn	3rd	
Trintignant	4th	
Collins	—	Radiator leak

NURBURGRING

Hawthorn	2nd	
Collins	3rd	
Musso	4th	

PESCARA

Musso	—	Engine After oil tank broke loose

MONZA

Von Trips	3rd	
Hawthorn	6th	
Musso	8th	
Collins	—	Broken valve

MODENA

Musso	2nd	V6-cylinder 1860-cc Dino
Collins	4th	V6-cylinder 1860-cc Dino

CASABLANCA

Collins	—	Crash V6 2.4-litre Dino
Hawthorn	—	Engine 2.2-litre V6 Dino

1958 Type V6 Dino
ARGENTINE GRAND PRIX

Musso	2nd	
Hawthorn	3rd	
Collins	—	Half shaft

MONACO

Musso	2nd	
Collins	3rd	
Hawthorn	—	Fuel pump
Von Trips	—	Engine

SILVERSTONE DAILY EXPRESS

Collins	1st	

SPA

Hawthorn	2nd	
Gendebien	6th	
Collins	—	Engine
Musso	—	Crash

ZANDVOORT

Hawthorn	5th	
Musso	7th	
Collins	—	Gearbox

RHEIMS

Hawthorn	1st	
Von Trips	3rd	
Collins	5th	
Musso	—	Fatal crash

PORTUGAL

Hawthorn	2nd	
Von Trips	5th	

BRITISH GRAND PRIX

Collins	1st	
Hawthorn	2nd	
Von Trips	—	Engine

NURBURGRING

Von Trips	4th	
Hill	9th	Formula 2, 4th in class
Hawthorn	—	Clutch
Collins	—	Fatal crash

MONZA

Hawthorn	2nd	
Hill	3rd	
Gendebien	—	De Dion bent in collision with Brabham
Von Trips	—	Crash

MOROCCO

Hawthorn	2nd	
Hill	3rd	
Gendebien	—	Crash

1959 Type V6 Dino
MONACO GRAND PRIX

Brooks	2nd	
P. Hill	4th	
Behra	—	Engine

ZANDVOORT

Behra	5th	
P. Hill	6th	
Allison	9th	
Brooks	—	Engine

RHEIMS

Brooks	1st	
P. Hill	2nd	
Gendebien	3rd	
Gurney	—	Broken radiator
Behra	—	Engine

AVUS

Brooks	1st	
Gurney	2nd	
P. Hill	3rd	
Allison	—	Clutch

PORTUGAL

Gurney	3rd	
Brooks	9th	
P. Hill	—	Crash

MONZA

P. Hill	2nd	
Gurney	4th	
Allison	5th	
Gendebien	6th	
Brooks	—	Clutch

U.S.A. GRAND PRIX SEBRING

Brooks	3rd	
Von Trips	6th	
P. Hill	—	Clutch
Allison	—	Clutch

1960
ARGENTINE GRAND PRIX
Allison	2nd	
Von Trips	5th	
P. Hill	8th	
Gonzales	10th	

MONACO GRAND PRIX
P. Hill	3rd	
Ginther	6th	(Rear engined type classified but not runner.)
Von Trips	8th	(Classified but not running at end.)

ZANDVOORT
Von Trips	5th	
Ginther	6th	
P. Hill	—	Engine

SPA
P. Hill	4th	
Von Trips	—	Clutch.
Mairesse	—	Engine.

RHEIMS
Von Trips	11th	(Classified but not running at end.)
P. Hill	12th	(Classified but not running at end.)
Mairesse	—	Transmission.

BRITISH GRAND PRIX SILVERSTONE
Von Trips	6th
P. Hill	7th

PORTUGAL
Von Trips	4th	
P. Hill	—	Clutch.

ITALY GRAND PRIX MONZA
P. Hill	1st
Ginther	2nd
Mairesse	3rd

1961 Rear engined 65 degree and 120 degree V6 engined cars
MONACO GRAND PRIX
Ginther	2nd	(120 deg.)
P. Hill	3rd	(65 deg.)
Von Trips	4th	(65 deg.)

SYRACUSE
Baghetti	1st	(65 deg.)

NAPLES
Baghetti	1st	(65 deg.)

ZANDVOORT
Von Trips	1st	
P. Hill	2nd	(All 120 deg.)
Ginther	5th	

SPA
P. Hill	1st	
Von Trips	2nd	
Ginther	3rd	
Gendebien	4th	(65 deg. all others 120 deg.)

RHEIMS
Baghetti	1st	(65 deg. all others 120 deg.)
P. Hill	9th	
Ginther	—	Engine.
Von Trips	—	Engine.

BRITISH GRAND PRIX AINTREE
Von Trips	1st	
P. Hill	2nd	
Ginther	3rd	
Baghetti	—	Crash (65 deg. all others 120 deg.)

GERMAN GRAND PRIX
Von Trips	2nd	
P. Hill	3rd	
Ginther	8th	
Mairesse	—	Crash (65 deg. all others 120 deg.)

ITALIAN GRAND PRIX
P. Hill	1st	
Von Trips	—	Fatal crash
R. Rodriguez	—	Engine (65 deg. all others 120 deg.)
Baghetti	—	Engine

1962
BRUSSELS GRAND PRIX
Mairesse	1st	(65 deg.)

PAU GRAND PRIX
R. Rodriguez	2nd	(120 deg.)
Bandini	4th	(65 deg.)

MONACO
P. Hill	2nd	(120 deg. central gearbox model.)
Bandini	3rd	(120 deg.)
Mairesse	6th	(120 deg.) Classified but not running at end

ZANDVOORT
P. Hill	3rd	(120 deg. wide rear track model.)
Baghetti	4th	(120 deg.)
R. Rodriguez	—	Crash (120 deg.)

SPA
P. Hill	3rd	(120 deg. central gearbox mod.)
R. Rodriguez	4th	(120 deg.)
Mairesse	—	Crash (120 deg.)

NURBURGRING
R. Rodriguez	6th	(65 deg.)
Baghetti	10th	(120 deg.)
P. Hill	—	Suspension (120 deg. 6 spd cent g/box mod.)
Bandini	—	Crash (120 deg. experimental)

BRITISH GRAND PRIX AINTREE
P. Hill	—	Engine (120 deg. 6 spd cent g/box mod.)

ITALIAN GRAND PRIX MONZA
Mairesse	4th	(120 deg. experimental.)
Baghetti	5th	(120 deg.)
Bandini	8th	(65 deg.)
P. Hill	11th	(120 deg. 6 spd cent g/box mod.)
R. Rodriguez	14th	(120 deg.) Classified but not running at end

PERGUSA
Bandini	1st	(120 deg.)
Baghetti	2nd	(120 deg.)

1963
DAILY EXPRESS TROPHY SILVERSTONE
Surtees	—	Engine
Mairesse	—	Crash

MONACO
Surtees	3rd	
Mairesse	—	Transmission

SPA
Surtees	—	Fuel injection
Mairesse	—	Crash

ZANDVOORT
Surtees	3rd
Scarfiotti	6th

BRITISH GRAND PRIX SILVERSTONE
Surtees	2nd

FRENCH GRAND PRIX RHEIMS
Surtees	—	Fuel pump.
Scarfiotti	—	Crash in practice.

NURBURGRING
Surtees	1st	
Mairesse	—	Crash.

PERGUSA
Surtees	1st	

MONZA
Surtees	—	Engine (monocoque 1964 car with
Bandini	—	Clutch. V6 engine).

WATKINS GLEN
Surtees	—	Engine.*
Bandini	5th	

*Surtees used monocoque with V6 engine in practice car
suffered from engine failure so Surtees used tubular chassis
practice car in race.

1964 V6, V8 and flat 12 cylinder cars
MONACO
Bandini	10th	V6.
Surtees	—	Gearbox (V8).

ZANDVOORT
Surtees	2nd	V8.
Bandini	—	Fuel injection (V6).

BRITISH GRAND PRIX BRANDS HATCH
Surtees	3rd	V8.
Bandini	5th	V6.

GERMAN GRAND PRIX NURBURGRING
Surtees	1st	V8.
Bandini	3rd	V6.

AUSTRIAN GRAND PRIX ZELTWEG
Bandini	1st	V6.
Surtees	—	Rear suspension (V8).

ITALIAN GRAND PRIX MONZA
Surtees	1st	V8.
Bandini	3rd	V8.
Scarfiotti	9th	V6.

U.S.A. GRAND PRIX WATKINS GLEN
Surtees	2nd	V8
Bandini	—	Engine (flat 12)

GRAND PRIX MEXICO
Surtees	2nd	V8.
Bandini	3rd	Flat 12.
Rodriguez	6th	V8.

1965
SOUTH AFRICAN GRAND PRIX
Surtees	2nd	V8.
Bandini	—	Ignition Flat 12.

MONACO GRAND PRIX
Bandini	2nd	Flat 12.
Surtees	4th	V8.

BELGIAN GRAND PRIX
Bandini	9th	Flat 12.
Surtees	—	Engine V8.

GRAND PRIX OF A.C.F. CLERMONT
Surtees	3rd	V8.
Bandini	8th	Flat 12.

BRITISH GRAND PRIX SILVERSTONE
Surtees	3rd	Flat 12.
Bandini	—	Engine Flat 12.

DUTCH GRAND PRIX
Surtees	7th	Flat 12.
Bandini	9th	V8.

GERMAN GRAND PRIX
Bandini	6th	Flat 12.
Surtees	—	Gear selection V8.

ITALIAN GRAND PRIX
Bandini	4th	Flat 12.
Vaccarella	12th	V8 engine
		— classified but not running at end.
Surtees	—	Clutch Flat 12.

U.S.A. GRAND PRIX WATKINS GLEN
Bandini	4th	Flat 12.
P. Rodriguez	5th	Flat 12.
Bondurant	10th	V8.

MEXICAN GRAND PRIX
P. Rodriguez	7th	Flat 12.
Bandini	8th	Flat 12.

1966 V12 cyl 3 litre and 2.4 litre V6
MONACO GRAND PRIX
Bandini	2nd	V6	2.4 lit.
Surtees	—	Rear axle	V12 3 lit.

INTERNATIONAL TROPHY SILVERSTONE
Surtees	2nd	V12	3 lit.

SYRACUSE GRAND PRIX
Surtees	1st	V12	3 lit.
Bandini	2nd	V6	2.4 lit.

GRAND PRIX OF A.C.F. REIMS
Parkes	2nd	V12	3 lit.
Bandini	—	V12	3 lit.
			running but not classified.

GERMAN GRAND PRIX
Bandini	6th	V12	3 lit.
Parkes	—	Crash	V12 3 lit.
Scarfiotti	—	Electrics	V6 2.4 lit.

DUTCH GRAND PRIX
Bandini	6th	V12	3 lit.
Parkes	—	Crash	V12 3 lit.

ITALIAN GRAND PRIX
Scarfiotti	1st	V12 3 lit.
Parkes	2nd	V12 3 lit.
Baghetti	10th	V6 2.4 lit.
Bandini	—	Ignition V12 3 lit.

BELGIAN GRAND PRIX
Surtees	1st	V12 3 lit.
Bandini	3rd	V6 2.4 lit.

U.S.A. GRAND PRIX WATKINS GLEN
Bandini	—	Engine V12 3 lit.

1967
SOUTH AFRICAN GRAND PRIX
No Ferraris

MONACO GRAND PRIX
Amon	3rd	V12
Bandini	—	V12 Fatal crash Lap 82.

DUTCH GRAND PRIX
Amon	4th	V12
Parkes	5th	V12

BELGIAN GRAND PRIX
Amon   3rd   V12
Parkes   —   V12   Crash Lap 1

GRAND PRIX OF THE A.C.T.
Amon   —   V12   Cable accelerator pedal Lap 48

BRITISH GRAND PRIX
Amon   3rd   V12

GERMAN GRAND PRIX
Amon   3rd   V12

CANADIAN GRAND PRIX
Amon   6th   V12

ITALIAN GRAND PRIX
Amon   7th   V12

U.S.A. GRAND PRIX
Amon   —   V12   Engine Lap 95

MEXICAN GRAND PRIX
Amon   9th   V12   Ran out of fuel but classified Lap 63

1968
SOUTH AFRICAN GRAND PRIX
Amon   4th   V12
de Adamich   —   V12   Crash Lap 13
Ickx   —   V12   Oil pipe Lap 51

SPANISH GP
Ickx   —   V12   Ignition Lap 13
Amon   —   V12   Fuel pump Lap 57

MONACO GRAND PRIX
No Ferraris

BELGIAN GRAND PRIX
Ickx   3rd   V12
Amon   —   V12   Oil radiator Lap 8

DUTCH GRAND PRIX
Ickx   4th   V12
Amon   6th   V12

FRENCH GRAND PRIX
Ickx   1st   V12
Amon   10th   V12

BRITISH GRAND PRIX
Amon   2nd   V12
Ickx   3rd   V12

GERMAN GRAND PRIX
Ickx   4th   V12
Amon   —   V12   Crash Lap 12

ITALIAN GRAND PRIX
Ickx   3rd   V12
Bell   —   V12   Fuel feed Lap 5
Amon   —   V12   Crash Lap 9

CANADIAN GRAND PRIX
Amon   —   V12   Transmission Lap 72

U.S.A. GRAND PRIX
Bell   —   V12   Overheating Lap 14
Amon   —   V12   Water pipe

MEXICAN GRAND PRIX
Ickx   —   V12   Ignition Lap 3
Amon   —   V12   Overheating Lap 16

1969
SOUTH AFRICAN GRAND PRIX
Amon   —   V12   Engine Lap 34

SPANISH GRAND PRIX
Amon   —   V12   Engine Lap 56

MONACO GRAND PRIX
Amon   —   V12   Differential Lap 17

DUTCH GRAND PRIX
Amon   3rd   V12

FRENCH GRAND PRIX
Amon   10th   V12   Engine Lap 30 DNF but classified

BRITISH GRAND PRIX
Amon   —   V12   Gearbox Lap 45
Rodriguez   —   V12   Engine Lap 61

GERMAN GRAND PRIX
No Ferraris

ITALIAN GRAND PRIX
Rodriguez   6th   V12

CANADIAN GRAND PRIX
Rodriguez   —   V12   Oil Pressure Lap 37

U.S.A. GRAND PRIX
Rodriguez   5th   V12

MEXICAN GRAND PRIX
Rodriguez   7th   V12

1970 Flat 12 B/1, B/2 and B/3
SOUTH AFRICAN GRAND PRIX
Ickx   —   Flat 12   Engine Lap 61

SPANISH GRAND PRIX
Ickx   —   Flat 12   Crash Lap 1

MONACO GRAND PRIX
Ickx   —   Flat 12   Drive shaft Lap 12

BELGIAN GRAND PRIX
Giunti   4th   Flat 12
Ickx   8th   Flat 12

DUTCH GP
Ickx   3rd   Flat 12
Regazzoni   4th   Flat 12

GP FRANCE
Giunti   14th   Flat 12
Ickx   —   Flat 12   Valve Lap 17

BRITISH GRAND PRIX
Regazzoni   4th   Flat 12
Ickx   —   Flat 12   Transmission Lap 7

GERMAN GRAND PRIX
Ickx   2nd   Flat 12
Regazzoni   —   Flat 12   Gearbox Lap 31

AUSTRIAN GRAND PRIX
Ickx   1st   Flat 12
Regazzoni   2nd   Flat 12

ITALIAN GRAND PRIX
Regazzoni   1st   Flat 12
Giunti   —   Flat 12   Engine Lap 15
Ickx   —   Flat 12   Clutch Lap 26

CANADIAN GRAND PRIX
Ickx   1st   Flat 12
Regazzoni   2nd   Flat 12

U.S.A. GRAND PRIX
Ickx   4th   Flat 12
Regazzoni   13th   Flat 12

MEXICAN GRAND PRIX
Ickx   1st   Flat 12
Regazzoni   2nd   Flat 12

1971

SOUTH AFRICAN GRAND PRIX

Andretti	1st	312B (1/002)	
Regazzoni	3rd	312B (1/004)	
Ickx	8th	312B (1/001)	

SPANISH GRAND PRIX

Ickx	2nd	312B (1/003)	
Regazzoni	—	312B (1/004)	Engine Lap 13
Andretti	—	312B (002)	Engine Lap 50

MONACO GRAND PRIX

Ickx	3rd	312B (006)	
Regazzoni	—	312B/2 (005)	Crash Lap 25
Andretti	—	312B (002)	Did not qualify

BRITISH GRAND PRIX

| Regazzoni | — | 312B/2 (No. 5) | Engine Lap 49 |
| Ickx | — | 312B/2 (No. 6) | Engine Lap 52 |

FRENCH GRAND PRIX

| Ickx | — | 312B/2 (No. 6) | Engine Lap 5 |
| Regazzoni | — | 312B/2 (No. 5) | Crash Lap 21 |

DUTCH GRAND PRIX

Ickx	1st	312B/2 (No. 6)	
Regazzoni	3rd	312B/2 (No. 5)	
Andretti	—	312B (No. 3)	Fuel system Lap 5

AUSTRIAN GRAND PRIX

| Regazzoni | — | 312B/2 (No. 5) | Engine Lap 9 |
| Ickx | — | 312B/2 (No. 6) | Engine Lap 32 |

GERMAN GRAND PRIX

Regazzoni	3rd	312B/2 (No. 5)	
Andretti	4th	312B/2 (No. 7)	
Ickx	—	312B/2 (No. 6)	Crash Lap 2

ITALIAN GRAND PRIX

| Ickx | — | 312B (No. 4) | Engine Lap 16 |
| Regazzoni | — | 312B/2 (No. 5) | Engine Lap 18 |

CANADIAN GP

Ickx	8th	312B/2 (No. 6)	
Andretti	13th	312B/2 (No. 7)	
Regazzoni	—	312B/2 (No. 5)	Crash

U.S.A. GRAND PRIX

| Regazzoni | 6th | 312B/2 (No. 5) | |
| Ickx | — | 312B (No. 4) | Alternator |

1972

ARGENTINE GRAND PRIX

Ickx	3rd	312/B2 (No. 6)	
Regazzoni	4th	312/B2 (No. 5)	
Andretti	—	312/B2 (No. 7)	Blackflagged, engine

SOUTH AFRICAN GRAND PRIX

Andretti	4th	312/B2 (No. 7)	
Ickx	8th	312/B2 (No. 6)	
Regazzoni	12th	312/B2 (No. 5)	

SPANISH GRAND PRIX

Ickx	2nd	312/B2 (No. 6)	
Regazzoni	3rd	312/B2 (No. 8)	
Andretti	—	312/B2 (No. 5)	Engine

MONACO GRAND PRIX

| Ickx | 2nd | 312/B2 (No. 6) | |
| Regazzoni | — | 312/B2 (No. 5) | Crash |

BELGIAN GRAND PRIX

| Ickx | — | 312/B2 (No. 6) | Throttle linkage |
| Regazzoni | — | 312/B2 (No. 5) | Crash |

FRENCH GRAND PRIX

| Ickx | 11th | 312/B2 (No. 6) | |
| Galli | 13th | 312/B2 (No. 7) | |

BRITISH GRAND PRIX

| Merzario | 6th | 312/B2 (No. 7) | |
| Ickx | — | 312/B2 (No. 5) | Oil pressure |

GERMAN GRAND PRIX

Ickx	1st	312/B2 (No. 5)	
Regazzoni	2nd	312/B2 (No. 7)	
Merzario	11th	312/B2 (No. 8)	

AUSTRIAN GRAND PRIX

| Ickx | — | 312/B2 (No. 5) | Fuel system |
| Regazzoni | — | 312/B2 (No. 7) | Fuel system |

ITALIAN GRAND PRIX

Andretti	7th	312/B2 (No. 8)	
Ickx	—	312/B2 (No. 5)	Crash
Regazzoni	—	312/B2 (No. 7)	Crash

CANADIAN GRAND PRIX

Regazzoni	5th	312/B2 (No. 7)	
Ickx	12th	312/B2 (No. 5)	
Merzario	—	312/B2 (No. 6)	Withdrawn before race

UNITED STATES GRAND PRIX

Ickx	5th	312/B2 (No. 5)	
Andretti	6th	312/B2 (No. 6)	
Regazzoni	8th	312/B2 (No. 7)	

1973

ARGENTINE GRAND PRIX

| Ickx | 4th | 312/B2 (005) | |
| Merzario | 9th | 312/B2 (008) | |

BRAZILIAN GRAND PRIX

| Merzario | 4th | 312/B2 (008) | |

SOUTH AFRICAN GRAND PRIX

| Merzario | 4th | 312/B2 (006) | |
| Ickx | — | 312/B2 (005) | Crash |

SPANISH GRAND PRIX

| Ickx | 12th | 312/B3 (010) | |
| Merzario | Withdrawn | 312/B3 (011) | |

BELGIAN GRAND PRIX

| Ickx | — | 312/B3 (010) | Oil pump |
| Merzario | Withdrawn | 312/B3 (011) | |

MONACO GRAND PRIX

| Ickx | — | 312/B3 (010) | Drive shaft |
| Merzario | — | 312/B3 (011) | Oil pressure |

SWEDISH GRAND PRIX

| Ickx | 8th | 312/B3 (010) | |

FRENCH GRAND PRIX

| Ickx | 5th | 312/B3 (010) | |
| Merzario | 7th | 312/B3 (012) | |

BRITISH GRAND PRIX

| Ickx | 8th | 312/B3 (010) | |

DUTCH GRAND PRIX

No Ferraris entered

AUSTRIAN GRAND PRIX

| Merzario | 7th | 312/B3 (011) | Forghieri modified |

ITALIAN GRAND PRIX

| Ickx | 8th | 312/B3 (010) | |
| Merzario | — | 312/B3 (012) | Crash |

CANADIAN GRAND PRIX

| Merzario | 15th | 312/B3 | |

USA GRAND PRIX

| Merzario | 16th | 312/B3 | |

FORMULA 2
1949 12-cyl 2-litre V12
BRUSSELS GRAND PRIX

Villoresi	1st	

LUXEMBOURG GRAND PRIX

Villoresi	1st	

GRAND PRIX OF ROME

Villoresi	1st	
Taruffi	2nd	
Cortese	3rd	
Bonetto	6th	

BARI GRAND PRIX

Ascari	1st	
Cortese	2nd	
Bonetto	3rd	
Villoresi	4th	
Vallone	5th	

NAPLES GRAND PRIX

Vallone	1st	
Bonetto	2nd	
Taruffi	— ret.	

FORMULA 2 GRAND PRIX FERRARIS
1950 — 12-cylinder cars
PAU

Ascari	—	Transmission Long chassis De Dion

MODENA

Ascari	1st	

MONS

Ascari	1st	

MONZA

Villoresi	1st	
Ascari	—	Transmission

SWISS GRAND PRIX FORMULA 2 EVENT

Sommer	1st	

ROME

Ascari	1st	
Villoresi	2nd	} Swing axle 1.5-litre chassis
Vallone	3rd	

RHEIMS

Ascari	1st	
Villoresi	—	Transmission

ERLEN

Villoresi	1st	Swing axle 1.5-litre chassis

BARI

Villoresi	—	Transmission

ZANDVOORT FORMULA 1 EVENT

Ascari	3rd	

GENEVA

Villoresi	—	Transmission
Serafini	3rd	

NURBURGRING

Ascari	1st	
Serafini	—	Transmission

METTET

Ascari	—	Transmission
Serafini	—	Transmission

GARDA

Ascari	**1st**	
Serafini	**2nd**	

1951 — 12-cylinder and 4-cylinder cars
MARSEILLES

Villoresi	1st	

MONZA

Ascari	1st	

ROME

Rafaelli	1st	
G. Marzotto	3rd	

ROUEN

G. Marzotto	1st	
Rafaelli	—	Transmission

NAPLES

Ascari	1st	
Villoresi	—	Transmission

MODENA

Ascari	1st	4-cylinder.
Villoresi	–	Engine 4-cylinder
Gonzales	2nd	12-cylinder

1952 — 4-cylinder cars
SYRACUSE

Ascari	1st	
Taruffi	2nd	
Farina	3rd	
Villoresi	7th	Caught fire at start

PAU

Ascari	1st	
Villoresi	—	Crashed
Scotti	—	Crashed

MARSEILLES

Ascari	1st	
Farina	—	Crashed
Villoresi	—	Engine

NAPLES

Farina	1st	
Taruffi	2nd	
Simon	—	Crash

SWISS GRAND PRIX

Farina	—	Engine
Taruffi	1st	
Simon	—	Car taken by Farina. Engine broke

PARIS

Taruffi	1st	
Farina	—	Crashed in Villoresi's car
Simon	2nd	
Villoresi	—	Handed car to Farina at start

MONZA

Ascari	—	Engine
Farina	1st	
Simon	2nd	
Villoresi	—	Engine

SPA

Ascari	1st	
Farina	2nd	
Taruffi	—	Crashed

RHEIMS

Ascari	3rd	With Villoresi
Villoresi	—	Engine
Farina	2nd	

ROUEN		
Ascari	1st	
Farina	2nd	} All long nosed types.
Taruffi	3rd	

SABLE D'OLONNE		
Ascari	—	Crashed
Villoresi	1st	
Farina	—	Crashed

BRITISH GRAND PRIX		
Ascari	1st	
Taruffi	2nd	
Farina	6th	

GERMAN GRAND PRIX		
Ascari	1st	
Farina	2nd	
Taruffi	4th	

COMMINGES		
Ascari		Engine
Farina	2nd	
Simon	1st	With Ascari

ZANDVOORT		
Ascari	1st	
Farina	2nd	
Villoresi	3rd	

MONZA		
Ascari	1st	
Villoresi	3rd	
Farina	4th	
Simon	6th	
Taruffi	7th	

MODENA		
Villoresi	1st	
Ascari	—	Engine.
Sighinolfi	3rd	With Ascari.

1953 — 4-cylinder cars

BUENOS AIRES		
Ascari	1st	
Villoresi	2nd	
Hawthorn	4th	
Farina	—	Crashed.

SYRACUSE		
Ascari	—	Engine.
Villoresi	—	Engine.
Hawthorn	—	Slight crash. Ascari took car. Engine.
Farina	—	Engine.

PAU		
Ascari	1st	
Hawthorn	2nd	
Farina	—	Crash.

BORDEAUX		
Ascari	1st	
Villoresi	2nd	
Farina	—	Gearbox.

SILVERSTONE		
Hawthorn	1st	

NAPLES		
Farina	1st	
Villoresi	4th	
Ascari	5th	

ULSTER		
Hawthorn	1st	

ZANDVOORT		
Ascari	1st	
Farina	2nd	
Hawthorn	4th	

SPA		
Ascari	1st	New carb layout siamesed
Farina	—	Engine New carb layout.
Villoresi	2nd	
Hawthorn	6th	Split fuel line after being 2nd.

RHEIMS		
Hawthorn	1st	
Ascari	4th	} All cars with new carbs
Farina	5th	
Villoresi	6th	

BRITISH GRAND PRIX		
Ascari	1st	
Villoresi	—	Axle.
Farina	3rd	
Hawthorn	5th	

GERMAN GRAND PRIX		
Farina	1st	
Ascari	8th	Changed cars with Villoresi.
Villoresi	—	Changed car with Ascari. Engine.
Hawthorn	3rd	

SWISS GRAND PRIX		
Ascari	1st	
Farina	2nd	
Hawthorn	3rd	
Villoresi	6th	

ITALIAN GRAND PRIX		
Ascari	—	Crash after leading on last lap.
Farina	2nd	
Villoresi	3rd	
Hawthorn	4th	
Carini	—	Engine New type Squalo
Maglioli	8th	New type Squalo.
Villoresi	—	Fuel feed.

1960

SYRACUSE GRAND PRIX		
Von Trips	1st	V6 Dino Front-engined

SOLITUDE		
Von Trips	1st	V6 Dino Rear-engined

ITALIAN GRAND PRIX		
Von Trips	5th	V6 Dino Rear-engined (1st in class)

MODENA GRAND PRIX		
Ginther	2nd	V6 Dino Front-engined
Von Trips	3rd	V6 Dino Rear-engined

APPENDIX 1A
FORMULA 2
1967 V6 Rear-engined Dino 166
ROUEN
Williams	—	Engine

1968 V6 Rear-engined Dino 166
BARCELONA GRAND PRIX
Amon	2nd	
Ickx	—	Crash

HOCKENHEIM
Amon	5th	

EIFELRENNEN
Redman	4th	
Ickx	—	Radiator

ZOLDER
Amon	2nd	
Ickx	4th	

CRYSTAL PALACE
Ickx	—	Crash

HOCKENHEIM RHEIN CUP
Ickx	5th	
Amon	8th	

MONZA
Casoni	7th	
Bell	—	Crash
Baghetti	—	Crash
Brambilla	—	Crash

FLUGPLATZRENNEN
Bell	7th	
Amon	—	Gearbox

ZANDVOORT
Bell	14th	
Brambilla	—	Steering

PERGUSA
Brambilla	3rd	
Bell	5th	
Ickx	6th	
Casoni	16th	

HOCKENHEIM WURTTEMBER GRAND PRIX
Brambilla	1st	
Bell	3rd	

VALLELUNGA
Brambilla	1st	
de Adamich	2nd	
Bell	6th	

BUENOS AIRES NO 1
Brambilla	1st	
de Adamich	2nd	

CORDOBA
de Adamich	1st	
Brambilla	—	Engine

ZONDA
de Adamich	1st	
Brambilla	—	Engine

BUENOS AIRES NO 2
de Adamich	5th	
Brambilla	—	Engine

1969 V6 Rear-engined Dino
THRUXTON
Brambilla	6th	
Regazzoni	10th	
Bell	—	Fuel pressure

HOCKENHEIM
Brambilla	—	Engine
Regazzoni	—	Disqualified

EIFELRENNEN
Bell	5th	
Brambilla	—	Illness
Regazzoni	—	Exhaust system

JARAMA
Brambilla	6th	
Bell	8th	
Regazzoni	11th	

MONZA
Bell	5th	
Brambilla	—	Engine
Regazzoni	—	Engine

APPENDIX 1B
PERFORMANCE OF FERRARI IN TASMAN SERIES AND SINGAPORE/MALAYA
1968 Formula 2 chassis with 2.5 V6 Dino Engine
NEW ZEALAND GRAND PRIX
Amon	1st	

LEVIN GRAND PRIX
Amon	1st	

LADY WIGRAM TROPHY
Amon	2nd	

TERETONGA
Amon	4th	

SURFERS PARADISE
Amon	—	Gasket

WARWICK FARM
Amon	4th	

AUSTRALIAN GRAND PRIX
Amon	2nd	

LONGFORD
Amon	7th	

1969
NEW ZEALAND GRAND PRIX
Amon	1st	
Bell	4th	

LEVIN
Amon	1st	
Bell	—	Exhaust

LADY WIGRAM TROPHY
Amon	3rd	
Bell	5th	

TERETONGA
Amon	3rd	
Bell	5th	

AUSTRALIAN GRAND PRIX
Amon	1st	
Bell	2nd	

WARWICK FARM
Bell	2nd	
Amon	—	Crash

SANDOWN PARK
Amon	1st	
Bell	5th	

1970
ROTHMANS INTERNATIONAL, LEVIN NZ
Graem Lawrence	1st	2.4 Dino V6	

NEW ZEALAND GRAND PRIX PUKEKOHE
Graem Lawrence	3rd	2.4 Dino V6	

WIGRAM TROPHY, CHRISTCHURCH, NZ
Graem Lawrence	—	2.4 Dino V6	Overheating

TERETONGA INTERNATIONAL, INVERCARGILL NZ
Graem Lawrence	4th	2.4 Dino V6	

SANDOWN PARK, AUSTRALIA
Graem Lawrence	2nd	2.4 Dino V6	

ROTHMANS INTL SURFER'S PARADISE, AUSTRALIA
Graem Lawrence	3rd	2.4 Dino V6	

SINGAPORE GRAND PRIX
Graem Lawrence	1st	2.4 Dino V6	

SELANGOR GRAND PRIX
Graem Lawrence	1st	2.4 Dino V6	

1971
LEVIN
Lawrence	—	Crash

NEW ZEALAND GRAND PRIX
Lawrence	6th	

LADY WIGRAM TROPHY
Lawrence	3rd	

TERETONGA
Lawrence	—	Engine

WARWICK FARM
Lawrence	—	Oil pressure

SANDOWN PARK
Lawrence	6th	

SURFERS PARADISE
Lawrence	4th	

Type 1500-cc single stage super-charged

Total entries	. . . . .	52
Total retirements	. . . .	18
Placings: 1st	. . . . .	7
2nd	. . . . .	6
3rd	. . . . .	7
4th	. . . . .	4
5th	. . . . .	5
7th	. . . . .	1
8th	. . . . .	1
9th	. . . . .	2
10th	. . . . .	1

Causes of retirement:

Engine	. . . . .	7
Transmission	. . . .	7
Crash	. . . . .	3
Driver's illness	. . . .	1

Type 1500-cc two stage supercharged

Total entries	. . . . .	8
Total retirements	. . . .	5
Placings: 1st	. . . . .	1
2nd	. . . . .	1
6th	. . . . .	1

Causes of retirement:

Engine	. . . . .	2
Transmission	. . . .	2
Crash	. . . . .	1

Type 2.5-litre 12-cylinder unsuper-charged

Total entries	. . . . .	10
Total retirements	. . . .	1
Placings: 1st	. . . . .	1
2nd	. . . . .	2
3rd	. . . . .	2
4th	. . . . .	1
6th	. . . . .	2
11th	. . . . .	1

Causes of retirement:

Steering	. . . . .	1

Types 3.3-litre and 4.1-litre unsuper-charged experimental

Total entries	. . . . .	4
Total retirements	. . . .	2
Placings: 3rd	. . . (4.1)	1
5th	. . . (3.3)	1

Causes of retirement:

Engine	. . . (3.3)	1
Crash	. . . (3.3)	1

Type 4.5-litre single ignition unsuper-charged

Total entries	. . . .	19
Total retirements	. . . .	8
Placings: 1st	. . . . .	7
2nd	. . . . .	4

Causes of retirement:

Engine	. . . . .	3
Transmission	. . . .	3
Crash	. . . . .	2

Type 4.5-litre twin ignition unsuper-charged

Total entries	. . . . .	38
Total retirements	. . . .	8
Placings: 1st	. . . . .	8
2nd	. . . . .	8
3rd	. . . . .	5
4th	. . . . .	5
5th	. . . . .	2
6th	. . . . .	1
12th	. . . . .	1

Causes of retirement:

Transmission	. . . .	5
Engine	. . . . .	2
Chassis	. . . . .	1

Type 4.5-litre twin ignition unsuper-charged Indianapolis and 'Thinwall'

Total entries	. . . . .	19
Total retirements	. . . .	9
Placings: 1st	. . . . .	8
2nd	. . . . .	2

Causes of retirement:

Engine	. . . . .	4
Transmission	. . . .	3
Crash	. . . . .	1
Split tank	. . . . .	1

Type 2-litre 12-cylinder unsuper-charged

Total entries	. . . . .	31
Total retirements	. . . .	10
Placings: 1st	. . . . .	14
2nd	. . . . .	3
3rd	. . . . .	4

Causes of retirement:

Transmission	. . . .	10

Type 2-litre 4-cylinder unsupercharged

Total entries	. . . . .	104
Total retirements	. . . .	29
Placings: 1st	. . . . .	29
2nd	. . . . .	18
3rd	. . . . .	9
4th	. . . . .	7
5th	. . . . .	4
6th	. . . . .	5
7th	. . . . .	2
8th	. . . . .	1

Causes of retirement:

Engine	. . . . .	15
Transmission	. . . .	2
Crash	. . . . .	12

Type 2-litre 4-cylinder unsupercharged Squalo

Total entries	. . . . .	2
Total retirements	. . . .	1
Placings: 8th	. . . . .	1

Cause of retirement:

Engine	. . . . .	1

Type 625 close angle valve engine

Total entries	. . . . .	43
Total retirements	. . . .	7
Placings: 1st	. . . . .	12
2nd	. . . . .	10
3rd	. . . . .	7
4th	. . . . .	2
5th	. . . . .	2
6th	. . . . .	2
7th	. . . . .	1

Causes of retirement:

Engine	. . . . .	4
Crash	. . . . .	2
Illness of driver	. . . . .	1

Type 625 wide angle valve and type 553 engine

Total entries	. . . . .	22
Total retirements	. . . .	12
Placings: 1st	. . . . .	1
2nd	. . . . .	4
3rd	. . . . .	1
4th	. . . . .	1
5th	. . . . .	2
6th	. . . . .	1

Causes of retirement:

Engine	. . . . .	8
Transmission	. . . .	4

Type 553 Squalo

Total entries	. . . .	10
Total retirements	. . . .	8
Placings: 1st	. . . .	1
7th	. . . .	1

Causes of retirement:

Engine	. . . . .	5
Crash	. . . . .	2
Transmission	. . . .	1

Type 555 Super Squalo

Total entries	. . . .	14
Total retirements	. . . .	6
Placings: 3rd	. . . .	2
4th	. . . .	1
5th	. . . .	1
6th	. . . .	1
7th	. . . .	3

Causes of retirement:
Engine 1
Transmission 4
Brakes 1

The V8 2.5-litre Ferrari
Total entries 74
Total retirements 33
Placings: 1st 10
2nd 10
3rd 5
4th 6
5th 3
6th 4
8th 2
10th 1

Causes of retirement:
Engine 10
Crash 6
Clutch 7
Steering 3
Transmission 2
Gearbox 1
Fuel leak 1
Magneto 1
Half shaft 1
Radiator leak 1

The V6 2.5-litre Ferrari
Total entries 38
Total retirements 15
Placings: 1st 3
2nd 8
3rd 5
4th 2
5th 3
6th 1
7th 1

Causes of retirement:
Crash 7
Engine 5
Clutch 1
Gearbox 1
Half shaft 1

The V6 1.5-litre Ferrari F.2
Total entries 4
Total retirements . . . . . —
Placings: 1st 2
2nd 1
4th 1

V6 Dino 2.5-litre (includes 1.9 and 2.2 prototypes)

Total entries 89
Total retirements 29

Placings: 1st 6
2nd 14
3rd 11
4th 6
5th 7
6th 7
7th 2
8th 2
9th 2
10th 1
11th 1
12th 1

Causes of retirement:
Engine 10
Clutch 7
Crash 8
Transmission 3
Broken radiator 1

V6 Rear engined 65 degree engine 1.5 litre F.1
Total entries 13
Total retirements 3
Placings: 1st 4
3rd 1
4th 3
6th 1
8th 1

Causes of retirement:
Engine 2
Crash 1

V6 Rear engined 120 degree engine 1.5 litre F.1
Total entries 57
Total retirements 20
Placings: 1st 7
2nd 9
3rd 8
4th 3
5th 3
6th 2
8th 1
9th 1
10th 1
11th 1
14th 1

Causes of retirement:
Engine 7
Crash 7
Suspension 1
Transmission 1
Fuel injection 1
Fuel pump 1
Clutch 1

APPENDIX IIIA SUMMARY OF RESULTS
Formula 1 year by year

1948
1.5 supercharged and 4.5 unsuper-charged
Total entries 7
Total retirements 6
Placings: 3rd 1
Causes of retirement:
Engine 1
Transmission 4
Driver's illness 1

2.5 unsupercharged
Nil

1949
1.5 supercharged and 4.5 unsuper-charged
Total entries 25
Total retirements 8
Placings: 1st 5
2nd 3
3rd 3
4th 2
5th 1
7th 1
8th 1
9th 1

Causes of retirement:
Engine 3
Transmission 3
Crash 2

2.5 unsupercharged
Nil

1950
1.5 supercharged and 4.5 unsuper-charged
Total entries 25
Total retirements 8
Placings: 1st 3
2nd 6
3rd 4
4th 2
5th 1
6th 1

Causes of retirement:
Engine 3
Transmission 2
Oil line 1
Crash 2

2.5 unsupercharged
Nil

1951

1.5 supercharged and 4.5 unsupercharged

Total entries	60
Total retirements	18
Placings: 1st	10
2nd	11
3rd	6
4th	4
5th	6
6th	3
9th	1
10th	1

Causes of retirement:

Engine	5
Transmission	7
Steering	1
Chassis	1
Crash	4

2.5 unsupercharged

Total entries	1
Total retirements	—
Placings: 3rd	1

1952

1.5 supercharged and 4.5 unsupercharged

Total entries	21
Total retirements	5
Placings: 1st	6
2nd	5
3rd	2
4th	2
12th	1

Causes of retirement:

Transmission	3
Crash	1
Split tank	1

2.5 unsupercharged

Total entries	1
Total retirements	—
Placings: 1st	1

1953

1.5 supercharged and 4.5 unsupercharged

Total entries	9
Total retirements	4
Placings: 1st	4
2nd	1

Causes of retirement:

Transmission	1
Oil leak	2
Magneto	1

2.5 unsupercharged

Total entries	7
Total retirements	1

Placings: 1st	2
2nd	3
3rd	1

Causes of retirement:

Engine	1

1954

1.5 supercharged and 4.5 unsupercharged

Total entries	5
Total retirements	2
Placings: 1st	3

Causes of retirement:

Plugs	2

2.5 unsupercharged

Total entries	52
Total retirements	20
Placings: 1st	9
2nd	9
3rd	5
4th	2
5th	3
6th	2
7th	2

Causes of retirement:

Engine	12
Transmission	3
Crash	4
Illness	1

1955

2.5-litre Ferrari unsupercharged

Total entries	25
Total retirements	11
Placings: 1st	1
2nd	1
3rd	3
4th	2
5th	2
6th	2
7th	3

Causes of retirement:

Engine	4
Transmission	6
Brakes	1

1956

2.5-litre Ferrari unsupercharged

Total entries	35
Total retirements	18
Placings: 1st	6
2nd	5
4th	2
5th	1
6th	1
8th	1
10th	1

Causes of retirement:

Crash	4
Engine	4

Clutch	3
Transmission	2
Fuel leak	1
Magneto	1
Steering	3

1957

2.5-litre Ferrari unsupercharged

Total entries	42
Total retirements	16
Placings: 1st	3
2nd	6
3rd	6
4th	5
5th	2
6th	3
8th	1

Causes of retirement:

Crash	3
Engine	8
Clutch	3
Half shaft	1
Water leak	1

1958

2.5-litre Ferrari unsupercharged

Total entries	35
Total retirements	13
Placings: 1st	3
2nd	7
3rd	6
4th	1
5th	3
7th	1
9th	1

Causes of retirement:

Crash	6
Engine	3
Half shaft	1
Gearbox	1
Clutch	2

1959

Total entries	28
Total retirements	9

Causes of retirement:

Engine	3
Clutch	4
Crash	1
Broken radiator	1

Placings: 1st	2
2nd	4
3rd	4
4th	2
5th	2
6th	3
9th	2

1960
Total entries 23
Total retirements 5
Causes of retirement:
  Engine 2
  Clutch 2
  Transmission 1
Placings: 1st 1
    2nd 2
    3rd 2
    4th 2
    5th 2
    6th 3
    7th 1
    8th 2
    10th 1
    11th 1
    12th 1

1961 *1.5-litre unsupercharged*
Total entries 28
Total retirements 7
Causes of retirement:
  Engine 4
  Crash 3
Placings: 1st 7
    2nd 5
    3rd 4
    4th 2
    5th 1
    8th 1
    9th 1

1962
Total entries 24
Total retirements 5
Causes of retirement:
  Crash 3
  Engine 1
  Suspension 1
Placings: 1st 2
    2nd 3
    3rd 3
    4th 4
    5th 1
    6th 2
    8th 1
    10th 1
    11th 1
    14th 1

1963 (note up to Watkins Glen 1963)
Total entries 18
Total retirements 11
Causes of retirement:
  Crash 4
  Engine 2
  Transmission 1
  Fuel injection 1
  Fuel pump 1
  Clutch 1
Placings: 1st 2
    2nd 1
    3rd 2
    5th 1
    6th 1

1964 *V6*
Total entries 6
Total retirements 1
Causes of retirement:
  Fuel injection 1
Placings: 1st 1
    3rd 1
    5th 1
    9th 1
    10th 1

1964 *unsupercharged V8*
Total entries 10
Total retirements 2
Causes of retirement:
  Gearbox 1
  Rear suspension 1
Placings: 1st 2
    2nd 3
    3rd 2
    6th 1

1964 *flat 12*
Total entries 2
Total retirements 1
Cause of retirement:
  Engine 1
Placings: 3rd 1

1965 *1.5-litre unsupercharged V8*
Total entries 8
Total retirements 2
Causes of retirement:
  Engine 1
  Gear selection 1
Placings: 2nd 1
    3rd 1
    4th 1
    9th 1
    10th 1
    12th 1

1965 *1.5-litre unsupercharged flat 12*
Total entries 14
Total retirements 3
Causes of retirement:
  Ignition 1
  Engine 1
  Clutch 1
Placings: 2nd 1
    3rd 1
    4th 2
    5th 1
    6th 1
    7th 1
    8th 2
    9th 1

1966 *2.4-litre 6-cylinder*
Total entries 5
Total retirements 1

Causes of retirement:
  Electrical system 1
Placings 2nd 2
    3rd 1
    10th 1

1967 *3-litre V12*
Total entries 14
Total retirements 6
Causes of retirement:
  Running not classified . . . 1
  Rear axle 1
  Ignition 1
  Engine 1
  Crash 2
Placings: 1st 3
    2nd 3
    6th 2

1968 *3-litre V12*
Total entries 23
Total retirements 13
Causes of retirements:
  Crash 3
  Ignition 2
  Overheating 2
  Oil pipe 1
  Water pipe 1
  Fuel pump 1
  Oil radiator 1
  Fuel feed 1
  Transmission 1
Placings: 1st 1
    2nd 1
    3rd 3
    4th 3
    6th 1
    10th 1

1969 *3-litre V12*
Total entries 12
Total retirements 5
Causes of retirement:
  Engine 2
  Gearbox 1
  Oil Press 1
  Differential 1
Placings: 3rd 1
    5th 1
    6th 1
    7th 1
    10th 1

1970 *3-litre flat 12*
Total entries 25
Total retirements 8
Causes of retirements:
  Engine 3
  Crash 1
  Drive shaft 1
  Transmission 1
  Gearbox 1
  Clutch 1

Placings: 1st 4
2nd 4
3rd 1
4th 4
7th 1
8th 1
13th 1
14th 1

1971 *3-litre flat 12*
Total entries 27
Total retirements 15
Causes of retirement:
Engine 7
Fuel pump 2
Rear susp 1
Crash 2
Transmission 2
Elect system 1
Placings: 1st 2
2nd 1
3rd 4
4th 1
6th 1
8th 1
13th 1

1972 *3-litre flat 12*
Total entries 30
Total retirements 10
Causes of retirement:
Crash 3
Fuel system 2
Elect system 1
Throttle link 1
Engine 1
Oil pressure 1
Black flag 1
Placings: 1st 1
2nd 3
3rd 2
4th 2
5th 2
6th 2
7th 1
8th 2
11th 2
12th 2
13th 1

1973 *3 litre flat 12*
Total entries 22
Total retirements 5
Placings: 4th 3
5th 1
7th 2
8th 3
9th 1
12th 1
15th 1
16th 1

Causes of retirement
Crash 2
Withdrawn 2
Oil pump 1
Drive shaft 1
Oil pressure 1

SUMMARY OF RESULTS
Formula 2
1948
Total entries 12
Total retirements 4
Placings: 1st 3
2nd 5

Causes of retirement
Illness 1
Unknown 3

1949
Total entries 15
Total retirements 1
Placings: 1st 5
2nd 3
3rd 2
4th 1
5th 1
6th 1

Causes of retirement
Unknown 1

1950
Total entries 22
Total retirements 8
Placings: 1st 9
2nd 2
3rd 3
Causes of retirement:
Transmission 8

1951
Total entries 11
Total retirements 3
Placings: 1st 6
2nd 1
3rd 1
Causes of retirement:
Engine 1
Transmission 2

1952
Total entries 55
Total retirements 16
Placings: 1st 16
2nd 11
3rd 6
4th 2
6th 2
7th 2
Causes of retirement:
Engine 8
Crash 8

1953
Total entries 49
Total retirements 13
Placings: 1st 12
2nd 7
3rd 4
4th 5
5th 3
6th 3
8th 2
Causes of retirement:
Engine 8
Transmission 2
Crash 3

1957
Total entries 2
Total retirements . . . . None
Placings: 1st 1
3rd 1
(1st in class)

1958
Total entries 2
Total retirements . . . . None
Placings: 1st 1
5th 1

1959
Total entries 3
Total retirements 2
Placings: 2nd 1
Causes of retirement
Crash 1
Engine 1

1960
Total entries 5
Total retirements . . . . None
Placings: 1st 2
2nd 1
3rd 1
5th 1
(1st in class)

1967
Total entries 1
Total retirements 1
Causes of retirement
Engine 1

1968
Total entries 17
Total retirements 8
Placings: 2nd 2
4th 2
5th 2
7th 2
8th 1
Causes of retirement
Crash 5
Engine 1
Gearbox 1
Radiator 1

1969
Total entries 32
Total retirements 11
Placings: 1st 4
2nd 2
3rd 2
5th 4
6th 4
8th 1
10th 1
11th 1
14th 1
16th 1
Causes of retirement
Engine 6
Steering 1
Fuel press 1
Disqualified 1
Illness 1
Exhaust system 1

ENGINE DATA — GRAND PRIX CARS

	1.5 SS	1.5 TS	2-litre SS	F2 4-cylinder 53	F2 Squalo	DS 50 Squalo	DS 50
Cylinders	12	12	12	4	4	8	8
Bore	55	55	60	90	93	73.6	73.6
Stroke	52.5	52.5	58.8	78	73.5	73.1	73.1
B/S Ratio	0.95	0.95	0.98	0.87	0.79	0.994	0.994
Engine capacity	1,498	1,489	1.995	1,980	1,998	2,489	2,489
B h p	225	300	300	180	190	250	275
R p m	7,500	7.500	7,500	7,000	7,500	7,000	7,000
B h p per litre	150	200	150	91.0	95.0	101	111
B m e p lb/sq in.	260	346	256	167	167	186	204
Piston speed f p m	2,600	2,600	2,890	3,600	3,610	3,360	3,360
Piston area sq in.	42.2	42.2	52.8	39.5	41.8	52.9	52.9
H p per sq in. piston area	5.35	7.23	5.70	4.57	4.56	4.73	5.21
Piston area sq in. per litre	28	28	26.5	19.95	20.9	21.2	21.2
Induction system	2.6 a t a	2.6 a t a	2.6 a t a	l a t a	l a t a	l a t a	l a t a

	2.5 US	3.3 US	2.5 Ptyp	625/54	Type 115
Cylinders	12	12	4	4	6
Bore	68	72	94	94	82.4
Stroke	58.8	68	90	90	78
B/S ratio	0.865	0.946	0.96	0.96	0.945
Engine capacity	2.560	3,300	2,490	2,490	2,495
B h p	200	260	200	230	250
R p m	7,500	6,500	6,500	7,000	6,500
B h p per litre	78.3	79.9	80.5	92.7	100
B m e p lb/sq in.	135	157	161	171	199
Piston speed f p m	2,890	2,900	3,850	4,150	3,340
Piston area sq in.	67.0	75.4	42.9	42.9	49.8
H p per sq in. piston area	2.99	3.44	4.68	5.38	5.02
Piston area sq in. per litre	26.2	22.8	17.2	17.2	20.0
Induction system	l a t a	l a t a	l a t a	l a t a	l a t a

	4.5 SI	4.5 TI	4.5 Indy	625/54 Inter.	553 Squalo	F. Libre
Cylinders	12	12	12	4	4	4
Bore	80	80	80	94	100	103
Stroke	74.5	74.5	74.5	90	79.5	90
B/S ratio	0.93	0.93	0.93	0.96	0.795	0.875
Engine capacity	4,498	4,498	4,498	2,490	2,496	2,999
B h p	330	380	430	250	250	290
R p m	7,000	7,500	7,500	7,500	7,500	6,500
B h p per litre	73.5	84.5	95.8	100.4	100.2	97.0
B m e p lb/sq in.	136	145	166	174	173	181
Piston speed f p m	3,420	3,660	3,660	4,430	3,920	3,850
Piston area sq in.	93.5	93.6	93.5	42.9	48.8	55.0
H p per sq in. piston area	3.53	4.06	4.59	5.85	5.13	5.28
Piston area sq in. per litre	20.8	20.8	20.8	17.2	19.5	18.3
Induction system	l a t a	l a t a	l a t a	l a t a	l a t a	l a t a

	F2 12-cylinder	F2 4-cylinder 52	625/55	555 S Squalo	Bardahl
Cylinders	12	4	4	4	6
Bore	60	90	100	100	102
Stroke	58.8	78	79.5	79.5	90
B/S ratio	0.98	0.87	0.795	0.795	0.865
Engine capacity	1.992	1,980	2,496	2,496	4,412
B h p	155	170	265	270	380
R p m	7,000	7,000	7,500	7,500	6,500
B h p per litre	77.5	85.9	106	108	85.9
B m e p lb/sq in.	144	158	183	186	165
Piston speed f p m	2,700	3,600	3,910	3,910	3,850
Piston area sq in.	52.8	39.5	48.8	48.8	79.0
H p per sq in. piston area	3.24	4.31	5.44	5.52	4.80
Piston area sq in. per litre	26.4	19.95	19.5	19.5	17.9
Induction system	l a t a	l a t a	l a t a	l a t a	l a t a

APPENDIX V

FERRARI ENGINES 1946 – 73

No	Year	Type	No Cyl	B/S	S/B Ratio	Unit c c	Total c c	C/R	b h p	r p m	No and Type carb	Ign	Cam
1	1946	125 GT	V12	55 × 52.5	0.95	124.7	1496.7	8	72	5400	3 30 DCF	Si 2 D	Si
2	1947	125 S	V12	55 × 52.5	0.95	124.7	1496.7	9	118	7000	3 30 DCF	Si 2D	Si
3	1947	159 S	V12	59 × 58	0.98	158.6	1902.8	8.5	125	7000	3 30 DCF	Si 2 D	Si
4	1948	166 S	V12	60 × 58.8	0.98	166.2	1995	8.5	150	7000	3 30 DCF	Si 2 D	Si
5	1948	166 MM	V12	60 × 58.8	0.98	166.2	1995	8.5	140	6600	3 32 DCF	Si 2 D	Si
6	1948	166 Inter	V12	60 × 58.8	0.98	166.2	1995	8	115	6000	1 32 DCF	Si 2 D	Si
7	1948	125 FI	V12	55 × 52.5	0.95	124.7	1496.7	6.5	230	7000	1 50 WCF	Si 2 M	Si
8	1948	166 F2	V12	60 × 58.8	0.98	166.2	1995	7	160	7000	3 32 DCF	Si 2 M	Si
9	1949	125 F1	V12	55 × 52.5	0.95	124.7	1496.7	10	260	7000	1 Weber TR Choke	Si 2 M	Tw
10	1949	125 FI DD	V12	55 × 52.5	0.95	124.7	1496.7	7	280	7500	1 50 WCF	Si 2 M	Tw
11	1949	166 FL Sc	V12	60 × 58.8	0.98	166.2	1995	6.5	310	7000	1 40 DO3C	Si 2 M	Si
12	1949	166 FL LC	V12	60 × 58.8	0.98	166.2	1995	6.5	310	7000	1 40 DO3C	Si 2 M	Si
13	1949	166 S	V12	60 × 58.8	0.98	166.2	1995	8	90	5600	1 32 DCF	Si 2D	Si
14	1949	166 MM	V12	60 × 58.8	0.98	166.2	1995	8.5	140	6600	3 32 DCF	Si 2 D	Si
15	1950	195 S (MM)	V12	65 × 58.8	0.90	195.1	2341	8.5	160	7000	3 32 DCF	Si 2 D	Si
16	1950	275 S	V12	72 × 68	0.94	276.8	3322.3	8	220	7200	3 40 DCF	Si 2 D	Si
17	1950	275 FI	V12	72 × 68	0.94	276.8	3322.3	10	300	7300	3 38 DCF	Si 2 M	Si
18	1950	340 FI	V12	80 × 68	0.85	341.8	4101.6	12	335	7000	3 42 DCF	Si 2 M	Si
19	1950	375 FI	V12	80 × 74.5	0.93	374.5	4493.7	11	350	7000	3 42 DCF	Si 2 M	Si
20	1950	166 Inter	V12	60 × 58.8	0.98	166.2	1995	7.5	105	6000	1 32 DCF	Si 2 D	Si
21	1950	166 MM	V12	60 × 58.8	0.98	166.2	1995	9.5	145	7000	3 36 DCF	Si 2 D	Si
22	1951	375 FI	V12	80 × 74.5	0.93	374.5	4493.7	12	384	7500	3 46 DCF3	Tw 4 M	Si
23	1951	166 F2	V12	63.5 × 52.5	0.83	166.2	1995.2	11	160	7200	3 32 DCF	Si 2 M	Tw
24	1951	500 F2	IL4	90 × 78	0.87	496.2	1984.9	12	170	7000	2 50 DCO	Si 2 M	Tw
25	1951	212 F1	V12	68 × 58.8	0.86	213.5	2562.6	12	200	7500	3 32 DCF	Si 2 M	Si
26	1951	195 Inter	V12	65 × 58.8	0.90	195.1	2341	7.5	135	6000	1 32 DCF	Si 2 D	Si

No	Year	Type	No Cyl	B/S	S/B Ratio	Unit cc	Total cc	C/R	bhp	rpm	No and Type Carb	Ign	Cam
27	1951	212 Export	V12	68 × 58.8	0.86	213.5	2562.6	8	150	6500	3 32 DCF	Si 2 D	Si
28	1951	342 American	V12	80 × 68	0.85	341.8	4101.6	8	230	6000	3 40 DCF	Si 2 D	Si
29	1952	212 Export	V12	68 × 58.8	0.86	213.5	2562.6	7.5	150	6500	1 36 DCF	Si 2 D	Si
30	1952	212 Inter	V12	68 × 58.8	0.86	213.5	2562.6	8	170	6500	3 36 DCF	Si 2 D	Si
31	1952	250 Europa	V12	68 × 68	1	246.9	2963.4	8	200	6300	3 36 DCF	Si 2 D	Si
32	1952	340 Mexico	V12	80 × 68	0.85	341.8	4101.6	8	280	660	3 40 DCF	Si 2 D	Si
33	1952	340 MM	V12	80 × 68	0.85	341.8	4101.6	8	280	6600	3 40 DCF	Si 2 D	Si
34	1952	342 America	V12	80 × 68	0.85	341.8	4101.6	8	200	5000	3 40 DCF	Si 2 D	Si
35	1952	375 Indy	V12	80 × 74.5	0.93	374.5	4493.7	13	384	7500	3 40 IF4C	Tw 4M	Si
36	1952	250 MM	V12	73 × 58.8	0.80	246.1	2953.2	9	240	7200	3 36 IF4C	Si 2 D	Si
37	1952	500 F2	IL4	90 × 78	0.87	496.2	1984.9	12	180	7200	2 50 DCO	Tw 2 M	Tw
38	1952	225 S	V12	70 × 58.8	0.84	226.3	2715.4	8.5	210	7200	3 36 DCF	Si 2 D	Si
39*	1952	735 S	IL4	102 × 90	0.88	735.4	2941.6	9	225	6800	2 50 DCOA	Tw 2 D	Tw
40	1953	212 Inter	V12	68 × 58.8	0.86	213.5	2562.6	8	170	6500	3 36 DCF	Si 2 D	Si
41	1953	250 Europa	V12	73 × 58.8	0.80	246.1	2953.2	9	240	7000	3 36 DCF	Si 2 D	Si
42	1953	275 MM	V12	72 × 68	0.94	276.8	3322.3	8.5	270	7000	3 40 DCF	Si 2 M	Si
43	1953	375 MM	V12	84 × 68	0.81	376.8	4522.9	9	340	7000	3 40 IF4C	Si 2 M	Si
44	1953	375 America	V12	84 × 68	0.81	376.8	4522.9	8	300	6300	3 40 DCF	Si 2 D	Si
45	1953	553 F2	IL 4	93 × 73.5	0.79	499.3	1997.2	13	190	7500	2 50 DCO	Tw 2 M	Tw
46	1953	340 Mexico	V12	80 × 68	0.85	341.8	4101.6	8.5	280	6600	3 40 DCF	Si 2 D	Si
47*	1953	625 FI	IL4	94 × 90	0.96	624.6	2498.3	13	240	7000	2 50 DCOA	Tw 2 M	Tw
48*	1954	700	IL4	99 × 90	0.91	692.8	2771.2	12	250	6800	2 45 DCOA	Tw 2 M	Tw
49	1954	250 Europa	V12	73 × 58.8	0.80	246.1	2953.2	8.5	220	7000	3 36 DCF	Si 2 Di	Si
50	1954	500 Mondial	IL4	90 × 78	0.87	496.2	1984.8	8.2	170	7000	2 45 DCOA/3	Tw 2 M	Tw
51	1954	750 Monza	IL4	103 × 90	0.87	749.9	2999.6	9.2	250	6000	2 58 DCOA/3	Tw 2 M	Tw
52	1954	625 FI	IL4	94 × 90	0.95	624.6	2498.4	12	240	7000	2 50 DCOA	Tw 2 M	Tw
53	1954	555 FI	IL4	100 × 79.5	0.79	624.4	2497.6	12	250	7500	2 52 DCOA	Tw 2 M	Tw
54	1954	625 Mondial	IL4	94 × 90	0.95	624.6	2498.4	9.2	220	6800	2 46 DCOA	Tw 2 M	Tw
55	1954	375 Plus	V12	84 × 74.5	0.88	412.8	4954.4	9.2	344	6500	3 46 DCF	Si 2 M	Si
56	1954	275 Spl	V12	88 × 68	0.77	413.6	4962.8	9	380	7000	3 46 DCF	Tw 4 D	Si
57	1954	375 Coupe America	V12	84 × 68	0.81	376.8	4522.9	9.2	350	7000	3 42 DCZ	Si 2 M	Si
58	1954	306 S	IL6	90 × 78	0.87	496.2	2977.2	8.5	240	7000	3 40 DCO	Tw 2 M	Tw

No	Year	Type	No Cyl	B/S	S/B Ratio	Unit cc	Total cc	C/R	bhp	rpm	No and Type Carb	Ign	Cam
59	1955	555 F1	IL4	100 x 79.5	0.79	624.4	2497.6	14	270	7500	2 52 DCOA	Tw 2 M	Tw
60*	1955	(115) 256 F1	IL6	82.4 x 78	0.95	416	2496	12	250	6500	3 45 DCOA	Tw 2 M	Tw
61*	1955	(116) 252 F1	IL2	118 x 114	0.96	1246.7	2493.4	13	174	4800	2 42 DCOA	Tw 2 M	Tw
62	1955	(118) 376 LM	IL6	94 x 90	0.95	624.6	3747.6	9	310	6000	3 45 DCOA	Tw 2 D	Tw
63	1955	250 GT	V12	73 x 58.8	0.80	246.1	2953.2	8.5	220	7000	3 36 DCF	Si 2 D	Si
64	1955	500 Mondial	IL4	90 x 78	0.87	496.2	1984.8	8.5	170	7000	2 40 DCOA/3	Tw 2 D	Tw
65	1955	625 Mondial	IL4	94 x 90	0.95	624.6	2498.4	9.2	220	6800	2 46DCOA	Tw 2D	Tw
66	1955	750 Monza	IL4	103 x 90	0.87	749.9	2999.6	8.6	260	6000	2 52 DCOA	Tw 2D	Tw
67	1955	410 SA	V12	88 x 68	0.77	413.6	4962.8	8.5	340	6000	3 40 DCF	Si 2 D	Si
68	1955	(121) 446 S	IL6	102 x 90	0.88	735.4	4412.5	8.5	330	6000	3 50 DCOA	Tw 2 D	Tw
69*	1955	(123)	IL6	100 x 90	0.90	706.8	4241.1	9	330	6000			
70*	1955	(124)	IL4	110 x 90	0.82	855.3	3421.2						
71*	1955	(127)	IL6	97.5 x 78	0.80	582.3	3494.2						
72*	1955	250 Sup	V12	68 x 68	1	246.9	2963.5	6	510	7000	1 40 IF4C	Tw 4 M	Tw
73	1955	857 S	IL4	102 x 105	1.03	857.9	3431.9	8.5	280	5800	2 58 DCOA	Tw 2 M	Tw
74	1956	625 F1	IL4	94 x 90	0.95	624.6	2498.4	12	250	7500	2 50 DCOA	Tw 2 M	Tw
75	1956	050/555 F1 Squalo	V8	76 x 68.8	0.90	312.1	2496.8	12	231	8600	4 40 DCS	Tw 2 M	Tw
76	1956	500 TR	IL4	90 x 78	0.87	496.2	1984.9	8.5	180	7000	2 40 DCO	Tw 2 D	Tw
77	1956	250 GT	V12	73 x 58.8	0.80	246.1	2953.2	8.5	240	7000	3 36 DCF	Si 2 D	Si
78	1956	410 SA	V12	88 x 68	0.77	413.6	4962.8	8.5	340	6000	3 42 DCF	Si 2 D	Si
79	1956	290 MM	V12	73 x 69.5	0.95	290.8	3490.3	9	320	6800	3 46 TRA	Tw 4 D	Si
80	1956	625 LM	IL4	94 x 90	0.95	624.6	2498.4	9	225	6200	2 42 DCOA	Tw 2 D	Tw
81	1956	860 Monza	IL4	102 x 105	1.03	857.9	3431.9	9	310	6200	2 58 DCOA	Tw 2 M	Tw
82	1956	446 Indy	IL6	102 x 90	0.88	735.4	4412.5	9	360	6300	3 50 DCOA	Tw 2 M	Tw
83	1956	500/ 750	IL4	100 x 95	0.95	746.1	2984.5	8.6	260	6000	2 52 DCO	Tw 2 D	Tw
84	1956	750/ 625	IL4	103 x 90	0.87	749.9	2999.6	9.5	280	6500	2 50 DCOA	Tw 2 M	Tw
85	1956	860/ 555	IL4	102 x 105	1.03	857.1	3431.9	9.5	310	6200	2 58 DCOA	Tw 2 M	Tw
86*	1956	(128) 260	V12	75 x 58.8	0.78	259.8	3117.2						
87*	1956	Exp	V8	74 x 72.2	0.98	310.5	2484.2	12					
88	1957	801 F1	V8	80 x 62	0.78	1311.8	2494.8	11	285	8800	4 40 DCS	Tw 2 M	Tw
89	1957	156 F2	V6	70 x 64.5	0.92	248.2	1489.3	10	180	9000	3 38 DCN	Tw 2 D	Tw
90	1957	156 S	V6	70 x 64.5	0.92	248.2	1489.3	9.2	170	8500	3 36 DCN	Tw 2 D	Tw
91	1957	410 SA	V12	88 x 68	0.77	413.6	4962.8	8.5	340	6000	3 42 DCF	Si 2 D	Si
92	1957	250 GT	V12	73 x 58.8	0.80	246.1	2953.2	8.5	240	7000	3 36 DCF	Si 2 D	Si

No	Year	Type	No Cyl	B/S	S/B Ratio	Unit cc	Total cc	C/R	bhp	rpm	No and Type Carb	Ign	Cam
93	1957	500 TRC	IL4	90 x 78	0.87	496.2	1984.9	8.75	190	7500	2 / 40 DCO	Tw / 2 D	Tw
94	1957	290 S	V12	73 x 69.5	0.95	290.8	3490.3	9	350	7200	6 / 42 DCN	Tw / 4 D	Tw
95	1957	315 S	V12	76 x 69.5	0.91	315.3	3783.5	9	360	7200	6 / 42 DCN	Tw / 4 D	Si
96	1957	335 S	V12	77 x 72	0.93	335.3	4023.3	9.2	390	7800	6 / 42 DCN	Tw / 4 D	Si
97*	1957	(139) 298 S	V8	81 x 72.8	0.90	375.1	3000.8	11.5			4 / Solex 40PJ		
98*	1957	196 S	V6	77 x 71	0.92	330.6	1983.7	10	225	8600	3 / 42 DCN	Tw / 1 M	Tw
99*	1957	226 S	V6	81 x 71	0.88	365.8	2195.2	10	235	8000	3 / 42 DCN	Tw / 1 M	Tw
100	1958	246 F1	V6	85 x 71	0.83	402.9	2417.3	11	270	8300	3 / 42 DCN	Tw / 1 M	Tw
101	1958	(326) 528 MI	V6	87 x 90	1.04	535	3210.1	9	330	7500	3 / 54 DCN	Tw / 2 D	Tw
102	1958	(412) 530 MI	V12	77 x 72	0.93	335.3	4023.3	9.4	415	8500	6 / 42 DCN	Tw / 4 M	Tw
103	1958	250 GT	V12	73 x 58.8	0.80	246.1	2953.2	8.5	240	7000	3 / 36 DCF	Si / 2 D	Si
104	1958	250 TRS	V12	73 x 58.8	0.80	246.1	2953.2	9.8	300	7200	6 / 40 DCN	Tw / 4 D	Si
105	1958	196 S (Dino)	V6	77 x 71	0.92	330.6	1983.7	9.8	195	7800	3 / 42 DCN	Tw / 2 D	Si
106*	1958	296 S (Dino)	V6	85 x 87	1.02	493.7	2962.1	9	300	8000	3 / 46 DCN	Tw / 2 D	Tw
107	1958	312 LM	V12	73 x 58.8	0.80	246.1	2953.2	10	280	8500	6 / 42 DCN	Tw / 4 D	Tw
108	1958	410 SA	V12	88 x 68	0.77	413.6	4962.8	8.5	340	6000	3 / 42 DCF	Si / 2 D	Si
109*	1958	196 GT	V6	77 x 71	0.92	330.6	1983.7	9	175	7500	3 / 38 DCN	Si / 1 D	Si
110*	1958	(144)	V12	75 x 65	0.87	287.1	3445.9	9			3	Tw	
111*	1958	256 F1	V6	86 x 71	0.82	412.4	2474.5	9.8	290	8800	3 / 42 DCN	Tw / 2 D	Tw
112*	1958	(152)	V6	84 x 72	0.87	399	2394	9			3 / 42 DCN	Si	
113*	1958	(153) 156 S	V6	72 x 64.5	0.90	262.6	1575.6	9	165	8000	3 / 38 DCN	Si / 1 D	
114	1959	256 F1	V6	86 x 71	0.83	412.4	2474.6	10	280	8500	3 / 42 DCN	Tw / 1 M	Tw
115	1959	250 TRS	V12	73 x 58.8	0.80	246.1	2953.2	9.8	300	7200	6 / 40 DCN	Si / 2 D	Si
116	1959	250 GT	V12	73 x 58.8	0.80	246.1	2953.2	8.5	240	7000	3 / 36 DCF	Si / 2 D	Si
117	1959	410 SA	V12	88 x 68	0.77	413.6	4962.8	9	400	6500	3 / 42 DCF	Si / 2 D	Si
118	1959	410 SF	V12	88 x 68	0.77	413.6	4962.8	9	400	6500	3 / 42 DCF	Si / 2 D	Si
119	1959	(154 S) 1500 Sport	V6	72 x 61	0.85	248.3	1489.9	9.6	150	7000			
120*	1959	(155)	V6	85 x 72	0.85	408.5	2451.1	9.8					
121*	1959	(159)	V12	77 x 75	0.98	349.2	4190.4	9					
122*	1959	(161) 854	IL4	65 x 64	0.98	212.3	849.5	7.5	68	7000	2 / 38 DCO	Si / 1 D	Si
123*	1959	(162) F. Inter Car	V12	75 x 71	0.95	313.6	3764						
124*	1959	(163) 330 GT	V12	77 x 71	0.92	330.6	3967.4	9.8	380	7000	6 / 40 DCN	Si / 2 D	Tw
125*	1959	(164) 950	IL4	67 x 69	1.03	243.2	973	9	80	7000	2 / 32 DCN	Si / 1 D	Si

No	Year	Type	No Cyl	B/S	S/B Ratio	Unit cc	Total cc	C/R	bhp	rpm	No and Type Carb	Ign	Cam
126	1959	850 Coupe	IL4	65 x 64	0.98	212.3	849.5	9	86	7000	2 32 DCO	Si 1 D	Si
127*	1959	156 F2	V6	73 x 58.8	0.80	246.1	1476.6	9.2	150	8000	3 38 DCN	Si 1 D	Si
128	1960	246 F1 LC	V6	85 x 71	0.83	402.9	2417.3	9.8	280	8500	3 42 DCN	Tw 1 M	Tw
129	1960	246 F1 SC	V6	85 x 71	0.83	402.9	2417.3	9.8	280	8500	3 42 DCN	Tw 1 M	Tw
130	1960	256 FI Si Cam	V6	85 x 71	0.83	402.9	2417.3	9.8	250	7700	3 42 DCN	Tw 1 M	Si
131	1960	296 FL	V6	87 x 83	0.95	493.4	2960.6	9.9	298	8200	3 42 DCN	Tw 1 M	Tw
132	1960	250 TRS	V12	73 x 58.8	0.80	246.1	2953.2	9.3	300	7500	6 42 DCN	Si 2 D	Si
133*	1960	250 Inj	V12	73 x 58.8	0.80	246.1	2953.2	9.2	300	7500	Bosch Inj	Si 2 D	Si
134*	1960	246 Inj	V6	85 x 71	0.83	402.9	2417.3	9.8	280	8500	Bosch Inj	Tw 2 D	Tw
135	1960	250 GT Coup Cabriolet	V12	73 x 58.8	0.80	246.1	2953.2	8.5	240	7000	3 36 DCF	Si 2 D	Si
136	1960	250 GT Spider	V12	73 x 58.8	0.80	246.1	2953.2	9	280	7500	3 36 DCF	Si 2 D	Si
137	1960	400 SA	V12	77 x 71	0.92	330.6	3967.4	9	400	7000	3 46 DCF	Si 2 D	Si
138	1960	F1 Rear	V6	86.4 x 71	0.82	416.3	2497.6	11	245	7600	3 42 DCN	Si 1 M	Tw
139	1960	F2 Front	V6	73 x 59.1	0.80	247.3	1484	9.8	180	9000	3 38 DCW	Tw 1 M	Tw
140	1960	F2 Rear	V6	73 x 59.1	0.80	247.3	1484	9.8	180	9000	3 38 DCW	Tw 1 M	Tw
141*	1960	(164 bis) 1000	IL4	69 x 69	1	258	1032	9	100	7200	2 38 DCOA	Si 1 D	Si
142*	1960	(165) 1600 GT	V6	73 x 62	0.85	259.5	1556.8	9.8	160	7500	3 42 DCN	Si 2 D	Si
143	1961	156 F1 650	V6	73 x 59	0.80	246.9	1481.4	9.8	180	9000	3 38 DCW	Tw 1 M	Tw
144	1961	156 F1 65°	V6	67 x 70	1.04	246.8	1480.7	9.8	185	9500	3 42 DCN	Tw 1 M	Tw
145*	1961	156 F1 65°	V6	81 x 48.2	0.60	249.4	1496.4	9.8	200	10,500	3 42 DCN	Tw 2 M	Tw
146*	1961	156 F1 120°	V6	73 x 58.8	0.80	246.1	1476.6	9.8	190	9500	2 40 IF3C	Tw 2 M	Tw
147	1961	250 S	V12	73 x 58.8	0.80	246.1	2953.2	9.8	300	7500	6 42 DCN	Si 2 D	Si
148*	1961	276 S	V6	90 x 71	0.79	451.7	2710.2	9.9	275	7700	3 42 DCN	Si 1 M	Si
149	1961	250 GT 2 + 2	V12	73 x 58.8	0.80	246.1	2953.2	8.5	240	7000	3 36 DCF	Si 2 D	Si
150	1961	250 Coupe Cabriolet	V12	73 x 58.8	0.80	246.1	2953.2	8.5	240	7000	3 36 DCF	Si 2 D	Si
151	1961	250 Berlinetta + Spider	V12	73 x 58.8	0.80	246.1	2953.2	9	280	7500	3 36 DCF	Si 2 D	Si
152	1961	400 SA	V12	77 x 71	0.92	330.6	3967.4	9	400	7000	3 46 DCF	Si 2 D	Si
153	1961	246 P	V6	85 x 71	0.83	402.9	2417.3	9.8	270	8000	3 46 DCN	Tw 2 D	Tw
154*	1961	296 P	V6	87 x 82	0.94	487.5	2924.9	9.8	310	7500		Tw 1 M	Tw

No	Year	Type	No Cyl	B/S	S/B Ratio	Unit cc	Total cc	C/R	bhp	rpm	No and Type Carb	Ign	Cam
155	1962	F1 120°	V6	73 x 58.8	0.80	246.1	1476.6	9.8	200	10,000	2 40 IFC3	Tw 2 D	Tw
156	1962	F1 65°	V6	67 x 70	1.04	246.8	1480.7	9.8	190	9400	3 40 DCN	Tw 2 D	Tw
157	1962	196 Sp	V6	77 x 71	0.92	330.6	1983.7	9.8	210	7500	3 42 DC	Si 1 D	Si
158	1962	248 Sp	V8	77 x 66	0.85	307.3	2458.4	9.8	250	7400	4 40 DC	Si 2 D	Si
159	1962	286 Sp	V6	90 x 75	0.83	477.1	2862.9	9.5	260	6800	3 46 DC	Si 2 D	Si
160	1962	250 Berl	V12	73 x 58.8	0.80	246.1	2953.2	9.8	300	7400	6 42 DCN	Si 2 D	Si
161	1962	246 Sp	V6	85 x 71	0.83	402.9	2417.3	9.5	275	7500	3 42 DC	Tw 2 D	Tw
162	1962	268 Sp	V8	77 x 71	0.92	330.6	2644.9	9.6	265	7000	4 40 DC	Si 2 D	Si
163	1962	330 TR	V12	77 x 71	0.92	330.6	3967.4	8.7	390	7500	6 42 DCN	Si 2 D	Si
164	1962	330 LM-B	V12	77 x 71	0.92	330.6	3967.4	8.7	390	7500	6 42 DCN	Si 2 D	Si
165	1962	400 Sp	V12	77 x 71	0.92	330.6	3967.4	8.8	340	7000	3 40 DCZ	Si 2 D	Si
166	1962	250 GT2 + 2	V12	73 x 58.8	0.80	246.1	2953.2	8.5	240	7000	3 36 DCF	Si 2 D	Si
167	1963	156 F1 Inj 120°	V6	73 x 58.8	0.80	246.1	1476.6	10	200	10,200	Bosch Inj	Tw 2 D	Tw
168	1963	158 F1 Mono	V8	67 x 52.8	0.76	186.1	1489.3	9.8	200	10,500	Bosch Inj	Tw 4 D	Tw
169	1963	156 F1 Mono	V6	73 x 58.8	0.80	246.1	1476.6	10	200	10,500	Bosch Inj	Tw 2 D	Tw
170*	1963	186 GT	V6	77 x 64	0.83	298	1788.1	9.2	156	7000	3 38 DCN	Si 1 D	Si
171	1963	196 S	V6	77 x 71	0.92	330.6	1983.7	9	200	7500	3 42 DCN	Si 1 D	Tw
172	1963	250 P	V12	73 x 58.8	0.80	246.1	2953.2	9.5	310	7500	6 38 DCN	Si 2 D	Si
173	1963	330 LM	V12	77 x 71	0.92	330.6	3967.4	9	400	7500	6 42 DCN	Si 2 D	Si
174	1963	250 GT 2 + 2	V12	73 x 58.8	0.80	246.1	2953.2	9.2	240	7000	3 36 DCF	Si 2 D	Si
175	1963	250 GTO + Spider	V12	73 x 58.8	0.80	246.1	2953.2	9.2	250	7500	6 38 DCN	Si 2 D	Si
176	1963	400 SA	V12	77 x 71	0.92	330.6	3967.4	8.8	340	7000	3 40 DCZ	Si 2 D	Si
177	1964	158 F1	V8	67 x 52.8	0.76	186.1	1489.3	9.8	200	10,500	Bosch Inj	Tw 4 D	Tw
178	1964	512 F1	F12	56 x 50.4	0.90	124.1	1489.6	9.8	220	12,000	Bosch Inj	Si 2 D	Tw
179	1964	500 SF	V12	88 x 68	0.77	413.6	4962.8	8.8	400	6500	3 40 DCZ6	Si 2 D	Si
180	1964	330 GT2 + 2	V12	77 x 71	0.92	330.6	3967.4	8.8	300	6600	3 40 DCZ6	Si 2 D	Si
181	1964	365 P	V12	81 x 71	0.87	365.8	4390.3	9.5	380	7200	6 38 DCN	Si 2 D	Si
182	1964	330 P	V12	77 x 71	0.92	330.6	3967.4	9	390	7500	6 42 DCN	Si 2 D	Si
183	1964	275 P	V12	77 x 58.8	0.76	273.8	3285.7	9.8	320	7700	6 38 DCN	Si 2 D	Si
184	1964	250 LM	V12	73 x 58.8	0.80	246.1	2953.2	9.7	300	7500	6 38 DCN	Si 2 D	Si
185	1964	275 GTB	V12	77 x 58.8	0.76	273.8	3285.7	9.2	280	7500	3 or 6 40 DCZ6	Si 2 D	Si
186	1964	275 GTS	V12	77 x 58.8	0.76	273.8	3285.7	9.2	260	7000	3 40 DCZ6	Si 2 D	Si

No	Year	Type	No Cyl	B/S	S/B Ratio	Unit cc	Total cc	C/R	bhp	rpm	No and Type Carb	Ign	Cam
187	1964	250 GTO/64	V12	73 x 58.8	0.80	246.1	2953.2	9.8	300	7700	6 38 DCN	Si 2 D	Si
188	1965	2TS P2	V12	77 x 58.8	0.76	273.8	3285.7	9.8	350	8500	6 40 DCN2	Tw 4 D	Tw
189	1965	330 P2	V12	77 x 71	0.92	330.6	3967.4	9.8	410	8200	6 42 DCN2	Tw 4 D	Tw
190	1965	166 Dino	V6	77 x 57	0.74	265.4	1592.7	9.8	180	9000	3 40 DCN	Tw 2 D	Tw
191	1965	206 SP Dino	V6	86 x 57	0.66	333.1	1986.7	12.5 9.8	218	9000	3 40 DCN2	Tw 2 D	Tw
192	1965	158 F1	V8	67 x 52.8	0.76	186.1	1489.3	9.8	210	11,000	Bosch Inj	Tw 4 D	Tw
193	1965	512 F1	F12	56 x 50.4	0.90	124.1	1489.6	9.8	220	12,000	Lucas Inj	Tw 4 D	Tw
194	1965	330 GT 2 + 2	V12	77 x 71	0.92	330.6	3967.4	8.8	300	6600	3 40 DCZ6	Si 2 D	Si
195	1965	500 SF	V12	88 x 68	0.77	413.6	4962.8	8.8	400	6500	3 40 DCZ6	Si 2 D	Si
196	1965	275 GTB	V12	77 x 58.8	0.76	273.8	3285.7	9.5	280	7600	3 or 6 40 DCZ6	Si 2 D	Si
197	1965	275 GTS	V12	77 x 58.8	0.76	273.8	3285.7	9.2	260	7000	3 40 DCZ6	Si 2 D	Si
198	1965	275 LM	V12	77 x 58.8	0.76	273.8	3285.7	9.7	320	7600	6 38 DCN	Si 2 D	Si
199	1966	F1	V12	77 x 53.5	0.69	249.1	2989.2	11	360	10,000	Inj	Tw 4 D	Tw
200	1966	330 GT	V12	77 x 71	0.92	330.6	3967.4	8.8	300	7000	3 40 DCZ6	Si 2 D	Si
201	1966	275 GTB	V12	77 x 58.8	0.76	273.8	3285.7	9.5	280	7600	3 or 6 40 DCN3	Si 2 D	Si
202	1966	275 GTS	V12	77 x 58.8	0.76	273.8	3285.7	9.2	260	7000	3 40 DCZ6	Si 2 D	Si
203	1966	275 LM	V12	77 x 58.8	0.76	273.8	3285.7	9.7	320	7600	6 38 DCN	Si 2 D	Si
204	1966	206 Dino/S	V6	86 x 57	0.66	331.1	1986.7	10.8	218	9000	3 40 DCN2	Si 1 D	Tw
205	1966	330/P3	V12	77 x 71	0.92	330.6	3967.4	11.4	420	8000	Lucas Inj	Tw 4 D	Tw
206	1966	330 GTC	V12	77 x 71	0.92	330.6	3967.4	8.8	300	7000	3 40 DFI	Si 2 D	Si
207	1966	500 SF	V12	88 x 68	0.77	413.6	4962.8	8.8	400	6500	3 40 DCZ6	Si 2 D	Si
208	1966	246 F1	V6	85 x 71	0.83	402.9	2417.3	9.5	275	8000	Lucas Inj	Tw 4 D	Tw
209	1967	F1 67	V12	77 x 53.5	0.69	249.13	2989.5	11	390	10,500	Lucas Inj	Tw 4 D	Tw
210	1967	330/P4	V12	77 x 71	0.92	330.6	3967.4	11	450	8000	Lucas Inj	Tw 4 D	Tw
211	1967	206 Dino SP	V6	86 x 57	0.66	331.1	1986.7	11	220	9000	Lucas Inj	Tw 2 D	Tw
212	1967	206 Dino GT	V6	86 x 57	0.66	331.1	1986.7	9	180	8000	3 40 DCN	Si 1 D	Tw
213	1967	Dino F2	V6	86 x 45.8	0.53	266.05	1596.3	11	200	10,000	Lucas Inj	Tw 2 D	Tw
214	1967	330 GT 2 + 2	V12	77 x 71	0.92	330.6	3967.4	8.8	300	7000	3 40 DCZ 6	Si 2 D	Si
215	1967	330 GTC	V12	77 x 71	0.92	330.6	3967.4	8.8	300	7000	3 40 DFI	Si 2 D	Si
216	1967	275 GTB	V12	77 x 58.8	0.76	273.8	3285.7	9.5	280	7600	6 40 DCN	Si 2 D	Si

No	Year	Type	No Cyl	B/S	S/B Ratio	Unit cc	Total cc	C/R	bhp	rpm	No and Type Carb	Ign	Cam
217	1967	275 GTS	V12	77 x 58.8	0.76	273.8	3285.7	9.2	260	7000	3 40 DCZ 6	Si 2 D	Si
218	1967	Can Am	V12	79 x 71	0.9	348.04	4176.5	11	480	8500	Lucas Inj	Tw 4 D	Tw
219	1968	F1/68	V12	77 x 53.5	0.69	249.13	2986.5	11.8	408	11,000	Lucas Inj	Si 2 D	Tw
220	1968	166 Dino F2	V6	79.5 x 53.5	0.67	265.6	1593.6	11.2	225	11,000	Lucas Inj	Si 1 D	Tw
221	1968	Tasman	V6	90 x 63	0.7	400.8	2404.8	11.5	285	8900	Lucas Inj	Tw 2 D	Tw
222	1968	P5/ 250	V12	77 x 53.5	0.69	249.13	2989.5	11	400	9200	Lucas Inj	Tw 4 D	Tw
223	1968	330 GTB	V12	77 x 71	0.92	330.6	3967.4						
224	1968	330 GTC	V12	77 x 71	0.92	330.6	3967.4	8.8	300	7000	3 40 DCN	Si 2 D	Si
225	1968	330 GTS	V12	77 x 71	0.92	330.6	3967.4	8.8	300	7000	3 40 DCN	Si 2 D	Si
226	1968	365 GT 2 + 2	V12	81 x 71	0.88	365.8	4390.3	8.8	320	6600	3 40 DCN	Si 2 D	Si
227	1968	206 Dino GT	V6	86 x 57	0.66	331.1	1986.7	9	180	8000	3 40 DCF	Dinoplex	Tw
228	1968	Can Am 612	V12	92 x 78	0.85	518.46	6221.6	10.5	620	7000	Lucas Inj	Dinoplex	Tw
229	1968	212E Expl	F12	65 x 50	0.77	165.9	1990.8	11	280	11,000	Lucas Inj	Si 2 D	Tw
230	1969	F1/69	V12	77 x 53.5	0.69	249.13	2989.5	11.8	436	11,000	Lucas Inj	Dinoplex	Tw
231	1969	166 Dino F2	V6	79.5 x 53.5	0.67	265.6	1593.6	11.2	230	11,000	Lucas Inj	Dinoplex	Tw
232	1969	246 Dino Tasman	V6	90 x 63	0.7	400.8	2404.8	11.5	290	9000	Lucas Inj	Dinoplex	Tw
233	1969	312/P Sport	V12	77 x 53.5	0.69	249.13	2989.5	11	420	9800	Lucas Inj	Dinoplex	Tw
234	1969	365 GT 2 + 2	V12	81 x 71	0.88	365.8	4390.3	8.8	320	6600	3 40 DCN	Si 2 D	Si
235	1969	246 Dino GT	V6	92.5 x 60	0.65	403.1	2418.4	9	195	7600	3 40 DCF	Dinoplex	Tw
236	1969	365 GTB/4	V12	81 x 71	0.88	365.8	4390.3	8.8	352	7500	6 40 DCNZO	Si 2 D	Tw
237*	1969	318 W	W18	65 x 50	0.77	165.9	2986.2	11	450	12,000	Lucas Inj	Si D	Tw
238	1969	365 GTC	V12	81 x 71	0.88	365.8	4390.3	8.8	320	6600	3 40 DCN	Si 2 D	Si
239	1969	365 GTS	V12	81 x 71	0.88	365.8	4390.3	8.8	320	6600	3 40 DCN	Si 2 D	Si
240	1969	212 E	F12	65 x 50	0.77	165.9	1990.8	11	300	11,800	Lucas Inj	Dinoplex	Tw
241	1969	612 Can Am	V12	92 x 78	0.85	518.46	6221.6	10.5	640	7700	Lucas Inj	Dinoplex	Tw
242	1970	512 S	V12	87 x 70	0.8	416	4994	11	550	8000	Lucas Inj	Dinoplex	Tw
243	1970	312 B-F1	F12	78.5 x 57.5	0.66	249.3	2991	11	450	12,000	Lucas Inj	Dinoplex	Tw
244	1970	365 GT 2 + 2	V12	81 x 71	0.88	365.8	4390.3	8.8	320	6600	3 40 DCN	Si 2 D	Tw
245	1970	365 Daytona	V12	81 x 71	0.88	365.8	4390.3	9.3	350	7000	6 40 DCN	Si 2 D	Tw
246	1970	246 Dino GT	V6	92.5 x 60	0.65	403.4	2418.4	9	195	7600	3 40 DCF	Dinoplex	Tw

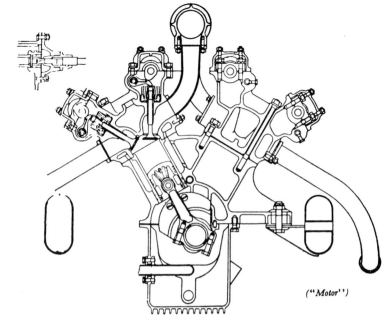

("Motor")

(*Top*) Section drawing of the Type 125 Formula 1 engine of 1949
(*Middle*) A 340 America engine on display. Note the low profile FISPA air cleaners
(*Bottom Left*) Silverstone, 5 May 1951. The 375 Formula 1 engine about to have its spark plugs changed
(*Bottom Right*) Two stage supercharging was used on Ascari's 1949 Formula 1 car

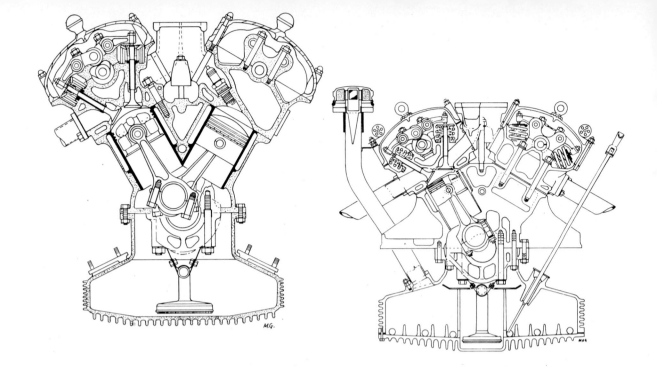

(Top Left) Early version of the Colombo V12. Spark plugs are mounted along the inside bank of the cylinder heads. Mousetrap valve springs were employed until circa 1960 on GT versions. Large water channel in centre of V distributed water to wet liners via metering holes. Round hole beneath main water channel is the central oil gallery. Angled connecting rod caps allowed them to be removed through the cylinders without interference
(Top Right) Late version of the Colombo V12. Coil valve springs are employed along with a revised cylinder head retention stud arrangement. Spark plugs are adjacent to exhaust porting. Note main bearings with four studs each, enlarged oil sump with detachable baseplate. Late engines have conventional connecting rods
(Bottom Left) The engine compartment of an early 340 Sport. Cooling fans were an unusual fitment
(Bottom Right) The Lampredi designed V12 was much larger than the Colombo design. This is the 342 or 375 America engine of 1953 - 1954

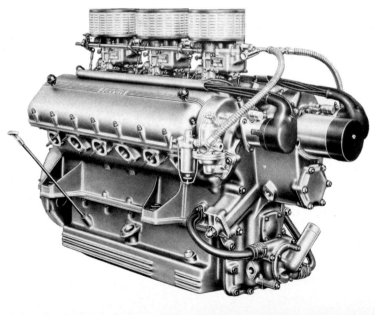

(*Top*) A corner in the Modena workshop in the early fifties. In the foreground is an early Type 500 with cambox covers and all but one of the single choke carburetters removed. The V12 is probably a Type 212. A completely dismantled Colombo V12 fills the shelves
(*Bottom Left*) Enzo Ferrari watches the engine dynamometer. Here a 250 MM engine is on test in 1953
(*Bottom Right*) The last of the series of Type 166 MM built in 1953

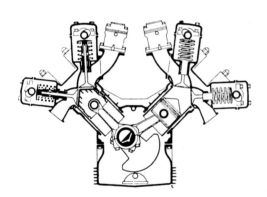

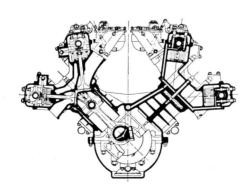

(*Top*) The Lampredi 375 MM
(*Bottom Left*) The Lancia V8 Formula
1 engine was subsequently modified by
Jano for Ferrari. These drawings illus-
trate those modifications
(*Bottom Right*) The Type 136 V12,
frontal aspect

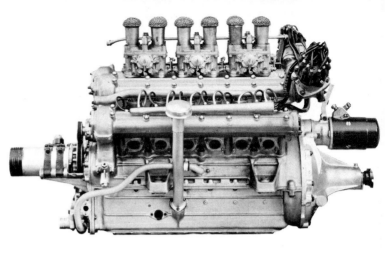

(Top Left) Formula 1 Dino 1958 on the test stand
(Top Right) The 1957 Type 136 V12, side view
(Middle) 1957 Testa Rossa prototype engine
(Bottom) 3 litre V12 engine as fitted to lightweight
Berlinetta Tour de France

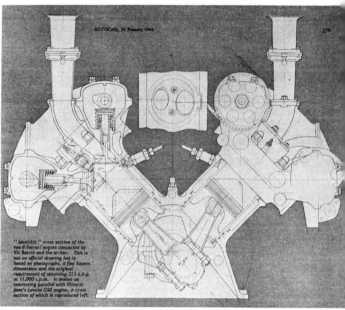

(Top) Vittorio Jano (right) discusses the prototype 196 Dino engine with Luigi Bazzi

(Middle) The internals of recent Ferrari racing engines have been guarded by the factory. This is a hypothetical cross-section of the 1965 Formula 1 V8. It is based on observations of the exterior, a few measurements, and the requirements of 215 bhp at 11,000 rpm. Note fuel injection direct to cylinder

(Bottom) Ferrari Dino Type 296 single cam per bank. This was the largest capacity Dino engine built at 2925-cc

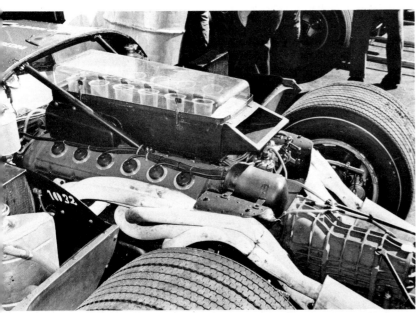

(*Top*) 1966 275 GTB4 engine
(*Middle*) The engine of the Squadra Picchio Rosso 512S at Daytona 1970. Note the clear plastic injector pipes under the airbox
(*Bottom*) The Chiti designed 248SP V8 of 1962

(*Above Left and Right*) Two views of the 2 cylinder Lampredi designed Grand Prix engine of 1953. Twin intake and exhaust manifold plus twin ignition had most people fooled into thinking that it was a 4 cylinder engine

(*Bottom*) The Ferrari 'Boxer' flat 12 engine in 1971

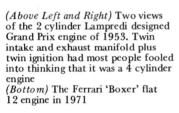

No	Year	Type	No Cyl	B/S	S/B Ratio	Unit cc	Total cc	C/R	bhp	rpm	No and Type Carb	Ign	Cam
247	1971	365 Daytona	V12	81 x 71	0.88	365.8	4390.3	9.3	350	7000	6 40 DCN	Dinoplex	Tw
248	1971	312 B-FI	F12	78.5 x 51.5	0.66	249.3	2991	11.5	480	11,500	Lucas Inj	Dinoplex	Tw
249	1971	312P Sport	F12	78.5 x 51.5	0.66	249.3	2991	11.5	450	10,800	Lucas Inj	Dinoplex	Tw
250	1971	246 Dino GT	V6	92.5 x 60	0.65	403.1	2418.4	9	195	7600	3 40 DCF	Dinoplex	Tw
251	1971	512 M	V12	87 x 70	0.8	416	4923	11.8	610	9000	Lucas Inj	Dinoplex	Tw
252	1971	365 GT 2 + 2	V12	81 x 71	0.88	365.8	4390.3	8.8	320	6600	3 40 DCN	Dinoplex	Tw
253	1971	365 GTC 4	V12	81 x 71	0.88	365.8	4390.3	8.8	340	6800	6 40 DCOE	Dinoplex	Tw
254	1972	BB	F12	81 x 71	0.88	365.8	4390.3	8.8	360	7500	4 40 IDL3C	Dinoplex	Tw
255	1972	312 B2-F1	F12	78.5 x 51.5	0.66	249.3	2991	11.5	480	11,800	Lucas Inj	Dinoplex	Tw
256	1972	312 P	F12	78.5 x 51.5	0.66	249.3	2991	11.5	450	10,800	Lucas Inj	Dinoplex	Tw
257	1972	246 Dino GTS	V6	92.5 x 60	0.65	403.1	2418.4	9	195	7600	3 40 DCF	Dinoplex	Tw
258	1972	246 Dino GT	V6	92.5 x 60	0.65	403.1	2418.4	9	195	7600	3 40 DCF	Dinoplex	Tw
259	1972	365 GTB 4	V12	81 x 71	0.88	365.8	4390	8.8	350	7000	6 40 DCOE	Dinoplex	Tw
260	1972	365 GTC 4	V12	81 x 71	0.88	365.8	4390	8.8	350	6800	6 40 DCOE	Dinoplex	Tw

Notes: The above are from the official Ferrari Record Book
*Denotes an Experimental Engine

KEY TO APPENDIX VI

Key to specifications

The following are in use throughout the specifications.

SS	. . . .	Single stage supercharged.
TS	. . . .	Two-stage supercharged.
US	. . . .	Unsupercharged.
S	. . . .	Siluminum light alloy.
LD	. . . .	Light alloy detachable.
H	. . . .	Hemispherical.
IO	. . . .	Inclined overhead.
HA	. . . .	Hairpin.
CO	. . . .	Coil
SI	. . . .	Single cam per bank.
TW	. . . .	Twin cam per bank.
CH	. . . .	Chain.
GE	. . . .	Gear.
R	. . . .	Rootes type supercharger.
W	. . . .	Weber.
So	. . . .	Solex.
M	. . . .	Magneto.
D	. . . .	Distributor.
Rv	. . . .	Reverse.
EN	. . . .	Unit with engine.
RA	. . . .	Unit with rear axle.
A & TL	. . . .	A arms (Wishbones) and transverse leaf spring.

A & CO	. . .	A arms (Wishbones) and coil springs.
SA & TL	. .	Swing axles and transverse leaf spring.
DD & TL	. .	De Dion and transverse leaf spring.
DD & CO	. .	De Dion and coil springs.
R & CO	. .	Rigid axle and coil springs.
HU	. . .	Houdaille shock absorbers.
FI	. . .	Fuel injection.
LPI	. . .	Lucas port injection.
BDI	. . .	Bosch direct injection.
DW & Co	. .	Double wishbones (A arms) and coil springs.
WeTwCh	. .	Weber twin choke carburettors.
DR	. . .	Drum brakes.
Dis	. . .	Disc brakes.
Du/Dis	. . .	Dunlop disc brakes.
Wi	. . .	Wire wheels.
Bo/Wi	. . .	Borrani wire wheels.
A1	. . .	Cast alloy wheels.
ARB	. . .	Anti roll bar.
CS	. . .	Channel section chassis.
MT.AS.FG	. .	Mixed construction chassis. Multi-tube/alloy sheet/fibreglass.
UL	. . .	Upper link.
LW	. . .	Lower wishbone.
TRA	. . .	Trailing arms.
UC	. . .	Unit construction chassis.
LS	. . .	Leaf spring.

Type abbreviations. Grand Prix Cars.

1.5 SS	1500-cc single stage supercharged.
1.5 TS	1500-cc two stage supercharged twin cam.
2.0 SS/SC	2000-cc single stage supercharged short chassis.
2.5 12/U/S	2500-cc unsupercharged 12-cylinder.
3.3 U/S	3300-cc unsupercharged prototype.
4.1 U/S	4100-cc unsupercharged prototype.
4.5 U/S/SI	4500-cc unsupercharged single ignition.
4.5 U/S/TI	4500-cc unsupercharged twin ignition.
4.5 U/S Indy.	4500-cc unsupercharged Indianapolis model.
1.5 TS/DD	1500-cc two stage supercharged De Dion chassis.
2.0 SS/LC	2000-cc single stage super. Long chassis.
2.5 U/S/DD	2500-cc unsupercharged De Dion chassis.
2.0 U/S/SC	2000-cc unsupercharged short chassis.
2.0 U/S/DD	2000-cc unsupercharged De Dion chassis.
2.0 U/S/LC	2000-cc unsupercharged long chassis.
2.0 4/52 Type 500	2000-cc 4-cylinder 1952.
2.0 4/53 Type 500	2000-cc 4-cylinder 1953.
2.0 4/SQ Type 553	2000-cc 4-cylinder Squalo.
2.5/4/PT	2500-cc 4-cylinder prototype.
2.5/625/54	2500-cc 4-cylinder 1954.
2.5/625/54	2500-cc 4-cylinder 1954 Interim model.
2.5/625/55	2500-cc 4-cylinder 1955.
2.5/555/54	2500-cc 4-cylinder Super Squalo 1954.
2.5/555	2500-cc 4-cylinder Super Squalo final version.
2.5/D50	2500-cc 8-cylinder Lancia/Ferrari 1st type.
2.5/801/57	2500-cc 8-cylinder Ferrari/Lancia derivative 1957.
2.5/246	2500-cc 6-cylinder Dino type.
750/625	3-litre Monza engine in type 625 chassis.
860/555	3.5-litre 4-cylinder engine in Super Squalo chassis.
121/Indy	6-cylinder Bardahl Indianapolis experimental.
D50/555	2.5-litre Lancia engine in Super Squalo chassis.
116/F1	Experimental 2-cylinder Grand Prix engine.
115/F1	Experimental 6-cylinder Grand Prix engine.
296/Monza	6-cylinder 3-litre 500 mile of Monza car.
412/Monza	12-cylinder 4.1-litre 500 mile of Monza car.
156/F2	V6 1500-cc Formula 2 car.
156/61/65	V6 Formula 1 car 1961 65 degree engine.
156/61/120	V6 Formula 1 car 1961 120 degree engine.
156/62/120 I	V6 Formula 1 car 1962 120 degree engine. Interim.
156/63	V6 Formula 1 car 1963.
158/53	V8 Formula 1 car 1963.
1512/63	Flat 12 Formula 1 car 1963.
166/F2	1.5-litre Formula II car 1967.
250/F1	3.0-litre V12 Formula 1 car 1966.

Type abbreviations. Sports and Touring cars.

125	1500-cc sports car.
166 MM	2000-cc Mille Miglia sports car.
166 Inter	2000-cc Touring model.
195 Inter	2300-cc Touring model.
212 Export	2500-cc Sports-Touring model.
212 Inter	2500-cc Touring model.
225 MM	2700-cc Mille Miglia sports model.
250 Export	3000-cc Sports Touring model.
250 MM	3000-cc Mille Miglia sports model.
250 Europa	3000-cc Touring model.
250 Eu/GT	3000-cc Europa Interim Gran Turismo model.
275 MM	3300-cc Experimental sports.
340 Mexico	4100-cc Mexican road race sports cars.
340 MM	4100-cc Mille Miglia sports model.
342 America	4100-cc Touring model.
375 MM	4500-cc Mille Miglia sports model.
375 America	4500-cc Touring car.
375 Plus	4900-cc Le Mans car.
410 Plus	4900-cc Twin ignition lightweight model.
410 SA	4900-cc Super America touring car.
500 MD/S1	2000-cc Mondial 4-cylinder series 1 sports.
500 MD/2S2	2000-cc Mondial 4-cylinder series 2 sports.
500 TR	2000-cc Testa Rossa 4-cylinder sports.

735 Monza	3000-cc Monza 4-cylinder sports prototype.
750 Monza	3000-cc Monza 4-cylinder sports.
118 Le Mans	3700-cc 6-cylinder in line sports car.
121 Le Mans	4400-cc 6-cylinder in line Le Mans sports car.
625 Le Mans	2500-cc 4-cylinder Le Mans sports car.
860 Monza	3500-cc 4-cylinder Monza sports car.
290 MM	3500-cc 12-cylinder Mille Miglia sports car.
315 MM	3800-cc 12-cylinder twin cam sports car.
412 MI	4100-cc 12-cylinder twin cam sports car.
250 TR	3000-cc 12-cylinder Testa Rossa sports car.
312 Le Mans	3000-cc 12-cylinder twin cam sports car.
206 Dino	2000-cc V6 cylinder sports car.
296 Dino	3000-cc V6 cylinder sports car.
246 SP	V6 2.4-litre rear-engined prototype.
250 TR/DD	Testa Rossa 3-litre De Dion.
250/TR/IRS	Testa Rossa 3-litre Independent rear suspension.
250/TR/61	Testa Rossa 3-litre 1961.
250/P	3-litre V12 rear-engined prototype.
268/SP	2.6-litre V8 rear-engined prototype.
248/SP	2.4-litre V8 rear-engined prototype.
330/LMB	3.9-litre V12 Le Mans Berlinetta.
330/LMB/63	3.9-litre V12 Le Mans Berlinetta 1963.
365 P2/3	4.4-litre rear-engined sports modified to P3 chassis specifications.
330 P3	4.0-litre rear-engined prototype 1966.
330 P4	4.0-litre rear-engined prototype 1967.
206/S	2.0-litre rear-engined Dino sports prototype.
275 GTS	3.3-litre touring car.
275 GTB/4	3.3-litre twin cam per bank touring car.
330 GTC	4.0-litre touring car.

GRAND PRIX CARS

TYPE	1.5 SS	1.5 TS	2.0 SS/SC	2.5/12 U/S	3.3 U/S	4.1 U/S	4.5 U/S/SI	4.5 U/S TI	4.5 U/S Indy
No of Cylinders	V12	V12	V12	V12	V12	V12	V12	V12	V12
B/S	55 × 52.5	55 × 52.5	60 × 58.8	68 × 58.8	72 × 68	80 × 68	80 × 75.5	80 × 75.5	80 × 75.5
Cubic Capacity	1498	1498	1995	2560	3322	4080	4498	4498	4498
Supercharged or Unsupercharged	SS	TS	SS	US	US	US	US	US	US
Compression Ratio	6.5/1	6.5/1	6.5/1	11/1	11/1	11/1	11/1	13/1	13/1
B h p	225	300	300	170	260	310	330	380	430
R p m	7500	7500	7500	6500	6500	6500	7000	7000	7500
Crankcase	S	S	S	S	S	S	S	S	S
Head	LD	LD	LD	LD	LD	LD	LD	LD	LD
Combustion Chamber	H	H	H	H	H	H	H	H	H
Crankshaft Bearings, No	7	7	7	7	7	7	7	7	7
Valves	IO	IO	IO	IO	IO	IO	IO	IO	IO
Valve Springs	HA	HA	HA	HA	HA	HA	HA	HA	HA
Camshaft	SI	TW	SI	SI	SI	SI	SI	SI	SI
Camshaft Drive	CH	GE	CH	CH	CH	CH	CH	CH	CH
Blower Type	1R	2R	1R	—	—	—	—	—	—
Carburettor Type	W/40 DO3C	W/50 WCF	W/40 DORC	W/36 DCF	W/38 DCF	W/38 DCF	W/40 DCF	W/40 IFAC	W/40 IFAC
No of Carburetters	1	1	1	3	3	3	3	3	3
Ignition	2M	2M	2M	2M	2M	2M	2M	1M	1M
Plugs per Cylinder	1	1	1	1	1	1	1	2	2
Gears	5 & Rv	5 & Rv	5 & Rv	5 & Rv	5 & Rv	4 & Rv	4 & Rv	4 & Rv	5 & Rv
Gearbox Mounting	EN	EN	EN	EN	EN	RA	RA	RA	RA
Front Suspension	A & TL	A & TL	A & TL	A & TL	A & TL	A & TL	A & TL	A & TL	A & TL
Rear Suspension	SA & TL	SA & TL	SA & TL	SA & TL	SA & TL	DD & TL	DD & TL	DD & TL	DD & TL
Shock-absorbers	HU	HU	HU	HU	HU	HU	HU	HU	HU
Frame	TLA	TLA	TLA	TLA	TLA	TLA	TLA	TLA	TLA
Wheelbase	7' 1"	7' 10"	7' 1"	7' 10"	7' 10"	7' 6"	7' 6"	7' 6"	7' 8"
Track	3' 11"	4' 2½"	3' 11"	4' 2½"	4' 2½"	F. 4' 2" R. 4' 0"	F. 4' 2" R. 4' 0"	F. 4' 2" R. 4' 0"	F. 4' 3½" R. 4' 3"

TYPE	1.5 TS/DD	2.0 SS/L/C	2.5 U/S DD	2.0 US/SC	2.0 US/DD	2.0 US/LC	2.0 4/52 Type 500	2.0 4/53 Type 500	2.0 4/SQ Type 553
No of Cylinders	V12	V12	V12	V12	V12	V12	4IL	4IL	4IL
B/S	55 × 52.5	60 × 58.8	68 × 58.8	60 × 58.8	60 × 58.8	60 × 58.8	90 × 78	90 × 78	93 × 73.5
Cubic Capacity	1498	1995	2560	1992	1992	19929	1980	1980	1998
Supercharged or Unsupercharged	TS	SS	US	US	US	US	US	US	US
Compression Ratio	6.5/1	6.5/1	13/1	11/1	11/1	11/1	11.5/1	12/1	12/1
B h p	315	300	200	155	160	160	170	180	190
R p m	7500	7500	7500	7000	7000	7000	7000	7200	7500
Crankcase	S	S	S	S	S	S	S	S	S
Head	LD	LD	LD	LD	LD	LD	LD	LD	LD
Combustion Chamber	H	H	H	H	H	H	H	H	H
Crankshaft Bearings. No	7	7	7	7	7	7	5	5	5
Valves	IO	IO	IO	IO	IO	IO	IO	IO	IO
Valve Springs	HA	HA	HA	HA	HA	HA	CO	CO	CO
Camshaft	TW	SI	SI	SI	SI	SI	TW	TW	TW
Camshaft Drive	GE	CH	CH	CH	CH	CH	GE	GE	GE
Blower Type	2R	1R	-	-	-	-	-	-	-
Carburetter Type	W/50 WCF	W/40 DORC	W/38 DCF	W/36 DCO	W/36 DCO	W/36 DCO	W/45 DOE	W/50 DCO	W/50 DCO
No of Carburetters	1	1	3	3	3	3	4	2	2
Ignition	2M	2M	2M	2M	2M	2M	2M	2M	2M
Plugs per Cylinder	1	1	1 $^{7}_{8}$	1	1	1	2	2	2
Gears	4 & Rv	5 & Rv	4 & Rv	5 & Rv	4 & Rv	5 & Rv	4 & Rv	4 & Rv	4 & Rv
Gearbox Mounting	RA	EN	RA	EN	RA	EN	RA	RA	RA
Front Suspension	A & TL	A & TL	A & TL	A & TL	A & TL	A & TL	A & TL	A & TL	A & TL
Rear Suspension	DD & TL	SA & TL	DD & TL	SA & TL	DD & TL	SA & TL	DD & TL	DD & TL	DD & TL
Shock-absorbers	HU	HU	HU	HU	HU	HU	HU	HU	HU
Frame	TLA	TLA	TLA	TLA	TLA	TLA	TLA	TLA	TSPA
Wheelbase	7' 8"	7' 10"	7' 8"	7' 1"	7' 6"	7' 10"	7' 2½"	7' 2½"	6' 10"
Track	4' 2½"	4' 2½"	4' 2½"	3' 10"	3' 11½"	4' 2½"	F. 4' 3½" R. 4' 1"	R. 4' 1"	F. 4' 1½" R. 3' 11½"

TYPE	2.5/4/PT	2.5/625/54	2.5/625/54I	2.5/555/54	2.5/625/55	2.5/555	2.5/D50	2.5/801/57	2.5/246
No of Cylinders	4IL	4IL	4IL	4IL	IL	4IL	8V	8V	6V
B/S	94 x 90	94 x 90	94 x 90	100 x 79.5	100 x 79.5	100 x 79.5	76 x 68.8	80 x 62	85 x 71
Cubic Capacity	2490	2490	2490	2496	2496	2496	2489	2490	2417
Supercharged or Unsupercharged	US	US	US	US	US	US	US	US	US
Compression Ratio	11/1	11/1	12/1	12/1	12/1	12/1	11.9/1	11.5/1	9/1
B h p	200	230	250	250	265	270	231	240	290
R p m	6500	7000	7500	7500	7500	7500	8600	9000	8300
Crankcase	S	S	S	S	S	S	S	S	S
Head	LD	LD	LD	LD	LD	LD	LD	LD	LD
Combustion Chamber	H	H	H	H	H	H	H	H	H
Crankshaft Bearings, No	5	5	5	5	5	5	5	5	4
Valves	IO	IO	IO	IO	IO	IO	IO	IO	IO
Valve Springs	HA	HA	HA	HA	HA	HA	HA	CO	CO
Camshaft	TW	TW	TW	TW	TW	TW	TW	TW	TW
Camshaft Drive	GE	GE	GE	GE	GE	GE	GE	CH	CH
Blower Type	—	—	—	—	—	—	—	—	—
Carburetter Type	W/50 DCO	W/50 DCO	W/50 DCOA3	W/58 DCOA3	W/58 DCOA3	W/58 DCOA3	S/40 PII	S/40 PII	W/42 DCNW
No of Carburetters	2	2	2	2	2	2	4	4	3
Ignition	2M	2M	2M	2M	2M	2M	2M	2M	1M
Plugs per Cylinder	2	2	2	2	2	2	2	2	2
Gears	4 & Rv	4 & Rv	4 &Rv	4 & Rv	5 & RV	5 & Rv	5 & Rv	5 & Rv	4 & Rv
Gearbox Mounting	RA	RA	RA	RA	RA	RA	RA	RA	RA
Front Suspension	A & TL	A & TL	A & TL	A & TL	A & CO	A & CO	A & CO	A & TL	A & CO
Rear Suspension	DD & TL	DD & TL	DD & TL	DD & TL	DD & TL	DD & TL	DD & TL	DD & TL	DD &TL
Shock-absorbers	HU	HU	HU	HU	HU	HU	TS	HU	HV
Frame	TLA	TLA	TLA	TSPA	TLA	TSPA	TSPA	TSPA	TSPA
Wheelbase	7' 2½"	7' 2½"	7' 2½"	7' 0"	7' 2½"	7' 0"	7'6"	7' 6"	—
Track	F. 4' 3½" R. 4' 1"	F. 4' 3½" R. 4' 1"	F. 4' 3½" R. 4' 1"	F. 4' 1" R. 3' 11½"	F. 4' 3½" R. 4' 1"	F. 4' 1" R. 3' 11½"	4' 2"	4' 2"	—

TYPE	750/625	860/555	121/Indy	D50/555	116/FI	115/FI	296/Monza	412/Monza	156/F2
No of Cylinders	4IL	4IL	6IL	V8	2IL	6IL	V6	V12	V6
B/S	103 x 90	102 x 105	102 x 90	76 x 68.8	118 x 114	82.4 x 78	85 x 87	77 x 72	70 x 64.5
Cubic Capacity	2999	3431	4412	2489	2493	2495	2962	4023	1489
Supercharged or Unsupercharged	US	US	US	US	US	US	US	US	US
Compression Ratio				11.5/1			9/1	9/1	9/1
B h p	290	310	380	250	174	250	316	447	190
R p m	6500	6200	6500	7000	4800	6500	7800	7700	9000
Crankcase	S	S	S	S	S	S	S	S	S
Head	LD	LD	LD	LD		LD	LD	LD	LD
Combustion Chamber	H	H	H	H	H	H	H	H	H
Crankshaft Bearings, No	5	5	7	5	3	7	4	7	4
Valves	IO	IO	IO	IO	—	IO	IO	IO	IO
Valve Springs	HA	HA	HA	CO	—	HA	CO	HA	CO
Camshaft	TW	TW	TW	TW	—	TW	TW	TW	TW
Camshaft Drive	GE	GE	GE	GE	—	GE	CH	CH	CH
Blower Type	—	—	—	—	—	—	—	—	—
Carburetter Type	W/50 DCOA3	W/58 DCOA	W/50 DCOA3	S/40 PII	W/42 DCOD	W/45 DCOA3	W/46 DCNW	W/42 DCNW	W/38 DCNW
No of Carburetters	2	2	3	4		3	3	6	3
Ignition	2D	2D	2D			2M	2D	2D	2M
Plugs per Cylinder	2	2	2	2		2	2	2	2
Gears	4 & Rv	4 & Rv	2	5 & Rv	—	—	3 & Rv	3 & Rv	4 & Rv
Gearbox Mounting	RA	RA		RA	—	—	RA	RA	RA
Front Suspension	A & TL	A & CO		A & CO	—	—	A & CO	A & CO	A & CO
Rear Suspension	DD & TL	DD & TL		DD & TL	—	—	DD & CO	DD & TL	DD & CO
Shock-absorbers	HU	HU		HU	—	—	HU	HU	HU
Frame	TLA	TSPA		TSPA	—	—	TSPA		TSPA
Wheelbase	7' 2½"	7' 0"		7' 0"	—	—			
Track	F. 4' 3½" R. 4' 1"	F. 4' 1" R. 3' 11½"		F. 4' 1" R. 3' 11½"	—	—			

SPORTS AND TOURING CARS

TYPE	125	166 MM	166 Inter	195 Inter	212 Export	212 Inter	225 Sport	250 Export	250 MM
No of Cylinders	V12	V12	V12	V12	V12	V12	V12	V12	V12
B/S	55 x 52.5	60 x 58.8	60 x 58.8	65 x 58.8	68 x 58.8	68 x 58.8	70 x 58.8	68 x 68	73 x 58.8
Cubic Capacity	1498	1995	1995	2340	2562	2562	2715	2963	2953
Compression Ratio	9/1	10/1	7.5/1	7.5/1	8/1	8/1	8.5/1	8.5/1	9/1
B h p	118	140	110	130	150	170	210	220	240
R p m	6500	6600	6000	6000	6500	6500	7200	7000	7200
Crankcase	S	S	S	S	S	S	S	S	S
Head	LD	LD	LD	LD	LD	LD	LD	LD	LD
Combustion Chamber	H	H	H	H	H	H	H	H	H
Crankshaft Bearings	7	7	7	7	7	7	7	7	7
Valves	IO	IO	IO	IO	IO	IO	IO	IO	IO
Valve Springs	HA	HA	HA	HA	HA	HA	HA	HA	HA
Camshafts	SI	SI	SI	SI	SI	SI	SI	SI	SI
Camshaft Drive	CH	CH	CH	CH	CH	CH	CH	CH	CH
Carburetter Type	W/30 DCF	W/32 DCF	W/32 DCF	W/32 DCF	W/32 DCF	W/36 DCF	W/36 DCF	W/36 DCF	W/36 IF4/C
No of Carburetters	1	3	1	1	1	3	3	3	3
Ignition	2D	2M	2D	2D	2D	2D	2D	2D	2D
Plugs per Cylinder	1	1	1	1	1	1	1	1	1
Gears	5 & Rv	5 & Rv	5 & Rv	5 & Rv	5 & Rv	5 & Rv	5 & Rv	R & Rv	4 & Rv
Gearbox Mounting	EN	EN	EN	EN	EN	EN	EN	EN	EN
Front Suspension	A & TL	A & TL	A & TL	A & TL	A & TL	A & TL	A &TL	A & TL	A & TL
Rear Suspension	R & SEL	R & SEL	R & SEL	R & SEL	R & SEL	R & SEL	R & SEL	R & SEL	R & SEL
Shock-absorbers	HU	HU	HU	HU	HU	HU	HU	HU	HU
Frame	T	T	T	T	T	T	T	T	T
Wheelbase	2.200	2.200	2.420	2.500	2.250	2.600	2.600	2.400	2.400
Track, Front	1.270	1.270	1.250	1.270	1.270	1.278	1.300	1.300	1.300
Track, Rear	1.250	1.250	1.200	1.250	1.250	1.250	1.320	1.320	1.320

TYPE	250 Europa	250 GT	275 Sport	340 Mexico	340 MM	342 America	375 MM	375 America	375 Plus
No of Cylinders	V12	V12	V12	V12	V12	V12	V12	V12	V12
B/S	68 x 68	73 x 58.8	72 x 68	80 x 68	80 x 68	80 x 68	84 x 68	84 x 68	84 x 74.5
Cubic Capacity	2963	2953	3322	4101	4101	4101	4522	4522	4954
Compression Ratio	8.5/1	8.5/1	8/1	8/1	8/1	8/1	9/1	8/1	9.25/1
B h p	200	220	270	280	300	200	340	300	344
R p m	7000	7000	7000	6600	6600	5000	7000	6300	6500
Crankcase	S	S	S	S	S	S	S	S	S
Head	L	LD	L	L	L	L	L	L	L
Combustion Chamber	H	H	H	H	H	H	H	H	H
Crankshaft Bearings	7	7	7	7	7	7	7	7	7
Valves	IO	IO	IO	IO	IO	IO	IO	IO	IO
Valve Springs	HA	HA	HA	HA	HA	HA	HA	HA	HA
Camshafts	SI	SI	SI	SI	SI	SI	SI	SI	SI
Camshaft Drive	CH	CH	CH	CH	CH	CH	CH	CH	CH
Carburetter Type	W/36 DCZ	W/36 DCZ	W/40 DCF	W/40 DCF	W/40 IFC	W/40 DCF	W/40 IFC/4	W/40 DCZ	W/40 DCF
No of Carburetters	3	3	3	3	3	3	3	3	3
Ignition	2D	2D	2M	2D	2M	2D	2M	2D	2M
Plugs per Cylinder	1	1	1	1	1	1	1	1	1
Gears	4 & Rv	4 & Rv	4 &Rv	5 & Rv	4 & Rv	4 & Rv	4 & Rv	4 &Rv	4 & Rv
Gearbox Mounting	EN	EN	EN	EN	EN	EN	EN	EN	RA
Front Suspension	A & TL	A & CO	A & TL	A & TL	A & TL	A & TL	A & TL	A & TL	A & TL
Rear Suspension	R & SEL	R & SEL	R & SEL	R & SEL	R & SEL	R & SEL	R & SEL	R & SEL	DD & TL
Shock-absorbers	HU	HU	NU	HU	HU	HU	HU	HU	HU
Frame	T	T	T	T	T	T	T	T	T
Wheelbase	2.800	2.600	2.500	2.600	2.500	2.650	2.600	2.800	2.600
Track, Front	1.325	1.354	1.325	1.278	1.325	1.325	1.325	1.325	1.325
Track, Rear	1.320	1.349	1.320	1.250	1.320	1.320	1.320	1.320	1.284

TYPE	410 Plus	410 SA	500 MD/S1	500 MD/S2	500 TR	735 Monza	750 Monza	118 Le Mans	121 Le Mans
No of Cylinders	V12	V12	4IL	4IL	4IL	4IL	4IL	6IL	6IL
B/S	88 x 68	88 x 68	90 x 78	90 x 78	90 x 78	102 x 90	103 x 90	94 x 90	102 x 90
Cubic Capacity	4961	4961	1984	1984	1984	2941	2999	3747	4412
Compression Ratio	9/1	8.5/1	8.5/1	8.5/1	8.75/1	8.5/1	8.6/1	8.75/1	8.75/1
Bhp	380	340	160	170	190	220	260	310	360
Rpm	7000	6000	7000	7000	7000	6000	6000	6000	6000
Crankcase	S	S	S	S	S	S	S	S	S
Head	L	L	L	L	L	L	L	L	L
Combustion Chamber	H	H	H	H	H	H	H	H	H
Crankshaft Bearings	7	7	5	5	5	5	5	7	7
Valves	IO	IO	IO	IO	IO	IO	IO	IO	IO
Valve Springs	HA	HA	HA	HA	HA	HA	HA	HA	HA
Camshafts	SI	SI	TW	TW	TW	TW	TW	TW	TW
Camshaft Drive	CH	CH	GE	GE	GE	GE	GE	GE	GE
Carburetter Type	W/42 DCZ/4	W/40 DCF	W/42 DCOA3	W/45 DCOA3	W/40 DCFA3	W/45 DCOA3	W/50 DCOA3	W/45 DCOA3	W/50 DCOA3
No of Carburetters	3	3	2	2	2	2	2	3	3
Ignition	2M	2D	2M	2D	2D	2D	2D	2D	2D
Plugs per cylinder	2	1	2	2	2	2	2	2	2
Gears	4 & Rv	4 & Rv	4 & Rv	5 & Rv	4 & Rv	5 & Rv	5 & Rv	5 & Rv	5 & Rv
Gearbox Mounting	RA	RA	RA	RA	EN	RA	RA	RA	RA
Front Suspension	A & CO	A & CO	A & TL	A & CO	A & CO	A & CO	A & CO	A & CO	A & CO
Rear Suspension	DD & TL	R & SEL	DD & TL	DD & TL	R & CO	DD & TL	DD & TL	DD & TL	DD & TL
Shock-absorbers	HU	HU	HU	HU	HU	HU	HU	HU	HU
Frame	T	T	T	T	T	T	T	T	T
Wheelbase	2.350	2.800	2.250	2.250	2.250	2.250	2.250	2.400	2.400
Track, Front	1.316	1.455	1.278	1.278	1.303	1.278	1.278	1.278	1.278
Track, Rear	1.286	1.450	1.284	1.284	1.250	1.284	1.284	1.284	1.284

TYPE	625 Le Mans	860 Monza	290 MM	315 MM	412 MI	250 TR	312 Le Mans	206 Dino	296 Dino	815
No of Cylinders	4IL	4IL	V12	V12	V12	V12	V12	V6	V6	8IL
B/S	94 x 90	102 x 105	73 x 69.5	76 x 69.5	77 x 72	73 x 58.8	73 x 58.8	77 x 71	85 x 87	63 x 60
Cubic Capacity	2498	3431	3490	3780	4023	2953	2953	1985	2962	1496
Compression Ratio	9/1	8.6/1	9/1	9/1	9/1	9.8/1	9.8/1	9/1	9/1	—
Bhp	225	310	350	380	447	300	356	225	316	75
Rpm	6200	6200	7200	7600	7700	7200	8600	8600	7800	5500
Crankcase	S	S	S	S	S	S	S	S	S	—
Head	L	L	L	L	L	LD	LD	LD	LD	
Combustion Chamber	H	H	H	H	H	H	H	H	H	—
Crankshaft Bearings	5	5	7	7	7	7	7	4	4	—
Valves	IO	IO	IO	IO	IO	IO	IO	IO	IO	—
Valve Springs	HA	HA	HA	HA	HA	HA	HA			
Camshafts	TW	TW	SI	TW	TW	SI	TW	TW	TW	OHV
Camshaft Drive	GE	GE	CH	CH	CH	CH	CH	CH	CH	
Carburetter Type	W/42 DCOA	W/58 DCOA	W/40 DCF	W/40 DCF	W/42 DCN	W/46 TR4/C1	W/42 DCNW	W/42 DCNW	W/46 DCNW	W/30 DR2
No of Carburetters	2	2	3	3	6	6	3	3	3	4
Ignition	2M	2D	2D	2D	2D	D	2D	2D	2D	—
Plugs per Cylinder	2	2	2	2	2	2	2	2	2	—
Gears	4 & Rv	4 & Rv	4 & Rv	4 & Rv	4 & Rv	4 & Rv	4 & Rv	4 & Rv	4 & Rv	4 & Rv
Gearbox Mounting	EN	RA	RA	RA	RA	EN	RA	RA	RA	EN
Front Suspension	A & CO	A & CO	A & CO	A & CO	A & CO	A & CO	A & CO	A & CO	A & CO	W & CO
Rear Suspension	R & CO	DD & TL	DD & TL	DD & TL	DD & TL	R & CO	DD & TL	R & CO	DD & CO	R & SELS
Shock-absorbers	HU	HU	HU	HU	HU	HU	HU	HU	HU	
Frame	T	T	T	T	T	T	T	T	T	—
Wheelbase	2.250	2.350	2.350	2.350	2.350	2.350	2.350	2.220	2.220	2.418
Track, Front	1.308	1.316	1.316	1.310	1.310	1.308	1.308	1.240	1.240	1.229
Track, Rear	1.250	1.286	1.286	1.286	1.286	1.300	1.300	1.200	1.200	1.224

SPECIFICATIONS OF CARS 1958 - 1968

TYPE	256/Dino	256M/Dino	246/RE	156/F2	156/61/65	156/61/120
No of Cylinders	6V	6V	6V	6V	6V	6V
B/S . . .	86 x 71	86 x 71	85 x 71	73 x 58.8	73 x 58.8	73 x 58.8
Cubic Capacity	2474	2474	2417	1476	1476	1476
B h p	295	305	290	175	180	190
R p m . . .	8600	9200	9000	9000	9000	9500
Camshaft . .	TW	TW	TW	TW	TW	TW
Carburetters	3WeTwCh	3WeTwCh	3WeTwCh	3WeTwCh	3WeTwCh	3WeTwCh
Chassis . .	MT	MT	MT	MT	MT	MT
Gearbox . .	5 & RvRa	5 & RvRa	5 & RvRa	5 & RvRa	5 & RvRa	5 & RvRa
Front Suspension	DW & Co	DW & Co	DW & Co	DW & Co	DW & Co	DW & Co
Rear Suspension	DD & Co	DD & Co	DD & Co	DW & Co	DW & Co	DW & Co
Brakes . .	Du/Dis	Du/Dis	Du/Dis	Du/Dis	Du/Dis	Du/Dis
Wheels . .	Wi	Wi	Wi	Wi	Wi	Wi
F. Tread . .	4' 0¾"	4' 0¾"	3' 11¼"	3' 11¼"	3' 11¼"	3' 11¼"
R. Tread . .	4' 0¾"	4' 0¾"	3' 11¼"	3' 11¼"	3' 11¼"	3' 11¼"
Wheelbase . .	7' 3¾"	7' 3¾"	7' 7"	7' 7"	7' 7"	7' 7"

TYPE	156/62/120/I	156/62/P	156/63	158/63	1512/63	296/Inter/R E
No of Cylinders	6V	6V	6V	8V	12V	6V
B/S . . .	73 x 58.8	73 x 58.8	73 x 58.8	64 x 57.8	56 x 50.4	87 x 82
Cubic Capacity	1476	1476	1476	1487	1489	2925
B h p	190	195	200	205	205	310
R p m . .	9500	9500	9800	7700	8000	7500
Camshaft . .	TW	TW	TW	TW	TW	TW
Carburetters	3TwChWe	3WeTwCh	F/Inj	F/Inj	F/Inj	3WeTwCh
Chassis . .	MT	MT	MT	MT	MT	MT
Gearbox . .	5 & RvRa	5 & RvRa	6 & RvRa	6 & RvRa	6 & RvRa	5 & RvRa
Front Suspension	DW & Co	DW & Co	DW & Co	DW & Co	DW & Co	DW & Co
Rear Suspension	DW & Co	DW & Co	DW & Co	DW & Co	DW & Co	DW & Co
Brakes . .	Du/Dis	Du/Dis	Du/Dis	Du/Dis	Du/Dis	Du/Dis
Wheels . .	Wi	Wi	Al	Al	Al	Wi
F Tread . .	4' 1"	3' 11¼"	3' 11¼"	3' 11¼"	3' 11¼"	3' 11¼"
R. Tread . .	4' 1"	3' 11¼"	3' 11¼"	3' 11¼"	3' 11¼"	3' 11¼"
Wheelbase . .	7' 7"	7' 6"	7' 6"	7' 6"	7' 6"	7' 9"

TYPE	250/246	555 Cooper/Cast	625LM/FL	246/SC	246/S/FE	206/S/FE
No of Cylinders	12V	4IL	4IL	6V	6V	6V
B/S . . .	73 x 58.8	100 x 79.5	98.5 x 90	85 x 71	85 x 71	77 x 71
Cubic Capacity	2953	2495	2730	2417	2417	1985
B h p	300	265	250	270	280	220
R p m . .	7500	7500	6200	8000	8300	8600
Camshaft . .	SI	TW	TW	SI	SI	SI
Carburetters	6WeTwCh	2WcTwCh	2WeTwCh	3WeTwCh	3WeTwCh	3WeTwCh
Chassis . .	MT	MT	TLA	MT	T	T
Gearbox . .	5 & RvRa	5 & RvRa	4 & RvRa	5 & RvRa	4 & RvRa	4 & RvEn
Front Suspension	DW & Co	DW & Co	DW & Co	DW & Co	DW & Co	R & Co
Rear Suspension	DD & Co	DW & Co	DD & TLS	DD & Co	DD & Co	R & Co
Brakes . .	Dr	Dis	Dr	Dr	Dis	Dis
Wheels . .	Wi	Wi	Wi	Wi	Wi	Wi
F. Tread .	4' 0¾"	3' 9½"	4' 3½"	4' 0¾"	4' 1½"	4' 1½"
R. Tread .	4' 0¾"	3' 11"	4' 1"	4' 0¾"	4' 0"	4' 0"
Wheelbase . .	7' 3¾"	7' 5"	7' 2½"	7' 2¾"	7' 4¾"	7' 4¾"

TYPE	206/S/FE/DD	246/SP	250TR/DD	250TR/IRS	250TRI/IRS	250/P
No of Cylinders	6V	6V	12V	12V	12V	12V
B/S . . .	77 x 71	85 x 71	73 x 58.8	73 x 58.8	73 x 58.8	73 x 58.8
Cubic Capacity	1985	2417	2953	2953	2953	2953
B h p . .	225	270	300	300	300	310
R p m . .	8600	8000	7200	7200	7200	7500
Camshaft . .	SI	TW	SI	SI	SI	SI
Carburetters .	3WeTwCh	3WeTwCh	6WeTwCh	6WeTwCh	6WeTwCh	6WeTwCh
Chassis . .	T	MT	T	T	T	MT
Gearbox . .	4 & RvRa	5 & RvRa	5 & RvRa	5 & RvRa	5 & RvRa	5 & RvRa
Front Suspension	DW & Co	DW & Co	DW & Co	DW & Co	DW & Co	DW & Co
Rear Suspension	DD & Co	DW & Co	DD & Co	DW & Co	DW & Co	DW & Co
Brakes . .	Dis	Dis	Dis	Dis	Dis	Dis
Wheels . .	Wi	Wi	Wi	Wi	Wi	Wi
F. Tread .	4' 1½"	4' 0½"	4' 4½"	4' 4½"	4' 4½"	4' 5¼"
R. Tread .	4' 0"	3' 11¼"	4' 4"	4' 4"	4' 4"	4' 3¾"
Wheelbase . .	7' 4¾"	7' 3¾"	7' 9"	7' 9"	7' 11"	7' 11"

TYPE	268/SP	248/SP	330/LMS	250GT/Calif	250GT/Fari	250GT/Fari./L
No of Cylinders	8V	8V	12V	12V	12V	12V
B/S	77 x 71	77 x 66	77 x 71	73 x 58.8	73 x 58.8	73 x 58.8
Cubic Capacity	2645	2458	3967	2953	2953	2953
B h p . . .	265	250	390	250	250	250
R p m . . .	7000	7400	7500	7000	7000	7000
Camshaft . .	TW	TW	SI	SI	SI	SI
Carburetters	4WeTwCh	4WeTwCh	6WeTwCh	3WeTwCh	3WeTwCh	3WeTwCh
Chassis . . .	MT	MT	MT	TLA	TLA	TLA
Gearbox . .	5 & RvRa	5 & RvRa	4 & Rv	4 & RvEn	4 & RvEn	4 & RvEn
Front Suspension	DW & Co	DW & Co	DW & Co	DW & Co	DW & Co	DW & Co
Rear Suspension	DW & Co	DW & Co	DW & Co	R & SELS	R & SELS	R & SELS
Brakes . .	Dis	Dis	Dis	Du/Dis	Du/Dis	Du/Dis
Wheels . . .	Wi	Wi	Wi	Wi	Wi	Wi
F. Tread . .	4' 0½"	4' 0½"	4' 1"	4' 5.2"	4' 6.2"	4' 6.2"
R. Tread . .	3' 11¼"	3' 11¼"	4' 2¾"	4' 5"	4' 6.2"	4' 6.2"
Wheelbase . .	7' 7¾"	7' 7¾"	7' 11¾"	8' 6.2"	8' 6.4"	8' 6.4"

TYPE	250GT/58	250GT/60	250GTO	250/2 + 2	410/SA	330/SA
No of Cylinders	12V	12V	12V	12V	12V	12V
B/S	73 x 58.8	73 x 58.8	73 x 58.8	73 x 58.8	88 x 86	77 x 71
Cubic Capacity	2953	2953	2953	2953	4962	3967
B h p . .	250	260	300	240	360	320
R p m . . .	7000	7000	7200	7000	6500	7500
Camshaft . .	SI	SI	SI	SI	SI	SI
Carburetters .	3WeTwCh	3WeTwCh	6WeTwCh	3WeTwCh	3WeTwCh	3S04Ch
Chassis . . .	TLA	TLA	TLA	TLA	TLA	TLA
Gearbox . .	4 & RvEn	4 & RvEn	4 & RvEn	4 & RvEn	4 & RvEn	4 & OD & RvEn
Front Suspension	DW & Co	DW & Co	DW & Co	DW & Co	DW & Co	DW & Co
Rear Suspension	R & SELS	R & SELS	R & SELS	R & SELS	R & SELS	R & SELS
Brakes . .	Dr	Dis	Dis	Dis	Dis	Dis
Wheels . . .	Wi	Wi	Wi	Wi	Wi	Wi
F. Tread . .	4' 5.2"	4' 5.2"	4' 5.2"	4' 6.2"	4' 10.4"	4' 6"
R. Tread . .	4' 5"	4' 5"	4' 5"	4' 10.6"	4' 10.2"	4' 5½"
Wheelbase . .	8' 6.2"	8' 6.2"	8' 6.2"	8' 6.4"	8' 6.3"	7' 11"

TYPE	330/LMB	330LMB/63	330LMB/I	854/1	854/2	854/3
No of Cylinders	12V	12V	12V	4IL	4IL	4IL
B/S	77 x 71	77 x 71	77 x 71	65 x 64	65 x 64	65 x 64
Cubic Capacity	3967	3967	3967	849	849	849
B h p . . .	390	400	395	64	72	84
R p m . . .	7500	7500	7500	6000	6500	7000
Camshaft . .	SI	SI	SI	SI	SI	SI
Carburetters .	6WeTwCh	6WeTwCh	6WeTwCh	1WeTwCh	2WeTwCh	2WeTwCh
Chassis . . .	MT	MT	MT	T	T	T
Gearbox . .	4 & Rv	4 & Rv	4 & Rv	4 & OD & Rv	4 & OD & Rv	4 & OD & Rv
Front Suspension	DW & Co	DW & Co	DW & Co	DW & Co	DW & Co	DW & Co
Rear Suspension	DW & Co	DW & Co	DW & Co	R & SELS	R & SELS	R & SELS
Brakes . .	Dis	Dis	Dis	Dis	Dis	Dis
Wheels . . .	Wi	Wi	Wi	ST	ST	ST
F. Tread . .	4' 8"	4' 8"	4' 8"	4' 0½"	4' 0½"	4' 0½"
R. Tread . .	4' 7¾"	4' 7¾"	4' 7¾"	3' 11.9"	3' 11.9"	3' 11.9"
Wheelbase . .	7' 9½"	8' 2¾"	7' 11½"	7' 2¼"	7' 2¼"	7' 2¼"

TYPE	ASA/Mille	ASA/Comp	158/64/FI	330/P	250LM/GT	
No of Cylinders	4IL	4IL	8V	12V	12V	
B/S	69 x 69	69 x 66.5	64 x 57.8	77 x 71	73 x 58.8	
Cubic Capacity	1032	995	1487	3967	2953	
B h p . .	97	110	220	400	310	
R p m . . .	7000	7200	11000	7500	7500	
Camshaft . .	SI	SI	TW	SI	SI	
Carburetters .	2WeTwCh	2WeTwCh	B/oFI	6WeTwCh	6WeTwCh	
Chassis . . .	T	T	MC	MT	MT	
Gearbox . .	4 & OD & Rv	5 & Rv	5 & RvRa	4 & RvRa	5 & RvRa	
Front Suspension	DW & Co	DW & Co	DW & Co	DW & Co	DW & Co	
Rear Suspension	R & Co	R & Co	DW & Co	DW & Co	DW & Co	
Brakes . .	Du/Dis	Du/Dis	Dis	Dis	Dis	
Wheels . . .	Wi	Wi	Al	Wi	Wi	
F. Tread . .	3' 9.9"	4' 1¹¹/₁₆"	3' 8"	4' 5¼"	4' 5¼"	
R. Tread . .	4' 0.7"	4' 2"	3' 7⁵/₈"	4' 4¾"	4' 4¾"	
Wheelbase . .	7' 2.6"	7' 4"	6' 4"	7' 11"	7' 11"	

TYPE	CAN/AM '67	CAN/AM '68	CAN/AM '69	Tasman '68	Tasman '69	512S	512M	312P/69	312P/71	312P/72
No of Cylinders	V12	V12	V12	V6	V6	V12	V12	V12	HO 12	HO 12
B/S	79 x 71	92 x 78	92 x 78	90 x 63	90 x 63	87 x 70	87 x 70	77 x 53.5	78.5 x 51.5	78.5 x 51.5
Cubic Capacity	4176.3	6221.6	6221.6	2404	2404	4993	4993	2989	2991	2991
Bhp	480	620	640	285	290	550	610	420	450	450
Rpm	8500	7000	7700	8900	9000	8000	9000	9800	10.800	10.800
Camshaft	TW	TW	TW	TW	TW	TW	TW	TW	TW	TW
Carburetters	LuF/Inj	LuF/Inj	LuF/Inj	LuF/Inj	LuF/Inj	LuF/Inj	LuF/Inj	LuF/Inj	LuF/Inj	LuF/Inj
Gearbox	5 & RvRa	4 & RvRa	4 & RvRa	5 & RvRa	5 & RvRa	5 & RvRa	5 & RvRa	5 & RvRa	5 & RvRa	5 & RvRa
Front Suspension	Ind Co	Ind Co	Ind Co	Ind Co	Ind Co	Ind Co	Ind Co	Ind Co	Ind Co	Ind Co
Rear Suspension	Ind Co	Ind Co	Ind Co	Ind Co	Ind Co	Ind Co	Ind Co	Ind Co	Ind Co	Ind Co
Brakes	Dis	Dis	Dis	Dis	Dis	DIs	Dis	Dis	Dis	Dis
Wheels	A1	A1	A1	A1	A1	A1	A1	A1	A1	A1
F. Tread	1488	1603	1603	1405	1405	1518	1518	1485	1425	1425
R. Tread	1450	1590	1590	1400	1400	1511	1511	1500	1400	1400
Wheelbase	2400	2450	2450	2220	2220	2400	2400	2370	2220	2220

TYPE	F1/67	F1/68	F1/69	312B F1/71	312B 2 F1/72	212E	246 DinoGT/71	246 DinoGTS/71
No of Cylinders	V12	V12	V12	HO 12	HO 12	HO 12	V6	V6
B/S	77 x 53.5	77 x 53.5	77 x 53.5	78.5 x 57.5	78.5 x 51.5	65 x 50	92.5 x 60	92.5 x 66
Cubic Capacity	2989	2989	2989	2991	2991	1990	2418	2418
Bhp	390	408	436	450	480	300	195	195
Rpm	10.500	11.000	11.000	12.000	11.800	11.800	7600	7600
Camshaft	TW	TW	TW	TW	TW	TW	TW	TW
Carburetters	LuF/Inj	LuF/Inj	LuF/Inj	LuF/Inj	LuF/Inj	LuF/Inj	3We 40DCF	3We 40DCF
Gearbox	5 & RvRa	5 & RvRa	5 & RvRa	5 & RvRa	5 & RvRa	5 & RvRa	5 & RvRa	5 & RvRa
Front Suspension	Ind Co	Ind Co	Ind Co	Ind Co	Ind Co	Ind Co	Ind Co	Ind Co
Rear Suspension	Ind Co	Ind Co	Ind Co	Ind Co	Ind Co	Ind Co	Ind Co	Ind Co
Brakes	Dis	Dis	Dis	Dis	Dis	Dis	Dis	Dis
Wheels	A1	A1	A1	A1	A1	A1	A1	A1
F. Tread	1488	1547	1550	1518	1425	1377	1425	1425
R. Tread	1450	1582	1561	1511	1420	1412	1430	1430
Wheelbase	2400	2400	2400	2400	2220	2340	2340	2340

TYPE	156/I/63	206/SP	1512/64/F1	330/GT 2+2	330/P3	330/P4
No of Cylinders	6V	6V	12 HO	V12	V12	V12
B/S	73 x 58.8	77 x 71	56 x 50.4 mm	77 x 71 mm	77 x 71 mm	77 x 71 mm
Cubic Capacity	1476	1985	1489	3967	3967	3967
Bhp	220	230	225	300	420	450
Rpm	11000	9000	9000	7500	8000	8000
Camshaft	TW	TW	TW	SI	TW	TW
Carburetters	Bo/FI	3WeTwCh	F/Inj	3WeCh40DCZ/6	Lucas FI	Lucas FI
Chassis	Mc	MT	MC	Tub.	MT/AS/FG	MT/AS/FG
Gearbox	5 & RvRa	5 & RvRa	6 & RvRa	4 & RvEn	5 & RvRa	5 & RvRa
Front Suspension	DW & Co	DW & Co	DW & Co	DW & Co	W & Co ARB	W & Co ARB
Rear Suspension	DW & Co	DW & Co	DW & Co	R & SELS & Co	W & Co ARB	W & Co ARB
Brakes	Dis	Dis	Du/Dis	Du/Dis	Girling/Dis	Girling/Dis
Wheels	A1	Wi	A1	Bo/wi	A1	A1
F. Tread	3' 8"	4' 0½"	3' 11¼"	4' 7"	4' 9.5"	4' 10.5"
R. Tread	3' 7⅝"	3' 11¼"	3' 11¼"	4' 6½"	4' 8.3"	4' 9.0"
Wheelbase	6' 4"	7' 7¾"	7' 6"	8' 6¼"	7' 10.5"	7' 9.5"

TYPE	Dino 206/S	275/GTS	275/GTB-4	330/GTC	166F/2
No of Cylinders	V6	V12	V12	V12	V6
B/S	86 x 57	77 x 58.8	77 x 58.8	77 x 71	86 x 46
Cubic Capacity	1987	3286	3286	3967	1596
Bhp	218	280	300	300	200
Rpm	9000	7500	8000	7000	10000
Camshaft	TW	SI	TW	SI	TW
Carburetters	3We40DCN2	3WeTwCh40DCL/6	6WeTwCh40DCH/17	3TwChWe40DCZ/6	Lucas FI
Chassis	MT/AS/FG	TLA	TLA	TLA	MM
Gearbox	5 & RvRa	5 & RvRa	5 & RvRa	5 & Rv	5 & RvRa
Front Suspension	W & Co ARB	DW & Co ARB	DW & Co ARB	DW & Co ARB	SiVa LW Co
Rear Suspension	W & Co ARB	DW & Co ARB	DW & Co ARB	DW & Co ARB	UL LW TRA Co
Brakes	Girling/Dis	Du/Dis	Du/Dis	Girling/Dis	Dis
Wheels	A1	Wi	A1	Wi	A1
F. Tread	4' 5.5"	4' 6.3"	4' 7.2"	4' 7.2"	4' 7.3"
R. Tread	4' 5.3"	4' 6.7"	4' 7.8"	4' 7.8"	4' 8.1"
Wheelbase	7' 5.8"	7' 10.5"	7' 10.4"	7' 10.4"	7' 2.6"

EXPERIMENTAL AND SPECIAL FERRARIS

TYPE	375/I	375/MI	121/I	296/MI	412/MI	625/PT	553/F2	D50/555
No of Cylinders	12V	12V	6IL	6V	12V	4IL	4IL	8V
B/S	80 x 75.5	80 x 75.5	102 x 90	85 x 87	77 x 72	94 x 90	93 x 73.5	76 x 68.8
Cubic Capacity	4498	4498	4412	2962	4023	2490	1998	2489
B h p	430	430	380	316	447	200	190	250
R p m	7500	7500	6500	7800	7700	6500	7500	7000
Cb No	3	3	3	3	6	2	2	4
Cb Type	W/401F1/4C	W/401F1/4C	W/50DCOA3	W/42DCN	W/42DCN	W/50DCO	W/50DCO	SO/40PII
Ignition	1M	2M	2D	2D	2D	2M	2M	2M
P.P. Cylinder	2	2	2	2	2	2	2	2
Gears	5 & Rv	5 & Rv	2	4 & RV	4 & RV	4 & Rv	4 & Rv	5 & Rv
Front Suspension	WB & TLS	WB & TLS	L & TB	DW & Co	DW & Co	DW & TLS	DW & TLS	DW & Co
Rear Suspension	DD & TLS	DD & TLS	L & TB	DD & Co	DD & Co	DD & TLS	DD & TLS	DD & TLS
Frame	TL	TL & SS	MT	MT	TL & SS	TL	TL & SS	TL & SS
Wheelbase	7' 8"	7' 6"	8' 0"	7' 3¾"	7' 8"	7' 2"	6' 10"	7' 0"
F. Tread	4' 3½"	4' 2"	—	4' 0¾"	4' 2"	4' 3½"	4' 1½"	4' 1"
R. Tread	4' 3"	4' 0"	—	4' 0¾"	4' 0"	4' 1"	3' 11½"	3' 11½"

TYPE	250/246	246/RE	206/PT	212/FI	212/FI.DD	275/FI	340/FI	375/FI.SI
No of Cylinders	12V	6V	6V	12V	12V	12V	12V	12V
B/S	73 x 58.8	85 x 71	77 x 71	68 x 58.8	68 x 58.8	72 x 68	80 x 68	80 x 75.5
Cubic Capacity	2953	2417	1985	2560	2560	3322	4080	4498
B h p	300	290	225	170	200	260	310	330
R p m	7200	8300	8600	6500	7500	6500	6500	7000
Cb No	6	3	3	3	3	3	3	3
Cb Type	W/42DCN	W/42DCNW	W/42DCNW	W/36DCF	W40DCF	W/38DCF	W/38DCF	W/40DCF
Ignition	2D	1M	2M	2M	2M	2M	2M	2M
P.P. Cylinder	2	2	2	1	1	1	1	1
Gears	5 & Rv	4 & Rv	4 & Rv	5 & Rv	5 & Rv	5 & Rv	4 & Rv	4 & Rv
Front Suspension	DW & Co	DW & Co	DW & Co	DW & TLS	DW & TLS	DW & TLS	DW & TLS	DW & TLS
Rear Suspension	DD & Co	DW & Co	DD & TLS	SA & TLS	DD & TLS	SA & TLS	SS & TLS	DD & TLS
Frame	MT	MT	MT	TLA	TLA	TLA	TLA	TLA
Wheelbase	7' 3¾"	7' 7"	7' 3¾"	7' 10"	7' 8"	7' 8"	7' 6"	7' 6"
F. Tread	4' 0¾"	3' 11¾"	4' 0¾"	4' 2½"	4' 2"	4' 2½"	4' 2"	4' 2"
R. Tread	4' 0¾"	3' 11¾"	4' 0¾"	4' 0"	4' 0"	4' 0"	4' 0"	4' 0"

TYPE	375/FI.TI	115/F	116/F	700/N	250 Exp	500 Exp	625 Exp
No of Cylinders	12V	6IL	2IL	4IL	12V SC.	4IL	4IL
B/S	80 x 75.5	82.4 x 78	118 x 114	99 x 99	68 x 68	90 x 78	100 x 79.5
Cubic Capacity	4498	2495	2493	2771	2963	1984	2496
B h p	380	250	174	250	510	170	245
R p m	7000	6500	4800	6800	7000	7000	7500
Cb No	3	3	2	2	1	TW	TW
Cb Type	W/401F1/4C	W/46DCNW	W/42DCOD	W/50DCOA3	W/50WCF	2WeTwCh	2WeTwCh
Ignition	1M	2M	1M	2M	1M	TLA	TLA
P.P. Cylinder	2	2	2	2	2	5 & RvRa	5 & RvRa
Gears	4 & Rv					W & Co	W & TLS
Front Suspension	DW & TLS					DD & TLS	R & SEL
Rear Suspension	DD & TLS					Dr	Dr
Frame	TLA					Wi	Wi
Wheelbase	7' 6"					4' 3"	4' 3"
F. Tread	4' 2"					4' 3¼"	4' 3¼"
R. Tread	4' 0"					7' 6¾"	7' 6¾"

APPENDIX IX
FERRARI FIRST PLACES IN FORMULA 1 AND 2 EVENTS

BRITISH GRAND PRIX
1951 Gonzales
1952 Ascari
1953 Ascari
1954 Gonzales
1956 Fangio
1958 Collins
1961 Von Trips

RHEIMS
1950 Ascari
1953 Hawthorn
1956 Collins
1957 Musso
1958 Hawthorn
1959 Brooks
1961 Baghetti

ROUEN
1951 G. Marzotto
1952 Ascari
1953 Farina
1954 Trintignant

ZANDVOORT
1949 Villoresi
1952 Ascari
1953 Ascari
1961 Von Trips
1971 Ickx

NURBURGRING
1950 Ascari
1951 Ascari
1952 Ascari
1953 Farina
1956 Fangio
1963 Surtees
1972 Ickx

MONZA
1951 Ascari
1952 Ascari
1960 P. Hill
1961 P. Hill
1964 Surtees
1966 Scarfiotti
1970 Regazzoni

MONACO
1955 Trintignant

SWISS GRAND PRIX
1949 Ascari
1952 Taruffi
1953 Ascari

SPA
1952 Ascari
1953 Ascari
1956 Collins
1961 P. Hill
1966 Surtees

AUSTRIA
1970 Ickx

MONZA C.I. MEETING
1949 Fangio
1950 Villoresi
1951 Ascari
1952 Farina

SYRACUSE
1951 Villoresi
1952 Ascari
1954 Farina
1956 Fangio
1957 Collins
1961 Baghetti
1966 Surtees
1967 Scarfiotti and Parkes
(dead heat)

NAPLES
1949 Vallone
1950 Cortese
1951 Ascari
1952 Farina
1953 Farina
1957 Collins
1961 Baghetti

MODENA
1950 Ascari
1951 Ascari
1952 Villoresi

DAILY EXPRESS TROPHY
1949 Ascari
1951 Parnell
1953 Hawthorn
1954 Gonzales
1958 Collins

ULSTER TROPHY
1950 Whitehead
1952 Taruffi
1953 Hawthorn

PAU
1951 Villoresi
1952 Ascari
1953 Ascari

COUPE DES PETITES CYL.
1948 Sommer
1949 Ascari
1950 Ascari

BARCELONA
1950 Ascari
1954 Hawthorn

BARI
1948 Landi
1949 Ascari

CANADA
1970 Ickx

MEXICO
1970 Ickx

SOUTH AFRICA
1971 Andretti

QUESTOR USA
1971 Andretti

AUSTRIAN GRAND PRIX
1963 Bandini

ROME
1948 Cortese
1949 Villoresi
1950 Ascari
1951 Rafaelli

TURIN
1947 Sommer
1952 Villoresi

GARDA
1948 Farina
1949 Villoresi
1950 Ascari

PESCARA
1951 Gonzales

PARMA
1947 Nuvolari

FLORENCE
1948 Sommer

SAN REMO
1951 Ascari

PERGUSA
1962 Bandini
1963 Surtees

BRUSSELS
1949 Villoresi
1962 Mairesse

GRENZALANDRING
1960 Von Trips

ALBI
1952 Rosier
1953 Rosier

MONS
1950 Ascari

PARIS
1952 Taruffi

CADOURS
1952 Rosier

ROUBAIX
1950 Sommer

COMMINGES
1952 Ascari

MARSEILLE
1950 Villoresi
1951 Villoresi
1952 Ascari

AIX LES BAINS
1951 Fischer

LA BAULE
1952 Ascari

SABLES D'OLONNE
1952 Villoresi

ANGOULEME
1951 Fischer

LUXEMBOURG
1949 Villoresi

EIFELRENNEN
1952 Fischer

PRIX DE BERNE
1950 Sommer

MASARYK GRAND PRIX
1949 Whitehead

PIRIAPOLIS
(*Note:* Several South American Auto clubs organized two events in the same year on the same circuit this accounts for the same year being quoted twice.)
1952 Fangio
1952 Fangio

MAR DEL PLATA
1950 Ascari

ROSARIO
1949 Farina
1950 Villoresi

SAO PAULO
1952 Fangio

RIO DE JANEIRO
1952 Gonzales

BOA VISTA
1952 Fangio

BUENOS AIRES AND ARGENTINE
GRAND PRIX
1950 Ascari
1950 Villoresi
1951 Gonzales
1951 Gonzales
1952 Fangio
1952 Fangio

FERRARI TEAM DRIVERS

Allison, Cliff (Br.) 1959, 1960.
Amon, Chris (N.Z.) 1967, 1968 1969.
Andretti, Mario (U.S.A.) 1971, 1972.
Ascari, Alberto (It.) 1949, 1950, 1951, 1952, 1953, 1954.
Baghetti, Giancarlo (It.) 1962.
Bandini, Lorenzo (It.) 1962, 1963, 1964, 1965, 1966, 1967.
Bell, Derek (G.B.) 1968.
Bondurant, Bob (U.S.A.) 1965.
Behra, Jean (Fr.) 1959.
Bira. B. (Sia.) 1948.
Brambilla, Ernesto, 1968 (FII only)
Brooks, Tony (Br.) 1959.
Castellotti, Eugenio (It.) 1955, 1956, 1957.
Carini, Piero (It.) 1953.
Collins, Peter (Br.) 1956, 1957, 1958.
De Adamich, Andrea (It.) 1967, 1968.
De Portago, Alfonso (Sp.) 1956, 1957.
Fangio, Juan Manuel (Arg.) 1956.
Farina, Guiseppe (It.) 1948, 1952, 1953, 1954, 1955.
Frere, Paul (Bel.) 1955, 1956.
Galli, Nanni (It.) 1972
Gendebien, Olivier (Bel.) 1956, 1957, 1958, 1959, 1961.
Ginther, Richie (U.S.A.) 1960, 1961.
Giunti, Ignazio (It.) 1970.
Gonzales, Froilan (Arg.) 1951, 1954, 1955, 1957, 1960.
Gregory, Masten (U.S.A.) 1957.
Gurney, Dan (U.S.A.) 1959.
Hawthorn, Mike (Br.) 1953, 1954, 1955, 1957, 1958.
Hill, Phil (U.S.A.) 1958, 1959, 1960, 1961, 1962.
Ickx, Jacky (Bel.) 1968, 1970, 1971, 1972, 1973.
Lauda. Nicki (Austrian) 1974.
Maglioli, Umberto (It.) 1953, 1954, 1955.
Mairesse, Willy (Bel.) 1960, 1961, 1962, 1963.
Manzon, Robert (Fr.) 1954.
Merzario, Andrea (It.) 1972, 1973.
Musso, Luigi (It.) 1956, 1957, 1958.
Parkes, Mike (Br.) 1966, 1967.
Perdisa, Cesare (It.) 1957.
Pilette, Andre (Bel.) 1956.
Pola, Julio (Spa.) 1948.
Regazzoni, Gianclaudio 'Clay' (Switz.) 1970, 1971, 1972, 1974.
Rodriguez, Pedro (Mex.) 1965, 1969.
Rodriguez, Ricardo (Mex.) 1961, 1962.
Scarfiotti, Ludovico (It.) 1963, 1966, 1967.
Schell, Harry (Fr./U.S.A.) 1955.
Scotti, Piero (It.) 1952.
Serafini, Dorino (It.) 1950, 1951.
Simon, Andre (Fr.) 1952.
Sommer, Raymond (Fr.) 1952.
Surtees, John (Br.) 1963, 1964, 1965, 1966.
Taruffi, Piero (It.) 1950, 1951, 1952, 1955.
Trintignant, Maurice (Fr.) 1954, 1955, 1957.
Vaccarella, Nino (It.) 1965.
Vallone, Roberto (It.) 1950.
Villoresi, Luigi (It.) 1949, 1950, 1951, 1952, 1953.
Von Trips, Wolfgang (Ger.) 1956, 1957, 1958, 1959, 1960, 1961.
Williams, Johnathan (Br.) 1967.

Total Drivers

Italian	. . . .	21
British	. . . .	8
U.S.A.	. . . .	6
French	. . . .	5
Belgian	. . . .	5
Spanish	. . . .	2
Argentine	. . . .	2
German	. . . .	1
Mexican	. . . .	2
Austrian	. . . .	1
New Zealand	. . . .	1
Siamese	. . . .	1
Franco/U.S.A.	. . . .	1
Swiss	. . . .	1
	Total	57

The above list only includes Grand Prix drivers. Sports car drivers are not listed as many so-called team drivers were without written commitment and a number were in the position of being sponsored by the factory without actually being a member of the team. Bandini takes the honours for the longest service to Ferrari with seven years. Ascari and Von Trips take second honours with six years apiece although in each case there was one year in which the two drivers drove once only for the team. Ascari in 1954 while he was actually under contract to Lancia and Von Trips in 1959 after he had been released from his Porsche contract. Villoresi, Hawthorn, Farina, Gendebien, Gonzales and Phil Hill take third honours with five years apiece.

The shortest careers with the Ferrari team went to Stirling Moss, Lewis Evans, Perdisa, Pola and Masten Gregory.

Moss was contracted to drive the 2.5-litre at the Bari G.P., but only got as far as testing the car and blowing it up at a test in Modena, as a result of which there was a rapid parting of the ways. Lewis Evans tested a G.P. car at Modena and actually drove a sports car at Le Mans but broke off his contract before he drove in a G.P. for Ferrari. Masten Gregory drove a few laps in the G.P. of Buenos Aires before Peter Collins took over the car, Perdisa drove thirty-three laps in the Argentine G.P. before his car was taken over and Julio Pola drove three-quarters of the Spanish G.P. before his car blew up.

Ferrari has six world championships to his credit, two by Ascari and one each by Fangio, Hawthorn, Phil Hill and Surtees.

The largest number of G.P. wins by a Ferrari driver goes to Alberto Ascari with the tremendous total of 32, Villoresi and Collins take second place with nine wins each, third goes to Farina with eight, fourth to Gonzales with seven, fifth to Hawthorn with six, sixth to Fangio and Surtees with five, seventh to Trintignant and Taruffi with four, eighth to Phil Hill and Baghetti with three, ninth to Brooks, Von Trips, Bandini and Parkes with two, and tenth to Scarfiotti with one.

If only the Grand Epreuve victories are counted the picture alters somewhat. Ascari is still way out front with fourteen first places. Following him are Fangio, Collins, Hawthorn, Phil Hill and Surtees with three victories, Farina, Gonzales, Brooks and Von Trips with two each, and Taruffi, Baghetti, Trintignant, Bandini and Scarfiotti with one each. By nationality the above drivers have totalled the following number of G.P. wins: Italian sixty, British twenty-two, Argentine twelve.

APPENDIX XI A
FERRARI SPORTS CAR PERFORMANCE IN MANUFACTURERS SPORTS CAR CHAMPIONSHIP

1957

BUENOS AIRES

Gregory–Castellotti–Musso	1st	(290 single cam 3.5-litre) Scuderia Buell
De Portago–Collins–Castellotti	2nd	(290 twin cam 3.5-litre)
Collins–Hawthorn	—	Engine (290 twin cam 3.5-litre)
Castellotti–Musso	—	Ignition (290 twin cam 3.5-litre)

SEBRING

Gregory–Brero	4th	(290 single cam 3.5-litre) Scuderia Buell
Collins–Trintignant	6th	(315 twin cam 3.8-litre)
De Portago–Musso	7th	(315 twin cam 3.8-litre)
Hill–Von Trips	—	Battery (315 twin cam 3.8-litre)

MILLE MIGLIA

Taruffi	1st	(315 twin cam 3.8-litre)
Von Trips	2nd	(315 twin cam 3.8-litre)
Collins–Klementaski	—	Rear axle (315 twin cam 3.8-litre)
De Portago–Nelson	—	Fatal accident (412 twin cam 4.1-litre)

NURBURGRING

Collins–Gendebien	2nd	(412 twin cam 4.1-litre)
Hawthorn–Trintignant	3rd	(315 twin cam 3.8-litre)
Gregory–Morolli	10th	(290 single cam 3.5-litre) Scuderia Buell

LE MANS

Lewis Evans–Severi	5th	(290 experimental 3.5-litre)
Collins–Hill	—	Engine (412 twin cam 4.1-litre)
Hawthorn–Musso	—	Engine (412 twin cam 4.1-litre)
Gendebien–Trintignant	—	Engine (250 prototype 3.0-litre)

SWEDISH GRAND PRIX

Hill–Collins	2nd	(412 twin cam 4.1-litre)
Hawthorn–Musso	4th	(412 twin cam 4.1-litre)
Gendebien–Trintignant	—	Engine (315 twin cam 3.8-litre)
Gregory–Seidel	—	Gearbox (315 twin cam 3.8-litre) Scuderia Buell

VENEZUELA

Collins–Hill	1st	(412 twin cam 4.1-litre)
Musso–Hawthorn	2nd	(412 twin cam 4.1-litre)
Von Trips–Seidel	3rd	(250/TR 3-litre)
Trintignant–Gendebien	4th	(250/TR 3-litre)

1958

BUENOS AIRES

Collins–Hill	1st	(250/TR)
Musso–Gendebien	—	Crash (250/TR)
Von Trips–Gendebien	2nd	(250/TR)

SEBRING

Collins–Hill	1st	(250/TR)
Musso–Gendebien	2nd	(250/TR)
Hawthorn–Von Trips	—	Gearbox (250/TR)

TARGA FLORIO

Musso–Gendebien	1st	(250/TR)
Hawthorn–Von Trips	3rd	(250/TR)
Collins–Hill	4th	(250/TR)

NURBURGRING

Hawthorn–Collins	2nd	(250/TR)
Von Trips–Gendebien	3rd	(250/TR)
Musso–Hill	4th	(250/TR)
Seidel–Munaron	5th	(250/TR)

LE MANS

Gendebien–Hill	1st	(250/TR)
Hawthorn–Collins	—	Clutch (250/TR)
Von Trips–Seidel	—	Crash (250/TR)

1959

SEBRING

Hill–Gendebien–Gurney–Daigh	1st	(250/TR)
Behra–Allison	2nd	(250/TR)
Gendebien–Daigh	—	Differential (250/TR)

TARGA FLORIO

Behra–Brooks	—	(250/TR)
Gurney–Allison	—	Rear axle (250/TR special)
Gendebien–Hill	—	Rear axle (250/TR)
Scarlatti–Cabianca	—	(206 Dino V6 front engined)

NURBURGRING

Gendebien–Hill	2nd	(250/TR)
Brooks–Behra	3rd	(250/TR)
Gurney–Allison	5th	(250/TR)
Cabianca–Scarlatti	—	Engine (206 Dino V6 front engined)

LE MANS

Behra–Gurney	—	Transmission (250/TR)
Gendebien–Hill	—	Water leak (250/TR)
Allison–Da Silva Ramos	—	Gearbox (250/TR)
Cabianca–Scarlatti	—	Fuel feed (206 Dino V6 front engined)

TOURIST TROPHY

Gendebien–Hill–Brooks-Allison	3rd	(250/TR)
Brooks–Gurney	5th	(250/TR)
Hill–Allison	—	Engine (250/TR)
Scarlatti–Scarfiotti	—	Rear suspension (206 Dino V6 front engined)

1960

BUENOS AIRES

Hill–Allison	1st	(250/TR)
Ginther–Von Trips	2nd	(250/TR)
Scarfiotti–Gonzales	—	Ignition (246 Dino V6 2.5 front engined)

SEBRING

Daigh–Ginther	—	Engine (250/TR) NART
Rodriguez–Rodriguez	—	Clutch (206 Dino V6 front engined) NART

TARGA FLORIO

Hill–Von Trips	2nd	(246 Dino V6 2.5-litre independent front engine)
Scarfiotti–Cabianca–Mairesse	4th	(246 Dino V6 2.5-litre front engine)
Rodriguez–Rodriguez	7th	(206 Dino V6 2-litre front engine) NART
Allison–Hill	—	Crashed by Allison in practice (250/TR. IRS)
Scarfiotti–Cabianca	—	Crashed by Frere in practice (250/TR. IRS)
Von Trips–Ginther	—	(246 Dino independent)
Mairesse–Frere	—	(246 Dino live)

NURBURGRING

Allison–Mairesse–Hill	3rd	(250/TR. De Dion)
Von Trips–Hill	—	Engine (250/TR. IRS)
Scarlatti–Cabianca	—	Fire at pits (246 Dino front engine)
Rodriguez–Rodriguez	—	Engine (206 Dino front engine) NART

LE MANS

Gendebien–Frere	1st	(250/TR. De Dion)
R. Rodriguez–Pilette	2nd	(250/TR. De Dion) NART
Von Trips–Hill	—	Out of fuel (250/TR. De Dion)
Scarlatti–P. Rodriguez	—	Out of fuel (250/TR. IRS)
Mairesse–Ginther	—	Gearbox (250/TR. IRS)

1961

SEBRING

Hill—Gendebien	1st	(250/TR61)
Baghetti—Mairesse—Ginther—Von Trips	2nd	(250/TR61)
Rodriguez—Rodriguez	3rd	(250/TR60) NART
Ginther—Von Trips	—	Steering (246/SP V6 rear engine)

TARGA FLORIO

Von Trips—Gendebien	1st	(246/SP V6 rear engine)
Hill—Ginther	—	Crash (246/SP rear engine)
R. Rodriguez—Mairesse	—	Broken tank (250/TR61)

NURBURGRING

Rodriguez—Rodriguez	2nd	(250/TR61)
Von Trips—Hill	3rd	(246/SP V6 rear engine)
Ginther—Gendebien—Von Trips	—	(246/SP V6 rear engine)

LE MANS

Hill—Gendebien	1st	(250/TR61)
Mairesse—Parks	2nd	(250/TR61)
Ginther—Von Trips	—	Out of fuel (246/SP V6 rear engine)
Baghetti—Tavano	—	Engine (250/TR/GT experimental)

PESCARA

Bandini—Scarlatti	1st	(250/TR61) Centro Sud
Ginther—Baghetti	—	(246/SP V6 rear engine)

1962

SEBRING

Bonnier—Bianchi	1st	(250/TR) S.S.R.V.
Rodriguez—Rodriguez	—	Engine (246/SP V6) NART
Grossmann—Connell	—	Oil pressure NART
Moss—Ireland	—	(250/TR) disqualified

TARGA FLORIO

Gendebien—Rodriguez—Mairesse	1st	(246/SP V6 rear engine)
Baghetti—Bandini	2nd	(206/SP V6 rear engine)
Hill—Gendebien	—	(248 V8 experimental) crash P

NURBURGRING

LE MANS

Hill—Gendebien	1st	(330/P V12 4-litre)
Baghetti—Scarfiotti	—	(268 V8) transmission
Rodriguez—Rodriguez	—	Transmission (250/TR)
Parkes—Bandini	—	Overheating (330/GT 4-litre coupe)

NURBURGRING

Hill—Gendebien	1st	(246/SP V6 rear engine)
Mairesse—Parkes	2nd	(330/GT V12 4-litre coupe)
Rodriguez—Rodriguez	—	(206/SP V6 2-litre rear engine)

1963

SEBRING

Surtees—Scarfiotti	1st	(250/P)
Mairesse—Vacarella	2nd	(250/P)
P. Rodriguez—G. Hill	3rd	(4-litre V12 front engined)
Parkes—Bandini	—	(4-litre coupe prototype)
Fulp—Buck	—	(248 V8 cylinder)

TARGA FLORIO

Bandini—Scarfiotti—Mairesse	2nd	(2-litre V6 rear engined)
Scarfiotti—Mairesse	—	Fuel pump (250/P)
Parkes—Surtees	—	Crash (250/P)
Lualdi—Bini	—	(2-litre V6 rear engined private entry)

NURBURGRING

Surtees—Mairesse	1st	(250/P)
Scarfiotti—Parkes	—	Crash (250/P)
Vaccarella Bandin.	—	Crash in practice (250/P)

LE MANS

Scarfiotti—Bandini	1st	(250/P)
Surtees—Mairesse	—	Fire (250/P)
Rodriguez—Penske	—	Engine (4-litre front engined NART)

1964

SEBRING

Parkes—Maglioli	1st	
Scarfiotti—Vaccarella	2nd	
Surtees—Bandini	3rd	
Rodriguez—Piper—Gammino	7th	GT
Grossmann—Thompson	15th	GT
Perkins—Eve	27th	GT
Heuer—Yenko—Cantrel	28th	GT

TARGA FLORIO

Ferlaino—Taramazzo	5th	GT
Norinder—Troberg	9th	GT
Bourillot—Bourbon Parma	10th	GT
Nicolosi—Zanardelli	12th	GT
Taormina—Tacci	13th	GT
Facetti—Guichet	—	Transmission
Terra—Toppetti	—	
"Ulisse"—Fortinbras	—	

NURBURGRING 1000 Km

Scarfiotti—Vaccarella	1st	
Parkes—Guichet	2nd	GT
Bianchi—Van Ophem	4th	GT
Piper—Maggs	7th	GT
Van Lysbeth—Gosselin	18th	GT
Ramminger—Schander	20th	GT
Koppchen—Bitter	26th	GT
Clarke—Margulies	28th	GT
Maglioli—Rindt	39th	Crash P classified
Surtees—Bandini	46th	Lost wheel P classified
Norinder—Amon	—	GT
"Beurlys"—Dumay	—	Suspension
G. Hill—Ireland	—	Disqualified

LE MANS

Guichet—Vaccarella	1st	
Bonnier—G. Hill	2nd	
Bandini—Surtees	3rd	
"Beurlys"—Bianchi	5th	GT
Ireland—Maggs	6th	GT
Grossmann—Tavano	9th	GT
Dumay—Langlois	16th	P
Piper—Rindt	—	Oil leak
Hudson—Rodriguez	—	Head gasket
Parkes—Scarfiotti	—	Oil pressure
Baghetti—Maglioli	—	Crash
Hugus—Rosinki	—	Transmission

1965

DAYTONA

Clark—Hurt	7th	GTO

SEBRING

Piper—Maggs	3rd	LM
Maglioli—Baghetti	8th	275 P
Hansgen—Donohue	11th	LM
O'Brien—Hugus—Richards	12th	275 P
Mairesse—Bianchi	23rd	275 P
Grossmann—Hudson	34th	330 P
G. Hill—Rodriguez	37th	275 P clutch, not running but classified
Lund—Clark—Scott	—	Clutch GTO
Fulp—McCluskey	—	Transmission 330 P

TARGA FLORIO

Bandini—Vaccarella	1st	275 P2
Taramazzo—Sigala	8th	LM
Ravetto—Starabba	12th	GTO
Nicodemi—Lessona	14th	LM
"Ulisse"—Marchesi	29th	GTO
Bourillot—Bourbon Parma	—	Crash GTO
Scarfiotti—Parkes	—	Crash 275 P2

Guichet–Baghetti	—	Short circuit 275 P2
Blonin–Sauer	—	Over time limit GTO
Biscaldi–Deserti	—	Over time limit GTB
Casoni–DeAdamich	—	Over time limit LM
Tagliavia–Semilia	—	Over time limit 2000SP

NURBURGRING 1000 Km

Surtees–Scarfiotti	1st	275 P2
Parkes–Guichet	2nd	275 P2
Bandini–Vaccarella	4th	Dino 206
Biscaldi–Baghetti	13th	LM
Sutcliffe–Lumsden	15th	GT
Piper–Maggs	16th	LM
Etmuller–Harper	22nd	LM
Lindermann–Ramminger	23rd	GT
Von Kothen–Kronenberg	30th	GT
Clarke–Fielding	—	Connecting rod GT
Gosselin–Dumay	—	Engine LM
G. Hill–Stewart	—	Short circuit
Langlois–Boulanger	—	Crash
Salmon–Kerrison	—	Engine
Mairesse–"Beurlys"	—	Engine

LE MANS

Gregory–Rindt	1st	250 LM NART entry
Dumay–Gosselin	2nd	250 LM
Mairesse–"Beurlys"	3rd	275 GTB
Rodriguez–Vaccarella	7th	365 P2
Bianchi–Salmon	—	Gearbox
Bonnier–Piper	—	Exhaust manifold
Langlois–"Elde"	—	Clutch
Bandini–Biscaldi	—	Valve
Surtees–Scarfiotti	—	Gearbox
Parkes–Guichet	—	Gearbox

1966
DAYTONA

Rodriguez–Andretti	4th	(365 P)
Rindt–Bondurant	9th	(250 LM)
Clarke–Konig–Hart	13th	(250 LM)
Piper–Attwood	15th	(250 LM)
Follmer–Wester	—	Generator (250 LM)
Epstein–Hawkins	—	Gearbox (250 LM)
Bianchi–Langlois–"Beurlys"	—	Piston (365 P2/3).
Fulp–Jennings	—	Wheel bearing (330 P)
Ireland–Hailwood–Drummond	—	Transmission (250 LM)
"Elde"–Ickx–"Beurlys"	—	Transmission (250 LM)
Wilson–Hulme	—	Transmission (250 LM)

SEBRING

Bandini–Scarfiotti	5th	(Dino 206)
Rodriguez–Andretti	—	Crash and fire (330 P2/3)
Parkes–Bondurant	—	Transmission (330 P3)
Slottag–Perkins	—	Crash (GTO)
Swanson–Ennis	—	Head gasket (250 LM)

MONZA 1000 Km

Surtees–Parkes	1st	(330 P3)
De Siebenthal–Peixinho	8th	(250 LM)
Bandini–Scarfiotti	10th	(Dino 206S)
Attwood–Piper	13th	(Dino 206S)
Pessina–Botalla	19th	(275 GTB)

SPA 1000 Km

Parkes–Scarfiotti	1st	(330 P3)
Attwood–Guichet	6th	(Dino 206S)
Epstein–Hawkins	7th	(250 LM)
Gosselin–De Keyn	8th	(250 LM)

TARGA FLORIO

Guichet–Baghetti	2nd	(Dino 206S)
Biscaldi–Casoni	14th	(Dino 206)
Vaccarella–Bandini	—	Crash (330 P3)

NURBURGRING 1000 Km

Scarfiotti–Bandini	2nd	(Dino 206S)
Rodriguez–Ginther	3rd	(Dino 206S)
Mairesse–Muller	9th	(330 P2/3)
Surtees–Parkes	—	Damper and clutch (330 P3)

LE MANS

Pike–Courage	8th	(275 GTB)
Noblet–Dubois	10th	(275 GTB)
Kolb–Follmer	—	Clutch (Dino 206)
Salmon–Hobbs	—	Final drive (Dino 206)
Vaccarella–Casoni	—	Water leak
Attwood–Piper	—	Engine
Parkes–Scarfiotti	—	Crash (330 P3)
Gregory–Bondurant	—	Gearbox
Mairesse–Muller	—	Gearbox

1967
DAYTONA

Bandini–Amon	1st	(330 P4)
Scarfiotti–Parkes	2nd	(330 P4)
Rodriguez–Guichet	3rd	(330 P3/4) NART

MONZA 1000 Km

Bandini–Amon	1st	(330 P4)
Parkes–Scarfiotti	2nd	(330 P4)
Vaccarella–Muller	4th	(330 P3/4) Scuderia Filipinetti
Siebenthal–Finiguerro	12th	(275 LM)
Gaspar–Vestey	14th	(GTB) 1st in class
Rodriguez–Guichet	—	Crash (330 P3/4) NART
Williams–Klass	—	Overheating (Dino 206)
Casoni–"Shangryla"	—	Crash (Dino 206)
Ravetto–Starabba	—	Engine (Dino 206)
Walter–Ditzler	—	Rear suspension (LM)
Zwimpfer–Sudan	—	(GTB)
Biscaldi–Pianta	—	Crash (Dino 206)
"Pam"–Lualdi	—	Not classified (Dino 206)
Bungerer–Blouin	—	Not classified (GTB/4)

SPA 1000 Km

Attwood–Bianchi	3rd	(330 P3/4) Maranello Conc
Parkes–Scarfiotti	5th	(330 P4)
Mairesse–"Beurlys"	—	Crash (330 P3/4) ENB

1968
DAYTONA

Ortega–Merello–Gunn	8th	275LM (No 34)
Kolb–Rodriguez	—	Dino (No 80), Cracked Head
Gregory–Piper	—	275LM (No 81), Crash.
Vesteley–Pike–Ridgeway	—	275LM (No 12), Roadholding

SEBRING

Gunn–Ortega–Merello	—	275LM (No 39), Clutch

BRANDS HATCH 500 MILES

Rodriguez–Pierpoint	5th	275LM
Vesteley–Pike	15th	275LM

WATKINS GLEN 6 Hr

Kolb–Rodriguez	7th	Dino, 1st in class
Grossmann–Bucknum	9th	GTB/4

NURBURGRING 1000 Km

Skailes–Liddell	—	250LM (No 63), Oil Pressure
Christofferson–Wangstre	—	Dino (No 30), Fire in carb

TARGA FLORIO
    Christofferson—
    Wangstre   22nd Dino (No 206)
MONZA 1000 Km
    Vesteley—Ridgeway   20th 275LM
LE MANS
    Piper—Attwood   7th 275LM (No 21)
    Chevalier—Ligier   —   Dino No 36), Oil
    Rey—Haldi   —   GTB/4 (No 17), Suspension
    Vesteley—Pike   —   275LM (No 19), Gearbox
    Gregory—Kolb   —   275LM (No 14), Crash
    Muller—Williams   —   275LM (No 2), Bearings

NOTE
Ferraris neither set fastest lap or won a race during the 1968 season.

1969
DAYTONA 24 Hrs
    Posey—Rodriguez   23rd (GTB)
    Merello—Maglioli   —   (275 LM), Transmission
    Biscaldi—Kolb   —   (Dino), Head gasket
SEBRING 12 Hrs
    Amon—Andretti   2nd (312P), 1st in class
    Rodriguez—Kolb   9th (Dino)
    Rodriguez—Parsons   —   Gearshift
ADAC 100 Km
    Amon—Rodriguez   —   (312P), Electrical system
    Wangstre—Christofferson   —   (Dino) engine
    Walton—de Cardenet   —   (Dino), differential
LE MANS 24 Hrs
    Zeccoli—R. Rodriguez   8th (250 LM)
    Amon—Schetty   —   (312 P), crash
    Rey—Haldi   —   (275 GTB), disqualified
    P. Rodriguez—Piper   —   (312 P), gearbox
BOAC 500
    Amon—Rodriguez   4th (312 P)
MONZA 1000 Km
    Amon—Andretti   —   (312 P), engine
    Rodriguez—Schetty   —   (312 P), crash
SPA 1000 Km
    Rodriguez—Piper   2nd (312 P)
    Rey—Berney   14th (275 GTB)

1970
DAYTONA 24 Hrs
    Andretti—Merzario—Ickx   3rd (512S) SEFAC
    Posey—Perkins   4th (312 P) NART
    Adamowicz—Piper   5th (312 P) NART
    Young—Chinetti Jr   7th (275 LM) NART
    Giunti—Vaccarella   —   Crash (512S) SEFAC
    Ickx—Schetty   —   Crash (512S) SEFAC
    Manfredini—Moretti   —   Crash (512S) Squadra P. Rosso
    Gurney—Parsons   —   Crash (512S) NART
    Bucknum—Pickett   —   Cooling (365 GTB) NART
    Cluxtum—Tatum   —   Cooling (GTB/4)
SEBRING 12 Hrs
    Giunti—Vaccarella—
    Andretti   1st (512S) SEFAC
    Parkes—Parsons   6th (312 P) NART
    Andretti—Merzario   —   Gearbox (512S) SEFAC
    Ickx—Schetty   —   Engine (512S) SEFAC
    Posey—Bucknum   —   (512S) NART
    Adamowicz—Chinetti Jr   —   (312 P) NART
BOAC 1000 Km
    Amon—Merzario   5th (512S) SEFAC
    Ickx—Oliver   8th (512S) SEFAC
    Parkes—Muller   13th (512S) Filipinetti
    Williams—Loos   —   (512S) Non starter
MONZA 1000 Km
    Giunti—Vaccarella   2nd (512S) SEFAC

Surtees—Schetty   3rd (512S) SEFAC
Amon—Merzario   4th (512S) SEFAC
Parkes—Muller   8th (512S) Filipinetti
Moretti—Manfredini   9th (512S) Squadra P. Rosso
SPA 1000 Km
    Ickx—Surtees   2nd (512S) SEFAC
    Giunti—Vaccarella   4th (512S) SEFAC
    Merzario—Schetty   7th (512S) SEFAC
    de Fierlant—Bell   8th (512S) Ecurie Francorchamps
ADAC 1000 Km
    Surtees—Vaccarella   3rd (512S) SEFAC
    Muller—Parkes   4th (512S) Filipinetti
    Giunti—Merzario   —   Fuel injection (512S) SEFAC
TARGA FLORIO
    Vaccarella—Giunti   3rd (512S) SEFAC
    Muller—Parkes   —   Crash (512S) Filipinetti
LE MANS 24 Hrs
    Posey—Bucknum   4th (512S) NART
    de Fierlant—Walker   5th (512S) ENB
    Adamowicz—Piper   10th (312 P) NART Not classified.
    Ickx—Schetty   —   Crash (512S) SEFAC
    Vaccarella—Giunti   —   Con rod (512S) SEFAC
    Regazzoni—Merzario   —   Crash (512S) SEFAC
    Bell—Peterson   —   Crash (512S) SEFAC
    Parkes—Muller   —   Crash (512S) Filipinetti
    Bonnier—Wisell   —   Crash (512S) Filipinetti
    Manfredini—Moretti   —   Gearbox (512S) Filipinetti
    Kellner—Loos   —   Handling (512S) NART
    Juncadella—Fernandez   —   Gearbox (512S) Escuderia Montjuich
WATKINS GLEN
    Andretti—Giunti   3rd (512S) SEFAC
    Ickx—Schetty   5th (512S) SEFAC
AUSTRIAN 1000 Km
    Loos—Pesch   7th (512S)
    Ickx—Giunti   —   Alternator (512M) SEFAC

1971
DAYTONA 24 Hrs
    Donohue—Hobbs   3rd (512M) Penske
    Chinetti Jr—Veiga   4th (312 P) modified NART
    Posey—Revson   —   (512M) Black flagged NART
    Young—Gregory   —   (512M) Con Rod, Young American
    Bucknum—Adamowicz   —   (512S) NART
    de Fierlant—Gosselin   —   (512S) Ecurie Francorchamps
    Juncadella—Merzario   —   (512S) Escuderia Montjuich
SEBRING 12 Hrs
    Donohue—Hobbs   6th (512M) Penske
    Chinetti Jr—Eaton   8th (312 P) Modified NART
    Grossmann—Chinetti Jr 12th GTB4
    Revson—Savage   —   (512M) NART, Transmission
    Bucknum—Posey   —   (512S) NART, Wheel and engine
    Parsons—Weir   —   (512S) Radiator
    Young—Gregory   —   (512M/S) Crash, Young American
    Ickx—Andretti   —   (312 P) SEFAC, Transmission
ADAC 1000 Km
    Loos—Pesch   9th (512M)
    Muller—Herzog   —   (512M) Crash, H. Muller Racing
    Wiesendanger—Kocher   —   (512S) Fuel pressure
    Ickx—Regazzoni   —   (312 P) SEFAC Engine
LE MANS 24 Hr
    Chinetti Jr—Grossman   5th (365GTB) Daytona
    Loos—Pesch   —   (512M) Piston
    Juncadella—Vaccarella   —   (512M) Clutch, Escuderia Montjuich
    Manfredini—Gagliardi   —   (512M) Gearbox
    de Fierlant—de Cardenet —   (512M) Gearbox, Ecurie Francorchamps
    Parkes—Pescarolo—
    Westbury   —   (512M) Crash, Filipinetti
    Donohue—Hobbs   —   (512M) Penske
    Posey—Adamowicz   —   (512M) NART

Gregory—Eaton	—	(512M)
Craft—Weir	—	(512M)

BUENOS AIRES 1000 Km

Juncadella—Pairetti	5th	(512S) Escuderia Montjuich
de Fierlant—Gosselin	6th	(512S) Ecurie Francochamps
Parkes—Bonnier	7th	(512M) Filipinetti
Posey—Veiga—di Palma	8th	(512S) NART
Guinti—Merzario	—	(312 P) SEFAC, Fatal crash

BOAC 1000

Ickx—Regazzoni	2nd	(312P) SEFAC
Muller—Herzog	4th	(512S/M) H. Muller Racing
Juncadella—Hobbs	5th	(512S/M)

MONZA 1000 Km

Muller—Herzog	6th	(512S/M) H. Muller Racing
Zeccoli—Moretti	8th	(512S/M) H. Muller Racing
Ickx—Regazzoni	—	(312 P) SEFAC, Crash
Juncadella—Merzario	—	(512M) Crash, Escuderia Montjuich
Manfredini—Gagliardi	—	(512M) Filipinetti
Parkes—Bonnier	—	(512S) Filipinetti, Engine

SPA 1000 Km

Ickx—Regazzoni	8th	(312 P) SEFAC, DNF crash
Manfredini—Gagliardi	13th	(512M) Filipinetti DNF con rod
Muller—Herzog	15th	(512M) H. Muller Racing, DNF con rod
Wiesendanger—Kocher	—	(512S) H. Muller Racing, DN Start

AUSTRIAN 1000 Km

Pasotti—Casoni	4th	(512S) Scuderia Brescia Corse
Ickx—Regazzoni	—	(312 P) SEFAC, Crash
Muller—Herzog	—	(512S) H. Muller Racing, Suspension
Gregory	—	(512M) H. Muller Racing, Non Start
Juncadella—Soler Roig	—	(512S) Escuderia Montjuicch Crash

WATKINS GLEN 6 Hr

de Cardenet— Montschenbacher	4th	(512M) Ecurie Francorchamps
Donohue—Hobbs	—	(512M) Penske, Steering
Ickx—Andretti	—	(312 P) SEFAC, Starter
Bucknum—Posey	—	(512M) Withdrawn NART
Muller—Eaton	—	(512M) H. Muller Rading, Crash
Young—Adamas	—	(512S)

1972

BUENOS AIRES 1000 Km

Peterson—Schenken	1st	(312P 082)
Regazzoni—Redman	2nd	(312P 086)
Ickx—Andretti	3rd	(312P 082)

DAYTONA 6 Hrs

Ickx—Andretti	1st	(312P 088)
Regazzoni—Redman	2nd	(312P 090)
Peterson—Schenken	4th	(312P 092)
Eaton—Chinetti Jr	—	(312P) NART V12, Holed Tank

SEBRING 12 Hrs

Ickx—Andretti	1st	(312P 082)
Peterson—Schenken	2nd	(312P 086)
Grossman—Chinetti Jr	8th	(GTB 4) Daytona NART
Regazzoni—Redman	—	(312P 084), Fire

BOAC 1000

Ickx—Andretti	1st	(312P 088)
Peterson—Schenken	2nd	(312P 089)
Regazzoni—Redman	5th	(312P 089)

MONZA 1000 Km

Ickx—Regazzoni	1st	(312P)
Peterson—Schenken	3rd	(312P)
Redman—Merzario	—	(312P) Crash

TARGA FLORIO

Merzario—Munari	1st	(312P 0884)

SPA 1000 Km

Redman—Merzario	1st	(312P 089)
Ickx—Regazzoni	2nd	(312P 088)
Peterson—Schenken	12th	(312P 090), Not Running

NURBURGRING 1000 Km

Peterson—Schenken	1st	(312P)
Redman—Merzario	2nd	(312P)
Ickx—Regazzoni	—	(312P), Crash

LE MANS 24 Hr

Ballot Lena—Andruet	5th	Daytona 1st Class Pozzi
Posey—Adamowicz	6th	Daytona NART

Parkes—Lafosse	7th	Daytona Filipinetti
Bell—Pilette	8th	Daytona Ecurie Francorchamps
Buchet—Jarrier	9th	Daytona NART
Laffeach—Doncieux	17th	(246 Dino) NART
Westbury—Hine		Engine Daytona Maranello Concessionaires

AUSTRIAN 1000 Km

Ickx—Redman	1st	(312P 096)
Pace—Marko	2nd	(312P)
Peterson—Schenken	3rd	(312P 0894)
Merzario—Munari	4th	(312P 0884)

WATKINS GLEN

Ickx—Andretti	1st	(312P)
Peterson—Schenken	2nd	(312P)
Jarrier—Young	6th	Daytona
Redman—Merzario	14th	(312P), Non Finisher
Posey—Hobbs	16th	Daytona, Non Finisher

1973

VALLELUNGA 6 HRS

Reutemann/ Schenken	2nd	312P
Ickx/Redman	3rd	312P
Pace/Merzario	4th	312P

DIJON 1000 KM

Ickz/Redman	2nd	312P
Merzario/ Pace	4th	312P

MONZA 1000 KM

Ickx/Redman	1st	312P
Reutemann/ Shenken	2nd	312P
Merzario/Pace	—	312P Gearbox

SPA 1000 KM

Pace/Merzario	4th	312P
Ickx/Redman	—	312P oil pipe

TARGA FLORIO

Merzario/ Vaccarella		312P Crash
Ickx/Redman		312P Crash

NURBURGRING 1000 KM

Ickx/Redman	1st	312P
Merzario/Pace	2nd	312P

AUSTRIAN 1000 KM

Ickx/Redman	3rd	312P
Pace/Merzario	6th	312P

LE MANS 24 HRS

Merzario/Pace	2nd	312P
Elford/ Ballot-Lena	6th	Daytona Pozzi (Class winner)
Dolhem/ Serpaggi	9th	Daytona Pozzi
Migault/ L.Chinetti Jr.	13th	Daytona
Andruet/ Bond	20th	Daytona Ecurie Francorchamps
Ickx/Redman	—	312P Engine
Reuteman/ Schenken	—	312P Engine
Garcia Veiga/ di Palma	—	Daytona NART
Posey/ Minter	—	Daytona NART
Grossman/ Guitteny	—	Daytona
Green/Corner	—	Daytona JCB Excavators

WATKINS GLEN 6 HRS

Ickx/Redman	2nd	312P
Pace/ Merzario	3rd	312P
Monaguzzi/ Garcia Veiga	13th	Daytona
Posey/ Migault	14th	Daytona
Grossman/ Yenko	15th	Daytona
Reuteman/ Schenken	—	312P Fuel pump

FERRARI SPORTS CAR PERFORMANCE

Fastest laps and race averages set by Ferrari sports cars

(R) Fastest lap in race   (RA) Race average by winning car

1956

BUENOS AIRES
(R) Collins. 3 min 26.4 secs (102.52 m p h).
SEBRING
(RA) Fangio—Castellotti. 194 laps.
MILLI MIGLIA
(RA) Castellotti. 11 hr 37 min 10 secs (85.40 m p h).
NURBURGRING
(R) Fangio. 10 min 5.3 secs (84.25 m p h).
SWEDISH GRAND PRIX
(R) Collins. 2 hr 26 min 2 secs (100.15 m p h).
(RA) Trintignant—Hill. 153 laps 6 hr 33 min 47.7 secs
(94.69 m p h).

1957

BUENOS AIRES
(RA) Gregory—Castellotti—Musso. 98 laps 6 hr 10 min 29.9 secs
(100.766 m p h).
MILLE MIGLIA
(RA) Taruffi. 10 hr 27 min 47 secs (94.84 m p h).
LE MANS
(R) Musso. 3 min 58.7 secs (126.2 m p h).
VENEZUELA
(RA) Collins—Hill. 101 laps 6 hr 31 min 55.4 secs (95.55 m p h).

1958

BUENOS AIRES
(R) Hill. 3 min 25.9 secs (102.937 m p h).
(RA) Hill—Collins. 6 hr 19 min 55.4 secs (98.568 m p h).
SEBRING
(RA) Hill—Collins. 200 laps (86.67 m p h).
TARGA FLORIO
(RA) Musso—Gendebien. 10 hr 37 min 58.1 secs (64.36 m p h).
LE MANS
(R) Hawthorn. 4 min 8 secs (121.3 m p h).
(RA) Hill-Gendebien (106.12 m p h).

1959

SEBRING
(R) Allison. 3 min 21.6 secs (92.85 m p h).
(RA) Hill—Gendebien—Gurney—Daigh. 188 laps (81.35 m p h).
LE MANS
(R) Behra. 4 min 0.9 secs (124.82 m p h).
TOURIST TROPHY
(R) Brooks. 1 min 31.8 secs (93.46 m p h).

1960

BUENOS AIRES
(RA) Hill—Gendebien. 106 laps 6 hr 17 min 12.1 secs (99.3 m p h).
LE MANS
(RA) Gendebien—Frere (109.2 m p h).

1961

SEBRING
(RA) Hill—Gendebien. 1,080.5 miles (90.412 m p h).
TARGA FLORIO
(R) Von Trips. 40 min 3 secs (76.015 m p h).
(RA) Gendebien—Von Trips. 6hr 57 min 39 secs (64.272 m p h).
NURBURGRING
(R) Hill. 9 min 15.8 secs (91.290 m p h).
LE MANS
(RA) Hill—Gendebien. 2,781.7 miles (115.904 m p h).
PESCARA
(R) Ginther. 9 min 55.5 secs (96.107 m p h).
(RA) Bandini—Scarlatti. 572.9 kil (88.995 m p h).

1962

TARGA FLORIO
(R) Mairesse. 40 min 0.3 secs (67.062 m p h).
NURBURGRING
(RA) Hill—Gendebien. 44 laps (82.39 m p h).

1964

SEBRING
(R) Surtees. 3 min 06.2 secs (100.54 m p h).
(RA) Parkes—Maglioli. 1,112.8 miles (92.36 m p h).
NURBURGRING 1000 Km
(R) Surtees. 9 min 09.0 secs (92.95 m p h).
(RA) Scarfiotti—Vaccarella. 44 laps (86.99 m p h).
LE MANS
(RA) Guichet—Vaccarella. 2,917.7 miles (121.6 m p h).

1965

DAYTONA
(R) Hansgen. 2 min 01.8 sec
TARGA FLORIO
(R) Vaccarella. 39 min 21.0 secs (68.22 m p h).
(RA) Bandini—Vaccarella. 7 hr 1 min 12.2 secs
NURBURGRING 1000 Km
(RA) Surtees—Scarfiotti. 6 hr 53 min 05.4 secs

1966

MONZA 1000 Km
(R) Surtees. 3 min 26.7 sec (109.24 m p h).
(RA) Surtees—Parkes 6 hr 5 min 11.6 secs (103.11 m p h).
SPA 1000 Km
(R) Parkes. 3 min 46.4 secs (145.52 m p h).
(RA) Parkes—Scarfiotti. 4 hr 43 min 24.0 secs (131.69 m p h).

1967

DAYTONA BEACH
(RA) Bandini—Amon. 666 laps, 2,537 miles (105.703 m p h).
MONZA 1000 Km
(RA) Bandini—Amon. 5 hr 7 min 43.0 secs (122.278 m p h).
(R) Bandini 2 min 55.8 secs (128.422 m p h).

1969

SEBRING 12 Hr
(R) Amon. 2 min 41.88 secs (115.64 m p h).

1970

OSTERREICHRING
(R) Ickx. 1 min 40.0 secs (132.24 m p h).
KYALAMI 9 Hr (Non Championship)
(RA) Ickx—Giunti. 370 laps, 9 hr 43 min 5 secs (104.833 m p h).

1971

24 Hr DAYTONA
(R) Donohue—Hobbs. 1 min 41.25 secs
ADAC 1000 Km
(R) Ickx. 7 min 40.8 secs (110.852 m p h).

1972

1000 Km BUENOS AIRES
(RA) Peterson—Schenken. 5 hr 45 min 58.22 secs (108.05 m p h).
DAYTONA
(RA) Ickx—Andretti. 6 hr 1 min 36.4 secs (115.81 m p h).
SEBRING
(RA) Ickx—Andretti. 12 hr 4 min 40 sec (111.47 m p h).
BOAC 1000
(RA) Ickx—Regazzoni. 5 hr 55 min 27.5 secs (104.95 m p h).
MONZA 1000
(RA) Ickx—Regazzoni. 5 hr 52 min 05.6 secs (109.608 m p h).
TARGA FLORIO
(RA) Merzario—Munari. 6 hr 27 min 48.0 secs (76.05 m p h).
SPA 1000
(RA) Redman—Merzario. 4 hr 17 min 19.1 secs (145.00 m p h).
ADAC 1000
(RA) Peterson—Schenken. 6 hr 1 min 40.2 secs (103.3 m p h).
AUSTRIAN 1000
(RA) Ickx—Redman. 4 hr 58 min 46.28 secs (125.44 m p h).
WATKINS GLEN 6 Hr
(RA) Ickx—Andretti. 6 hr 1 min 11.27 secs (109.39 m p h).
IMOLA 500 (Non Championship)
(R) Merzario. 1 min 40.2 secs (116.12 m p h).
(RA) Merzario. 1 hr 7 min 56.2 secs (112.09 m p h).

FERRARI SPORTS CAR PERFORMANCE
Placings in Manufacturers World Championship

1957
FERRARI	30
Maserati	25
Jaguar	17
Aston Martin	8
Porsche	7
OSCA	1

1958
FERRARI	38
Porsche	19
Aston Martin	18
Lotus	3
OSCA	2

1959
Aston Martin	24
FERRARI	22
Porsche	21
Maserati	2

1960
FERARRI	30
Porsche	26
Maserati	11
Aston Martin	4

1961
FERRARI	30
Maserati	16
Porsche	13
OSCA	1

1962*
FERRARI	45
Jaguar	16
Chevrolet	9
Lancia	4
Aston Martin	1

*After 1961 the style of sports car Manufacturers' Championship changed. For 1962 through to 1964 a GT car championship was substituted although prototype cars often ran. For those three years Ferrari came out on top at the end of the year, often winning handsomely.
For 1965 through to 1973 there were individual yearly championships, always of marques, which catered for 'prototype' cars which may, in some years, have been defined as sports cars. They may have varied from 3 to 7 litres.
1965 was won by Ferrari, 1966 by Ford while Porsche won each year from 1967 through to 1971. 1972 was the next Ferrari year but 1973 went to Matra.

FERRARI IN THE EUROPEAN HILLCLIMB CHAMPIONSHIP

1965

TRENTO-BONDONE
Scarfiotti	1st	Dino V6 2 litre

CESANA-SESTRIERE
Scarfiotti	1st	Dino V6 2 litre

FREIBURG-SCHAUINSLAND
Scarfiotti	1st	Dino V6 2 litre

OLLON-VILLARS
Scarfiotti	1st	Dino V6 2 litre

GAISBERG
Scarfiotti	5th	Dino V6 2 litre

1965 European Hillclimb Championship
Scarfiotti Ferrari Dino V6	1st	38 points
Mitter Porsche	2nd	33 points
Herrmann Abarth	3rd	23 points

1969

MONTSENY
Schetty	1st Type 212 E Flat 12

ROSSFELD
Schetty	1st 212 E

MONT VENTOUX
Schetty	1st 212 E

TRENTO-BONDONE
Schetty	1st 212 E

FREIBURG-SCHAUINSLAND
Schetty	1st 212 E

CESANA-SESTRIERE
Schetty	1st 212 E
Codonex	2nd V6 Dino

OLLON-VILLARS
Schetty	1st 212 E

1969 European Hillclimb Championship
Schetty	Ferrari Type 212 E	1st 56 points
Merzario	Abarth	2nd 38 points
Weber	Alfa Romeo	3rd 21 points

APPENDIX XII A

ENZO FERRARI'S PERSONAL RACING RECORD

1919 Parma Poggio di Berceto 4th (C.M.N.).
    Targa Florio 9th (C.M.N.).
1920 Targa Florio 2nd (Alfa Romeo).
    Aosta Grand St. Bernard 1st (Alfa Romeo).
1921 Mugello 2nd (Alfa Romeo).
1923 Savio 1st (Alfa Romeo).
1924 Pozzo Circuit 2nd (Alfa Romeo).

    Pescara 1st (Alfa Romeo).
    Gargano 1st (Alfa Romeo).
    Savio 1st (Alfa Romeo).
    Polesine 1st (Alfa Romeo).
1927 Modena 1st (Alfa Romeo).
1928 Modena 1st (Alfa Romeo).
1929 Pozzo circuit 5th (Alfa Romeo).
    Mugello 8th (Alfa Romeo).
1930 Alessandria 3rd (Alfa Romeo).
1931 Montenero 2nd (Talbot).
    Pescara 2nd (Talbot).

APPENDIX XII B

MOTORCYCLE SUCCESSES BY SCUDERIA FERRARI
1933

ALESSANDRIA

Aldrighetti	1st	500 cc Rudge.
Pigorini	1st	350 cc Class Rudge.
Aldrighetti	2nd	250 cc Class Rudge.

CARATE

Aldrighetti	1st	500 cc Class Rudge.

MODENA

Aldrighetti	2nd	500 cc Class Rudge.
Pigorini	1st	350 cc Class Rudge.

STRADELLA

Aldrighetti	1st	500 cc Class Rudge.
Pigorini	3rd	500 cc Class Rudge.

TORINO

Aldrighetti	1st	500 cc Class Rudge.
Fagnani	3rd	500 cc Class Rudge.
Aldrighetti	1st	250 cc Class Rudge.

BIELLA—GRAGLIA

Aldrighetti	—	Retired.
Fagnani	—	Retired.

LIVORNO

Aldrighetti	2nd	500 cc Class Rudge.
Lama	2nd	250 cc Class Rudge.

RIMINI

Aldrighetti	1st	500 cc Class Rudge.
Fagnani	3rd	500 cc Class Rudge.

ACERBO

Aldrighetti	1st	500 cc Class Rudge.
Lama	3rd	350 cc Class Rudge.

FOGGIA

Aldrighetti	1st	500 cc Class Rudge.

ROMA (Velocita)

Pigorini	1st	500 cc Class Rudge.
Lama	1st	250 cc Class Rudge.

ROMA (Campionato)

Pigorini	2nd	350 cc Class Rudge.

Scuderia/Ferrari Motor Cycle Team

Enzo Ferrari formed his motorcycle team in 1932 and raced for two years, after which the team was disbanded. He chose the British Rudge over several available Italian machines and the team raced in the 500, 350, and 250 cc categories. His riders were Giordano Aldrighetti, Carlo Baschieri, Giuseppe Fagnani, Aldo Pigorini, Francesco Lama, Piero Taruffi, and Guglielmo Sandri.

Of the riders, I only came into contact with three of them. At the time of my residence in Modena, Carlo Baschieri was the local Alfa Romeo dealer. I saw him quite frequently and in fact at one time I was involved with him and ex Alfa Romeo dealer 158 driver Francesco Severi, in an attempt to buy the Scuderia Marzotto Grand Prix and sports racing Ferraris.

Guglielmo Sandri I met through Hans Ruesch, the ex-Alfa Romeo driver. Sandri was living in Bologna and running a general hardware store. He was full of memories of his motorcycle days.

Piero Taruffi I naturally knew from my Ferrari racing days, and only a month ago I had dinner with him and his wife at Rene Dreyfus' Chanteclair restaurant in New York. We spoke about his motorcycle days, but I must confess we spent more time discussing the fantastic 4-cylinder Rondine motorcycle which was the predecessor of the 4-cylinder Gilera and with which Taruffi set world records.

Giordano Aldrighetti was the star of the Scuderia Ferrari Motorcycle Team. Part of Ferrari's reasoning was that he would, through motorcycle racing, develop new automobile racing drivers. Aldrighetti accordingly turned to 4 wheels and made his debut at Livorno in 1934. In 1939, Aldrighetti gave up motorcycle racing completely and joined the Alfa Romeo team racing at Tripoli and Livorno. In practice for the Coppa Acerbo at Pescara, his car caught fire and he died from his injuries.

In 1932 Aldrighetti won at Alessandria, Pontedera, Faenza in both 250 and 350, the Coppa del Mare, Circuito Tre Monti, Avellino, and in the International 6 Day Trial, he won the Gold Medal with a 175 cc Bianchi. Aldrighetti's closest friend was Aldo Pigorini, who with the Scuderia Ferrari 350 Rudge, became Champion of Italy for that class in 1939. Pigorini was killed in 1937 at the Circuit of Rome riding a Guzzi.

(Top) Pesaro 1932. Left to right: Fagioli, Taruffi (on bike), and Enzo
Ferrari
(Middle) Coppa del Mare 1932. Scuderia Ferrari, Aldrighetti (20),
Pigorini (56), Nazzaro (26) and Colobattisti (12)
(Bottom Left) Minister Leonardi, head of the Royal Italian Motorcycle
Association congratulates Pigorini, the winner for the Scuderia Ferrari
of the 350-cc class of the Coppa del Mare
(Bottom Right) Coppa del Mare 1932, Aldrighetti (20), Pigorini (56)

BARACCA

Enzo Ferrari, in his memories *Le Mie Gioie Terribili*, states The story of the Prancing Horse is simple and fascinating. The "Cavallino" was the badge used on the fighter plane of Francesco Baracca, the Italian ace of aces and World War I hero who was killed at Montello.

When I was competing at the first Circuit of Savio near Ravenna in 1923 I made the acquaintance of Count Enrico Baracca. From this resulted my acquaintance with the mother, Countess Paolina.

She was the one who said to me "Ferrari, put the prancing horse of my son on your cars. It will bring you luck." I still have a photo of Baracca dedicated by the parents and giving the emblem into my keeping. The "Cavallino" was and remains black. I added the canary yellow background as this is the colour of Modena."

While the story of Enzo Ferrari is well known, that of Francesco Baracca has faded with time, nevertheless it deserves retelling in conjunction with the history of Ferrari.

Francesco Baracca was born at Lugo di Romagna near Ravenna on May 9th 1888. He was the son of a family that had been farming in that region for generations.

He reveived part of his education at the Liceo Dante in Florence and at that institution he determined to attend the Military Academy in Modena.

This was a move that was very unpopular with his parents and friends as there was a wave of anti-militarism sweeping through the country at the time.

Nevertheless he enrolled in the Scuola Militare at Modena in October 1907 and graduated with honors as a sub lieutenant of the Cavalry in 1909.

He continued his cavalry training until he heard of an opportunity to join the fascinating new field of flying and volunteered for aviation training in 1912. He was immediately sent to Rheims, in France, which at that time was the most famous flying school in Europe. There, in a 35 hp Hanriot, he learned to fly and in July 1912 received his pilot's license No. 1037. Baracca flew extensively in Italy and became an advanced instructor. He was a member of the panel of judges for the Military Aircraft Competition at Mirafiore in 1913. More and more he became convinced that Italy would be involved in War so he took every opportunity to fly any new type of aircraft available. When Italy finally declared war on Austria in May 1915, the declaration found Baracca in Paris on a military mission testing the latest French Nieuports, Moranes and Voisins.

He immediately returned to Italy and joined a Squadron flying Nieuports purchased from France and was posted in the Udine region to cover the Austro-Italian border.

Baracca's first encounter with the Austrians happened on September 7th 1915 when he engaged an enemy two seater but repeated stoppages of his machine gun forced him to give up the fight.

Three more times he failed to get his victims because of troubles with machine guns and it was not until the following year 1916, when his squadron was re-equipped with the Type eleven Nieuport that Baracca claimed his first victory. This he achieved on the night of April 17th and, typical of the chivalry of the time, he landed near to his victim, shook his hand and made certain that he was properly escorted to prison camp.

On May 14th another victory followed but his score remained low as he was involved in a series of daring attacks on enemy ground installations.

On August 23rd 1916, his list of victories increased once more but machine gun problems still dogged him and it was not until November 25th 1916 that he scored his fifth victory. On this occasion he was honored by a special investiture and was given the unofficial right to call himself a Knight of the air and as such entitled to put his crest the Cavallino Rampante on the fuselage of his Nieuport.

1917 was a great year for Baracca. He began New Year's Day by shooting down an Albatros. On February 11th he shot down another in the presence of King Vittorio Emmanuele who congratulated Baracca in person, awarded his a silver medal and a considerable sum of money and promoted him to Captain on the spot.

Baracca donated the money to the Red Cross. After his 8th victory on April 26th he was awarded the Cross of Officer of the Military Order of Savoia with the citation: A pilot of exceptional merit, already decorated three times with the "Medaglia al Valore Militare," consistently directing all his efforts to the successful prosecution of the war in the air.

Part of the 70a Squadriglia was formed into the 91a Squadriglia with Baracca leading the first flight newly equipped with Spad S 7s. With the Spad more victories followed quickly and Baracca was given command of the 91a and based at Istrana.

On October 21st he scored his first double, shooting down two two-seater Austrian aircraft in one day, a feat that he was destined to repeat several times. However, German pilots were backing up the Austrians and the opposition stiffened, Baracca himself being badly shot up and losing two of his squadron pilots in one day. The following day after this disaster he determined to avenge the situation and proceeded to shoot down two German Aviatiks before making a forced landing with a bullet hole in his fuel tank.

The Spad 7s were replaced by Spad 13s about the time of the disastrous Italian retreat from Caporetto and Baracca's Squadriglia found themselves up against the Austrian Ace Capt. Brumowski.

Baracca took time out from the front to test the new Ansaldo fighters but was never destined to use the Italian products in combat.

After returning to battle, a special investiture was held for him in the presence of the kings and queens of Italy and Belgium where he was awarded a high Belgian decoration. This was followed by an investiture in the famous La Scala Opera House where he received Italy's highest military honor, the Medagila d'Oro al Valore Militare.

His score of victories increased steadily through May and June of 1918 and on June 19th at 18.30 hours the 91a Squadriglia sent a patrol to Montello. Baracca led the flight out for the urgent job of ground support and began strafing the enemy lines. The Austrians returned heavy fire and Baracca's two companions lost sight of their leader.

There was no sign of him despite a long search by his companions and it was not until the Austrian ground troops retreated that the wreckage of Baracca's Spad was found with the body of Italy's Ace of Aces nearby with a bullet hole in his forehead.

Francesco Baracca remained undefeated in aerial combat his career having been ended by a lucky shot from the ground.

Francesco Baracca. Note the prancing horse emblem on the side of his Spad

SOME FERRARI LAP TIME COMPARISONS

RHEIMS

1949	Peter Whitehead	(125 V12)	2.46.2
1951	Alberto Ascari	(375 V12)	2.28.1
1952	Alberto Ascari	(375 V12)	2.26.2
1954	Froilan Gonzales	(555 IL4)	2.34.3
1956	Peter Collins	(D50 V8)	2.23.3
1958	Mike Hawthorn	(246D V6)	2.21.7
1959	Tony Brooks	(256D V6)	2.19.4
1960	Phil Hill	(256D V6)	2.18.2
1961	Phil Hill	(156 V6)	2.24.9
1963	John Surtees	(156/63 V6)	2.21.9
1966	Lorenzo Bandini	(V12)	2.07.8

NURBURGRING

1951	Alberto Ascari	(500 IL4)	9.55.8
1954	Mike Hawthorn	(625 IL4)	9.53.3
1956	Juan Fangio	(D50 V8)	9.51.2
1957	Mike Hawthorn	(801 V8)	9.14.0
1961	Phil Hill	(156 V6)	8.55.2
1962	Ricardo Rodriguez	(156 V6)	9.14.2
1963	John Surtees	(156/63 V6)	8.47.0
1964	John Surtees	(V8)	8.38.4
1965	John Surtees	(Flat 12)	8.27.8
1966	Lodovico Scarfiotti	(2.4 V6)	8.20.2
1967	Chris Amon	(V12)	8.20.4

MONZA

1951	Alberto Ascari	(375 V12)	1.55.1
1952	Alberto Ascari	(500 4IL)	2.05.7
1954	Alberto Ascari	(625 4IL)	1.59.2
1957	Peter Collins	(801 V8)	1.45.3
1958	Mike Hawthorn	(246D V6)	1.41.8
1959	Tony Brooks	(256D V6)	1.39.8
1960*	Phil Hill	(246D V6)	2.41.4
1961*	Von Trips	(156 V6)	2.46.3
1962	Willy Mairesse	(156 V6)	1.42.8
1963	John Surtees	(156 V6)	1.37.3
1964	John Surtees	(V8)	1.37.4
1965	John Surtees	(Flat 12)	1.36.1
1966	Mike Parkes	(V12)	1.31.3
1967	Chris Amon	(V12)	1.29.3

* Combined Road and Banked circuits.

SPA-FRANCORCHAMPS

1951	Luigi Villoresi		
1952	Alberto Ascari		
1954	Friolan Gonzales		
1956	Juan Fangio	(D50 V8)	4.09.8
1958	Mike Hawthorn	(246 V6)	3.57.1
1960	Phil Hill	(246D V6)	3.53.3
1961	Phil Hill	(156 V6)	3.59.3
1962	Phil Hill	(156 V6)	3.59.6
1963	John Surtees	(156 V6FI)	3.57.9
1964	John Surtees	(V8)	3.55.2
1965	John Surtees	(V8)	3.49.5
1965	Lorenzo Bandini	(Flat 12)	3.54.0
1966	John Surtees	(V12)	3.38.0
1966	Lorenzo Bandini	(2.4 V6)	3.43.8
1967	Chris Amon	(V12)	3.34.3

SILVERSTONE

1949	Alberto Ascari	(125 V12)	1.56.0
1951	Froilan Gonzales	(375 V12)	1.43.4
1952	Giuseppe Farina	(500 4IL)	1.50.0
1954	Froilan Gonzales	(555 4IL)	1.50.0
1956	Juan Fangio	(D50M V8)	1.42.0
1958	Mike Hawthorn	(246D V6)	1.40.4
1960	Von Trips	(246D V6)	1.37.0
1962†	John Surtees	(156 V6)	1.36.2
1963*	John Surtees	(156/63 V6)	1.35.2
1965	John Surtees	(V8)	1.31.3

ZANDVOORT

1951	Rudolf Fischer	(212 V12)	1.55.4
1952	Alberto Ascari	(500 4IL)	1.46.5
1958	Mike Hawthorn	(246D V6)	1.39.1
1959	Jean Behra	(256D V6)	1.36.6
1960	Richie Ginther	(246D V6)	1.36.3
1961	Phil Hill	(156 V6)	1.35.7
1962	Phil Hill	(156 V6)	1.35.0
1963	John Surtees	(156/63 V6)	1.33.0
1964	John Surtees	(V8)	1.32.8
1966	Mike Parkes	(V12)	1.29.0
1967	Chris Amon	(V12)	1.26.9

MONACO

1956	Juan Fangio	(D50M V8)	1.42.5
1957	Eugenio Castelotti	(801 V8)	1.44.2
1958	Mike Hawthorn	(246D V6)	1.42.6
1960	Von Trips	(246D V6)	1.39.2
1961	Richie Ginther	(156 V6)	1.39.3
1962	Willy Mairesse	(156 V6)	1.36.4
1963	John Surtees	(156 V6)	1.34.5
1964	John Surtees	(V8)	1.34.5
1965	Lorenzo Bandini	(Flat 12)	1.33.0
1965	John Surtees	(V8)	1.33.2
1966	John Surtees	(V12)	1.30.1
1966	Lorenzo Bandini	(2.4 V6)	1.30.5
1967	Lorenzo Bandini	(V12)	1.28.3

BERNE-BREMGARTEN

1949	Alberto Ascari	(125 V12)	2.54.7
1951	Luigi Villoresi	(375 V12)	2.39.3
1952	Guiseppe Farina	(500 4IL)	2.47.5
1954	Froilan Gonzales	(625 4IL)	2.39.5

ARGENTINA

1956	Juan Fangio	(D50M V8)	1.42.5
1957	Eugenio Castelotti	(801 V8)	1.44.2
1958	Mike Hawthorn	(246D V6)	1.42.6
1960	Von Trips	(246D V6)	1.39.2

U.S. GRAND PRIX WATKINS GLEN

1964	John Surtees	(V8)	1.12.7
1965	Lorenzo Bandini	(Flat 12)	1.11.7
1965	Bob Bondurant	(V8)	1.12.9
1966	Lorenzo Bandini	(V12)	1.08.6
1967	Chris Amon	(V12)	1.06.6

† Daily Express Trophy meeting.
*British Grand Prix.

SOUTH AFRICA (Kyalami)

1968	Andrea de Adamich	(3 Lit V12)	1.23.6
1969	Chris Amon	(3 Lit V12)	1.20.5
1970	Jacky Ickx	(312/B)	1.10.0

1971	Clay Regazzoni	(312/B)	1.18.2
1972	Clay Regazzoni	(312/B2)	1.17.3
1973	Jacky Ickx	(312/B2)	1.17.16

MONACO

1969	Chris Amon	(3 Lit V12)	1.25.0
1970	Jacky Ickx	(312/B)	1.25.5
1971	Jacky Ickx	(312/b)	1.24.4
1972	Jacky Ickx	(312/B2)	1.21.6
1973	Jacky Ickx	(312/B3)	1.28.7

BRITISH SILVERSTONE

1969	Chris Amon	(3 Lit V12)	1.21.9
1971	Clay Regazzoni	(312/B)	1.18.1
1973	Jacky Ickx	(312/B3)	1.18.9

BRITISH (BRANDS HATCH)

1970	Jacky Ickx	(312/B)	1.25.1
1972	Jacky Ickx	(312/B2)	1.22.2

GERMAN (NURBURGRING)

1968	Jacky Ickx	(3 Lit V12)	9.04.0
1971	Jacky Ickx	(312/B)	7.19.2
1972	Jacky Ickx	(312/B2)	7.07.0

GERMAN (HOCKENHEIM)

1970	Jacky Ickx	(312/B)	1.59.5

ITALIAN (MONZA)

1968	Chris Amon	(3 Lit V12)	1.26.21
1969	Pedro Rodriguez	(3 Lit V12)	1.28.47
1970	Jacky Ickx	(312/B)	1.24.14
1971	Jacky Ickx	(312/B)	1.22.82
1972	Jacky Ickx	(312/B2)	1.35.63
1973	Andrea Merzario	(312/B3)	1.36.37

BELGIAN (SPA)

1968	Chris Amon	(3 Lit V12)	3.28.6
1970	Jacky Ickx	(312/B)	3.30.7

BELGIAN (NIVELLES)

1972	Clay Regazzoni	(312/B2)	1.11.58

BELGIAN (ZOLDER)

1973	Jacky Ickx	(312/B3)	1.23.10

U.S.A. WATKINS GLEN

1968	Chris Amon	(3 Lit V12)	1.04.37
1969	Pedro Rodrigues	(3 Lit V12)	1.05.94
1970	Jacky Ickx	(312/B)	1.03.07
1971	Clay Regazzoni	(312/B2)	1.43.00
1971	Jacky Ickx	312/B	1.43.84
1972	Clay Regazzoni	(312/B2)	1.41.95
1973	Andrea Merzario	(312/B3)	1.41.45

MEXICO

1968	Chris Amon	(3 Lit V12)	1.45.62
1969	Pedro Rodrigues	(3 Lit V12)	1.49.46
1970	Clay Regazzoni	(312/B)	1.41.86

DUTCH (ZANDVOORT)

1968	Chris Amon	(3 Lit V12)	1.23.54
1969	Chris Amon	(3 Lit V12)	1.22.69
1970	Jacky Ickx	(312/B)	1.18.93
1970	Jacky Ickx	(312/B)	1.17.42

AUSTRIA (ZELTWEG)

1970	Clay Regazzoni	(312/B)	1.39.7
1971	Clay Regazzoni	(312/B)	1.37.9
1972	Clay Regazzoni	(312/B2)	1.36.04
1973	Andrea Merzario	(312/B3)	1.36.42

ARGENTINE

1972	Clay Regazzoni	(312/B2)	1.13.28
1973	Jacky Ickx	(312/B2)	1.11.01

FRANCE (ROUEN)

1968	Jacky Ickx	(3 Lit V12)	1.57.7

FRANCE (CLERMONT)

1969	Chris Amon	(3 Lit V12)	3.04.2
1970	Jacky Ickx	(312/B)	2.58.2
1972	Jacky Ickx	(312/B2)	2.55.1

FRANCE (PAUL RICARD)

1971	Clay Regazzoni	(312/B)	1.51.53
1973	Andrea Merzario	(312/B3)	1.51.17

SPAIN (BARCELONA)

1968	Chris Amon	(3 Lit V12)	1.27.9
1969	Chris Amon	(3 Lit V12)	1.26.2
1971	Jacky Ickx	(312/B)	1.25.9
1973	Jacky Ickx	(312/B3)	1.23.5

SPAIN (JARAMA)

1970	Jacky Ickx	(312/B)	1.24.7
1972	Jacky Ickx	(312/B2)	1.18.43

CANADA (MONT TREMBLANT)

1968	Chris Amon	(3 Lit V12)	1.33.8
1970	Jacky Ickx	(312/B)	1.31.6

CANADA (MOSPORT)

1969	Pedro Rodrigues	(3 Lit V12)	1.20.5
1971	Jacky Ickx	(312/B2)	1.16.5
1972	Clay Regazzoni	(312/B2)	1.14.5

SWEDEN (ANDERSTORP)

1973	Jacky Ickx	(312/B3)	1.25.60

BRAZIL (INTERLAGOS)

1973	Jacky Ickx	(312/B2)	2.32.0

FASTEST LAPS BY FERRARI DRIVERS IN WORLD CHAMPIONSHIP EVENTS

1956

ARGENTINA
Fangio 1.42.5
Castellotti 1.44.7
Musso 1.44.7
Collins 1.47.7
Gendebien . . . 1.50.4

MONACO
Fangio 1.44.0
Castellotti 1.44.9
Musso 1.46.8

SPA
Fangio 4.09.8
Collins 4.15.3
Castellotti 4.16.7
Frere 4.32.8
Pilette 4.51.9

RHEIMS
Collins 2.23.3
Castellotti 2.24.6
Fangio 2.24.9
De Portago . . . 2.32.8
Gendebien . . . 2.34.5

SILVERSTONE
Fangio 1.42
Collins 1.43
Castellotti 1.44
De Portago . . . 1.47

NURBURGRING
Fangio 9.51.2
Collins 9.51.5
Castellotti 9.54.4
Musso 10.20.3
De Portago . . . 10.37.1

1957

ARGENTINA
Castellotti 1.44.2
Collins 1.44.6
Musso 1.44.8
Hawthorn 1.44.8
De Portago . . . 1.46.8

ROUEN
Musso 2.22.7
Collins 2.23.3
Hawthorn 2.25.6
Trintignant . . . 2.25.9

AINTREE
Hawthorn 2.01.2
Collins 2.01.8
Musso 2.03.4
Trintignant . . . 2.03.2

NURBURGRING
Hawthorn 9.28.4
Collins 9.34.7
Musso 9.43.1

PESCARA
Musso 10.00.0

MONZA
Collins 1.45.3
Von Trips 1.45.5
Musso 1.45.7
Hawthorn 1.46.1

1958

ARGENTINA
Collins 1.42.6
Hawthorn 1.42.6

Musso 1.42.9

MONACO
Hawthorn 1.41.5
Collins 1.42.4
Musso 1.42.6
Von Trips 1.44.3

ZANDVOORT
Hawthorn 1.39.1
Collins 1.39.3
Musso 1.39.5

SPA
Hawthorn 3.57.1
Musso 3.57.5
Collins 3.57.7
Gendebien . . . 3.59.3

RHEIMS
Hawthorn 2.21.7
Musso 2.22.4
Collins 2.23.3

SILVERSTONE
Hawthorn 1.40.4
Collins 1.40.6
Von Trips 1.42.0

NURBURGRING
Hawthorn 9.14.0
Collins 9.21.9
Von Trips 9.24.7
P. Hill 9.48.9
(F2 car)

OPORTO
Hawthorn 2.34.2
Von Trips 2.37.0

MONZA
Hawthorn 1.41.8
Gendebien . . . 1.42.5
Von Trips 1.42.6
P. Hill 1.42.7

CASABLANCA
Hawthorn 2.23.1
P. Hill 2.24.1
Gendebien . . . 2.24.3

1959

MONACO
Behra 1.40.0
Brooks 1.41.0
P. Hill 1.41.3
Allison 1.44.4
(F2 car)

ZANDVOORT
Behra 1.36.6
Brooks 1.37.9
P. Hill 1.39.2

RHEIMS
Brooks 2.19.4
P. Hill 2.19.8
Behra 2.20.2
Gendebien . . . 2.21.5
Gurney 2.21.9

AVUS
Brooks 2.05.9
Gurney 2.07.2
P. Hill 2.07.6
Allison 2.05.8

LISBON
P. Hill 2.08.0
Gurney 2.08.0

Brooks 2.11.0

MONZA
Brooks 1.39.8
P. Hill 1.41.2
Gurney 1.40.8
Gendebien . . . 1.41.4
Allison 1.41.8

SEBRING
Brooks 3.05.9
Von Trips 3.06.2
Allison 3.06.8
P. Hill 3.07.2

1960

ARGENTINA
Von Trips 1.39.2
P. Hill 1.39.3
Allison 1.39.7
Gonzales 1.41.0

MONACO
Von Trips 1.38.3
Ginther 1.38.6
P. Hill 1.38.6

ZANDVOORT
Ginther 1.36.3
P. Hill 1.36.4
Von Trips 1.36.7

SPA
P. Hill 3.53.3
Von Trips 3.57.8
Mairesse 3.58.9

RHEIMS
P. Hill 2.18.2
Mairesse 2.19.3
Von Trips 2.19.4

SILVERSTONE
P. Hill 1.37.8
Von Trips 1.37.0

MONZA
Mairesse 1.42.8
R. Rodriguez . . . 1.43.1
Bandini 1.44.3
Baghetti 1.44.4
P. Hill 1.43.4

OPORTO
Von Trips 2.28.4
P. Hill 2.28.4

MONZA
P. Hill 2.41.4
Ginther 2.43.3
Mairesse 2.43.9
Von Trips 2.51.9
(F2 car)

1961

MONACO
Ginther 1.39.3
P. Hill 1.39.8
Von Trips 1.39.8

ZANDVOORT
P. Hill 1.35.7
Von Trips 1.35.7
Ginther 1.35.9

SPA
P. Hill 3.59.3
Von Trips 4.00.1
Gendebien . . . 4.03.0
Ginther 4.06.1

RHEIMS
P. Hill	. . . . .	2.24.9
Von Trips	. . . .	2.26.4
Ginther	. . . .	2.26.8
Baghetti	. . . .	2.30.5

AINTREE
P. Hill	. . . .	1.58.8
Ginther	. . . .	1.58.8
Von Trips	. . . .	1.58.8

NURBRGRING
P. Hill	. . . .	8.55.2
Von Trips	. . . .	9.05.5
Mairesse	. . . .	9.15.9

MONZA
Von Trips	. . . .	2.46.3
R. Rodriguez	. . . .	2.46.4
Ginther	. . . .	2.46.8
P. Hill	. . . .	2.47.2
Baghetti	. . . .	2.49.0

1962
ZANDVOORT
P. Hill	. . . .	1.35.0
R. Rodriguez	. . . .	1.36.1
Baghetti	. . . .	1.36.3

SPA
P. Hill	. . . .	3.59.6
Mairesse	. . . .	3.59.8
R. Rodriguez	. . . .	4.01.0
Baghetti	. . . .	4.08.0

AINTREE
P. Hill	. . . .	1.56.2

NURBURGRING
R. Rodriguez	. . . .	9.14.2
P. Hill	. . . .	2.24.7
Baghetti	. . . .	9.28.1
Bandini	. . . .	9.39.7

1963
MONACO
Surtees	. . . .	1.34.5
Mairesse	. . . .	1.35.9

SPA-FRANCORCHAMPS
Mairesse	. . . .	3.55.3
Surtees	. . . .	3.57.9

ZANDVOORT
Surtees	. . . .	1.33.0
Scarfiotti	. . . .	1.35.6

G.P. A.C.F. RHEIMS
Surtees	. . . .	2.21.9

BRITISH G.P. SILVERSTONE
Surtees	. . . .	1.35.2

GERMAN G.P. NURBURGRING
Surtees	. . . .	8.46.7
Mairesse	. . . .	9.03.5

ITALIAN G.P. MONZA
Surtees	. . . .	1.37.3
Bandini	. . . .	1.40.1

U.S.A. G.P. WATKINS GLEN
Surtees	. . . .	1.13.7
Bandini	. . . .	1.15.8

MEXICAN G.P.
Surtees	. . . .	2.00.5
Bandini	. . . .	2.02.4

S.A. G.P. EAST LONDON
Surtees	. . . .	1.29.8
Bandini	. . . .	1.30.2

1964
MONACO
Surtees	. . . .	1.34.5
Bandini	. . . .	1.35.5

DUTCH G.P.
Surtees	. . . .	1.32.8
Bandini	. . . .	1.35.0

BELGIAN G.P. SPA
Surtees	. . . .	3.55.2
Bandini	. . . .	3.58.8

G.P.A.C.F. ROUEN
Surtees	. . . .	2.11.1
Bandini	. . . .	2.12.8

BRITISH G.P. BRANDS HATCH
Surtees	. . . .	1.38.7
Bandini	. . . .	1.40.2

GERMAN G.P.
Surtees	. . . .	8.38.7
Bandini	. . . .	8.42.6

AUSTRIAN G.P. ZELTWEG
Surtees	. . . .	1.10.1
Bandini	. . . .	1.10.6

ITALIAN G.P.
Surtees	. . . .	1.37.4
Bandini	. . . .	1.39.8
Scarfiotti	. . . .	1.41.6

U.S.A. G.P. WATKINS GLEN
Surtees	. . . .	1.12.78
Bandini	. . . .	1.13.83

MEXICAN G.P.
Bandini	. . . .	1.58.60
Surtees	. . . .	1.58.70
Rodriguez	. . . .	2.00.90

1965
SOUTH AFRICA
Surtees	. . . .	1.28.1
Bandini	. . . .	1.29.3

MONACO
Bandini	. . . .	1.33.0
Surtees	. . . .	1.33.2

BELGIAN G.P.
Surtees	. . . .	3.49.5
Bandini	. . . .	3.54.0

G.P. A.C.F. CLERMONT FERRAND
Bandini	. . . .	3.19.1
Surtees	. . . .	3.19.1

BRITISH G.P. SILVERSTONE
Surtees	. . . .	1.31.3
Bandini	. . . .	1.33.1

DUTCH G.P.
Surtees	. . . .	1.31.0
Bandini	. . . .	1.33.1

GERMAN G.P.
Surtees	. . . .	8.27.8
Bandini	. . . .	8.33.8

ITALIAN G.P.
Surtees	. . . .	1.36.1
Bandini	. . . .	1.37.2
Vaccarella	. . . .	1.38.9

U.S.A. G.P. WATKINS GLEN
Bandini	. . . .	1.11.73
Bondurant	. . . .	1.12.90
Rodriguez	. . . .	1.13.00

MEXICAN G.P.
Bandini	. . . .	1.57.31
Scarfiotti	. . . .	1.58.93
Rodriguez	. . . .	1.59.06

1966
MONACO
Surtees	. . . .	1.30.1
Bandini	. . . .	1.30.5

ZANDVOORT
Parkes	. . . .	1.29.0
Bandini	. . . .	1.30.0

BELGIAN G.P.
Surtees	. . . .	3.38.0
Bandini	. . . .	3.43.8

GERMAN G.P.
Scarfiotti	. . . .	8.20.2
Bandini	. . . .	8.21.1
Parkes	. . . .	8.21.7

RHEIMS G.P. A.C.F.
Bandini	. . . .	2.07.8
Parkes	. . . .	2.09.1

ITALIAN G.P.
Parkes	. . . .	1.31.3
Scarfiotti	. . . .	1.31.3
Bandini	. . . .	1.32.0
Baghetti	. . . .	1.35.5

WATKINS GLEN
Bandini	. . . .	1.08.67

1967
MONACO
Bandini	. . . .	1.28.3
Amon	. . . .	1.30.7

DUTCH G.P.
Amon	. . . .	1.26.9
Parkes	. . . .	1.27.0
Scarfiotti	. . . .	1.27.9

BELGIAN G.P.
Amon	. . . .	3.34.9
Parkes	. . . .	3.36.6
Scarfiotti	. . . .	3.37.7

BRITISH G.P. SILVERSTONE
Amon	. . . .	1.26.9

A.C.F. G.P. LE MANS
Amon	. . . .	1.38.0

GERMAN G.P.
Amon	. . . .	8.20.4

CANADIAN G.P.
Amon	. . . .	1.23.3

ITALIAN G.P.
Amon	. . . .	1.29.3

U.S. G.P. WATKINS GLEN
Amon	. . . .	1.06.6

MEXICAN G.P.
Amon	. . . .	1.48.03

1968
SOUTH AFRICAN G.P.
De Adamich	. . . .	1.23.6
Amon	. . . .	1.23.8
Ickx	. . . .	1.24.9

SPANISH G.P.
Amon	. . . .	1.27.9
Ickx	. . . .	1.29.6

MONACO G.P
No Ferrari

BELGIAN G.P.
Amon	. . . .	3.28.6
Ickx	. . . .	3.34.3

DUTCH G.P.
Amon	. . . .	1.23.54
Ickx	. . . .	1.24.42

FRENCH G.P. ROUEN
Ickx 1.57.7
Amon 1.57.8
BRITISH G.P. BRANDS HATCH
Amon 1.29.5
Ickx 1.31.0
GERMAN G.P.
Ickx 9.04.0
Amon 9.14.9
ITALIAN G.P.
Amon 1.26.21
Ickx 1.26.41
Bell 1.26.90
CANADIAN G.P.
Amon 1.33.8
U.S.A. G.P.
Amon 1.04.37
Bell 1.07.06
MEXICAN G.P.
Amon 1.45.62
Ickx 1.49.24

1969
SOUTH AFRICAN G.P.
Amon 1.20.5
SPANISH G.P.
Amon 1.26.2
MONACO G.P.
Amon 1.25.0
DUTCH G.P.
Amon 1.22.69
FRENCH G.P. CHARADE
Amon 3.04.2
BRITISH G.P. SILVERSTONE
Amon 1.21.9
Rodriguez 1.22.6
GERMAN G.P.
No Ferraris
ITALIAN G.P.
Rodriguez 1.28.47
CANADIAN G.P.
Rodriguez 1.20.5
U.S.A. G.P.
Rodriguez 1.05.94
MEXICAN G.P.
Rodriguez 1.49.46

1970
SOUTH AFRICAN G.P.
Ickx 1.20.0
SPANISH G.P.
Ickx 1.24.7
MONACO G.P.
Ickx 1.25.5
BELGIAN G.P.
Ickx 3.30.7
Giunti 3.32.4
DUTCH G.P.
Ickx 1.18.93
Regazzoni 1.19.48
FRENCH G.P. CHARADE
Ickx 2.58.22
Giunti 3.01.85
BRITISH G.P. BRANDS HATCH
Ickx 1.25.1
Regazzoni 1.25.8
GERMAN G.P.
Ickx 1.59.5

Regazzoni 1.59.8
AUSTRIAN G.P.
Regazzoni 1.39.7
Ickx 1.39.8
Giunti 1.40.3
ITALIAN G.P.
Ickx 1.24.14
Regazzoni 1.24.39
Giunti 1.24.74
CANADIAN G.P.
Ickx 1.31.6
Regazzoni 1.31.9
U.S.A. G.P.
Ickx 1.03.07
Regazzoni 1.04.30
MEXICAN G.P.
Regazzoni 1.41.86
Ickx 1.42.41

1971
SOUTH AFRICAN G.P. KYALAMI
Regazzoni 1.18.7
Andretti 1.19.0
Ickx 1.19.2
SPANISH G.P.
Ickx 1.25.9
Regazzoni 1.26.0
Andretti 1.26.9
MONACO G.P.
Ickx 1.24.4
Regazzoni 1.26.1
Andretti (DNQ) . . 1.29.1
BRITISH G.P. SILVERSTONE
Regazzoni 1.18.1
Ickx 1.19.5
FRENCH G.P. CASTELLET
Regazzoni 1.51.53
Ickx 1.51.88
DUTCH G.P.
Ickx 1.17.42
Regazzoni 1.17.98
Andretti 1.20.32
AUSTRIAN G.P.
Regazzoni 1.37.90
Ickx 1.38.27
GERMAN G.P.
Ickx 7.19.2
Regazzoni 7.22.7
Andretti 7.31.7
ITALIAN G.P.
Ickx 1.22.82
Regazzoni 1.23.69
CANADIAN G.P.
Ickx 1.16.5
Andretti 1.16.9
Regazzoni 1.17.5
U.S.A. G.P.
Regazzoni 1.43.002
Ickx 1.43.843

1972
ARGENTINE G.P.
Regazzoni 1.13.28
Ickx 1.13.56
Andretti 1.13.61
SOUTH AFRICAN G.P. KYALAMI
Regazzoni 1.17.3
Andretti 1.17.5

Ickx 1.17.7
SPANISH G.P. JARAMA
Ickx 1.18.43*
Andretti 1.19.39
Regazzoni 1.19.71
GRAND PRI OF MONACO
Ickx 1.21.6
Regazzoni 1.21.9
BELGIAN G.P. NIVELLES
Regazzoni 1.11.58
Ickx 1.11.83
FRENCH G.P. CLERMONT
Ickx 2.55.1
Galli 3.00.7
BRITISH G.P. BRANDS HATCH
Ickx 1.22.2*
Merzario 1.23.7
GERMAN G.P. NURBURGRING
Ickx 7.07.00*
Regazzoni 7.13.4
Merzario 7.30.0
AUSTRIAN G.P. ZELTWEG
Regazzoni 1.36.04
Ickx 1.37.33
ITALIAN G.P. MONZA
Ickx 1.35.63
Regazzoni 1.35.83
Andretti 1.36.32
CANADIAN G.P. MOSPORT
Regazzoni 1.14.5
Ickx 1.14.7
Merzario . . . . No time
UNITED STATES G.P.
Regazzoni 1.41.95
Andretti 1.42.48
Ickx 1.42.60

1973
ARGENTINE GRAND PRIX
Ickx 1.11.01
Merzario 1.12.39
BRAZILIAN GRAND PRIX
Ickx 2.32.0
SOUTH AFRICAN GRAND PRIX
Merzario 1.17.16
Ickx 1.17.64
SPANISH GRAND PRIX
Ickx 1.23.5
BELGIAN GRAND PRIX
Ickx 1.23.10
MONACO GRAND PRIX
Ickx 1.28.7
Merzario 1.29.5
SWEDISH GRAND PRIX
Ickx 1.25.60
FRENCH GRAND PRIX
Merzario 1.51.17
Ickx 1.51.44
BRITISH GRAND PRIX
Ickx 1.18.19
AUSTRIAN GRAND PRIX
Merzario 1.36.42
ITALIAN GRAND PRIX
Merzario 1.36.37
Ickx 1.36.99
CANADIAN GRAND PRIX
Merzario 1.17.35
U.S.A. GRAND PRIX
Merzario 1.41.45

*Indicates Pole postion on starting grid.

APPENDIX XV
FERRARI ROAD TEST DATA

Type 212 Inter
Speeds attainable at 6500 r p m with 6.40 x 15 tyres m p h

Rear Axle Ratio	1st	2nd	3rd	4th	5th	4th x 1000 r p m
8/40	33.5	55.0	75.0	105.5	115.5	26.10
9/42	36.0	58.0	80.5	113.0	123.5	28.00

Type 250 Mille Miglia
Speeds attainable at 7200 r p m with 6.00 x 16 tyres m p h

Rear Axle Ratio	1st	2nd	3rd	4th	4th x 1000 r p m
9/40	50.5	75.5	102.5	129.0	
10/40	56.5	84.0	114.5	143.5	
11/40	62.0	93.15	126.0	157.5	

Type 340 Mexico
Speeds attainable at 6600 r p m with 6.50 x tyres m p h

Rear Axle Ratio	1st	2nd	3rd	4th	5th	4th x 1000 r p m
10/40	40.0	65.0	90.5	127.0	139.0	
11/40	44.0	71.5	99.5	139.5	153.0	
12/42	50.5	82.0	114.0	160.0	175.0	

Type 250 Grand Turismo
Speeds attainable with 6.00 x 16 tyres m p h

Rear Axle Ratio	1st	2nd	3rd	4th	4th x 1000 r p m
7/32	54.0	76.0	102.0	126.0	18.00
8/34	58.0	82.0	110.0	135.0	20.00
9/34	65.0	92.0	124.0	153.0	22.00
9/33	67.0	95.0	128.0	157.0	23.00

Type 375 Plus
Speeds attainable with 7.50 x 18 tyres m p h

Rear Axle Ratio	1st	2nd	3rd	4th
13/51 x 15/16-4.185	73.20	92.50	130.4	162.3
16/48 x 13/16-3.692	83.21	104.30	145.9	182.2
16/48 x 15/16-3.2	96.25	118.85	174.7	210.2

m p h	Type 212 seconds	Type 250 seconds	Type 340 seconds	Type 375 seconds
0–40	5	3.5	4	3.1
0–60	7	5	6	4
0–70	9	6	8	5.5
0–90	14	10.5	12.5	9i
0–100	19	12.5	16	11.5
0–110	24	17	20	13.5
0–120	31	23	25	18.0

Type 342 America
Speeds attainable at 5000 r p m with 6.40 x 15 tyres m p h

Rear Axle Ratio	1st	2nd	3rd	4th	4th x 1000 r p m
10/40	40.0	59.0	80.5	104.5	
12/42	45.0	67.5	92.0	115.5	

Type 750 Monza
Speeds attainable at 6000 engine r p m with 6.00 x 16 tyres m p h

Rear Axle Ratio	1st	2nd	3rd	4th	5th	5th x 1000 r p m
12/52 x 20/20-4.34	43.0	59.0	78.0	103.0	113.0	18.95
13/55 x 20/20-3.92	48.0	65.0	86.0	114.0	125.0	20.94
14/50 x 20/20-3.57	52.0	71.0	95.0	125.0	137.0	23.00
15/49 x 20/20-3.26	57.0	78.0	103.0	137.0	151.0	25.17
16/48 x 20/20-3.00	63.0	85.0	112.0	149.0	164.0	27.34

With 6.50 x 16 tyres these speeds are increased 1.73%.

Type 500 Mondial
Speeds attainable at 7000 engine r p m with 6.00 x 16 tyres m p h

Rear Axle Ratio	1st	2nd	3rd	4th	5th	5th x 1000 r p m
14/50 x 12/17-5.06	43.0	59.0	78.0	103.0	113.0	16.28
12/52 x 20/21-4.55	48.0	65.0	87.0	114.0	126.0	18.02
12/52 x 20/20-4.34	50.0	68.0	91.0	120.0	132.0	18.95
13/51 x 20/21-4.12	53.0	72.0	95.0	126.0	139.0	19.88
13/51 x 20/20-3.92	56.0	75.0	100.0	133.0	146.0	20.94

Type 250 Testa Rossa
Speeds attainable at 7200 r p m with 6.00 x 16 tyres m p h

Rear Axle Ratio	1st	2nd	3rd	4th
7/34	56.0	78.0	103.0	123.0
7/32	56.0	31.0	109.0	131.0
8/34	60.0	89.0	117.0	140.0
8/32	64.0	94.0	124.0	149.0
9/34	68.0	99.0	132.0	158.0
9/32	76.0	106.0	140.0	167.0

Type 335 Sport 4.1-litre four cam
Speeds attainable at 7000 r p m with 7.00 x 16 tyres m p h

Rear Axle Ratio	1st	2nd	3rd	4th
14/16 10/43	49.0	72.0	98.0	124.0
15/15 10/43	56.0	83.0	112.0	141.0
15/15 11/42	63.0	94.0	126.0	159.0
15/15 12/41	70.0	104.0	141.0	177.0

Type 250 Gran Turismo 1958
Speeds attainable at 7000 r p m with 6.00 x 16 rear tyres m p h

Rear Axle Ratio	1st	2nd	3rd	4th
7/34 = 4,858	46.6	69.6	93.8	118.0
7/32 = 4,57	49.7	74.0	100.0	125.5
8/34 = 4,25	53.5	79.5	107.5	135.8
8/32 = 4	56.5	84.5	114.3	143.6
9/34 = 3,778	60.3	89.5	121.2	152.2
9/32 = 3,666	62.1	92.0	124.3	156.6

Type 250 Gran Turismo 1959
Speeds attainable at 7000 r p m with 6.00 x 16 tyres m p h

Rear Axle Ratio	1st	2nd	3rd	4th
7/32	53.0	76.0	102.0	125.0
8/34	58.0	81.0	109.0	135.0
8/32	61.0	84.0	114.0	143.0
9/34	64.0	92.0	123.0	152.0
9/33	66.0	94.0	127.0	156.0

4.9 litre Superamerica
Acceleration
From zero to:

30 m p h	2.8 seconds
40 m p h	3.6 seconds
50 m p h	4.5 seconds
60 m p h	5.6 seconds
70 m p h	7.1 seconds
80 m p h	8.3 seconds
90 m p h	9.8 seconds
100 m p h	12.1 seconds

Standing ¼ mile: 13.9 seconds
Speed at end of ¼ mile: 108 m p h
Fuel consumption: 11.8 m p g
Speed ranges in gears (900–6,500 as tested, 7,000 permissible)

1st	9–65 m p h	(70)
2nd	13–93 m p h	(100)
3rd	18–128 m p h	(138)
4th	22–top	

Transmission ratios:

(1)	2.44
(2)	1.71
(3)	1.24
(4)	1.00

Final drive ratio: 3.44 (3.66, 3.22, 3.11)
Rating factors
Specific power output: 1.26 b h p/cu in
Piston speed at 60 m p h: 1,100 ft/min
Speed at 1,000 r p m in top gear: 24.4 m p h

400 Superamerica
Acceleration
From zero to:

30 m p h	3.5 seconds
60 m p h	9.2 seconds
90 m p h	16.9 seconds

Standing ¼ mile: 17 seconds
Fuel consumption: 12–20 m p g

Transmission ratios:	(1)	2.54
	(2)	1.70
	(3)	1.26
	(4)	1.0
	(OD)	0.78

Final drive ratio: 3.77
Torque: 235 lb/ft at 4,500 rpm

250 GT 2 plus 2
Acceleration
From zero to:

30 m p h	3.8 seconds
40 m p h	5.0 seconds
50 m p h	6.3 seconds
60 m p h	8.0 seconds
70 m p h	10.5 seconds
80 m p h	13.4 seconds
100 m p h	22.8 seconds

Stand ¼ mile: 16.3 seconds
Speed at end of ¼ mile: 88 m p h

Transmission ratios:	(1)	2.45
	(2)	1.72
	(3)	1.24
	(4)	1.00
	(OD)	0.778

Torque: 181 lb/ft at 5,000 rpm
Lb/h p: 14.5
m p h/1,000 r p m (in o/d): 28.0

ASA "Mille"
Acceleration
From zero to:

30 m p h	4.0 seconds
40 m p h	6.6 seconds
50 m p h	10.2 seconds
60 m p h	13.8 seconds
70 m p h	18.6 seconds
80 m p h	23.8 seconds
90 m p h	32.2 seconds
100 m p h	42.0 seconds

Standing ¼ mile: 19.2 seconds
Speed at end of ¼ mile: 72 m p h

Transmission ratios:	(1)	3.33
	(2)	2.12
	(3)	1.38
	(4)	1.00

Torque: 97 lb/ft at 6,000 rpm
b h p per cu in.: 1.57

Type 166 MM
Acceleration
From zero to:

30 m p h	3.8 seconds
40 m p h	5.7 seconds
50 m p h	7.3 seconds
60 m p h	10.0 seconds
70 m p h	12.6 seconds
80 m p h	16.2 seconds
90 m p h	20.0 seconds
100 m p h	25.0 seconds

Gear Ratios:

1st	(2.41)	11.2:1
2nd	(1.74)	8.11:1
3rd	(1.27)	5.92:1
4th	(1.00)	4.66:1

5th	(0.85)	3.96:1

Speeds in Gears:

1st	(7500)	51 m p h
2nd	(7500)	70 m p h
3rd	(7500)	96 m p h
4th	(7500)	122 m p h
5th		125 m p h

Type 212
Acceleration
From zero to:

30 m p h	3.4 seconds
40 m p h	4.0 seconds
50 m p h	5.2 seconds
60 m p h	7.05 seconds
70 m p h	9.2 seconds
80 m p h	11.8 seconds
90 m p h	14.2 seconds
100 m p h	18.1 seconds

Gear Ratios

1st	(overall)	11.23:1
2nd	(overall)	8.11:1
3rd	(overall)	5.92:1
4th	(overall)	4.66:1
5th	(OD)	4.28:1

Speeds in Gears

1st	53 m p h
2nd	74 m p h
3rd	102 m p h
4th	118 m p h

250 TRC/4 Cyl
Acceleration
From zero to

30 m p h	2.8 seconds
40 m p h	3.6 seconds
50 m p h	4.7 seconds
60 m p h	5.8 seconds
70 m p h	6.9 seconds
80 m p h	8.6 seconds
90 m p h	10.2 seconds
100 m p h	12.0 seconds
110 m p h	15.4 seconds

Gear Ratios

1st	11.3:1
2nd	6.78:1
3rd	5.13:1
4th	4.25:1

Speeds in Gears

1st	(6500)	47 m p h
2nd	(6500)	78 m p h
3rd	(6500)	103 m p h
4th		130 m p h

250 GT Lusso
Acceleration
From zero to:

30 m p h	3.9 seconds
40 m p h	5.1 seconds
50 m p h	6.2 seconds
60 m p h	8.0 seconds
80 m p h	12.5 seconds
100 m p h	19.5 seconds
120 m p h	29.4 seconds

Gear Ratios

1st	(2.45)	10.16:1
2nd	(1.70)	7.20:1
3rd	(1.26)	5.03:1
4th	(1.00)	4.00:1

Final drive ratio 4.00:1

Speed in Gears

1st	(7500)	55 m p h
2nd	(7500)	84 m p h

3rd	(7500)	117 m p h
4th	(7500)	150 m p h

275 GTS/4 Nart
Acceleration
From zero to:

30 m p h	3.0 seconds
40 m p h	4.0 seconds
60 m p h	6.7 seconds
80 m p h	9.8 seconds
100 m p h	15.0 seconds
120 m p h	21.6 seconds
140 m p h	34.2 seconds

Gear Ratios

1st	(3.08)	10.9:1
2nd	(2.12)	7.54:1
3rd	(1.57)	5.58:1
4th	(1.25)	4.45:1
5th	(1.04)	3.70:1

Speed in Gears

1st	(8000)	44 m p h
2nd	(8000)	64 m p h
3rd	(8000)	87 m p h
4th	(8000)	109 m p h
5th	(8000)	155 m p h

330 GTS
Acceleration
From zero to:

30 m p h	3.0 seconds
40 m p h	4.0 seconds
50 m p h	5.5 seconds
60 m p h	6.9 seconds
80 m p h	10.3 seconds
100 m p h	17.1 seconds
120 m p h	26.4 seconds

Gear Ratios

1st	(3.077)	10.60:1
2nd	(2.119)	7.30:1
3rd	(1.582)	5.45:1
4th	(1.250)	4.30:1
5th	(0.961)	3.31:1

Final drive ratio 3.44:1

Speed in Gears

1st	(7000)	49 m p h
2nd	(7000)	71 m p h
3rd	(7000)	97 m p h
4th	(7000)	124 m p h
5th	(6300)	146 m p h

365 GTB 2 + 2
Acceleration
From zero to:

30 m p h	2.9 seconds
40 m p h	4.0 seconds
50 m p h	5.7 seconds
60 m p h	7.1 seconds
80 m p h	11.2 seconds
100 m p h	16.5 seconds
120 m p h	26.6 seconds

Gear Ratios

1st	(2.54)	10.80:1
2nd	(1.70)	7.22:1
3rd	(1.26)	5.78:1
4th	(1.00)	4.25:1
5th	(0.797)	3.39:1

Final drive ratio 4.25:1

Speed in Gears

1st	(6600)	44 m p h
2nd	(6600)	68 m p h
3rd	(6600)	94 m p h
4th	(6600)	122 m p h
5th	(6450)	152 m p h

365 GTB/4 Daytona
Acceleration
From zero to:

30 m p h	. . . . .	2.4 seconds
40 m p h	. . . . .	3.3 seconds
50 m p h	. . . . .	4.3 seconds
60 m p h	. . . . .	5.9 seconds
70 m p h	. . . . .	7.0 seconds
80 m p h	. . . . .	8.3 seconds
100 m p h	. . . . .	12.0 seconds
120 m p h	. . . . .	18.3 seconds

Gear Ratios

1st	(3.08)	10.16:1
2nd	(2.12)	7.01:1
3rd	(1.57)	5.18:1
4th	(1.25)	4.12:1
5th	(0.95)	3.16:1

Speeds in gears

1st	(7700)	59 m p h
2nd	(7700)	86 m p h
3rd	(7700)	116 m p h
4th	(7700)	148 m p h
5th	(7000)	173 m p h

Final Drive Ratio 3.30:1
Fuel Consumption (Normal) 12.0 mpg
Range (Cruising) 317 miles

Dino 308/GT4
Speed in Gears

1st	43.5 m p h
2nd	62.7 m p h
3rd	86.9 m p h
4th	118.0 m p h
5th	115.2 m p h

Berlinetto Boxer
Speed in Gears

1st	54 m p h
2nd	80 m p h
3rd	108 m p h
4th	138 m p h
5th	188 m p h

APPENDIX XVII
VALVE TIMING OF VARIOUS FERRARI ENGINES

Model	Intake		Exhaust	
	Open BTDC	Close ABDC	Open BBDC	Close ATDC
125 Sport	15°	54°	54°	15°
125 F 1 (SS)	18°	58°	54°	22°
212	20°	55°	60°	15°
342 AM	25°	55°	58°	14°
340 MEX} MM }	24°	68°	70°	20°
375 F1	24°	68°	70°	20°
250 MM } GT }	22°	66°	67°	17°
500 F2	50°	80°	78°	48°
760 M	50°	80°	78°	48°
860 M	51°	75°	77°	47°
250 TR[1]	27°	65°	74°	16°
250 GT/E } GT/L }	27°	65°	74°	16°
250 GTO	45°	76°	74°	43°
275 GTB	34°	72°	66°	28°
275 GTB/Comp.	35°	62°	66°	32°
275 GTB/4	45°	65°	60°	41°
330 GT	27°	65°	74°	16°
330 GT (late)	14°	62°	62°	14°
275 LM[2]	46°	75°	70°	40°
365 GT	13°	59°	59°	13°
365 GTB/4	45°	46°	46°	38°
365 GTC/4	43°	38°	38°	34°
246 GT	40°	52°	53°	31°

*As specified by factory. Production allows for variations by a few degrees either plus or minus. Considerable variation will be found in specific examples of early cars.
[1] Variations will be found in competition cars.
[2] Some GTO engines have this timing sequence.

CHASSIS NUMBERS OF THE FIRST CARS BUILT EACH YEAR

1947	166 Inter	002		1967	330 GTC	9251
1948	166 Inter	001/S			275 GTB	9463
1949	166 Inter	003/S			330 GT 2+2	9471
1950	166 Inter	035/S				
1951	195 Inter	0123/S		1968	275 GTB/4	10855
1952	212 Inter	0189/EL			365 GT 2+2	11291
1953	212 Inter	0265/EU			330 GTC	11153
1954	250 GT	0357/GT				
1955	250 GT	0385/GT		1969	Daytona (Oct)	12827
1956	250 GT	0503/GT			365 GT 2+2	13009
1957	250 GT	0649/GT			365 GTC	12107
1958	250 GT	0845/GT1959			Dino 206	00152
1959	250 GT	1245/GT				
1960	250 GT	1735/GT		1970	Daytona	12841
1961	250 GT	2385/GT			365 GT 2+2	12109
1962	250 GT	3319/GT			365 GTC	12165
1963	250 GT	4359/GT			Dino 246 (Oct)	01134
1964	400 Superamerica P/F	5093				
				1971	Daytona	14103
	250 GTB Lusso	5255			365 GT 2+2	13835
	330 GT P/F 2+2	5263			365 GTC	12715
	250 LM	5149			365 GTC/4 (Oct)	14555
					Dino 246	01302
1965	330 GT P/F 2+2	6593				
	250 LM	5975		1972	Daytona	15023
	275 GTB	06609			365 GTC/4	14883
	275 GTS	06315			Dino 246	02962
	500 Superfast	6351				
				1973	Daytona	16349
1966	275 GTB	08111			365 GTC/4	16237
	330 GT p/F 2+2	7917			Dino 246	05468
	275 GTS	07583			365 GT/4 2+2	17127
	500 Superfast	8083				

GENERAL INDEX

Page numbers are not given for every repetition of a name, this would make for an impossibly long index, but only where it first appears in each significant part of the story, ie the single seater chapters and the sports car chapter. Enzo Ferrari and Dino Ferrari do not feature in the index because they appear throughout the book in a very consistent manner.

FERRARI

FERRARI